PILGRIMS OF THE VERTICAL

PILGRIMS OF THE VERTICAL

Yosemite Rock Climbers and Nature at Risk

Joseph E. Taylor III

HARVARD UNIVERSITY PRESS

Cambridge, Massachusetts • London, England • 2010

Many of the designations used by manufacturers and sellers to distinguish their products are
claimed as trademarks. Where those designations appear in this book and Harvard University Press
was aware of a trademark claim, then the designations have been printed in initial capital letters.

Library of Congress Cataloging-in-Publication Data
Taylor, Joseph E.
   Pilgrims of the vertical : Yosemite rock climbers and nature at risk / Joseph E. Taylor III.
      p.   cm.
   Includes bibliographical references and index.
   ISBN 978-0-674-05287-1 (alk. paper)
   1. Rock climbing—California—Yosemite Valley.   2. Mountaineering—California—Yosemite
Valley.   3. Rock climbing—Environmental aspects—California—Yosemite Valley.
4. Mountaineering—Environmental aspects—California—Yosemite Valley.   I. Title.
   GV199.42.C22Y67985   2010
   796.52′230979447—dc22   2010021578

for Lara

CONTENTS

1 Adventurers   1

2 Victorians   15

3 Pioneers   44

4 Members   62

5 Soldiers   91

6 Individualists   107

7 Experientialists   133

8 Moralists   148

9 Entrepreneurs   175

10 Dirtbags   190

11 Traditionalists   218

12 Consumers   233

13 Survivors   259

Abbreviations   279

Notes   281

Acknowledgments   355

Map and Illustration Credits   359

Index   361

PILGRIMS OF THE VERTICAL

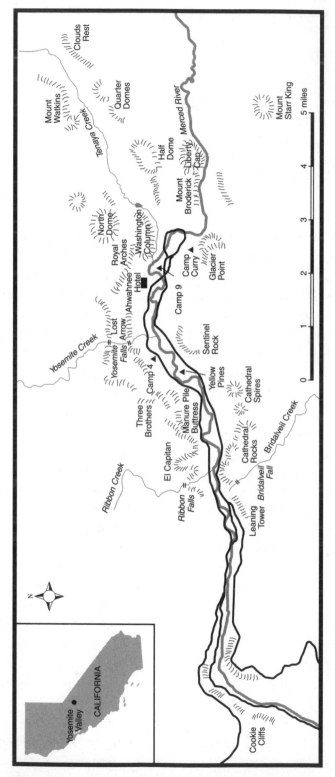

Map 1.1. Yosemite Valley climbing locations.

1. ADVENTURERS

I have a low opinion of books; they are but piles of stones set up to
show coming travelers where other minds have been, or at best signal smokes to call attention. . . . No amount of word-making will
ever make a single soul to *know* these mountains.
—JOHN MUIR

The March air is warm. Soft breezes carry a luxuriant aroma of new growth
up Yosemite's cliffs. The waterfalls thunder. A blue sky dazzles. I am sur-
rounded by the sensations of spring. By any metric this is a glorious day, but
I don't give a damn. All I can think right now is, *I'm in trouble.* I am spread
eagled across an intersection of two vertical faces of rock, and enough adren-
alin surges through me to resuscitate the dead because I am about to fall. My
right foot tiptoes on a nubbin, my right hand grasps at nothing, my left hand
is slipping from a crack, and my left foot is sliding off an alleged bulge. The
bucket hold that will save me remains twenty inches beyond reach. Worse
still, I am losing focus. This is partly because I am berating myself for growing old and out of shape, partly because my partner is saying distracting
words of encouragement. It is the wrong tactic. He should be barking like a
football coach, telling me I'm not worthy or something, anything to make
me angry enough to focus. Instead, I supply the insult: *Move it, fat man.*

I am trying to climb a popular route called *Nutcracker Suite,* but I am
stuck on the route's hardest, most committing move, the crux upon which
everything turns. The longer I hang here the more certain failure becomes. I
must go for it. I adjust my left foot and lie to myself that it is fine. I shove my
left hand into the crack and clench to increase friction. *Huh? Not sure I can
extract that.* Then I make the move, but as my fingers touch the bucket, my
left foot peels and two sounds follow: first "splat," then "phhhlbbbbsss." I
have the hold, but it is not much of an improvement. I now hang from my
right hand, my face plastered to the rock, breathing like a rhino. The sole
consolation is that my partner sees only the four fingers of my right hand.
The rest of me remains below the ledge and out of sight. I retrieve my left
hand, now bleeding freely, and reach up. With both hands I treat the bucket
like a pull-up bar and lean back to create more friction for my feet. *Pretend
for a moment you know what you are doing.* I walk my feet up and over the

lip, return my partner's smile, and impassively scan the terrain ahead. Outside, I'm a picture of cool, as if this was casual; inside my brain a confused party has erupted: *Yeah! Ow! Yeah! Ow! Yeah! Ow!* . . .

Looking back on that moment is a double-edged experience. I had completed my hardest climb in fifteen years, and a warm glow followed me the rest of the day. That feeling still comes back like a friendly March wind, but it is bittersweet. Even then I was feeling ever more distant from climbing and the other outdoor pursuits that had shaped me. Some changes were physical. After decades on mountains and oceans, my body was a wreck. My ankles were horror shows, my elbows had chronic tendonitis, and my right shoulder needed a surgery that has ended my ability to make that crux pull. Other changes were social. Family and friends were complicating the calculus of my life. Married and planning a kid, the risks I took when single no longer made sense. I already knew the technical climbs planned for the coming weeks would be my last, so as I scrambled toward the final belay, I knew I was nearing the end of the adventure in a larger sense.

I want to be clear. Ending my days as a rock climber was no small thing. I had read the literature since the mid-1960s. As a boy I consumed issues of *Ascent* in a sitting and pawed copies of *Mountain* and *Climbing* in local gear shops. I followed debates about bolts, competition, publicity, and conservation. Preserving adventure, maintaining fairness, and protecting nature resonated strongly. Even then I knew this had been the sport's constant thread. The ability to discover new ground, much like an explorer beyond the frontier, was a sublime aesthetic experience, and being first to ascend a route by fair means was considered the epitome of sporting performance. For decades my ideal of adventure had been defined by Maurice Herzog's *Annapurna* and Thomas Hornbein's *Everest: The West Ridge,* two classics about men venturing beyond the known on difficult terrain. I dreamt of vast walls and desperate moments, and I yearned to be in one of those dramatic photos that garnished climbing journals. I wanted, as Patrick McManus wrote of his own youthful fantasies, a great epic in which I would "face great hardship and overcome terrible obstacles." For a very long time I wanted to be an adventurer.[1]

Thus ceasing to be a "pilgrim of the vertical," to use Royal Robbins's phrase, represented a massive psychic transition. My very presence in Yosemite was less to climb than to research how people have related to nature through sport. Few people believe that modern society has "been seriously affected by the small band of visionaries climbing has produced." Even the Victorian climber Leslie Stephen admitted that "when history comes to pronounce a final judgment upon the men of the time, it won't put mountain-climbing on a level with patriotism, or even with excellence in the fine arts." I disagree. Like the historian Maurice Isserman, I see climbers as "products of their own eras; the way they climb, and the way they feel about climbing, can help map a larger cultural, political, and social terrain." Revisiting the books and essays of my youth confirmed this. It no longer made sense to think of climbing, or surfing and skiing for that matter, as "an individual sport" in which athletes escaped "the formless tangle of sounds that distinguish life in the city" for a timeless, noncompetitive "communion with nature." Mountaineers have been narrating their adventures for audiences since the late 1700s, and their exploits, like those of other outdoor sports, have been part of a prominent conversation about how people should interact with nature.[2]

In other words, outdoor sports were always social activities, and many athletes went on to influence environmental and social politics across the planet. The question is why. The answers are not simple, and they force us to adjust our thinking. A pastime long considered escapism was actually intensely engaged with the broader world. But this raises another issue. While it is always preferable to let historical actors speak for themselves, the past has rarely been as simple as athletes portrayed it. Imbedded in their stories are lessons about the relationship of individuals to groups, sport to society, and nature to culture. These bonds are not transparent, however, nor were climbers eager to examine the complicating details of their lives. Geoffrey Winthrop Young once said that each adventure was idiosyncratic to the individual, yet Young had a complicated sexuality and shied from "the relationship called into being by the meeting of characteristics in ourselves" when it came to himself. Similarly, Warren Harding admitted that he did not want to think "deep and heavy when it's deep and heavy," yet he out-debated an entire generation of moralists about the balance between the individual and the community. We cannot simply rely on athletes themselves to tease apart the complexities of their avocations. That requires a different perspective and methodology. Thus I read this literature not as a climber but as a historian, and I am less concerned with recounting great deeds than telling a story about what climbers' stories reveal. They have played many games, with many goals, and created many, ever-shifting ways of relating to nature across time and space.[3]

Although I cannot match the authenticity or drama of a first-person account—those who lived adventures will always tell their stories better, and John Muir was right that "word making" cannot fully capture the sublimity of nature—I can place stories in context to illustrate the connections between climbers and their times, and I can do this more dispassionately than people whose identities remain intrinsically bound to their play. Moreover and unlike Muir, who was actually a prolific writer of books, I have a high opinion of writing. Climbers' words are fascinating and illuminating, albeit not always in the ways intended. Thus this is a different sort of an adventure: it is an intellectual quest, and I am a peculiar sort of guide—an academic historian. So let's just get this out of the way as well. Although I used to climb, that is not the basis of my expertise. I have trained not with pull-ups and boulders but with reading and that most precious resource nowadays: time. I have pored over texts in libraries and archives around North America. I have ruminated for years, and I am sure Yosemite's pilgrims of the vertical have much to teach us about nature, sport, and culture.[4]

To draw out these lessons, we need to consider not only the thrilling feats but the contexts and contingencies. We need to pay attention as people ventured into the wild but also as they returned to society, because recreation was inextricably linked to identity. The tales adventurers told were partly about who they thought they were. For centuries the mere possession of leisure was exceptional, and each form of play helped further distinguish recreationalists from their cohort and other classes. Activities such as tourism, which emphasized visual senses, produced meanings distinct from games requiring physical exertion. Participants of each pastime were deeply invested in these distinctions. Play was about fun and about social positioning. Different games emerged across society, each reflecting the peculiar talents and resources of communities. One familiar example is golf. Those who played at country clubs cultivated different contacts and status than those at public courses or driving ranges. Similarly, sports like mountaineering appealed in part because they enabled athletes to distinguish themselves in a world of expanding leisure. Ascending distant peaks offered "maximum distinction" by "simultaneously mastering one's own body and a nature inaccessible to the many," or as Leslie Stephen put it, "Mountain scenery is the antithesis not so much of the plains as of the commonplace." For Dorothy Pilley Richards climbing offered "a compassable world with classic boundaries to it, something you could belong to as you cannot to an expanding universe." Rather than an escape, these sports were forms of belonging and even conformity.[5]

This is a key point. Sports were not only activities but contexts. To climb well meant disciplining oneself to rules that, while unwritten, were clear to participants. Before I could try *Nutcracker Suite,* I had to internalize Royal

Robbins's account of his first ascent as an ethos of adventure. He pioneered the route in 1967 to demonstrate that passive protection was safe. Using only hands and feet to move upward—what climbers call "free climbing"—he refused to hammer metal pitons into cracks, instead inserting small wedges, called *artificial chocks,* and linking them to his safety rope with loops of cord and carabiners. While these "nuts" are now standard tools, many viewed them then as edgy, even irresponsible. In the event of a fall, Robbins's partner would have wrapped the rope around her waist—a *body belay*—to create enough friction to hold the fall, but it was an open question whether chocks could hold such forces. If they had failed, Robbins might have fallen twice the distance from himself to his belayer or, worse yet, hit a ledge. He took a calculated risk. He was an elite, by which I mean someone who climbed in a self-consciously didactic manner, and *Nutcracker Suite* was his attempt to redefine the game. Robbins knew that sporting culture disciplined climbers to abide by the standards of a first ascent. This is why I had to equal Robbins's style. I had to climb using only hands and feet, and place only the technologies Robbins had used, or I had to abstain. Put another way, sport structured my behavior. The freedom of the hills, to quote a famous book, meant submitting to a lot of rules.[6]

These were some of the ways that sport influenced how people interacted with nature. Robbins did not invent this culture. He merely inherited and refined a set of historical practices. To comprehend the beliefs guiding him and others, we must examine the sport's roots. We have to begin not in Yosemite but in London's Alpine Club, consider when the sport was founded and by whom, and how it evolved and came to North America. This is the only way to understand Yosemite climbers' peculiar ideas about technology, style, competition, and publicity, because none were home grown. All were well established by the time technical climbing reached the Sierra Nevada in 1930. By then climbing was already eighty years old with considerable cultural inertia. Mastering its logic will lead us to its basic assumptions. And as surely as we must study the Victorians, we must also attend to the Sierra Club. The members who brought technical climbing to Yosemite honored the sport's history and culture, yet they reshaped the rules to suit their own social and environmental contexts. These innovations later framed the options for Robbins's, my, and later generations, but each cohort also further refined the game to accommodate new techniques, technologies, and motives. This is why sport must be considered in a historical context.[7]

The same holds for the social and cultural contexts in which climbing developed. As a climber, I knew my pastime offered intoxicating rewards,

both in the endorphins that coursed through my body and in the empowerment that came from mastering vertical nature and my inner self. Hanging
there at the crux of *Nutcracker Suite,* I knew that more than my body would
be bruised by a fall because this was never simply between me and nature.
Climbing was part of how I identified myself, and my sporting labors were
how I staked claims to nature. As a scholar I know my actions flowed from
a gendered code that was also historical.[8] Sport grew popular in the nineteenth century as a way to develop manly habits, what William James called
the "moral equivalent of war." Climbing's rules were developed by upper-
middling Victorians who borrowed aristocratic traditions of chivalrous masculinity to create a tempering contest with nature. That game has now attracted young men for 150 years. As Edward Whymper wrote, "We who go
mountain-scrambling have constantly set before us the superiority of fixed
purposes or perseverance to brute force. . . . we know that where there's a
will there's a way; and we come back to our daily occupations better fitted to
fight the battle of life, . . . strengthened and cheered by the recollection of
past labours, and by the memories of victories gained in other fields." A century later, Robbins remarked, "I think most of us who are climbers recognize
that we have a deep-seated need for some sort of battle as part of our lives."
Rarely was climbing simply about getting to the top.[9]

Social and cultural contexts are critical for understanding how the sport
evolved, what participants thought they were doing, and why they cared.
Consider the sexual and imperial connotations of being first. Nineteenth-
century mountaineers saw nature as "sensuous and feminine" and competed for her "virgin" summits. Edward Whymper likened the Aiguille de
Trélatête to "a beautiful coquette," and Simon Beisheuvel called climbers'
conquests "a unique consummation." When John Tyndall "pressed the very
highest snowflake" of the Weisshorn, he declared its "prestige . . . forever
gone." Whymper agreed. Although he, too, had lusted after the virgin summit, once Tyndall defiled it "My interest . . . abated." Men's gendered and sexualized language sometimes went over the top, yet women occasionally expressed remarkably similar attitudes. Nearly eighty years later, Ruth Dyar
Mendenhall wrote that standing atop Monument Peak, "where no man-ever-
had stood before . . . was our Matterhorn." If some sexualized these feats,
others saw them no less as conquests. Mendenhall described first ascents as
"the acme of most climbers' dreams—and sort of a last frontier in a well
explored civilized world." Men could experience mountain sport differently
from women, and for both gender was expressed in distinct patterns, but it
is crucial to recognize that there was as much diversity among men and

women as between them. We can find male and female athletes at each point on the spectrum of sport, and they always channeled broader social attitudes.[10]

Ideas about risk revealed similar lessons. Middle-class mountaineers derived value not just by reaching the top but by overcoming difficulty with dignity. At first uncertainties about thin air meant that simply getting up and back was celebrated, but by 1870 many peaks seemed unchallenging or, as Stephen put it, "an easy day for a lady." This is when climbers began to discuss fair play. Like Robbins on *Nutcracker Suite*, they nurtured uncertainty by rejecting techniques and tools that unduly favored success. They also valorized being first on the rope because the leader at the "sharp end" above a belay risked greater falls. Mendenhall admired "the glory of leading," but because she rarely led Robbins called her "a good climber—competent, experienced, and canny—but not a great one in the sense of leaving her mark on posterity through her first ascents." The same held for Elizabeth Robbins, who accompanied Royal on many climbs, including *Nutcracker Suite*, but by her husband's standard did not leave her mark.[11]

This reflects the sport's basic gendering, yet we should note that men and women alike defended risk-taking, sharing Stephen's view that "those love [the mountains] best who have wandered longest in their recesses, and have most endangered their own lives . . . in the attempt to open out routes." This is why risk is associated with environmental sensitivity in outdoor sports. The line of propriety has shifted, but the basic equation has not. When the feminist mountaineer Arlene Blum explained in 1990 that having "experiences that are on the edge of life and death" is why the sport "is the real ultimate activity," she essentially echoed Alfred Mummery's 1895 observation that "the essence of the sport lies, not in ascending a peak, but in struggling with and overcoming difficulties. The happy climber, like the aged Ulysses, is one who has 'Drunk delight of battle with his peers,' and this delight is only attainable by assaulting cliffs which tax to their utmost limits the powers of the mountaineers engaged." Women's and men's shared values, and their remarkably similar backgrounds, suggest that race and class may be more central than gender to explaining community attitudes about sport and nature.[12]

Assumptions about risk also clarify the cultural and material implications of technology. All sports limit the tools that players can use. Much as I may wish otherwise, I cannot park a ladder under a basketball hoop, nor use a howitzer from the golf tees. The prestige of hunting and angling tools are inversely related to efficiency. A treble hook is not as sporting as a dry fly; bows and arrows are more admirable than punt guns. Climbers' disdain for gear that eased ascent paralleled such examples, but there was more to it. Like genteel hunters and anglers, climbers wanted to give nature "a fair chance," but they also regarded technology as impeding their connections to nature and to each other. Arnold Lunn argued that "the more we interpose mechanisms between our natural sense and their rhythmic lines and plane the less chance is there of a real interplay being established or . . . uncovering its pleasures." Charles Houston complained that climbers did not mention "the fellowship of the rope, perhaps because hardware has blurred that bond." Others said fixed gear "spoil[ed] the fun" and preferred routes "in as 'wild' a state as possible." Many climbers were powerfully ambivalent about their tools.[13]

In this sense they were also unrepresentative. Skiers and surfers said their boards and skis connected them to nature. Hang gliders and kayakers could not experience nature without their technologies. Not even all climbers shared this purist view. Far from feeling alienated, some said tools enhanced the environmental experience. Louise Shepherd explained that "the process of discovering an unclimbed line and brushing and bolting it . . . made the ascent even more personally rewarding." Over time gear refinements revealed a nuanced knowledge about the nature of rock, tools, and bodies, yet every change also aroused resistance. Pitons, carabiners, crampons, tennis shoes, bottled oxygen, bolts, chocks, cams, and sticky soles triggered heated debates about fair play. Every clash revealed an intense desire to preserve risk.[14]

There were also ecological implications. Some impacts were obvious, such as holes drilled for bolts or cracks gouged by pitons. Even the movement of rope could leave a permanent mark. Other effects were more subtle but no less consequential. First ascenders often scoured dirt and plants to create holds or place protection. Those who followed viewed Yosemite's clean walls as natural rather than denuded ecosystems. Every climber scraped lichen, slowly creating barer pathways that contrasted starkly with surrounding cliffs. The human body also altered the rock. On *Nutcracker Suite* several crucial moves are now more difficult because thousands of slipping feet have polished surfaces smooth, and holds have been greased by the oil of countless sweaty hands. Rebecca Solnit is thus right that obsessions with "geological time scales and natural wonders" make it "easy to believe that Yosemite has no significant human history; and thereby that human history is not part of the landscape," but climbers find it ever harder to ignore the accumulated material and cultural baggage of their very human and historical nature.[15]

So while technological moralists did simplify relationships between sport, technology, and ecology, some of their fears were just. Each choice did alter how climbers interacted with nature. Free climbers sought different vertical environments than aid climbers, chocks and pitons worked in differently configured cracks, as did iron and chrome-molybdenum pitons, and bolts opened terrain unprotectable by other gear. The purists were correct—technology was a structuring context—but they were also caught by this conundrum. Climbers idealized an unmediated environmental experience, yet mountaineering was as technologically intensive as it got. Even early Victorians employed specialized ropes, tents, axes, clothes, and footwear. They also developed associations, journals, and books to disseminate information and discipline participants. There was no escaping technology, and since most climbers did not make their equipment, the sport also fostered forms of consumption and complex relationships between producers and consumers. Climbers adapted construction bolts, machine nuts, and gymnastic chalk. Nylon stockings inspired the first safe ropes, and pile carpets became the foundation of modern outdoor apparel. Manufacturers devised and refined protective gear that climbers altered and consumers appropriated for their own ends. Technology mediated athletes' relations to nature and society, but climbers were hardly passive agents in this process.[16]

This also applies to the literally massive subject of Yosemite Valley. Any discussion of "The Valley" must include geology. A vast plutonic batholith formed during the Cretaceous around 120 million years ago. This firm granitic plain, composed of quartz, potassium feldspar, and plagioclase, then tilted into the present Sierra Nevada along a major fault at its eastern edge. Uplifting created joint fractures in the batholith, while wind, water, heat, and at least three glacial periods sculpted the present landscape. What distinguishes Yosemite Valley from most places in the Sierra, and in fact the world, is first its scale. Many cliffs vault 1,500 to 3,000 feet above the valley floor. The most daunting faces—Leaning Tower, Sentinel Rock, Yosemite Falls, Half Dome, Mount Watkins, and the massive monolith of El Capitan—are vertical to overhanging. This alone would attract ambitious climbers, but there is more. As erosive processes exposed the batholith, the pressure of the earth released, leading to a peculiar process of *sheet jointing,* often called *exfoliation,* in which granite breaks apart like a drying onion. As a result, Yosemite's cliffs are distinguished by long, vertically oriented cracks, and because the cliffs tended to shed in very large blocks, the rock is solid and unusually reliable. Second, the valley is at the relatively low altitude of 4,000 feet. It shares California's warm, dry climate, and because large urban areas cluster nearby,

Figure 1.1. Yosemite Valley from the Wawona Tunnel, by Ansel Adams. At near left is the southwest face of El Capitan and *The Nose* route in profile. At far center is the northwest face of Half Dome, at near right center the Cathedral Rocks, and near right Bridalveil Fall and the Leaning Tower. The photograph also exemplifies the sublime aesthetic defined by John Ruskin and refined by later photographers such as Carleton Watkins, Eadweard Muybridge, Vittorio Sella, and Adams.

and most features are less than a five-minute walk from the road, Yosemite is, as François Matthes remarked, "a paradaisical [*sic*] spot" for climbers.[17]

What paradise means has long been contested. As climber Lynn Hill observes, "If you take a secular view of existence, then Yosemite is a wonderfully sculpted geologic accident; if you believe in a cosmic master plan, then it is among the Creator's greatest works." Yosemite has always inspired. In 1855, James Hutchings called it a "singular and romantic valley" of "wild and sublime grandeur." Thomas Starr King likened his reaction to that "which the Israelites felt amid the passes of Sinai with the Divine glory on the mount." John Muir wrote simply, "Born again!" All this raving encouraged something extraordinary. In 1864, Congress declared Yosemite a preserve to be managed by California, and when the state faltered, Congress declared it North America's third national park. In the meantime stewards systematically erased the valley's human history, evicting Ahwahneechees, Miwoks, and Paiutes and renaming features to fit their image of place. They attached "cathedral" to no less than seven formations, named one to honor George Washington, and sprinkled the rest with romantic and personal titles. Many helped rescript space, but one of the most forceful and sustained efforts was by a group of mountaineers and environmental advocates who had institutionalized John Muir's vision in the Sierra Club. The SC has long dominated Yosemite's history, yet from the beginning there were others who valued the valley for different recreational and entrepreneurial interests, including the valley's first hotelier, James Hutchings.[18]

Outdoor athletes expressed similarly diverse views. Some nurtured spiritual relationships. The usually jaded Stephen likened the Oberland Alps to "the Pyramids or a Gothic cathedral, it throws off the taint of vulgarity by its imperishable majesty." Twelve decades later, a similarly worldly Daniel Duane compared El Capitan to the Hagia Sophia in terms of "cosmic" significance. Although their language echoed that of tourists, outdoor athletes believed that "the qualities which strike every sensitive observer are impressed upon the mountaineer with tenfold force and intensity." Grappling with stone turned hands and feet into data receptors, and sporting labor produced information that sightseers never acquired from afar. Feeling rock, breathing air, gardening cracks, pounding metal, and studying the "peeled, blistered and swollen faces" of fellow climbers generated unique insights about vertical nature. As Arnold Lunn asked, "Does anybody really suppose that 'the child, the cripple, and the man of grey hairs' even see the same mountain as the man who has climbed it?"[19]

Similarly, when Mendenhall walked out of the Canadian Rockies into a busload of tourists, she wrote, "We had seen the mountains not as a pretty scene to be looked at through a glass window while a uniformed bus driver said 'That is Fortress Peak.' We had lived the mountains." Outdoor athletes engaged nature with peculiar intensity, yet it was also their stage. Climbing, skiing, and surfing were almost always social performances. Play was about experiencing nature but also about defining oneself in relation to others. This is why Mendenhall needed to explain that she possessed knowledge not available to those autobound tourists, and it is why some athletes became important environmental advocates. The caveat is that advocates covered the sporting spectrum and expressed many different agendas.[20]

Yosemite is thus a perfect place to examine the links between outdoor sport and environmental culture. For a century it has inspired climbing excellence and environmental values that were more than coincidentally related. Consider for a moment a few events. In 1915, Theodore Roosevelt eulogized John Muir as one of the "few nature lovers . . . able to influence contemporary thought and action on the subjects to which he had devoted his life." In the 1920s, Francis Farquhar's San Francisco apartment was "the unofficial western headquarters of the National Park Service." In 1968, Secretary of the Interior Stewart Udall called Sierra Club Executive Director David Brower "the most effective single person on the cutting edge of conservation in this country." In 1971, the Sierra Club created the Ansel Adams Award to honor the photographer's aesthetic contributions to conservation, and in 1984 it gave that award to Galen Rowell for his oeuvre of images and writings. In 1985, George Sessions gave the philosophy of deep ecology its guiding text. In 1999, *Time* deemed Yvon Chouinard one of its "Heroes for the Planet." And in 2008, Allen Steck was honored for founding the modern ecotourism and geotourism industry. The two things they all had in common were a love of wild nature and a history of climbing in Yosemite.[21]

Many pilgrims shared these passions, but values were not essences acquired merely by touching nature. Culture is a learned thing, sustained and transformed through social processes. As Marjorie Hope Nicholson wrote, "we see in Nature what we have been taught to look for, we feel what we have been prepared to feel." The social networks within which learning occurred are critical for understanding how sporting and environmental culture interacted. I did not pick up my values through immaculate inspiration or by tying a rope around my waist. Mine came from reading books, taking lessons, climbing widely, and debating issues. Two lessons from those experiences shape this study. First, outdoor play does not occur in a vacuum. A matrix of influences always shape it, including but not limited to talent, psychology, identity, social contacts, education, pop culture, drug preferences, sexual orientation, and environmental contingencies. Athletes' cultural attitudes are always shaped by time and place.[22]

The other insight is that there has never been a homogeneous climbing or environmental culture, yet simply tracing these plural social and cultural systems is not sufficient either. Culture is specific to context. Climbers developed dynamic orientations to nature, technology, and each other based on where they were and whom they were with. There are so many examples of climbers pushing themselves in some situations and being uncompetitive in others that we must pay particular attention to how contexts influenced them. Outdoor sports were neither timeless nor did they evolve in any simple or predictable way. I use two terms in this book to highlight these key social contexts. The first is *homosocial.* Sometimes this refers to the single-sex demographics that shaped climbers from the early Alpine Club through the Yosemite campsite favored by climbers after World War II, Camp 4, but it also applies to culturally homogeneous groups that held similar views about sport or nature, such as the complexly segmented climbing gym. The second, *heterosocial,* applies to demographically or athletically heterogeneous groups, or groups that tolerated a range of views about sport or nature. We see this in the early climbing clubs of North America, especially in the Sierra Club's Rock Climbing Sections. Beyond the labels is a crucial point: these categories were not hermetic. Climbers regularly moved among groups, and as they did so we see how values about sport and nature shifted depending upon social contexts. This ultimately provides a historical way to think about identity and people's interactions with nature and each other.[23]

As Claire Engel observed, "one of the striking aspects of mountaineering" is that "one can hardly find two climbers who indulge in it for identical reasons," yet a conceit heard widely from climbers is that there is such a thing as a "real climber." According to Louise Shepherd, "By 'climber' I mean one who leads. The perpetual seconders-cum-portable-belayers that one sees especially in Europe, I do not count as climbers." This is heard not only from elites but moderates and beginners. Authenticity rests on the assumption that one has not had a genuine experience until one has risked and suffered. Such posturing, an attitude I held fervently in my teens and which remained latently powerful enough to goad me over *Nutcracker Suite*'s crux, is easy enough to unmask, but its legacy has long privileged a tiny percentage of outdoor athletes at the expense of the broader community. Panning out from the narrow focus on elite climbers in most mountaineering histories reveals not just many other ways of relating to nature through sport but also how all these climbers—elites, weekend warriors, wannabes, and beginners—were bound together by networks of technology and consumption.[24]

Access to this new world is the adventure I offer. As I waded through archival documents, letters, diaries, essays, and more books than I care to admit, it opened up like a promising mountain route. Passage was challenging, and I was tested intellectually and emotionally. It was an adventure, but not of the standard type. The sociologist Georg Simmel once defined adventure as a basically insular experience. Separate and unto itself, it had the "mysterious power to make us feel for a moment the whole sum of life," or as George Mallory wrote, "every mountain adventure is emotionally complete. The spirit goes on a journey just as does the body, and this journey has a beginning and an end, and is concerned with all that happens between these extremities." Eighty years later Gabriela Zim still thought Yosemite's Camp 4 "had separated itself from the popular culture." I see a different story. The longer I studied Yosemite climbers, the more I saw connection, not separa-tion, as the basic theme. Thus the story found in these pages is not about solitary quests but the relentless bonds between the individual and group, sport and society, and nature and culture. Pilgrims' errands into the vertical, and the values they infused in sport and wild nature, were inseparable from the ever-shifting social and cultural currents of the broader society. There were no timeless truths, nor can this history have a tidy ending. The story stretches back as far as we care to look, and it will run forward in ways we cannot predict. Come explore.[25]

2. VICTORIANS

[T]o ask for a tug on the rope, or to employ it as a handhold, as beginners are always tempted to do, is to make use of artificial assistance which the leader himself did not possess and which destroys
the value of the climb.
—Robert L. M. Underhill

In tale after tale by climbers and historians, the birth of Yosemite climbing has had biblical overtones. The time is summer 1931, the place Garnet
Lake in the Sierra Nevada. Francis Farquhar has brought fellow Harvard man
and celebrated American mountaineer Robert Underhill to teach European
techniques to the Sierra Club. Underhill treads the holy Range of Light like a
mountaineering Moses, and the followers of John Muir listen reverently. He
teaches these pilgrims to tie knots, manage ropes, belay climbers, and rappel. He also discusses ethics, counseling that peaks "must be surmounted by
one's own unaided abilities" or risk destroying "the value of the climb." His
disciples learn the art of technical climbing and begin to ascend safely and—
of equal importance—in good style. Underhill then leads a few acolytes into
the vertical wilderness, culminating with the first ascent of the east face of
Mount Whitney, tallest mountain in the contiguous United States. They then
disperse to proselytize climbing, form clubs, collect converts, and build the
sport. From Farquhar's and Underhill's seminal labors flows a storied chronicle of vertical adventure. According to Ed Webster, Underhill "deserves full
accolades for awakening California climbers to the vast, untouched potential of technical routes in the Sierra. His brief trip precipitated a flurry of
subsequent exploration, including the first probes upon Yosemite's vertical
walls."[1]

This tidy story has become a legend climbers invoke to assert a pecu-
liarly American pedigree in which Underhill and Muir father modern American climbing. Life is messy, however, and the dawn of Yosemite climbing
was more complicated. Underhill was but one of many influences in western North America. Technical manuals in several languages had circulated
for half a century. In Alaska an Italian prince bagged Mount Saint Elias in
1899 and local miners climbed Mount McKinley in 1910. People had scrambled over the Sierra Nevada for generations, the Mazamas (a climbing club

founded in 1894 atop Mount Hood) had reached every summit in Oregon, and Seattle's Mountaineers were taking the flower of the last virgin peaks in the Cascade and Olympic ranges. Even Underhill's techniques were known. Americans had used roped belays on Grand Teton as early as 1898. In 1910 the Mazamas made an ascent of North Sister "by means of the Swiss Alpine rope." John Case used similar methods in the Adirondacks in 1916, as did Albert Ellingwood on Colorado's Lizardhead in 1920, and Joe and Paul Stettner on Longs Peak in 1927. In California, easterners had climbed Sierra peaks in 1926 using modern techniques, Sierra Club members John Mendenhall and Max Von Patten had used belays on Mount Laurel in 1930, and Farquhar had instructed club members in rope work the week before Underhill arrived. California was not quite a *tabula rasa,* yet the genesis myth is repeated so often that it and Underhill deserve sustained scrutiny.[2]

Underhill did influence climbers, through both what he did and did not do and say. Fully comprehending his visit thus demands a richer rendition of the past. Underhill was born in 1889 to a successful New York lawyer and raised in relative comfort and privilege. He grew up in the pastoral splendor of the Hudson River Valley. His first climbs were in New Hampshire's White Mountains, and by the time he went abroad after graduating from Haverford College in 1909, he was fluent in German and European travel. That summer he made his first climb in the Alps, returning to the Dolomites in 1914. Underhill belonged to a community of upper-middling young men who had long before worked out how to distinguish themselves through outdoor play. Thoroughly representative of his era and social circumstances, he learned to follow particular rules, and those rules followed him to Garnet Lake.

Exploring Underhill's cultural contexts, we can begin to recognize how his lessons bore traces of nationalistic and class biases. His ideas on amateurism revealed Victorian influences. His instruction on technique censored many of what became the most salient tools in Yosemite. Although it seems counterintuitive, even sacrilegious, Underhill did as much to obscure as to enlighten. Under his tutelage modern Yosemite climbing should have become an Anglican pastime, but that was at odds with both the environment and ambitions of his students, who from the start made brilliant ascents on terms that conflicted with Underhill's counsel. But we are jumping forward. For now the challenge is to understand why Underhill visited the Sierra Nevada and what he revealed about the roots of serious play.

Yosemite's prehistory is easy to trace. The literature on early mountaineering is outsized in relation to its participants, and whether one reads little or prodigiously, the story is the same. Alpine climbing evolved into modern mountaineering during the middle third of the nineteenth century as intrepid men rapidly conquered the major peaks of western Europe. This golden age ended in 1865, when four men died while descending from the Matterhorn, supposedly the last great challenge. An ensuing, less lustrous silver age extended to 1877, 1885, or 1910, depending on whom you read, and it was dominated by the pursuit of final virgin summits and new, more challenging routes up peaks and pinnacles. At least one author has posited a third, more debased epoch, the iron age, which extended into the twentieth century. This era featured the refinement of technologies, including ropes, pitons, carabiners, and bolts, that enhanced climbers' safety and ability but damaged the sport's historical values.[3]

Coupling a fall from grace with rising technical trends and safety equipment is just one of mountaineering's many paradoxes. Why is it, for example, that the sport of climbing mountains was born in cities? Why did British climbers consider an 1854 climb of the Wetterhorn, likely its fifth or sixth ascent, the beginning of the golden age? Why did they embrace risk yet decry recklessness, or consciously ignore guides when crediting first ascents? And why, given this myopia, did they object when climbers went guideless? Ironies abound. An activity associated with nature and loners was ruled by urban joiners. A sport celebrating self-control and iconoclasm was dominated by the insecure and self-conscious. A culture that stresses action was shaped most by authors. Such contradictions can inspire cynicism, but they are also instructive.[4]

Mountaineering's inconsistencies mirrored the tensions of modernity. Urbanization and industrialization reshaped life in western Europe and eastern North America. Work and life were increasingly experienced inside buildings, factories, and offices that restructured human activities through the artificial frameworks of clocks and contracts. Success, especially for those middling professionals like Robert Underhill, was measured by one's place in corporate structures, the accrual of property, and the display of trinkets produced for the emerging consumer economy. The basis of identity that had dominated agrarian society was quickly fading, and with it access to the pastoral and wild places that were the focus of the popular landscape painters of the time. Very simply, the old ways of measuring success were losing meaning, the old paths to manhood fading.[5]

This was the environmental and cultural context in which sport erupted as an important masculine activity. Organized play offered young men a way to perform socially acceptable acts of dominance. The vigorous but orderly games of rounders, baseball, and soccer blossomed in culturally confusing cities, and rugby, football, and basketball thrived in anxiety-drenched schools. Many young men eagerly embraced these forms of play because they performed "an important role in redefining the criterion of middle-class masculinity, moving beyond the man's relationship to his work and family to include his character and physical self." As bringing home the bacon and counting coup became increasingly abstract, unpleasant, and impossible, sober feats of athleticism emerged as suitable surrogates for building character. They opened new avenues to moral masculinity, especially in cities and especially among young men from middling backgrounds who could not yet make propertied or matrimonial claims to manhood. Interest in mountain climbing was one expression of these trends. Peter Hansen notes that climbing "was preeminently a masculine sport. Scrambling among the Alps provided exposure to bodily risk and danger for men whose daily lives were governed by the rhythms of safety and security," yet mountaineering's role as a bourgeois sport and hearth of Victorian values came later.[6]

Climbing mountains was a rare, even bizarre activity in the early 1800s, but the paucity of historical attention to this era has less to do with rarity than the sport's shifting trajectory after 1850. Early mountaineering is largely treated as a prelude. There is friendly debate about the first mountaineer. Some cite Antoine de Ville for climbing Mont Inaccessible with ladders in 1492, others cite Petrarch for scaling Mont Ventoux in 1336, or various monks for wandering up peaks and over passes, or Hannibal for crossing the Alps in 218 BC, or even Ötzi, the unfortunate Bronze Age traveler found frozen in a Tyrolean glacier in 1991. All agree, however, that the first ascent of 15,782-foot Mont Blanc was a pivotal event. Briefly told, in the 1760s two wealthy Genevans, Horace Bénédict de Saussure and Marc Théodore Bourrit, became obsessed, and for twenty-five years each encouraged efforts to reach the mountain's top. Bourrit advocated incessantly, and Saussure offered a two-guinea reward. By the 1780s Saussure's bounty had enticed Michel Paccard, Jacques Balmat, and others from nearby Chamonix, and in August 1786, Balmat and Paccard reached the highest point in Europe. Although it was, like Mount Everest's South Col route, not technically difficult by later standards, the highly publicized climb, couched in unknown danger and spiced with ambition and envy, lent mountaineering romantic appeal.[7]

What followed was, if not a rush, at least a rising interest. Climbing remained a "minority taste" because few could afford or were willing to make the grueling trek to the remote villages of Chamonix, Grindelwald, Breuil, or Zermatt. Moreover, most readers who followed such exploits in the papers regarded these people as "an unclassified species of idiot." Nonetheless, mountaineers' motivations provide a useful reference for gauging changes by mid-century. The first principled rationale for climbing was science. To ascend in quest of knowledge, to measure the air, ice, and earth, was eminently respectable during this era of scientific exploration. Saussure made the third ascent of Mont Blanc and stayed on top for hours to conduct atmospheric experiments. James Forbes, Louis Agassiz, and John Tyndall followed this example, and some of their research was extraordinary. By the 1850s, though, the scientific merit of measuring temperature and pressure was losing credibility as a justification for further ascents.[8]

Whether science was ever more than a pretext for thrill seekers, more and more left their instruments behind and simply climbed for pleasure or sport. As early as 1792, four Englishmen admitted that they had climbed Mont Blanc for fun, and by the 1820s some treated the mountain like a race track, competing for times. Climbers also gained audiences. The Alps had been part of the Grand Tour of the wealthy and powerful since the 1700s, but by 1830 they were also populated by a growing legion of more modest tourists following word of mouth and John Murray's new *Handbook for Travellers to Switzerland*. Some climbers played to the crowd. On the advice of Jacques Balmat, a peasant girl named Marie Paradis ascended Mont Blanc in 1809 reputedly to market herself as "Marie Mont-Blanc," first female to reach the top. She was hardly alone. The Jungfrau and Bosses Ridge of Mont Blanc were sites of prolonged contest over their first ascents, and upon descent the first act of many more was to notify the London *Times* of their feat. Pleasure, sport, and fame infiltrated the sport very early, but the Alps' growing popularity requires a broader explanation.[9]

The growth of tourism draws us back to the consequences of modernity. Industrialization remade not only cities but their inhabitants. Accelerating productivity had concentrated wealth, improved transportation, and increased leisure time. In Europe and America, the emerging middle class had for the first time the means to pursue play, and railroads enabled them to reach Europe's inner sanctums. But while industrialization explains *how* massing tourists could gawk at and clamber over mountains, it does not tell us *why* they chose the Alps. For that we need to remember the importance of class consciousness. By the 1830s an increasingly self-confident bourgeoisie was defining itself in opposition to both the poor and the wealthy. Middling folk viewed themselves as superior to the working class by reason of their material success, and morally superior to both the lower and upper classes by virtue of their self-made and sober lifestyles. By Victoria's reign they had come into their own as an economic and cultural force. Recreation was one way they set themselves apart, and nature was a favored setting. Common wisdom says that Europeans regarded mountains as ugly and uninspiring until romantics redefined mountains as naturally sublime in the early 1800s. In fact this process began in the 1600s, and inclusion of the Alps in the Grand Tour of the upper classes suggests that they had recalibrated their Alpine sensibilities long before Rousseau, Turner, Wordsworth, Byron, and Ruskin. What changed by the mid-1800s was that the middle classes also thought it important to be sensible to the morally uplifting qualities of pastoral and wild landscapes. This is why so many urbanites were making pilgrimages to Alpine resorts by the 1830s.[10]

Climbers took these impulses further. For all the adoration of mountains, romantics such as John Ruskin preferred the Alps at arms' length. Like women, the sublime heights were most nobly loved from afar. Ruskin damned mountaineers for treating summits like soaped-pole contests, but they demurred. Climbers' physical engagement with nature produced an intimate knowledge unobtainable through distant gazes. They knew vertical nature in a way no passing tourist could ever grasp, yet their motives went beyond mere acquisition of special knowledge. As the sports craze gained steam, upper-middle-class Brits rejected the gentrified play of rowing, tennis, golf, and blood sports for activities that better expressed their sober values. Although mountaineering was not very popular, it did reinforce their views about class and gender. The expense of climbing—in Britain only elite angling, hunting, and yachting cost more—helped set participants apart as exceptional, and the physical and mental demands of climbing snow and ice, and costs of failure, served as a sporting equivalent of martial discipline. Mountaineering was serious play; it enabled young men to represent themselves as desert saints in contrast to the effete dandies of the salon. Mountaineering was "one of the ways in which a broadly defined middle class culture represented itself to itself," and the Alps provided the stage. Ruskin's restrained romanticism alone did not suffice. Growing interest in sport and material prosperity pushed many upper-middle-class men to penetrate Europe's virgin peaks in search of physical and psychic conquest.[11]

By the 1850s, the steady assault on the Alps became a British rush. Like Mont Blanc, most major early ascents had been made by continental climbers: Mont Perdu (1802) in the Pyrenees; the Jungfrau (1811), Finsteraarhorn (1829), and Wetterhorn (1844) in the Bernese Oberland; the Kleinglockner (1799), Grossglockner (1800), and Piz Bernina (1850) in the eastern Alps; and Mount Elbrus (1829) in the Caucasus. Victors were both very wealthy and very poor because early pilgrims of the vertical relied on impoverished locals

Figure 2.1. Edward Whymper's etching of two climbers *(lower left)* below the Dent du Géant, literally "the giant's tooth," conveys the sense of overwhelming nature that dominated early mountain art. Where Whymper and other climbers departed from Ruskin was in believing that the sublime was best known and loved through tactile engagement rather than distant contemplation.

to break paths and carry supplies. Like twentieth-century Himalayan Sherpas, nineteenth-century European peasants accepted this fitful and dangerous work because it was extraordinarily profitable. To gain greater control of this burgeoning economy, guides created the Compagnie des Guides de Chamonix in 1821, and in 1823 the Sardinian government sanctioned their monopoly. In the next three decades the guiding business grew steadily. Then peak bagging gained new energy from a new source. From 1854 to 1865 mountaineers conquered thirty-nine peaks over 13,000 feet plus many smaller peaks and passes. The British were responsible for at least thirty-one ascents. This quantum leap effectively eclipsed the past. Modern mountaineering history seemed instead to erupt all at once in 1854, as if time had rushed forward from Paccard and Balmat atop Mont Blanc to Alfred Wills astride the Wetterhorn, conveniently ignoring the fact that the latter peak had already been climbed several times.[12]

The resulting Anglophilic shadow over climbing history stems less from great ascents than the sport's institutionalization in London. By mid-century, hotels and chalets in Chamonix and other Alpine villages were catering to a stampede of British tourists with English-speaking staffs and Anglo-friendly fare. These were part of a regular circuit for upper-middling tourists, including climbers such as John Ball, Charles Hudson, Leslie Stephen, John Tyndall, and Alfred Wills. These accommodations were bastions of homogeneity amid exotic peoples and mountains, offering a warm welcome for anyone of like mind and background. Ironically, British mountaineers had no similar refuge back home, so in 1857 they invented one. Once established, London's Alpine Club was by default mountaineering's governing body. For six years the AC was the only organization in the sport, and its restrictive membership and publications made it a gatekeeper to mountaineering respectability. For many years reputations hung on admittance and publication by the AC. *Alpine Journal* was the authoritative voice of English-speaking climbers, and its style reinforced the linkage between adventure and genteel masculinity.[13]

Like the Alpine chalets, the AC was a nexus both for climbing and social advancement. Although the sport "enabled middle class men to make social and professional contacts in the Alps which were beyond their reach at home," most AC members were already poised to shape society. Climbing historian Arnold Lunn bragged that the club was dominated by Oxford and Cambridge graduates—hardly marginal figures in nineteenth-century England. The AC was "a cross-section of upper class England, and . . . its particular ethos was the creation of many men distinguished in other walks of life." Composed of professionals and entrepreneurs, the stereotypical AC member was urban, well educated, and dedicated to the Victorian status quo. This is why the club "exerted a strong grip on the cultural climate of the day, despite its small numbers, because the fingers of its members extended into every nook and cranny of British society." If the Alps was like a "giant country club for British professionals," then the AC was British mountaineering's equivalent of the Rotary Club. The AC's social and cultural contours matter because it was a force in defining the rules of the sport as a genteel pastime. Climbing's very liminality made it a badge of distinction, and climbers' play set them apart from the masses. Maintaining that distance was a principal and principled concern, and while being first or fastest was important, comportment and motives were also crucial.[14]

No subject was more central to the minds of Victorians than the question of risk. A signal quality of genteel manhood was responsibility. No matter how spectacular the feat, no gentleman gained respect if he seemed to abandon his duty to keep others safe. Mountaineering very obviously placed these two impulses in tension. The *Edinburgh Review* asked rhetorically, "Has a man a right to expose his life, and the lives of others, for an object of no earthly value, either to himself or his fellow creature? If life is lost in the adventure, how little does the moral guilt differ from that of suicide or murder?" Conversely, even that reticent romantic, John Ruskin, understood that much of the value of mountaineering derived from its manly tests:

> That question of the moral effect of danger is a very curious one; . . . if you come to a dangerous place, and turn back from it, though it may have been perfectly right and wise to do, still your *character* has suffered some slight deterioration; you are to that extent weaker, more lifeless, more effeminate, more liable to passion and error in future; whereas if you go through with the danger though it may have been apparently wrong and foolish to encounter it, you come out of the encounter a stronger and better man, fitter for every sort of work and trial, and *nothing but danger* produces this effect.

Risk had become—and remains—a double-edged element of the sport. Danger was a precondition for demonstrating nerve and virility, yet embracing such challenges imperiled masculine respectability.[15]

Victorian climbers tried to balance this contradiction with an ethic of safe climbing. Their solution exposed the cultural foundations of social and sporting legitimacy. The AC insisted that members train properly, avoid dangerous conditions, and use experienced guides. In 1870 it damned ascents that ignored such precautions as "totally unjustifiable and calculated to produce the most lamentable results." Professional guides were integral to proper climbing, but they were not equals. Like laborers and mercenaries, their work was crucial yet suspect because of their pecuniary interests. In Victorian thinking, professionalization tainted sport because money degraded labor; only the amateur possessed pure motives. First articulated by the eighteenth-century gentry to exclude working-class athletes from tournaments, Victorians educated in public schools appropriated this formulation to "develop their own social exclusivity." Lunn remarked that climbers "thought of guides much as an African explorer thought of natives. It was the function of the explorer to plan the expedition and to decide on its objective. It was the function of the native to relieve him of all unnecessary labour. 'I do not myself cut steps', wrote mountaineer Leslie Stephen, 'when I can get a guide to do it for me, first because a guide can do it much better; and secondly because he is paid to do it.'" Thus when it came time to recognize achievements, "it was the amateur, not the guide, who was the real leader" and deserved sole credit.[16]

Mountaineering history has been deeply influenced by these Victorian assumptions. Perhaps as Edward Whymper complained, many guides were merely "pointers out of paths and large consumers of meat and drink," but when it came to the most celebrated ascents of the nineteenth century, the record suggests otherwise. Whymper conquered the Pointe des Écrins only because of his guides' relentless efforts, and even at the height of his mountaineering proficiency, he seemed psychically dependent on Michel Croz. Horace Walker would not have climbed the Grandes Jorasses without brilliant help from Melchior Anderegg, Johann Jaun, and Julien Grange. Clinton Dent and J. Walker Hartley only scaled the Grand Dru because they were literally dragged up by Alexander Burgener and Kaspar Maurer, as was that paragon of ethics, Geoffrey Young, up the Grépon by Swiss, French, and Austrian guides. The most conspicuous case of this double standard was the Mummery Crack on the Grépon. Named for Albert Mummery, the pitch was first climbed by his guide, Benedikt Venetz, who then hauled up Mummery. Middle-class Victorians contrasted their love, that of the enlightened amateur, with the base lusts of prostitute guides. The former basked in the historical alpenglow of genteel conceits, while the latter, along with many European rivals and a number of women who climbed beside men and on their own, lingered in asterisked shadows. The only guides the AC deigned to acknowledge were those who had "already conformed by temperament or socialization to the standards of behavior and culture which the climbers expected." It is one of climbing's weirder paradoxes that a sport which champions the deed above the word has a history which celebrates identity as much as effort.[17]

The social and cultural biases of mountaineering might be debatable if early climbers had not been so explicit about their prejudices. For years the AC tried to break the Compagnie des Guides de Chamonix—Alfred Wills had once called it "rankest Communism"—so foreign tourists, not guides, controlled the price of services. Guides were not their sole annoyance. The AC was also alarmed by the growing horde of déclassé tourists. John Ruskin complained of "a Cockney ascent of Mont Blanc." Herman Merivale railed about Chamonix being overtaken by "the Cockneyism, the Albert Smithery, the fun, the frolic, and the vulgarity" that accompanied the masses. The strains of a Cockney accent at an Alpine hotel struck William Brockedon with "disbelief that such vulgarity could have reached the Great St. Bernard." As Leslie Stephen illustrated in the 1880s, though, Victorians were equal-opportunity snobs, as put off by "a genuine king" as by "the genuine British cockney in all his terrors." Both were "very objectionable neighbours at an hotel. They raise prices and destroy solitude and make an Alpine valley pretty nearly as noisy and irritating for the nerves as St James's." Victorian climbers mirrored John Muir in defining mountains as refuges from the commonplace.[18]

A similar candor attended climbing's role in masculinity. A common assumption was the necessity, as Charles Hudson wrote in 1853, of possessing "physical strength, moral strength, personal courage, and a good head." What did not need stating was that these were manly attributes. One reason Alfred Wills despised the Compagnie des Guides de Chamonix was that it crushed the "public spirit, independence, and self-respect" mountaineering offered. "It is only surprising that any manliness is left." Climbing made John Tyndall "feel in all my fires the blessedness of perfect manhood." Leo Amery wrote that mountaineering opened "a new and delightful chapter . . . in life, full of fresh air and strenuous exertion with just enough savour of adventure and risk to spice the whole." Novelist George Meredith made climbing a prescription for neurasthenics. "Carry your fever to the Alps, you of minds diseased: not to sit down in sight of them ruminating . . . but mount, rack the limbs, wrestle it out among the peaks; taste danger, sweat, earn rest: learn to discover ungrudgingly that haggard fatigue is the fair vision." A real man needed to "hang upon the crags at a gradient that makes your next step a debate between the thing you are and the thing you may become. . . . You are the man of your faculties, nothing more." Thus although most modern climbers balk at the subject of masculinity, Victorians had no such qualms. For them climbing was not simply intrinsic to masculine identity but a rationale they proudly broadcast.[19]

Perhaps the best exemplar was Edward Whymper. A lower-middle-class artisan whose life foreshadowed Royal Robbins a century later, Whymper understood as well as anyone how mastery in the Alps could result in advancement in London. Climbing was an inherently masculine pursuit, "essentially adapted to the young or vigorous, and not to the old or feeble." It was also preparation for bourgeois success. "We who go mountain-scrambling have constantly set before us the superiority of fixed purposes or perseverance to brute force. . . . [W]e know where there's a will there's a way; and we come back to our daily occupations better fitted to fight the battle of life, and to overcome the impediments which obstruct our paths, strengthened and cheered by the recollection of past labours, and by the memories of victories gained in other fields." As Fergus Fleming notes, when Whymper "strode into [Zermatt] he knew what he was worth." Moreover, he knew how to make his sport fungible through speaking engagements and by leading expeditions to Canada and South America.[20]

Yet the fulcrum for Whymper's fame was an ambivalent event. Rising starkly above the villages of Zermatt, Switzerland and Breuil, Italy, the Matterhorn (Il Cervina in Italy) was a coveted prize. Many tried its rocky and icy flanks, but three rivals stood out: Jean-Antoine Carrel, John Tyndall, and Edward Whymper. All sought the summit for personal and national glory, and each made repeated attempts to climb the seemingly easier ridge from the Col du Lion above Breuil. Victory came only when Whymper's party of three guides and four Englishmen shifted to the steeper but more feasible Hörnli Ridge above Zermatt. Whymper's favorite guide, Michel Croz, led the way, and on top they planted Croz's shirt as a victory flag and launched stones toward the Col du Lion to let Carrel's all-Italian team know they had been beaten. As the party began its descent, however, the inexperienced Robert Hadow stumbled and pulled Croz, Charles Hudson, and Lord Douglas to their deaths. The only reason Whymper and two other guides did not fall was that their "safety" rope broke. What should have been the crowning event of English mountaineering instead became an object lesson about the sport's omnipresent risks.[21]

The Matterhorn tragedy, combined with six other climbing fatalities that season, unleashed a storm of protest. Climbers defended themselves with talk of personal quests and manly testing, but the public and press were unimpressed. The London *Times, Chambers's Journal, Saturday Review,* and *Edinburgh Review* published editorials decrying irresponsibility. The *Times* likened mountaineering to "a succession of desperate adventures," and Charles Dickens remarked that when "'great and noble devotion,' as displayed in the Charge of the Light Brigade, was replaced by 'secondary and selfish interests and advantages, then, indeed, may we take leave of the glory of England.'" Even the Queen wondered whether Parliament should outlaw the sport. There had been similar rumblings in 1860 after three deaths on the Col du Géant, but criticism in 1865 was acute "because the cultural norms of Victorian death and mourning had been so completely violated" by Lord Douglas's death and disfigurement from his four-thousand-foot fall. Enrollment in the AC declined, and British mountaineers began to seem defensive and uncomfortably estranged from society.[22]

Climbing's rapprochement with Victorian respectability was halting and incomplete. The repairs that did occur took their cue from Dickens, elaborating mountaineering's social contributions in a literary genre that exploded in the decade after the Matterhorn and, perhaps because of the context, has always been obsessed with self-justification. Climbers re-emphasized the romantic, even transcendental power of mountains. A few such as Charles Hudson had long spoken of religious conversions on high peaks. More and more they began to describe mountains as a surrogate of religion. Sounding much like John Muir, John Tyndall thought there was "surely morality in the oxygen of the mountains. . . . Spirit and matter are interfused; the Alps improve us *totally.*" Leslie Stephen said mountains had a "mystic" voice that spoke "in tones at once more tender and more awe-inspiring than any mortal teacher." Many regarded themselves as explorers who contributed to Britain's imperial goals. Like quests to reach the poles, mountain ascents spread British influence and produced crucial geographical knowledge. By eschewing sensational aspects in favor of a "dry and obsessively factual" literary style, mountaineers also perfected a breathtakingly understated style of writing—what one writer has called the "and-so-we-climbed-to-the-top" school. Alpine Club members used these rhetorical strategies throughout the later nineteenth century in an attempt to persuade the public that climbers were agents of empire rather than thrill junkies.[23]

The Matterhorn accident ushered in that seeming transition. For more than a century historians have cited it as punctuating a golden age, the first and greatest period of Alpine climbing, but this break in continuity is overstated. The crusade against virgin peaks, including the Meije, Dent du Géant, and Blanche de Peuterey, took two more decades to complete, while the creation of new, more challenging routes up previously ascended peaks was already well underway, beginning with the 1855 Saint-Gervais route on Mont Blanc. Guideless climbing also began in the 1850s with A. G. Girdlestone, Charles Hudson, T. S. Kennedy, and the Parker brothers, and British climbers had ventured farther afield since Charles Packe explored the Pyrenees in the 1850s. Still, unclimbed peaks *were* rarer, the ambitious *had* to shift from summits to ridges and pinnacles to gain new firsts, and climbers *did* begin to climb rock as well as snow and ice. As Clinton Dent noted wryly in 1876, older climbers had "picked out the plums and left us stones." Wealthy Brits began to travel to Spitsbergen, the Caucasus Mountains, the Rockies, New Zealand's Alps, and the Himalaya to distinguish themselves, while middling climbers worked out new relationships with the Alps and joined a community whose demography and fealty to Victorian values were rapidly evolving.[24]

The first major challenge to the AC's dominance in the Alps was the surge of humanity. Shortly after mid-century English entrepreneur Thomas Cook began to capitalize on the interest in the Alps that Ruskin and other romanticists had fueled in the previous decades. Each year Cook shuttled more and more tourists to Alpine resorts. By the early 1870s the Cockney twang that Leslie Stephen so reviled was muffling Oxbridge accents. More significantly, British dominance was drowning under a tsunami of European visitors as well. Then in 1863 the AC's exclusive status ended when both Swiss and Italian climbers formed national clubs, followed in 1869 by Austria and in 1874 by Germany and France. Like the AC, these new clubs were populated by upper-middling professionals from industrial cities with blossoming sports cultures, but that was nearly all they had in common. While the AC never topped 300 members, the Deutscher und Österreichischer Alpen-Verein alone counted 18,000 members in 1874, and Club Alpin Français, Club Alpino Italiano, and Schweizer Alpen-Club totaled nearly 12,000 members by 1884. The rank and file of these clubs were also more diverse, including not only elite mountaineers but casual scramblers and hill walkers from a much broader cross section of society. All were swarming over the Alps and some were beating the British to the best mountaineering prizes.[25]

When British mountaineer Arthur Cust surveyed these events in 1870, he prophesied a growing spectrum of climbing styles. At one extreme was a modest approach to mountain enjoyment emphasizing "a community-oriented sharing of scientific and recreational activity in the Alps, or *Alpenkunde.*" Like the AC, continental clubs tried to regulate guides, but they also offered insurance for guides, constructed huts for travelers, and placed ropes on popular routes to enhance safety. Unlike the AC, they wanted to expand the definition of and participation in mountaineering. At the spectrum's other end a few Europeans were even more dedicated to imperial mountaineering than the British. Jean-Antoine Carrel had dreamed of conquering the Cervina (Matterhorn) for Italy years before Whymper thought to climb it, and the Sella and Maquingnaz families waged a similar but more successful campaign to beat English climbers to the top of the Dent du Géant. The continental counterpoint to Victorian climbing was by turns both more democratic and more explicitly nationalistic.[26]

Continental climbers also pushed the edges of mountaineering individualism. At a time when Victorians roundly criticized guideless climbing, a few German, Austrian, and Swiss climbers embraced soloing. Stephan Steinberger and J. J. Weilenmann made solo first ascents before 1860; after 1870 Hermann von Barth, Paul Güssfeldt, Ludwig Purtscheller, Otto and Emil Zsigmondy, Eugen Guido Lammer, and Georg Winkler refined soloing into an art. This was not always intentional. Many climbed first as students, when soloing was simply a practical response to fiscal and time constraints. By the 1880s, though, some such as Lammer and the Zsigmondys began to see sport as a poignant expression of their will to power or, as Wilhelm Lehner remarked, a way to awaken the climber's "dormant sense of mastery." In their quest to realize the inner self, they were as much at odds with their own national clubs as with the AC, opposing not only guides but huts, ropes, even partners—anything that intruded between man and mountain. Widely criticized, these antiestablishmentarians found few like Arthur Cust, who prophesied that "the only way real mountaineers would be able to [continue to] differentiate themselves would be by banding together to go without guides."[27]

Most Victorians reacted as if the barbarians were at the gates. For romantics like Leslie Stephen, the mountains were the "antithesis not so much of the plains as the commonplace. . . . There we can breathe the air that has not passed through a million pair of lungs." Devotion was a meritocracy. Those who loved the Alps best "have wandered longest in their recesses, and have most endangered their own lives and those of their guides in the attempt to open out routes amongst them." Having earned a claim through risk, Victorians were loathe to share their rarified playground with the unworthy. As with the fight to preserve the English Lake District several decades earlier, the AC lobbied against railways and even commercial photographers. Yet their rants against Cockneys, peasants, and soloists revealed an aesthetic as much concerned with social exclusion as Alpine preservation. Learning of plans to build a funicular railway up the Jungfrau, a British minister complained that the Swiss were "vulgarising the 'playground of Europe,'" and A. F. Mummery regarded a proposed tramway up the Matterhorn as a class affront. "To ascend the Matterhorn in a steam lift, and all the time remember that brave men have been killed by mere stress of difficulty on its gaunt, ice-bound cliffs, will be to the Cockney and his congeners unmixed delight." Very simply, the AC "did not like to share the Alps with the 'mob of trippers.'" The mountains were private shrines. With no hint of irony, H. E. M. Stutfield wrote, "Our Holy of Holies lies ensconced somewhere in the recesses of the everlasting snows. Their invasion by unorthodox people, or in unorthodox ways, is to us a profanation of hallowed mysteries."[28]

Growing heterogeneity exposed rifts between continental and British traditions that the life of Alfred Mummery only underscored. Born wealthy but slightly hunchbacked, Mummery never looked it but was Britain's leading mountaineer in the 1880s and 1890s. He could walk forever and climb superbly. By the mid-1880s he was making audacious ascents with his guide, Alexander Burgener, setting bold new standards with an 1886 route up the Grépon. His merchant background offended some members, however, and he was initially blackballed. The scorn was mostly misplaced. Mummery shared many Victorian sensibilities. His writings were typically understated and celebrated mountaineering's imperial, romantic, and spiritual facets. He used guides, distrusted technology, and exemplified that late-Victorian merger of cerebral and physical masculinity, arguing that climbing allowed man to gain "knowledge of himself, a love of all that is most beautiful in nature, and an outlet such as no other sport affords for the stirring of energies of youth." Like his peers, Mummery counseled the importance of safety, of physical and mental fitness, of never thrusting "into places where he is hopelessly mastered and dominated by his environment."[29]

Yet in crucial ways he broke with Victorian mountaineering, and in the end his career spoke more to emerging continental traditions. While others downplayed risk, Mummery insisted it was integral to the value of sport. There was "an educative and purifying power in danger that is to be found in no other school, and it is worth much for a man to know that he is not 'clean gone to flesh pots and effeminacy.'" "Our best efforts," he believed, "must sometimes be seconded by the great goddess of Luck," and any "increase in the skill [of the climber] involves, *pari passu* an increase in the difficulties grappled with." It was incumbent to embrace risk. The "aesthetic value of an ascent generally varies with its difficulty," so "the most difficult way up the most difficult peaks is always the right thing to attempt." Any less was only "worthy of the fibreless contents of fashionable clothes, dumped with all their scents and ointments, starched linen and shiny boots, at Zermatt by the railway." By 1890 even guides seemed "destructive of all proper self-respect and of every feeling of self-reliant manliness." Only the independent climber was "free from all these baneful and blighting influences." Thus he cut the cord to Burgener and repeated the Mummery Crack alone. He then joined a growing imperial army of British mountaineers in the Caucasus and Himalaya. In 1895, Mummery published *My Climbs in the Alps and Caucasus* and died on India's 26,657-foot Nanga Parbat. The AC eulogized him as "a gymnast of almost unique skill," "'reckless'—but in no evil sense." They even claimed his audacious style as "essentially English," but they did not emulate him. In reality, Mummery had mocked the staid AC and shared much more in common with continental climbers such as the Zsigmondys, Purtscheller, and Lammer.[30]

The more Europeans framed their preferences in spiritual terms, the more their differences seemed like sectarian spats over motives, comportment, and aesthetics, a set of issues later oversimplified as "climbing ethics." One church disdained anything that mediated between man and nature. Their prophets were Mummery and the Austrian scientist Paul Preuss, who made over 1,200 climbs, 300 of which were solos and 150 of which were first ascents. Preuss even codified his theology with six theorems that argued safety was paramount and that mountaineers must be superior to any route attempted, able to ascend and descend without help from tools, ropes, or partners. As his eulogist noted, Preuss articulated not so much a personal ethics as a "mountaineering morality" with nonnegotiable terms. Geoffrey Young and the AC led an equally strident sect of British and French climbers who agreed with Preuss about the importance of safety and disdain for technology, but they were torn by guideless ascents and could not abide the practice of soloing. Both denominations regarded free climbing (ascending only by means of hands and feet) as the only true form of sport, and their bêtes noires were the agnostics who were increasingly using new gear to aid the ascent of challenging routes. This is why Arnold Lunn portrayed the 1883 first ascent of the Dent du Géant, a rock pillar on Mont Blanc, with pitons and fixed ropes as climbing's moment of original sin.[31]

These techniques have come to be called modern *aid climbing,* and the hearth of this approach was the Dolomites of northeastern Italy. This range of sheer limestone walls had little snow or ice and required excellent rock climbing skills on small holds with few places to use standard protection. British climbers were put off, so Germans, Austrians, and Italians dominated by default. Purtscheller and the Zsigmondys first used pitons in the 1880s, and by 1900 Hans Dülfer, Otto Herzog, and Hans Fiechtl had refined and systematized aid climbing. They forged harder pitons for the thinner cracks, steel snap-links (*carabiners*) to connect pitons to the rope, and rope ladders (*etriers*) to attach to pitons. They also created new techniques such as a body belay to hold falls, a way to wrap the rope around a body and rappel downward, and a method of penduluming past holdless areas. The result was "a self-consciously modern practice that dramatically changes the cultural meanings of mountaineering"—one quickly scorned by the English. Young prided himself for using only two pitons, and R. L. G. Irving famously derided carabiners as "un-English in name and nature." Yet Victorian disdain also reflected geological contingencies. The western Alps were broken ranges with many outcroppings around which climbers could drape their bodies and ropes. English climbers did not need new tools and techniques to climb safely, so like contemporary hunters and anglers, they saw valor in limiting one's resources. Elite sportsmen had long regarded inefficient weapons as superior tools because they gave their quarry a fighting chance. Similarly, English mountaineers eschewed aid climbing to "give the mountain a chance," as though it was a sentient opponent. As Young argued, "Getting to the top is nothing. How you do it is everything."[32]

By the early 1900s modern technical climbers were pushing new routes up the biggest, most dangerous faces in the Alps. In 1907, Tita Piaz ascended the sheer, 1,200-foot southeast face of Torre Est. In 1910 Angelo Dibona, Luigi Rizzi, and Guido and Max Mayer scaled the 2,600-foot north face of Cima Una. After the Great War continental climbers pushed the envelope on precipitous routes ranging from the 1,000-foot *Ha-He Dihedral* on the Dreizinkenspitze to the Marmolata's 1,800-foot south pillar. Then they turned to the ice-encrusted, storm-ravaged north faces of the Matterhorn, Cima Grande di Lavaredo, Drus, Piz Badile, Grandes Jorasses, and Eiger. In 1931, Franz and Toni Schmid bagged the Matterhorn, and in the next seven years Austrian, French, German, and Italian climbers threw themselves at the other *nordwands*. The resulting toll—three dead on the Grandes Jorasses, eight on the Eiger—horrified the British, who dismissed this "hysterical frenzy" as mere engineering, "heresies," "perversions" and "appalling" "imbecile variants" by "mentally deranged" "extremists." The AC howled with outrage, but they could not stanch the trend toward ever greater risk and ever more aid.[33]

Principles of style hardened into nationalistic fault lines, yet in the mountains sweeping moralisms often reverted to personal ethics—that is, *thou*

Figure 2.2. European rope technique. This study reveals the limitations of European safety practices in the 1890s: the belayer is in an insecure stance, and the rope is not clearly anchored to anything other than an ice axe.

shalt became *if reasonable.* Extremists such as Barth, who once exclaimed that "Who goes with me must be ready to die," were not all that different from the Zsigmondys, Winkler, and Preuss, all of whom died young and alone on mountains. Most mountaineers, though, were more flexible. The pale of style was instead a contingent threshold of acceptable risk. Technological tolerance hinged on one's comfort level. Although still couched as a moral failure, even Preuss allowed for "the use of artificial aids . . . in case of sudden threatening danger." The line between free and aid climbing was similarly subjective. When Young made the first ascent of the east face of the Grépon with H. O. Jones, Ralph Todhunter, and guides Joseph Knubel and Henri Brocherel, they used no pitons but, to pass a difficult overhang, Knubel stood on Brocherel's shoulders, jammed his ice axe in a crack, and pulled up to pass the crux. "The Knubel Crack" was celebrated as the hardest pitch in the Alps, yet similarly difficult climbs by European rivals were derided because they had used pitons to protect their belays. Climbing ethics was not so much a fixed set of values as a personal and provincial sliding scale.[34]

Genteel principle thrived within the homosocial confines of the Alpine Club, but beyond London the sport grew increasingly diverse, especially with a rash of clubs formed at the turn of the century: national organs in South Africa (1891), the United States (1902), Canada (1906), Japan (1906), and Norway (1908), and local groups like the Climbers Club (1898), Cambridge University Mountaineering Club (1905), Oxford Climbing Club (1906), and Fell and Rock Climbing Club (1906). The latter, for example, were rock climbers from the Lake District who shared little with the Alpine Club's snow and ice enthusiasts. Every club's exclusion of guides also exacerbated the estrangement of professionals from amateurs. Even more extreme were the self-consciously elitist Munich Academic Alpine Club, Groupe des Rochassiers, and Groupe de Haute Montagne. Members further distinguished themselves with pins, ties, and buttons, while internal schisms tore clubs apart. When merchants began to outnumber professionals in the AC, the latter initiated a prolonged discussion over whether social status should influence membership. Club Alpin Français endured repeated rifts between cultural elites, sporting elites, and recreationists, and "modernists" and "traditionalists" squared off in many clubs over the virtue of technology and climbing in local or distant ranges. By 1930, mountaineering was so diverse it was silly to speak of a single culture, yet that is exactly what Robert Underhill did when he met the Sierra Club in 1931.[35]

To understand Underhill's significance, we must place him in context. He was arguably the most influential American climber to come out of Europe before 1930, but he was hardly the first. By 1878 there were at least nine American ascents of Mont Blanc, and enough countrymen climbed in the Alps for Arthur Cust to dismiss the lot as vulgar peak baggers. The two exceptions were wealthy expatriates Meta Brevoort and her nephew William Coolidge, who lived in England, climbed extensively, and made many first female and first winter ascents. Coolidge eventually joined the AC (Brevoort was excluded by sex) and became the sport's leading historian, mastering minutiae and passing judgment with Victorian zeal. By 1900, Americans Edward Arthur Fitzgerald, Samuel Turner, Annie Peck, Fanny Bullock Workman, and William Hunter Workman trod the great ranges of South America, New Zealand, South Asia, and Siberia with the same mix of personal ambition and nationalistic hubris that marked European contemporaries. Well before Underhill entered the Alps, American climbers already ranged from casual funseekers to egotistical imperialists, and the spectrum broadened when Fritz Wiessner, a German engineer who had accomplished extreme aid and free climbs in Europe in the 1920s, emigrated to the United States in 1927. Underhill was not blind to this diversity. Wiessner was a regular partner, but Underhill's background had prepared him to omit what did not please his Anglophilic sensibilities.[36]

Put another way, Robert Underhill's attitudes reflected the times. As in Europe, industrialization remade America in the nineteenth century. The urban Northeast became a cultural hothouse. Cities grew more polyglot, opportunity expanded yet became more elusive, and political machines overwhelmed a Protestant and patrician order that had dominated America for nearly three centuries. Unease infected even that bastion of privilege and power, Harvard. The college's leading symbol of manliness was William James, America's premier man of letters and a firm believer that success stemmed from conquering the self through a martial dedication to physical and moral fitness. James represented the quest for muscular self-possession. He was a walking example of the self-made man for students such as G. Stanley Hall, Theodore Roosevelt, Owen Wister, and, eventually, Robert Underhill, all of whom would proselytize primitiveness, the vigorous life, and muscular Christianity as cures for a perceived malaise of neurasthenic effeminacy among middle-class men. And like their counterparts in England and on the continent, middle-class Americans self-consciously distinguished themselves through modes of consumption and social activities that included vigorous physicality. As one historian notes, "many middle-class men, faced with lowered career expectations, [found their] identity in leisure instead of work."[37]

When leisure blossomed as a vehicle for American masculinity, middling and wealthy Americans mirrored Europeans by developing forms of play that were as much about identity as leisure. They infused athletics with ideals of manliness, but the popularity of the new sports created a double bind. As more young men embraced games like baseball and football, the less athletically gifted turned to more esoteric activities to distinguish themselves. Some practiced conspicuous consumption at Saratoga or Newport, others attended Chautauquas, hunted and fished for rare game, or visited dude ranches and national parks. When primitive life emerged as a manly ideal in the 1890s, young men were urged to recapitulate racial evolution by stripping away their civilized selves. Thomas Higginson told affluent Bostonians to return, at least briefly, to the forest and discover their Indianlike pasts. Enthusiasts followed Ernest Thompson Seton and embraced woodcraft, scouts, and back-to-the-land fads such as recreating the Voyageur culture of Canada's early history. One man remarked admiringly that a friend "was never so truly himself as when looking into the bright face of danger." Others such as Wister, Roosevelt, and Frederic Remington compensated for their Ivy League backgrounds by heading west to emulate that great manly symbol of the nineteenth century, the cowboy.[38]

Only rarely did Americans turn uphill. In the 1870s, William James was one of few who climbed mountains to merge vigorous sport with a romantic appreciation of nature. More spectacularly, Clarence King and John Muir, educated at Yale and the University of Wisconsin, respectively, roamed the Sierra for adventure and for science. Although bitter rivals, they told remarkably similar tales about wild nature. Both relayed exhilarating experiences of death-defying acts in prose that fused identity with adventure. Both also practiced Tyndall's scientific approach to mountain study—King even named a Sierra peak for him—and Whymper's masculine form of narration, and both adventurers attracted cults of admirers. King's accounts would lubricate his way into Washington's inner circles of power, while Muir's works propelled him to scientific respectability and the forefront of nature advocacy.[39]

Early American mountaineers were disparate and idiosyncratic, yet they were highly compatible with British mountaineers of their era. When AC member H. E. M. Stutfield declared that "We seek by mountaineering to improve our minds and morals as well as our muscles; and a likeness of muscular Christianity may be said to be the result," he shared the same cultural ground as when American climber John Case boasted that he never used a piton because they were crutches for incompetents. No less than Europeans, middling Americans yearned to escape the commonplace, but all their desires were so entwined with everyday life that it is impossible to understand their drive toward the peaks outside that broader, more mundane context. Rather than an escape, mountain play accented modernity through experiences that distinguished participants even as they continued to navigate their middle-class lives. The quest for vigorous respites actually laid bare their connection to an urban, highly educated society of consumers.[40]

American clubs institutionalized the links between play, identity, and modernity. Settlers had scaled peaks since the 1600s, but only after 1850, when wealthy Americans began to follow Brits into the Alps, did mountaineering become a sport. In 1863 Professor Albert Hopkins formed the Alpine Club of Williamstown, Massachusetts, and in 1876 Bostonians started the Appalachian Mountain Club (AMC). Out west William Gladstone Steel founded the Oregon Alpine Club in 1887 and, more elaborately, the Mazamas formed on the summit of Mount Hood in 1894. Other clubs followed, including Muir's Sierra Club in 1892 and the Seattle Mountaineers in 1906. Historians have characterized these clubs as middle-class organs that stressed scientific enlightenment, sober adventure, and cultural propriety. While accurate in its parts, the description fails to capture the sense of elitism that guided members. Lists of club officers mirrored the social register. As Michael Cohen notes, the Sierra Club was filled with "prominent Bay Area professors, scientists, politicians, and business leaders." The few Americans who visited the Alps were considered even more extraordinary because only the very wealthy could afford the time and expense of an overseas holiday. Based in Chamonix and Zermatt, they rubbed elbows with the AC, Club Alpin Français, and Schweizer Alpen-Club, and their experiences distinguished them when they returned home. Their stories spread rapidly among North America's rapidly growing climbing clubs, many of which shared members and publications, ensuring that lessons learned in one corner of the continent quickly made the rounds.[41]

It was also around the turn of the century that these clubs merged sport and environmental politics. John Muir was the most famous mountaineer advocate, but at the time the most influential club was the AMC, and the most networked climber was Charles Fay. Like the Sierra Club and other American climbing organizations, the AMC melded play and advocacy into a paternalistic agenda consciously aimed at social uplift. Fay, who was a Tufts University professor and AMC president, championed these cultural politics. He lured new members on any grounds because a growing club's "power for wider good becomes incalculable." Like Muir, Fay believed that the "cultivation of the love of nature is an aesthetic education, and like that of music and art contributes to the higher level of civilization." Environmental culture was a central concern of many mountaineering clubs. "A love of wild nature," Fay argued, "presupposes a profound interest in those movements that look to the preservation for public enjoyment and health of those naturally beautiful places in our immediate surroundings for which the spirit of commercialism cares nothing and would not scruple to destroy." Like the Victorians, Fay, Muir, and other American mountaineers viewed clubs as recruiting organs for quests that were as much about nature, identity, and consumerism as about climbing.[42]

Fay spoke widely and effectively for those who had sacralized peaks as private *and* civic shrines. Many regarded the mountains as refuges for spiritual and physical rejuvenation. Fay "stressed the special value of climbing to develop for the benefit of the state a staunch physique and moral stamina in the citizenry." The Mazamas' C. H. Sholes remarked that the "great charm of mountain-climbing in America, and especially in our magnificent ranges on the Pacific Coast, is the fact that the mountains are free to those who seek to derive from them the joy of unaided conquest." Muir, who was councilor and president to the American Alpine Club (AAC) that Fay formed in 1902, implored the "tired, nerve-shaken, over-civilized people . . . to find out that going to the mountains is going home; that wilderness is a necessity." In other words, many American mountaineers had cast mountains as stages for private and national advancement long before Robert Underhill became a leading proponent of moral mountaineering in the late 1920s.[43]

Underhill epitomized the genteel American who climbed for personal pride and pleasure. Although he made his first technical climb in the Alps in 1909, academia diverted him after 1914. Not until 1925, when his academic career began to stall, did he turn back to the peaks. That year he studied with Swiss and Italian guides, and then in 1926 forged the first of his own routes in the White Mountains, Adirondacks, and Rockies. He joined the Harvard Mountaineering Club, Appalachian Mountain Club, Schweizer Alpen-Club, and Club Alpino Italiano, assumed editorial duties for the AMC journal *Appalachia*, wrote essays on technique, and founded a rock climbing group. Although less talented than the top Europeans of the era, by 1931 Underhill was regarded as North America's preeminent mountaineer. He had achieved major ascents on the Mont Blanc Massif and Bernese, Pennine, Dauphine, Grisons, and Dolomites Alps, including the first traverse of the Aiguilles du Diable in 1928 with his future wife Miriam O'Brien and their mutual guide Armand Charlet. Then only weeks before he traveled to the Sierra, Underhill made the first ascent of Grand Teton's North Ridge, at the time the most committing route in North America. If Underhill's talents and tenacity distinguished him among American mountaineers, his privileged background had also opened opportunities few others could enjoy and contributed to a distinctly genteel perspective of the sport.[44]

Underhill's advantages matter because his social networks were crucial to Yosemite history. He climbed a wide arc of peaks with but a narrow range of companions. Early partners Willard Helburn, Ken Henderson, Lincoln

O'Brien (brother of Miriam), and Leland Pollock were fellow Harvard men who used the same European guides: Franz Josef Biner, Armand Charlet, and Adolf Rubi. This small circle developed a strong bias for free climbing over aid climbing. As climber Roger Frison-Roche noted, Charlet "respected the traditions of his elders; he did not trouble himself with pitons, ignored the potential of carabiners, was able to free climb pitches of over thirty meters in nail-soled shoes with no protection and, when the overhang became too extreme, used risky ice axe holds" rather than pitons. Underhill recalled Biner fondly as "a true lover of the mountains. He was a guide, but he wasn't [tainted as] a strict professional." At a time when bold climbers were rushing Europe's last virgin walls, Robert Underhill instead gravitated toward the resilient values of Victorian amateurism. Like Young and the AC, he viewed mountains as refuges of masculine adventure that technology only demeaned.[45]

Indeed and ironically, it was Underhill's insularity that led him to the Sierra Nevada. In 1930, the Harvard Mountaineering Club traveled to the Selkirks, a jagged range in the interior of British Columbia whose very remoteness, like the Alps, underscored these visitors' exceptional resources. The outing, which included Underhill and an accountant from San Francisco named Francis Farquhar, ascended many peaks, but long weeks in the backcountry also forced members to exercise social skills. Underhill and Farquhar found much in common. Nearly the same age, both hailed from affluent eastern families and had earned degrees from Harvard—Underhill an A.M. in 1910 and Ph.D. in 1916, Farquhar an A.B. in 1909. Both had also started climbing in the White Mountains and were active in their clubs—Farquhar in the SC and AAC—as officers, writers, and editors. Finally, both were forty-something bachelors, and mountains were their principal passion. If Farquhar had found greater professional success as an accountant than Underhill had attained in academia—the latter was nearing his end as a Harvard tutor—Underhill was the more honored climber and author. They were thus peers and rough equals. Farquhar admired Underhill's climbs and essays, so it was no surprise that as the editor of the *Sierra Club Bulletin* he would ask Underhill to write a treatise on technique; and it seemed natural, given all they had in common, that Underhill would accept an invitation to instruct the Sierra Club during its 1931 outing.[46]

It seemed equally natural that Underhill would handpick a few Sierrans for special training. At the end of the outing, he and Farquhar headed south with what amounted to the founding pillars of the holy church of Sierra mountaineering. The select included Lewis Clark, Norman Clyde, Elmer Col-

BODY BELAY
A—Hip Belay   B—Sideways Shoulder Belay
C—Forward Shoulder Belay (incorrect)   D—Forward Shoulder Belay (correct)

Figure 2.3. This illustration from 1931 shows the belayer in a more stable stance with greater rope friction for climbers ascending from below, but none of this was much good for a climber leading above. Richard Leonard would soon revise these techniques.

lett, Glen Dawson, Jules Eichorn, Bestor Robinson, and Neill Wilson. They visited the Minarets and Palisades, scaling the hardest routes yet in the Sierra, including a first ascent of Thunderbolt Peak, so named because lightning zapped Eichorn during a hurried retreat from the summit. As they moved southward to the range's highest peaks, the group shrank to Underhill, Farquhar, Clyde, Eichorn, and Dawson. The ascent of Mount Whitney's east face marked the technical and cultural apogee of the trek. Underhill called it "our culminating effort." The expedition's greatest impact was on its youngest member, nineteen-year-old Glen Dawson, who wrote that of all the things Underhill conveyed about "the art of correct climbing with a rope," the most important lesson was that the "rope is intended for safety and not as a physical aid." As obvious as his point may seem to modern climbers, Dawson's simple explanation contained a much broader history of the culture of serious play.[47]

Although western climbers already knew that European methods existed, likening Underhill to Moses still makes sense. Farquhar gave him a chance not just to teach technique but to define the parameters of sport. Consider that for a moment, and his Sierra visit gains new depth. Underhill had already written much about technique, and Farquhar had already instructed members the week before Underhill arrived at Garnet Lake. Underhill did not *need* to visit California to teach knots or rope work, and in hindsight his belay lesson, which taught climbers to wrap the rope around a rock projection or an arm, was potentially harmful. Similarly, his essay parroted advice from many earlier tracts, including Geoffrey Young's *Mountain Craft*. What was novel, at least to readers of the *Sierra Club Bulletin*, was his cultural agenda. His exhortations to eschew technological aids, that "*the purpose of the rope is protective only;* under ordinary conditions, *it may never, with propriety, be used as a direct help in climbing,*" had less to do with safety than with genteel sport. Likening climbers to military comrades and ascribing leadership to the "virtue" of "natural capacity" and "inborn talent and natural instinct," Underhill echoed Victorian beliefs about the innate nature of masculine, physical superiority. In many respects he simply echoed Alpine Club wisdom when he told readers that, "According to amateur standards . . . no pitch has really been climbed where the direct aid of the rope has been resorted to, and since failure to climb any single pitch generally means failure to make the peak itself, no peak where this has occurred can properly be included in a climbing record." In fact, Underhill did less to assure safety than to preserve the moral purity of sport.[48]

Historical perspective suggests that the context and contingencies of Underhill's audience were also crucial. If he had spoken to a different group of climbers, especially someone as talented and experienced as Fritz Wiessner, Underhill might have tempered his Victorian enthusiasms. There *were* rival ideas about technology and ethics among his peers, and he knew it. Western climbing was thus not predestined to embrace one particular set of values. Nothing was inevitable, but the networks that carried Underhill to the Sierra—his personal and educational connections to elite climbers in the East and Europe—had shaped him in peculiar ways. In this sense the man and the message were inextricably linked because Underhill's genteel roots had predisposed him to endorse some values but not others. And by being the first to proselytize to the Sierra Club, a group with little exposure to the nuances of eastern and European climbing, he was able to convert technical prowess into moral authority. In a way few climbers consider, Underhill *was* the lawgiver, defining for future generations not only how one should climb but what climbing should mean.

Few climbers consider the genealogy of their ideals. They instead believe culture to flow organically from a physical encounter with nature or patron saint rather than from a tortuous and sometimes tortured social history. For example, many assert that John Muir inspired modern Yosemite climbing. As early as 1939 Dick Jones claimed that the "Sierra Club's first president, John Muir, was a master at solo climbing . . . , so rock climbing for the Sierra Club is rooted deep in its past."[49] More recently Royal Robbins and Yvon Chouinard have portrayed Muir as a "true mountaineer," and Gary Arce has called Muir "Yosemite's original climbing bum." All of them simplify the past. Robbins has said Muir's "biggest impact upon the American climbing world" was "his message of the sacredness of the natural order and the desirability of leaving it natural and unsullied," while Chouinard has celebrated Muir's philosophy of "going into the wilderness but leaving no trace of having been there." Both transform Muir into a spiritual visionary, a nineteenth-century Dharma Bum who reveled in wild nature and lived like a preternatural biocentrist. The historical Muir complicates these claims.[50]

In many ways Muir was unexceptional. Recent biographers view his "orthodox Christian values" as paralleling American Protestantism at the time, and his evangelical temperament stemmed from his Campbellite Presbyterian roots. Even his rebellious shift from the Bible to nature was part of a broader trend at the time, as was his selective defense of nature. Although he adored cathedral-like Hetch Hetchy, he endorsed re-engineering the Tulare Basin as an industrial livestock fiefdom. And although Muir completed solo ascents, like other ambitious climbers he converted private adventures into social events through writings that delineated who did and did not belong in nature. The chosen included "tired, nerve-shaken, over-civilized" urbanites, while rural laborers and Indians had "no right place in the landscape." At moments Muir was anything but exceptional in the history of how people related to nature through outdoor sport, and he never quite stood for the ideals that Robbins and Chouinard attribute to him.[51]

We should recognize that modern debates about techniques and tools derive less from Muir than from genteel Victorians and later sporting contexts. Muir wanted to ban sheep and Indians from his mountains, yet in 1875 he nearly burst with ethnic pride when a fellow Scot "resolutely drilled his way" up on the first ascent of Half Dome. The source of Yosemite climbers' ideas about ropes, pitons, and bolts comes not from the mystical Muir but from the staid Alpine Club of London. The principles that frame modern climbing and other outdoor sports still echo Victorian obsessions about class, gender, and national prestige. Muir did tie together wilderness climbing and environmental mysticism—and modern climbers are still inspired by his writings—yet Muir was hardly the only one to draw such links. King, Zsigmondy, and Mallory expressed similar emotions, but even acknowledging this broader group misses the key point. Ultimately, it was genteel easterners such as Roosevelt, Wister, and Underhill who carried modern sporting ethics westward. In battling for the wild, they sought to preserve both the world, as Henry David Thoreau put it, and genteel manhood. Thus while Muir inspired people to embrace wild nature, how they interacted with it and each other exposed a far more complex history.[52]

Thus the history of Yosemite climbing involves more than a retelling of Underhill's errand into the wilderness. The apostles who accompanied Underhill to the High Sierra and then converted to his Victorian theology were key figures in the sport's future. Yosemite climbing did begin as a genteel masculine endeavor, yet once Clyde, Dawson, Eichorn, Farquhar, Lewis, and Robinson left the mountains at the end of that summer, they had to accommodate social and environmental factors Underhill never accounted for in his brief visit to California. Moreover, the most influential climber of the coming era was about to draw upon a much broader array of influences as he initiated technical climbing in Yosemite Valley. Put another way, an already intricate cultural genealogy of sport only grew more complicated the moment Robert Underhill departed, and like his visit, the next generation offers far richer stories than we have so far recognized.

3. PIONEERS

As the spirit of adventure or the spirit of the pioneer pushed the
49r's West, so the 39r's in the Club today are pioneering up.
—DICK JONES

Although Robert Underhill is an important figure in the history of American
climbing, the celebration of him has eclipsed the continuity and innovative-
ness of western climbers at the time. For one thing, Underhill's impact depended considerably on his audience already possessing certain skills. Thus
his "students," several of whom were noted mountaineers in their own right,
also deserve recognition. Norman Clyde was the preeminent peak bagger
of the 1920s. He had collected more than 250 ascents and forty firsts just
since 1925. Francis Farquhar had been climbing for decades, and he, too,
had made several important first ascents. Lewis Clark had grown up in the
Sierra Club and regarded climbing as a normal part of every summer, while
Bestor Robinson was emerging as one of the most ambitious climbers of the
era. Even the youngest members of the expedition had been climbing since
1927 and had accrued their own firsts. Jules Eichorn had been taught to
climb at fifteen by his piano teacher, Ansel Adams, while Glen Dawson, another second-generation SC member who regularly attended the summer
outings, had joined his father "on a pre-[D]epression Grand Tour of Europe
including an ascent of the Matterhorn."[1]

Californians were not neophytes, nor were they overwhelmed by Underhill's authority. Clyde was proud of the Whitney ascent, but he reckoned it
was just "another outstanding climb to the many already discovered in the
Sierra Nevada." Likewise, Dawson wrote to his parents during the trip that
he was "learning a great deal," yet he realized that "I can climb as well as the
best of them." All he lacked was "experience to equal them in leading ability." Dawson honored Underhill in public, but his private comments suggest
that what he most valued was climbing with any seasoned partner, including Clyde and Farquhar. Dawson was, after all, a veteran of the Matterhorn,
so little of what Underhill said on technique or ethics was completely new.
In fact, Underhill's main contribution might have been that his knowledge
and skills were *not* superior to those that the SC members already possessed.
Private musings by expedition members suggest as much, and it helps to

explain the major qualification of Underhill's impact: the most influential climber in the Sierra Club during the 1930s did not even attend the 1931 club outing.[2]

In modern climbing history, Richard Leonard is the equivalent of a red-headed stepson: in mixed company he can inspire awkward questions. Leonard entered the sport idiosyncratically and was a top climber only briefly, yet his impact was profound. Underhill inspired a number of acolytes, but the decade's leading figure was busy reading law while Underhill sermonized. It was a bookish student who ultimately moved the sport of American rock climbing beyond its Anglican roots. Founder of the Cragmont Climbing Club and, by extension, the Sierra Club's Rock Climbing Sections (RCS), Leonard was a key member of three of the most important North American ascents during the 1930s. He also devised a method of training and certifying climbers that altered the technical and cultural parameters of the sport, chaired key committees for the Sierra Club and American Alpine Club, and maintained strong links between clubs and the National Park Service. No American mountaineer had a greater impact on the sport's techniques and institutions. Leonard and other RCS pioneers, not Underhill, created the foundation for not only a far more technologically sophisticated approach to climbing but one that was far more socially and culturally inclusive as well.

In one sense Leonard's youth was typical. Born to an officer in the Signal Corps, at fourteen Richard (called "Dick" by his friends) moved with his mother and sisters to Berkeley after his father's untimely death in the Philippines. Seeking male fellowship, Dick joined the Boy Scouts, explored local hills, and scrambled in the Sierra. Scouting introduced him to wild places, and summit registers placed by the Sierra Club acquainted him with the club. In 1930, his neighbors sponsored him for club membership, where he soon met other budding climbers. Like many later climbers, Leonard came from a broken home and compensated for his father's absence with homosocial activities. Scouting and climbing became his models for masculinity, and like Edward Whymper, Alfred Mummery, Bob Marshall, David Brower, Royal Robbins, Jim Bridwell, John Long, and many others, Leonard found in mountains a means to identity and a connection to community.[3]

In most respects, though, Leonard was extraordinary. A good athlete and disciplined polymath, at the University of California he studied geology, chemistry, and electronics before taking up law. Leonard specialized in business law, and eventually he sat on the boards of several corporations. For more than four decades he was also on the board of directors for both the SC and Wilderness Society. During that time he served in several offices, including president of the Sierra Club from 1953 to 1955. Well before Pearl Harbor, the Army recruited Leonard to develop an Alpine training program and to refine the military's climbing equipment. During the war he spied behind enemy lines in Burma, and after the war he trained in emergency first aid. Leonard was one of those omnicompetent people who inspire awe and self-loathing. It seemed there was nothing he could not do, and measuring oneself against his accomplishments is a humbling experience.[4]

What linked Leonard's many interests was rock climbing. If scrambling drew him to the Sierra Club and environmental activism, it was the pressures of graduate school that attracted him to stone. Although he grew up near several of Berkeley's famed outcroppings, not until he entered Boalt Hall did he find any use for boulders. The faces of Cragmont Rock, Indian Rock, and Pinnacle Rock—all within blocks of his Berkeley hills home—became convenient sites for cathartic exercise. Clambering and sweating, testing muscles and refining skills, his workouts began as a recess from reading law. Climbing was at first ancillary to the more important work of education and career, yet while his initial impulse was to blow off steam, he soon applied the same work ethic to his climbing.[5]

Leonard was incapable of half-measures. What began as idle recreation soon evolved into another way to discipline the body and mind. Having learned a move or route, Leonard tackled the next challenge. Unfortunately, his previous climbing experiences had not prepared him for what he encountered on boulders. He knew little about technique or safety, so true to form he descended on the Sierra Club's library to voraciously consume the writings of Underhill, Geoffrey Young, the *Alpine Journal,* and other English and European texts. In contrast to law, which stressed precedence and rote learning, climbing literature inspired interpretation and dissent. The more he read about ethics and technique, the more heterodox Leonard's views became. He later remarked that the "British considered since you could not hold the fall of a leader, and since the leader knew that, if the leader fell then he had violated his duty to the other two on the rope and therefore you should simply cut the rope over a sharp point of rock and get rid of him." Appalled, Leonard concluded that "there must be some better way." His ensuing quest laid the foundation for Yosemite Valley's very different legacy.[6]

Like many contemporaries, Leonard said Underhill inspired modern climbing, yet in practice he rejected Underhill's theses. During practices he and Kenneth May used top ropes, a technique of stringing a rope from above to insure they fell only the length of slack. They also altered how climbers managed rope by devising concise verbal signals to enhance communication and safety, and they turned belaying from an art to a science. Leonard and May dissected techniques, analyzed body positions and anchor points, tested technology, and simulated falls. Many knew that technology and technique were weak links. Manila and cotton ropes could not withstand the forces of even minor falls, but nobody had devised an alternative to holding tight and hoping for the best. Geoffrey Young noted that long ropes had greater elasticity, and he advised belayers not to grab a rope firmly until in a secure position. He never systematically linked these measures, however, and always maintained that as "a protection to more than the *morale* of the leader, the [piton] is futile."[7]

It was left to Leonard to figure out that forces could be reduced significantly if belayers intentionally let the rope slip. He explained in 1934 that "Mathematically, if a falling body is stopped infinitely quickly, the force required will be infinitely great. Conversely, if the fall is stopped more slowly, the checking force need be proportionately less." Wrapping the rope around the hips was also easier to hold, added elasticity to the system, and was more secure than looping it around the shoulder or forearm, as Young and Underhill advised. Leonard tested this by taking ever higher falls at Cragmont until friends "realized that it was getting to a point where, if anything went wrong, and you were dropped the full thirty-three feet, it would probably kill you." Within a year he had the rudiments of the "dynamic belay," an advance in safety that altered climbing. He told an editor that his "experiments clearly show the fallacy of Young's predictions that pitons could never protect the leader." Ironically, this Anglophile's greatest contribution to climbing was demonstrating the shortcomings of Britain's leading climbing critic.[8]

Such innovations enabled climbers to remain safe even when pushing their limits far above ground, and that produced a major technical *and* philosophical departure in the sport. The mantra of the era of natural fiber ropes was that falling equaled death. Echoed by many others, Young admonished readers that a "leader or a last man [on a rope] . . . must not fall," and because falling imperiled everyone, taking risks was a breach of trust and thus a moral infraction as well. Technology and technique created a context in which many climbers assumed that they had achieved the outer edge of human performance. Young claimed that "the standard of difficult rock climbing has now been forced up to a point that practically represents the limit of human possibility." "Beyond that point lies not danger . . . but impossibility." Underhill encouraged training programs yet believed "climbing ability is very largely a matter of inborn talent and its use the result of natural in-

Figure 3.1. In 1932 the Cragmont Climbing Club sought a better way to protect climbers. Conducting tests in which members leapt from ever higher perches, the club found a way to protect climbers on lead by moving the rope from shoulders and arms to torsos. Belayers also allowed the rope to slip through their hands at first to lower the forces on the era's fragile natural fiber ropes. This "dynamic belay" was a major safety advance in the era before nylon ropes.

stinct." Leonard, by contrast, devised a training system that advanced safety by effectively rewarding the individual for attempting "problems considerably beyond the present ability of the climber." In doing so, he revolutionized North American climbing through a belief that climbers were made, not born, and that risk was neither necessary nor unavoidable.[9]

Leonard's technical and cultural innovations redefined basic assumptions in ways that opened outdoor sports to many more people regardless of their physical talent or psychological commitment. The effect was almost immediate. In early 1932 Leonard invited May, James Archer, Beverly Blanks, Elliot Sawyer, Richard Ray, and several others to Cragmont Rock. By March, those still climbing decided to call themselves the Cragmont Climbing Club (CCC). They met every Sunday at a local rock, and to ensure safety they imposed a set of standards. Applicants gained membership only after they had demonstrated an ability to belay a fall and to rappel over an overhanging section of rock. They also had to climb up and down the "Qualification Crack." "C1," as it was dubbed, was a thirty-foot route on Cragmont Rock. While not difficult with modern footgear, ascent was a challenge in tennis shoes or hobnail boots. Descent was even trickier, but being able to downclimb was mandatory. Geoffrey Young had written "that the neglect of the art of *climbing* down is a definite bar to achieving success." Even with improved belays, leader falls were decidedly dangerous, especially on Leonard's questionable ropes, yet the emphasis on downclimbing also reflected the sport's persistent moral and gendered concerns. Young commented that, aside from unforeseen emergencies, he could "imagine no other cases where a climber should not feel that he is confessing to incapacity or some misjudgment if he has to fall back upon pegs and aids to help him to come down what he, or some other man, has ascended." Downclimbing, then, was also a way to avoid the stigmatizing effects of technological reliance.[10]

Through the spring of 1932 the CCC attracted a steady stream of the curious. Berkeley friends and neighbors jelled into a committed core at several locations. It was a local affair with the modest assets of two "climbing" ropes —really half-inch cotton line for sailboats—and several challenging boulders. Cragmont was a squat outcropping of soda rhyolite with sides that varied from easy inclines to severe overhangs. Several blocks downhill Indian and Mortar Rocks were of the same material and features. All offered short, steep face climbing on rock "very similar to granite in texture and holds." A block uphill rose Pinnacle Rock—actually two outcroppings of acid rhyolite, a soft material weathered into an "abundance of deep, sharp-edged holds" for high-angle face climbing. Wildcat Caves were farther and visited less frequently. By the end of May the CCC had five full members—Archer, Blanks, Leonard, May, and Ray—and two prospective members still struggling to complete their qualification tests.[11]

We know these details because of another feature of the club: systematic records. The records reflected Leonard's penchant for cataloguing . . . everything. Like many obsessive climbers, he paid meticulous attention to club issues. From the beginning he kept notes on attendance, training, and climbs. He even coded boulder routes. "C-1" was the qualification crack at Cragmont, while "P-1" was the first route at Pinnacle and "I-3" the third at Indian Rock. Late that summer he typed and distributed his notes as the first edition of the *Journal of the Cragmont Climbing Club*, earnestly advising readers to "Preserve it carefully because in the future it will be as valuable as first numbers of 'The Alpine Journal', or 'Appalachia', or 'The Sierra Club Bulletin.'" In many respects Leonard was a historian's dream. He was an earnest scribe of early technical climbing in California, conscientiously recording the facts for posterity, and through him we can discover many subtle facets of the sport's history.[12]

We know, for example, that in June 1932 the CCC founded the custom of taking a summer hiatus. For years climbers from the Bay Area would meet regularly from fall through spring, but the moment the passes cleared, they headed for the hills. That first year Leonard, Blanks, and Ray enjoyed a busman's holiday. Ansel Hall, a senior naturalist and forester for the National Park Service and a member of the American Alpine Club, had asked these three to create an instructional film on mountaineering, while the geologist François Matthes needed them to assist with botanical and geological research during a Scout Naturalist Expedition. In the process, the trio swarmed over many Sierra peaks that summer, including three first ascents as a group and one solo by Ray. In retrospect, the summer of 1932 was a period of transition. The CCC used it to perfect their techniques on standard climbs and a few untried routes in the high mountains, but when they hit Yosemite Valley, they dared scramble only to the edge of falls or features along nontechnical routes. It was a measure of their respect or fear that they avoided Yosemite's walls. No one felt ready.[13]

These self-styled pioneers nevertheless wanted to test their mettle on what everyone recognized as the premier rock climbing landscape. Serious preparation began on 18 September 1932. That Sunday the CCC reconvened as a broader, more experienced group. Existing members had enjoyed a summer of technical climbing, and seasoned mountaineers from around the Bay Area also showed, including Jules Eichorn and Jean Husted, a UC student who had recently become the first woman to free-climb Yosemite's imposing Mount Starr King. Within a month Marjory Bridge, Lewis Clark, Francis Farquhar, Kenneth Hazelton, Stewart Kimbal, Carl Sharsmith, Barbara Welch, and others further swelled the ranks, but growth brought novel problems. Members now had to wait their turn to use the club's limited supplies, sometimes standing around for extended periods. Eichorn and Farquhar responded by donating new ropes, the group jelled, and an esprit de corps took hold.[14]

On its surface, this club era seemed idyllic. Morgan Harris remembered it as a time of innocence, insisting there "was no competition, probably because we weren't smart enough to be competitive." Leonard's notes suggest a different tale. Everyone took their turn at belay practice, working to master the skill and teach novices, but some members engaged in other games as well. Leonard recorded not only who climbed what but also how fast they climbed. First ascents were coveted, and a core group competed to be first up the most difficult problems. Once a line was ascended the others rushed to prove that they were equal to the challenge. To evaluate progress, Leonard scored members' ability, technique, experience, judgment, and theoretical knowledge. This table also reveals that a pecking order quickly emerged. Not surprisingly, the three most ambitious members—Leonard, Eichorn, and Robinson—ranked highest, while Blanks, Bridge, Clark, Oscar Kehrlein, May, and Hervey Voge were slightly behind. Women had their own complex games. Many vied to be the best woman member, with Bridge rising to the top in the Bay Area and Ruth Dyar priding herself for outclimbing other women in Southern California. Early club climbers *were* competitive, but the larger point is that all these activities were facilitated by Leonard's training system, which enabled climbers safely to push themselves and each other.[15]

Eichorn's arrival at Cragmont was a turning point, yet the timing forces us to reconsider the genealogy of Yosemite climbing. Steve Roper has portrayed Eichorn as a principal historical agent of change, placing him both with Underhill in summer 1931 and with Leonard the following winter. For Roper the process of cultural dissemination was clear: like Philip in Samaria, Eichorn carried Underhill's words to the Bay Area. The problem is that Leonard's documents do not support this. He first mentioned Eichorn in a September 1932 cover letter for the club journal, and all he wrote was that he had invited Eichorn to the CCC's September 18 meeting. There is no evidence the two met previously. Rather, Leonard's wife remarked at how shocked Dick was by Eichorn's youth when they met that September. Similarly, Chris Jones and Gary Arce portray the CCC as an insular organization,

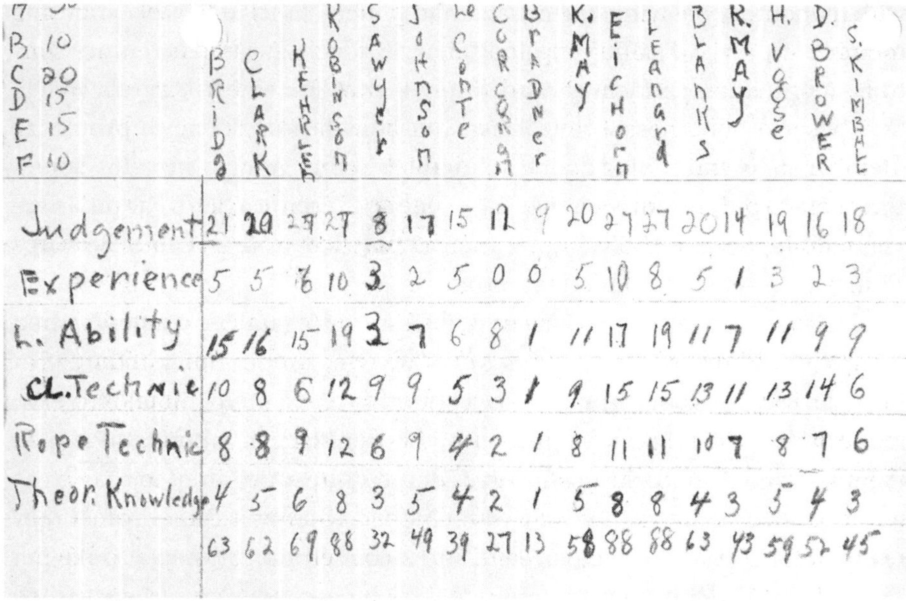

	BRIDGE	CLARK	KEHRLEN	ROBIN	SAWYER	JOHNSON	LeCONTE	CORKRAN	BROGAN	K. MAY	EICHORN	LEONARD	BLANKS	R. MAY	H. VOBOSE	D. BROWER	S. KIMBALL
Judgement	21	20	27	27	8	17	15	12	9	20	27	27	20	14	19	16	18
Experience	5	5	6	10	3	2	5	0	0	5	10	8	5	1	3	2	3
L. Ability	15	16	15	19	3	7	6	8	1	11	17	19	11	7	11	9	9
Cl. Technic	10	8	6	12	9	9	5	3	1	9	15	15	13	11	13	14	6
Rope Technic	8	8	9	12	6	9	4	2	1	8	11	11	10	7	8	7	6
Theor. Knowledge	4	5	6	8	3	5	4	2	1	5	8	8	4	3	5	4	3
	63	62	69	88	32	49	39	27	13	58	88	88	63	43	59	52	45

Figure 3.2. This score card from about 1933 is one example of Richard Leonard's inclination to systemize. Leonard tried to tabulate the merits of each RCS member using a set of categories largely related to safety.

yet this ignores the many texts that influenced Leonard's thinking, not to mention the key role of the SC library in his research. If casting Underhill as the patriarch overly simplifies, so does the immaculate conception at Cragmont. In evolutionary terms, neither monogenesis nor polygenesis captures the unique synthesis of many traditions that developed within the head of Dick Leonard in late 1931 and early 1932. To a greater extent than climbers recognize, the modern sport owes its North American forms and techniques to the mind of a pent-up law student and how those ideas blossomed within the Bay Area club culture of the 1930s. The result altered the technical and social parameters of climbing and, eventually, many other outdoor sports.[16]

The enrollment of Clark, Eichorn, and Farquhar was also the downfall of the CCC. Leonard, May, and Archer were members of both the CCC and SC, but by October the CCC seemed a bit limited. There were not enough ropes to go around, and, more important, no financial base for replacing equipment. As a result, Leonard and Clark, who chaired the SC's Bay Area Chapter Executive Committee, discussed a formal association with the SC. Clark raised the idea with the Executive Committee, and Farquhar, at the time the club's president-elect, encouraged a merger. The SC officers agreed, once they visited practices and saw a disciplined group that made safety routine with mandatory belaying, falling, and rappelling drills. Each week a rotating member supervised all training and safety. The club also had inventory controls, maintenance practices, and first-aid supplies. Everything about the CCC bespoke soberness. They further alleviated liability concerns by issuing member cards and adding qualification rules to enable less athletically gifted members to progress at their own pace. The CCC courted the SC by performing middling respectability. Safety, which had always been Leonard's obsession, fairly screamed from every rule and drill.[17]

On November 17 the SC Executive Committee established a new outing group called the Rock Climbing Section of the Bay Area Chapter of the Sierra Club, or RCS for short. The RCS instantly enhanced the climbers' funding and exposure. The Executive Committee established an annual budget so members could regularly replace ropes and acquire specialized tools such as pitons and carabiners. An Executive Committee member even wrote an essay on the RCS for the *Oakland Tribune,* which sent its photographer to the November 27 outing at Cragmont Rock for a front-page feature with photos of Eichorn, Leonard, and Barbara Welch climbing, rappelling, and belaying. Quite suddenly, hanging out at Cragmont was hip. Three weeks later the RCS drew even more attention when it held a joint meeting with the Sierra Club's Local Walks group. This was the section's coming-out party. RCS members demonstrated skills to ninety-six members of the SC, an audience several-fold more than any CCC meeting. Institutional support and publicity ensured the RCS was off to a roaring start by the end of 1932.[18]

Doris Leonard remarked that when the RCS came in "the C.C.C. passed out," but club records actually show considerable overlap in these institutions. The scene at Cragmont did evolve. The RCS continued to grow and diversify. There were not only more men but many more women at practices, and the range of talent widened, including many more novices. The merger thus confirmed the RCS as a heterosocial climbing community that was neither simply elitist nor simply egalitarian. Leonard and other climbers had to accommodate a spectrum of abilities and ambitions, but this was not new. The range of talent had been an issue since April 1932, and it was a key reason why Leonard had stressed safety and made everyone follow the same rules and drills. Thus while the SC essentially swallowed the Cragmont Climbing Club, it also absorbed its spirit and, in the process, expanded its vision of mountain play. By November 1932 the SC was in name and resources formally supporting the sport of modern technical climbing. Yet the CCC lived on, even after the RCS dissolved it in February 1933. Despite the rush of enrollments, attendance records continued to record who had been a CCC member, and CCC members continued to lead the RCS for decades. Memory of the CCC remained strong enough that Bay Area climbers resurrected it in the 1980s after the SC terminated all its Rock Climbing Sections for liability reasons. If the CCC was midwife to the modern climbing club, then the midwife outlived the child.[19]

In the meantime the RCS blossomed. By 1933 future stars such as Jack Arnold, Raffi Bedayan, David Brower, Morgan Harris, and Bestor Robinson had joined. Members hailed from more towns around the Bay, and practice destinations were added to accommodate this growth. They began to frequent Miraloma Rocks in San Francisco, Devils Slide near Pacifica, Mount Tamalpais and Dutchmans Rock in Marin County, Mount Diablo in Contra Costa County, and Hunters Hill in Solano County. Most were accessible by public transportation. In the 1930s the Bay Area had an extensive system of streetcars, trains, and ferries. Thus like many other sportsmen and nature lovers around North America, England, and Australia, mass transit carried Bay Area climbers to outdoor recreation. Southern Pacific and Key Route ferries steamed from San Francisco to the East Bay. The No. 4 Key Route streetcar ran by Cragmont, and the Muni K-Line went past Miraloma. Members carpooled from the end of the Muni line to Devils Slide, while Northwestern Pacific Railroad Company ferries sailed to Marin and company trains stopped at Mill Valley and Fairfax, from which members hiked to Tamalpais and Dutchmans. Public transit alleviated the necessity of private cars, while the club subsidized ropes, pitons, and carabiners. A climber needed little more than good shoes and the right attitude. The aura of the mountains drew people to the Bay Area Chapter's RCS, but the social contexts of urban transit and club-subsidized gear helped sustain their play during the Great Depression. The result was a communal climbing culture which contrasted sharply with the individualistic and consumerist orientation of postwar recreation.[20]

Social preferences and geography also illuminate differences between the Bay Area and Southern California RCS. After his Mount Whitney ascent, Glen Dawson climbed with Norman Clyde for several weeks before matriculating at UCLA. Back in Los Angeles, Dawson shared his experiences with Dick Jones and Mark Scott so they could work on skills together. Unfortunately, college would curb their free hours. Not until summer 1934, and then only after much cajoling, did Dawson hold a clinic for members of the Southern Chapter. Having heard about the RCS, Arthur Johnson asked Dawson to start a local section. Dawson was swamped, so Johnson formed an RCS in Los Angeles. Emerging separately, the two sections had different rhythms. While Bay Area climbers met from fall to spring, southern members liked to

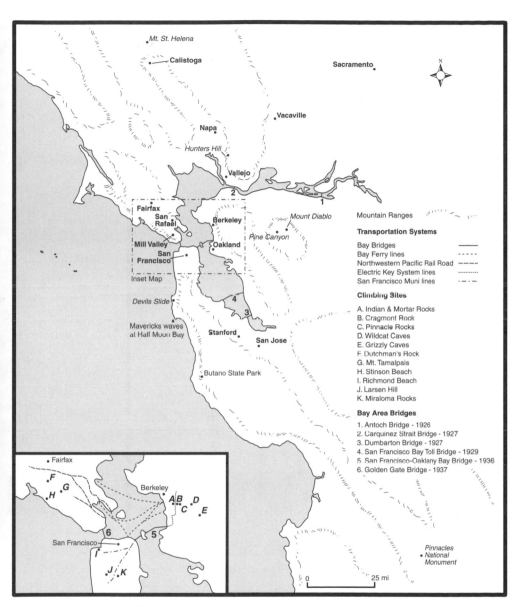

Map 3.1. Bay Area climbing sites and transportation systems.

ski. They met from April or May to October or November and then reconfigured as Ski Mountaineers to pursue the European sport of climbing mountains with skis and then making long runs. The Bay Area RCS and Ski Mountaineers were similarly entwined but ran parallel programs. The landscape of Southern California also distinguished the section. Initially there were but three practice sites—Eagle Rock at Occidental College, Devils Gate in

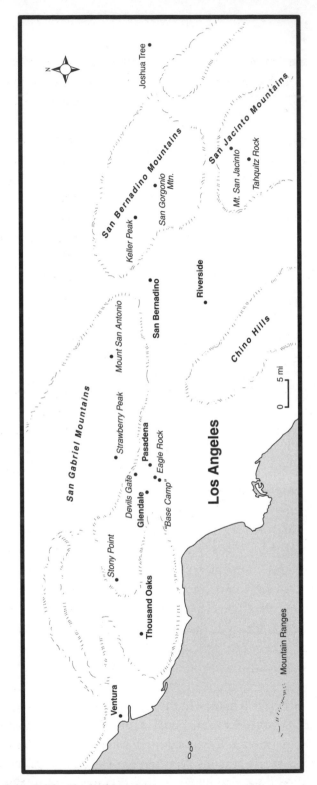

Map 3.2. Southern California climbing sites.

La Canada, and Stony Point in Chatsworth—and Los Angeles's attenuated public transit forced members to rely on private cars. The Southern RCS was thus geographically and socially more dispersed and less fixated on rock climbing.[21]

Still, the two sections had much in common. Members met regularly at the Sierra Club's annual outing, and officers corresponded and occasionally visited each other's practices. Ideas about logistics, technology, and technique flowed freely. Training and membership requirements varied only slightly and values even less. Foremost for all was the role of safety. As Dick Jones explained, the joys of climbing depended on an unwavering commitment to the ideal that "We must play safe." RCS members' thoughts about the sport underscored their ties to the wider mountaineering culture. They read all the same journals and books about the latest technological innovations, bold ascents, and ethical debates. They were familiar with English criticisms of competition, rating systems, and nationalism, yet they knew that British mountaineers had been driven by these same motives since the 1850s, and that British fatalities on the Matterhorn and Mount Everest had much in common with German and Italian deaths on the Eiger and Nanga Parbat. The RCS was aware that more complex perspectives were emerging even among the British. Lilian Bray had argued that there was "a good deal to be said for" the safety provided by pitons, while Joseph Henry Doughty mocked purists for censuring rubber-soled shoes and crampons for "making things too easy" yet embracing ice axes and ropes. There was no consensus on recent sporting innovations, even among the supposedly tradition-bound British. The old rules were changing in the eastern United States and Europe, and the urge to pioneer led to similar convulsions in Yosemite.[22]

The RCS and other organizations re-enacted these debates as they contemplated the prospect of using pitons and direct aid on Yosemite's steep walls. On one side were concerns about safety and the desire to scale technically challenging routes, on the other an abiding respect for British tradition. Marjory Bridge noted that "a great discussion would come up—would you use pitons only for safety, or should you use them as direct aid? And then of course you'd hear, 'Well, the British school doesn't believe in anything like that—you should have a natural climb.'" This ran to the heart of what motivated climbers. Some emphasized romantic and mystical rewards, the sublime nature of grand vistas and warm fellowship. Ansel Adams cautioned that while "it is rarely the case of the complete ascendancy of acrobatics over esthetics, we should bear in mind that the mountains are more to us than a mere proving-ground of strength and alert skill." Others stressed more secu-

lar and gendered impulses. Mountains were playgrounds, and virgin summits beckoned manly conquest. For example, H. C. Sholes championed "Adventure—the great heights—the appeal of danger—desire to conquer
obstacles—the wide outlook—the thrill of victory—the starry depths of
Heaven in midday." Positions were rarely rigid, however. Most climbers emphasized different values at different times. David Brower, Norman Clyde,
and Robert Marshall could be romantics one day and obsessive peak baggers the next. Dick Jones spoke for most, though, when he declared that "I
climb, in the first place, for fun." The pioneers charted not only new routes
but a new, more flexible climbing culture.[23]

The debates have never ceased, and no generation has ever drawn a de-
finitive and lasting line. This is largely because when faced with dilemmas
on actual climbs, most climbers adopt a pragmatic approach to ethics. One
pole can be represented by the examples Dick Leonard set in the early 1930s
when he and several friends twice hiked to the southwest face of Half Dome.
Despite an approach that involved steep scrambling and bushwhacking
through manzanita brush, on both occasions they concluded they "couldn't
climb it without more pitons than we thought we wanted to put in. . . . We
still kinda had the British reluctance to do so." Leonard can thus embody the
persistence of British fealty to free climbing and technological minimalism,
yet—and this is why it is important not to reify individual legacies—Leonard
can also represent the other pole. When the Bay Area RCS finally ventured to
Yosemite Valley in September 1933, Leonard, Eichorn, and Robinson began a
yearlong assault up two massive pillars on the valley's south side called the
Cathedral Spires. Neither the use of an unprecedented number of pitons for
direct aid nor the deliberate defacement of rock deterred the trio's efforts to
pioneer routes up these uncharted pinnacles.[24]

Ambition and nature were critical in shaping the emerging ethics of
Yosemite climbing. The first visit to the spires—Leonard called it a reconnaissance, but it was really an eight-hour failed attempt—revealed that
while both spires were steep, the granite was solid and there were many
ledges and trees from which they could rappel. In other words, the nature of
the spires was challenging but not overly risky. The first taste only whetted
their appetite. The team queried others for details and studied photos "under microscope and protractor" to refine their route. Their preparations remind us that most modern climbs began in the mind, not on the rock, and
that success often owed more to relentless planning than spontaneity. In November the trio tried again, but now the nature of their "pitons" intruded.
Until then neither Leonard nor the RCS had cared much about piton tech-

nology, instead improvising with whatever was handy, including industrial nails: "great big, long spikes about ten inches long. We would drive them into a crack, and then we would tie a loop of rope to the nail." This worked well in the horizontal cracks of Berkeley's boulders, but the nails tended to pivot in the vertical cracks that predominated in Yosemite Valley. Even when their pitons did hold, the higher they ventured the less secure they felt. Fittingly it was safety that drove the RCS team back to the drawing board.[25]

The nature of granite and iron had clarified priorities. Confronted by Yosemite's parallel vertical cracks, Leonard, who had read about piton technique, at last realized why special gear was necessary. The iron blades of European pitons conformed to cracks when driven, and some designs transformed vertical into torsional force, providing better grip than cylindrical nails. But with no local manufacturers, the RCS had to place orders through the only known dealer: Sporthaus Schuster in Munich. By mid-April the team was back at Higher Spire with their new gear. They had hoped to use the pitons only for protection, but several times Eichorn and Leonard had to rely on one piton above another for direct aid on the steep, smooth walls. In all they carried fifty-five pitons with them, the final headwall alone requiring twelve aid pins to enable them to reach the summit. Matters grew more extreme on Lower Spire, which they scaled in August. The crux was a twenty-foot by thirty-foot exfoliated flake of granite that leaned precariously. The team could neither free climb nor drive pitons behind it, so Leonard created holds by chipping its razor-thin edge with a hammer, a technique that would later scandalize a top climber in 1981. In 1934, however, the team boosted each other to handholds and pendulumed past blank areas. In the end safety mattered more than tradition, and making it to the top mattered most of all.[26]

The RCS tactics scandalized some climbers, but the primary reaction within the club was pride. Eichorn explained to Dawson that "this type of climbing is entirely different from the higher Sierra and much more difficult. We used pitons for safety rather freely." Leonard felt no shame about admitting that the team had maintained safety "by practically nailing ourselves to the solid granite wall with spikes of steel," while Robinson wrote that "we find our greatest satisfaction in having demonstrated, at least to ourselves, that by the proper application of climbing technique extremely difficult ascents can be made in safety. . . . there was no time on the entire climb, but that if any member of the party had fallen, his injuries would, at the worst, have been a few scratches and bruises." Critics, including members of London's Alpine Club, insisted "that the summit of the Cathedral Spires had been reached . . . by the use of pitons, but it had not been climbed." Their intent was to shame, but the RCS was "quite amused." British disdain had bared British ignorance. Yosemite Valley was a different game on a grander scale, and Higher Spire was in retrospect "the most technical aid climbing in North America at the time." From the beginning the nature of Yosemite Valley forced technical climbers to adopt a more ecumenical approach to the game. As Leonard later explained, "Anyone who knows anything about climbing would know that the Spires were climbed using the techniques gleaned from books on rock-climbing, principally German." The RCS had "taken bodily from them," transporting European tools and techniques to a uniquely American landscape.[27]

The social, technological, and environmental contexts of the first ascents of the Cathedral Spires force a reconsideration of basic assumptions about how people have related to nature through outdoor sport. Peter Hansen argues that climbers "never developed an appreciation for what has been called the 'technological sublime,' in which 'the awe and reverence once reserved for the Deity and later bestowed upon the visible landscape is directed toward technology or, rather, the technological conquest of matter.'" This is mostly incontestable. It is true that climbers "never admired the technological sublime because the tenets of their own faith were premised on the unmediated physical contact between man and mountain. They were trying to escape the reach of contemporary urban civilization, not to celebrate it," yet it was only because of modern technologies that climbers reached the summits they had idealized as natural others, and clubs, journals, photography, cartography, transportation, metallurgy, textiles, and other technologies were integral to their pursuits. Thus while climbers' condemnation of dams and railways do matter, we must also note the books, cameras, maps, pitons, and carabiners that they carried with them to nature. Geology and technology complicate our understanding of the environmental and social contingencies that shaped sporting culture in the 1930s.[28]

This is why Yosemite matters not only to mountaineering history but to the history of sport, technology, gender, and environmental culture. In the preface to a report by the Sierra Club committee on mountain records, Leonard called 1932 a turning point in the sport. The RCS's "development of modern climbing technique"—not simply Underhill's sermon on the mount—had "added much stimulus and interest to climbing, greatly increased the numbers, reduced the hazard, and made possible, by the use of artificial aid, climbs that once had been considered impossible."[29] The pioneers had institutionalized a novel blend of tradition and innovation. They cultivated

a goal-oriented, even competitive milieu that was nevertheless safety conscious and socially and culturally inclusive. Dick Leonard's management of
the CCC and RCS created a trove of information about this formative period.
Through him we learn how a marginal sport was embraced by an environmental organization *and* by the National Park Service, yet we cannot take
Leonard's word as the final word. While he recorded many facts about those
early years, they tended to be the bits most germane to an ambitious young
man who valued conquest. Yet other events, some of which would shape his
future as a husband, father, and club leader—he simply ignored. We must
rely on others for a broader understanding of this heterosocial climbing culture. There was much more to club climbing than just boulders, belaying,
and first ascents. The gendered nature of these activities not only offers a
fuller picture of the social and cultural parameters of outdoor sport but a
more nuanced view of participants' dynamic relations to nature and to each
other at the time.

4. MEMBERS

The community pants were much in use that day as there is a splendid roping down place about 55 feet high. Once when I happened to look up it seemed to me that a pair of pants were roping down, but upon closer observation I saw that a Miss Helen LeConte was supplying the necessary weight, but I couldn't keep myself from saying, "Pants where yo' all goin' with Helen?"
—DORIS CORCORAN

In an era when top climbers test themselves by leaving ropes at home, we should remember the very different social and cultural orientation of Yosemite's first technical climbers. The valley was originally about group fun, and the RCS's priorities differed greatly from later climbers. To understand why, we have to shift our gaze from individual achievements to social context. In some ways the pioneers did help shape the modern, extreme sport. They carried Robert Underhill's moral vision to urban centers, trained athletes to challenge vertical frontiers, and made Yosemite the object of their ambition. If there was a moment when Yosemite climbing could have become a "hypermasculine" endeavor, this was it, yet club members were remarkable for how little they resembled earlier or later generations. The valley's sheer cliffs, smooth granite, and vertical cracks were indeed tests, but most members most of the time saw a social playground. Until the 1960s, most climbers preferred moderate fun to extreme risk. For every effort on Higher Cathedral Spire, there were many fun climbs of *Lunch Ledge, Monday Morning Slab, Sunnyside Bench,* and the *West Face of Lower Brother.* Indeed, club members valued the sport because it was *not* a life-and-death struggle. Few sought the edge for its own sake.[1]

Why was Yosemite climbing at first about sober fun? Robert Underhill's vision of genteel sport actually conflicted with the entrenched assumptions of existing clubs. The Sierra Club (SC) had climbed for forty years, others for even longer. The American West had a vibrant climbing culture well before Underhill, and the communal nature of outings was part of the appeal of the mountains. Thus Underhill preached safety to the choir, but his ethics tended to inspire ambivalence. His ideals resonated with some members, but they saw this as a personal choice. Clubs had to balance many views.

Mountaineering was only one of many pursuits, and comity required accommodation. Demography also mattered. Unlike the old Alpine Club, American clubs recruited women and men. Membership was relatively open, and public transportation enabled many to participate. As a result, American clubs were demographically broader, and their members had a wider range of abilities and interests. Leaders facilitated diversity by suppressing personal agendas. Through mid-century, climbers acted differently from later generations because acculturation worked both ways. If Underhill's apostles fostered climbing in the West, their clubs tended to domesticate both the idealists and the sport by establishing standards and a social context that were critical for legitimating it in the eyes of society and the government.

Clubs thus open a largely ignored topic in climbing, one that focuses on men and women less for what they did on rock than how they interacted with nature and each other through sport. When discussed at all, historians have tended to segregate women as if they either had no impact or were so very different as to be *sui generis*. Neither is tenable in historical light. The women who joined clubs embraced an activity already inscribed with masculine values, and internalizing those gendered norms was part of mastering the sport. Conversely, women's participation drew men into more complex social and cultural experiences that, before 1960, were more communally oriented than later. The individual and imperial competitiveness that had long marked mountaineering remained, but it was muted by the expectation that experienced members teach, encourage, and lead the less talented. There was also an intimate side to club life. While mostly implied, evidence of romances, marriages, births, divorces, and deaths permeates club records. Clubs were venues for socializing as well as climbing, and tracing their history complicates how we view the interplay of recreation and nature. At moments the history of Yosemite rock climbing is more a biography of an extended family than a chronicle of great climbs and climbers.[2]

We need only shift our perspective slightly. Thumb through any history of western mountaineering and you will encounter an image of mob climbing: one of those black-and-white photos of darkly clad people set against an overexposed field of snow. They wear hats, gloves, jackets, pants, bloomers, dresses, and high-ankle boots. Inevitably, someone leans on an alpenstock. Photographs of genteel mountaineers plodding toward summits are a staple of the literature, and researchers have noticed that they include many women who "took a simple, basic pleasure" in the mountains. But look again. There is more afoot than "Wimmin is everywhere." The pleasures were not singular, nor was history so easily bifurcated. At a time when climbers are

Figure 4.1. Edward Parson's summit shot of a Sierra Club climb on Mount Brewer in 1902. The adventure was important, but so was socializing. Clubs accommodated women and men with a range of abilities and ambitions, so members had to temper their individual views about sport.

canonized for untying from partners, William Gladstone Steel's 1894 ascent of Mount Hood with 160 people, or the Sierra Club's 1914 ascent of Mount Lyell by seventy-seven members, seem downright exotic. The rope was both a safety device and a symbol that bound men to women and club to club across the continent. Such ties contained social dimensions that single-sex analysis cannot convey. The communal implications of clubs help remind us that early Yosemite climbing took place in an explicitly, often emphatically heterosocial context.[3]

In this sense Victorian climbing culture was a miserable failure. London's Alpine Club was a fraternal organization, an all-male enclave that excluded women until the 1970s. British women climbers had to form a separate Ladies Alpine Club in 1907, which essentially confirmed their second-class status. As one historian notes, when "women climbed mountains they undermined the masculine power of the Alps, and thereby changed them from mountains into molehills." Leslie Stephen's stages of mountaineering— "'inaccessible,' 'the most difficult point in the Alps,' 'a good hard climb, but nothing out of the way,' 'a perfectly straightforward bit of work,' and finally, 'an easy day for a lady'"—neatly encapsulated gendered assumptions of risk. Auxiliaries protected the AC by segregating it from women's polluting influence, yet their Victorian anxieties were not representative. The Lake District's Fell and Rock Club enrolled women from its founding, and clubs outside Britain were normally inclusive. The Club Alpin Français accepted women in 1874, the Mountain Club of South Africa in 1894. In other words, most climbers did not follow the Alpine Club's misogynistic lead.[4]

North American clubs were normally inclusive. The Alpine Club of Williamstown admitted women and men "on equal terms" in 1863, as did the Appalachian Mountain Club (AMC) in 1875, American Alpine Club in 1902, and Alpine Club of Canada in 1906. London's Alpine Club did publish an article by Meta Brevoort in 1872, but only because her nephew signed it. By contrast, the AMC published the work of many women climbers in the late nineteenth and early twentieth centuries. The Portland-based Oregon Alpine Club (OAC) was a brief exception. The first mountaineering club in the West, it was a male enclave of western power. Its members included senators, congressmen, judges, newsmen, robber barons, explorers, and scientists. Most of Portland's leading lights also belonged. More than any other club, the OAC was an explicitly exclusive organization. They behaved more like "social climbers" than mountaineers, however, and like the London AC, the OAC was an anomaly.[5]

Like other prominent Oregonians, William Gladstone Steel was originally from elsewhere. Scion to a wealthy family of pro-Union, abolitionist New Englanders, Steel went west to seek his fortune but spent more time organizing people than earning money. The Oregon Alpine Club was his attempt to form a western analog to the Boone and Crockett Club, a powerful group of eastern sportsmen who lobbied for causes such as New York's Adirondack State Park. His goal was to turn Crater Lake into a national park, but the OAC proved too self-centered. He complained that a "great many very wealthy men in Portland" were "lazy" posers, little more than "telescope mountaineers." Frustrated, he arranged a mass climb of Mount Hood. The 1894 ascent started with 250 climbers, 160 of whom made it to the top and forty of whom stuck around to form a new club. The Mazamas was the West's first performance-based mountaineering club. Applicants had to climb a glaciated mountain to qualify, but by stressing action over identity the club opened itself to anyone. By 1899 it had nearly 300 members, fifty-two of whom were women. By 1917 it had 366 members, 118 of whom were women.

Steel formed the first of what became many western mountaineering clubs, including the Sierra Club (1892), Seattle Mountaineers (1906), BC Mountaineers (1907), and Colorado Mountain Club (1912).[6]

Many clubs have published histories of early members and ascents, but few have discussed their social networks. One metric of such links is the club libraries brimming with journals from regional, national, and international organizations. Another is the club reports published in other journals. Sometimes ties were more personal. Famed geologist Joseph LeConte was a charter member of the OAC, Sierra Club, and Mazamas. Edward Taylor Parsons belonged to the Mazamas and helped start the SC's outings program. Seattle photographer Asahel Curtis climbed with the SC and Mazamas before founding the Seattle Mountaineers as a Mazamas auxiliary. All had ties to eastern clubs. The AMC had joint outings with the Mazamas and SC in 1906, 1918, and 1925, and all gave an open invitation to the Iowa Mountaineers, a widely beloved group from what Greg Child called "a Siberian gulag of flatland." Some members transcended any one club. Geologist François Matthes, for example, did not climb challenging peaks, yet he belonged to the American Alpine Club, Appalachian Mountain Club, Mazamas, and Sierra Club.[7]

Such ties were prerequisite to a broadly shared climbing culture, and women's experiences illustrate the continuity. Women had ascended European peaks since the early 1800s, and many were as ambitious as their male counterparts. Some like Marie Paradis, Lucy Walker, and Meta Brevoort specialized in categorical firsts: the first woman to climb a peak or route, or first to make a winter ascent. Others accompanied and even led family and friends on important ascents, including Elizabeth Hawkins-Whitshed, Mary Mummery, and Katherine Richardson. North Americans forged their own achievements, from Julia Archibald Holmes's first-female ascent of Pikes Peak in 1858 to the many firsts by Marjory Bridge, Phyllis Munday, and Miriam O'Brien. Many more resembled Margaret Griffin Redman, who gained fame by climbing Oregon's Rooster Rock shortly after its first ascent, than Fanny Bullock Workman or Annie Peck, who competed for the coveted title "highest woman in the world." The spectrum of talents and motives spanned continents. Climbing was often an expression of physical equality and even liberation, yet it did not make women revolutionaries. Away from the rock, most embraced domesticity and middle-class values.[8]

Only a few explicitly equated climbing with equality and independence. Annie Peck said "being always from the earliest years a firm believer in the equality of the sexes, I felt that any great achievement in any line of endeavour would be of advantage to my sex." Upon reaching a summit she and Bullock unfurled banners proclaiming VOTES FOR WOMEN. Others preferred to climb exclusively with women. The first all-female first ascent in 1869, by Anna and Ellen Pigeon and their uncredited guides, was crossing the Sesia Joch, highest pass in the Pennine Alps, but when Elizabeth Le Blond and Evelyn McDonnell climbed Piz Palu without guides in 1900, they scandalized society. Women-only ascents were unprecedented, yet by 1920 *la cordée feminine* had become a trend.[9]

The most famous American practitioner was Miriam O'Brien. Daughter of a wealthy newspaperman, O'Brien was in many respects the typical eastern American alpinist. She had made a grand tour of Europe just before the Great War, and after the war she took up climbing, joined the AMC, and visited the Alps regularly. O'Brien distinguished herself as an alpinist, her personal guide Angelo Dimai even naming a route for her on Torre Grande. She thrived under Dimai's tutelage yet eventually concluded that climbing with any man had retarded her. If "women were really to lead," she argued, "that is, to take the entire responsibility for the climb, there couldn't be any man at all in the party." In 1929, O'Brien with Winifred Marples climbed the Aiguille du Peigne. Three days later O'Brien and Alice Damesme astounded the climbing world by ascending the Grépon. Soon other women rushed the Aiguilles Mummery-Ravenel, Blaitière, Charmoz, Droites, Matterhorn, Meije, Mönch, Torre Grande, and Grépon again. Then in 1932, O'Brien published an essay in *Appalachia* titled "Without Men: Some Considerations on the Theory and Practice of Manless Climbing."[10]

Historical research offers important insights about the gendering of climbing. Leslie Stephen's stages of mountaineering, the Alpine Club's bar against women, and auxiliaries such as the Ladies' Alpine Club in 1907, Ladies Scottish Climbing Club in 1908, and Pinnacle Club in 1921 bared a misogynistic strain among English climbers. Perhaps the most infamous case was not that of an English climber but a Chamonix guide named Étienne Bruhl. Shortly after O'Brien and Damesme had descended from the Grépon, Bruhl allegedly mourned: "The Grépon has disappeared. . . . Of course, there are still some rocks standing there, but as a climb it no longer exists. Now that it has been done by two women alone, no self-respecting man can undertake it." A more clearer link between masculinity and sport is hard to find, yet we can make too much of it. The Club Alpin Français had always admitted women, and not every Brit loathed women climbers. The London *Times* rejoiced when an English lady climbed Mont Blanc in 1854, and *Punch* gave "three cheers" for Lucy Walker. Moreover, if we take Bruhl seriously, if we think him representative, then what are we to make of the many thousands of men who did climb the Grépon after 1929? Did they fail to realize the pinnacle's degraded state or did they just lack self respect? If neither seems likely, then perhaps we overstate the significance of Bruhl's complaint. O'Brien, in fact, was climbing exclusively with her fiancé, Bob Underhill, by the time her essay on "manless climbing" appeared in 1932. Women matter intrinsically to the histories of sport and environmental culture, both for their participation and absences, so segregating their tales as gender-specific events deflects us from a more representative view of climbing culture.[11]

We need to reconsider clubs and to take much more seriously the cultural and environmental implications of group fun. Most climbing associations had no problem with mixed outings, and most women and men enjoyed each other's company in the mountains. In North America clubs were bastions of families and friends, and sociability was guaranteed because applications had to be endorsed by two members, sometimes only after an interview confirmed a candidate's respectability. This vetting process was buttressed by club structures. Annual outings were not terribly expensive, but their two-to-four-week duration limited participation. Dress codes reinforced conformity. The result was a wilderness version of the Greek system: demographically narrow and culturally homogeneous groups that filled their days with rugged adventure and nights with campfire parties, pantomime, and song. These were the figures in those photos of mob climbing. Seattle Mountaineers and Portland Mazamas climbed northwestern volcanoes en masse. The Sierra Club and Colorado Mountain Club gave awards for bagging 14,000-foot peaks. Members held induction ceremonies and weddings on summits. Their rites remind us not only that mountains were sacred places for western climbers but that their communions with nature were often social, even crowded, affairs.[12]

This was the milieu Robert Underhill encountered in 1931. He taught technique to people already acculturated to climbing as a social activity, and by December 1932 the Cragmont Climbing Club was linked to a society that regularly marched hundreds of people up mountains. Socialization was an integral part of sport, though we might never have known it from the dry, matter-of-fact reports of Dick Leonard and others in the first volume of the *Journal of the Cragmont Climbing Club*. For all his athletic, intellectual, and logistical gifts, Leonard, and his pals too, had blind spots that can obscure our vision. The last entry of that volume differed little from the first, and it mattered not whether Leonard, Kenneth May, Elliott Sawyer, or Jules Eichorn wrote the report. Their précis read like police blotters. The details they offer about attendance, practice drills, and routes climbed are as dryly objective as it gets, but, again, the journal reflected what mattered most to a few guys who were rather obsessed with rocks. Nothing they wrote prepares us for the journal's second volume.[13]

But for her relationship with Leonard, Doris Corcoran may well have remained a shadowy figure in the RCS, one of many names that pepper records but never emerge as fully fleshed individuals. Corcoran first attended practice in November 1932 with Leonard and his sister Claire, who may have played chaperone. It is not clear whether Dick and Doris dated before November, but thereafter she was a regular at weekly meets and Yosemite outings. Still, she is never more than a name in his prose. By her own admission she did not climb until May 1933. Only when Doris took over the RCS journal in April 1933, largely because Dick was studying for the bar, do we gain a sense of her as a person. Then our world changes. Her editorial hand profoundly alters our view of climbing culture. She humanized the sport, revealing textures and experiences that, while always present in the RCS, remained buried under Leonard's Joe Friday prose. Through Doris Corcoran we witness both athleticism and community formation. The humor, joy, sassiness, and camaraderie of group fun erupt from journal pages. Friendships, courtships, and families blossom, and with them a far more complex vision of climbing unfolds.[14]

Clambering over rocks was indeed the tie that bound, yet, paradoxically, it was not how the club spent most of its time. One entry for a trip to Mount Tamalpais reveals the proportional treatment Corcoran gave to the parts of the day:

TAMALPAIS—May 14, 1933.

Present: Leader Dick Leonard, Dick Johnson, Dorothy Bradner, Asta Selchau, Damina Zaro, Jules Eichorn, Cedro and Doris Corcoran.

We met at the Ferry at 8:15 A.M. There was a high wind blowing but the air was warm. We walked via Te-mel-pa Trail to the Summit where we had lunch. Excellent climbing was found on the East Peak. Several present were beginners, including myself, it being my first attempt at Rock Climbing. We practiced belaying and falling and we beginners did a few of the preliminary climbs. The two Dicks and Jules and Cedro then paired off and tackled the heavier climbing while the female members basked in the sun as long as it lasted. The fog rolled in around 3:30 and we all expe-

Figure 4.2. Richard and Doris Leonard, shown here in the early 1930s, perhaps on their honeymoon climbing trip in the Sierra, had very different climbing temperaments. Richard was extremely ambitious; Doris loved the social aspects of club climbing. Their different voices and priorities emerged in the Cragmont Climbing Club and RCS newsletters, yet both became influential members of the Sierra Club's board of directors in later years.

rienced a real treat in witnessing a 'Spectre of the Brocken', something rarely seen. By 5:30 we girls, pretty nigh to starvation and
freezing, hailed the boys and dinner was started. What a dinner
too! The fog had cleared by now and we had a magnificent view of
the Valley and surrounding country. After a conglomeration of
Pepper Pot Soup, Potatoe Salad, Hot dogs, Fried Chicken, Pickles,
Olives, Cake, Cookies, Beans, Coffee and Tea, we proceeded to
get under way. We missed the 8:40 train and had to wait till 9:10.
During the wait the boys reconnoitered the climbing on the West
face of the Mill Valley Station. During the ride home the time was
spent in dislodging ticks from one Jules Eichorn, much to the dis-
may of the writer.

The Ferry Building became the parting of the ways and we all
went home tired and happy.

Corcoran's light banter exposes a different facet of the RCS, one in which play
and recreation are essential components of outdoor sports. Play gains nuances never revealed by players at the elitist end of the climbing spectrum.[15]

Within the club, climbing was a social activity. Although the sport was
archetypically individualistic, seemingly obsessed with the imagery of lone
figures intensely engaged with stone, club climbing had many more dimensions. Individuals were intensely engaged with nature, but they pursued
their quests in an explicitly social setting. Climbing was performed; onlookers were an assumed presence. Corcoran's account reveals an interplay between those climbing and those spectating. Many times the "surrounding
rocks became box seats as we all gathered around to lend moral support."
"It was really marvelous," she added, "to watch the powerful muscles be-
neath the fingernails in the tiny ledges that existed." Climbing's voyeuristic
side was a communal and sensual experience that members both participated in and recorded for posterity with pen and camera. Moreover, climbers were willing accomplices, consciously, even outlandishly playing to the
crowd. Boulders were stages, climbers were performers, and clubs were audiences.[16]

The range and meaning of play only expands as we watch the crowd.
Climbing was important, yet not equally for all members nor at all times. It
instead shared the spotlight with swimming, talking, resting, picnics, Easter egg hunts, and listening to the radio. A steady banter ran between those
presently climbing and those presently watching. On one occasion Johnson
wrote, "Randy and Doris both practiced what Robert L. M. Underhill criti-

cizes very strongly, that is, coming out to climb, but sitting on the sidelines and watching others climb. However, the various pointed remarks aimed at them went for naught, and they continued to enjoy the view." Where teasing ended and flirtation began is not always clear. RCS records are peppered with a verbal form of footsies. Corcoran liked to call Johnson, a high-school classmate, the "skin you love to touch." Olive Dyer and Kenneth Adam traded playful barbs over her habit of knitting during practice. Ruth Dyar told her family that "More important than for me to fall in love with one of the Mountaineers, is for one of the more worthy to fall in love with me." It was all part of the mix of the RCS.[17]

Climbing culture neither began nor ended with the rock. Barbara Norris remarked, "It isn't all belays, pitons and rope—this rock-climbing business. One of its better points is the dinner and discussion that follows, when pleasantly tired and with whetted appetites, the group dash off to some member's house in time for dinner." Après-climbing dinners were regular events. The host watched as RCS members laid waste to bathrooms, ransacked kitchens (usually spaghetti and pot luck on a scale to feed the Cossack Army), and settled into circles on living-room floors. Then members became friends. Through the evening they talked, danced, sang, and even lovingly tolerated Dick Leonard's penchant for yodeling. They pored over photographs, watched home movies, played records, held scavenger hunts, and occasionally returned to the rock for late-night bouldering by flashlight. Flirtations matured. Occasionally someone deviated from the norm by dressing up, which was a sure way to draw attentions that soon escalated into pillow fights and wrestling matches, all of which only underscored the wonderful tensions of social climbing.[18]

Southern Chapter members developed a unique tradition. In 1939 Joan and Ruth Dyar, Howard Koster, John Mendenhall, Olga Schomberg, and Glen Warner needed somewhere to live, so they rented a house . . . together. Cohabitation was still scandalous, and the landlords would have balked had they not already known the six through the Sierra Club. Even so, they lived in an apartment on site for several months to watch for hanky panky. Neither the landlady nor the parents ever quite accepted the arrangement, yet nothing untoward occurred. Instead, they brought the club home with them. When they first moved in to 4343 Griffin Avenue, Mendenhall and Koster were RCS officers. To simplify their lives, they ran the RCS from the living room rather than the SC office, quickly dubbing it "Base Camp." As residents rotated, the house itself became the most stable presence in the RCS. It was where ropes were stored, meetings held, events organized, and newsletters

written, mimeoed, and mailed. Base Camp was where members met, socialized, and became couples.[19]

The social aspects of climbing were underscored by the time members
devoted to various activities. Except for outings to the Pinnacles, Tahquitz
Rock, Mount Whitney, and Yosemite Valley, the most anticipated event was
the annual banquet. The Southern RCS organized its first dinner in 1937,
the Northern RCS two years later. These evenings were filled with speakers,
movies, contests, and a lot of planning, including the renting of halls, send-
ing of invitations, organizing of meals, and managing of budgets. Somebody
brought a record player, others donated records, and everyone danced. So
much fun was had that practices the day after devolved into slumber parties.
There were also many lesser functions. Members gathered to watch theatri-
cal releases such as *The Challenge,* a dramatization of Whymper's 1865 ascent of the Matterhorn, and amateur films on RCS practices, ski trips, and
the 1939 American expedition to K2. They hooked up for lunches, sympho-

Figure 4.3. The announcement for the 1938 annual banquet of the Southern RCS gives a
sense of the warmly intimate nature of heterosocial climbing. Sport, fun, and romance
blended easily during this period.

nies, and exhibits, and Base Camp residents celebrated the one-year anniversary by reenacting the first meal: split-pea soup, crackers, and peanut
butter. The RCS functioned as both a climbing *and* social club, so trying
to separate these elements only obscures how members regarded them as
seamlessly connected.[20]

Newsletters were particularly attentive to these dynamics. Leonard began his journal to document club history for a few friends, and Corcoran
greatly expanded the scope of that history. Not until 1937, however, did the
RCS institutionalize this report. That year the Southern RCS founded the
Mugelnoos, named as a pun on a skiing term, and the next the Northern RCS
began *The Yodeler.* As newsletters documented club events on a regular basis, a much wider audience gained a view of the sporting and personal sides
of club climbing. Articles featured prominent individuals, relayed gossip,
and teased members mercilessly. Jack Riegelhuth was soon known simply as
"The Slug," while Daisy Miller was lampooned for using her chin as a "third
hand" during a climb. Scholars note that clubs used journals to establish authority and "provide a forum in which the values of the climbing community are developed and reinforced." Club publications did abet institutional
power, but the RCS newsletters contained a lot of information that was never
instrumentally about sport or authority. Rather, much of the energy members expended, and most of the content of these publications, was very simply and innocently about group fun.[21]

The most obvious evidence of these priorities were the many intimate
relationships which blossomed within clubs. In spring 1934 Leonard and
Corcoran married, and that fall Francis Farquhar, who mostly attended practices to watch, married Marjory Bridge. By 1936 the RCS was quite the domestic scene. During one outing eight of the fourteen attendees were married to each other. John Mendenhall and Ruth Dyar had to leave Base Camp
when they married, and Ruth's sister Joan, another Base Camp resident, had
to move out when she married Nathan Clark. Club genealogies grew tangled
when Jack Pionteki married Therese Kehrlein, youngest daughter of long-
time SC member Oliver Kehrlein. Other RCS marriages included Raffi Bedayan and Barbara Norris, Ellen Beaumont and Chuck Wilts, and Joe Firey
and Joan Wilshire. Elizabeth Lewis spoofed the frequency of these hitchings
when she assured her mates that they would "probably Get your Man. . . . I
notice practically all the girl rock-climbers do!" Ruth Dyar's letters revealed a
competition to draw and hold men's attention, but men were no different.
Several once explained that they were not married but "if they were, their
wives would not forbid them to climb, but would no doubt be right there

climbing with them." Although members were mostly drawn separately to the RCS by their interest in climbing, there were times, as with Corcoran, when women were pulled in by boyfriends or, as with Ivan Weeks, guys followed their girlfriends. For many members, especially those who found mates, there was no separation between play and life.[22]

Clubs thoroughly entwined sporting and social intercourse. Bob and Luella MacConaghy were "a typical S.C. romance. Boris Edgehill introduced the two at a Friday night dinner, next, Bob drove Luella home from a rock climbing trip; on their first date they went hiking, and led a trip to Crestview Lodge on their honeymoon—thus introducing the Mass Honeymoon." On their honeymoon, Dick and Doris Leonard wandered in and out of the SC outing and discovered a wedding cake left atop one pinnacle by friends. At such moments clubs turned climbing into a shivaree. Early climbers never lost sight of the intrinsically social nature of the RCS, nor was it the only club to behave this way. The Mazamas also "served as a social club for single men and women, where couples might meet and get married," and in 1941 an article in *The Woman* titled "You Needn't Be Lonely" recommended "among other measures, joining the Sierra Club." Climbing clubs were created to support climbing, yet that did not preclude activities that deepened the experience. By focusing solely on great climbs and climbers, we shortchange the social aspects of this and other outdoor sports.[23]

Although clubs could be intensely intimate, they also engaged with the wider world. Members were always meeting, recruiting, and training new members. Senior RCS members wrote articles, gave lectures, and aired films. The Bay Area Chapter spoke at schools. The Southern Chapter ran a Friday lecture series at Boos Brothers Café and offered to instruct "proselytes in tying knots, belaying, etc." During practices accomplished members helped novices, literally teaching them the ropes and guiding ascents. Richard Johnson described one session on Tamalpais: "Our boys had their hands full in teaching those who wanted to learn how to tie bowlines, how to belay from standing and sitting positions and how to fall." The students included some "very eager" Boy Scouts who happened by. It made for more work, but Johnson crowed "that we probably will have a few new recruits." Metaphorically and functionally, the RCS acted like an evangelical church. It transformed private enthusiasm into public appeals by preaching the gospel of adventure to the masses. Although members longed for paradise on high, they spent most of their time in the flatlands proselytizing experience and collecting converts.[24]

Keeping clubs going demanded major investments of energy. Even seemingly mundane things like weekly practices presupposed a schedule of locations and leaders. Such issues quickly exhausted even the indefatigable Leonard. The problem of where to meet on Sundays, and who to lead, was soon delegated to a Scheduling Committee, while a Locations Committee identified practice areas and, when needed, negotiated access with owners. Leaders tracked gear, counted heads, trained novices, and tempered elites. The Bay Area Chapter also struggled with finding locations that would satisfy their scattered membership. Committees balanced outings to San Francisco, East Bay, and Marin sites, and equalized committee representation. The Southern RCS in the 1930s had far fewer meeting places. Site prospecting was belated and conducted individually, and members voted with their feet. When John Mendenhall and Ruth Dyar scouted Strawberry Peak in the San Gabriel Mountains, a large turnout for the first outing ensured repeated visits, but when only four people attended a trip to Bonita Falls near Fontana, the site was dropped. The RCS's varied contexts thus also produced diverging organizational cultures.[25]

At times the sections seemed starkly opposed. The Southern RCS was stereotypically individualistic and automobile-bound, whereas the Bay Area Chapter showed Soviet tendencies, forming committees for seemingly everything, including banquet, knapsack, location, membership, mountaineering, movie, pin, publications, rescue, rope, and scheduling, not to mention a committee of chairs known as the Rock Climbing Committee (RCC). This was less a sign of incipient socialism, however, than a practical response to institutional demands on overcommitted, deeply bourgeois members. Such pressures were not new. In the 1920s the Portland Mazamas and Seattle Mountaineers dealt with members' diverging interests by forming mountaineering committees, just as the Sierra Club did with the RCS, yet these committees were but the opening wedge of institution building. In late 1936 Dick Leonard jotted down a few notes before yet another RCC meeting. His list of nagging issues amounted to a structural crisis. Club records were scattered and incomplete. There was little information on the extent, age, and location of gear. Committees met irregularly, and notes were random. This haphazard state posed several threats, including fiscal insolvency and unsafe conditions. If the club did not systematize practices, it might unravel like a worn rope.[26]

The main impulse for systematization was, again, the double-edge of growth. By 1941 the Bay Area RCS had surpassed five thousand attendees. Outing participation waxed and waned, but by 1939 the club had forty-nine regular members. Most lived in San Francisco or the East Bay, with outliers in

Salinas, Tracy, Modesto, and Boston. *Yodeler* distribution was even broader. Of its 304 subscribers, most lived in the Bay Area, but forty-three were scattered elsewhere in California, on the East Coast, or "Down Mexico Way." Paired with growth, however, was the problem of turnover, which ultimately underscored how similar the two clubs were. Each summer the Southern RCS performed a ritual putsch, expelling those who had not attended at least four outings the preceding year. In 1939 they voted in two members and dumped twenty-four laggards; in 1941 they added six, dropped nineteen, and still had over fifty members. The Bay Area RCS also tried to discipline members with mass meetings and threats of expulsion. It commissioned a club pin that, like the Sierra Club's badges for ascending 14,000-foot summits, rewarded achievement, reinforced camaraderie, and helped trip leaders identify members. The most important efforts to systematize, though, involved safety and technology.[27]

Not surprisingly, Leonard was the driving force behind safety consciousness, but his concern was widely shared. Accidents and deaths had plagued the SC for decades, beginning with the fall of a climber during the first ascent of the west couloir of El Capitan in 1905. There were more in the 1920s, including a fatal fall near Tuolumne Meadows on an annual outing and the time-consuming rescue of Charles Michael, another SC member, after he fell while soloing Yosemite's North Dome. It was the loss of a favored son, though, that most rocked the club. In August 1933 a young lawyer from San Francisco began a weeklong solo expedition in the eastern Sierra. When he missed a scheduled rendezvous, friends initiated a massive search with elite climbing teams and a plane. Weeks later the body was found on a remote ledge in the Minaret Range.[28]

The death of Peter Starr was a personal and sporting shock. He was from a prominent family long active in the SC. Honored in polite society and the mountaineering fraternity, Starr had been compiling a guide for the John Muir Trail, which ran along the spine of the Sierra from Yosemite Valley to Mount Whitney, the longest unbroken stretch of roadless area in the American West. Few could match his skills, which made his death all the more chastening. At the memorial Francis Farquhar eulogized Starr as a manly hero: "It is a grand company, those who have not come back. There are Englishmen—Mummery, of Nanga Parbat, Mallory and Irvine, of Everest; and the Americans—Allen Carpe and Theodore Koven, of Mount McKinley, Norman Waff, of Roberson, and now, Pete Starr, of the Minarets. The young men of today know them, and the young men of tomorrow will not forget them." Farquhar saluted the fallen climber, but he and others must also have worried that if even Starr could be stilled by a solitary misstep, then their own ventures were all the more risky.[29]

The RCS responded by trying to eliminate risk, or at least to increase control of "untoward occurrences." The desire to master chaos fed a widely held belief that proper discipline was the key to safety and success. Climbers everywhere were "quick to search for plausible causes of any mishap and to reassure themselves that had the relevant rules been followed the untoward event could have been avoided." Hoping to learn from others' mistakes, the RCS tracked climbing accidents around the world, while Dick Leonard monitored local accidents and climbers in a notorious black book. Training was another means. Although John Muir was a spiritual muse, RCS leaders frowned on his brand of solo climbing, instead setting time limits for routes and insisting that members pack extra gear, learn first aid, and follow protocols. Dick Jones captured this ethos of control when he instructed an audience that "Self-control, knowledge of knots and technique, and the increased knowledge gained from each experience, together with common sense, will all help to determine the necessary margin of safety."[30]

The RCS further evaluated members with qualification tests. The Appalachian Mountain Club first instituted tests in the 1920s. The RCS tried to transplant the system, but it did not address all the necessary skills. Members continually debated what should be tested, but a few things were commonly agreed. Ascent and descent of C-1 was mandatory in the Bay Area, as were standards for belaying, falling, and rappelling. The RCS also charted experience and certified leaders after climbing a list of routes officers deemed indicative of mastery. The Southern RCS established similar strictures. In addition to attendance and belay, fall, and rappel tests, members could climb at Tahquitz Rock only after ascending Eagle Rock and two routes at Devils Gate. They only gained access to Yosemite's walls or Mount Whitney after climbing one of "the more difficult Tahquitz routes." As will be discussed more later, the club was effectively a gatekeeper controlling people's access to public spaces through a regulatory structure that reflected both the technical and social concerns of responsible play. Later on the RCS added readings, including several of Underhill's articles, and additional climbs to its ever-evolving prerequisites for club membership and, at least for a time, easy access to more difficult climbs.[31]

The RCS monitored members' attendance and work ethic, but officers also issued instruments for members to police themselves. Called "climbing records," these single-sheet forms had a grid of practice sites and routes so climbers could record when and what they ascended. On the back were sections for their fall, belay, and rappel tests, a running bibliography of readings, and climbs made in the mountains. These document a spectrum of experiences. Some such as Ken Adams and Jack Arnold earnestly maintained their forms, diligently noting every practice, route, or text consumed. Of course, Dick Leonard had the most detailed sheet. He claimed twenty-three first ascents on local boulders and nine more in Yosemite Valley, and he had exhausted all the routes at fifteen practice sites. He knocked off readings with the same alacrity. Although busy building a law career, Leonard nevertheless had time to read twenty-six major works on mountaineering, the entire runs of *Appalachia* and the *Sierra Club Bulletin,* and many back issues of *Alpine Journal* and *Trail and Timberline.* Near the other end of the spectrum were Doris Leonard and Ed Koskinen, who practiced regularly but charted a decidedly modest list of climbs. There were also people who attended a few meetings and vanished, and members such as Artur Argiewicz, Raffi Bedayan, and David Brower, who climbed enthusiastically but had zero interest in forms.[32]

The more officers tried to control their sport, the more limits they encountered. There were the disorderly inconveniences such as a housing development that destroyed part of Miraloma Rocks, and outings cancelled by rain or, in one case, a herd of pregnant cows. More disturbing were the moments when nature revealed its instability. In 1940 the Southern RCS had to expand its list of concerns after a falling rock lacerated a member's scalp. Later that year the Bay Area RCS learned that their safety belay station at Devils Slide had itself slid into the sea. Even worse, the club's first major accident involved a fall during a rappel. The officers at first blamed incompetence, but their investigation "revealed the strong possibility that the rock itself had failed." Even the most experienced could falter. In October 1940 the mountaineering world was shocked when Don Babenroth, an officer of the AMC, died when he and four others fell during a practice climb. Two years later Clyde Nelson Jr. and Bill Rice, both from the Southern RCS, fell descending Grand Teton. As with Peter Starr, the fate of these respected climbers exposed the limits of control. Climbers tried to blame accidents on lapses of self-control, but experience showed they could never account for all contingencies. Later on risk became more appealing, but the climbing culture of the 1930s sought to minimize it as much as humanly possible.[33]

Technology thus commanded great attention. Safety hinged on reliable equipment, so RCS committees invested considerable effort to ensure gear was not a source of worry. Members probably spent the most time, certainly the most money, on ropes. Hemp, sisal, and cotton ropes degraded quickly, so the RCS replaced ropes annually to ensure safety. The Bay Area RCS spent $197.65 from 1933 to 1940, $140.57 of which went to ropes. New line was reserved for outings, while aging coils were rotated into practices. Members also debated rope length. Unlike modern line which is sold in predetermined lengths, the RCS bought spools and cut to size. They used half-inch ropes for climbing, and doubled a nine-sixteenths-inch line for rappelling. Some members preferred 150-foot lengths for ascent and 240-foot lengths for rappel; others favored 120-foot and 200-foot lengths. The issue was flexibility in climbing versus the number of ropes for outings. Economy took precedence in the club. To avoid confusion about provenience each lot was wrapped with a different-colored thread, and caretakers—Dick Leonard or Raffi Bedayan in the Bay Area, Base Camp in the south—stored gear. The RCS also lent texts such as Underhill's essays or articles translated from German and Italian journals to members. Even with a tracking system, caretakers begged for return of items, and occasionally practices were cancelled because of missing gear.[34]

Members themselves also investigated the nature of their gear. As with sports such as hunting and fishing, formal and tacit innovation had produced considerable advances in climbing equipment since the Great War. Just as guns grew more powerful and hunters learned to fine-tune equipment for particular goals, woven ropes grew stouter and more consistent and better carbon steel strengthened pitons and carabiners. Natural-fiber ropes were nevertheless fragile, and members had to ventilate them diligently to prevent mildew. They also had to figure out capacities. The Union Internationale des Assocations D'Alpinisme (UIAA) did not systematically test ropes until after World War II, so the RCS, like other clubs, did their own ad hoc research. A committee tabulated rope strengths based on information supplied by a ship chandler, concluding that four-stranded ropes were on average 10 percent stronger than three-stranded ropes. Then in 1934, Hans Leschke, an engineer, ran stress tests on ropes, pitons, and carabiners at Stanford University. The RCS repeated these tests in 1939 and 1942, and with the AMC at Massachusetts Institute of Technology in 1941. Members learned that the strongest four-strand ropes could hold loads of 3,400 pounds, but the slings through which climbing and rappel ropes were laced broke at 1,400 pounds. Worse yet, carabiner designs allowed gates to open at 1,050 pounds, enabling ropes to slip out. Iron pitons could hold loads to 10,000 pounds, but the steel rings welded onto pitons broke at 4,500 pounds and ropes run through those rings broke at 2,700 pounds. The nature of their ropes was also unstable. New line was quite safe, but under normal loads it stretched and rapidly lost effective strength.[35]

This was not comforting. Studies suggested that the nature of gear was as mutable, perhaps even more so, than the rock they climbed. Testing also left unresolved the question of the forces experienced in actual climbing. Leschke ran static-load tests, measuring steadily applied loads. He wanted to use a ballistic scale to simulate kinetic forces, believing it "quite possible that pulls of over 1050 pounds can occur" on leader falls, which later research would confirm, but the scale cost more than the club could afford. Nevertheless, they already knew that the nature of climbing ropes changed under normal use, and all carabiners were unreliable. Leonard also doubted "horizontal pitons," in which eyes were perpendicular to blades. He thought "vertical pitons," in which eyes were parallel to blades, worked as well and were less expensive. Morgan Harris and David Brower disagreed, arguing that perpendicular eyes added torsional strength and could be placed in more situations. Leonard resisted, and for once he took the losing side, but the main significance at the time was how little all those climbers knew about their gear.[36]

Historians of technology like to debate whether innovation is driven by internal or external factors. Does the internal logic of a design drive refinement, or is necessity really the mother of invention? Mountaineering history reveals both processes at work. In pursuit of the Matterhorn, Edward Whymper had his blacksmith fabricate special hooks, and other climbers devised pitons for local environments. By the early twentieth century a range of designs circulated across Europe. Sporthaus Schuster in Munich effectively narrowed the selection for American consumers by selling one of each type of piton—vertical, horizontal, and ring. The range sufficed on Cathedral Spires and other early climbs, but was insufficient later on. The RCS faced three emerging problems finding reliable gear in the late 1930s. First, Nazi militarism throttled the export of metal. By the end of the decade European pitons and carabiners had grown scarce and costly. Second, although German pitons worked well in quarter-inch fissures, Yosemite's cracks varied in width, forcing climbers to innovate. Finally, no existing carabiner inspired confidence, so the RCS experimented with designs and materials to resolve problems with strength and insecure gates. Thus external factors such as war, cultural acceptance of aid climbing, and geological contingencies combined with the internal limitations of existing technology to foster a domestic supply source.[37]

Making and refining gear posed challenges. Like sportsmen's grassroots efforts to create better gunsights, fishing lures, and birding glasses, members tried to build better equipment locally. Tom Rixon created a "wafer piton" for cracks thinner than normal, and Raffi Bedayan offered a galvanized piton that resisted rust. The problem in 1938 was less whether someone could make this gear than why anyone would bother. There was a demand. Inquiries about West Coast suppliers came from as far away as the East Coast, but local fabricators resisted. The work could be done, but there was no economy of scale. The cost per item was exorbitant because manufacturers could not sell enough units to offset initial costs for dies and stamps. RCS designs also posed problems. Galvanized pitons were so brittle Bedayan later warned climbers they "should *not* be trusted." Similar problems plagued the carabiner research. George Dondero made a much lighter design that passed stress tests, but it had the same unreliable gate. Bedayan tinkered as well, but when he, Bob Hansen, and Tom Rixon looked into making carabiners, they, too, learned that the milling machine ($500) and die ($35) were prohibitive. Then World War II intervened.[38]

The RCS eventually devised better tools, but even their failures, from the folly of nails to the sophisticated efforts of Dondero and Bedayan, said much about who was most interested in advances in gear, and for what type of climbing. Clubs invested lots of time and energy in technology because it was central to the game. It was no coincidence that the main producers of gear were also its most avid consumers. The last RCS order to Sporthaus Schuster in 1938 requested ninety-three pitons, sixty of which were for three people: Bedayan, Brower, and Ed Koskinen. Leonard and Dawson were also major consumers, and Hansen, Rixon, Bedayan, and Artur Argiewicz were among the most active climbers and consumers of gear by 1940. Of course this gear was used by everyone in the RCS, but the most aggressive climbers paid greatest attention to technology, and all were young men strongly committed to the sport.[39]

Women also cared about equipment, however. They were no less dependent on gear for safety, but within the RCS the committees primarily concerned with technical issues were dominated by men while women stereotypically attended to membership, banquet, and secretarial tasks. This gendered pattern held for other clubs as well, and it underscores the domestic tenor of the heterosocial club. Superficially, it also seems to suggest that serious climbing was a guy thing. The accomplishments of Marjory Bridge, Ruth Dyar Mendenhall, Phyllis Munday, Miriam O'Brien, and Betsy Cowles

Partridge belied that notion, yet it was a woman who first mocked the nascent gearheads. May Pridham was a design student at Pasadena Junior College, and in 1938 she deployed her sense of humor in a series of cartoons for the imaginary Little Gem Invention Corporation. Ads for things like "the famous Little Gem parachute," suction cups, a "piton gun," and "rubber pitons" adorned the pages of the *Mugelnoos* through early fall, and Arthur Johnson carried on with his own "panacea piton forge and forks." Lampooning lacked the moralistic edge of the 1920s or postwar era, however, because both artists depended on the gear they satirized. Johnson pioneered the first major aid route at Tahquitz, called *Piton Pooper,* while Pridham made manless first ascents in the Sierra and climbed a route at Devils Gate called *Pridham's Predicament.* Teasing members about gear was fair game because no-

LITTLE GEM RUBBER PITONS

Guaranteed to fit any crack. As they can be pushed in with the fingers, no hammer is needed. They can be used over and over again.

CAUTION : Due to the ease with which the Little Gem Rubber Pitons are inserted, they also come out rather easily. It is best to be equipped with a Little Gem Parachute when using these pitons.

Figure 4.4. May Pridham's satirical "Little Gem" cartoons were a great hit with RCS members in both Southern California and the Bay Area. Her gentle ribbing of club climbers' obsessions with technology lacked the moralistic edge of later eras in part because everyone still believed that safety trumped risk.

body disputed its importance. Advances in gear may have appealed most to the most adventurous climbers, but safe gear also enabled a safer climb for all club members.[40]

Safety and heterosociality were the core features of club climbing in the 1930s. Nothing better illustrates how these were integrated than the RCS outings to Tahquitz Rock, Pinnacles National Monument, Mount Whitney, and Yosemite Valley. Members prepared all year for these exotic locales, yet wilderness climbs remained intrinsically linked to the drills on boulders around urban northern and southern California. The mountains were not a world apart, and the early RCS outings gain additional texture when viewed as extensions of the club context.

These trips were compressed versions of the annual outings the SC had conducted since 1901. Instead of two- or four-week treks through the Sierra Nevada, the RCS exploited three-day weekends around Memorial Day, the Fourth of July, Labor Day, and Veterans Day. Instead of hiking amid sublime scenery with all the amenities, the RCS ran low-budget affairs at public sites. If the SC trips epitomized the genteel wilderness experience, RCS outings were the essence of car camping, yet they had much in common. Both depended on elaborate infrastructures. Summer SC outings needed laborers and animals to cut trails, pack gear, and fix meals, while the RCS relied on carpools, roads, parks, and campgrounds. Clubs also contributed. The Mazamas, Mountaineers, and Colorado Mountain Club all built lodges, and the SC erected a string of buildings from San Gorgonio to Donner Pass, including three in Yosemite National Park. These were refuges and social centers. Clubs even altered mountains by installing cable ladders on Longs Peak and Half Dome to aid ascent and by plumbing running water and digging outhouses at lodges. The simple climbing trip relied on resources ranging from the very personal to services by county, state, and federal agencies.[41]

One major difference between RCS outings and other trips was the terms of admittance. Both the Bay Area and Southern chapters insisted that members demonstrate competence before traveling to Yosemite, and both scheduled special trips so members could prove themselves. For the Bay Area RCS, the volcanic outcroppings at Pinnacles National Monument were a test site. About 130 miles south of San Francisco, the area became a regular stop for the RCS because these brecciated rhyolite pinnacles, some over 150 feet in height, posed challenges beyond the Bay Area boulders yet were less intimidating than Yosemite. By 1938, the RCS made visits in both spring and fall to evaluate members. About 120 miles east of Los Angeles, Tahquitz Rock served the same purpose for the Southern RCS. Although made of tonalite,

Tahquitz was called "granite U-ropia" by climbers because its cliffs resembled the Sierra stone. The Southern RCS made Tahquitz a prerequisite for bigger ventures, insisting that members ascend the technically moderate *Angel's Fright, Piton Pooper,* or *Mechanic's Route* before climbing in Yosemite. Unlike the older SC trips, RCS outings were earned, but that still allowed many people to play in Yosemite Valley.[42]

Planning began months in advance. A committee arranged food, accommodations, and rides. If it was a joint outing with another section, coordination work began even earlier to accommodate mail service. Once arrangements were finalized, members received a postcard with the date, estimated commissary (under $2.50 during the 1930s), and ride-sharing costs (about $3.50 from the Bay Area, more from Los Angeles). The few things members were expected to bring—sleeping rolls, shoes, silverware, knapsacks, canteens, flashlights, and sunglasses—underscored how much clubs subsidized sport before World War II. The National Park Service furnished the rest. Members usually squatted at Camp 9, the "Organization Camp," because it was reserved for large groups, but when the RCS arrived in late fall, they used Camp 4, also known as the "Winter Camp," because it was the only all-year site in the valley with a heated bathroom and running water. The first RCS trip in 1933 over Labor Day weekend was a modest venture by seventeen members from the Bay Area. By 1941, nearly 500 people attended, consuming over 3,000 meals. As the *Yodeler* explained in 1940, managing food, money, and reservations, not to mention the nightly battles with bears, was a major chore. The editor asked "the hundreds who enjoyed the trip" whether they realized "that their joy was the result of successful planning, and much HARD work?"[43]

The RCS applied the same systematic management to climbers. The first fall trip to Yosemite took place a week after Peter Starr's memorial service, so safety was on everyone's mind. The ledgers used to record commissary payments were also used to chart members' climbs. Trip leaders met each evening to arrange parties and record everyone's plans for the next day. The aim was to know that all had returned at the end of the day, and when to worry and where to look if someone went missing. The forms also enabled leaders to assess competence: what members were capable of and how fast they could climb. Now these ledgers and newsletters are our best evidence of the scope and tenor of prewar climbing. They tell us about the ambitions and values that shaped club climbing. Through them we learn not only who climbed what, and how fast, but the range of interests. The first day of the first trip, for example, four members tried to ascend Washington Column, while three began a route up Royal Arches. As during practice sessions, these ascents were attempted before an audience because both routes were within earshot of Camp 9. Most of the group shied from hero climbs, content to hike or scramble less technical ground. This became a trend. The ledgers reveal that well over half the RCS members preferred to enjoy scenery or follow qualified leaders up moderate routes. Thus in May 1936 thirty-three RCS members went to Yosemite, but only twelve did technical climbs. By 1940 the club accommodated this range of ambitions by arranging trips "each day for those of all ages, abilities or creeds."[44]

The patterns of Sunday practices thus migrated to Yosemite. Much as on the boulders, a few emerged as an elite contingent in the valley, foremost being none other than Dick Leonard. Although he was later an adamant voice for diversity, Leonard initially argued that the "purpose" of these trips was to "explore new rock climbing possibilities" on the "walls, pinnacles and domes." He and other driven members pioneered technical routes, spending much of the decade scaling the valley's remaining untrod summits such as Cathedral Spires, Church Tower, Pulpit Rock, Split Pinnacle, The Rostrum, and Kat Pinnacle. They also made a sustained effort to ascend several walls from floor to rim. Washington Column, Royal Arches, and Glacier Point were eventually climbed, but the 1,200-foot Lost Arrow Chimney was too difficult. Although Leonard and Brower failed repeatedly, they kept their humor, christening one high point *The First Error*. While most RCS members regarded climbing as but one element of their Yosemite experience, a core of diehards were extremely adventurous and competitive. They wanted, as Leonard put it, "to solve an unsolved problem." Their preparations were scaled-down versions of militaristic Himalayan expeditions, leaving little to chance. Like the Cathedral Spires, each route required extensive reconnaissance, detailed planning, and intensive aid. Major ascents revealed stereotypical strains of ambition, but the social aspects of the RCS diverged sharply.[45]

The heterosocial nature of the RCS fostered a novel climbing culture. Historians often treat the pioneers as a group apart—even some SC members felt this way—but RCS documents again reveal a more complex story. Even the hardest climbs were social events. On the first ascent of Higher Spire, four RCS members and the chief naturalist of Yosemite National Park climbed a nearby ridge to watch Leonard, Robinson, and Eichorn. There was no pretense of isolation. Spectators yelled encouragement, and climbers shouted and waved in reply. Both groups carried cameras to document the event. The "gallery" was on hand for other ascents as well, including The

Pulpit and The Rostrum in Yosemite, and Moro Rock in Sequoia National Park. Steve Roper suggested that women practiced an "unspoken avoidance of the major routes," but this too begs nuance. It was true that few women made major first ascents, but then relatively few of either sex did this. Conversely, men and women alike followed on these routes, and a few women were top climbers by any standard. Marjory Bridge made the third ascent of Higher Spire. Ruth Dyar completed the third ascent of the East Buttress and the first ascent of the Third Needle on Mount Whitney. Virginia Greever was on the first ascent of Washington Column and made an early ascent of Lower Spire. Olive Dyer, Ethel Mae Hill, Helen LeConte, Dorothy Markwad, and Harriet Parsons were as active as any male member of the RCS. More to the point, the RCS climbing records reveal a sporting culture in which men and women were anything but separate.[46]

Members sought escape neither from civilization nor each other. Climbing and spectating went hand in hand, a prime example being the first route on Washington Column. The first attempt to climb the column failed halfway up the western face. The team dubbed their turnaround point *Lunch Ledge,* an indistinct alcove barely visible from below with no great vista. Nevertheless, very quickly it became the valley's most popular route. Technically, it was moderately challenging and very secure. The rock was solid, the moves interesting and diverse, and there were many intervening ledges and trees from which to rappel. And because both the column and *Royal Arches*—another favorite—were near Camp 9, friends could follow the action. But watching had its risks. During Leonard's and Brower's ascent to the *First Error,* Doris Leonard kept watch from below. Unbeknownst to her, the two had to make a pendulum. When they did, "Dick gave an abbreviated wolf-call, Doris looked up to see why, and Dave launched a circling traverse through space. Too far below to discern the rope, Doris imagined the hurtling body to be the start of a 350-foot fall" and lost her lunch. When Eichorn dropped a rock off Higher Spire in 1934, several people feared someone had fallen, but instead of experiencing queasiness, Marjory Bridge reflexively reached for a camera. And when someone did fall off Lower Spire two years later, Brower, who was supposed to be taking photos, could only gawk in horror.[47]

All these experiences were fodder for an equally important event, the nightly gathering. As sociologist Richard Mitchell observes, "the climb is not over till the tale is told." So it was with the RCS. The return to camp initiated a series of formal and informal debriefings. Trip leaders were notified that members were safe and sound, and stories were traded over washtubs, meals, and campfires. Camp was a three-day version of the après-practice party, waxing and waning with the rhythms of eating, sleeping, and climbing. Members bragged and mocked good-naturedly. Sometimes RCS officers lectured on the sport's technical aspects, or invited rangers to speak on the history or ecology of Yosemite. Other times members performed skits recreating a funny moment such as a bear chase or climbing fiasco. They yodeled in the morning and sang at night. Their fondness for folk songs occasionally inspired them to rework a tune to tease, as happened when John Dyer and Joan Dyar were stranded on the Diving Board by nightfall:

> Oh, Johnny! Oh, Johnny!
>   out for the night
> Oh, Johnny! Oh, Johnny!
>   gave us a fright;
> We thought your gang was gone for good,
> But later on we understood
> 'twas Dyar necessity—but
> Oh, Johnny! Oh, Johnny!
>   please set us right
> About those long, dark nights
>   'til the dawn's early light
> Eased those Dyers' sad plight
> Oh, Johnny! Oh, Johnny! Oh!!![48]

"A Night on the Diving Board" was a bit of fun at the expense of well-liked members from the Bay Area (Dyer) and Southern (Dyar) chapters, but its humor skirted the edge of a submerged feature of heterosocial climbing: sex. The fact that Joan Dyar was part of the fiasco seemed portentous because her sister, the former Ruth Dyar, had been stranded overnight on Mount Banner with John Mendenhall only weeks before they were engaged. Members did not imagine romance. Just as at Sunday evening gatherings, in Yosemite members lost no opportunity to pinch a bottom. One morning Eichorn almost toppled the bacon tray "while dodging a pass made by one of the chef's helpers." Single members slept in sex-segregated groups throughout the 1930s, but boyfriends and girlfriends attended trips in growing numbers, as did whole families. Sometimes as much energy was spent on the dance floor as the rock walls. Bob Hansen remarked that members seemed to be "wooing the pitches all day and pitching the woo all night." This was a great appeal of the heterosocial club. Sport and life merged in a seamless web of relationships.[49]

7

THE ROCK-CLIMBERS

JAM CRACK JOE
By "Hoofin' Herb" Conn

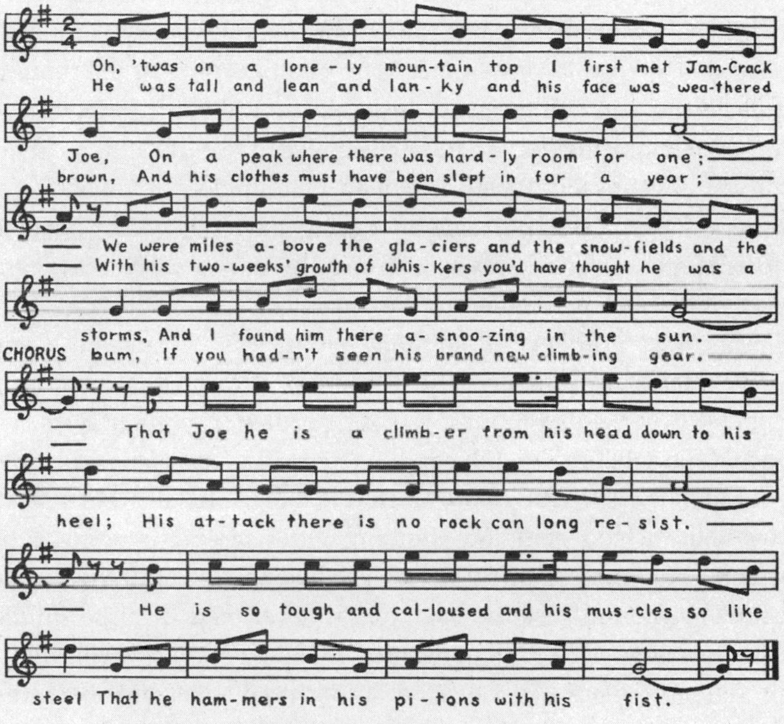

Oh, 'twas on a lone-ly moun-tain top I first met Jam-Crack
He was tall and lean and lan-ky and his face was wea-thered

Joe, On a peak where there was hard-ly room for one;
brown, And his clothes must have been slept in for a year;

We were miles a-bove the gla-ciers and the snow-fields and the
With his two-weeks' growth of whis-kers you'd have thought he was a

storms, And I found him there a-snoo-zing in the sun.
CHORUS bum, If you had-n't seen his brand new climb-ing gear.

That Joe he is a climb-er from his head down to his

heel; His at-tack there is no rock can long re-sist.

He is so tough and cal-loused and his mus-cles so like

steel That he ham-mers in his pi-tons with his fist.

If, as one sings the exploits of Jam Crack Joe, he catches a little of the spirit of rock-climbing and the true feel of the mountains it is because the words were written by a real rock-climber. "Hoofin' Herb" definitely knows his way around on the rocks. He has the unique distinction of being the only person to make a successful ascent of Herbie's Horror, a climb which is possibly too difficult even for Jam Crack Joe himself. When pressed by his associates to make a statement as to what prompts him to spend his spare time writing songs and climbing rocks Herbie grins forth with the philosophy of a true rock-climber: "It's all for fun and fun for all."

Figure 4.5. Herb Conn's "Jam Crack Joe" and impromptu campfire songs were a regular feature of club outings. This one circulated quickly among other clubs. First printed in the January 1944 issue of the *Potomac Appalachian Trail Club Bulletin,* by late fall it was already being reprinted on the other side of the continent in the *Sierra Club Bulletin.*

Yosemite Valley was less an escape from than an extension of civilization. The RCS transplanted to it a climbing culture that had developed both on the boulders and in the living rooms of the Bay Area and Southern California. Members carried with them attitudes that saw climbing and granite as intrinsically linked not only to each other but to values of safety and sociality that were, in retrospect, remarkably different from both the Victorians and later generations. Most members were more interested in fun than immortality. Their modesty explains their anonymity in history, yet it exposes a conceit that simply does not hold. Most climbers portray the mountains as worlds apart, and risk as an intrinsic element of sport. Robert Macfarlane thinks climbing reflects an innate impulse to test one's limits, that it is a confrontation between the individual and the shadow of "oblivion." He is an astute observer of the sport, but in arguing that it has *always* been about "the search for an entirely new way of being," he simply misses the degree to which climbers once strived for just the opposite.[50]

The historical influence of climbing clubs deserves greater attention. Whymper, Mallory, Mummery, and Underhill were mythical figures who drew attention to the sport, but it was the peculiar way the RCS integrated nature and sport that made club climbing appealing and acceptable to middling sensibilities. The club domesticated the sport. Its blend of safety and heterosociality helped legitimate climbing in the eyes of the Sierra Club and the National Park Service, and it is very possible that without the RCS those few climbers who did seek the edge might never have been permitted on Yosemite's walls. Rock climbing was initially valued because civilization and nature were not separate, risk was not a fetishized state, and sport was explicitly proestablishment. It was also emphatically heterosocial. Later in life Ruth Dyar Mendenhall remarked that there had not been enough women climbers in the 1930s to pursue manless ascents, but club records suggest that men and women, including the ambitious Ruth Dyar, climbed together by choice, not necessity. Moreover, this milieu enhanced the outing for all concerned. The archetypal Yosemite climber was not a loner pitted against vertical wilderness but instead a rather modest, fun-loving group of men and women climbing together as men and women together. Tensions between these visions did emerge in the final years before World War II, but full-fledged conflict did not become widely apparent until the late 1950s. Besides, in fall of 1941 other issues took precedence. War was brewing, and even Yosemite rock climbers were being drawn into the conflict.[51]

5. SOLDIERS

The knowledge thus gained over so many years will now be of great
value to the Country in time of war. Nearly all who participated in
those fine studies in difficult rock climbing are now serving with the
Armed Forces.
—RICHARD LEONARD

The New Deal and World War II transformed the American West. Public
works projects and war preparation created a vast industrial and recreational
infrastructure. They also drew new people to the region, including African
Americans from the South and rural refugees from the western South and
Great Plains, yet older residents were forced to the margins, especially people of Indian and Japanese descent. The economy accelerated after two bad
decades, but wartime rationing constrained all this newfound prosperity. It
got harder to run off and play, even compared to the Depression years. Visits
to Yosemite plummeted, and the face of the climbing club changed. Many
members enlisted as soldiers, pilots, seamen, WACs, and WAVs; most of the
rest went to work or became more deeply engaged in wartime research—so
many, in fact, that some feared the RCS would implode.[1]

This did not happen. Instead, clubs thrived as members transformed
its social and technical functions into wartime resources. The Sierra Club
helped recruit soldiers, and the RCS and Ski Mountaineers mobilized bodies and expertise to refine military equipment, all well before Pearl Harbor.
The RCS also provided important social and cultural services. As members
dispersed around the globe, the club maintained a sense of community, and
as members' knowledge of the world expanded, club newsletters became
forums for discussing the future of climbing and conservation. War revolutionized climbing gear, and overseas service transformed soldiers into wilderness warriors. By war's end neither was quite the same. No one was more
profoundly changed by these events than David Brower.

Brower's example offers a variation on why marginal boys gravitated to
the self-empowering world of mountaineering. Born to parents with post-
graduate training in mechanical drawing and literature, Brower grew up in a
well-educated but awfully snake-bit family. His mom lost her sight when he
was eight, and his dad was denied tenure and eventually lost his teaching job

at the University of California, Berkeley. To make ends meet the family sub-divided their lot and rented rooms. David helped by delivering papers, work-ing odd jobs, and nurturing his parents. He also grappled with his own inse-curities, including a ten-year span without two front teeth and then, in what must have been an extremely traumatic moment, an aborted visit by the UC Berkeley rush committee that ended when the visitors did not even bother to knock on the door of his modest home. Soon after Brower left college for a clerking job. Although he grew up with a father at home, unlike Dick Leon-ard, like many other climbers Brower seems to have lacked a strong male role model or cohort in his youth.[2]

In his twenties Brower transformed himself via climbing. His most pre-cious boyhood experiences were family camping trips, and he hiked and scrambled ever more in early adulthood. By fall 1933 he had completed a long list of nontechnical ascents in the Sierra. That summer he also met An-sel Adams and Norman Clyde, who introduced him to basic climbing tech-nique and to Dick Leonard. Leonard invited Brower to join the RCS and sponsored his application to the Sierra Club. Looking back, Brower marked this moment as the beginning of his "ego trip." In climbing he found an iden-tity and community. Within months he was one of the better climbers in the RCS, besting the boulder problems in Berkeley and the hard routes in Yosemite Valley. He was promising enough to be invited on a 1935 expedi-tion to British Columbia's unclimbed Mount Waddington.[3]

The trip cost Brower his job, but it was also a segue into a life increas-ingly framed by the Sierra Club. At loose ends, he moved to Yosemite to hike, climb, and ski. Friends inside the SC helped him find work first as an accoun-tant and publicity agent for the Yosemite Park & Curry Company and then as a darkroom assistant. When he returned to the Bay Area in 1938, friends again helped him find part-time work as an editor for the *Sierra Club Bul-letin* and *Yodeler* and then full-time work at the University of California Press. Drawn in by climbing, Brower's SC mentors, including Ansel Adams, Art Blake, Marjory Bridge, Francis Farquhar, Oliver Kehrlein, Dick Leonard, and Bestor Robinson, channeled him toward an intersection of sport and en-vironmental activism. His jobs honed literary and photographic skills that proved critical when Brower turned to advocacy, and Adams and Blake stoked his evangelical passion for wilderness. Very soon Brower was "lectur-ing the rest of us," Bernice May remembered. Climbing turned a shy, inse-cure boy into a confident firebrand. By fall 1941, Brower was a Yosemite and Sierra Club insider.[4]

Nowadays we equate U.S. involvement in World War II with the attack on

Pearl Harbor. Sunday, December 7, 1941, shattered our innocence, starkly dividing peacetime activities from war, yet RCS records reveal a longer relationship between sport and war. By 1939 many members suspected that war was coming when they had to shift from European to domestic suppliers for their pitons and carabiners. It seemed imminent when all climbing rope was withdrawn from the wholesale market in September 1941. By then the Army had also enlisted several members to redesign mountain equipment and prepare an Alpine fighting force. The attack on Pearl Harbor was a shocking moment, but in a very real sense the war had already begun for some in the RCS.[5]

Militarization of American climbing started in 1940 when members of the American Alpine Club (AAC) and the National Ski Association urged officials to develop a training program for mountain warfare. Charles Minot Dole, chair of the National Ski Patrol Committee, was a relentless lobbyist, and historians have foregrounded his role in creating the 10th Mountain Division and the war's influence in shaping postwar skiing. Dole's history tells half the story. While Dole lobbied politicians, the AAC formed a committee to write an Army report on modern mountaineering. In early 1941 some committee members, including Bestor Robinson and Leonard, joined the Army as advisors. In retrospect both men seemed destined for service—Robinson was a leading innovator of winter mountaineering, and Leonard was considered *the* technical expert on belaying and rappelling. Their posting at the Cold Climate Technical Unit may seem inevitable, but we must remember that their expertise came from pursuing fun. It was only the unforeseen contingencies of war that propelled them and other climbers into these roles, and no one suspected then that military service would alter postwar climbing as profoundly as it did postwar skiing.[6]

By mid-1941, RCS officers were less concerned about belay practice than national defense. At the banquet Robinson urged members "to perfect and standardize mountaineering techniques for military use," and to experiment "if necessary in an attempt to determine the minimum essential equipment for mountain use." By fall the RCS and Ski Mountaineers were recruiting soldiers. In October they encouraged early enlistment at a Commonwealth Club meeting in San Francisco, and in November they screened an Army film for members. After Pearl Harbor the Ski Mountaineers and RCS began to distribute questionnaires for the 87th Infantry Mountain Division, and in January 1942 club officers took over the Defense Committee of the California Ski Association, which coordinated training for prospective mountain soldiers. In the next two years the *Yodeler* and *Mugelnoos* relentlessly promoted

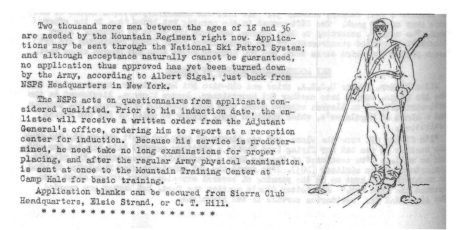

Figure 5.1. This ad encouraging club climbers to enlist in the Army's new mountain regiments came near the end of a year-and-a-half recruitment effort that began well before the United States entered World War II. Clubs would continue to make the war a central concern of their activities through VJ Day in September 1945.

enlistment. The club boasted its success at channeling men into mountain-fighting units in hopes of drawing more people to the RCS. Members even patrolled the backcountry for a regionally coordinated U.S. security network.[7]

Meanwhile, Robinson and Leonard joined the Quartermaster's Corps in Washington with a mission to develop better technology. Robinson headed a team researching textiles for mountain and arctic warfare, while Leonard refined climbing gear with researchers at MIT and the National Bureau of Standards. They were kids in a candy store. As one friend noted, "Anyone who knows Dick will know that working on a problem of *testing equipment* would be seventh heaven for Mr. Leonard!" After a decade of frustration, the RCS was now ordered to create the very things they desired—stronger pitons, trustier carabiners, lighter clothing, drier tents, warmer bags—and they had access to the most advanced textiles and metallurgy in the world. Robinson and Leonard led research, but the entire RCS contributed. Lab work was done in Cambridge and Washington, while practical testing took place in the field. In October 1941 the RCS formed a committee to conduct rope tests at Cragmont Rock and Indian Rock. Other research occurred in an Alabama swamp, a California desert, an Alaska mountain, and the cliffs of the Potomac and Yosemite.[8]

The war had widespread effects on sport. It revolutionized surfing and kayaking through advances in fiberglass the same way the space program would later contribute light alloys, synthetic fabrics, and freeze-dried food.

For the most part these were trickle-down benefits. Climbing was different; the intent was to make better ropes, pitons, and carabiners and lighter, warmer clothing and sleeping bags. The goal was still to produce a more effective killing force. Lightweight gear and clothing reduced a soldier's burden. A Garand rifle and a bandolier of forty-eight rounds weighed 9.48 and 3.25 pounds, respectively, and these were light weapons. A .50 caliber machine gun weighed 54.38 pounds, a 37 millimeter cannon 912 pounds. Antitank and mortar rounds ran 3 to 91.5 pounds each. Mountain troops lugged this materiel wherever they went, so eliminating even grams from carabiners and pitons, or ounces from jackets and tents, had strategic value. Similar concerns shaped manuals on climbing and skiing. Each innovation was initially a technology of war.[9]

The research and design program had its greatest impact on rope technology. The RCS spent the 1930s studying natural-fiber rope, but in 1940 the Potomac Appalachian Trail Club's RCS hinted at a new rope "reputedly . . . having a tensile strength 8 times that of Manila hemp." The mystery fiber was soon known as Nylon, a polymer created by DuPont. Leonard's first task from the quartermaster was to test every rope material imaginable, and now he could conduct static *and* kinetic tests with the help of Arnold Wexler, an engineer at the National Bureau of Standards who also climbed in the D.C. area. The results were dramatic. Nylon was three to four times stronger than sisal or manila under a range of wet and dry conditions, and far more resilient during destructive tests. It was also more elastic; "a considerable aid," Leonard noted, "with troops who are not fully trained in the technique of holding a fall." By fall 1942, "ropes, carabiners, and other equipment to be used by our Army [were] already far superior to anything ever imported from Europe." National security kept this secret, but in 1943 Leonard leaked a memo. Francis Farquhar was told not to publish it until after the war, but Leonard wanted to ensure his research was not "lost to posterity," a grim request reflecting the fact that many key innovators were about to go overseas.[10]

The natural-fiber era did not end suddenly in 1942. Nylon was expensive and, at times, hard to acquire, so for practical reasons clubs still used manila, sisal, and cotton for practice and rappels. Nevertheless, the Army's adoption of nylon opened a new era in sport, one in which industrial synthetics played an ever greater role. Cotton, crepe, manila, rubber, silk, sisal, and wool gave way to Kevlar, Nylon, Perlon, Spandex, and other petroleum-based synthetics, while aluminum and exotic alloys replaced iron and steel. War mobilized resources to empower soldiers, and the results eclipsed gear that had shaped recreation for a century. Such innovation set off revolutions in many sports because technology so altered outdoor experiences that participants had to redefine their rules to account for new, fundamentally changed contexts. The new gear made adventure objectively safer, a crisis even Dick Leonard did not foresee.[11]

Total war also reshaped how clubs functioned. Fighting a global conflict required sacrifices from everyone. Many went to war; the rest did without. When the government withdrew rope from the market in fall 1941, Leonard tried to balance concerns about war and safety by advising RCS members that, when "war ends, mountaineers will have available far better lightweight equipment of all kinds." The patriotic thing was neither to hoard nor "postpone getting articles that you will really *need* in the next few months." In August 1942, the government released "Victory Cordage," a hemp product that was slightly better than aging manila and sisal ropes, but its rough texture and uneven quality did not boost morale. Climbing grew more difficult as rubber and gasoline rationing curbed mobility. By July 1942, the RCS had come full circle. The Bay Area RCS had effectively reverted to the old CCC, meeting every other week only at sites near public transit, which meant Cragmont, Pinnacle, and Indian Rocks. The Southern RCS met biweekly at Stony Point, Devils Gate, and Eagle Rock. Scheduling accommodated most members, but some like Morgan Harris, who lived beyond public transportation in Palo Alto, resigned for the duration of the war.[12]

The greatest pressure came from enlistments. Of the SC's four thousand members in 1941, over one thousand women and men joined the military, an inordinate number coming from the RCS and Ski Mountaineers. Many enlisted immediately after Pearl Harbor, but a few such as Brower joined only when it was clear that a draft would nab them. In practical terms the military could not handle so many recruits at once, so the impact was gradual. Members left in ones and twos. Committees shuffled repeatedly to manage losses, often with women assuming roles usually held by men. Within months Base Camp had disintegrated and the bi-weekly *Mugelnoos* was put on a tri-weekly schedule. By fall 1942, the Regional Pacific Testing Committee needed complete replacement because "100% of this committee are now in the Service." The drain did not end until October 1943, when the Army stopped recruiting mountain troops. Clubs worried about the losses. In the Bay Area, Brower suggested tightening participation rules to ensure qualified leaders in his absence, but Leonard prevailed in keeping the existing policy of dropping members "only when it became apparent that active interest . . . shall have ceased." Climbers in the service would remain in good standing until the end of hostilities.[13]

Members enlisted, equipment aged, and resources shrank, but the RCS's persistence revealed its centrality to people's lives. Climbing and skiing initially grew more popular as prospective soldiers tried to learn or polish skills necessary for a more desirable assignment in the mountain troops, but by summer 1942 participation waned. A core group carried on, but morale began to falter due to the drain of bodies. Into this vacuum stepped older, less active members. In the Bay Area, Kenneth Adam and Virginia Greever Romain were once again running committees and practices. Down south Jim Gorin, Bill Pabst, and Chuck and Ellen Wilts seized the reins. Most were too old for service or had strategic deferments as chemists, engineers, or physicists. Buoyed by occasional visits by members on military leave, the RCS ground on through 1942 and 1943, meeting at old haunts or joining other sections to clean trails and support the war by, for example, picking fruit.[14]

A few even visited Yosemite. Park attendance fluctuated between 296,000 and 228,000 during the worst years of the Depression from 1933 to 1936, then rose to a half million into the early 1940s. By 1943 gas rationing reduced visits to 228,723, with 122,618 in 1944 and 139,701 in 1945. The RCS made a joint trip over Memorial Day in 1942, and the Bay Area RCS returned over Labor Day weekend. They already knew it was "the last [visit] officially scheduled for the duration" of the war. Thereafter members only made private trips "to the climbers' mecca." A few snuck off one warm weekend in November 1942 to make their last climbs before enlisting. Five returned in March 1943 to test gear for the Quartermaster Corps, and two on leave briefly visited in January 1944. With the best climbers in uniform, no new routes were blazed until fall 1945. Yosemite was simply too far away for the Southern RCS. In spring 1942 they chartered a bus to Tahquitz. After that only private parties visited, and even this was rare. A few tried other ventures. Helene Glass asked *Yodeler* readers for "any takers" on a backpacking trip in the Sierra. There were none. Few had the time or resources for such an adventure in summer 1943.[15]

Most members took it in stride, but not John and Ruth Mendenhall. Although others may have felt similarly pent up but left no paper trail, Ruth Mendenhall's wartime correspondence bristles with the frustrations of domestic life, the war, and the South. John had a deferment because of his engineering expertise, so he and Ruth took on assignments related to defense industry production. It was, his daughter explained, a fate that "disappointed

him the rest of his life." Ruth shared his discontent. Cooped up in the flatlands, both yearned for mountains, cliffs, even an old quarry, and both individually and together arranged leaves of absence to climb. One time they left
their year-old daughter with a "paid babysitter" in Alabama to make a first
ascent in Wyoming's Teton Range. If climbing grew less important for RCS
members directly involved in the war, the Mendenhalls' case suggests that
war only underscored the importance of outdoor sports for people trapped
in white-collar work.[16]

Although actual climbing declined, the RCS continued to function. Practice and attendance declined, but hanging out increased. Members sought
reasons to socialize, and the smaller the gathering, the more dear they were
to each other. The annual banquets persisted, but the "real highlights," one
member noted, "were the incomparable evenings at the Leonards. Rafters
groaned and walls resounded as squirming masses of assorted climbers"
sang, danced, and talked. Those out of sight were never out of mind. Newsletters kept tabs with good news and bad. They noted assignments and pro-
motions, engagements and marriages, births and deaths. Clubs may have
begun as sporting organizations, but by the 1940s members shared a history that went beyond play. These relationships mattered, and the *Yodeler*
and *Mugelnoos* were no longer just about climbing. They helped maintain a
community literally scattered across the globe.[17]

Club rags were coveted in military camps. Soldiers became avid consumers and producers of gossip, relaying bits about Army life and fellow members. Their letters reveal that, aside from the irritations of regimented life,
the first year of service was sometimes a lark. Paul Estes bragged that he had
"formed a climbing club" at Fort Lewis in Washington state, and later that
he had "been skiing for 10 weeks now and will keep on until the snow disap-
pears. Am going on a eight-man, two weeks expedition to the top of [Mt.]
Rainier soon, supplies to be dropped by parachute." Others with college degrees were made officers and assigned to lab, desk, or teaching jobs. Robinson and Leonard shared a forty-seven-foot yacht on the Potomac, climbed
on weekends with a local club, and lived with their wives for months. More
were reunited when the Army expanded the 87th Mountain Regiment into
a full division of 15,000 and concentrated the mountain soldiers, including
most of the country's top climbers and skiers, at Camp Hale in Colorado. The
newly formed 10th Mountain Division was a homecoming, and by early 1943
many RCS members were at Hale.[18]

Letters during this period bore a carefree, seemingly arrogant air, but
there was a deadly seriousness to Hale. The RCS were among the country's

best climbers, and sometimes they needed all their will to cope with the ignorance and officiousness. Early months were marred by near disasters. Two regiments from the South and Plains had few soldiers with mountain experience, and officers did not realize they should adjust packs and marches to avoid exhaustion at high elevations. A two-week maneuver in −25°F temperatures and heavy snowfall inflicted frostbite and pneumonia, and morale did not rebound until the original officer corps was reassigned. Poor performances underscored the role of proper conditioning, so the Army placed the most fit in charge of training. By mid-1943 the skiing and climbing schools were directed by members of the National Ski Patrol, American Alpine Club, Sierra Club, Colorado Mountain Club, and Mountaineers. Put another way, the enlisted were running the show.[19]

Club alliances in the 10th Mountain Division were critical to this shift in control. By the time Brower enlisted in October 1942, many climbers were in position to protect his file from the bureaucracy. At the Quartermaster General's Office, Leonard attached a telegram from the Adjutant General so Brower went to Camp Carson for basic training with the mountain troops, then to Fort Benning for Infantry School, and finally to Camp Hale. At Carson, Capt. John Woodward, friend to some "skiing associates," assigned Brower to work on a mountain training manual. Then at Brower's entrance exam for Officer Candidate School, Major Paul Lafferty, who first met Brower while snow camping, intervened to ensure the poorly prepared Brower passed. Lafferty then sent Brower and other RCS members to the Assault Climbing School at the West Virginia Maneuver Area at Seneca Rocks. When the Army disbanded the school and scattered the instructors, Brower and others phoned Leonard, Robinson, and Dole to get their orders countermanded. Within hours they were reassigned to Camp Swift in Texas, where Lafferty saved Brower again from duties he could not perform by making him an intelligence officer.[20]

In this manner many regular officers at Camp Hale and elsewhere ended up taking orders from lower-ranking soldiers on how to ski, climb, and survive the mountains. It was awkward for everyone. Most instructors were not built for regimentation. Donning a uniform was difficult enough, but giving orders to officers induced waves of irony in all concerned. Artur Argiewicz was as unlikely a commander as ever existed. A bookish introvert, he nevertheless had strong ideas about how to train climbers and, with support from Leonard and Robinson, he, Brower, and others rewrote the Army manual and shepherded thousands of soldiers through intensive, two-week courses at Hale and Seneca Rocks. Conscripts and officers alike spent one week inside, the other on the cliffs. Occasionally an officer balked at the arrangement, but most saw that their lives depended on what they learned. Brower noted that most "soldiers would never, had they been asked, admit to any affinity for rock-climbing, but you didn't have to ask." They took to it with such alacrity their "skilled instructors [shuddered] at the abandon with which they took to holdless pitches and nauseating overhangs."[21]

Most historians have focused on the links Camp Hale created between soldiers and the postwar skiing industry, but in terms of the war itself, climbing mattered more. The 10th was not sent overseas until November 1944, when it was thrown against heavily fortified Nazi units in Italy's Apennine Mountains. Few troops skied because gear was late and then spring was early, but many climbed steep cliffs or used Tyrolean traverses, crossing a rope between two points, during assaults on Riva Ridge and Lake Garda. Heavy attrition exposed problems. In retrospect training at Hale and Seneca Rocks was impersonal and shortsighted. Soldiers were run through by the company. Even worse, there was no backup, so new troops were trained in Italy during the winter at "a battalion an hour." Robert Bates taught officers in the lobby of a spa, while H. E. Link and John Clement lectured in a theater and "Sergeant Duke performed an hilarious strip-tease [of the relevant gear] which riveted attention on the stage." With an hour of training, replacements entered the brutal campaign. In five months the 10th suffered an extraordinary 37 percent casualty rate, with 992 dead and 4,154 wounded. The lark gave way to a short but harrowing war.[22]

Keeping members abreast of events overseas was wrenching. In 1943, Dick Leonard joined a "newly organized Observations Section" and went to Burma as, essentially, a fashion spy. His mission was to identify the materials Japanese soldiers wore and learn how to improve Allied clothing for jungle warfare. It was a perfect job for someone with his interest in technology, but members lost track of him. A year later he wrote from an Assam hospital to say a tropical disease made him lose thirty-five pounds. Members waited another month to learn of his recovery. Other delays were more excruciating. Not until spring 1943 did members learn Leland Chase, Dick Peterson, and John Wiggenhorn were captured when Japan invaded Manila in January 1942. Word of their release came only in October 1945. Emotions vacillated in the extreme. The *Yodeler* and *Mugelnoos* spread joy when Robin Hansen earned the Distinguished Flying Cross, and sorrow when Argiewicz and Jack Benson died in Italy. For better and worse newsletters maintained a community in offices, planes, prisons, trenches, and hospitals across four continents.[23]

Figure 5.2. Members of the 10th Mountain Division did most of their mountain training at Camp Hale in western Colorado, but rock climbing skills were honed at the Assault Climbing School in the West Virginia Maneuver Area at Seneca Rocks. Training was designed to represent actual wartime conditions, so climbers wore full field dress and even carried packs and arms.

In the early 1940s, news of the war eclipsed other issues in climbing newsletters, but even during the conflict, in fact because of the war, climbers gave thought to wild nature. Newsletters provided a platform for their concerns. Climbers had advocated for mountains for a century. The Alpine Club mobilized to bar rail projects from the Alps in the 1880s. American climbers battled for nearly as long to save Crater Lake and Yosemite Valley. The Mazamas and Sierra Club had used recreational outings as political recruiting programs since 1900, and in the 1920s North American climbers founded the Associated Mountaineering Clubs of North America and Federation of Western Outdoor Clubs to save the environment. These were modern political networks, yet they held no single vision. Although Sierra Clubbers shared John Muir's hatred of sheep as "hoofed locusts," the Mazamas nearly self-destructed over an effort to stop grazing in the Cascades. Similar tensions split the Sierra Club during campaigns to dam Hetch Hetchy Valley and improve a road through Yosemite National Park. Outdoor clubs were neither culturally nor politically homogeneous.[24]

Climbers were equally diverse. After Robert Underhill's 1931 visit, Ansel Adams said rock climbing "should be accepted with the greatest enthusiasm, yet I feel that certain values should be preserved in our contact with mountains. While it is rarely a case of the complete ascendancy of acrobatics over esthetics, we should bear in mind that the mountains are more to us than a mere proving-ground of strength and alert skill. Rock-climbing should be considered a thrilling means to a more important end." For Adams, that end was best expressed by Walt Whitman: "while the great thoughts of space and eternity fill me/I will measure myself by them." Like John Ruskin, Adams stressed the importance of contemplation. Leonard and Robinson were equally sure that exertion enhanced appreciation. Brower was an extreme example of how some climbers even sexualized the mountains, believing "a peak that had been climbed would rate, on a scale of one to ten, hardly more than a one. An unclimbed peak, especially if many attempts on it had failed, rated the full ten." For some of the most ambitious climbers, conquering virginity still eclipsed other motives and emotions.[25]

Adams and Brower might seem fundamentally opposed, yet both articulated a selective and anthropocentric regard for nature. Neither objected to "gardening" plants and dirt from piton cracks, nor to killing any rattlesnake they encountered. Both opposed road and tram projects that opened primitive areas to the masses, yet both helped build and plumb club huts in those same areas. For Adams, Brower, and other club climbers, even Robert Marshall and Aldo Leopold, wilderness values reflected human concerns.

Throughout the 1940s, the wild mountains were still primarily refuges from civilization, landscapes for manly testing, and places to encounter the sublime. Concerns for these refuges' ecological health gained traction only in the 1950s.[26]

The postwar transition was part of a generational shift in politics that began before the war, to which the RCS supplied an inordinate number of leaders. Brower, Leonard, and Robinson had already tweaked the annual outings by giving greater consideration to fragile environments, young families, and recreational trends. Along with Marjory Farquhar, Braeme Gigas, Howard Koster, and John and Ruth Mendenhall, they became organization leaders, working on key committees and joining the board of directors. As Michael Cohen notes, it "was not clear to anyone that technical climbs produced conservation warriors, yet a list of the active Club climbers in the early 1930s doubles as a list of the men [and women] who became the Club's most energetic campaigners for conservation." After the war they emerged as political forces.[27]

Sport and war were central to shifting attitudes toward nature and our place in it. To a considerable extent Americans related to nature through sport. They valued mountains primarily as sites for fun and self-discovery. Play was the pretext of their attraction to nature, and war was the contingent event that changed this relationship. In taking up climbing, members did not intend to become literal or figurative warriors, but special skills channeled them into special units. Those units then carried them to exotic places, and their experiences altered their perspectives of the West. Brower journeyed through the Alps, Leonard traversed the Himalaya, but the Sierra remained the prism through which they viewed these foreign destinations. Brower wrote, "Italy is a good example of what can happen to mountains. At the front we see lots of piton country, including scenes that could be wild and beautiful. But in addition to war damage, there is the wrecking of scenery that Italians have been indulging in . . . for centuries." The damage was a litany of progress: "Roads, trails, railroads, houses, shacks, stone walls, terraces and power developments." "As a result," he warned, "country almost as rugged and potentially as beautiful as some Eastside Sierra localities is cut up beyond relief." Leonard added, "the Jeep which doesn't need roads, and the helicopter and other small planes are matters that we must be thinking about very seriously now." Brower ended: "Spare us."[28]

In the midst of war, a debate broke out over the future of wilderness politics. Brower and Leonard were only two of many members contemplating postwar environmental politics. Marion Randall Parsons "kept her spirits up by thinking about the undesecrated American earth." Kenneth May argued that "the proper development" of skiing and climbing were "of importance to far more people than those happy few who fully appreciated the mountains and are eager to preserve them for the use of all likeminded people." Dick Riegelhuth broadened perspectives by rhapsodizing about Texas's Big Bend country. Arthur Blake fanned discussion by reporting on plans to defile California's peaks with trams, roads, and resorts. Stationed in the Alps at war's end, the mountain troops took time to climb and ski, yet like George Perkins Marsh eighty years before, they regarded the Old World as an object lesson about how not to ruin the New World.[29]

Their worries stemmed from many issues, but a basic concern was the cultural implications of nature in outdoor recreation. Wilderness was not only a representation of the sublime but a space that had long been the ground upon which people had tested themselves physically and spiritually. From Moses and Jesus to the Puritans, pioneers, and knapsackers, it had been a "proving ground" of character and identity. Since recreation's rise as a preferred way to express manhood, wild nature had been a stage for extreme performances of manliness by climbers and skiers. By the early 1900s war was the only experience that still trumped reaching a pole or climbing a virgin peak. A wartime debate about wilderness thus crystallized issues as few contexts could. Wilderness was becoming an ever more precious physical and cultural resource.[30]

Peace was also why most pioneers stopped climbing. The reunions began in May as members straggled home in ones and twos. Excitement rose in July when the Army announced the 10th was headed home to prepare for the Pacific Theater. Japan's surrender on September 2 meant loved ones would become civilians within weeks. Attendance at Sunday practices and parties grew throughout spring and summer. Easing gas rationing even allowed the first club trip to Yosemite in three years. The RCS was not alone. July visitations almost doubled those of 1944. Total war relaxed, and Americans exhaled. RCS members assured themselves "that climbing was, after all, an unchanging thing," but one *Yodeler* writer admitted that "No, it wasn't really like old times." The face of the club had changed. A new generation had emerged, and older members' priorities had shifted. The *Mugelnoos* took a census. The Southern RCS had seen ten marriages and forty births since 1941. Bay Area RCS members were no different. Adulthood seemed to close a chapter, but endings were not so neat.[31]

Vital statistics were not always reliable predictors of participation. Parenthood did not necessarily slow climbers, but then climbing had not slowed

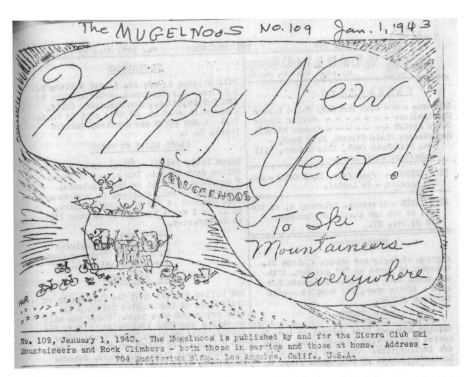

No. 109, January 1, 1943. The Mugelnoos is published by and for the Sierra Club Ski Mountaineers and Rock Climbers — both those in service and those at home. Address — 704 Auditorium Bldg., Los Angeles, Calif., U.S.A.

Figure 5.3. Phoebe Russell's banner for the New Year's edition of the *Mugelnoos* in 1943 shows how climbing clubs evolved during the war. The swarm of bicycles and baby carriages reflect the effects of rationing and of maturing relationships. The greeting to "ski mountaineers everywhere" speaks to how members had been scattered across the globe by the war.

the growing families of several RCS pioneers before the war, including those of Dick Leonard and Bestor Robinson. Marjory Farquhar did blame "the baby production business, and . . . the war" for her retreat from the sport, and Leonard said his own declining participation was "because the war came along." In fact his break was longer and more complex. Leonard explained that he "started to lead the Sierra Club [summer outings in] 1937, so that took up my entire summer," yet he completed a major ascent of Glacier Point in 1939. He did spend far less time on the rock, but as a Sierra Club officer he continued to influence Yosemite climbing for two more decades.[32]

Peace itself was the decisive event. For many members the sport had been a surrogate rite of passage, a way to demonstrate something to oneself and one's peers in the absence of other resources. As Richard White notes, the middle class had embraced forms of play that made it seem "as if [their] lives depended on it." Climbing was exceptional in that lives really could hang in the balance, but it was still a form of risk that was both totally voluntary and had no purpose beyond self-satisfaction. War put play in its place;

sport paled in cultural significance. Having risked their lives for truly great stakes, older RCS members reassessed their willful courting of risk. Climbing seemed like child's play, perhaps in some cases even foolish. The pioneers had grown up, and like most of their generation, the war became the defining event of their lives. Climbing no longer mattered so much. The telling exception were individuals such as the Mendenhalls, who had not gone through the tempering fires of war in the same way. For them, climbing would continue to form the basis of their identity for decades to come.[33]

6. INDIVIDUALISTS

Vigorous discussion [ensued] about independent parties scuttling
the scheduled trips, and apparently avoiding them when possible.
[It was a]dmitted that those involved attended some scheduled
trips, but seemed to like going elsewhere, and did so at every opportunity. . . . The section cannot become stronger or grow if the strongest climbers and most active are not willing to give some of their
time and patronize the scheduled climbs if possible.
—MINUTES OF THE ROCK CLIMBING COMMITTEE

For all the fun and camaraderie, a basic tension lurked at the heart of climbing clubs. The Sierra Club's Rock Climbing Sections disciplined members to
an ethos of sober fun. The most and least talented were equal members so
long as they mastered basic safety procedures. This policy empowered all
climbers by legitimizing the sport with key institutions, but for those few
who had ability and ambition, the RCS increasingly represented a tyrannical
force that restrained and even coerced. How clubs and individualists negotiated this conflict bared the radiating forces within the elite sport and the
modern environmental movement.

At first only wealthy climbers could afford to own their equipment *and*
travel independently to mountains. Others had to pool resources, especially
during the 1930s. Thus when Eichorn, Leonard, and Robinson traveled to the
Cathedral Spires as a private party, they went with several friends and borrowed club equipment. Clubs subsidized early technical climbs in Yosemite. They were a necessity, yet clubs and members did not necessarily share
agendas. Clubs needed talent to train and lead the less capable; talent
needed club resources. Tensions existed between them from the beginning,
even over seemingly mundane issues like tracking down borrowed equipment or enlisting outing leaders. Over time conflicts proved more vexing.
The more ambitious top climbers became, the more club officers were compelled to rein in their stars. By the late 1940s, the escalating difficulty of
routes drove the best to associate separately and skirt duties. By the mid-
1950s youths went their own way. Slowly, inexorably, the club ceased to be
the center of Yosemite's climbing culture.

Institutions produce inertia, however, and because of its special setting,

Yosemite was shaped by both the SC and the National Park Service. The NPS had long accepted climbing in the high mountains, but park officials feared Yosemite's walls. Several spectacular accidents illustrated the risks of rescuing the scared, tired, injured, and dead, and rangers were rightly leery of people who intentionally scaled these cliffs. As a result the RCS battled impressions of recklessness for decades with only partial success. Some officials dismissed the sport as a stunt, but climbing *was* dangerous. The SC and NPS nevertheless built a working relationship in which club training became the basis for climbing legitimacy. The entente made the RCS the de facto governing body of Yosemite climbing, and served both the RCS and NPS for several decades. Their interactions also offer an intriguing glimpse of personalities that later tore apart the Sierra Club.

Before the advent of clubs, climbing alone was often the only option. In the 1860s, Clarence King was lucky to have Richard Cotter and Jim Gardner as partners. In the 1870s, John Muir claimed that "No mountaineer is truly free who is trammeled with friend or servant, who has the care of more than two legs," yet he usually had no choice. Climbing Mount Ritter in 1872, Muir found himself in a vertical cul-de-sac, "suddenly brought to a dead stop, with arms outspread, clinging close to the face of the rock, unable to move hand or foot either up or down." Panic seized him. Trembling and "nerve shaken" as he imagined "a lifeless tumble," his "mind seemed to fill with a stifling smoke." Of course, Muir did regain his composure and did reach the summit. His tale, recounted many years later, now inspires mountaineers who regard him as the first existential climber, but this was not always so. Pre-war climbers, some of whom knew Muir directly, "frowned upon" his soloist inclinations.[1]

The RCS rejected Muir's example and instead established a tradition of safety. They cherished adventure no less, but they rigorously avoided undue risk, favoring the easier routes or turning away. Original SC members Joseph N. LeConte, Theodore Solomons, and others climbed portions of the Sierra that even Muir could not reach, yet they almost always did so with company. Only two dared to emulate the old man. The first was Charles Michael, a postmaster in Yosemite Valley who pioneered many airy routes in the valley and high country. Often climbing with his wife Enid, when things got dicey he went on alone. One time Charles left Enid on a ledge and completed a winding ascent of an unclimbed pinnacle now called Michael Minaret. He returned unscathed from what even he admitted was a risky endeavor. Later on the slabs of North Dome, Michael fell hard, but that story must wait.[2]

The other soloist was Norman Clyde, a classically educated midwesterner who began climbing in 1914, joined the SC, and went on a fifteen-year tear. Like Underhill, Clyde at first focused on things other than mountains. He married and taught school, but when his wife died he sought solace in the backcountry. In the 1920s he became the most accomplished climber in the Far West. By 1928 he had amassed over three hundred Sierra ascents, forty-six of which were firsts. That fall he brandished a gun before several students, and parents made him resign his teaching and principal positions. It was his last steady job. Clyde retreated to the mountains, carrying legendary packs filled with everything from skillets and anvils to firewood, cameras, and classics in the original Greek. David Brower dubbed him "the pack that walks like a man," and Clyde climbed so often that the *Sierra Club Bulletin* published a separate section for his ascents each year.[3]

By 1930 Clyde was a singular figure in mountaineering, yet he was no longer alone in the mountains. A horde of climbers, many of whom joined the RCS, were swarming over the Sierra. In addition to Glen Dawson, Jules Eichorn, and Dick Leonard, the *Bulletin* reported on William Horsfall, Oliver Kehrlein, Nelson Nies, John Nixon, John Pearne, Bestor Robinson, Paul Roberts, Howard Sloan, and Carl Sharsmith. In the early 1930s, Brower and Hervey Voge joined the rush. So many people entered so quickly that a generational shift was already underway before Robert Underhill's visit, but the changes were at first slight.[4]

In most respects there had been considerable aesthetic continuity since Muir. All mountaineers tended to marry romanticism and masculinity in their prose. Muir described Ritter's "savagely hacked and torn" aspect, his "inexhaustible" strength, and the sublime view: "How truly glorious the landscape circled around this noble summit!—giant mountains, valleys innumerable, glaciers and meadows, rivers and lakes, with the wide blue sky bent tenderly over them all." Such moments led Muir to counsel "tired, nerve-shaken, over-civilized people" that "going to the mountains is going home; that wilderness is a necessity." Clyde likewise loved being free of "the distractions and restrictions of the city; the enjoyment of superb scenery; the appreciation of plant and animal life." A mountain tarn was "a beautiful sheet of limpid blue shining like a mirror in the dawn," and exercise and ultraviolet rays produced an "almost immediate increase in the number of red corpuscles" of "a city-jaded tramper." Everyone from Muir to the tyros of the early 1930s wrote this way, including Geoffrey Young, Alfred Mummery, and Leslie Stephen. Muir stood apart only in his mystical moments, as when he "shouted and gesticulated in a wild burst of ecstasy" at the upper Merced basin, or crept to the lip of Yosemite fall to sense the water's power, or climbed a

Douglas Fir to experience "the passionate music and motion" of a summer storm.[5]

Michael Cohen argues that "mountaineering was an aesthetic experience; the men who opened up routes on the high peaks were expressing their love for the mountains," yet we should realize that this was a covetous love. Muir boasted to Jeanne Carr, "Give me a summer and a bunch of matches and a sack of meal and I will climb every [peak] in the region." Brower titled his climbing résumé the "First 1300 Miles in the Sierras." Many others kept astonishingly meticulous accounts of their trysts. Brower's list began facetiously with an "ascent" of Founders Rock on the UC Berkeley campus at the age of five and went on for three pages until 1933. The next summer he added many more on an epic, seventy-three-day trip through the Sierra with Voge. As accomplished as he was, Brower was not among the top five climbers of the RCS. Helen LeConte had kept a three-page résumé of her own since 1918, Voge's was four pages, Ken May's six, and Peter Grubb's eight. The longest, unsurprisingly, was Dick Leonard's eleven-page, single-spaced account of hikes and climbs since 1908. No one seemed to share Wilderness Society founder Bob Marshall's habit of tabulating both mountains climbed and women dated, but the impulse to record conquests was essentially the same for Don Juans, peak baggers, birders, hikers, hunters, and anglers. Such lists expose the social implications of wilderness escapes.[6]

Preeminent climbers were individualists, men and women who distinguished themselves with daring ascents, yet in breaking from the pack they paradoxically joined a group of like-minded individualists. All read widely about European traditions, and their experiences and values tended to conform to their heroes. A journalist noted that Brower "often invited comparison with John Muir," yet his writings suggest more varied influences. Brower once crossed between Mount Winchell and Agassiz Needle in the eastern Sierra. To give this otherwise nondescript journey meaning, he "dubbed it 'Agassizjoch.'" There is little that is Germanic about that pass. Looking eastward, the Owens Valley and White Mountains are as un-Alpine as it gets in North America. Brower's inspiration was not natural; it came from "having read about such places in a mountaineering book." He did share Muir's passion for climbing and defending mountains as if they were possessions, but that was where commonality ended. Muir did not keep lists, his mysticism went unmatched, and Brower and others imbibed their climbing values from the Victorians, not Muir. Both Muir and Brower were peak baggers, and their hunger for the journey *and* the summit differed little from other mountaineers.[7]

The RCS techniques changed how individualists climbed. By 1932, cars and all-year roads had improved access to Yosemite, but carabiners, pitons, and ropes made climbing more social. Top climbers could visit Yosemite independently, but difficult routes required help. Individualistic climbing was both more dependent on others yet increasingly at odds with clubs. A similar trend emerged in the Pacific Northwest, one that officers of the Mazamas and Mountaineers labeled "outlaw climbing" because it took place beyond, often in defiance of, club sanctions.[8]

Change was at first tentative. The first attempt on the Cathedral Spires was during an official outing, and later tries were hardly solitary. In November 1933 and again in April and August 1934, Eichorn, Leonard, and Robinson traveled with a band of friends and rangers. The gatherings reflected the political implications of climbing as much as friendships. Less demanding ascents rarely garnered such crowds, and climbers often avoided audiences. Leonard and Oliver Kehrlein tried the southwest face of Half Dome repeatedly without fanfare, as did climbers in Tenaya Canyon, Rodgers Peak, and Mount Shasta. In each case their break from the club was temporary, however. We ultimately know about these journeys because individualists reported to members through letters and articles. Individualists remained attached to the club, yet each success inspired more private quests.[9]

RCS members soon extended beyond the Sierra. By 1935 they had visited Arizona, Baja California, Nevada, Oregon, and Utah. By the outbreak of World War II they had first ascents in most western North American ranges, scaling so many peaks they lost track of where they had been. In 1939 ten Southern RCS members claimed the first ascent of Telescope Peak's 11,000-foot east face only to learn that four Bay Area members had climbed it in 1927. Ambition finally exceeded ability on Mount Waddington. In the early 1930s Robinson learned of a huge spike of unclimbed rock and ice in the Coast Range of British Columbia, an intriguing challenge Don Munday had titled "Mystery Mountain." Robinson recruited Leonard, Eichorn, and Brower for what seemed like just another spire: "We figured we could rock climb there as well as anywhere else." Instead they spent weeks in 1935 slogging through rain forests and waist-deep snow or enduring storms. The following year they were overawed by the mountain's unremitting avalanches.[10]

Waddington exposed American mountaineering's diversity. The RCS seemed unstoppable. Their philosophy of safety first empowered them to try hard routes in a deliberate manner, but Waddington's uncontrollable nature stymied them. The fastest route to the top was a 3,000-foot couloir, but the team "stayed out of it because we decided that it wasn't safe." Instead, they chose a ridge because "it is the soundest rock." It did, he admitted, have "fewer hand and foot holds than usual. But it is safe, since anything that falls passes by either side." The group's inexperience on snow and ice limited them, but so did their safety ethic, which had channeled them onto more difficult terrain. Attitudes about risk were highlighted two days later when Fritz Wiessner and William House rushed the couloir for the first ascent. Wiessner's experience in the Alps taught him that speed was a legitimate way to reduce risk on unstable mountains. Leonard never accepted this. Four decades later he still dismissed House and Wiessner as "just lucky they weren't hit."[11]

The sport Leonard had liberated rapidly moved beyond him. First was the matter of maturity. By 1937, work and family were deflecting him. With a wife, daughter, and law practice, he did not have the energy to remain atop the RCS hierarchy. Even his logistical talents on Waddington backfired when the SC asked Leonard to run the summer outing program. Eichorn and Dawson were similarly hemmed in by families and backcountry scouting programs. In the final four years before the war, Leonard would manage just two significant routes: Split Pinnacle and the east face of Glacier Point. Age and maturity drew the RCS founders in new directions, and younger climbers filled the vacuum.[12]

The next generation did not so much emerge as erupt. Dick Leonard's training system enabled athletes to develop so quickly that younger climbers soon ran circles around Leonard and other founders, scampering over boulders and cliffs that repulsed the "old guard." No longer did climbers need long seasoning. They could train locally on weekends and dash off in elite teams for quick conquests at Pinnacles National Monument, Sequoia National Park, and Yosemite. The *Yodeler* reported breathlessly: "Scramming to the Valley Saturday night, Torc Bedayan and Fritz Lippmann dashed up Arrowhead chimney for a fine first ascent." The new cohort also repeated the classics in faster times, even ascending both Cathedral Spires in a day. They pushed new and harder routes near Lost Arrow and Washington Column and mastered the unclimbed Pulpit Rock, Kat Pinnacle, and K. P. Pinnacle.[13]

Pioneers mostly took it in stride. For Leonard and Marjory Bridge, climbing had been a cherished phase of life, but family was a natural maturation. If their eclipse stung, they did not show it. After the ascent of The Pulpit, for example, Leonard and Brower engaged in obtuse self-mockery by insisting that it could not have been climbed because their own failures proved it was prima facie impossible. Everyone had a good chuckle, but the laughter faded when Bob Hansen hinted that the RCS had declined once his peers entered service. Lobbing a gendered insult, he called one outing "below standard for a good rugged grandmother trip." The retort was swift. Brower bitterly denied that stateside climbers were less accomplished than Hansen's now "middle-aged" generation, which, as Art Argiewicz noted, had been too self-absorbed to train climbers to fill their void. The spat was brief and left no scars, but its heat revealed a level of frustration simply absent until the transition.[14]

The flames were fanned by a second rift over commitment and competition. In 1936 the RCS team wanted to beat two rivals to the top of Waddington, but it made a deliberate choice and their slow progress forced a decision to hunker or retreat. Unwilling to risk a high, unplanned bivouac, the RCS backed off, tipped their hat to Wiessner's party, and conceded: "It's all yours." Four years and a cohort later, roles reversed in the Bugaboos, a dramatic set of granitic fins that rise from glaciers in eastern British Columbia's Purcell Range. In 1938, Glen Dawson led the Southern RCS to the popular Bugaboo Spire. When he saw the unclimbed Snowpatch Spire, he said it "looked so tough we did not even make a formal attempt." Wiessner did try later that year, but he thought it could not "be climbed without extensive use of artificial means" and did not "care much about nailing my way up a peak." Here was the essence of genteel mountaineering: restrained competition and a rejection of untoward methods.[15]

In 1940 four members of the Bay Area RCS shrugged off these precedents. Raffi Bedayan, Jack Arnold, Ed Koskinen, and Fritz Lippmann were determined to finish the job. An initial attempt winnowed them to Bedayan and Arnold, who soon passed Wiessner's high point and, contrary to predictions, summited using only two pins for direct aid rather than Wiessner's six in failure. What most distinguished Bedayan and Arnold was not their technique but commitment. More than any previous RCS expedition, they were willing to bivouac high and use aid to succeed. Younger climbers were also more willing to crow. The *Yodeler* framed the team's superiority with a litany of quotes from previous parties on the impossibility of Snowpatch Spire. The next year Lippmann, Arnold, Koskinen, and Jack Pionteki returned to climb Howser Spire in a manner they made clear was faster and more proficient than their Seattle-based rivals. Their overt competitiveness rankled. Harriet Parsons criticized speed records and asked, "Is that what we are training young climbers for? . . . I know you're all good, and this proves you are even better . . . but still—I wonder."[16]

The next generation did not. In the final years before World War II, their confidence led them to the unconquered plums of Alaska, Canada, and the

American Southwest. The most famous of these highlighted a new relationship to technology. Old qualms about ironmongery were fading. Although Arnold and Bedayan did climb Snowpatch in better style than Wiessner, they were ready to use many more pitons. This attitude was even more evident in northwestern New Mexico. Near the edge of the Navajo Reservation, a 1,700-foot core of fluted basalt pierces the desert floor. Navajos have revered it as Tsé Bit'a'í, or winged rock, while settlers likened it to a ship sailing across the San Juan River plateau. By 1935 climbers called Shiprock "America's toughest climbing problem." Many brooded over the "volcanic monster." Dick Leonard was flat-out obsessed. In 1938 he dubbed himself the RCS "Intelligence Officer," turned his den into a war room, and systematically collected data for what became the crowning ascent of American mountaineering during the interwar period.[17]

Perhaps a dozen parties had tried, including a 1937 attempt by the Colorado Mountain Club (CMC) that ended in near disaster and a thrilling *Saturday Evening Post* essay. Robert Ormes, a member of the CMC climbing party, said they were spurred to action by "a sudden fear . . . some other party would be the first to conquer its summit," but the author of the widely distributed article insisted they "were surely not seeking fame." Victorian platitudes sounded hollow. Competition was intrinsic to elite climbing, and climbers' actions belied their words. The article also bared a voyeuristic fascination with sporting risks. Ormes had a near-fatal fall, saved only by a single piton he called "a piece of bent iron." The *Post*'s story included a photo of him dangling upside down after the critical slip. Still, no one had climbed higher, and everyone knew Shiprock's steep, rotten rock posed an extreme challenge. Most American climbers were neither technically nor psychically prepared in 1939, and the RCS was, as historian Chris Jones notes, "probably the only group on the continent capable of making the climb." Jones calls them "a home-grown group, owing no allegiance to hallowed traditions," but emphasizing their independence does not do justice to the aid they received from other clubs.[18]

The RCS's Shiprock ascent exposed the delicate balance of tradition and competition. In his usual way, Leonard left nothing to chance. He queried all previous parties, yet his letters show not that "the military metaphor predominated," as Michael Cohen suggests, but that genteel codes still facilitated sharing of information among rivals. They researched and plotted for a year. Only in October 1939 were they ready to try "the Ship." Brower, Raffi Bedayan, and John Dyer set sail with Bestor and Florence Robinson. Dick and Doris Leonard followed. Two days later they asked the Navajos' permission to climb and rendezvoused with several CMC members. The rival club's assistance only underscored the gentlemanly rules still informing the sport. Wandering around the rock the first day, everyone concluded that previous routes were dead ends. The RCS took a different tack. They followed the CMC route for several pitches, then descended over a ridge to skirt the headwall that had nearly killed Ormes and persisted even after gaining only twelve feet the second day.[19]

The RCS's familiarity with technology was crucial to their success. They carried 1,400 feet of rope, the largest supply of pitons in North America, and expansion bolts, which were a new tool in American climbing. Normally used in building construction, these metal rods required pounding holes in the rock with a handheld drill. The Bay Area RCS had used bolts as "bomb-proof" anchors locally and at Pinnacles National Monument. The RCS preferred routes with cracks, ledges, and trees, however, because they had qualms about bolts. In contrast, a hole could be drilled anywhere and, thus, anything could be climbed with enough drills and persistence. Using machines to pierce and penetrate pristine nature, with all its sexualized connotations, also exposed questions about the proper use and meaning of the vertical wilderness.[20]

Bolts threatened to negate nature's challenges, but in this case the concerns were muted by the nature of Shiprock, whose flaky breccia and unstable piton cracks offered more than enough risk. Without compunction the RCS placed 54 pitons and 4 bolts, and once again raised the ire of purists, who damned them as blasphemers. Many more were impressed. Shiprock was one of the hardest routes ever. The whole club felt pride. Brower mocked his "Rocking-Chair"-bound critics. Robinson boasted: "I am a rock engineer and proud of it," and he called critics' bluff. If they "really wish to eschew all artificial aides, let them abandon ropes and shoes for surely these are products of a mechanized society. Let them establish a 'Nudist Climbing Club' if that is the way they enjoy climbing." Reading the exchanges, the CMC's Carl Melzer anticipated "little further from the 'purists' and 'nudists.'" By spring 1940, the RCS had expanded the legitimate uses of technology in adventure.[21]

Bedayan, Brower, Dyer, Leonard, and Robinson gained instant fame. Brower wrote an essay for the *Saturday Evening Post,* and all were accepted into the prestigious American Alpine Club. The only thing was: Dick Leonard did not climb Shiprock. As John Dyer made the final scrambling moves to the summit, Leonard was hundreds of miles away, already assuming a new role within the climbing community. As four RCS individualists reached the pinnacle of interwar climbing, Leonard began to forge a new relationship that became critical to the postwar sport.[22]

While the climbers set camp, Dick and Doris sped southeast to a regional conference of NPS superintendents in Santa Fe, New Mexico. They were specially invited as SC representatives. Doris was an authority on many issues, and Dick was an expert on safety. Both spoke about the need to build stronger alliances between clubs and the NPS to enhance the safe enjoyment of national parks, but they and Harlean James, who represented the Federation of Western Outdoor Clubs and was the only other non-NPS official at the meeting, argued most strenuously for the acceptance of recreation as a legitimate activity in the parks.[23]

That they had to make such an argument might seem odd given the RCS's safety record, but the NPS was justifiably skeptical. Rangers had rescued visitors from dire situations for decades. The problem was not that it had to conduct rescues. The NPS dealt with everything from nose bleeds and snake bites to body recoveries. This included unintentional climbers, typically hikers who lost their way or tried to shortcut the steep trails to the northern or southern rims of Yosemite Valley. Rangers spent hours or days searching for lost souls, often assuming great risk to retrieve victims of accident or stupidity. In 1935, Robert Tate and Elizabeth Lorimer were hiking back from Half Dome when they took a shortcut down a steep gully abutting the northwest face. The "trail" ended on a ledge, and when Tate sought escape he fell, injured his shoulder, and lacerated his head. Lorimer stayed put, yelled for help, and was rescued after a twenty-four-hour, hair-raising operation. Similar accidents had happened for decades, but they were growing more frequent with more, and more adventurous, visitors.[24]

Intentional climbers also caused havoc. Tourists fell from Yosemite's cliffs and boulders with distressing regularity. One died in 1924, another in 1926, two in 1927, and two in 1928. The most famous rescue took place in December 1928, when Charles Michael broke a leg soloing North Dome. Rangers hiked eight circuitous miles to reach him on a long winter's night. The superintendent described the ordeal as "rough and dangerous," but later rescues made it look simple. In 1930 rangers "had to use ropes and extension ladders and first aid" to lower a boy from a cliff next to Yosemite Falls. A month later they lowered another boy 400 feet. The superintendent bragged how rangers "functioned excellently in emergencies—scaling the cliffs to lower down the over-adventuresome, searching for lost visitors, and in the innumerable and sometimes almost fantastic episodes that enliven official existence here." Unstated was that they had no training. The result was frightening when Al-

Figure 6.1. This photo of Alfred Soares, Octavio Camara, and several rangers after a harrowing rescue from a gully high on the northwest face of Half Dome in 1934 reveals the physical and emotional costs of such crises. Park rangers found themselves responding to ever more calls by the late 1920s, and the prospect of allowing climbers to scale even more technical faces filled many rangers with dread.

fred Soares and Octavio Camara climbed the route Lorimer and Tate had descended. Stalled "high up on the northwestern face of Half Dome," their "signal fires and muffled cries" once again "exposed rescue forces to unusually arduous and hazardous effort."[25]

Most crises involved unaffiliated individuals, but the SC was also implicated. Soares confessed that Oliver Kehrlein had inspired his attempt, and SC hikers had to be rescued from North Dome the same fall. The RCS tried to insulate itself. Robinson had emphasized safety in his essay on the first ascent of Higher Spire, and Francis Farquhar defended the RCS to superintendents. Officials were not impressed, especially after the Southern RCS bragged that Phoebe Russell climbed the same route that stopped Soares, Camara, Tate, and Lorimer. One ranger asked a newsreel team to film the Tate-Lorimer case, hoping that showing "the dangers of wandering off trails would be beneficial." When not reckless, climbers merely annoyed. Rangers at Sequoia had to manage "gawking crowds" when Southern RCS members climbed Moro Rock. The *Fresno Bee* said the "unvarnished truth . . . is that most of these acts are stunts inspired by bravado. They permit the climber, if he is successful, to gain momentary fame but they contribute little or nothing to the world's advancement." Little wonder the Leonards had to defend climbing in Santa Fe.[26]

The NPS did not universally oppose climbing. It rebuilt the Half Dome cable route each spring, and rangers acknowledged major climbs, socialized with the RCS, and occasionally climbed with them. That said, some park officials did rue climbers, and some rangers could be obstructionist. Just before the Santa Fe meeting NPS director Frank Kittredge heard mountaineering clubs complain that "rangers sometimes know nothing about mountain climbing and yet dictate to those who do." The RCS joked about one ranger who allowed a Bay Area hiker on Mount Rainier but barred a Himalayan veteran because the ranger did not know that K2, Kanchenjunga, and Nanga Parbat were the second, third, and ninth highest peaks in the world. The way Leonard and the RCS responded to this political landscape resulted in new institutional relationships between the NPS and climbing clubs that quickly became critical in sustaining the sport in national parks.[27]

It was not enough to argue that members of the RCS were different from those who needed to be rescued. The NPS had already proved it could not distinguish competence, so Leonard proposed a two-pronged strategy to help sort bodies. The first was to use climbers as seasonal rangers. This would place experts on staff as liaisons and key personnel in emergencies. The NPS agreed and, fittingly, hired Jules Eichorn as its first climbing ranger. Eichorn in turn got the NPS to purchase climbing equipment and to allow him to teach rangers technical climbing and high-angle rescue. When Eichorn left to teach music, Tom Rixon took over, and when Rixon became a permanent ranger in 1945, Jack Riegelhuth got the job. In the next decade several more members served as climbing rangers.[28]

Their main duty was managing the other policy: a climber registration system. Leonard argued that a register tracking climbers' movements would at the very least "facilitate any rescue work that might be necessary," but he went further. The RCS already tested member competence, so it was a small step to let rangers use RCS lists as screening devices. By requiring climbers to register before climbing, NPS officials could, in theory, control access and prevent accidents. Rangers adopted both measures, and the system began propitiously. Club climbers did register, and relations between the NPS and RCS stabilized. No policy could stop all accidents. Tourists still wandered off trails, and boys convinced of their immortality continued to prove themselves wrong. How rangers responded underscored the impact of the system. When a convalescing Navy officer was trapped on a ledge in 1945, the "efficiency with which the rangers executed the rescue" deeply impressed officials."[29]

The policy changes also increased the authority of the RCS. While Leonard had charted proficiency since 1932, he had never used these lists to restrict access. Formal classification thus signaled a new level of intervention. Morgan Harris objected in principle because he doubted any such list could fairly assess or improve climbing ability. He also feared the rankings would erode a communitarian spirit by encouraging "an individualistic struggle for recognition." RCS officers listened politely, but their main concern was how to refine tests. In 1946, they even suspended the entire club until members passed a new test. When complaints followed, officers explained that it was "a 'safety' test rather than 'proficiency' test." This was hair splitting. Safety was philosophically linked to proficiency, and in the next decade leaders expanded standards to assess an ever-wider range of skills. They also imposed a mandatory list of Yosemite routes members had to climb to be qualified leaders. By 1950, climbers had to go through the RCS to climb in Yosemite Valley.[30]

The RCS classification and NPS registration systems were mutually constituted systems of power. RCS lists helped the NPS patrol climbers, and NPS reliance on RCS endorsement made it the de facto gatekeeper to Yosemite. There was nothing sinister in this. Leonard wanted to ameliorate tensions, and the NPS wanted to reduce risks. Nor was Yosemite unique. Similar arrangements emerged on Mount Rainier with the Seattle Mountaineers, in Rocky Mountain National Park with the CMC, and on Mount Hood with the Mazamas. Everyone involved wanted safety, but their tradeoff reshaped the sport. By war's end individualists' access to mountains was increasingly mediated by land managers coordinating with clubs.[31]

Because these systems drew clubs into co-management roles, they enhanced the club's ability to aid or punish climbers, a power the RCS used for both purposes with individualists. In April 1941, the Rock Climbing Committee met to discipline Bob Hansen, Fritz Lippmann, and Jack Pionteki. The ostensible issue was an unsanctioned ascent of Lower Spire with several climbers judged insufficiently experienced. Leonard lectured that

> formerly when climbs like that were planned, the R.C.C. passed on the competence of climbers (informally), as not only the personal safety of the climbers was involved, but the reputation of the Sierra Club. There has always been cooperation with the park service in connection with climbing once the S.C. was able to

show its good faith and prove by safe climbing that it would always be responsible for its climbers. The continuance of this trust and the consequent freedom given to S.C. climbers in the Valley, rests on the continued care with which the climbing parties pick their men or women, and the responsibility they take in ensuring in every way as safe a climb as is possible. Without the full cooperation of the climbing parties with the Sierra Club principles of safe climbing this faith in the S.C. may not continue.[32]

Tensions went beyond arguing over competence. Lippmann and Hansen also planned to skip an upcoming RCS outing in favor of a private run to Yosemite. Fearing the implications of "independent parties scuttling the scheduled trips," and that the RCS could not "become stronger or grow if the strongest climbers and most active are not willing to give some of their time and patronize the scheduled climbs," officers pressed the pair to give way for the sake of the RCS. Under threat of an unspecified but obvious punishment the two conceded. The RCS disciplined individualists by curbing access to equipment for private trips. More efforts to "crack down" occurred in the late 1940s and 1950s, and as late as 1961, RCS officers were still explaining to members that the screening process was "for your protection—and for ours."[33]

Under different circumstances the RCS used its leverage to support individualists. The club did still subsidize climbers by purchasing and loaning gear. Through Leonard it also lobbied on their behalf, resulting in the NPS announcing in 1950 that "mountain climbing is a legitimate activity in the national parks and one which need not be discouraged." When Yosemite's superintendent threatened in 1952 to ban "stunt or spectacle climbing" due to onlookers and poor rescue capabilities, Leonard said relations "must be handled very delicately." Although keen not to "endanger the good relations" that existed, he had the SC board of directors pressure the NPS. Leonard intervened again in 1954 when the NPS insisted that the only way the San Diego RCS could attempt a major ascent was if a support party waited below with a rescue litter, and in 1957 when the NPS barred more climbers. Brower took over in 1959 when the NPS director briefly prohibited all "stunt" climbing. Wayne Merry and Warren Harding later confessed that without such assistance the first ascent of El Capitan "might never have been successful." The RCS did support individualists, but only after it vetted them.[34]

Dick Leonard was the heart and soul of the system. Rangers and registers had been his inspiration, and his reputation with the SC and NPS legitimized arrangements. He was simply the most influential climber of his era. The system was supposed to be objective and impersonal, yet when problems arose both the NPS and RCS turned to him. There was a built-in limit, however. These policies were ultimately products of, and thus limited by, the context. The stress on safety was borne of a necessity to appear responsible, and its regulatory solutions flowed from a genteel assumption that institutions knew best. The small world that made this work was crumbling by the early 1950s, however. Outdoor recreation was growing rapidly, and individualists were becoming the norm. By 1960 the club itself would begin to seem an anachronism.[35]

Postwar changes began with Yosemite. In 1884 a tourist complained that Yosemite was already lost because 2,000 people had visited the valley that year. This seemed quaint and funny when the NPS announced that 700,000 had passed through in 1947. By 1954 attendance had topped 1 million and was accelerating. Growth placed huge pressures on the park. Budgets strained to accommodate unprecedented numbers and demands. By the

Figure 6.2. The sign-out ritual innovated by Richard Leonard and the RCS was a regular part of technical climbing in Yosemite and other national parks from the 1940s to the early 1960s. In this instance Corky Cortherell signed the register for fellow Stanford Alpine Club members Jim Carl and Dick Irvin while Ranger Murray and President Eisenhower look on. Registers enabled the National Park Service and clubs to monitor members and individualists, while climbers were assured faster rescues when things went bad.

1950s it was even more true than in 1931 "that the majority of visitors to Yosemite are keenly interested in wholesome out-of-door sports." People drove, hiked, and climbed seemingly everywhere, and the NPS struggled to balance tourism and conservation. Some such as Brower and Ansel Adams charged the NPS with ignoring the environmental and aesthetic consequences, yet the superintendent in 1946 warned of the need for "constant vigilance and careful planning . . . to protect the park and preserve a cathedral-like atmosphere." Unfortunately, the NPS had neither the resources for proper planning nor the authority to restrain the masses.[36]

Clubs exacerbated the task. The dominant image of postwar culture is omnipresent domesticity, with women and men rapidly settling down to families and careers. The fate of most pre-war climbers seemed to confirm this, as did fictional pieces such as a short story in *American Magazine* that had the heroine swear off risky sports after a close call, yet club memberships grew rapidly. The number of young women and men pursuing mountain adventure increased worldwide, especially in the American West. In May 1946, the Southern RCS experienced a "mild explosion" when 150 people showed up for its first meeting. Enthusiasm built elsewhere as well. The SC's Loma Prieta, Mother Lode, Redwood, Riverside, and San Diego chapters established their own rock climbing sections, and new recruits showed "up in large numbers" through the mid-1950s. The media took notice. *Time* magazine covered Alpine climbing in 1949, the *Los Angeles Times* featured the Southern RCS in spring 1951, and *National Geographic* devoted its June 1954 issue to the SC's remarkable growth and energy. The postwar RCS was mobile, domestic, and multigenerational. Expanded car ownership delivered growing crowds to practices and outings, and parents and kids swarmed over rocks, hosts' houses, and group camps. The parties and romances also continued. On its surface little changed. Clubs still stressed safety and group comity. When the Bay Area RCS visited Pinnacles National Monument in 1945, they hailed the park's "hospitality and lack of commercialism," yet something clearly had changed when the RCS set camp, threw old tires in a pit, and enjoyed, as one member put it, "the pleasures of a rip-roaring white man's fire."[37]

Demography and culture had changed in subtle but key ways. Bedayn, Brower, and Leonard still participated, but when Brower resigned from the climbing committee in 1946 "because of the urgency of other Club duties," others were drawn away as well. The "old guard" of the RCS were the "Young Turks" of the SC board. Brower chaired the editorial board, Leonard was secretary, and Robinson was president. Four of five presidents from 1946 to

1955 were early RCS members, as was the executive director, both secretaries from 1946 to 1959, and nine of fifteen on the board. The political rise of the RCS might suggest increased support for recreation, but just the opposite happened. Most officers had been radicalized by their wartime experiences. Leonard and Brower pushed the board to adopt a purist wilderness philosophy and to oppose recreational development. In shifting to the SC board, though, they ceded the RCS to a generation taking the sport in the opposite direction. New tensions appeared between the recreationalist and preservationist orientations to nature.[38]

Like the founders, the new RCS leaders included ambitious climbers, but far fewer of them participated in SC governance. The reasons were many. In part the founders were still young when they joined the board, and some served until the end of the 1960s, precluding advancement of younger RCS members at a time when the club was growing much larger and more environmentalist. By the time an ambitious climber such as Will Siri entered SC governance in the mid-1950s, recreationalists were outnumbered by wilderness advocates, but young climbers also had different priorities. Leaders of the Southern RCS made climbing more central, and Bay Area climbers were even more ambitious than Leonard and Brower. Rock climbing sections traveled and interacted more often, and Yosemite was their common ground.[39]

RCS outings to Yosemite suggested in microcosm the mounting pressures on parks. The club's first postwar visit took place, appropriately, on Armistice Day. A horde descended on Camp 4 with great enthusiasm and then spent two days devising ways to keep rain out of tents. It was the least well-attended visit before 1960. In May 1946 the Bay Area and Southern RCS took over Camp 9 for four days of climbing, hiking, "horseback riding, bicycling, and swimming." The demand on services only grew. In 1948, the NPS set aside a portion of Camp 11 for the SC's Memorial Day outing, and the park superintendent gave a special talk "on a long-term plan to spread the Valley population over a larger area" with the goal of "reducing the number of campers on the floor of the Valley to 5,000 instead of 12,000 as at present." It never happened, and the RCS illustrated why. In 1949 they visited four times, and the 1950 Memorial Day outing brought together six sections. The rest of the decade went similarly. Thus even as the club began to resist development, members strained existing services and demanded more.[40]

Other clubs behaved similarly. By war's end the Mazamas, Mountaineers, and Appalachian Mountain Club had their own rock climbing sections. The Federation of Western Outdoor Clubs coordinated joint meetings to advocate recreational interests, and the RCS interacted with the American Alpine

Club and groups from other countries. There were also campus clubs. Students at Cal Tech, Stanford, UC Berkeley, and UCLA formed clubs. By 1955 the UC Hiking Club had several top climbers. UCLA's Mountaineers were an offshoot of the Ski Club that had inspired the Ski Mountaineers. Chuck Wilts ran Cal Tech's club. Across California institutional and social boundaries between college clubs and the RCS blurred considerably.[41]

The Stanford Alpine Club's early years reveal the vexing nature of postwar growth. The SAC was born when Larry Taylor and Fritz Lippmann, both already RCS members, plotted a school club, and then Taylor saw Alfred Baxter carrying climbing boots across campus. The student union approved a charter, and the trio recruited in the dorms. Some members were experienced, but most were novices. From the start the SAC relied on the RCS for many things. They worked closely to order gear, set training programs, and hold joint practices. Baxter fondly remembered après-practice meals with the RCS founders: "they were ten, fifteen years older so they were starting families and it was very impressive to have dinner at their houses after practice climbs. They'd play chess with you or they'd argue over mountaineering history and so on. It was not just climbing but climbing set in a kind of larger social and domestic circumstance." Ties held on the road. The RCS invited the SAC to outings in Yosemite, and private SAC trips included RCS members. "There were," Baxter said, "no sharp boundaries" between the clubs.[42]

Like the RCS the SAC was a heterosocial group that did much more than climb. The "primary purpose," wrote Paul Revak, was "to provide relaxation for members during the course of the regular school year." The SAC was a refuge in which members supported each other on and off the rock. On campus there was "pressure to dress up, date, make an impression, play a role," Bea Vogel remembered. "In the club we were comfortable being ourselves." Members met for meals and parties. Few dated then, but several paired later. At the time they liked to climb or talk climbing. At lunch and parties members pored over photos and essays, sought partners, and planned. They cultivated a sense of the possible. "We weren't told that there were limits on our ability or 'you can't do such-and-such,' because 'you aren't strong enough' or 'because you're a woman.' There was a wonderful spirit of camaraderie and cooperation." When women made manless ascents, they were encouraged and celebrated, yet the goal was fun, not liberation. The SAC was in some ways stereotypically domestic. President and vice-president were always men, while women served as secretary and treasurer. In other ways the gendered distinctions faded. Jane Nobel Hogan remembered some "boys were stronger climbers than most girls, some girls were better climbers or trip leaders than some boys. People were appreciated for their merits and friend-ships."[43]

The SAC was nevertheless burdened by structural weaknesses. First and foremost, the itinerant nature of college clubs meant they rarely kept "mem-bers for more than four years. . . . As a result, the influence of long term mem-bers is sorely needed." Rhythms of school also worked against much season-ing, but the gravest problem was "summarized in one word, youth." One member admitted they were often "ambitious and impetuous." This drove the RCS to distraction. When *This Week Magazine* featured a SAC member climbing without a rope, the *Mugelnoos* editorialized against the sensation-alism. For decades it had educated people, "especially young folks, for the enjoyment of safe" climbing. The SAC finally got the message two years later when it punished two members for climbing without a rope, but it never mastered its shortcomings. Disaster hounded its early years, and broader trends in Yosemite climbing exacerbated these weaknesses.[44]

Reviewing seventeen years of RCS history in 1962, Ed Morse remarked that since 1945 "the new generations of club climbers have continued the endless effort to surpass the accomplishments of the past." Postwar climb-ers not only attained new heights but reshaped climbing culture. In twos, threes, and fours the individualists fanned across Yosemite and the world. By 1946 ascents of the Cathedral Spires were related as though they were noth-ing special. Private trips were the preferred way to put up new routes on Pul-pit Rock, Watkins Pinnacle, Rixon's Pinnacle, Phantom Pinnacle, Sugar Loaf, and El Capitan. Most pushed the limits of free and aid climbing, or their lo-cation and length were serious. Three ascents stood out for all these factors: the southwest face of Half Dome, the Lost Arrow Chimney and Lost Arrow, and the north face of Sentinel Rock.[45]

They had something else in common as well: John Salathé. Salathé is a quixotic figure in Yosemite history. In a club run by young, well-educated secularists, he was a forty-something Swiss blacksmith who believed that angels directed his ascents; and while his partners published notices on even minor outings, Salathé never wrote a word. He was a modest member who assisted practices and ameliorated friction. He also was an innovator. Some of Yosemite's cliffs, such as the southwest face of Half Dome, had not been climbed because they needed too many pitons. This had been a key limita-tion in the pre-war years. Sporthaus Schuster pitons could be pounded into cracks with little problem, but extraction required whacking them back and forth until loosened, and that usually bent the pitons beyond further use. Thus climbers had to carry many pitons on long, technical routes. Salathé substituted alloyed steel, and his pitons revolutionized the sport. They were both flexible enough to create springlike tension inside cracks and resilient enough to be hit repeatedly. Climbers could carry far less gear and still find a way up. Climbers later quoted a remark Salathé made in a heated meeting when, exasperated by a debate about how to regulate climbers, he quietly muttered, "Vhy can't ve chust go out und climb?" It perfectly captured his legacy.[46]

In a brief, six-year span Salathé made five of the hardest, most committing ascents in North America. In November 1946 he and Anton Nelson returned to a crack on Half Dome's southwest face which had twice repelled Leonard. Salathé and Nelson used the new pitons 150 times on a two-day ascent. The next spring, Salathé accompanied the RCS to Pinnacles National Monument and free-climbed The Hand, a steep and loose pinnacle none would dare. It was so hard his seasoned belayers climbed the rope instead, calling the lead "one of the best ever seen." That fall Salathé and Nelson spent five days in the 1,200-foot Lost Arrow Chimney, a feature that had stymied Leonard, Brower, and others since the mid-1930s. They topped it off by climbing the Lost Arrow Spire, an obelisk so smooth few thought it possible. Salathé and Nelson were unfazed. Two elements marked this ascent. First, the team tried to be self-contained, carrying all their water, food, and gear for most of the climb. Second, they used an unprecedented number of pitons and bolts. Never had climbers used so much direct aid, and never had such a route been so universally admired.[47]

If Salathé had stopped then, his spot in climbing's pantheon would have already been secure, but in the summer of 1950, a fifty-something Salathé teamed with a twenty-something Allen Steck on Sentinel Rock's north face. Like many Yosemite features, Sentinel was first reached from the southern rim by scramblers, but its sheer face had repulsed all attempts since 1936. The wall got more attention after Salathé and Nelson showed how to do multi-day ascents. Steck, Phil Bettler, Bill Long, and Jim Wilson tried repeatedly, but then the angels sang again, and Steck decided to hitch his star to the old man. In two hot days they reached the previous high point. The next three were an ordeal of hard leads in "agonizing" heat. The dehydrated pair placed ten bolts for aid, squeezed through hidden tunnels, and topped out while hallucinating about orange juice. A San Francisco headline blared, "51-Year Old Conquers the Sentinel Rock." Everyone was in awe. A year later Salathé made his final climb on Sugarloaf in the Yosemite backcountry. Then his angels quieted.[48]

There were other important climbs in these years, including a bold as-

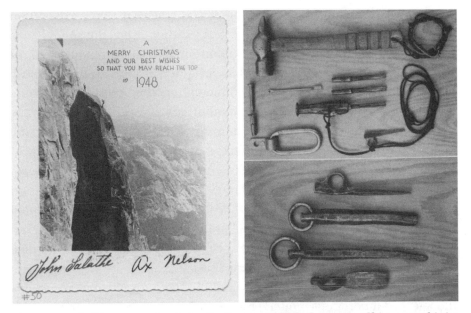

Figure 6.3 a & b. Like most early climbs, the first ascent of the Lost Arrow Chimney and Spire was documented by many club members. In this case John Salathé and Anton Nelson turned one photo of their rappel from the Lost Arrow Spire summit into a Christmas card celebrating the season and their climb. Another photo of Salathé's revolutionary pitons and bolts used on that climb was published in the 1948 *Sierra Club Bulletin*.

cent of Castle Rock Spire in Sequoia National Park that Salathé and Nelson regarded as "better than the Lost Arrow," but it was Salathé's trilogy of Half Dome, Lost Arrow, and Sentinel that altered the game. The RCS had at first feared the walls, but after the war climbers learned to live in the vertical. Steck proclaimed a new "technical age," and growing acceptance of aid liberated the ambitious to seek routes without ledges or trees. In 1952, Steck and Bob Swift ascended the barren Yosemite Point Buttress, and with Siri and Bill Dunmire reached a tree on El Capitan. The next year Steck, Siri, Long, and Willi Unsoeld climbed El Capitan's east buttress. Individualists redefined the possible, often making older routes seem less intimidating. Ultimately, that abetted disaster.[49]

In many respects SAC outings to Yosemite stand out for how little they differed from the RCS. The clubs were a seamless culture. Ellen Searby Jori remembered waking up in Camp 4 one Sunday to see RCS member Bob Swift planting a nest of Easter eggs atop Columbia Boulder. For Searby, the most remarkable thing was that, if "there's anybody who doesn't look like an Easter bunny, it's Bob Swift." Members traveled, climbed, and played together just like any other club, and Yosemite's walls were just as much "an ever present challenge." They climbed the same routes and made the same "exploration for new routes." Only their lack of experience distinguished the SAC.[50]

Time and again the club drew attention for its mistakes. In July 1947, Al Baxter and two SAC partners tackled Lower Cathedral Spire. Thirty feet above his belayer, he slipped while clipping into a piton, then pulled two more as he fell, hit a ledge, and plummeted another thirty feet. Baxter's legs broke in nineteen places. Taylor and Ulf Ramm-Erickson had to lower him to the base, an amazing feat given their limited experience. Rangers helped evacuate Baxter's broken body, but one ranger broke his ankle while descending the steep talus and another was badly cut. The SAC responded by devising a classification system in 1948, but trouble followed. In 1949, two unaffiliated Stanford students were found dead below Lower Yosemite Fall, having plummeted 200–300 feet while roped together. In 1953, Edgar Werner-Hoff died from head injuries sustained on Mount Shasta.[51]

Each incident drew concern, and combined with several minor accidents the SAC had a notorious reputation even before the terrible spring of 1955. Within fifty days the SAC lost three members. In March, the bodies of Fred Hadden and Bert Woodburn were found at the bottom of Scotland's Ben Nevis. Hadden was the club vice-president. Then on April 17 Jack Weicker, Irene Beardsley, and Anne Pottinger started up Higher Spire. Cold weather threatened, but they were acceptably dressed and made fair time through the hardest pitches. Wet snow began to fall, but the trio pushed on, reaching the summit after noon. Trouble began when they tried to rappel. Frozen ropes slowed them to a crawl. Weicker had to dislodge and cut line repeatedly. Not until they reached the base did anyone notice that Pottinger was exhausted. She slept little the previous night, and the toll set in rapidly. Night overtook a desperate attempt to evacuate her. Slippery conditions slowed movement. Then hypothermia set in and Pottinger collapsed. There was no shelter or fuel, so Weicker bolted downhill. Beardsley tried to rally her friend, but Pottinger died before help could arrive.[52]

Anne Pottinger's death was the last straw in a mounting pile of troubles involving much more than one college club. Unaffiliated climbers had harried the NPS for years. From 1947 to 1955 rangers rescued eighteen and recovered six bodies. As bad as this was, club climbers were worse. In May 1948 a member of the California Alpine Club broke a foot and cut his head in a fall on Arrowhead Spire. The previous December, Salathé had skidded his car into the Merced River, and in 1952 Royal Robbins fell asleep at the wheel while returning from an aborted attempt on Lost Arrow. The same year Dunmire hurt his shoulder and head on the east buttress of El Capitan. In April 1954, Larry Lackey broke a leg in two places while descending Higher Spire. During RCS outings in spring 1955, Dick Miechal scraped himself badly, Don Tocher broke a leg, and Helen Von Rykervorsel cracked both arms and her skull. An unprecedented number had also injured or killed themselves dur-

Figure 6.4. Richard Leonard's last major innovation was the creation of a climbing ranger position. Beginning in 1940, these seasonal rangers served as liaisons between the climbing community and the National Park Service and directed rescues. They also organized ranger training such as this rock climbing school in 1955 that involved regular rangers and several California clubs.

ing practices and outings from Tahquitz to the Bugaboos. Assessing the car-
nage, one member called their record "impressively bad."[53]

The RCS and NPS had to act, but their responses exposed the limits of
institutions in an age of individualists. Five days after Pottinger's death, the
RCS Safety Committee summoned SAC leaders to "a room filled with all the
leading lights of the Sierra Club" to debrief and adjust policies. Members offered many suggestions on how to restrict access to gear and routes. Then
tempers flared, Salathé said something about just wanting to climb, and everyone went home. In the coming years the NPS, RCS, and SAC bolstered
the institutional approach by refining training, qualification, register, ranger,
and rescue systems. They discussed safety and republished Leonard's "Belaying the Leader" essay as a pamphlet, but they were fighting the tide. Leonard's entente was losing relevance because clubs could no longer discipline a
building wave of individualists.[54]

Rarely does history turn on one moment. The climbing world did not
suddenly change because of an RCS meeting in April 1955, but that meeting
did reveal the sport's shifting social and cultural lines. Resituated in its original context, Salathé's remark reveals that he was not simply calming the wa-
ters but expressing an increasingly popular belief that climbers should not
be regulated. One SAC leader at the meeting later observed that the members "finally recognized that . . . calculated risk was part of climbing." This
was undoubtedly true, but more was implied by that realization than a simple acknowledgment of risk. For some in the room, and for more each year,
risk was a fact and a value, and clubs were irrelevant. Individualists believed
that clubs neither could nor should protect climbers from themselves. Four
days later another RCS meeting conceded this when it agreed that "Safety
depends upon the action of the individual." This was the beginning of the
end of the club as a regulatory force in outdoor sports.[55]

The Pottinger tragedy bared climbing's fractures, but these plagued
broader environmental culture as well. The entire SC was fragmenting. The
more Ansel Adams, David Brower, and Dick Leonard persuaded and cajoled
the board toward "purism," the more they alienated conservative members.
Looking back, there is a tendency to bifurcate the disagreements, but members' opinions were more diverse. Robinson favored recreational development, Adams and Brower resisted, and Leonard and the Farquhars tried to
find middle ground. The same divisions strained the RCS. One member tried
to balance the diverging views, insisting that all members were "aware that
the basic purpose of the Sierra Club is to fight to the last ditch to preserve
places to have fun in. Everybody also knows that an equally basic purpose of

the Sierra Club is to have fun in the wilderness." Problem was, members no longer agreed that these were in fact equal concerns. As Brower said to the NPS director, "it was a different Sierra Club now."[56]

This could be said of climbing clubs in general. By the 1950s climbers were more and more segmented. One cohort specialized in the great ranges. In the late 1940s, Baxter and Steck traveled to Europe to test themselves on the classics, then lit out for Canada, Alaska, the Andes, and the Himalaya. Each trip drew them more into the imperial, hypermasculine game that had been a hallmark of European mountaineering since the 1850s and Canadian climbing since formation of the Alpine Club of Canada. It culminated in 1958 when a small team, mostly composed of SAC and RCS members, accomplished the first ascent of Gasherbrum I—the only American first ascent of an 8,000-meter peak, and in 1965 when Steck, Wilson, John Evans, and two others completed a thirty-day ascent of the six-mile, 14,000-foot Hummingbird Ridge on Canada's massive Mount Logan, one of the most committing routes in the world.[57]

Another cohort turned provincial, focusing exclusively on Yosemite. In 1955 the SAC's Paul Revak criticized the "tendency for people trained in Yosemite to become one-sided in their climbing interests," but others thought its "potentialities as a gymnasium are infinite." In the next decade some members were so cliquish that their reports read like briefs from a foreign club of top climbers doing only severe routes. The *Yodeler* gave inordinate press to Yosemite stars, so much so officers worried that the RCS was "more or less separate from the rest of the club," yet in 1958 a few members asked the newsletter to focus even more exclusively on climbing. In early 1959 they got their wish when *The Rotten Log* was published solely to cover club climbing. Its first feature was on the *Royal Arches* route, but the newsletter did not and could not last. The club itself was shrinking.[58]

The RCS carried on until liability concerns finally drove the SC board to terminate the sections in the 1980s, but the heterosocial club that bound elites to novices had already splintered by 1960. The causes included not only specialization but a youth culture less inclined to join organizations and more grating to older members. The RCS struggled to keep recruits, and established members exacerbated matters by grousing about "young climbers who feel that they can break into the 'elite' by doing harder climbs." They complained about whelps "'hero' climbing." They ventured "close to the margin of their ability" on the "'ragged edge' most of the way," yet would "downgrade difficult climbs" as if they were a breeze. Members even talked about an age limit to ensure maturity. Generational alienation had become a circular problem. Each cohort annoyed the other so much that the shrinking list of qualified leaders ensured the club could not train future climbers. For nearly three decades it had been a resource for individualists, providing training, gear, and legitimacy, and individualists had repaid their debt by helping to sustain the RCS. By 1960 the ties no longer held. And with the decline of club climbing Yosemite's future looked very different.[59]

7. EXPERIENTIALISTS

Experiences are the only things that are really important.
—JACK ARNOLD

Warren Harding likened him to "a lean, mean, tigerish climbing machine." Gary Arce called him "a dominating force on the Yosemite climbing scene during the mid 1950s." Steve Roper just called him "God." He was Mark Powell, and in his own way Powell influenced climbing and environmental culture as much as John Salathé, David Brower, Dick Leonard, or Robert Underhill by providing an alternative model of being for a generation that identified less with the RCS and Camp 9 than with the individualists in Camp 4. The new cohort viewed climbing less as an avocation than a calling, and they transformed the valley into a globally important center for the sport. Equally important, some became environmental leaders. How this happened is anything but a straightforward tale.[1]

The men and women who built this society were fundamentally different in motive and outlook from previous generations. They developed a novel philosophy, one that simultaneously honored tradition and championed a countercultural quest for authentic experience. They were Beats, part of a cohort who defied conformity in an era seemingly captured by *The Lonely Crowd* and *The Organization Man*. Some moved to the Left Bank, hit the road, or joined biker gangs; others sought more elemental experiences. Climbers believed that bodily engagement with nature produced a truer reality, what William James called "pure experience." They were, to be sure, just as invested in sport's ties to masculinity—in some ways more so—yet they dropped the equation of respectability to responsibility. Beats wanted unmediated reality, and to achieve it they discarded, among other things, the assumption that risk must be avoided. Well before Timothy Leary, a generation of climbers, surfers, and Dharma Bums tuned in, turned on, and dropped out to commune with nature as an alternative to the 1950s buttoned-down hegemony.[2]

Mark Powell was among the first. Born near Fresno, he grew up in the San Joaquin Valley, camped in the Sierra, and ascended Mount Lyell in the Yosemite backcountry. Although he read climbing literature, he did not seriously embrace the sport until after serving in the Air Force. When Powell returned to Fresno in 1954 to work as an air traffic controller, he joined the local RCS. He was enthusiastic, but at first Powell's only remarkable trait was his over two-hundred-pound frame. After struggling up Lower Cathedral Spire, a partner declared the gasping Powell hopeless. That should have been the end, but the ascent sparked a hunger.[3]

Powell vowed to literally and figuratively remake himself. He started a crash diet and training program. Then, when he was transferred to Bakersfield, Powell quit his job, left the RCS, and moved to Los Angeles to train all winter. By June 1955 he had lost fifty pounds and had enough money to quit working altogether and move to Yosemite, largely because it was warm, dry, and cheap. Until that moment, no one had climbed in Yosemite full time. He went on a tear, climbing anything with any partner, but his spartan lifestyle had costs. He lost too much weight, and by September he was the only climber left. Powell was hungry, lonely, and broke, so he returned to Los Angeles and began a seasonal rhythm of working in winter, saving money, and climbing all summer.[4]

In 1955 all this really amounted to was a quirky story of self-discovery. What made it historically significant was how Powell's body and mind responded. By climbing all summer, he rapidly built muscle and refined technique. Then in October he joined Don Wilson for the fourth and fastest ascent of Castle Rock Spire. The following spring they and Jerry Gallwas, who in 1954 had deemed Powell a wash, made the first ascent of Spider Rock in Canyon de Chelly. Months later they made a first ascent on Lower Cathedral Rock, and in September, Powell, Royal Robbins, and Mike Sherrick made the first ascent of Liberty Cap's south face. Powell distinguished himself on each climb as stronger, faster, and bolder. He pushed mates and built an aggressive style of rushing routes without much reconnoitering. He also showed how living in Yosemite could transform an aspirant into an elite. By the time he returned to Yosemite in 1957, Powell was simply the best. Ambitious rivals had to recalibrate. By dedicating himself to the pursuit of experience, Powell changed the sport. Chuck Pratt later wrote that he "showed us all that climbing can be a way of life and a basis for a philosophy."[5]

Although Powell blazed the path, he was not the first. In the 1920s the Bergavabonden cut loose from increasingly anti-Semitic and authoritarian Alpine clubs in Weimar Germany, and then several Americans committed themselves more fully. In the 1930s, Jack Durrance trained on boulders and set standards of boldness in the Tetons and Alps before turning to pulmonary medicine. In the 1940s, Herb and Jan Conn refitted an Army Jeep and pursued a vagabond life of cross-country climbing and partying. Fred Beckey was the original American climbing bum. Starting in the late 1930s and continuing past 2000, Beckey toured the continent in beat-up cars, staying long enough to climb something audacious and then departing for the next prize. Each helped develop the idea of climbing as a way of life, but Powell diverged in a crucial respect. Like Durrance, he made training central to his identity as a full-time climber; like the Conns, he never let climbing get in the way of a good time; like Beckey, he climbed with clubs but never identified with them. Unlike anyone, Powell settled in one place, in effect becoming Yosemite's first resident climber.[6]

Powell's presence also altered Yosemite's social geography. Bay Area climbers, especially the RCS, had dominated the valley since 1933. A few Southern Californians such as Jerry Ganapole, Roy Gorin, and Chuck and Ellen Wilts also participated, but they climbed as individuals rather than as regional representatives. That changed with Powell. The RCS, SAC, and Berkeley Hiking Club still contributed climbers, and Gallwas, Robbins, Sherrick, and Wilson were regulars in the valley. Most other Southern Californians were a bit intimidated, though, preferring Tahquitz Rock and the eastern Sierra.[7]

Powell changed that attitude largely through the force of his personality. By late 1955 he was not only a top climber but one of those prototypically Californian icons. A "tall, blond man with an angular face and sparkling, ultra-blue eyes," he "radiated charisma and enthusiasm." While training at Tahquitz and Stony Point during the winter, Powell befriended many climbers and persuaded them that Yosemite was within their reach. His summer-long residence in the valley also provided a social anchor. Yosemite ceased to be alien territory. Powell was a sort of mountaineering Paul in Damascus. He brought the word and encouraged such young talents as Yvon Chouinard, Bill Feuerer, Joe Fitschen, Don Goodrich, TM Herbert, Bill Loughman, Wayne Merry, and Lito Tejada-Flores. He also welcomed central Californians like Rich Calderwood, Warren Harding, George Sessions, and George Whitmore. Within two years the Bay Area had lost its monopoly. A younger, more diverse cohort had laid claim to the valley.[8]

As more climbers arrived, the community center shifted from Camp 9 to Camp 4, a dusty, boulder-strewn area west of Yosemite Creek. The glacial erratics were useful for honing technique and hiding from rangers when camp permits expired, and many have since assumed it was this that first attracted climbers. In reality, Camp 4 was originally called "The Winter Camp" because it was the only all-year site with water and toilets. The RCS first used it in October 1939 because Camp 9 was closed for the season. For similar

Figure 7.1. When not climbing Yosemite's walls, a tightly knit, overwhelmingly male community practiced on and slept among the boulders of Camp 4 in the 1960s. Here John Evans cooks while Jim Bridwell and Chris Fredericks eat and socialize.

reasons many individualists slept there in late fall and early spring. Low fees were another attraction, but the resulting assemblage of "trailers, dogs, and climbers" was a problem when climbers decided to party. Doug Robinson recalled awakening one evening "to see a climber, carrying a lantern and loudly calling directions, leading from the campground a ragged procession of figures clutching wine bottles. Bringing up the rear of the long line, quieter and rather more sure-footed than the rest, were two figures in Smokey-the-Bear hats" herding them away from others.[9]

Such moments were emblematic of broader changes. Compared to Camp 9's heterosocial clubs, Camp 4 was a narrowly homosocial band. Nearly all male and committed to pushing the edge, those who settled in were a tribe of the very talented and committed, what Penny Carr called "the elite section." They were obsessed with climbing and Yosemite, their lives revolving around these priorities. Chuck Pratt vowed not "to change or modify my basic way of life in the slightest." He and others thought "the Valley is the greatest" place on earth. Layton Kor obsessed over the "white granite [that reached] for hundreds & hundreds of feet." El Capitan was "the most beautiful thing in the world." By the early 1960s climbing had become a calling.[10]

Climbing drew them to Yosemite, but there were also things driving them from elsewhere. Many were extraordinary athletes, possessing not only great strength, balance, and stamina but a rare ability to keep cool in potentially lethal circumstances. Some had played ball, run track, sailed, skied, or wrestled, but others were incapable of catching anything or performing before people. In a postwar world where masculinity was closely tied to sporting prowess, many Beats did not make the grade. Camp 4 was, in Kor's words, "populated . . . by various risk-takers, oddballs, misfits, and other escapees from social convention." They often shared little more than a love of climbing, a sense of alienation, and a yearning for authenticity.[11]

Like other Beats, they sought "modes of living that would allow a man to live passionately, true to himself in a larger culture that seemed anything but genuine." Marginal sports such as climbing and surfing appealed because participants could say "the hell with the ordinary ways of making it." "[P]ractically taking vows of poverty and chastity," they pursued experiences that resonated with authenticity. First and foremost was contact with nature, which produced "a bodily statement of what they felt. They were looking for the limits of control—the edge where you feel out of control but are really in control." What they did not do was articulate this very coherently.[12]

It took the prophesying of Jack Kerouac to merge life and art into what became an out-of-doors Beat revolution: "see the whole thing is a world full of rucksack wanderers, Dharma Bums refusing to subscribe to the general demand that they consume production and therefore have to work for the privilege of consuming. . . . I see a vision of a great rucksack revolution thousands or even millions of young Americans wandering around with rucksacks, going up to the mountains to pray."[13] Kerouac perfected "the rhetoric of rebellion," offering a vision of change through existential play. Footloose and stricken by wanderlust, by the end of the decade many Beats had "a dogeared copy of *The Dharma Bums* in their back pocket." Kerouac's self-confident, carefree, and promiscuous Japhy, a hyper-masculine caricature of poet Gary Snyder, himself a high-Sierra scrambler, proved extremely appealing. Japhy's lifestyle was a gendered antidote to postwar ennui, and places like Yosemite and Oahu were the cure. Both were sporting meccas and retreats from the world—at once stunning sites to test one's mettle and refuges from the oppression of work, school, family, and marriage. Makaha and Camp 4 were rustic analogs of San Francisco's North Beach, cultural retreats peopled by elite adventure athletes.[14]

These communities were filled with loners and outcasts by chance and design. Oahu's North Shore was pioneered by surf-hungry dropouts from Southern California. Camp 4's demography was remarkably similar. Chouinard was a surfer, and along with Harding and Robbins, they were working-class kids, blessed with athletic talent but at odds with peers. Each found in the sport something they could physically and culturally master. Rare were individuals such as Gary Hemming, a troubled kid from a broken home who never fit. More common were some very well-educated young men rebelling against a world that had groomed them. Nearly all attended college, most had degrees, and a few were in graduate school before choosing climbing instead. As in the past, Beats embraced sport as a way to construct the self, but they turned from bourgeois values, idolizing Europeans such as Herman Buhl, Walter Bonnati, Joe Brown, and Don Whillans, all of whom endured intense privations to pursue their passion. Like their heroes, Camp 4's denizens were poor, but not by necessity reclusive. Now there was a community.[15]

Camp 4 was an odd place. Residents pursued a weird version of the self-made man, yet their goal was rather conservative. Their lifestyles were indeed radical departures from accepted norms. Underneath, though, was a familiarly gendered, very American belief about the need to control one's destiny. Each climber yearned, as much as their fathers, to be their own man. Robbins liked to quote labor leader Dean Alfange's "To Be an American": "I do not choose to be a common man. It is my right to be uncommon. . . . I seek opportunity . . . not security. . . . I want to take the calculated risk; to dream and to build, to fail and to succeed." Chouinard quoted Robinson Jeffers's "The Cruel Falcon": "A man who knows death by heart/Is the man for that life." Climbing was not the most socially respectable way to self-possession, but manly individualism remained the goal.[16]

Pursuit of "the ecstatic possibilities of male adventure" could take many forms. Kor noted that the "interludes between climbs saw parties, drugs, and women, all supplementing the escapism that propelled me and many of my contemporaries in our upward drive on the vertical walls." The "bacchanalian orgies" were a key Yosemite attraction for Powell. Beer, wine, and Teton Tea, a stew of juices and wine—whatever was available—were favorite poisons, but drugs were also consumed. Marijuana was a Beat favorite. By the early 1960s they also experimented with mescaline, peyote, and LSD. Although chemical preferences evolved, drugs were not new. Clubs used caffeine (coffee, tea) and alcohol (beer, wine) as lubricants for socializing, and other climbers had self-medicated with stimulants (amphetamines, brandy) and depressants (sedatives, barbiturates) for a century. What changed were the motives and consequences. As highs became another adventure, the costs of intoxication took greater tolls. Beats tolerated drunkenness more

than clubs, and their parties became enabling environments for several notorious abusers.[17]

Less noticed was the role of the military. For all their rebelliousness, Beats
were also part of the Service Generation, a cohort that came of age at the
same time the draft became a regular practice, not just for wartime. Being
one of the oldest members in camp, Robbins was first to be inducted. Chouinard, Pratt, Dave Dornan, Joe Fitschen, Art Gran, Dick Long, George Marks,
and Roper followed. Beats resisted regimentation with a number of strategies. Robbins forged passes and jumped flights for weekend trips to Southern California and Yosemite. Others hitchhiked or hopped trains to climb in
Arkansas, North Carolina, Georgia, and Korea. Several conspired to obtain
early discharges. Pratt schemed for an economic hardship release so he
could be a seasonal instructor for "a completely fictitious climbing school."
Thoroughly miserable in Korea, Chouinard tried hunger strikes, acting suicidal, voluntary isolation, and writing insults like "Fuck the Army!" and
"GEN. D. McCARTHER & McNAMERA PISSWATER" [sic] on envelopes. Eventually he got a legitimate hardship discharge to restart his gear business.[18]

Chouinard's letters revealed how the group bonded through service. By
the time Roper was inducted in 1964, many climbers could relate, albeit not
always usefully. Some commiserated. Pratt assured Roper the Army would
"never be mentioned" once he got out. Others suggested it was an opportunity for personal growth or warned, "don't get any false illusions or hopes
about the army being not so bad. . . . Wait until you have nothing *but* time to
think, when you see day after valuable irrecoverable day completely wasted.
Things will get *infinitely worse!*" Another vowed: "I shall not give myself up
willingly. I shall employ every trick of treachery. . . . No, I shall flee to the farthest corners of the earth. I shall rack my body and vilify my soul so as to be
unfit. Dollar for degeneration but not one cent for tribute." He signed off,
"Semper Defecatus (Always shitty)." Though well intended, many friends
only underscored Roper's misery. Stationed to Phenix City, Alabama, it was
the Berkeleyite's first encounter with intense bigotry in the South. Pals sympathized, yet when Robbins suggested H. L. Mencken's "The Sahara of the
Bozart," or Dave Dornan shipped a copy of *Catch-22*, they only highlighted
how out of place Roper felt.[19]

The longer Roper served, the more his duty marked the end of an era.
The pattern had been for a climber to complete boot camp and endure a
godforsaken assignment. Boredom and useless regimentation were the principal foes. That changed when Roper was sent to Vietnam. The tone of letters
careened from advice to pleas not to "get your ass shot up." Roper was the

last climber of the service generation. His wartime duty defined the limits of shared experience. Thereafter climbers discovered a new interest in school, marriage, or any other means to avoid the draft. The only other climbers to visit Vietnam were Warren Harding and Dick Long, the former on a construction project and the latter in a medical unit during the Tet Offensive. In ways that can only be gauged through Roper's private correspondence, Army service was critical for defining a distinct cohort.[20]

Climbing, parties, and the Army created community. It was a tightly knit yet fluid society, with members coming and going through the year: spring in Yosemite and the Southwest, summer in the Tetons, Rockies, and Alaska, and fall back in the valley. It was also overwhelmingly young, single, and male. Sport had structured them into a homosocial hierarchy with the strongest enjoying the greatest prestige. They called themselves a "brotherhood," a term alien to the heterosocial club era, and membership was a huge honor. Pratt boasted that he chose not "to mix with people beyond my own narrow little circle of climbers. . . . we are not ordinary men and so we do not lead common-place lives." When Layton Kor, one of the world's top climbers from Colorado, was called a Yosemite climber, "it made me feel like I finally belonged to this elite group." Tom Frost called it "a rare privilege, a sacred privilege, a great thing." In practice, "gang" more accurately described Camp 4's social dynamics. Members were awarded nicknames—some loving, some not—and special status. Formerly faceless young men became "Christ," "Frog," "God," "Ropero," "Korini," "Sank Fracker," "Sparrow," and "Tex." Yosemite Valley was their turf in the same way surfers claimed waves and skateboarders staked pools.[21]

Although Camp 4 could be atomized and ephemeral, its bonds were powerful. The rituals of campfire debates, sorting gear, and "joyfully scaring themselves" on climbs gave texture and meaning to life. Yosemite became a home that was psychically difficult to leave. Commenting on mediocre climbers who could not give it up, Eric Beck noted that "climbing irrevocably captures those who fall within its grasp." The community kept tabs on those away and rendezvoused at pads and parties in the Bay Area, Tetons, and elsewhere. Beck cruelly related one winter reunion in Mazatlan while Roper was stuck in Alabama. He ended his postcard: "Wish you were here, sucker!" It was a friendly taunt full of affection in a properly masculine vein, but it also hinted at the darker side of Camp 4's closeness.[22]

Yosemite could be a mean place for those who did not fit. In 1963 Chouinard warned that an "outsider is not welcomed and accepted until he proves that he is equal to the better climbs and climbers. He is constantly on trial to prove himself." The lowly wannabe and storied hero alike endured a hazing process as the gang put them through the paces of climbing and drinking to gauge worthiness. Those who performed poorly were subjected to withering criticism. The insufficiently adept were dismissed with a laugh. Gaffs were mocked, and those lacking drive were humiliated, even beaten. Robbins and Sacherer were fanatics, and Roper famously railed against "a group that seems to live in torment in Camp 4. . . . they suffer from 'mind problems,' a euphemism for fear and uncertainty." Neither could he stand those "caught between . . . the parental ideal that one must go to college and become successful, and the instinctive desire of all animals to be free and wild and to do what they want." All were disciplined to "Valley values," even the disciplinarians. Stricken by anxiety while soloing, Roper revealed masculinity's dependence on group approval when he forced himself upward to avoid "the hoots of laughter that would greet me back in Camp 4" and, even worse, the possibility that his girlfriend "might refuse to mate . . . with a known coward." Roper was not irrational. After watching one climber struggle, Penny Carr wrote, "It's sort of embarrassing to see a man so vulnerable."[23]

The astonishing thing is how many climbers were vulnerable. Climbing at the highest levels required not only superb physical conditioning but the ability to keep one's wits when slips could be fatal. From the outside, climbers seemed prime examples of masculine self-possession, but roiling inside were storms of insecurity. Roper remembered that "many of us, including the more active ones, were lost souls waiting for something to happen." Kor could not cope with loneliness, Robbins hated crowds. Belonging to the gang ameliorated some anxieties, but there were costs. Being an insider required making the valley central to one's life. Climbing elsewhere or associating with others cast a shadow. Chouinard, who had a love-hate thing with Yosemite, once warned Roper, "THE VALLEY WILL DESTROY YOU! GET OUT! BEFORE ITS TOO LATE." The prospect of death haunted many, and they reacted with sadness and disappointment when a climber bought it. When friends chose girls over sport, there was a sense of shame, and when Powell and Herbert married, or Kor took up religion, it was as if they had fallen from grace or died.[24]

As these reactions suggest, women were a problem in Camp 4, as they were for Beats in general. Climbers' primary attachments "were deeply, if intermittently . . . to each other. Women and their demands for responsibility were, at worst, irritating and more often just uninteresting." Except, of course, when it came to sex. Getting laid was the second most frequent topic in letters. Who was getting it, who was not, and how they would explode if they did not get some. Coitus was mostly another conquest, however, and like climbing, a competitive hierarchy existed. Top dog was Kor, "the Great

American Don Juan" for his ability to seduce women. Others, most of whom were "painfully shy, with a poor track record in the dating game," were awed. The inept got no sympathy. Their frustration was attributed to a "defeatist attitude" that echoed climbers' faith in willpower. What went unconsidered was the spectrum of sexuality. One climber was later described as neither hetero nor gay but "sexless; he was never interested in anything beyond his work and mountains." At least two others were closeted, one perhaps to himself. Camp 4 was a hetero-centric culture. All else was not simply abnormal but unimaginable.[25]

Beyond sex women were often afterthoughts. Climbers rarely discussed wives or girlfriends except to brag or to complain. Otherwise, women represented a threat to the gang, their worth a function of their support for climbing. Evoking the domesticity of the era, one climber was relieved his wife was pregnant. She needed "fulfillment as a women [sic] just as I do as a man. I think this baby is the way for her to find it." Patriarchal values were also applied to women climbers. Steve Roper has argued that "Wives and girlfriends tried climbing, of course, but they usually did it because their men were doing it—not for any particular love of the sport." There was truth in this. Most women were not competitive in the same way as elite men, and even clubs were seeing a decline in female participation. The few women in Camp 4 were usually wives or dates. Independents such as Jan Baker were always exceptional, but none were equal. Camp 4 climbers were shallow and self-centered, mostly concerned with finding and keeping climbing partners. Their treatment of women was at times harsh. Dave Rearick remembered how Janie Taylor "struggled and tried to be a good sport" on climbs beyond her ability, and another caustically called one climber's wife "a haul bag."[26]

It did not follow that women were simply acted upon. Jan Baker, Irene Ortenberger, Dorene Frost, Beverly Powell, Janie Taylor, and Ellen Wilts were respected, dedicated climbers, and many wives and dates were as eager for adventure as their beaus. Neither were they passive about personal relationships. Many of the guys were, to put it charitably, young and clueless. Coming home from Korea, Chouinard remarked in an offhand way that he was returning to "work on carabiners and get married." Later he bragged that after "Dec 29, sex is no longer one of my major problems." He was wrong, and both he and Robbins were divorced by their first wives in short order. Roper argued that "men set the agenda," but few women put up with this sort of thinking. Some found supportive ties among wives and girlfriends in this community, or they stopped dating, broke engagements, moved out, and divorced when mates proved narrow and undependable.[27]

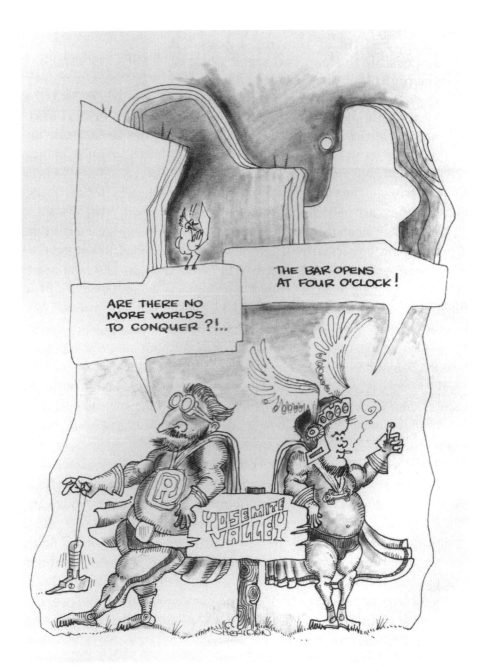

Figure 7.2. No Beat climber more ably captured the tenor of the late 1960s than Sheridan Anderson. His pen-and-ink drawings deftly mocked the sometimes too-serious tenor of Camp 4's homosocial world. Here caricatures of Royal Robbins and Chuck Pratt expose the tensions between hyper-competent climbers' sporting ennui and their perpetual quest for sexual conquest.

For one woman, though, Camp 4's Beat culture became a fatal trap. Penny Carr was first drawn to climbing as a student. She joined the Stanford Alpine Club and spent considerable time in Yosemite. She was a good climber, making a first ascent at the base of El Capitan and even reaching Sickle Ledge on *The Nose*. She had the same hunger for the valley, but her priorities were dramatically different. Unlike the men of Camp 4, Carr yearned most for human connection, and her sense of community included not only climbers but wives and girlfriends. She remarked that "All these more-or-less casual friends I have are the only really good & important things in my life. . . . I'm almost content just to be here & listen to them."[28]

Among Beat climbers, just being was not enough. Camp 4 valued action. Thus as more strangers arrived, Carr moved to the margins. By fall 1965 she was "uncomfortable and out of place." The "walls, trees, streams, and waterfalls are still willing to let me come," but the social bonds faded. Carr had mentioned suicide, but friends could not or would not recognize her seriousness. In May 1966, she piped the exhaust into her car and quietly, shockingly killed herself. Camp 4 did not kill Penny Carr, but her belated realization that Yosemite's climbers could not give her what she craved, that she would never be an equal among those who most mattered, was fatally devastating. Camp 4 was filled with charismatic and smart men who were indeed interesting company, but they were uninterested in the kind of relationships Carr needed.[29]

Climbers instead looked to each other and to nature. They obsessed and fantasized about Yosemite. All Kor could "think of is [El Capitan.] The [West Buttress] and the nose are my life. I think of them constantly." Walls and women blurred in a sexualized discourse of things "to do." The walls drove them "wild" with "desire." They were "hot for" any "virgin" line. It was fitting for Robbins to call Layton Kor the "Don Juan of Mountaineering," but that title fit a number of climbers. Denny proposed "a fine expedition of adventure into the pure smooth vertical." He was giddy about "living climbing as a climactic orgasm." Robbins likened one wall to "Aphrodite's thigh" and felt a powerful "lust to tattoo my name in indelible ink" in its "flesh." Such remarks revealed how sexual tensions slipped into the language of violence, and they reinforce the impression that climbers maintained emotional distance. Different metaphors were available. Tom Higgins remembered Bob Kamps's "witty love for those soaring virgin walls" and how they had embraced him "like a mother," but gendering nature as mother did not diminish climbers' desire to conquer and claim. Rather, it suggested sloppy writing and an unresolved environmental philosophy.[30]

Still, the confusion of analogies retained a certain logic. Climbers' relations with nature were usually more intense and rewarding than anything they gave or received from others. Many yearned for intimacy, but their words and actions revealed self-absorption. Robbins spoke warmly of his climbing partners, yet he remained distant and distancing, as aloof as he was talented and competitive. Chouinard yearned for a "oneness with fellow man," yet his letters dwelled on manly self-possession. Some focused on conquering inner demons and virginal walls. Others such as Chuck Pratt sought liberation from responsibility. Like a true Beat, he thought "freedom means the right to travel, to participate unmolested in any [goddamn] activity you want and the freedom to choose your own manner of death. I cannot imagine a sport other than climbing which offers such a complete and fulfilling expression of individuality." Sport, nature, and masculinity were inseparable. The Beats' intense focus on the self, and their utter commitment to climbing, made Camp 4 less a departure than a complete rupture of heterosocial climbing.[31]

No one was more explicit about the gendered implications of this philosophy than Yvon Chouinard. Drafted into the Army, he invaded the military library system and read everything from the Tao and French philosophers to D. H. Lawrence and the Bible. He wanted to explain "why a small group of the total field of climbers must climb—of those that climbing is their life." For this Beat, the goal was nothing less than reversing the decline of manhood. "In the beginning," he intoned, "Earth, Sun and Sky and all living things were one. Man was part of Nature. He was close to the Mother Earth. He belonged. He could identify himself and could communicate with all things. The Earth was a vast all encompassing womb and man was one with the 'Mother' Nature." That bond was severed by civilization. Men's intimacy with nature declined because of modernity's "unquenchable thirst for security." Every society suffered, but "western society has gone the farthest and is the sickest."[32]

Chouinard's language can sound like a feminist yearning for the great goddess, but he was actually crafting a manly vision of cultural decay and redemption. Society had been effeminized by a debilitating urge for soft living. The only way to reverse it was through "necessary *violence*." Men had to embrace risk as a cleansing force. Climbing was a way to restore the masculine self. Resurrecting a theme articulated by George Mallory, Chouinard poured out his ideas to Roper: "Climbing is an art (or *can* be)[. T]herefore it is love (or can be). It is possible for climbing to be the highest form of art attainable because you can *combine* oneness with the medium (the mother rock), loss of the narcissistical 'I', and oneness with fellow man."[33] One accomplished this by deliberately seeking existential risk. Chouinard's ideals were wrapped in a Beat orientalism but largely echoed things Mallory, Geoffrey Young, and James Ramsey Ullman had said. The key difference was how he redefined risk and death as integral to adventure, radically inverting the RCS's guiding philosophy. Echoing instead the fatalist Germans of the late nineteenth century and Bergvagabonden of the 1930s, Chouinard embraced the climb-or-die view: "This is *IT* dad, this is truth, this is our Way out of the 'dark night of the soul.'"[34]

Not everyone shared Chouinard's fetish with manly violence, but many, each for his own reasons, did see the advancement of climbing as a moral imperative, and greater objective risk as a necessary step. Robbins had challenged club rules since his teens, using less protection and even climbing unroped on easy routes. The more the Beats did this, the more they irritated the RCS; and the more the clubs complained, the more Beats knew they were onto something vital. Camp 4's spiraling estrangement from the clubs only accelerated. By 1960, Beats pursued a game that was effectively divorcing them from heterosocial climbers.[35]

Climbing had become more than a pastime. Robbins called it "searching for adventure, searching for ourselves, searching for situations which would call forth our total resources." Denny valued the "smiles and handshakes and looks from real friends who knew what it was like—why that spark was in my eyes, why my grin was 10" wide." He yearned to sit "on the summit with this great thing, this experience, between us, and [communicate] in the phrases and actions of our own relationship through climbing." Pratt was "completely sure that the life I have been leading and the life I intend to . . . lead is right. I will continue to climb until I am killed or until I am no longer physically capable of doing even the easiest routes." Frost called it "the real thing." Place also mattered. Only in Camp 4 was Beck at home. Everyone else "bug[s] me with their middle class ambitions and chickenshitedness." Yosemite was where Powell escaped the "façade of middle class righteousness," and why Kor regarded the walls, meadows, and river, along "with Yosemite's more civilized amenities and the social life of Camp Four . . . [as] not just a climbing area, but a way of life."[36]

Rarely does history reveal sharp generational breaks, but Mark Powell's move to Yosemite in 1955 marked the end of one era and the beginning of another. Through 1954, Yosemite was a bastion for members; by 1956, individualists had taken over. Some were also members, but in Camp 4 they were free agents. Generations did interact, but in practical terms they were distinct. Older climbers hewed to the heterosocial vision, but numbers of club members continued to fall at a time when youth lost interest in joining any organization. Raffi Bedayn, David Brower, and Dick Leonard remained liaisons between climbers and the NPS, most notably in the aftermath of Harding's ascent of El Capitan, but Camp 4 increasingly looked to the American Alpine Club and to other climbing centers rather than to the Sierra Club. This contributed significantly to the cultural eclipse of the RCS. Heterosocial climbers never went extinct, but they grew invisible to Camp 4 and to later historians.[37]

Clubs were displaced by a small group of hugely influential Beats. Yvon Chouinard, Glen Denny, Tom Frost, Warren Harding, Chuck Pratt, Royal Robbins, Steve Roper, and Frank Sacherer, spurred by Mark Powell, redefined the sport's core values. Climbing evolved from a heterosocial avocation that stressed safety and group fun into a quest that reflected the concerns of extremely ambitious individuals in homosocial enclaves. Individualism and risk distinguished this game. One result was more challenging routes; another was a more challenging milieu. Depending upon perspective, Camp 4 was an edgy community, a harsh gang, or a bunch of rivals. In no sense was it still the warm, broadly embracing scene the RCS had cultivated. By 1960, Yosemite climbers pursued a rawer form of experience. Penny Carr was an extreme example of the costs of these changes, but it was Mark Powell who most effectively illustrated the new reality.

Powell's presence faded in the late 1950s, partly due to a terrible injury, partly because he married and became a teacher, but mostly because he no longer climbed routes that made rivals notice. Camp 4 never rejected him, but neither was he a vital part of the community. Fun at parties and filled with exciting opinions, by 1963, Powell was also a figure from the past. Like Carr, he had drifted to the margins, but as she accelerated toward tragedy, he both understood the terms upon which the community operated and possessed the means to reverse his slide. To reclaim the center, there had to be "a resurgent Mark Powell, previously known as God." As in 1954, he vowed to remake himself. Powell mastered Camp 4 in a way Carr could not, because he understood that climbing was the only thing that truly mattered. Each was his own man, and the only way to make others notice was to force the issue. Beginning in 1955, this cultural equation reshaped how climbers interacted with nature, each other, and the rest of society. Camp 4 residents increasingly defined themselves solely through climbing, and their intensity remains critical to understanding Beats' sporting values and their commitment to wild nature.[38]

8. MORALISTS

The climber elevates his opinions into dogmas, which he maintains
fiercely against all comers: there are occasions when he shows
traces of that bigotry, a spice of that persecuting spirit, without
which no true religion would ever be complete.
—H. E. M. STUTFIELD

Yin and yang, dark and light, good and evil: an elemental tension underlies drama, and all great tales have it, including Yosemite's morality play of Royal Robbins versus Warren Harding. The antagonists are inextricably linked, having dominated Yosemite Valley in the same era, but more was always at stake than simple ego. Each championed a significantly different interpretation of the sport and, by extension, of what counted as a legitimate climb and relationship with nature. Each drew inspiration as much from the other as from Yosemite, and their rivalry—itself equal parts philosophy and envy—was as crucial as any ascent. Their legacy was thus not just some truly awesome climbs but how they personified some irresolvable tensions concerning technology, ambition, and publicity. Through them we can see how the Beats altered sporting and environmental culture.[1]

The main theme is by now familiar, involving that ancient conflict over the aesthetics of adventure. Just like Victorians the Beats rued their reliance on technology. They needed ropes, pitons, and bolts to ascend, yet their tools cheapened victory. They tried to reconcile the contradiction by erecting an ethical approach to adventure that honored tradition yet accommodated innovation. Situational ethics reigned on rock, but in camp personal aesthetics reified into absolutes. The laid back got uptight, and even countercultural-ists acted like grand muftis. Then things got really weird. A self-professed champion of diversity went medieval with a cold chisel, a blue-collar iron smith spat at the hoi polloi, and a carefree iconoclast ranted about the Spanish Inquisition. Camp 4 lost its sense of humor. Climbing lost its joie de vivre, and the Beats beat a retreat.[2]

By then, though, they had redefined how outdoor athletes and environmentalists related to nature. More than any previous generation, the Beats turned their sport into a competitive and existential endeavor. They climbed so much and so well that the impossible was probable, and that was a crisis. Their talent had undermined adventure. Many looked inward for new ways to maintain difficulty, yet they still measured themselves against rivals. Their actions exposed ambiguous attitudes about the past and future. Some echoed C. F. Meade, that competition "will be the ruin of the pure tradition of mountaineering"; others invoked liberty, arguing that climbing was about individual freedom. Philosophical differences seemed clear but tended to blur on the rock because, when the going got tough, all climbed rather similarly. Thus the development of a uniquely Yosemite style really was a group effort. Yvon Chouinard, Tom Frost, TM Herbert, Bob Kamps, Chuck Pratt, Steve Roper, and Frank Sacherer played key roles, but Robbins and Harding were always at the center. Without them, this story loses coherence.[3]

To understand Royal Robbins's place in climbing history, we must begin with the parable of how he came to be. Born in West Virginia to Royal Shannon and Beulah Robbins, the boy had a father who was unfaithful and unreliable. Beulah divorced and married an even more violent man who insisted the boy adopt *his* name. They moved to Southern California for the wartime opportunities, but the abuse continued and Beulah divorced again. Like Dick Leonard, the fatherless boy found male companionship hiking with scouts. Then in one of those rare moments of true definition, he renamed himself, choosing his original name. Unlike anyone else in this history, Royal Robbins really was the architect of his own identity. In a childhood that often spun out of control, the story of Royal Robbins's name became the first chapter of an autobiography about self-fashioning. He was close to his mom and distant from others. He yearned to distinguish himself but struggled to find a niche. He excelled at sports but was out of place in school and church. He read adventure tales for escape, but the plot of his own life remained vague until he happened upon an image of a lone climber in James Ramsey Ullman's *High Conquest*.[4]

Robbins's reaction to that photo linked him to a long line of people seduced by mountaineering imagery. Albert Smith first demonstrated this in the 1850s. Smith dramatized his ascent of Mont Blanc by festooning London's stages with animals, plants, pictures, and people. What made it work was how he "encouraged his audience to imagine themselves in Switzerland, making their own ascent of Mont Blanc." His visual triggers were probably more responsible for the ensuing rush to the Alps than any other climb or climber. Panoramas, etchings, and photos had lured men to mountains for a century before Robbins fixated on a "man clinging by his fingers and toes." Robbins was not the last. Harding was hooked by *The White Tower,* Layton Kor by a film on the Matterhorn, Yvon Chouinard by a man on rappel, Scott

Davis by photos of Chouinard, and John Long by Spencer Tracy in *The Mountain*. The imaginative ability to transpose oneself into an image was a critical step, but imagery takes us only so far.[5]

What gave the photo meaning was Ullman's text. Without it the source of Robbins's values is less clear. Ullman was one of many mid-century climbing historians. Most were English and all were Anglophiles. They praised sturdy Brits and scorned those who perverted sport with pitons and carabiners. Some authors even equated aid climbing with Nazi zealotry, especially those 1930s assaults on the Nordwands and Nanga Parbat. To Ullman it was all "suicidal insanity." "Aflame with the hero-philosophy of Nazi-Fascism and egged on by flag-wavers and tub-thumpers . . . brown- and black-shirted young climbers began vying with one another in what they conceived to be feats of courage and skill. All or nothing was their watchword—victory or death. No risk was too great, no foolhardiness to be condemned, so long as their exploits brought kudos to *Vaterland* or *patria*." Fascism was anathematic in the late 1940s, and Ullman tapped that stigma to create a philosophical touchstone for Robbins.[6]

Ullman honored a masculine form of climbing that stressed mastery of the self. "The history of mountaineering," he wrote, "is not merely a story of the conquest of mountains, but of the conquest of fear. It is not merely the record of stirring deeds, but of a great adventure of the human spirit." Ullman contrasted brown-skinned monks, cowering in superstitious fear of Chomolungma, with the undaunted will of the British climber Geoffrey Bruce, who even in defeat quietly vowed to Mount Everest, "We'll get you yet!" Such men saw "a great challenge to their own qualities *as men;* a chance to conquer their own weakness, ignorance and fear; a struggle to match achievement to aspiration and reality to dream." For Ullman and ultimately for Robbins, this was the harder but higher road. The emphasis on self-testing merged physical rigor with dignified manhood. Here was a recipe for an uncommon life and, as John Cleare argues, "a pastime which was both romantic and personal . . . and which demanded total commitment both physical and mental." Robbins's passion for these values helps explain the intensity with which he helped form and patrol the homosocial world of Camp 4.[7]

Over time Robbins would actually become as technologically oriented and ambitious as Ullman's bêtes noires. He even idolized some figures, yet he never abandoned his Anglophilia. Robbins always honored the ideals first imbibed from Ullman, and always defended a sporting ethos he compared favorably to bullfighting. He probably saw no choice. In a way matched by few others, his values and ascents merged with his identity. His reputation was a product not just of his great climbs but of how he inscribed them with a particular sporting and environmental sensibility.[8]

Robbins came out of nowhere in the late 1940s. Scrambling with the scouts led to meetings with the Southern RCS, which saw an incredible but raw talent. He did not know even basic rope work, so John Mendenhall and Chuck Wilts tutored Robbins and he progressed rapidly. His first trip to Yosemite resulted in the first 5.9 free climb on Higher Cathedral Spire. The feat was astounding yet accidental—Robbins had wandered off route—but the next year he did it intentionally by freeing an aid route at Tahquitz Rock called *Open Book*. Except for maybe Mendenhall, no one in California matched Robbins's skill, and only one other North American climber had ever ascended a more difficult route.[9]

Robbins's talents were unrivaled, but his social skills were wanting. Since the early days of the RCS Yosemite climbers had been freeing pitches—essentially free climbing sections that had formerly required aid. There was at first a friendly rivalry in these efforts, but Robbins added a sense of righteousness. In 1953 he, Jerry Gallwas, and Don Wilson made the second ascent of Sentinel's north face, passing most of the aid Salathé and Steck had used. The climb was impressive, but they soured it by claiming Salathé and Steck had exaggerated difficulties to save face. Within a community that still observed genteel customs, this was poor form. Criticizing two highly esteemed members made the assault even worse. All conceded Robbins's strengths, but his brashness and habit of boasting every time he climbed something in better style was off-putting.[10]

Robbins's personality was always a double-edged force. His aloofness, itself largely due to shyness, awed and inspired some but irritated and alienated others. His awkwardness might even have bolstered his rivals' popularity. Whatever his strengths, Robbins's pious views about technology, style, and revelry were alienating. He treated the sport less as an avocation or way of life than as a cause. Climbing was a noble endeavor, a way for a high-school dropout to build a respectable identity on his own terms. For some, this was too serious. Climbing was supposed to be fun, and afterward they wanted to let loose. But Robbins disdained Camp 4's wild side, and his Victorian sensibilities drove as many away from him toward the licentious Powell and Harding as those charismatic climbers attracted on their own. It was a testament to his climbing prowess that so many admired Robbins despite himself.[11]

Thus for all his talent, Robbins was not at first highly regarded. One problem was that his job as a bookkeeper kept him in Southern California during most of Powell's run. Another was that his only first ascent in Yosemite Valley was Liberty Cap, which Powell had dominated. Robbins had not yet made his mark, and by 1957 the only remaining plums were Half Dome, El Capitan, and Mount Watkins. Of those, only Half Dome's northwest face seemed feasible; the rest were too big and blank. Robbins had tried Half Dome in 1955 with Gallwas, Harding, and Wilson, but Wilson called a halt because of slow progress. It was a turning point. Robbins and Harding were eager to continue and bridled at Wilson's authoritarianism. Their frustrations precipitated change.[12]

Robbins's responses cast light on his personality. The first thing he did was assert greater control of his projects. He formed a team, inviting Gallwas and Mike Sherrick, a friend from Southern California, but discarding Wilson and Harding. Like most climbers, he relied on a small circle of friends, most of whom were Southern Californians. Robbins was also extremely ambitious. Several teams coveted Half Dome, including one led by Harding. Robbins admitted competitiveness later, but his obsession with speed on Half Dome suggests that besting others was always important. As soon as the NPS consented, Robbins moved onto the wall and hid, timing communications with friends when tourists gazed elsewhere. He also made a telling maneuver by leaving a rope across a key traverse to facilitate retreat, but tying the line so only his team could use it.[13]

Robbins's penchant for control—over himself, his team, and eventually Camp 4—would increasingly warp his actions, but the 1957 ascent of Half Dome seemed pure. He had merged aesthetics and technique to make Half Dome a nearly flawless expression of his vision. An ascent of 2,000 feet of dead vertical granite, the route was the longest and steepest not only in Yosemite but in all of North America. Moreover, Robbins was the driving force behind the Half Dome climb, unlike Liberty Cap. He climbed the tough leads, did the hard work, and made the daring pendulums. In a literal swoop he elevated himself to elite status in Yosemite and, soon, the world.

He also became the sport's conscience. Despite his earlier remarks, he respected Salathé. The old iron smith had committed to his routes, climbing bottom to top in single, self-contained efforts. The way Salathé limited himself increased the risks and, therefore, the adventure. Robbins similarly rationed food, water, rope, and, crucially, bolts. Half Dome was more than an ascent—it was a statement on style. He insisted they climbed "as safely as possible," yet argued that even "enthusiasts must admit a certain amount of calculated risk on a climb of this kind." This was the key to Robbins's ethos: a real climber was an adventurer who dared to fail.[14]

Robbins had begun a lifelong effort to make adventure an aesthetic standard. Like Salathé, he showed men how to find themselves. Half Dome was a vertical *Pilgrim's Progress*. Like the hero Christian, Robbins surmounted many challenges, only his landscape was not early modern England but a sheer wall in an incomparable valley. Both protagonists sought a state of grace, and both endured a masculine process of self-testing. Christian resisted Vanity Fair, Robbins cheap fame. Technology was an issue, however. Robbins tried to follow natural crack systems, but blank sections of Half Dome required twenty bolts, which contradicted his sporting and environmental ideals. Drilling violated the rules of natural protection because it altered the rock and could be done anywhere. Such acts required justification. He reasoned that "bolts (which can be placed only after arduous hammer-and-drill preparation of holes to receive them) were used only where they seemed essential for progress or safety." Like the Anglophiles he read as a boy, Robbins would accept bolts only under extraordinary circumstances.[15]

If Royal Robbins was Camp 4's new philosopher king, then Warren Harding was its jester. They were perfect foils. Both had been blue-collar misfits who made climbing their identity, yet their views differed so starkly that it is hard to imagine them as anything but rivals. The more Robbins proselytized, the more Harding apostasized. Their routes became counterpoints in a debate about aesthetics and ethics, and the two were so good that each new climb made everyone consider the broader stakes. Robbins was a serious aesthete, always advocating high ideals, while Harding pursued hard climbing and hard drinking with equal commitment. Playing the fool, though, was a double-edged game. He could speak truth to power, but only by acting in ways that allowed people to dismiss him.[16]

In retrospect, Harding was born a decade too early. Raised in northern California during the Depression, he was "undersized . . . unambitious and aimless," a wiry boy who could run forever but was otherwise uncoordinated. Like other Beats, he was also adrift. After the war he took a job as a surveyor "to keep the wolf from the door," but work never defined him—play did. For a time Harding raced sports cars for glamour and excitement, but then a friend took him climbing. He had fun. The sport was edgy, and he was good. Then, fittingly, he read Ullman's heroic *The White Tower,* saw the movie, and was hooked. By 1950 he had joined the Bay Area RCS, found partners, went climbing, and improved rapidly. However, by the time he visited Yosemite in 1953, two years after Robbins had done the valley's first 5.9 at age sixteen, Harding was nearly thirty.[17]

Harding's age did not become an issue until later in his career. In 1954 he made the first ascent of Middle Cathedral Rock's North Buttress and East Buttress and the second ascent of Lost Arrow Chimney. Many more followed, and although he was later known for aid climbing, these were distinguished by his free-climbing ability. Harding wormed up a fearsome tunnel in the Lost Arrow Chimney, an airy slot called *The Worst Error,* and a bottomless pitch on Washington Column. Yosemite was his candy store. By the end of the 1950s he had seventeen first ascents with fourteen partners; Robbins had three firsts with six rope mates. The two did share partners such as Mark Powell, Chuck Pratt, and Wayne Merry, but mostly they went separate ways and showed little interest in climbing with each other.[18]

Their estrangement developed in the aftermath of Robbins's Half Dome climb. Left off Robbins's team, Harding joined Powell and Bill Feuerer, but by the time they reached Yosemite, Robbins was well up the face. Harding hiked to the top to congratulate the victors, but his disappointment festered. He had lost the prize and felt snubbed. His team "grumbled around the valley for a couple days. . . . There were plenty of attractive routes to be done, but everything else seemed to represent some sort of 'put down' compared to Half Dome." All, that is, except the 3,000-foot face of El Capitan. With typical self-deprecation, he explained that his team got lubricated on cheap wine, gazed in awe at a prominent corner where El Capitan's southwest and southeast faces meet, and screwed up their courage. Harding's girlfriend, Bea Vogel, recalled things differently. Harding was "pouting and moaning because he had been left out," so she shamed him: "'Oh Hell! There are lots of other walls. Why don't you do El Capitan'" and then pointed out the route. Whatever the true inspiration, the climb that followed changed the game again.[19]

Climbers had contemplated El Capitan for twenty years, but it was all talk. Everyone was appalled by the amount of aid and especially bolts that it required. After Art Argiewicz lost a bet in 1943, The *Yodeler* teased that he would have to bolt his way up El Cap as payment. Five years later the Washington Rock Climbers wrote a futuristic "night mare" in which an eight-man team built a 500-gallon water tank and used 6,500 feet of rope and ten fifty-pound crates of bolts to engineer their way up. In some ways reality matched fantasy. Powell, Feuerer, and Harding rushed the first third in July 1957, but then they got mired in a route that took 45 days over 18 months, with 675 pitons, 125 bolts, and 2,000 feet of rope.[20]

The amount of gear and hype were unprecedented, and some called Harding a self-aggrandizing engineer. Several ascents drew this charge, but critics oversimplified in 1958. The line, called *The Nose,* was by far the most demanding in North America. Its length and problems were unprecedented,

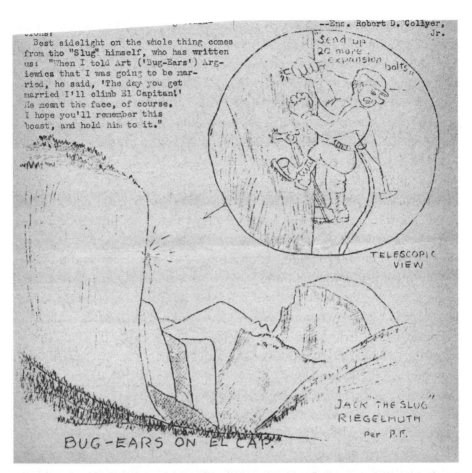

Figure 8.1. As this teasing cartoon from the early 1940s shows, climbers had considered climbing El Capitan long before the first ascent team started up *The Nose* in 1957, but everyone had assumed that it could only be done by incessant drilling and bolt placements. Here Artur "Bug-Ears" Argiewicz supposedly requests "20 more expansion bolts" because he had to climb El Cap after losing a bet with fellow member Jack "The Slug" Riegelhuth. Sadly, Argiewicz died less than a year later while fighting in Italy with the 10th Mountain Division.

and as Robbins said later, the team adopted "the only possible tactics for those days." Critics also assumed Harding's leadership and the media attention were intended, but both were as much due to accident as assertion. The original trio were a true team. Powell was the driving force, Feuerer the technical genius, Harding the indefatigable will. But by fall 1957, Powell had shattered an ankle and Feuerer lost interest. That left Harding in charge.[21]

Harding seemed to need El Capitan, but he also needed help. His first invitation went to none other than Robbins, who was put off by the siege-style tactics. Harding then enlisted a platoon of friends including Powell,

Feuerer, Rich Calderwood, Wally Reed, Ellen Searby, George Sessions, Allen Steck, and John Whitmer. Sessions dealt with traffic, Searby with the press. The rest ferried food, water, and gear. Then attrition set in. Steck was out of shape, Reed distrusted the gear, and Calderwood lost his nerve. Only Harding stuck it out from the start, and only Wayne Merry and George Whitmore accompanied him to the top. The group dynamic was captured by a vignette on the final night: Whitmore perched atop a granite spike, Merry on endless belay, and Harding relentlessly drilling twenty-eight holes into the summit overhangs. As he "staggered over the rim," Harding wrote that "it was not at all clear to me who was conqueror and who was conquered: I do recall that El Cap seemed to be in much better condition than I was." Humor was easy because he had succeeded.[22]

The ensuing notoriety was more complex. Harding and Merry always credited everyone who contributed labor or gear, but the guidebook writers, some of whom detested Harding, followed a protocol of honoring only the summit trio. Thus his opponents helped foreground Harding, and his fame became an issue. Critics dwelled first on the "publicity." The climb drew coverage from the start, but this was mostly due to geography. El Capitan is the biggest thing in Yosemite Valley. The NPS still bills it as the "largest exposed granite monolith" in the world, and whatever its actual rank, it *is* huge. Driving west, El Capitan fills the windshield and beyond. Its two main faces meet in a prominent buttress *(The Nose)* that forces the road left, and this is the only feature with cracks from bottom to top. Thus the trio were climbing the closest feature to the road on the most conspicuous thing around, and because it was easy to park and gawk, roads clogged in July 1957. El Capitan Meadow was a mob scene, so the chief ranger ordered the team down after seven days. It was the first time the NPS had intervened in a climb.[23]

The rangers' main concern was a wholly preventable traffic jam. The chief ranger was none too thrilled with climbers in general, but the sport was deeply entrenched. So, with support from another timely letter by Dick Leonard, he let them resume from Labor Day to Memorial Day. By then Harding was in charge, which meant he also bore responsibility for the circus. A year later his evanescent team was still stuck in the middle of the face, and gawkers now included reporters. This is when Searby became press liaison, and Sessions, later a philosopher who defined deep ecology as a long-term, nonconsumerist engagement with nature, began to direct traffic. As the spectacle grew the chief ranger issued another ultimatum: finish by Thanksgiving . . . or else. Harding later dismissed the threat, but it had an effect. The team made four assaults that fall, culminating in a marathon, twelve-day push covered nationwide.[24]

Unlike Robbins, whose Half Dome ascent was widely admired, Harding divided Yosemite. The park superintendent and the American Alpine Club hailed his expertise and attention to safety, but the NPS director called it a "trick or stunt." Conrad Wirth decried the spectacle and vowed to end all technical climbing in parks. Many defended Harding's techniques, and though not known then, the chief ranger even ordered Harding to place fixed ropes for rescue. Others were less supportive. Powell and Feuerer resented Harding's fame, and Robbins hated the Himalayan-style siege. A rumor spread that Robbins wanted to steal the route. Some also felt Harding's publicity debased the sport. Searby did sell photos to *Life,* and Harding and Merry did sell a story to *Argosy,* but profit was not the motive. Harding told Leonard that his "very slight financial gain" would barely pay for the ropes, and it "was not what prompted us to make the attempt. There certainly must be easier ways to earn 10¢ an hour and get one's picture in the paper!" Making money was not the issue. Even David Brower publicized his Shiprock climb in the *Saturday Evening Post.*[25]

The problem was how *The Nose* contributed to the erasure of risk. Robbins noted that Harding was "the first to break that fear" of El Capitan. He pierced a psychic barrier by proving that even the most intimidating faces could fall. Climbers remained wary, but now they knew they could succeed. *The Nose* was thus another blow in what Reinhold Messner called "The Murder of the Impossible," and the new cohort, all of whom trained at Tahquitz or Berkeley, redefined the limits. Frost, Kamps, Pratt, and Sacherer freed pitches with zeal, and by 1961, Pratt, Robbins, and Dave Rearick had free climbed three routes, each so significantly harder than anything before that the rating system had to include a previously unimagined level of difficulty. Climbers also did harder aid climbs. Harding and Pratt ascended Washington Column's overhanging east face. Frost, who was an aeronautical engineer, and Chouinard, who knew the working end of a hammer better than anyone since Salathé, made postage-stamp-sized pitons called "RURPs," or "Realized Ultimate Reality Pitons," that they smashed into incipient cracks on the southwest edge of Kat Pinnacle and the *West Face* on Sentinel. Joe Fitschen and Robbins used RURPs on *Royal Arches Direct.* Again, these routes were so difficult they warranted a new aid grade.[26]

Although difficult routes were nothing new, the rate at which unprecedented climbs were successfully attempted in Yosemite around 1960 redefined the valley as a globally important climbing center. As a result, things done there and the climbers who did them were by definition important. Just being there mattered. "What could be finer," Kor asked, "than to spend our strength, minds & desire toward the greatest thing in the world, the nose of El Capitan." The AAC agreed. In 1961 it opened membership to climbers who stayed on one continent in order to lure Yosemite climbers, and officers celebrated when Chouinard applied, noting "it has been hard for the Club to seem to offer much to many of the best Western climbers." Then in 1963, the *AAJ* featured the valley. The Beats were now insiders. Steve Roper boasted, "No one can seriously deny . . . that Yosemite Valley is the most influential and important rock climbing area of this country." A European called Yosemite the "Mecca of American rock climbers," and the label "Yosemite climber" became a mark of distinction. For Kor it meant "I finally belonged to this elite group." No one was more responsible for the valley's stature than Robbins *and* Harding.[27]

The Nose also clarified positions on sporting aesthetics. On one side stood Robbins, who personified a style of adventure steeped in natural lines, restrained methods, and decorum. On the other was Harding, who flinched at neither the spotlight nor critics. Whereas Robbins hid behind a rock in 1955 to avoid curious tourists, Harding hammed it up for reporters; and while Robbins said a mea culpa for his twenty holes on Half Dome, Harding was unapologetic about his 125 holes on El Capitan. He called Wirth's complaints about drilling "ridiculous" and explained matter-of-factly that bolts were "just a standard procedure of climbing where there are no natural holds." Robbins viewed issues through a moral prism; Harding was agnostic. By 1960, Yosemite's two stars seemed to inhabit polar positions about the ethics of adventure.[28]

Appearances were partly deceiving. In practice Harding and Robbins approached technical problems very similarly, but their rivalry was real. In the game of climbing second ascents are also important because they serve as a peer review. Subsequent parties confirm or critique pioneer performances, and repeated routes gain respect. *The Nose* showed how this worked. After the Army, Robbins prepared to repeat *The Nose* in one push without fixed ropes, as a comment on Harding's performance. His team, composed of Frost, Pratt, and Fitschen, aimed to begin in fall 1960, but the route complicated their agenda. The length, multiple pendulums, and difficulty of retreat forced them to carry many supplies, and hauling became a problem. The team ultimately proved that they did not need an umbilical cord, but they did need all of the labor Harding had put into his bolts. The ascent, completed in seven days, produced contradictory messages. Robbins made his point about fixed ropes, but he also legitimated Harding and the route. Their rivalry was cemented. Thereafter Robbins was cool to Harding, granting his "abundance of energy and determination" but rarely complimenting his abilities.[29]

Robbins regarded his aesthetic of adventure as timeless, but it actually depended on a rapidly changing technological context. Climbers had innovated gear since the 1930s. The RCS developed designs that the Quartermaster Corps perfected during the war. Plymouth Cordage Company began to produce nylon ropes while the Ames Shovel Company made horizontal and angle pitons. Civilians acquired this gear after the war, but the pitons often performed poorly in Yosemite granite. Salathé made more resilient blades using vanadium. Raffi Bedayn designed stronger, lighter carabiners from aluminum. Chuck Wilts forged very thin "knife-blade" pitons from chromium-molybdenum. Each resulted from the close study of granite and metal, and all significantly diminished Yosemite's technical and environmental challenges.[30]

Other climbers produced an array of devices. Most, such as members of the Stanford Alpine Club who used the campus foundry, or Jerry Gallwas who made gear for the 1957 ascent of Half Dome, copied the work of Salathé and Wilts. Others followed unique paths, such as Bill Feuerer who turned aluminum into everything from bolt hangers to wide-angle pitons. The most famous effort is now enshrined in El Capitan's climbingscape. In 1956, Frank Tarver and Harding discussed Half Dome's challenges, including cracks too wide for the three-quarter-inch angles made by Ames. Tarver later roamed a dump and spied a stove from which he took three legs—he would have had to buy the stove if he removed all four. Then with roommate John Thune, he crimped, drilled, and braised the legs into the widest pitons ever. When Tarver went to Alaska in 1957, he offered his gear to Harding for Half Dome, and when Robbins got there first, Harding used them on a series of two- to four-inch fissures on El Capitan now known as the Stoveleg Cracks.[31]

In retrospect the long era of vernacular piton craft closed with the second ascent of *The Nose*. Some pre-1960 gear was very good, some very dangerous. Feuerer's efforts failed often, and Harding had so few stove legs that, even after Calderwood made more, he had to leap-frog gear, removing pitons from below to reinsert them above. At times he was so far above reliable protection that bolts were necessary just to gain some measure of safety, and the more he pounded the untempered gear, the more crumpled and unreliable it became. By the top of the Stoveleg Cracks, the pitons were useless.

In contrast, Robbins's team used Chouinard's RURPs to bypass some bolts, and Frost created wide-angle pitons, called "bong bongs" for the noise made when hammered, that were far more reliable than Tarver's gear. The result was an ironic turning point. Climbers called the first continuous ascent an aesthetic breakthrough, yet it was facilitated by technologies, including Harding's bolts, that meant Robbins's team actually faced less objective risk than Harding had just two years earlier.[32]

The nature of climbers also changed. The Beats were the strongest, most agile cohort ever as a result of the revolution Powell began. Leonard marveled at how they spent "the entire summer climbing every single day, so that their muscles get to be extremely powerful. . . . When we were climbing, we were quite proud that we used the side of our foot when climbing on little ledges because it would have less of a strain, but nowadays these climbers put the tip of their toe on the ledges. That puts a terrific leverage on the ankle. . . . They have the strength, and that forces the body in closer to the rock and gives better balance." Even those not climbing built strength with training programs. This was not new. To prepare for their ascent of Lost Arrow Chimney, Salathé and Anton Nelson practiced living on a pint of water per day, and Harding worked out with weights before *The Nose,* but by 1960 many Yosemite climbers had formal regimens of running, lifting, and calisthenics.[33]

Climbers also sharpened their minds. Published articles in the *Sierra Club Bulletin* and *Summit Magazine,* and private route descriptions, were part of a vast database on nature, climbers, and technology. This began in 1934 when Leonard made climbers' maps, now called "topos," of Upper and Lower Cathedral Spire. By the 1960s this data had become a significant part of vertical experience. Kor remembered how Steve Roper gave "me a selection of pitons for the Lost Arrow Tip. . . . He knew precisely which pitons were necessary to climb the final section [and] even told me which piton to use where." Robbins similarly climbed halfway up *The North America Wall* just to reconnoiter the other half. However, the more Beats mastered the variables, honing body and mind, the more elusive uncertainty became. They had fetishized risk. Danger was integral to their sense of adventure, yet each advance eroded the thing that they craved most: doubt. Yosemite had ceased to be terra incognita. Something had to give.[34]

As the most intrusive and safest form of protection, bolts seemed the most threatening impediments to sport. In 1960, Chouinard revived this already well-worn issue by warning that abuses were "very real and grave" and that they derived from "the problem of ethics in the use of bolts in climbing."

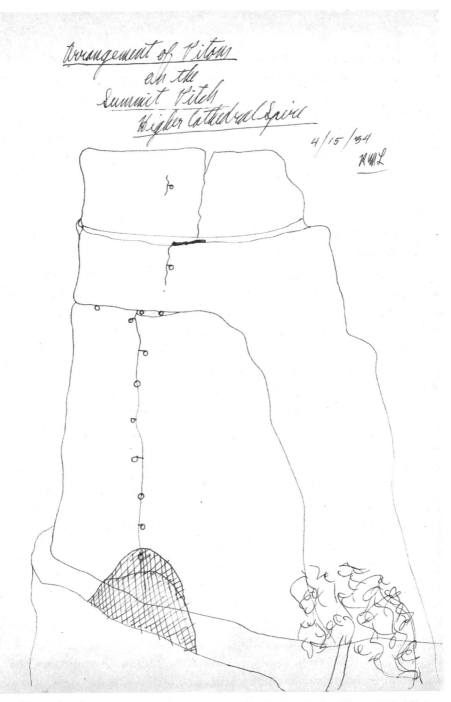

Figure 8.2. Although graphical representations of climbing routes had been produced since this mid-1930s drawing by Richard Leonard of the final pitch of Higher Cathedral Spire, these invaluable and closely guarded "topos" circulated only among small circles of friends. When entrepreneurs began to publish refined topos of popular routes in the early 1970s, Steve Roper, Royal Robbins, and others protested, claiming that publication would make climbing too easy and draw in the masses.

For Chouinard ethics was a communal issue. He argued that bolts "must be treated in the same manner as social morals. The problem is not one of individual taste, but rather one which must be determined by the entire climbing fraternity and adhered to by everyone who climbs." As always his metric was risk: a climber was "only justified" in placing a bolt "if he thinks that [a move] would be very dangerous even for a better climber than himself." Practically speaking, however, the "fraternity" was unfit to judge. Only "the very experienced and expert climber should even own a 'bolt kit.' It is incomprehensible for the average climber to know just what can be climbed safely by the expert on either free or artificial ground." Chouinard's sermon inspired a flood of responses. Robbins seconded his sense of crisis and the need for "a change in values." He, Fitschen, and others began to enumerate the bolts they used, including the odd notation of "no bolts were placed," while others began to remove or "chop" superfluous bolts from existing routes.[35]

Chouinard and Robbins were inventing tradition and, through it, the means of regulation. British climbers had long treated the sport as more than a pastime. H. E. M. Stutfield remarked that "mountaineering had in our day ceased to be a mere sport, an agreeable relaxation for jaded workers. . . . our attitude towards it was marked with a fervour and an intensity of purpose characteristic of the genuine devotee." Climbing was "a joy, a passion, an inspiration—one might say 'a religion' . . . tinged with veneration that at times savours of worship." Some zealots even harbored "sectarian" bigotries. One British group known as "The Squirrels" regularly patrolled routes to "remove all pitons they regard as superfluous." Everyone else belonged to the "outside world." In broader perspective, Beat rants about bolts and culture change belonged to a longer tradition of local rule.[36]

Such attempts at community regulation were extremely divisive, and many climbers resisted. Several noted that Chouinard had equated physical talent with moral authority. He wanted to regulate climbing by elitist principles, even proposing an invitation-only "Yosemite Climbing Club" for those of "outstanding climbing ability" interested in "raising the standards." Even some who sympathized, including Wilts and Robbins, saw no practical way to police climbers. Steve McCrory wrote that "the question of ethics regarding the use of bolts remains solely to the individual climber." Others, most of whom were moderate or club climbers, rejected the notion that climbing was in crisis. Bolts enhanced safety, and that was a good thing. Some routes were even improved by the addition of bolts where pioneers had taken too many risks. This was one of the implications of peer review, and even Robbins participated when he placed an extra bolt on *The Nose* in a state of fear and on *The Muir Wall* in a state of exhaustion. As for the environmental implications, David Brower noted that the 125 holes on *The Nose* meant "a total approximate excavation of a two-inch cube of granite, under more awkward circumstances than the highway excavator!" Critics were echoing Bestor Robinson's plea after Shiprock to "drop this childish prattle about the immorality of artificial aides."[37]

As a practical matter, the argument was moot. Only elites carried bolt kits because only they chose hard routes. From 1960 to 1965, many older routes were free climbed for the first time. Sacherer freed twice as many as anyone, but many participated in, as Chouinard put it, "raising the standards." The other key effort was the creation of "big wall" routes. In 1961, Robbins, Frost, and Fitschen climbed the 1,100-foot outside face of Higher Cathedral Spire, and with Pratt that fall a second, circuitous line up the southwest face of El Capitan. Named in honor of the old blacksmith, *The Salathé Wall* required fixed ropes but hewed close to Robbins's ideal by using only nine bolts. As with the second ascent of *The Nose,* it was an aesthetic statement, and combined with routes such as the *Direct North Buttress* on Middle Cathedral Rock by Chouinard and Roper, and two on Sentinel by Robbins and Frost and by Chouinard and TM Herbert, philosophies jelled. Robbins took great risks, including an irreversible decision to climb free where failure would have resulted in a "long and thrilling" fall. Chouinard and Herbert so limited their bolts that they once had to retreat. The big boys were walking the walk, showing the rest how to climb in style.[38]

There were outliers, though, great and not-so-good climbers who ignored the moralists. In 1961, Harding countered Robbins by pushing a line straight up the Leaning Tower, which lurches 110 degrees over the south side of the valley. He, Glen Denny, and Al MacDonald fixed ropes and drilled holes up the severely overhanging cliff. As with *The Nose* there was no other way, but Harding's stature shielded him from criticism. This was not so for outsiders such as Ed Cooper and Jim Baldwin. Arriving in 1962 to try a line on El Capitan's southwest face, Cooper was marked as a Northwesterner who Camp 4 residents judged unproven and thus unworthy. He also had a reputation for unwarranted bolting and publicity, or as Denny wrote, of being "ruthlessly materialistic and sensationalistic." Baldwin befriended others with bawdy behavior, but Cooper was aloof and therefore suspect. When the two fixed ropes up disconnected cracks, locals heaped scorn. Robbins took it as a personal affront after his declarations on siege climbing, and even those who helped, including Roper and Denny, called Cooper calculating and cold natured.[39]

Tensions boiled over in petty cause célèbres. Despite the criticism, Cooper pushed a difficult route that, in retrospect, was impossible without fixed ropes. How he finished was another matter. Waiting on top was a prearranged phalanx of reporters. Denny was crushed: "We all could have sat on the summit with this great thing, this experience, between us, and could have communicated in the phrases and actions of our own relationship through climbing. . . . But it could not happen, and the summit was dead. Cooper had contacted the world of sensationalism and the god damn thing ruined the summit." Robbins fumed, and even after seconding the route and conceding its quality, he did not compliment Cooper. The publicity was intolerable, so when Al Macdonald proposed a route on El Capitan done in similar style, locals made every effort to stop him. In a letter to a friend, Denny called Macdonald a "maniac" evincing a *"kind of climbing schizophrenia"* who "must be stopped before he rapes El Cap and its significance to the world of rock climbing." This pained Denny because he liked Macdonald and did not want to hurt him. Others were less considerate, berating in person and in letters until Macdonald quit in disgust.[40]

The moralists were reacting to apostasy. Climbing was a spiritual quest, Yosemite the temple, and Camp 4 the monastery where Victorian and Beat ideals melded in a new religion. Denny argued that the *"climbs on El Cap should be the particular expression of climbing that Yosemite contributes to the climbing world: amazing virtuosity in pure technical rock climbing of the greatest difficulty and magnitude."* The problematic climbers, as he saw it, were those who *"cannot approach this goal."* But what to do with the infidels and who exactly were they? The answers had everything to do with the homosocial world of Camp 4. Cooper, Macdonald, and even Harding to a degree were suspect outsiders; insiders got a pass. In 1963, for example, Kor started up El Capitan's 2,000-foot West Buttress in a manner much like Harding's early ascents. He fixed ropes, drilled holes, and dragooned many, yet Kor never faced criticism. He was not climbing with much more style than Cooper or Harding. It was not his expertise that distinguished him; rather, he was one of the boys and, thus, he was worthy.[41]

This was not the case with Cooper, and it was only a matter of time before there was a confrontation. When Cooper and Galen Rowell began a new route on Half Dome's northwest face in June 1963, all eyes were on them, and when they descended after a few days to attend to school and work, the attack came. The team left ropes in place to signal their intentions, and most climbers recognized their claim. Robbins perceived an incipient siege, however, so he asked Kor to help him pirate the route. When Kor balked, he turned to Dick McCracken, who agreed that Cooper deserved no quarter. It was Yosemite's first route theft. Robbins did not apologize. He snubbed a hated rival and kept control of Half Dome. When Cooper told the press about another route, locals expelled him. Cooper's only response was an impotent remark that "the spirit of competition in the Valley brings out weaknesses in some."[42]

By 1963, Robbins had become *the* moral authority of Camp 4, and along with a few others that one climber uncharitably called "Robbins' clique," they turned tribal. Except for Kor, Robbins was the best all-around climber in North America. He was also the most competitive of a very competitive group. If a route was climbed quickly or a boulder done with style, he immediately climbed it faster or better. Robbins kept tabs on new arrivals and seconded as many routes as possible, even his own, to assert himself as the reigning peer of aesthetic merit and moral fiber. He had to know who his rivals were and whether they were worthy. There was too much at stake. Yosemite was a treasure, and he and others wanted to ensure that their values would rule.[43]

Camp 4 was a rough place. Roper warned that if a climber "arrives in Yosemite with even a faint trace of arrogance, he is in for an unpleasant time: not only will he not gain the respect of the Valley climbers, but it is unlikely that he will ever fulfill his ambitious climbing schedules." Outsiders had to suppress their "desire for notoriety" and emulate "'normal' climbers, who pertinaciously cling to their belief that climbing is pure and noble." The bolt debate also continued to rage. Kamps wrote about the "obligation to a purity of climbing" and criticized how bolt chopping was personalized as "a symbol of superiority—person above person, area over area." His protégé Tom Higgins emphasized "the moral side" of competition, or as Robbins put it after citing Geoffrey Winthrop Young, "the *way it is done.*" Most lurked or discussed issues privately, but Ross Petrie was "a little tired of reading this 'Ethics in Mountaineering' garbage. . . . a very small vocal minority, jealous of each other's accomplishments, is trying to create a tempest in a tea pot." He suggested a "shoot out with bolt guns at twenty paces to settle the question." Another privately regretted "the petty bickerings and rivalries in Camp 4. The mountains are big enough to accommodate all talents and interests. It's a pity the people who go into them are not."[44]

The rancor finally faded in late 1965, and in the end the only arguments that mattered were on the rock. By 1964 no one, not even Robbins, had climbed a major wall without fixed ropes, so it was no small irony that the author of this aesthetic feat was Warren Harding. That spring he spied a line in the roadless Tenaya Canyon. In July he recruited Pratt and Chouinard to tackle the untested 2,800-foot face of Mount Watkins, accessible only by a backcountry approach, far from watchful eyes and without an umbilical cord. Big-wall ascents were usually begun in spring or fall. Watkins would reveal why. Temperatures soared over 100 degrees. The south face became a convection oven. Then cracks dead-ended. Bolts and water ran low. Dehydration set in. The climb became an epic. Harding lassoed a tree to avoid the drill, then donated his water so the others could reach the top. Pratt, who translated the climb into a gripping tale, showed readers how far the elite were willing to push themselves.[45]

That November they went even further. Unlike the gleaming polish of its southwest face, El Capitan's southeast face was dark and rotten. Brittle diorite intrusions formed a hazy map of North America that was intriguing to view but frightening to climb. So much material had fallen away that the upper wall overhung. It was literally disintegrating, and the base was a vast blast zone of talus running hundreds of yards downhill. The technical challenges were extreme, and the proposed route wandered up some of the nastiest, most sustained difficulties. Balanced against this were Frost, Pratt, Chouinard, and Robbins, perhaps the four finest climbers in North America. They began in a heat wave and ended in a foot of snow. Robbins noted that "there were at least a dozen pitches which on almost any other climb would be the crux," yet they ascended relentlessly in ten days. Robbins called *The North America Wall* the hardest route ever, and his team claimed the valley's penultimate "virgin."[46]

By suasion and intimidation a core group had narrowed the valley's acceptable techniques and couched them in a strongly gendered aesthetic of adventure. Chouinard noted at the end of one climb that he and Frost felt "purified and happy; happy that for a few hours we had been free and happy to take some of this freedom back with us." Pratt remarked that for "five days the south face of Mount Watkins had dominated each of our lives as only nature can dominate the lives of men. With the struggle over and our goal achieved I was conscious of an inner calm." His mates were "united by a bond far stronger and more lasting than any we could find in the world below." Robbins described *The North America Wall* as an existential quest: "We climbed onward, searching, always searching. Searching for handholds and footholds, for piton cracks and the right piton. And searching ourselves for the necessary human qualities to make this climb possible. Searching for adventure, searching for ourselves, searching for situations which would call forth our total resources." Many guffawed at the prose, but most agreed that big walls were ultimates. By 1964 a climber had to succeed by the Beat rules or start over to "preserve his own dignity."[47]

There were costs to this approach. At the comical end was an ascent of the 1,800-foot face of East Portal. Pratt described how he, Steck, John Evans, and Dick Long, "aided by a small band of porters [who] transported our tonnage to the Ribbon Falls amphitheater," hoped "to succeed by sheer weight of numbers." Hewing to the code of continuous ascent, they carried food for a week, but their loads reduced them to exercises in "hauling and tangling." Then they pelted themselves with stones, damaged ropes, and lost most of their food, water, and gear. Despite the mishaps, or perhaps because of them, the team had a blast as they struggled to the top. For others the rules were a torment. Famous for a rigorous opposition to technology, Frank Sacherer would climb unroped, expect similar commitment from partners, and punish any relaxation of principle. Occasionally he turned his climbs into ordeals, cursing partners' weaknesses and fraying at the seams. One noted that Sacherer refused "to plan hardware. When he does it is very bad. He is poor at getting it out. When under pressure there is a certain amount of hysteria in his voice and actions. . . . No wonder [TM Herbert] is psyched out." The rest of Camp 4 felt similarly.[48]

Sacherer was an extreme example of a general problem. The game was turning insidious. Each individual success heightened a general sense of crisis. By late 1964, valley climbers were feeling victimized by their skill. Even *The North America Wall* seemed anticlimactic. Chouinard remarked that climbing with Robbins was no fun: "He was like a crutch. You knew you were going to make it." To cure this plague of über competence, he upped the ante by pursuing a new El Capitan route with only two people and thirty bolts. They hoped to cleanse their souls. "This purer form of climbing," he wrote, "takes more of a complete effort, more personal adjustment, and involves more risk, but being more idealistic, the rewards are greater." But this was a conundrum. If the struggle was indeed everything, then the more they did this the rarer adventure would become. Like an addict, climber highs grew ever more elusive. Robbins wrote, "a climber needs stronger brew. He needs to edge close to the edge of the pit so a glance therein will rekindle his taste for the sunrise. He needs to face terror, and control it, to remind himself that he is more than the pawn of the forces around him, more than an expendable piece in a monstrous chess game."[49]

During eight days in fall 1965, Chouinard and Herbert found their fix. Their ascent of *The Muir Wall* devolved into a modern spirit quest of bad weather, dwindling resources, and borderline hallucinations. Doug Robinson called it "visionary." Chouinard and Herbert had achieved a Beat ideal, first voiced in Kerouac's *Dharma Bums* and Gary Snyder's poetry, of the ecstatic state. Better yet, their method was replicable. One "need only copy the ingredients and commit," Robinson remarked. The recipe was actually first concocted in 1945 when Nelson and Salathé endured eerily similar hallucinations during their dehydrated, two-day ascent of Half Dome's *Southwest Face* in intense heat. The major change was that Yosemite climbers now sought such suffering.[50]

Logic thus dictated that the only reasonable response was more paring. Valley climbers began to emulate top Europeans such as Herman Buhl and Walter Bonatti, both of whom were noted soloists. There had been several valley solos, including two first-free ascents by Frost and Robbins. They had also soloed several big walls. Robbins followed the *Steck-Salathé* route on Sentinel and made the second ascent of *The West Face* of Leaning Tower, Roper the *Lost Arrow Chimney*, and Eric Beck *The Northwest Face* of Half Dome. Still, no one had dared El Capitan, so in 1968 Robbins made the second ascent of *The Muir Wall*, solo. With allusions to Bonatti and Hemingway, he called it the "fullest expression of the climbing egoist." At age 33, it was also the greatest challenge he could find. He faced both the technical difficulties and psychic barriers of being alone in the vast vertical. Without backup, it really was his show. But no climber was better prepared, and as Chouinard said, few doubted he would "make it." Nine days, a few crises, and a bit of talking to himself later, Robbins did succeed, attaining a rarified stature. In 1970 he followed with a solo first ascent of *In Cold Blood* on Sentinel Rock.[51]

Elite climbing had effectively turned inward, testing by divesting, and each success escalated the game of one-upmanship. Some eschewed partners, others equipment, but all did a sort of technical and psychic striptease, discarding one crutch after another and all the while redefining the margins of reasonable risk. Underlying this self-imposed deprivation was that old British assumption, articulated most baldly by C. F. Meade in 1936, that minimalism would "recover some of the spirit of their predecessors and understand better the pioneers' feeling for the hills." Unlike skiers and surfers who connected to nature through equipment, climbers assumed their tools were impediments, yet evidence suggests the opposite. Achievements in fact revealed an ever more nuanced knowledge of the nature of gear, granite, bodies, and minds. The Beats had grown so in touch that the game seemed predictable.[52]

Yet the inward turn, it turned out, did not prohibit bolts. Huge cliffs still beckoned, and one of the loudest critics of bolts was also one of the most ambitious drillers. The lure of "virgin" lines was too strong for Robbins. Time and again he hammered up challenging faces, including Royal Arches, Washington Column, Sentinel Rock, Cathedral Spires, and three more routes on Half Dome. His efforts on *Tis-sa-ack,* a sketchy line up Half Dome's northwest face, were particularly notable for pissing off two partners and leaving 110 holes, but he was unapologetic. He owned Half Dome, having pioneered all four of its major routes. He even "took a weird delight" in placing what he called the best and worst bolt ladders ever, but his transgressions still paled before those of his old rival.[53]

Quietly, Harding had refined a different aesthetic. If Robbins looked to British tradition and European aesthetes like Buhl and Bonatti, Harding seemed to emulate the Italian Emilio Comici, who argued that the most elegant route was as straight as "a falling drop of water." Harding chased this ideal on *The Nose,* Leaning Tower *West Face, Lost Arrow Direct,* and *Southwest Face* of Liberty Cap, even though it resulted in unrivaled hole counts of 125, 111, 55, and 29 respectively. The toll included not only bolts but a new device called the BAT Hook, short for "Basically Absurd Technology." Harding was mocking both himself and Chouinard's pretentious acronym for RURPs, but his device, essentially an altered hook, lessened the use of the drill. The filed hook required only a shallow depression, and because it was a temporary placement, it accelerated ascent and elevated risk.[54]

By 1970, the now forty-something Harding's hallmarks of *direttissime,* relentlessness, and aid directly contradicted Robbins's values. Since 1965, Harding had labored in figurative and literal obscurity on Half Dome's less known and unscaled 2,200-foot south face. The route followed a massive, 800-foot arch and then wandered up a longer, blanker wall. Several tries resulted in one injured and two freaked-out partners, interludes in Vietnam and an emergency room after a hit-and-run accident, six storms, and the second major rescue. Nothing deterred him. Drill firmly in fist, Harding and Rowell plugged away, finally summiting in July, five years, six attempts, and 180 holes later. Camp 4 reactions revealed that Harding could still push limits. Most considered *The South Face* an achievement, but many were appalled by the methods. Robbins derided Harding's "penchant for great smooth walls," which underestimated the team's ability to free climb and use hooks on rugosities to pass areas without cracks. Roper feared that "with nearly all the more obvious crack systems climbed in the past decade, the inevitable trend is toward even more tenuous lines, ever more blank walls . . . ever more bolting."[55]

This distress set the stage for Harding's next route. *The Dawn Wall* traced a line between *The Nose* and *The North America Wall,* and it was a classic Harding ascent: 2,800 feet of overhanging and intimidating granite. All understood it would need many bolts. There had been two previous attempts, and most viewed any attempt as unnatural. Thus when Harding and Dean Caldwell roped up on 23 October 1971, they were trying something nearly everyone had dismissed. The team nevertheless lurched onto what became the valley's longest continuous climb. After twenty-seven days, 330 drilled holes, four storms, and one refused rescue, Harding clambered up to another swarm of cameras. He was once again a sensation, and this time he cashed in with an impromptu national tour.[56]

When the media tired, critics took over. Many flinched at the number of holes. Echoing his views of Robert Underhill's visit, Ansel Adams called Harding's ascent a "super-spectacular 'engineering' achievement [with] little relation to the spirit of mountaineering." TM Herbert likened him to Cesare Maestri, who had scaled Patagonia's Cerro Torre with a pneumatic drill. Chouinard called him the "mad bolter," and Robbins foresaw a future of bolt guns and "suction pads." The publicity also rankled. Robbins mentioned "Harding's adroit use of the press," which Rowell called "almost shameful," while Adams condemned the "obvious publicity effort." Herbert "felt like screaming, 'But they bolted the damned thing, and then they sold it to millions on television!'" For all the heat, the sin now seems unclear. Some critics were among Yosemite's most ambitious entrepreneurs. Robbins and Rowell wrote prolifically, Chouinard had equipped most of the community, and no one sold Yosemite's beauty longer or more effectively than Adams.[57]

The media's involvement revealed just how convoluted things got. Critics were correct that Harding sought publicity. While surprised at the number of reporters on top, he and Caldwell had schemed to sell photos, but editors were uninterested in another El Cap climb until the two were caught by a storm on Day Twenty. Then they saw a hook in raw endeavor amidst comfort. Interest heightened when the team refused a rescue initiated by critics who claimed they were overmatched and by a ranger who did not want climbers dying on his watch. This is when national media crews arrived, but Harding was hardly a publicity genius. He had failed to pique interest until nature made things dicey and his opponents intervened.[58]

The tempest was a brew of many contingencies, but climbers' opinions tended toward black and white. Some celebrated Harding's tenaciousness; others vilified his sensationalism. Robbins was all mixed up. He began by praising Harding's "eccentric individualism," saying it was "good to have a man around who doesn't give a damm [*sic*] what the establishment thinks." He cherished Camp 4's diversity and cautioned, "we can better spend our energy than ripping and tearing." What followed was bizarre. Like a mountaineering Carrie Nation, Robbins took chisel in hand and seconded *The Dawn Wall* with the intent of "erasing" it. Observers were stunned. Not only had Robbins contradicted his recent remarks but nearly everything he had written. In 1965 he had lectured, "reckless bolt chopping is just as irresponsible as indiscriminate bolting. . . . [I]f we respect the established nature of routes, and refrain from bolt chopping and placing, there will be plenty of climbs for all shades of abilities and tastes—and much less bitterness." Three years later he railed at NPS restrictions, asking "Who are those who would police climbing?" Now he was playing judge and jury and looking like a hypocrite, and he knew it. When asked afterward to justify himself, Robbins replied, "It will be difficult."[59]

Even worse, he did not finish the job. Robbins began with righteous fervor, chopping every bolt regardless of whether he had used it—a breach of his own "First Ascent Principle" in his instruction manual—but his indignation faltered. Partner Don Lauria recalled that "Royal really began questioning his reasons for erasing the route. He was having difficulty rationalizing his behavior. . . . He decided that the quality of the aid climbing was much higher than he had ever expected." Robbins admitted "there was one good lead after another. And that, of course, complicated the whole thing enormously." The upshot was obvious. Robbins called bolts a "blot" and drilling "rape," but his metaphors backfired because of his own routes. Ultimately he conceded that "Harding won," which frustrated TM Herbert, who had lobbied for the aborted rescue and then called the erasure "one of the most important events I have witnessed."[60]

Outwardly Harding was merely annoyed. He did not "give a rat's ass what Royal" and the other "Valley Christians" did. "If all or most other climbers feel a need for the comfort and shelter of structured thinking—if there are those who feel a need to establish and promulgate these principles and lead the masses to a better 1984-ish life, fine with me! . . . As long as the V.C. don't get their own secret police and employ Spanish Inquisition methods, I won't worry about being imprisoned, stretched on a rack, and forced to confess my sins." He again played the clown. Mixing Vietcong and religious symbols in the farcical journal *Descent* and an autobiography titled *Downward Bound,*

"... A bolt eh? ... Say twenty five Hail Mary's and do Half Dome free."

Figure 8.3. Eventually the moralists began to wear on climbers, and more and more pleas to drop the sermonizing made their way into journals and magazines, such as this caricature of Royal Robbins as father confessor.

Harding mocked his peers but also had the better end of the argument. "I've always played the basic climbing game to the best of *my* ability," he wrote. It was not "a matter of . . . morals" because there was no way to patrol the mob. It really was about individual ethics because there were simply too many contingencies of nature, talent, and technology, even on a day-to-day basis, to realize Robbins's and Chouinard's idealized order.[61]

Unfortunately for Harding, his joking style allowed critics to dismiss him. Some shared a weariness of righteous posturing, but most balked at his crude humor. Nor did they believe he did not "give a damn." Nobody seriously engaged his insights about the unresolvable tension between the individual and the group. Instead, Robbins made him a fetishist of blank walls. Chouinard said he trampled risk and inspired "the average Joe to do climbs that are normally over his head and . . . experts to do incredibly hard climbs without having to stick their necks out." Harding led "the common man" to bring "the Art down to his own level of values and competence." Roper called him "the master bolter," a selfish man driven by "glory" who cared "little what his peers thought." But on this point even Robbins demurred. Harding may have avoided thinking "deep and heavy when it's deep and heavy," but he did care. His routes were his legacy, and he was proud that none had "been criticized by the 'big boys'" once they had climbed them. He tried to shrug off the controversy but ended up writing an open letter wishing for "nothing better than to forget" the hardest, most important climb of his life.[62]

The conclusion was straight out of T. S. Eliot. Robbins made one last bid in 1972, soloing a new, even edgier line on El Capitan's southeast face. He got 700 feet before the prospect of continuous bolting forced retreat. In 1975, Harding climbed another smooth, overhanging wall west of Half Dome called *The Porcelain Wall*. The route was unexceptional, but Harding, Steve Bosque, and Dave Lomba committed the ultimate self-effacement by chopping their own bolts, summarily erasing the route to preempt critics. Harding climbed two last routes, and then both were done. Their era ended with a whimper, but the values inscribed in their climbs and writings had already reshaped the sport.[63]

Robbins and Harding did not invent the debates that framed them. Rather, they came to embody longstanding rival principles and, as such, became place holders other climbers invoked in their own arguments. As contexts evolved, though, they were extracted from their Beat heritage and mythologized as timeless warriors of tradition and liberty. Some regarded adventure and risk as transcendent values that buttressed a singular morality. Others saw these as highly contingent concepts with no consistent mean-ing given the mutable talents, ambitions, and nature even within the narrow confines of Yosemite Valley. Either way, the historical Robbins and Harding often faded into irrelevance.[64]

But their passions were critical contingencies. The Beats risked their lives for their ideals, and that fervor sometimes led them to see disputes in abso-lutes. As Daniel Duane observes, Robbins desired "a coherent way of being in the world, an orderly philosophy . . . a means to self-improvement and self-mastery." He felt so strongly about this that at times he could see no right place in this upright, self-made man's world for a Warren Harding, who rev-eled in the dissipation and relativity Robbins rejected. Thus Robbins could not agree when Harding insisted they were "really saying [and doing] the same thing." At a basic level their estrangement *was* personal. Passion helps illuminate this human dimension. It also helps explain how a group of mis-fits created "not just the modern culture of rock-climbing, but . . . contempo-rary outdoors California." The Beats remade themselves through climbing, and a few became famous and wealthy. As avocations became vocations, each success reshaped not only the game but how future athletes and envi-ronmentalists interacted with nature. The Beats created a context in which people increasingly related to nature through consumption, because the Beats did much more than just climb. They sold themselves and their way of life, and many people bought the product: a new environmental culture.[65]

9. ENTREPRENEURS

I have begun my campaign to wipe out CMI and Long and Leeper
too. Fuck them all. Leeper gets fucked up for even *thinking* he can
make a better pin than I can.
—YVON CHOUINARD

The Beat movement was a reaction to middle-class values, but Beat climbers rejected the style more than substance of normative society. Their pursuit of success and acceptance was thoroughly bourgeois, and their pursuit of virtuous sport flowed from conservative ideals about amateurism that were deeply rooted in middle-class culture. Reconciling these contradictions was awkward and, ultimately, impossible. Beats remade their avocation into a vocation, and the most zealous purists were also most responsible for turning climbing into a consumable activity. They literally "sold out," but the underlying reasons were more complex than greed or hypocrisy.[1]

One motive was simple: climbers had to eat. In the 1950s they developed new strategies to keep food on the picnic table. Some followed Mark Powell's lead and relied on off-season work. Layton Kor, Steve Komito, Chuck Pratt, and Steve Roper served as temporary laborers or clerks, saving up for extended periods of play. The seasonal rhythms of education appealed to Powell, George Sessions, Willi Unsoeld, and other teachers and students. Dave Dornan and Wayne Merry joined the Park Service so they never had to leave. A number also made goods and sold services to the sport's growing consumer base.[2]

The Beats were the first generation of outdoor athletes to make a living from play, and chief among these mongers was Yvon Chouinard. His journey from bum to businessman to environmental guru mirrored that of many entrepreneurial climbers. There was no grand plan, and in many ways he was indeed a reluctant success story. In other respects, though, no one was more cutthroat. Each move was calculated to raise his profile in the sport and industry. Each essay marked him as an elitist among elites. Each product distinguished him among a growing field of competitors. He was extremely ambitious, but the broader story is less about his immense ambition than the contexts and contingencies. It is how serendipity helped Yvon Chouinard be in the right place at the right time to influence, with help from many others, how outdoor athletes and environmentalists interacted with nature.[3]

If anyone seemed predestined to embrace an individualistic sport peopled by outsiders, it was Chouinard. Born to French Canadians in southeastern Maine, Chouinard would always be an outsider. A French-speaking Catholic in a region dominated by Anglo Protestants, he inherited a hard blue-collar life. His dad worked at a local mill, and when he needed dentures, he slugged some whiskey and pulled his own teeth. To escape this life, Chouinard's family joined the rush to California after the war. Yvon was seven, short, and spoke no English. He spent most of his time with his mom and sisters, and like other Beats he was athletic but a misfit. Chouinard hated school and avoided peers, froze in front of spectators, and liked to hunt and fish alone in the area's vanishing wildlands. He even took up the truly idiosyncratic pastime of falconry. Descending cliffs to band birds led him to the Southern RCS and some of Yosemite's budding stars. Chouinard liked the sport and had a gift for it, so he pushed off in this new direction.[4]

After high school Chouinard attended junior college and took odd jobs, but mostly he surfed and climbed. Although he met many like-minded people, he remained a solitary figure, among, but not of, a larger group that visited Baja in winter, the Tetons in summer, and Yosemite in spring and fall. Climbing was costly and money tight, so in 1957 he got a forge and anvil from a junkyard to make his own gear. He pounded steel any time he had to wait for the surf or partners, and soon he was improving on existing pitons, including Salathé's work. In 1958 he turned to aluminum carabiners, acquiring a drill press, grinder, and die to refine Raffi Bedayn's design. In 1959, he and Tom Frost devised the RURP for their Kat Pinnacle ascent.[5]

This was mostly a solitary quest to refine gear. Chouinard simply reacted to perceived gaps in the technological suite, but he was also entrepreneurial. He was not the only gear maker. Jerry Gallwas crafted pitons like Salathé's for Half Dome. Bill Feuerer made many items for El Capitan. Unlike them, Chouinard had an eye for the market. The only commercially available gear in the mid-1950s were from Sporthaus Schuster, Army surplus, and house brands of like provenience from stores such as Holubars in Boulder. Chouinard saw a niche for pitons crafted from 4130 chrome-molybdenum. Early pieces were for himself and partners, but soon he was also selling at climbing areas. Some complained about his $1.50 price tag—German pitons were 20¢—but Chouinard was firm: his gear was more versatile and resilient. Yosemite also entered the pitch. The more his gear was used on the big routes, the more caché they gained. To climb like the best, one needed his equipment. Little by little Chouinard became a businessman.[6]

His induction into the Army profoundly changed the scope and scale of his business. Chouinard has remembered this as a time of rebellion. He was not built to salute uniforms, and he spent much of his stint resisting authority, trying every tactic imaginable to obtain an early discharge. Driving this was not just his deeply contradictory anti-authoritarianism but an urgent desire to build the business. Prior to induction Chouinard was "reportedly very bitter" and desperate for a "6 months delay to take care of his business." Once in uniform he decided to mine the Army library. He threw himself "into studying Engineering and working on developing new pitons and manufacturing processes. . . . I've gotten hold of every book on metallurgy, mechanical drawing, strength of materials, manufacturing, machine shop practice etc that I could get my hands on. So now I finally know what the hell is coming off with the hardware business." He redesigned his gear with "new super iron," made "blueprints for every piton from the rurp to the 4" angle," and acquired a new die for RURPs. "Perhaps if I had not been in the Army," he reflected, "I couldn't of thought up all of these new ideas. It's something to think about."[7]

When Chouinard was transferred to San Francisco, he went back to work, spending "almost every evening" in a friend's garage making "biners and stuff." He bragged about RURPs that went "into solid concrete sidewalks—no cracks." As he built inventory he also began his "campaign to wipe out" competitors who were also friends. By the early 1960s, Gregg Blomberg, Bill Feuerer, Ed Leeper, and Dick Long also made equipment for the gear market. Chouinard worried most about Long, who had borrowed his designs and product names. It was a problem made for a lawyer, but in 1964 the "industry" was intimate enough that Chouinard instead invited Long to dinner and chewed him out. The rest he battled in the market. Chouinard issued order sheets, business grew, and he moved from his parents' backyard to a Burbank shed. When he added capital and expertise by taking Doreen and Tom Frost as partners in 1966, they moved to Ventura so Chouinard Equipment could expand and its workers could be close to the surf.[8]

Chouinard worked very hard, but his success also hinged on fortuitous timing. Outdoor sports grew rapidly in the 1950s. By 1960 the *Wall Street Journal* counted 100,000 U.S. consumers of climbing equipment. The time was long gone when Sporthaus Schuster was the only supplier. Western firms such as Holubars, Recreational Equipment Co-Op, Eddie Bauer, The Ski Hut,

Figure 9.1. The sort-out. Laying out gear before an ascent was a Camp 4 ritual. Here Yvon Chouinard puts together a gear rack before attempting a major aid route in 1969. Note the prevalence of pitons, the pair of mechanical rope ascenders *(lower left),* and the kernmantle ropes, core ropes with braided sheaths, instead of the three-strand twist ropes.

Bedayns Market, and Vandegrift's were thriving storefront and mail-order operations. The rush to the mountains fueled a market of one to two million dollars, with Californians the main consumers. Chouinard had entered a booming economy with few competitors, and he set up shop at ground zero. Whether the result of pure luck or savvy timing, he was in the right place at the right time.[9]

Sport became business. In Seattle, Recreational Equipment Co-Op incorporated as REI. In Boulder, Gerry Cunningham opened Gerry's. In Southern California, Dick Kelty opened a shop to sell his packs. In the Bay Area, The Ski Hut added product lines and Doug Tompkins founded North Face. Meanwhile, The Sport Chalet in La Canada, Alpenhaus in Sacramento, Barry Corbet's The Outhaus in Jackson, and Robbins's Mountain Paraphernalia in Modesto were a few of the many specialty stores opening one after another. The commercial thrust did not immediately change climbing's insular world. When producers needed gear testers, they gave friends prototypes and asked for feedback. When merchants needed labor, they hired buddies. Allen Steck joined The Ski Hut in 1951 and employed pal Steve Roper each winter during the latter's annual retreat from Yosemite. Commercial practice followed sporting culture, but that was seldom a good business model. Employees bridled at rules, and employers suffered flaky friends. Chouinard initially relied on climbers and surfers, but a need for reliable and timely products led him to hire real blacksmiths, which strained some friendships. The market created these tensions, but it also enabled Beats to pursue amateur ideals as semi-professionalized athletes.[10]

Conversely, Steve Komito's experiences revealed the limits of Beat entrepreneurship. Komito was Kor's rope mate on some especially sketchy desert climbs and widely liked in Camp 4. As with his peers, he was an athletic misfit who found "a sport in which I could perform at a passable level and a group of friends who accepted me as an equal." He dropped out and labored in the industry, enjoying some jobs and suffering others. His Rubicon was typical of many Beats. In summer 1965, Steve and his wife lived in a tent while he managed The Outhaus. The store closed as usual at the end of the climbing season. Steve was again out of work, but now Peggy was pregnant. They moved to Leadville so Steve could work at the Climax molybdenum mine. It was a short-term gig to pay bills and obtain insurance, and he soon switched to Alpine Designs in Boulder. Steve wanted to be his own boss, however, so he took shoe repair classes and hung a shingle.[11]

Komito learned that independence was illusory. Business meant bills, he told a friend, and credit had to be repaid: "This is the winter of my discontent. I have my balls in a vise and my own hand is turning the handle. In order to pay my rent and the bills for my increased machinery and inventory, I am working in my fucking shop every fucking day of nearly every fucking weekend. . . . Every day I feel more like the withered old Jewish shopkeepers who were my predecessors. This shit must end." It did not. Komito had replaced the yoke of wage labor with the burdens of debt. Ironically, starting a climbing business stole time from climbing. It took years to repay loans from friends. His frustrations were compounded by a problem that plagued many entrepreneurs: flawed workmanship. Komito was mortified when customers had soles delaminate, but this was endemic to learning on the job. Nor was he alone. Early piton manufacturers feared gear failures. Chouinard obsessed about his heat treater or any process he did not personally oversee. The Beat ideal of carefree adventure vanished rapidly for Beat entrepreneurs.[12]

Komito wove his identity into business correspondence. With friends he joked about running "the Chosen People Shoe Corporation" or "Jap-Jew fix-a-shoe," but business names were serious business. To customers he was "Steve Komito Bootmaker Alpine Footwear." His moniker represented a widespread approach to commerce. Komito and others branded themselves and traded on their climbing reputations. Robbins teamed with the French boot manufacturer Galibier to create a shoe called the RR. Ed Leeper and Bill Forrest sold gear under their names. Bill Feuerer used his nickname, "The Dolt," while Komito worked his handle "Frog" into signage and stationery. Chouinard's identity was unusually complicated. He called his gear company Chouinard Equipment and fumed about brand infringement, yet his Diamond-C mark mimicked John Salathé's P-inside-a-diamond brand and his first products were essentially refinements of Raffi Bedayn's RCS carabiner and Salathé's pitons, which he called "Lost Arrows" to honor the old blacksmith's revolutionary ascent.[13]

Another way to capitalize was to open a guide service. This had been the bread and butter of Chamonix since the 1820s, and guides commodified Mount Hood in the 1870s, the Canadian Rockies in the 1890s, Mount Rainier in the 1910s, and the Tetons in the 1920s. The famous American mountaineer John Harlin was sports director for the Leysin American School and ran the International School of Modern Mountaineering. High-end clients could learn to climb and ski with mountain stars such as Royal Robbins and Don Whillans. When Harlin quit Robbins took over as sports director and then started his own school in California, called Rockcraft. Others worked for outfits such as Glen Exum's school and guide service in the Tetons, but all Beats learned that guiding was, as the Chamonix mountaineer Gaston Rébuffat observed, not "foolhardy" adventure but a "job" that stressed Victorian responsibility. The guide "loves difficulty," he wrote, "but abhors danger." This meant Beats espoused one ideal personally and another professionally, and how they interacted with nature depended on which identity they were inhabiting.[14]

Another casualty of entrepreneurship was the bias against publicity. Talk has always been integral to climbing culture. Climbers' "private physical accomplishments" only truly "become public" when their "tale is told." The process began around campfires, but by the 1850s it had already evolved into public lectures and journal essays. Lectures were central to club culture. As a member of London's Alpine Club explained, "If the Club could not go to the Himalayas or the Rockies, then the Himalayas and the Rockies could come to the Club." The adoption of cameras made talk an increasingly visual exercise, and by 1900 lantern shows were de rigueur. This was also true for the RCS. When visiting Los Angeles, Dick Leonard and Bestor Robinson showed home movies to the RCS, and southern members reciprocated at Mills Tower in San Francisco. Lecturing helped build reputations, but there was little remuneration except for elites such as Whymper in the 1890s, Mallory in the

1920s, and Rébuffat and Hillary in the 1950s. Their international tours were exceptional, yet their audiences revealed a growing body of mountaineering consumers.[15]

By the 1960s the ability to entertain with images and tales was fungible. Ed Cooper, Dennis Hennek, Robbins, and Steck were selling photos, showing slides, and telling stories on the club circuit. This was significant income for some. Kor said talks helped "pay my way out to the Valley." Others made movies. In 1932, Dick Leonard filmed *Mountaineering in the Sierra Nevada* for the AAC, and David Brower shot *Sky-Land Trails of the Kings* in 1939 for one of the SC's first wilderness battles in the Sierra Nevada. The RCS also staged ascents of Upper and Lower Spires for the two-reel *Climbing Cathedral Spires*. During the war members produced *The Taking of Seneca Rock* for the Army, and after the war they produced many more RCS training films.[16]

Aside from the pure entertainment of studio releases such as *White Hell of Pitz Palu* and *The White Tower*, climbing films were didactics on techniques and values. In *Climbing Cathedral Spires*, for example, the lens lingers on the art of belaying, placing pitons, and rappelling while text counsels: "Careful Preparations Provide Security." The film captures the safety ethos of the club era, ending with Francis Farquhar's eulogy, "And lest we forget those who did not come back—Mummery of Nanga Parbat, Mallory of Everest, Peter Starr of the Minarets." By the 1960s, very different films were emerging. The Canadian mountaineer Hans Gmoser traveled widely to promote his films and guide service in the Canadian Rockies. Chouinard and Robbins worked with Frost, Pratt, Corbet, and Roger Brown on *Sentinel: The West Face*. The film follows Chouinard and Robbins partly to demonstrate modern Yosemite techniques but also to promote the Beat aesthetic: "Nowhere is man more dependent upon his fellow man, and nowhere more isolated. Each pitch echoes a recurring cycle of separation and reunion." If RCS films reproduced the heterosocial ideal of safe fun, then *Sentinel* captures a homosocial ideal of manly individualism. "The mood," the narrator intones, "is one of transcendency, agony, or ecstasy."[17]

Selling values was never simple. Like many films, *Sentinel* was a controversial venture. One Camp 4 resident said Robbins's involvement was "certainly a hypocritical thing . . . after all he has said about [Ed] Cooper['s self promotion]." The amateur bias against self-promotion, the contempt of "extravagant hero-worship" and "star performers" that C. F. Meade described in the 1930s, still fired many Beats. Jerry Gallwas was proud that he did not record some first ascents, and Dave Rearick was bothered that one of his routes was called a "hero climb." Anything smacking of self-aggrandizement scandalized. Thus Beat entrepreneurs were always focused on more than vanity and greed. If *Sentinel's* commercial nature exposed contradictions in how Robbins treated rivals, he and Chouinard still sought more than money. They were selling a novel approach to adventure, one emphasizing empowerment and liberation, and they saw no inconsistency in profit. *Sentinel* had a higher purpose: it was about culture change.[18]

Beat writings also merged aesthetics and entrepreneurship. For a century climbers had written restrained narratives for peers and sensational tales for the public. By the time Warren Harding published his *Argosy* article in 1959, the climber-author was a genre. Journals had been the primary outlet for most of the era, while periodicals like the *Saturday Evening Post* added the occasional thrilling tale. The surge outdoors changed this literary landscape. *Ski* was the first commercial periodical for an outdoor athletic sport in 1936. *Skiing* followed in 1948, and *Summit* and *American Whitewater* appeared in 1955. Enthusiasts began to use these and other publications to tell tales, build reps, and debate values. The Beats' homosocial adventure ethos tapped a literary network largely outside heterosocial clubs.[19]

The talk was also increasingly complex. Before 1955 the three most prolific California climber-writers were John Muir, Norman Clyde, and Francis Farquhar, each for different reasons. Muir was the mystic, Clyde the aesthete, Farquhar the historian. Most of Yosemite's early technical climbers published little. Brower wrote three essays, Bedayan, Leonard, and Bestor Robinson one each, and Jules Eichorn none. Likewise, Salathé published nothing, Cooper and Kor wrote only two essays each on Yosemite, Steck three, and the master publicist Harding wrote four. The output of the moralists was thus a fascinating departure. While Frost and Bob Kamps wrote one essay each, and Sacherer none at all, Pratt wrote six, Chouinard over ten, and Robbins more than forty. The loudest critics of publicity were also the era's most published writers. Again, this was not hypocrisy. There was ideological purpose behind their verbosity. Robbins was legendary for his espousal of high principles, and Chouinard made him look like a moral slacker. Their messages were rarely singular, however. The moralists sold both values and themselves.[20]

No climber wrote with greater partisanship than Chouinard. Beginning in 1961, he railed against any technique that reduced risk. By 1972 he had vented so often that one essay was titled, "Coonyard Mouths Off." Identity, ideals, and technology fused in his prose. In the Army he wrote "Modern Yosemite Climbing" for the *AAJ* as a "completely biased and prejudiced" promotion. Yosemite was "one of the most important schools of rock climbing in the world" with "techniques, ethics and equipment all of its own." He fore-grounded his generation with photos of himself, Frost, Herbert, Pratt, and Robbins, and pitched his own gear, noting "that since 1958 every major rock climb in North America has used my equipment." The essay was an ego trip, but it was philosophically consistent. Chouinard's gear had reduced the need for bolts, and because they were removable, the rock remained seemingly pristine and, thus, "cleaner." Like Robbins, Chouinard merged identity and ideals. His philosophy, ego, and business were thoroughly entangled.[21]

The ultimate advocacy vehicles were guidebooks. Originally for members, they always did more than offer route descriptions. Erik Weiselberg notes that collecting and publishing climbers' feats made clubs the "arbiters of the climbing world." Journals and summit registers were the means of authority. Californians had to publish their exploits in eastern-based journals until the SC founded its *Bulletin* in 1900. Thereafter it became the journal of record for much of the American West, tracking first ascents, variations, and histories. As ascents multiplied in the 1930s, Bay Area RCS members lobbied for a more comprehensive reference text. Already mapping RCS practice sites, Leonard became the chair of the SC Mountain Records Committee and began to direct an effort to compile information for a climber's guide of the entire Sierra Nevada. In the process the SC became the gatekeeper of climbing information and, thus, the repository of legitimacy.[22]

Authority was at first narrowly situated, resting solely in the SC and—through its relationship with the NPS—at sites like Yosemite, but as the loose-leaf binder grew into unwieldy reams, the guide evolved into the 1954 hardbound *A Climber's Guide to the High Sierra*. In 1956 the SC published Leigh Ortenburger's guide to the Tetons, and the RCS issued guides for Pinnacles National Monument, Tahquitz Rock, Joshua Tree National Monument, and New York's Shawangunks. These were popular texts, both for their spatial information and, as the *Yodeler* admitted, because climbers liked to "read their names in print." Yosemite was at first subsumed within the Sierra guide, but it was an awkward fit. The valley was technically distinct, and by 1960 route creation had outpaced other areas, which had also grown popular, so Yosemite climbers hived off to publish separately.[23]

This set the context for *A Climber's Guide to Yosemite Valley*. From the start it was conceived as a tool for promoting Yosemite's uniqueness, and its author, Steve Roper, pulled no punches. In practical terms most of Roper's work amounted to compiling and refining route descriptions written by others, yet in key ways he made the guide a personal expression. He added a section on Yosemite history, a feature Ortenburger pioneered in the Teton guide, but Roper's essay was far more opinionated. It foregrounded heroes, derided the NPS and weekenders, and warned outsiders to obey local mores or "never gain the respect of the Valley climbers." He also wrote mini-histories for routes and formations that aggrandized allies and slighted rivals. He let it all hang out, and Brower backed him by arguing that Roper came "uncomfortably close" to spilling "the secret" about "the *real* reason" men climb. Roper also erased Yosemite's heterodox past. "Normal" climbers were now only those "who pertinaciously cling to their belief that climbing is pure and noble." All others were by implication inauthentic.[24]

For all his moralizing, much of which he tempered in the 1971 second edition, Roper's greatest impact was on a technical issue. All guidebooks use rating systems to standardize route comparisons. The German alpinist Willo Welzenbach proposed the first numerical system in the 1920s, devising Grades I to VI for overall difficulty. Purists balked, fearing that quantification fostered a "spirit of competition," or as R. L. G. Irving sneered, "sporting-heroic-arithmetic climbing." The RCS tried scales of 1–5 and A–C, but the SC Mountaineering Committee substituted Welzenbach's I–VI grades for overall difficulty plus Class 1–6 for technical difficulties that ranged from walking (1–2) to scrambling (3), roped climbing (4), protected free (5) and aid (6) climbing. The SC system was the Yosemite standard through the 1954 *A Climber's Guide to the High Sierra*, but Robbins, Don Wilson, and Chuck Wilts refined it at Tahquitz, subdividing 5th and 6th class to define difficulty more precisely. This "Decimal System," as it was known, originally ranged from 5.0 to 5.9, but a mathematically weird yet systemically logical 5.10 was added after 1960 for even harder climbs.[25]

At the time Roper wrote his guide, most Beats used a hybrid of the SC and Decimal systems, but a few preferred a new system. Ortenburger first balked in 1956 while compiling his Teton guide because he thought the SC emphasized technology over difficulty. The mountaineering committee disagreed. They regarded the use of ropes and protection as intrinsically related to difficulty, plus they valued continuity with European practices. Rebuffed, Ortenburger persisted and by 1963 had a system that would deal with a spectrum of climbing and environmental challenges from pure rock to pure ice. He and other reformers published their National Climbing Classification System in *Summit*. The NCCS embodied all the era's ideals. It was like climbing Esperanto, "a common language" that would facilitate "understanding and appreciation" across the continent. Ortenburger even included a table to translate no less than eight regional systems into one unified structure.[26]

The timing of publication was intended to preempt several forthcom-

ing guidebooks, and lobbying was intense. Many influential western climbers drummed up support in letters to *Summit* and clubs. They also pursued
institutional backing in the AAC, and worked relentlessly on guidebook authors. Chouinard and Robbins practically begged Roper, but he and Brower
were set in their ways. The contest had many dimensions. Egos and values
did matter, not to mention all the work already completed on manuscripts,
but there were also substantive disputes. The reformers desired a universal
schema, while resisters thought it meaningless to compare the icebound
"Liberty Ridge on Mt. Rainier with the Higher Spire in Yosemite." Even more
basic was the problem of inertia. Ortenburger might have been correct that
a national system would erode provincialism, but most climbers were already invested in local schemas. Regional sporting and environmental cultures were not so easily erased.[27]

The outcome bared Yosemite's ironic impact on continental culture. The
NCCS group had star power, but authors had final say. Robbins admitted to
Roper, "In reality you have the big stick, and I believe that whatever system
you use in the Yosemite guide will become the national system." Reformers
hoped to convert Roper, but when it was clear he would stick with custom,
Chouinard pleaded to add a conversion table for the Tetons, since Ortenburger was already revising his guide with the NCCS. Robbins was correct
about Yosemite's impact. Other authors took Roper's cue and adopted the
Decimal System, now renamed the Yosemite Decimal System. Thus a supposedly regional system became the continental standard, while the supposedly national system framed only a few mountains. Still, there were no
clear-cut victories. Roper did adopt the NCCS aid scheme of A1 to A5, and
both Ortenburger and Roper retained Welzenbach's grades for overall difficulty. The resulting impact of Roper's guide, dubbed the "red book" for its
cover, cast light on why he took a hard line. Yosemite was indeed the most
important climbing area in North America, so more was at stake there. Grading schemes mattered less in other places, and Roper's other guidebooks
were less dogmatic.[28]

The 1964 edition of *A Climber's Guide to Yosemite Valley* is arguably the
urtext of modern rock climbing, but it was hardly the only one shaping the
sport. Guidebooks and training manuals had been produced since the early
1900s, and by 1930 there were many how-to articles as well. During the war
the AAC published its *Handbook of American Mountaineering,* and afterward
the SC issued long-planned manuals on ski mountaineering and climbing.
In 1960 the Seattle Mountaineers published *Mountaineering: The Freedom of
the Hills,* now in its seventh edition. Later Beats made their own individual

contributions. Some were strictly methodological, such as essays by Chouinard on rock and ice technique, or by Robbins on haul systems, but some were quite self-serving, such as Royal Robbins's climbing manual *Basic Rockcraft,* the title of which advertised his Rockcraft Climbing School.[29]

In reality authorial and entrepreneurial agendas were inseparable. As publication of the red book approached, Denny told Roper that he would "really have it made." In a sense this was true. Roper evolved from a fast climber to an authoritative voice. While still in the Army, he finished a second guide on Pinnacles National Monument, strategized sales, and outlined a history of Yosemite. The latter project took decades. In the meantime he wrote or edited seven guides, three picture books, and two anthologies. With Steck he also co-authored *Fifty Classic Climbs in North America* and co-edited *Ascent.*[30]

The latter was a path-breaking journal and culmination of many independent factors. By 1965 there was still no journal dedicated to the Beat perspective. RCS members had tried and failed to publish *The Rotten Log,* and even after Robbins became *Summit's* rock climbing editor in 1965, the magazine owners kept Beat values at arm's length, sometimes begging climbers not to discuss ethics. The SC was also changing. Recreation-oriented members were increasingly marginalized by the club's narrowing focus, especially in projects directed by Brower. The SC press ignored climbers, and conservation-oriented members questioned their dedication. By 1963, Glen Denny noted that many climbers were "pissed off about there being no Yosemite notes" in the *Bulletin,* which for sixty years had been the sport's journal of record. Roper sympathized as Brower's committee repeatedly delayed publication of his Yosemite and Pinnacles guidebooks.[31]

Steck tried to break the impasse by proposing *Ascent,* a new journal "devoted entirely to mountaineering matters." Brower balked, partly to maintain proprietary access to plum essays for the *Bulletin,* and partly because of the fiscal implications. He was already in hot water with members, officers, and the federal government because his publishing agenda had created budgetary and taxation problems. A new journal would only deepen the debt. The more he resisted, though, the more support swung to Steck. Will Siri, both a climber and club president, admonished Brower, "During the past two years I have defended you . . . on a good many occasions. Let us now give Steck a free hand, just like the one you insist on having." Brower had to yield, but he had never been hostile to climbers. He continued to care about the sport. Once the publications committee endorsed *Ascent,* he encouraged the editors to make it unique: publish literature, take stands, and use color to highlight the Beat aesthetic. The last suggestion was particularly significant.[32]

Mountaineering art had two aesthetic traditions. One came from John Ruskin and the Hudson Valley School and stressed the sublime through distant, usually unpeopled landscapes. This had long informed climbing and environmental culture, especially the mountain photography of Vittorio Sella, Ansel Adams, and Bradford Washburn. The other strain, seen in Edward Whymper's etchings in *Scrambles Amongst the Alps,* emphasized men clawing and hacking at nature. One adored from afar; the other zoomed in. They finally merged when Stanford Alpine Club member Henry Kendall carried his 35mm camera up El Capitan in the late 1950s. Climbing the East Buttress, Kendall began to blend Whymperian action with jaw-dropping scenery. Then in 1960, Frost completed the transition with shots on *The Salathé Wall,* later published in the red book, of intensely private moments, suffused with action, in sublime settings. Other Beats elaborated these existentially masculine themes into a truly novel aesthetic.[33]

Ascent brought it together as a distinctive expression of "the total Alpine

Figure 9.2. In the late 1950s and early 1960s, Ed Cooper, Glen Denny, Tom Frost, Henry Kendall, Steve Roper, and Galen Rowell redefined the aesthetics of mountain art, merging John Ruskin's sublime with the physical dynamism of Edward Whymper's nineteenth-century etchings. Glen Denny captures that new sensibility as Layton Kor begins to crest a swell of granite above Camp 6 on *The Nose* in 1963.

experience." Joe Fitschen and Roper shaped the literary style, recruiting poetry, fiction, humor, technical, and opinion pieces. They reinstated the *Bulletin's* climbing notes section, issued guides to new areas, and reprinted such
classics as A. Phimster Proctor's account of the second ascent of Half Dome,
a Dolomite solo by Giusto Gervasutti, and satire from *Punch, Strand,* and
MAD Magazine. Denny, who was a gifted photographer, nurtured *Ascent's*
appearance. For the first time mountain art stood alone rather than as il-
lustrative dressing. The journal became a platform for photographers such
as Cooper, Denny, Barry Hagen, Ken Wilson, and, most notably, Galen Rowell.
It also featured cartoonist Sheridan Anderson, whose ribald wit took the
stuffing out of stars. Nothing had ever looked like *Ascent,* and nothing after
could afford to look like what came before.[34]

Ascent was a hit, but that was true of the entire sport. Beat climbers point
to 1970 as a watershed year, but the sport's popularity had grown ever since
the 1950s. The Beats were part of this boom, and Roper's guidebook, which
sold "like hotcakes," only fueled interest. In 1964, Robbins noticed "more
climbers were signing out on weekdays than ever before." The following
spring Pratt told Roper, "Everyone plans to hit Yosemite this year. Your guide
has really sparked a lot of interest in the Valley. . . . Climbers from Canada,
SLC, Boulder and England are definitely going to arrive this spring." By year's
end the NPS had recorded a 50 percent increase. By 1968, Robbins felt pride
and apprehension that Yosemite was growing "ever more popular" with "the
pilgrims of the vertical." When the AAC president in 1970 noted that American climbing was growing "at a tremendous rate," the trend was already over
a decade old.[35]

Entrepreneurs knew this as well. Roper was but one of many Beats who
had turned play into work. Chouinard's business grew rapidly. In 1964 he issued an order sheet, and in 1965 he made his buddy Doug Tompkins's new
store in San Francisco, The North Face, the exclusive wholesaler for Chouinard Equipment. Annual sales doubled well into the 1970s. Across the bay
Steck left The Ski Hut, founded Mountain Travel with Leo Le Bon and Barry
Bishop, and inaugurated modern ecotourism. Former employees of Tompkins and Steck started Sierra Design, and a former employee of Gerry started
Alp Sport and Alpine Designs. In some ways it was a Beat triumph. They had
learned how to sell themselves and their ideals without destroying the small
circles that coalesced first around campfires in Camp 4, Jenny Lake, and
Mazatlan.[36]

There were costs, of course. Chouinard would later long for fall days
"when I and one other guy were the only climbers in the valley," yet no one

had a greater hand in annihilating that solitude. His essays and gear informed and enabled the bustling mob. He and other entrepreneurs had tried to instill values, but the industry's growth rested on an increasingly diverse consumer base. Camp 4's homosocial world was overrun by its success. Some resulting tensions stemmed from social and cultural shifts in the 1960s, but some problems were structural. As with previous climbing generations, the next cohort had to push boundaries to make their mark, and that required physical and mental commitments that necessarily strained tradition. What emerged in the later 1960s was a new class of climbers, self-styled "dirtbags," who tested the limits of nature, the NPS, each other, and ultimately themselves. This was not a matter of barbarians at the gates, however. The Beats not only invited them in but gave them the keys to paradise.[37]

10. DIRTBAGS

The vandals have arrived.
—ROYAL ROBBINS

The end is always the hardest part of an athletic career. There is nothing worse than that undeniable moment when the body fails, when other bodies rush past and even Herculean will can no longer summon an adequate response. Getting older or frailer is hard on everyone, but it is especially cruel for those whose identities have hinged on bodily performance. The Beats had intellectualized climbing like no previous generation, yet none had so dedicated themselves to the cult of the body. They had conflated identity with sport and underwent rigorous moral and physical training to achieve idealized performances. Thus their last days as top climbers were an existential crisis, and the seeming coincidence of their decline with *The Dawn Wall* debacle in 1971 led some to blame that event as the moment of the fall.[1]

This is problematic, for the facts do not fit. Unlike in 1955, when Mark Powell initiated a major transition in Yosemite, the ensuing decades were a time of constant infusions of new blood, ideas, and techniques. Thus bounding the Beat generation in Camp 4 is a historically muddy problem. Some new arrivals such as Eric Beck were embraced, while others like Jim Bridwell were distanced. We glimpse the process of social segmentation through public climbs and private asides. The result is dissonance between the evidence and explanations of Yosemite history. Although athletic and cultural change was continual, the Beats posited a sharp divide. They personalized climbing history, conflating their individual feats with the collective good. Thus it was perhaps inevitable that they saw their era as the "Golden Age of Yosemite climbing," and as they went so did the sport.[2]

This idealized past still matters because its rhetoric has privileged one generation above others. Framing the Beat era as an apogee also made Beat values normative and, by implication, relegated other views and groups to signs of declension. Any departure was backsliding. Defining their age as a golden age also helped Beats distance themselves from professionalization, dissipation, and a woeful legacy toward Native Americans. A before-and-after view emerged in which idealistic amateurs gave way to waves of ever baser "dirtbags." Like ancient Arcadia, Yosemite's golden age is mythic, yet it casts light on changes in sport, culture, and identity. The world morphed in messy ways, and that disorder illuminates how a simplified history shaped outdoor recreation and environmental culture in the late twentieth century.

As their era closed, the Beats began to sound like codgers. Warren Harding declared, "Yosemite has just about played its part—it's become a sort of granite gymnasium." His ascent and Royal Robbins's descent on *The Dawn Wall* became a confirmation. Jim McCarthy said they had rung "down the curtain" on another frontier. "Our society and culture are catching up with us just as the wagon trains followed the first mountain men." Galen Rowell cried, "the creaking door has suddenly closed." Manly opportunities were vanishing, the good times were gone. Steve Roper wrote that the ascent "was another nail in the coffin of the once-idyllic Valley scene." Pat Callis felt "sorry for the young climbers." Chris Jones said that while his generation was "inner directed . . . Tomorrow's may be out directed, influenced by advertising and external forces."[3]

Awed by the Beats, younger climbers largely conceded their sorry state. After all, the "virgin rock" had vanished. Callis said "unplowed ground . . . doesn't exist." Tom Higgins wrote, there "just don't seem to be more good lines between lines between lines between lines." Nature had been overrun. Between 1961 and 1967, Yosemite's annual visitation doubled from one to two million. By 1972 there were 50,000 "serious" U.S. climbers, a stunning growth since 1955. Lito Tejada-Flores concluded that the "source of our nebulous but very real malaise is invariably found in numbers: there are too many of us." Even skeptics of the Beats agreed that reform was necessary. Yosemite seemed less an inspiration than a microcosm of the world's woes. A population bomb had exploded, technology's noose was closing, and a tragedy of the commons gripped the campgrounds and walls. When even dammed and degraded Hetch Hetchy Valley seemed to Rowell a pristine and inviting refuge compared to the insanity of Yosemite Valley, something had gone terribly wrong.[4]

Social and ecological developments had merged to signal the passing of another Arcadian idyll. In classical Greece, Arcadia was a pastoral retreat inhabited by poets and artists who "dwelt in an Eden-like state of innocence." Its decline punctuated the world's first golden age. In the late nineteenth century two British climbers concluded that mountaineering's golden age ran from Alfred Wills's 1854 ascent of the Wetterhorn to Edward Whymper's cataclysm on the Matterhorn in 1865, a period that just happened to encompass British dominance in the sport. Not coincidentally, although the first usage of "golden age" came in 1887, the phrase gained its widest usage at a highpoint of anticontinental feeling among Anglophiles in the mid-twentieth century. Not coincidentally, these were the texts through which Beats discovered mountaineering history.[5]

Other climbers defined golden ages for Norway, Canada, the Cascades, and Sierra Nevada, all of which became mythic claims to "alpine paternity." Like Arcadia, each age celebrated a few men for planting and husbanding mountaineering's seed, and all implied that the good times were over, that "there was no glory left." Generational self-congratulation was thus a well-worn habit by the time Robbins sighed: "Those were the golden days." Taking the opposite side of Clinton Dent's frustrated remark in 1876, the Beats smugly admitted that, yes, they had taken the plums and left only stones. They then marketed the Beat era by republishing past glories to modest profit and immodest laurels, and historians accepted "the golden age of Yosemite climbing" as a temporal and analytical framework.[6]

Not that the basic argument is wrong. Climbing did change socially, culturally, technologically, and environmentally, but the timing had little to do with *The Dawn Wall* or any other lone event. Wherever climbers claimed golden ages, the term operated primarily to distinguish an "us" from a "them." In the valley it separated Beats from both clubs and dirtbags, but it did not illuminate actual processes of change, all of which began well before 1971.

Take for example the issue of how generations were limned. An important implication of Robbins's remark about "pilgrims of the vertical" is that Camp 4 grew steadily throughout the 1960s, not in a sudden rush after 1970. The relatively sharp social and cultural divide of 1955 simply did not repeat itself, but this did not prevent Beats from delimiting themselves. When Jim Baldwin, Frank Sacherer, and others arrived in the early 1960s, they were incorporated into the Beat community. But when Bridwell, Dennis Hennek, Don Lauria, and Kim Schmitz arrived a year or two later, they were kept at arm's length. Roper facetiously recalled that "we 'elders,' approaching twenty-five, found them vulgar and arrogant," yet group identity was a serious, deliberate process.[7]

The Beats were deeply suspicious of these kids. Outlining his history of Yosemite climbing, Roper added a chapter titled "The Future" because he doubted their sincerity or commitment. "To what extent," he asked, "do these young climbers climb for the reasons we do? Are they in it just for kicks, to impress other people? Insecure? All of this must be brought out." Chuck Pratt agreed. He labeled one group "Bridwell's puppets" and said "the next real generation has not made its appearance," implying not that these climbers were part of the Beats but that they were nobody at all. Both Roper and Pratt were astonishingly unreflective. Most of the supposed unworthies had been in the valley less than two years, and their progress was not significantly slower. As Powell noted, one up-and-coming climber had achieved "the difficult leads" yet lacked "that indefinable knowledge and experience which is so necessary for big-time climbing and which takes a couple of years of solid climbing to attain."[8]

The rise of Jim Bridwell is a case in point. Like Richard Leonard, Bridwell grew up a military brat, another typical loner who, like Robbins, was a gifted athlete but distant from peers. He kept to himself, read, explored, and even shared Chouinard's attraction to falconry. Like so many, he was first drawn in by a photo of El Capitan and an essay on Layton Kor's ascent of Utah's The Titan. Bridwell lived in San Mateo, so he joined the Loma Prieta RCS, learned the ropes, and fell in love. What he "liked best about climbing was that I was accepted as myself." What he did not like was club conservativism, so at seventeen he drove to Yosemite and "found in Camp 4 the neighborhood he had never known as a child." He began to cut college classes, and at nineteen gave up a track scholarship at San Jose State for Camp 4, where he climbed regularly with Baldwin, Kor, Pratt, and especially Sacherer, who impressed upon him the principle of eschewing technology to explore the edge.[9]

Contrary to the dour views of Pratt and Roper, Bridwell and other newbies *were* making their mark. By 1965, Steck was amazed at the activity taking place by "new climbers from everywhere." Bridwell was one of the best free climbers, and Lauria, Schmitz, Ken Boche, and Jim Madsen made very fast ascents of El Capitan. Then in 1968, Hennek and Lauria halved the time of *The North America Wall*'s first ascenders, who in 1964 had called themselves the world's four best rock climbers. In 1965, Pratt said the "big climbs seem to be running out." Five years later Stanford Alpine Club members Chuck Kroger and Scott Davis quietly climbed a new route on El Capitan with little reconnaissance or bolting. The line, called *Heart Route*, stunned the Beats. They never saw it coming, yet it was simply an extension of the decades-long one-upmanship they had practiced. The biggest difference was that younger climbers seemed more modest. While Robbins and Rowell published thirty-three pages on *Tis-sa-ack* and *South Face*, both of which were shorter than *Heart Route*, Kroger wrote four funny pages on what was, with Chouinard and Herbert's *Muir Wall*, one of the two most stylish big-wall routes ever attempted in Yosemite.[10]

There was no divide in 1971. The hardest free-climbing moves had reached 5.11 as early as 1967, and then in the 1970s literally reached new ceilings with *Owl Roof, Separate Reality, Hang Dog Flyer, A Dog's Roof,* and *Phoenix,* all of which followed lone cracks under severe overhangs. These were short test pieces, usually less than one hundred feet, but the difficulties forced Bridwell to fine tune the Yosemite Decimal System with plus and minus signs (5.9+ or 5.10−) and lowercase suffixes (a, b, c, d). The quest to free pitches extended to big walls. Sacherer had freed *The Southwest Face* of Half Dome, *Lost Arrow Chimney,* and *East Buttress* and *Direct North Buttress* on Middle Cathedral Rock. Then in 1969, Bridwell free climbed the Stoveleg Cracks. This was a different game from test pieces, one that required far greater commitment. It was one thing to climb eighty feet at the edge of ability and then rappel to the ground, quite another to try the same with thousands of feet to go. Freeing the *Steck-Salathé* route on Sentinel in 1970 was thus part of an incremental escalation of physicality that had continued without break since the 1930s, and long stretches of El Capitan, Half Dome, Mount Watkins, and Sentinel were also being freed.[11]

Aid climbing was also evolving. To reduce bolting in the late 1960s Harding, Rowell, Callis, and Dean Caldwell perfected the BAT Hook, and Jim Madsen used short aluminum rods in shallow holes as insecure pegs. BAT Hooks and "rivets" or "dowels," as they were called, still required drilling, but they used gravity and balance instead of mechanical friction to hold a climber. By 1970 these riskier techniques had been used on many routes, so when Schmitz and Bridwell used them in 1971 on the *Aquarian Wall* on El Cap, it was not quite the breakthrough Daniel Duane claims. True, "the incipient, elusive lines that were left to Bridwell's generation required more imaginative . . . almost perverse" methods in an "increasingly strange game," but the techniques themselves had a longer history.[12]

This held for an entire suite of tools that were extreme in function and value. Several gear makers built tools to exploit neglected features. Hooks had been used in the Alps since Edward Whymper and in Yosemite since Salathé, but new designs exploited the tiniest purchases. Like BAT Hooks and rivets, Cliffhangers, Beaks, and Crack'n-Ups relied on friction. Copperheads and bashies were chunks of soft metal swaged onto wire and molded to the rock with hammer and chisel. All were unstable. Climbers had to weight moves precisely or gear would pop and bodies would fly. All these devices were significant departures, yet they revealed the enduring influence of Beat ideals. In an era when proficiency seemed to kill adventure, the very insecurity of these new tools contributed to the process of testing by divesting.[13]

The most significant innovation was for sleep. Until the late 1960s climbers had to descend by dark or suffer. Bivouac options ranged from the rare commodious ledge to standing in slings as limbs went numb. This led to such classic moments as George Whitmore straddling a granite shaft as Harding bolted the last pitch of *The Nose*, or *The North America Wall* team hanging in hammocks while a snowstorm raged. Locations for a two-point hammock were rare, so in the late 1960s Harding designed a tent that could be hung from a single bolt or piton. The body still pressed against the rock, and fabric could tear or collect rain. Truly reliable comfort was still a dream. Then in 1972, Greg Lowe built an aluminum-framed platform, and he and Rob Kiesel completed a proof of concept in an icy storm on the first winter ascent of Half Dome. By the 1980s climbers used weatherproofed "portaledges" to scale previously inaccessible walls in Baffin, Norway, and Pakistan. Sleeping platforms and Robbins's haul system, which used pulleys and body weight to raise loads, were perhaps the two most empowering innovations for aid climbers after 1950.[14]

The new tools enhanced edginess by enabling climbers to exploit the subtlest features. Weathered wrinkles, tiny edges, and pinholes could be used instead of the drill. The blank walls were less blank, but most devices barely held a climber's weight, let alone the force of a fall. When used in series they tested physical and psychic limits. In 1972, Charlie Porter pushed a new line up the southwest face of El Capitan. *The Shield* mostly retraced older ground, but a new section revealed a stark game. On one pitch Porter used thirty-five RURPs in a row, descending repeatedly—like Harding on the Stoveleg Cracks—to reuse his limited supply. The result was a harrowing pitch. A fall would have "zippered" all his gear, and the belay was so poor that cutting the rope "might have been the only thing [to prevent both climbers] from going to the deck." The RCS would have thrown a fit, but climbers now marveled. Robbins called Porter "more than just an aid specialist, he is a connoisseur. . . . He has gotten inside the rurp and is looking out."[15]

The gendered and sexualized implications of aid climbing shifted. The best were now regarded as "super-sensitive" to the capacities of their tools and nature. Porter was "an artist." Aid specialists were "determined not to let technology mediate [their] direct experience of the wall." Each first ascent was "an artistic creation." Greg Child explained, "We were modern Michelangelos [who] worked gently and carefully, regarding each placement like a crucial work of art, of copper and steel on granite." The old aspersions no longer stuck. Critics "may think that climbing is a sort of forced entry, a violation, a pounding of spikes and smashing of the rock into submission," but

Child "wasn't doing anything that El Cap didn't let me do. Every move and placement flowed as naturally as the stone that accepted it." This was not rape; it was consensual.[16]

No one pushed the art more than Jim Bridwell. Since 1962 he had developed an ethos merging climbers' faith in self will with Frank Sacherer's embrace of the edge. Bridwell believed that he had "the power to form at least a part of [his] own reality," not simply for motivation but perhaps even to control weather. "If I could imagine a route," he insisted, "I could climb it. Climbing had become a cause to live for—a way to prove the freedom of my mind"—but he was also certain that "if you're not scared, you're not having fun." In 1975 he returned to the liminal terrain of El Cap's southeast face to ascend a line west of *The North America Wall. The Pacific Ocean Wall* was the first of four routes on which Bridwell redefined the elite game. Extremeness came from not only new tools and poor rock but pitches where falls ensured injury. The stakes were bared when a partner suffered permanent brain damage. Three years later his team upped the ante on *Sea of Dreams* by limiting themselves to forty bolts used only for belay anchors. One evening they hung from fourteen barely inserted pitons. Bridwell punctuated another lead by belaying from six RURPs, although in this case a partner insisted on adding a bolt. By the end, two pitches had earned the unofficial rating of "fall-and-you-die." By 1980 difficulty had taken a quantum leap upward, and new routes were no longer comparable to earlier ratings.[17]

A new sport had emerged. One climber noted that Bridwell's "obsession with minimizing bolts [was] less about ethics than playing dice with the limits of possibility," but that applied widely. More and more routes had death pitches, and many took astonishing risks. John Bachar soloed without a rope. Bill Denz preferred BAT Hooks to rivets *because* of their insecurity. Rob Slater rappelled from hooks and hoped the friction of his weight would keep anchors in place. Older aesthetic arguments imploded, replaced by a crushingly simple philosophy of pushing risk as far as possible.[18]

An endless parade of young climbers flailed at the hardest routes in the world, flogging themselves daily to stay in shape. Camp 4 added a makeshift gym of boulders, balance chains and ropes, pull-up boards, bars, and ladders worthy of the Marquis de Sade. The more that elite climbers pulled on tiny edges and very thin cracks, the more their training focused on strengthening first knuckles. They were "pumping granite." Wandering through the camp, Trip Gabriel was struck by the sheer athleticism. All were "crackerjack athletes." This is why Yosemite remained an epicenter of sport. Englishman John Sheard admitted that "only Americans" were "capable of both very hard free climbs and A5 nightmares." Another declared "the best climbers in the world were American," and Bridwell "was the best climber in America."[19]

Much indeed had changed, but from a technical perspective little pointed to 1971 as a turning point. The same held for Camp 4's social and cultural milieu, which evolved well before Harding and Robbins duked it out on *The Dawn Wall.* Climbers had bent NPS rules for decades. In the 1950s, Nick Clinch slept in Camp 4's bathroom because it was the only heated room he could find, and Yvon Chouinard and Ken Weeks ate wildlife that visited their abandoned incinerator in the Tetons. Kor slept in caves and Roper and Sacherer shoplifted, but it was Eric Beck who made these tactics a low-road lifestyle. To stay and climb, which was increasingly the only way to be an elite, Beck hunkered in caves, scarfed discarded food, snuck showers, and mined trashcans for returnable cans and bottles. In the process this intermittent college student revised Thorstein Veblen's statement by demonstrating that "at either end of the economic spectrum lies a leisure class."[20]

By the mid-1960s a new society was emerging that seemed an embodied set of contradictions. Propelled by a vast library of essays promoting Yosemite as a global standard, climbers from around the world converged on the valley, each sensing they were incomplete without an El Cap ascent, and all dedicated in equal measures to stoic discipline on rock and sybaritic dissipation in camp. Climbers valued fellowship yet viciously criticized any weakness. They espoused high ideals yet broke laws as a matter of course. They honed their bodies to a fine edge yet ingested a stunning range of intoxicants. They wanted to get close to nature yet carried with them, sometimes literally, the pop culture they criticized. Camp 4's chronically impoverished denizens reveled in a natural paradise, yet caving, scarfing, and canning were how they survived.[21]

Much of this crossed generational lines. Climbers had defied the NPS and scammed the Yosemite Park & Curry Company since the individualists moved into the valley, and no one escaped camp culture. Nor did the dirtbags introduce drugs. According to Bridwell, "almost every climber I knew used" drugs in the 1960s, but they "didn't use them on routes. . . . We were using hallucinogens to help us understand what we were experiencing from a point of view seldom visited by the western mind." True to the Beats, they "were trying to make sense of this new awareness. To unfold the mysteries. Drugs were equipment." What set the dirtbags apart was a lack of "any philosophical agenda to getting stoned. It was recreation, pure and simple." Like the rest of society, Camp 4 lost its idealism. Youthful "rebelliousness remained knowing, jaded, circumspect" but without its "utopian naiveté."[22]

Instead, as John Sheard remarked, waking early could seem "a waste of a day" because of the "inevitable night-time epics." Many still self-medicated with caffeine and alcohol, but pot, hash, mescaline, and acid were also popular. Kroger remembered a mid-1960s visit when everyone was "sitting in Camp drinking red wine" while friends were stuck on walls. By 1970 a clique of Southern Californians formed "The Stonemasters" as a double entendre about their free-climbing and recreational prowess. By the late 1970s some were on a "Three Day Plan" of preparation, "free soloing on LSD," and recuperation. Others ingested pot, wine, and hallucinogens at bivouacs. Yosemite climbers in fact kept pace with the rest of society in questioning authority, consuming intoxicants, and using leisure to define themselves. Even in the climbing world dirtbags were largely a continental composite of irreverent Vulgarians from the Shawangunks in New York state, ribald partiers from Squamish, British Columbia, and a California hippie culture that led surfers also to believe "the 'ideal' lifestyle . . . was one of joblessness and 'self-sufficiency.'"[23]

Camp 4 became a complex society of climbers, crowds, and parties in the 1960s. Its base was composed of two rather anonymous groups. The weekenders were a longstanding if ephemeral presence. Carrying Coleman lanterns, stoves, ice chests, and tents, a few families always squatted. Gawkers were the other nameless pack of amiable, sometimes knowledgeable tourists fascinated by the sport. More noted, if not respected, were the hippies and lower caste climbers. Swarms of high-school and college kids hung out, played music, got stoned, and drove to distraction the NPS and Beats, while a growing knot of minor climbers came and went without note. All were, as the local epithet went, "campers," and their sin was twofold. Their very presence reminded Roper "that we weren't doing anything unique any longer." They also crowded cliffs and forced locals to queue up. On the next rung were outsiders, often climbers with reputations elsewhere but lacking local cred. On top were the Brahmins, an inner circle who had climbed the most difficult free and big-wall routes and, as a result, enjoyed special privileges in camp and got first crack at the valley's unclimbed lines.[24]

Camp 4 burst with "neighbors, love affairs, slums, parties, gymnasiums, loonies, territorial disputes, degeneration, and inspiration." Lording over all was Bridwell. Only 24 in 1969, he already had one of the longest tenures as a full-time climber. His power derived not only from his climbing talents but from a sure vision of the future, itself largely an internalized version of Sacherer's devotion to risk. Bridwell's faith led him to remake Yosemite. John Long called him the "Sorcerer," and John Roskelley deemed him the "grandfather

Figure 10.1. Although Yosemite climbers had engaged in physical training since the 1930s, by the 1970s the demands of elite routes were so difficult that residents of Camp 4 assembled an outdoor gym complete with weights, pull-up bars, rope ladders, and slack lines to hone strength and skills. Rock climbing had become a full-time occupation, and dirtbagging was the only way most aspirants could afford to pursue their sport.

of American rock climbing," but the better simile was Fagin. Bridwell ruled Camp 4 with a scary combination of cunning charm and ruthless coercion. Some he cajoled to greater feats, others he bullied to abandon climbs. Apprentices and veterans alike knew who was in charge. All bent to Bridwell.[25]

As the 1960s closed, Camp 4 seemed maddening and chaotic. The NPS was at wits' end, confronted by the same challenge to authority that plagued campus administrators and cops. It was hard to sort climbers from hippies, and the national park no longer seemed a timeless refuge. These problems had festered for some time. Indeed, in 1968 both rangers and climbers would acknowledge a "long-standing friction." In 1962 the NPS said it would accommodate conflicts with camping limits, but in August 1963 rangers summarily evicted all climbers from Camp 4 and in 1966 they imposed a seven-day camp limit. The hippie invasion only exacerbated matters. By summer 1969 there were conspicuous tensions between rangers, climbers, freaks, and other visitors, and confrontations resumed over Memorial Day weekend in 1970.[26]

Tensions finally exploded in July. Hippies had taken over a meadow near Camp Curry, trampling plants, reading poetry, playing music, consuming drugs, and defying curfew. At night they roamed the adjacent Camp 14, disturbing vacationers and distracting rangers from nocturnal bears. The issue divided climbers. Some such as Harding wanted to live and let live. Roskelley and others had only contempt for drugged-out, lice-ridden hippies. Confrontations escalated, both sides growing more rigid. The denouement on Saturday, July 4, surprised no one. Crowds and the media had gathered all day, closing in as the 7 P.M. curfew approached. When NPS forces, batons and mace in hand, charged the meadow on foot and horseback, the hippies had no escape. The authorities surged, the kids countered, a "riot" ensued, and the freaks won. Rangers later admitted they "didn't do it right" and that negotiation would have been more prudent, but at the time hippies seemed a threat. However, when federal, state, and local police systematically harassed all youths the rest of the summer, even self-professed redneck Roskelley began to wonder, "Are we still in America"?[27]

Equally relevant was whether they were still in nature. National parks were supposedly environmental icons, but hotels, stores, cafeterias, crowds, and smog spoiled it. Climbers and environmentalists felt besieged. The riot, purchase of the park concession by Music Corporation of America (MCA), and a proposed tramway from the valley to Glacier Point were alarming. The Beats, some of whom had followed in the footsteps of older climbers to become officers in climbing and environmental organizations, protested with the same indignation with which Alfred Mummery vented on the "cockney and his congeners" in 1895. Rowell raged at the MCA's lack of "environmental awareness" and willingness to unleash a "flood of people in Yosemite [that] has damaged the wilderness character of far more terrain than has the quiet reservoir in Hetch-Hetchy Valley." Robbins likened the hordes to invading "vandals," and Bridwell declared "Paradise Lost" after real vandals damaged his gear. All wanted to turn back the clock.[28]

Although riven with similar divisions, the NPS ultimately saw things differently. Administrators investigated the riot to prepare for Labor Day, but the resulting report cast a much longer shadow. It concluded that communication had failed completely. Even minor changes in tactics would likely have prevented conflict on July 4, but problems ran deeper. The recommendations revealed an agency out of step with its public. Rangers were ill-prepared for a clientele that had fewer clubs and more hitchhikers, backpackers, and runaways. Ranger training needed to emphasize law enforcement, and the interpretation programs needed to speak to youths. Slide shows for kids were fine, but young adults wanted laser and rock shows and talks for a more ecologically minded audience. To curry rapport, male rangers were even encouraged to grow facial hair.[29]

Administrators also responded to youth demands for their own place. In the first shakeup in a century, the NPS totally reconfigured its campgrounds. Camp numbers were dropped in favor of organic names such as Upper and Lower Pines. Camp 4 became Sunnyside. It also shrank in size as a walk-in site, and fees doubled to $4 per day, forcing even more climbers to adopt dirtbag tactics. Rangers tried to ameliorate tensions with climbers by starting an annual softball game (the "Pine Pigs" won in 1973), and they rehired a seasonal ranger to "rap" with climbers. New policies were supported by Beats in the AAC. Even Raffi Bedayn played a liaison role. The park also established a new camp called Yellow Pines to segregate hippies in a laxly patrolled walk-in area down valley. The riot was not the sole trigger of change, but it was the most "obvious symptom of the social pressures which forced the re-evaluation of the goals and responsibilities of those guarding the parks."[30]

The NPS tried to enhance the park experience, but their unintended consequences were equally unsettling. In the short term the new training and camp system eased tensions. Arrests fell in 1971 and 1972, partly because there were no riots and partly because rangers focused on narcotics instead of marijuana and underage alcohol possession, but one lesson was that the vast majority of people arrested were under thirty and "that all future efforts should be devoted to this age group." Caseloads soon quadrupled. The superintendent noted ruefully that the "implication of these statistics are possibly that we have opened 'Pandora's Box.'" The ranger corps was becoming a law enforcement agency. The new emphasis warped budgets. There was "a very real manpower crunch with a conservation of funds until the big rush in the summertime" that drained resources from the park's infrastructure, research, and rescue operations.[31]

Climbers were appalled. Roskelley began to camp illegally to escape Camp 4's "transient climbers and drugged-out 'flower children.'" The climbing journal *Off Belay* mourned the changes in articles titled "Ah Wilderness!" and "John Muir Turns Over in Grave." Regardless of whether Roskelley was right that "the dream [had] ended," weird stuff was happening. In 1972 the "Nation's first 'helicopter hijack'" occurred inside Yosemite. By 1977 rangers had christened a $70,000 jail, endured a wave of arson and tire slashings, and guarded the crash scene of a World War II bomber crammed with marijuana. The accident drained NPS coffers, but it was a boon to dirtbags. Rangers confiscated several thousand pounds and then left until spring. Meanwhile a parade of dirtbags mined the remaining contraband. Before rangers finally shut down the bonanza, several Camp 4 residents had acquired new bags, packs, tents, ropes, gear, and cars.[32]

The story of "Airplane," as pot smokers dubbed the product, is told often, but few notice how the incident revealed the degree to which Yosemite
climbers were connected to the rest of the world. The NPS had no choice
but to admit this in 1970, but climbers, as their remarks about Vandals, lost
paradises, and ended dreams attested, kept their heads firmly in the sand.
The reason had everything to do with a desire for distinction. Since the 1850s
there had been a firm link between climbing and prestige. Part of why climbers climbed, even in Yosemite, was to mark themselves via some astonishingly bourgeois principles. And therein lay a paradox. The entire development of American sport was a "quest for subcommunities." Climbing drew
some athletes for the same reason baseball, bicycling, fly fishing, and surfing
drew others, and complex social systems emerged in each sport. Dirtbags
were one manifestation of a "climbing lifestyle" with its own hierarchies. At
the pyramidal apex of Camp 4 was a "gang," complete with special status
and privilege, but similar societies with "stratification along status lines," a
"reigning orthodoxy" of sporting behavior, and consequences for those "who
failed to abide" operated at Joshua Tree, the Tetons, and Shawangunks. Nothing about Yosemite was unique.[33]

Much like high school, sports functioned as "relatively autonomous social space[s]" that structured identity. The environmental preferences of participants were important. Scaling cliffs, riding waves, and descending slopes
were not the same, yet their private meanings and social dynamics were
quite comparable. Thus when John Jay said powder skiing could make nature "your domain, your copperplate, your will," he was not so different from
when Tom Blake viewed surfing as, for "brief and fleeting moments," a way
to master the "laws of time and tide" or Eric Jacobsen claiming that ice
climbing gave "the feeling that you can control your own destiny." Outdoor
sports empowered young men and women to imagine themselves as masters of destiny, and their communities were essentially self-selected tribes of
like-minded, even politicized, individuals.[34]

The nature of these sports did matter. Surfers, kayakers, and skiers were
dependent upon weather, but in each case the medium was reproducible.
Whenever the Aleutian Low obliged, waves rolled into the North Shore, powder reigned in Utah, and rapids roared in the New River Gorge. Vertical nature was different. Although ice climbers depended on weather, rock climbers could play in drought or deluge. Conversely, although the individual
wave or slope was ephemeral, another soon replaced it. Rock was not a re-
newable resource. Torn away spectacularly or chipped away subtly, climbers
accelerated Yosemite's demise. The RCS first recognized this when Art Blake

in 1940 complained that "Rock Engineering . . . hastens the erosion of our noblest peaks and spires," and Robin Hansen not long after feared an exfoliated slab on Lower Cathedral Spire would soon fall. Like hunters, anglers, and even birders, climbers inexorably degraded their environments.[35]

Through the 1960s the pace of destruction accelerated. By 1962 a crack on Arrowhead Spire had taken so many pitons "that it was a real problem to find a solid placement." By the end of the decade a key flake had fallen from Higher Spire, and the NPS closed two areas to climbing. Ironically, the culprit was the chrome molybdenum piton first devised by Salathé. Carbon 4130's high tensile strength made for strong yet springy pitons that could better hold parallel-sided cracks. Their stiffness also meant they could be removed and reused, thus preserving a pioneerlike experience. However, removal required whacking pitons back and forth in the crack until they were loose enough to extract, usually after grinding a bit of rock as well. The technology of the no-trace ethic did leave permanent traces.[36]

In the early 1970s climbers reacted with the Clean Climbing Revolution. Paralleling concerns about damage by well-meaning backpackers, Chouinard and Frost flinched at the impact of their pitons. Inspired by artificial chockstones from England, they introduced lines of Stoppers and Hexcentrics with the 1972 Chouinard Equipment catalog. Their foreword decried the sport's ecological and "moral deterioration," arguing that preservation of "vertical wilderness" and adventure hinged on a technological shift. The artificial chock became the ecologically and morally superior tool. Like natural chockstones, "nuts" required wise placement in constrictive fissures and thus demanded greater attunement to nature. The new word, Doug Robinson wrote in an essay titled "The Whole Natural Art of Protection," was "clean," and "clean climbing demand[ed] increased awareness of the rock." This was a more ecologically sensitive and adventurous way to climb, and the Chouinard catalog was a cultural watershed. The *American Alpine Journal* even reviewed it in its book section, and many scholars cite its appearance as a turning point in the sport.[37]

What goes unsaid in this tale of ecological and spiritual enlightenment is Chouinard's own late conversion. The English had used real chockstones since the 1920s. Climbers gathered rocks en route to cliffs, placed them in cracks, and attached slings as a more natural substitute to a piton. In the 1930s the RCS published a note on how to use pitons as chocks. Then in the 1950s British climbers adapted machine nuts (thus the nickname "nuts") found on railways near cliffs. Steel had several advantages. Climbers could taper the metal, drill holes, and thread rope for faster, more secure placements. By the early 1960s Brits were making nuts from polymers, steel, and aluminum, at least one of which was sold in the United States. The turning point for U.S. climbers arrived in 1966 when Royal Robbins visited Great Britain and, as Frost recalled, "caught the vision." The appeal had much to do with how they reinforced Robbins's equation of risk, adventure, and masculinity. He wrote, "Rockclimbing is a man's sport in England, somewhat like bullfighting. . . . I think we can learn a lot from the British, and I see a place in the U.S. for the concept that placing a lot of pitons is not good style, and also for the use of nuts at places like Tahquitz Rock, where years of placing and removing pitons have worn the cracks so much as to change the routes."[38]

Robbins became the most forceful advocate for technology change. As rock climbing editor at *Summit*, he chided readers that the English "are forced to learn the craft more thoroughly in order to climb safely," but the typically weaker American "brings the climb down to his level with ironmongery." He then published a series of essays on technology and technique. He also demonstrated their applicability by protecting climbs with only chocks. In fall 1966, Robbins, his wife Elizabeth, and two English friends climbed a route called *Chockstone Gorge*. The next spring Royal and Elizabeth climbed a line on Ranger Rock, now called Manure Pile Buttress, christened *Nutcracker Suite*.[39]

The backlash was immediate. Chocks were not hammerless pitons. Although pitons scarred the rock, the rising tone when driven in properly comforted climbers with the knowledge that the piton was seated well. Nuts were "silent protection" that offered no audible assurance. When placed they could also dislodge with rope movement. In one article a photo of a chock in a parallel-sided crack seemed to reinforce impressions of precariousness. Many were leery, including a usually easygoing Pratt, who told Robbins, "Nuts to you!" Debates raged, but the most intriguing resistance came from the reigning piton maker. Chouinard never categorically opposed chocks. He made his own for a 1959 Teton trip and even told Robbins that they gave him a "satisfying" feeling. But he never substituted "a nut for a piton in a normal situation." Robbins was a "nut fanatic," and Chouinard finally commented on Robbins's evangelizing by climbing a line next to *Nutcracker Suite* that, with Pratt's prodding, he christened *Cocksucker's Concerto*, later shortened in guidebooks to *C. S. Concerto*.[40]

Whether it was weariness with Robbins, defensiveness about his pitons, or something else, Chouinard's role in the clean climbing revolution has an ironic subtext. Robbins converted many valley regulars before 1970, including Bill Feuerer, who hocked his own line of chocks by 1969, but most did not

Figure 10.2. Another sort-out in 1969 reveals the big-wall climber's expanding arsenal of tools, ranging from tiny RURPs to three-inch bongs but also hooks, beaks, bashies, and, at both the lower left and upper right, wired chocks.

seem to switch until after the publication of the 1972 Chouinard Equipment catalog. "Seem" is the operative word, however, because there is little way to document this ecologically and culturally critical event except through anecdotal remarks. Journals published essays on clean climbing but also, albeit more rarely, complaints about chocks and clean-climbing fanatics. In general, and in stark contrast to golden-age rhetoric, climbers regendered technology so "there was rejoicing in Nature for Man had joined the eternal harmony of the Earth-song." They even invented a new class of firsts. The intrepid and ecologically sensitive could now make "first hammerless" ascents, rating clean aid pitches C1 to C5. The most notable was Bruce Carson, who in 1973 clean climbed the Rostrum, Washington Column, Rixon's Pinnacle, Sentinel (twice), and *The Nose* (with Chouinard). Meanwhile, Hennek, Rowell, and Robinson climbed Half Dome's *Northwest Face* for a *National Geographic* essay. The Shawangunks and Alps soon followed.[41]

"Clean" was narrowly defined. As Bart O'Brien ascended Half Dome in the late 1970s, he began by congratulating himself on joining an environmentally attuned tribe, but soon he found a legacy of worn trails, deserted campsites, garbage dumps, and ledges littered with cans "and useless old slings." "We were following in the footsteps of hundreds of great climbers and considered ourselves part of the climbing-wilderness community exemplified by John Muir and David Brower," but something was awry. By the 1970s ever more outdoor enthusiasts, many of whom were dedicated wilderness defenders, were trashing the nature they loved. Climbers had to establish annual litter patrols in Yosemite, the Shawangunks, Alps, and Himalaya. Other problems remained intractable. Multiday climbs forced climbers to excrete *in situ,* resulting in urine- and feces-drenched ledges or filled paper bags that were dropped and exploded upon impact. By summer's end talus smelled like cesspools and water seeps were septic. Eventually rangers required climbers to carry PVC pipe, called "poop tubes," but even this caused trouble when an exhausted climber mistakenly left a tube beside the road. When rangers could not identify the sealed tube's contents, they called in the bomb squad.[42]

The nature that climbers idealized was a complex subject. Some piton scars stymied chock placement but opened formerly holdless routes to free climbers. The nature inside cracks went largely unexamined. Climbers before the 1970s had the secret joy of discovering insects, frogs, rodents, and birds found nowhere else. These moments were so integral to the ecological vision of clean climbers that Mike Hoover made the discovery and care of a frog a key thread in his 1973 film *Solo.* The ecological reality of rock climbing

Figure 10.3. Sheridan Anderson's drawing for the March 1973 cover of *Summit* magazine trumpets the clean climbing revolution, with the chock knocking out the piton. The actual transition began before 1972 and was never complete, especially among big-wall climbers. Moreover, while artificial chocks significantly slowed the erosional pressures on cracks, they did not alleviate other ecological impacts, including the practice of "gardening" and the general destruction of lichen systems.

was less sensitive. Forty years of concerted "gardening" had deracinated the vertical wilderness of soil and plants, and the inclination of some climbers to ascend trees or vines to avoid aid merely hastened the death of more vegetation. For all their good intentions, clean climbers did not, indeed could not, escape this legacy because they also used cracks for protection. Ironically, the only technology that did not threaten vertical ecology was the bolt, but that, too, would change. By the end of the 1970s, some routes were regulated by the Endangered Species Act to protect DDT-damaged peregrine falcons and, later, a rare salamander population on Half Dome.[43]

Climbing had never been clean or easy. During ascent climbers could sometimes spare little thought to protecting the natural world, and some forms of vertical nature were downright threatening. The logistics of big-wall routes forced people to starve on meager rations. Summers were desiccating; winters froze. Even the environmentally attuned Chouinard flinched at the nature of Yosemite: "I have always abhorred the tremendous heat, the dirt-filled cracks, the ant-covered foul-smelling trees and bushes which cover the cliffs, the filth and noise of Camp 4. . . . The climbing as a whole is not very esthetic or enjoyable; it is merely difficult." Big walls were a form of masochism. One scene in Fred Pedula's award-winning film *El Capitan* shows climbers on a ledge, looking stunned and silently passing food. One climber said "big wall climbing was more work than he'd ever done on a construction site." Another "said you got so tired on big walls you couldn't think about ecology if you wanted to: you just sat on your ledge like a chain-gang worker with the flu and moaned. Garbage dropped out of your hands. Paper bags full of human shit burst on the ground."[44]

Degradation included human injury. On one route climbers "risked serious falls trying to avoid fixed pitons . . . to earn a spot in the coveted 'first clean ascent' registry." Elsewhere they tackled features that were unavoidably injuring: thin, razor-sharp cracks that accepted perhaps a finger knuckle or "off-width" cracks too wide for a hand but too narrow for a body. Climbers shoved themselves in and grunted, thrust, and thrashed upward. John Long noted that Yosemite's "stupendous hand-cracks . . . had begotten me a host of lifetime scars, and the finger-cracks . . . had over the years ripped away every cuticle from my hands." A climbing area in Utah was touted as having cracks "in every conceivable size . . . just waiting to draw blood." Aid climbers donned work gloves, lugged tons of gear, and wielded chisels, while free climbers applied athletic tape to lessen abrasion, gymnastic chalk to eliminate moisture, and tincture of benzoin to toughen skin. Some scorned

this "chemical courage," but it was integral to the growing technological so-
phistication and increasingly self-abusive nature of elite-level climbing.[45]

Even the rise of clean climbing is overstated. Chouinard recalled that
"Frost and I decided we would phase out the piton business," and within
"a few months of the catalog's mailing, the piton business had atrophied;
chocks sold faster than they could be made." By all accounts climbers began to favor chocks, but they did not give up pitons. Chouinard, Leeper, and
others kept forges burning at steady but lower paces, and Chouinard Equipment and Great Pacific Ironworks catalogs continued to sell Lost Arrows until Chouinard sold his hardware business in 1989. The very catalog introducing clean climbing also featured a new hammer that had "a long, thin, blunt
pick" for "cleaning dirt and vegetation from prospective nut cracks." Wide-
angle "bongs" were not dropped until after 1980, and they were replaced in
1982 by bashies, which had a reputation for breaking in place and leaving
useless bits of aluminum welded to the rock. It was not that Chouinard was
deceptive or hypocritical. Rather, the gear market reflected a broader sporting culture than writers often recognize. There were no sharp befores and
afters.[46]

Everything depended on perspective. In one corner were the faithful
who, with monastic devotion, pursued a spiritual quest. With proper dedication and training, they felt "nothing to be impossible" in "the Mecca of
rock-climbing." They could transcend normative consciousness for an ecstatic attunement with "the cosmic scheme." Brits such as Aleister Crowley
and George Mallory had hinted at it, and Chouinard explored it in private
letters, but it was Pratt who baldly stated the case: "Rockclimbers have their
religion." The vertical was indeed a spiritual experience for some; others revealed secular motives. Some sought psychic catharsis. Billy Westbay
spoke of being "extremely focused. Awareness of things external to my own
immediate space ceases." Tucker Tech "wanted nothing more than to feel
nothing." Some thought risk could counter emasculating modernity. Roger
Breedlove said it "signifies to a climber that he is confident and in control."
Most, though, were mute or maddeningly inarticulate, like the guy who remarked: "I just like being vertical." As always, adventure was a means to ends
that diverged widely across the climbing community.[47]

The spectrum was evident in climbers' radiating ambitions. One group
settled into Camp 4 for the long haul; another, as Chouinard put it in 1963,
ventured "forth to the high mountains of the world to do the most esthetic
and difficult walls on the face of the earth." Although some regard Choui-

nard's remarks as prophecy, in many senses he simply noted an already established trend. Valley climbers had tackled the continent's walls since Shiprock, and a wider arc of climbers had challenged even more difficult walls since the 1950s, including Mustagh Tower, Longs Peak, the Dru, and the *"El Cap of the Caucasus,"* the 1,500-meter southwest face of Uschba. Yosemite did shape this progression. Locally developed skills enabled climbers to move quickly in the wilderness. In 1963, Kor, McCarthy, Robbins, and Dick McCracken climbed the Proboscis in the Yukon. In 1971, David Roberts and Ed Ward climbed Shot Tower deep in the Brooks Range. In 1975, Charlie Row trudged thirty miles across Baffin Island to solo Mount Asgard while Bridwell rushed Patagonia's Cerro Torre, then the hardest climb in the world. By the end of the 1970s, small teams had ascended several massive shafts in Baltistan, faces much bigger and at much higher altitudes than anything in North America: Trango Tower, Great Trango Tower, and Uli Biaho. All routes were very technical and topped out at over 20,000 feet.[48]

Wherever they went, younger climbers would inscribe their lifestyles on the rock. Hugh Burton, Darryl Hatten, and Steve Sutton thrived on a regimen of risk and drugs, and named their psychochemically fueled routes *Magic Mushroom* and *Mescalito*. The commemoration of intoxication began in 1966 with Ken Boche and Dennis Hennek's *Psychedelic Wall.* In the 1970s Carlos Castaneda's peyote novels inspired *Separate Reality* and *Tales of Power,* and the 1980s produced *Stoner's Highway, Free Bong,* and *Bad Acid.* The Australian Greg Child dreamed of a route called *Heart of Darkness,* but westerner Rob Slater climbed the line first and called it *Wyoming Sheep Ranch.* Climbers also carried boom boxes blaring adrenalin-tweaking heavy metal and punk music. They named routes for Jimmy Hendrix's *Little Wing,* Bob Dylan's *Positively 4th Street,* and The Police's *Zenyatta Mondatta.* Trango Tower's *Eternal Flame* was inspired by a Bangles album. Some walls became palimpsests. Harding's *East Face* of Washington Column, the lower part of Robbins's *Salathé Wall,* and Frost and Chouinard's *North Face* of Quarter Dome were all freed and renamed *Astroman, Free Blast,* and *Pegasus.*[49]

These cultural threads merged in a quintessential moment born of two inspirations. Frank Sacherer seeded the idea of climbing audaciously fast in 1965, and a 1971 *Mountain* magazine cover featuring four European climbers in matching sweaters before the north face of the Eiger provided the impetus. Bridwell had long worked on climbing lighter and faster, and the cover crystallized why Yosemite was aesthetically and technically significant. One night in June 1975, he, Westbay, and Long donned polyester pants, hippie vests, and paisley and African print shirts and climbed *The Nose.* By dawn

Figure 10.4. This photograph of Billy Westbay, Jim Bridwell, and John Long in the outfits they wore during the first one-day ascent of *The Nose* underscored the degree to which the climb was as much an aesthetic statement as a technical feat. The hippie clothes and cigarettes rebutted a *Mountain* magazine cover of four climbers in matching guide sweaters before the north face of the Eiger, then considered one of the most challenging climbs in the world. The objective dangers of El Capitan were significantly less than the Eiger, but no one could dispute the technical breakthrough the one-day ascent represented.

they had reached a team on Dolt Tower still recovering from the day before. Rubbing their eyes, it was not clear whether the team members were more taken by the early arrival, style of dress, or missing haul bag. In any event they were only the first team on *The Nose* to encounter the trio. By 7 P.M. the three had topped out. Posing the next day in costume, cigarettes on lower lips, *their* photo sent a message which "etched in the collective mind that American climbers were surly and irreverent, at a station confidently distinct from their European contemporaries."[50]

Beyond the idea that Yosemite climbers were badass, though, the message was muddled. Like the rest of the 1970s, Camp 4 was individualistic, inarticulate, and jaded. Robbins and Roper saw only declension in routes celebrating sex, drugs, and rock and roll. Robbins regarded these as lesser achievements because the technology and technique made "climbing El Capitan easier than it once was." The end was still too raw, the frustrations too fresh. Only time would temper. Visiting Camp 4 in 1990, Roper fumed about "unkempt kids fiddling with their earrings and listening mindlessly to what charitably might be called music." He called them "Wretched punks," but then he realized "that kid sitting there is me, thirty years earlier." By then it was too late. Bridwell had long since declared the sport the province of "the new generation." The Beats were history; dirtbags were the future, but this was less about regime change than community atomization. When Slater irked locals with *Wyoming Sheep Ranch,* he admitted he was not one of "the most popular guys in the Valley," but neither did he care. By the 1980s the only thing most climbers shared was a sense of entitlement.[51]

One measure of this was the evolution of Yosemite's search and rescue program. Most rescues still involved hikers, but more intentionally scrambled beyond their limits. Good climbers also got into more trouble. In March 1958 a winter expedition went spectacularly wrong, requiring two rescue flights in terrible weather. In 1960, Irving Smith fell 500 feet into Lost Arrow Chimney, prompting rangers to close the route for a year. A month later a rock crushed the skull and bones of another Beat climber. In 1961, one climber had to be rescued from Cathedral Spires, six from the high country, and Roper nearly killed himself ice climbing. In 1962, Glen Denny and John Weichard were pulled from the Lost Arrow in a snowstorm. There were several tricky rescues in 1963. In 1964, Beck broke an arm on Middle Cathedral Rock, and Jim Baldwin rappelled off his rope on Washington Column. There were several accidents in 1965, one of which involved winching an injured climber up Sentinel's face, and in 1966, Jim McCarthy broke an arm in the Stoveleg Cracks, requiring the first major rescue on El Capitan.[52]

Thus venerable RCS member Morgan Harris erred when he said there was a "tremendous safety record which has accompanied all this flowering growth of extremely difficult climbing." Rangers knew better. They trained continually, but a big-wall rescue seemed ever more likely and scary. Practically speaking, most rescues were still done by Camp 4 climbers, so in 1965 rangers selectively ignored the camping limit so some top climbers were always "on hand in case of rescue." Thus began what became YOSAR, or Yosemite Search & Rescue. In 1967 rangers asked Bridwell to handpick a team. In exchange for their readiness, they could squat in Camp 4 indefinitely. At first rescuers used their own gear, and operations remained ad hoc until late summer 1970, when an arson fire enabled the newly established director of Search & Rescue to equip and house YOSAR in a separate space. Training grew more regular and professional, but Camp 4 climbers remained the backbone labor.[53]

This had several unintended consequences. The team's very existence meant more rescues. Most were low-tech, involving an array of calls from crashes to drownings, missing persons, animal bites, sore feet, turned ankles, bad backs, and at least one bunk-bed incident. Each siphoned funds from other possible operations. There was also a steep learning curve. Jim Madsen hiked to the top of El Capitan to check on a storm-besieged team but rappelled off his rope. Jack Dorn went to look for stranded climbers but walked off a ledge. In 1968 a team helicoptered to the top of Half Dome for a nighttime, winch-aided rescue in icy conditions. In 1972, Bridwell lowered a climber 2,800 feet down El Capitan. In 1976, Dale Bard descended 1,300 feet on Mount Watkins at night, illuminated by a 9 million candlepower light suspended from a hovering Coast Guard helicopter.[54]

These cases alarmed rangers and climbers, and concerns were voiced after each incident. The stakes had grown extreme. By 1979 there were "hundreds of climbers who have done routes harder than any in the world in 1970." Old routes were passé, and fresh terrain was scarce. Lito Tejada-Flores noted, "if you want to be a hero, it's not that easy any more. First ascents no longer come cheap." "The main commitment," George Meyers added, "lies in a technical difficulty that asks: how far do you want to fall?" Many discounted the peril, and critics began to fear a perverse effect: the more adept YOSAR became, the more climbers felt it gave them license to screw up. After one bad stretch in 1977, YOSAR director Tim Setnicka railed at the "Unthinking and unaware" who endangered rescuers and wasted taxpayer funds. He foresaw a time when YOSAR would charge for rescues. Dick Leonard advised a return to the safety-first values of *Belaying the Leader*.[55]

These expressions were sincere yet flawed. There were more rescues, but most involved unintentional scramblers. Records on technical climbers reveal that, with the exception of the very bad year of 1975, accidents hovered within remarkably stable parameters for over a decade even though the number of climbers grew steadily. Thus while impossible to prove because there are no reliable numbers on participation, YOSAR statistics suggest that, demographically speaking, climbing grew safer after 1967.[56]

So why the fuss? One look around Camp 4 usually sufficed. The rescuers offended just about everyone. The deal the NPS cut produced an elite among elite, a group of exceptionally talented dirtbags who seemed hardwired to abuse privilege. Bridwell's team was "a clique." Kauk felt like he had joined "a gang" when invited onto the Search & Rescue site. All members were tops, but not all top climbers were members. Kauk noted, "Even if you were the best climber from Colorado, you didn't have a hope of getting on the site. . . . If you hadn't done a wall with someone on the site, no way." Another observed that "how hard you climbed and the quality of your vibe" both mattered in the sorting process. The selection process and YOSAR members' behavior vexed many. They drank to excess, shirked duties, and defiled corpses. Bridwell bragged about stealing electricity from a Camp 4 restroom: "For the remainder of that summer we bathed in the amplified sounds of our favorite bands, and in the enthusiastic approval of our friends and neighbors. We hosted an almost continuous party and were very pleased with ourselves. Not only had we scored a social success, but we had done so at the expense of the hated Park Service." Dirtbags were Brahmins and Untouchables all in one, but their righteous sense of entitlement was common.[57]

Consider climbers' relationships with Native Americans. Ever since 1939 at Shiprock, there has been little evidence that climbers cared what Indians thought about invasions of The Res. The *Yodeler* remarked, "Nearby Navajos . . . shunned the summit—superstition, the white men say, but perhaps they knew better." Perhaps, but no one asked. Climbers in the 1950s almost never mentioned Indians. The only exception was Don Wilson, who did ask permission from the Canyon de Chelly superintendent before climbing Spider Rock. More typical was a 1960 Shiprock article that instructed climbers to carry "a plentiful supply of water" and hard hats but ignored Navajos who controlled access to Tsé Bit'a'í through grazing permits. Indians were superstitious, invisible, and irrelevant, pretty much like all the other locals climbers had derided or ignored since mountaineering began. Camp 4 loved to mock the nationalistic twits who planted flags in Africa and Asia, but their invasion of Indian territory was every bit as imperialistic and arrogant.[58]

The parallels grew more obvious in the 1960s. The American Southwest held stunning geology. The region's tall, isolated spires of sandstone were vertical, rotten, scary, and coveted. Two of the most ambitious suitors were Chuck Pratt and Layton Kor, both of whom yearned to tread "where no human had been." Both invaded regularly to bag towers, needles, and spires. By 1959, though, Navajos and Hopis objected to trespasses of these spiritually significant places. Shiprock, Canyon de Chelly, and Monument Valley were sacred ground. From the beginning Pratt and Kor knew they were not wanted. Their response was to evade. Pratt and Bob Kamps made the second ascent of Spider Rock in 1960, plotting to avoid detection and feigning ignorance when caught. Kor admitted that "I wanted to climb [Monument Valley's Totem Pole] very badly and, less concerned about matters of conscience . . . we decided to ignore the ban and sneak in." When caught on Spider Rock, he lied as surely as Pratt. Only at the end did Pratt admit that he "had to learn to put our pitons and ropes away and to go exploring in silence." Only then did he gain "any lasting worth from what the desert has to offer."[59]

Pratt's point was mostly lost. Fed up with trespassers in 1968 the Navajo Nation notified journals that it did not permit climbing. Climbers merely considered this a challenge. Bridwell wrote, "It's illegal to climb on Navaho [*sic*] land and Shiprock is the central power-point of the Navaho Indian religion, just as Mecca is for the Moslem, definitely taboo for us infidels. We needed the cloak of stealth to perform our sacrilege." In another essay he dwelled less on climbing than fooling Indians. The Navajos were not alone. Entitled climbers also contested an array of restrictions at Hueco Tanks in Texas, Baboquivari Peak in Arizona, Cave Rock at Lake Tahoe, Devils Tower in Wyoming, and buildings, churches, and holy sites around the world.[60]

The blinders even applied to Yosemite. Greg Child blithely "wondered what the Native Americans, who must have revered [El Capitan] as something sacred, would think of" modern Yosemite. "Whatever happened to the Valley's original inhabitants anyway?" Camp 4 had been a gathering site for Miwoks, some of whom still lived in the park, but Child was not really interested in living Indians, nor were climbers in general. When stymied by tribal opposition, climbers griped about not being able to "pursue our sport on the Reservation[.] Isn't it part of the United States?" A few counseled "respect" for "mystical" spirituality. More insisted that their climbing religion gave them a right to sites such as Devils Tower. Only in 1995 did the AAC finally advise climbers to respect "the law of diplomacy and basic human interaction": ask permission and heed the answer.[61]

Dirtbags were contemptuous and contemptible, but pinning down who

Figure 10.5. With his usual wit, Sheridan Anderson broached the racial homogeneity of climbing through a clever juxtaposition of James Ramsey Ullman's *The White Tower*. Not all racial issues were equal, however. It would be decades before climbers examined their assumptions about invading Native American reservations.

qualified was tricky. For one thing, while the term now applies widely to climbers at the edges of respectability, words like "grovelers," "park bum," or "PB" were also invoked. Not until the late 1980s did "dirtbag" gain wide usage, if not precision. Child caved and canned with the best. Downing beer one day, he bitched about "Dirtbags, misfits, and oddballs" who spoiled the local vibe. "We agreed that we were dirty but not Dirtbags, that we didn't fit into society at that point in our lives but we weren't misfits, that though we were oddities we weren't oddballs. . . . Climbers, we agreed after another six-pack, were as indigenous to Yosemite as bears, and we belonged there just as much as any Winnebago." Other climbers nodded "in agreement with our diatribe. . . . They had no idea we were talking about them. I realized then that 'dirtbag' is a relative term."[62]

Dirtbagging was also a strategy as much as a lifestyle. To climb at the sharp edge was ever more demanding, and Yosemite an ever harsher place. Aspiring climbers had to abandon school and work. For anyone without trust funds, this meant a descent into scarfing, caving, canning, and shoplifting. The Beats flinched. The dirt, depravity, and *Dawn Wall* suggested declension, but the fear was unwarranted. Tom Higgins erred that an "entire way of being, seeing, thinking [was] forever gone." Some Beat values actually flourished, but the coarsening trends and terrible toll in injuries, poverty, and drugs allowed disruptions to eclipse continuities. The golden age was really more about one cohort saying "this was our time" than a reliable metric of before and after. Soon, dirtbags of the 1970s would grouse about dirtbags of the 1990s. Dirtbagging was a means, a cul-de-sac of arrested development, and a reformulation of the culture wars.[63]

11. TRADITIONALISTS

$10,000 reward for anyone who can follow me for one full day.
—JOHN BACHAR

Dirtbags was a hopelessly subjective term that could serve as epithet or badge of honor, and climbing style was endlessly debated, but in some ways an abiding consensus settled over Camp 4. A timeless view emerged—as though climbing had always been this way—which prevailed well into the 1980s, yet at the same time, people were arriving who would sunder the sense of continuity. These transformative figures did not seek to destabilize. Every last one respected precedent, and many were remarkably conservative, even traditional in their views about sport and life. But their actions, at times their very presence, worked like a chemical catalyst to speed change. In different ways women and innovators transformed how climbers related to nature and to each other. By the mid-1980s mounting turmoil and fragmentation forced all of Camp 4 to reassess what *tradition* meant.

This tale properly begins with Beverly Johnson. Born to a peripatetic Navy family, Johnson grew up in a middle-class household that stressed education and athletics. She attended Kent State and the University of Southern California on gymnastic scholarships, fell for the mountains in a geology class, and joined the Trojan Peak Club. In summer 1969 she traversed the continent to climb in the Shawangunks and Yosemite. The following spring she moved to the valley. Her path paralleled other contemporary and former climbers: like Michael Cohen, John Gill, and Florence Humphries, gymnastics had honed her body; like Julie Brugger, Carla Firey, and Judy Lovelace, she learned with a college club; and like Gwen Moffat, Britain's first female guide, Johnson entered climbing as a lone woman. Unlike anyone, however, she was the first full-time resident in Camp 4 who had also been a debutante at a Virginia cotillion. There was no one quite like Bev Johnson.[1]

Gymnastics translated well to rock, and through it Johnson became a leading edge of change. She liked the creativity in contrast to the rote exercises of the gym. There was more than one way to succeed. This was key because Johnson could not do even one pull-up. In gymnastics she devised clever and daring techniques to perform moves competitors did with arm strength. In Camp 4, where guys were muscling up, her 5′ 5″, 120-pound body did not seem a cutting-edge phenotype. Her flexibility and balance did make a difference, but many saw only stereotypical weakness. Jim Bridwell explained that "We'd take girls over to climb on [the relatively low-angled] Glacier Point Apron . . . and I'd tell guys, 'Climb over there too much and you'll grow tits. That's where girls climb.'" In one sense Johnson agreed. Her style of "good balance" and choreography was "girl climbing."[2]

This should have reinforced Camp 4 tradition, but Johnson had a way of undermining things. She arrived able to free climb well, so Bridwell treated her as a gender metric. "If she could do it," he remarked, "it must be only 5.9." Then in fall 1970, Johnson climbed Chuck Pratt's *Crack of Doom,* the first Yosemite route to be rated 5.10. She was already known for tenacity; now she had a nickname: "5.10 Bev." Bridwell began to take Johnson on first ascents, but it was a back-handed compliment. "If I get up," she noted, "it's 5.10, and if I don't it's 5.11." The glass ceiling moved but did not break. Camp 4's homosocial boundaries were resilient, but they did not contain Johnson. She worked up to big walls and then largely erased the gender barrier by being the first woman to ascend El Capitan as an equal participant on *The Nose* and then first to do a first ascent on *Grape Race.* Tom Carter noted that by fall 1973 she had become "the first woman to command the respect of the men in [the] male dominated kingdom" of Camp 4.[3]

Johnson's quest to become one of the boys was paralleled by her drive to be first among girls. By the mid-1970s many women had arrived, and a race ensued for what Lawrence Hamilton calls "categorical achievements," in this case a gendered distinction of "first woman" to climb a route or formation. The two biggest prizes were the first all-women ascent of El Capitan and first woman solo of El Capitan. Johnson coveted both. In September 1973 she tried *The Nose* with Donna Pritchard, but an endemic problem on big walls stymied them: neither was large enough nor strong enough to haul the hundreds of pounds of gear, food, and water for their ascent. Johnson regrouped, chose a route that required fewer supplies, and tapped Sibylle Hechtel, whom she had groomed. The two prepared quietly, keenly aware, as Hechtel remembered, that "failure of the first women's attempt on El Cap would be a fiasco we could never live down." The stakes were so high Hechtel nearly psyched herself out. The night before she admitted to a friend: "I'm so afraid."[4]

They nevertheless prevailed in a reputable eight days, and in the next few years the sex divide eroded further. By 1974, Johnson, Hechtel, and others had climbed 5.11. The following year Hechtel became the first woman to climb *The Salathé Wall,* and Molly Higgins began a campaign of all-women

ascents on El Cap, Half Dome, Sentinel, the Column, and Colorado's Longs
Peak. In 1978, Johnson trumped these climbs by soloing *The Dihedral Wall*.
The valley was a microcosm of broader changes. The era of manless ascents
begun by Miriam O'Brien in the 1920s never stopped. In 1955 three intrepid
Scots trekked to Nepal's uncharted Jugal Himal to make the first ascent of
Gyalzen Peak. Like most previous manless climbs, their expedition, Claude
Kogan's 1959 attempt on Cho Oyu, and Junko Tabei's 1970 ascent of Mount
Everest had few pretensions, but that too was changing. Beginning in 1970
with an all-women expedition to Denali and a fifteen-month peak-bagging
tour of Africa, Asia, and New Zealand, Arlene Blum politicized her climbs.
She resented being rejected for expeditions because of her sex. Her feminism
was explicit while soliciting for the 1978 all-women expedition to Nepal's Annapurna, selling t-shirts that read: "A Woman's Place Is On Top."[5]

 Despite its gendered and sexualized implications, being on top had no
consistent meaning. By becoming what Sherry Ortner calls "gender radicals"
and "questioning or breaking gender rules," women drew praise and criticism. Johnson and others endured hazings but were mostly accepted into
Camp 4, but the path never cleared for a few. A string of disasters since the

"Guess what us girls did today?!"

Figure 11.1. As Beverly Johnson began to destabilize long-held assumptions about gender
and sport, Sheridan Anderson found new ways to prod Camp 4's increasingly fragile homosocial world.

late 1950s, including the deaths of all eight members of a women's Soviet team in the Pamirs, Willi Unsoeld's daughter on her namesake Nanda Devi, two women on Annapurna, and one woman on Dhauligiri, sparked outrage. Critics said all-women expeditions suffered a confusion of goals, that they promoted underqualified climbers for gender's sake, and that all-female claims were fraudulent and racist because women had relied on male Sherpas. The shrillest remarks came from Galen Rowell and John Roskelley, both of whom spent time in Camp 4, but there was no gender solidarity in this debate.[6]

Women and men aligned on both sides. Men accused critics of overemphasizing accidents and posing double standards because men also relied on Sherpas, yet some women maintained distance. Johnson and Higgins had declined to go to Annapurna because they were leery of incompetence and, as Johnson put it, even a week with women was "a drag." Nevertheless, Johnson did join the all-women international guild Rendez-vous Hautes Montagnes. Others belonged to regional clubs like Women Climbers Northwest. These were in one sense atavistic throwbacks to the old auxiliaries, yet they served a purpose. Many women noted the importance of knowing top women climbers. Gender models were morale boosters in this male-dominated sport. Clubs were "wonderfully free of the sex-related complications of male/female relationships," "a special bond," and "one of the rare times when we could speak woman-to-woman without a bunch of guys hanging around." Or it could just be "fun." Any way one looked at it, these homosocial organizations empowered, especially when Rowell huffed that women were "conspicuously absent" from history because there "simply were no major first ascents in Yosemite done by women."[7]

Camp 4 was not usually oppressive, but it was edgy. Living among what Tom Carter called "the merry men in Sherwood Forest" took some getting used to. It helped that Hechtel grew up among climbers, that Johnson called herself a "little jock," and that Lynn Hill had been a "tomboy." They knew how to handle bluster, but Elaine Matthews was frustrated. Her talents threatened some men, and it was "really difficult to find partners. Very often I wound up going out with someone on their day off." Hechtel resented the relentless surveillance. There was "always a certain pressure to prove that women can do things." Even Hill, a Camp 4 insider, said climbing was run "by a fraternity of men, and there was little encouragement or, frankly, inclination for women to participate." Nor did it help when Robbins proclaimed women's limits, or Chouinard said "women climbers now are all really proud of themselves for being very close to the standards of men, but all they're do-

ing is following these chalk trails," or Bridwell compared the valley's "schizoid" weather to "a woman's prerogative," or others thought the "luscious
chicks" were a local attraction. Women had to contend with an army of men
trying to maintain Camp 4 as a guy's domain.[8]

There were ways to blend in, but each had a cost. Higgins and Johnson
partook in Camp 4's intoxication rituals and paid the usual price. Being female enabled friendships. Tom Carter said "it was easier . . . bonding with
[Johnson] than with the guys who would look at you sideways and judge you
more on your ability than your enthusiasm." Being pretty and heterosexual
also had its perks. Johnson inspired many crushes that she took in stride,
letting femininity charm sometimes, at others teasing men for their pornography, yet she also pursued a vigorous sex life in a setting with little intimacy.
A lover noted that "she was not a one man woman," and her biographer details complex and overlapping relationships. This caused problems. A tent-
mate remembered that "Bev slept with her climbing rack as her pillow. . . .
Whenever there were scary noises she would reach down and throw a hand-
ful of pitons. She said they were good for man or beast." Hechtel confessed
that one of the motives for climbing El Capitan was sex. Johnson "had two
boy friends, one of whom was usually in the East Coast and the second in
Mammoth," but by "an unfortunate coincidence" both were in Yosemite at
the same time. Johnson needed an out. Hechtel "had the opposite problem,"
hoping that the ascent would arouse her current infatuation.[9]

The homosocial and heterosexual tensions within Camp 4 were increasingly inscribed on Yosemite's walls. Gordie Smaill and Neil Bennett tied a
pair of panties to belay bolts on *The North America Wall*, and Randy Leavitt
placed a double-headed dildo on *Wyoming Sheep Ranch*. These tokens
served as double evidence, of having been there and somewhere else. Others
left their mark in the guidebooks. The female body was objectified with *Jugs*,
"The Cuntress," and at least three "Nipple"s. Climbers celebrated male anat-
omy with *Pink Banana* and *Short But Thick*, and Hechtel wrote an essay titled "Walls Without Balls" about the first all-women ascent of El Capitan. The
deed inspired *Dog Dick Lik*, *Gang Bang*, *Handjob*, *Jump for Joy*, *Liz Is Tight*,
The Opening of Misty Beethoven, *The Shaft*, *Sloppy Seconds*, and *Siberian
Swarm Screw*, which included Johnson on the first ascent. Squamish sported
the *Black Dyke*, and the Vulgarians contributed *Dick's Prick*, *Swinging Cunt*,
and *Vulga-Tits*—the latter an all-women's ascent—at Shawangunks. By the
mid-1970s the epoch of romantic route names had slid into an earthier era
in which bodies and psyches collided publicly in spectacularly violent metaphors.[10]

So how did women change the sport? Some hailed the "emancipatory potential" of women's participation, and, as Hechtel put it, women could indeed do great things when given a chance. They *did* chart an independent and equal course, yet this poses more issues. Was there a female culture of climbing? There are hints, as when Johnson paused during her solo of *The Dihedral Wall* to read, sunbathe, or botanize, or when Arlie Anderson walked away from the risks of her own solo. Yet there was "no homogeneous experience or set of values on the part of women athletes, no fixed or monolithic 'femininity'. . . . variation and contradiction [were] common." This was acutely so in Camp 4, where experiences varied widely and inclusion hinged on acculturation. Johnson's most striking trait was her conservatism. She minimized the issue of gender, insisting that "Rocks make no compromise for sex" and that she was "sort of an antifeminist. I do think women are weaker." Women also invoked the same metaphors as men. Haul bags were "pigs," Jeanne Panek called herself "a machine, calculating and methodical," and Hill laid out her "arsenal of gear and supplies . . . like arraying the ranks of one's army before charging into the foe." There were many gendered ways of climbing, and women and men could be found all along the spectrum.[11]

Another question concerns the content of emancipation. The simple presence of single, independent women broadened the sport's social history, and ever more women were encouraged to climb because of Johnson, Higgins, and others. Gender models mattered, yet this female version of liberation was also physically degrading. Sports have long stressed the masculine value of performing when injured. Pain was intrinsic to the sporting ethic, its mastery a sign of merit, and women were expected—by men, other women, and themselves—to accept it. Real climbers ignored discomfort. Cuts, tears, breaks, let alone constantly shredded skin, were part of the game. Malinda Chouinard said Johnson "was always one of the girls, but to make her career she had to be better than all the guys. . . . As a woman her legendary injuries were badges of pride; proof of accomplishment." Sociologists call this "positive deviance." Athletes call it "being tough," but notice how "tough" made pain normative. It was as if success required scars, and this appealed to some. Australian Louise Shepherd admitted that the "amalgamation of physical, mental and psychological stresses" attracted her to rock climbing. Attitudes like Shepherd's are why Kevin Young and Philip White view sports as "ambiguously empowering" for women and men alike.[12]

Rather than being feminized, Camp 4's hypermasculine values seemed to spike in the late 1970s, especially with John Bachar. Bachar was that rare cross of nerd and jock. By 1974, when the 5' 11", 185-pound math major and pole vaulter entered UCLA, he was already one of Yosemite's best. He spent more time on the rock than in school, but he had not truly distinguished himself. He had to make a choice, so in 1976 he decided to put "the same effort into climbing as I was going to put into being a professor." He lived in a van and moved seasonally from Joshua Tree to Yosemite to Tuolumne. Unlike previous top climbers, he also decided to focus only on pure rock. "It was," he said, "about becoming a legend." The nerd boned up on kinesiology and devised exercises that isolated climbing muscles. The athlete built an outdoor gym with a balance chain, fingertip hangboard, and rope ladder, and, like Mark Powell in 1955, pushed himself to new levels. Bachar could do two-arm pull-ups with an extra 140 pounds, and one-arm pulls with an extra twelve pounds.[13]

Bachar was a superb free climber, able to make the highest grades, but this was true of at least a dozen Yosemite regulars. What set him apart was a fundamentalist's dedication to tradition and his mental acuity. Like most in the valley, his philosophy came from Bridwell. There was a moral order and deviation was sinful. A climber started at the bottom, placed protection on lead, and returned to ground after falls. Above all, risk was good. Most climbers followed the scripture, but this proselyte was more zealous than even the Sorcerer. He held himself to the highest standard. The stronger he became, the more he had to shave the margins. Then one day John Long egged Bachar: "If you toprope this route a hundred times, how many times will you fall?" He replied, "zero." "Being a math guy, that totally clicked." Risk was preserved only by untying. Bachar "was hooked," and he had that rare ability in "the coffin zone" to focus on what-next instead of what-if.[14]

Bachar was not the first free soloist, but he made it his marque like no one else. Beat climbers climbed ropeless on occasion, and Henry Barber had stunned Camp 4 in 1973 by soloing Sentinel Rock before breakfast. Then in 1976, Bachar tried to "blow some minds" by soloing *New Dimensions,* a sustained 5.11 test piece. In the broader mountaineering world, this paled in comparison to the daring ascents of superalpinists at altitude in sketchy weather, but within the narrowing culture of Camp 4, Bachar stunned. "People looked at me very weird for a couple months. They thought I was crazy or something." Rather than back off as others had, he soloed more, evolving from "a master of difficulty to a master of boldness." He reached a peak with *The Nabisco Wall,* a route with pitches rated 5.10c, 5.10c, and 5.11a or 5.11b. It was "like going to a new continent, the moon or something. . . . A new frontier. It's someplace no one belongs." Some shouted "God, you're fucking *nuts.*" Others emulated Bachar but only underscored his superiority.

Charlie Fowler felt "sort of spaced out. Like I'd gotten away with something." Ron Kauk roamed for two nights "in an extremely altered state of awareness." Long "wandered listlessly through dark desert corridors, scouting for turtles, making garlands of wildflowers, relishing the skyscape, doing all those things a person does on borrowed time." Bachar shrugged.[15]

He was a legend, and like any demigod he toiled to maintain that distinction. Even on roped ascents he cultivated the edge by placing little protection. In 1981, he forged three routes that epitomized his ethic. *Body and Soul* posed certain injury if one fell, and the "runouts" between bolts on *You Asked for It* ensured a shredded body if one slipped. Then he and Dave Yerian forged a long, sparsely bolted 5.11c called *Bachar/Yerian*. The route was widely admired yet no one followed. Bachar had fixed his ideals in the climbingscape, but principles and ego mixed in toxic ways. The implied message seemed clear, but just the same he posted a reward offering $10,000 to "anyone who can follow me for one full day." It was a lark. "It was stupid," he said, "It was such an easy bet," but the rest of the community laughed uneasily. They knew who was the butt of the joke.[16]

The more Bachar explored the edge, the more he seemed to embody a "Yosemite tradition," yet none of it was timeless. His moralizing was an echo of Victorian idealists, his fetishization of risk derived from Chouinard, and his ascent rules came from the heated brain of Frank Sacherer. Moreover, none of this was static. Technology had continually reshaped outdoor sports. Fiberglass boards, composite skis, urethane wheels, and polymer kayaks had liberated athletes to go faster and maneuver better, but each innovation changed the game. Similarly, bolts, alloy pitons, aluminum carabiners, mechanical rope ascenders, and sleeping platforms expanded climbers' options, and spring-loaded cams, portable drills and sticky-soled shoes were creating new instabilities. Novel ideas and materials again redefined the game, but so did culture and nature. Advocates had driven the clean climbing revolution, but they did not eliminate pitons or other hammered devices from aid climbing. Nor did chocks work well in Yosemite's parallel and flared cracks or on routes without cracks. There were still gaps in the climbing toolkit.[17]

This is why Ray Jardine matters. Jardine was a tenacious free climber in the early 1970s, and like Tom Frost and many surfing innovators, he had worked in the aerospace industry. He applied his knowledge of design and materials to a tool first developed in the 1930s by Soviet climber Vitaly Abalakov and patented in 1973 by Utah native Greg Lowe. In theory a cam placed in a crack will, when loaded, transform linear force into rotational force, turning a falling climber's kinetic energy into holding power. Abalakov and Lowe refined a logarithmic spiral shape, much like a conch shell, so cams fit a range of widths with constant pressure. They had imagined the cam as a chockstone, something that rested passively. Jardine instead doubled the cams in opposed alignment and integrated another Lowe idea called the "Crack Jumar," which used springs to engage rock. His new design was compressed before insertion and then, when released, two sets of cams expanded inside the crack.[18]

Jardine's cams provided unprecedentedly fast and stable protection, but their impact was eclipsed by a shoe. Climbers had obsessed about shoes since the 1850s because—and unlike all other forms of gear—their soles connected them to nature. At first they pounded spikes through shoe leather, and the initial challenge was to find a better nail. By the 1870s climbers also tried soles of crepe, felt, rope, or rubber, with uppers of leather or canvas. They tested materials ad nauseum, and by 1920 the tennis shoe was the sport's cutting-edge technology. Then in the 1930s Italian mountaineer Vitale Bramani lost six friends when they had to switch from heavy boots to light rock shoes and were caught by a storm. Bramani and the Italian tire manufacturer Pirelli responded by devising a rubber sole that was durable and flexible. They called it Vibram.[19]

By the 1950s boot makers such as Bourdonneau, Galibier, Kronhofer, Pivetta, and Zillertal made specialized rock shoes. Most featured narrow, toe-crushing uppers to eliminate internal slippage, with lug or smooth soles to enhance traction. More brands followed, often known only by an abbreviation: Cortinas, EBs (Eduard Bourdonneau), Masters, PAs (Pierre Alain), RDs (René Desmaison), RRs (Royal Robbins), Shoenards, and Spiders. Rubber soles differed in stiffness and consistency, and each influenced climbing style. Stiff soles enabled climbers to weight the toe instead of the instep. This posture required greater strength but resulted in better balance, and it was fundamental to the modern style of pushing away rather than clinging like a limpet. Soft, smooth soles like that of a boat shoe allowed climbers to place more rubber on rock. Known as "smearing," they were crucial on slick surfaces such as Yosemite's glacially polished walls, but each advantage had a tradeoff. Stiff shoes were poor for smearing; soft shoes were hell in aid slings. Occasionally the dizzied climber, unsure which trait was best, donned a different brand on each foot.[20]

Then came Miguel Angel Gallego. In fall 1982, the Spanish climber asked Bachar to try a prototype made by Boreal. Bachar put the Firé through its paces on Camp 4's boulder circuit. He was impressed. They "were a half size too big. My foot never slipped." *Why* was and remains a trade secret, but a few things seem at least as clear as mud. Rumors circulated of Formula 1 tires and industrial espionage—nothing was certain—but Gallego was inspired by racing tires that grew sticky when driven. The basic principle was well known. Heat and sulfur cure naturally sticky and formless latex into the smooth, dynamically elastic material we call rubber. In technical terms, vulcanization triggers chemical reactions that make polymer chains cross-link, creating ever greater structure and rigidity. Conversely, interrupting this process preserves stickiness at the cost of structural stability. The trick is balancing properties, and two decades later no one is talking because the Firé was golden. The shoe lowered ratings—A 5.11 was like a 5.10. Bachar struck a deal for exclusive U.S. distribution rights. Word spread. In spring 1983 the first 265 pairs arrived in Yosemite. They sold out in two hours flat. Sticky soles changed the sport again.[21]

Some complained. As with bolts and topos, new tools made climbing easier, perhaps too easy. Friends, the brand under which Jardine's cams were marketed, meant climbers no longer had to fiddle with tricky chock placements or needed a stance to place gear. They could slap cams anywhere, and Firés elevated anyone. Risk eased, ratings lost context. Chouinard said "technological development is killing the sport" and likened Firés to cheating. Ansel Adams again called drilling "a desecration." Something had indeed changed. Even younger climbers such as Lynn Hill admitted that although "we were climbing harder routes, I doubt we were climbing with more boldness." Complaints felt like déjà vu. Lawrence Hamilton had already observed that any time "a significant new climbing invention is introduced, there are two predictable responses. . . . One is negative: it will make all the existing routes easier; it's unfair and unethical; it will ruin climbing. The other is positive: it makes new routes possible," or as Allen Steck remarked even earlier, "every generation that comes along wants to be original and have new avenues to explore." Technology was again providing an untested pathway.[22]

The implications were not obvious. Contradictions hounded everyone, but the contours of the period are best followed through Jardine, Bachar, Kauk, and Hill, each of whom reacted in a different way. By the mid-1970s Jardine had climbed a series of very hard 5.12 routes. All else being equal these would have been praised, but Jardine's use of his cams seemed to ease and, thus, diminish his ascents. Even more suspect were his tactics. Instead of returning to ground after falls, he rested on the rope, studying holds and refining sequences. This "hang-dogging" was alien to the valley. He called it "working the route." Others called it cheating, but Jardine persisted on a leaning crack called *Phoenix* and made Yosemite's first 5.13.[23]

Jardine was also freeing El Capitan. In 1979 he made the first free ascent of the *West Face* with Bill Price, and by 1981 he was on *The Nose*. Even by Jardine's fluid ethics, however, what came next crossed a line. Normally, a climber must make several spectacular pendulums to link the route's disconnected cracks. This had stymied free climbers because the intervening rock was blank. Jardine would engineer a traverse, preplacing bolts on rappel with a battery-powered drill that cut holes one-handed in two minutes instead of two-handed in twenty minutes. He also mashed pitons to widen cracks and chiseled holds where none existed. He rationalized these transgressions by arguing, at least to himself, that a free climb, even one artificially crafted, was preferable to aid. The result was a disaster. He "didn't realize how blatantly [the chisel marks] would stand out. Like everyone else, I was pretty appalled."[24]

That Jardine's objection was less the principle than the aesthetics of chiseling underscored a growing rift in climbing. Jardine was singled out repeatedly for his apostasy, but he was hardly alone. Chris Cantwell, Vern Clevenger, Tim Harrison, Max Jones, and Mark Hudon had also strayed, though they merely emulated Europeans who had hang-dogged, rap-bolted, and altered rock for decades. These were standard practices on the cliffs of Buoux, Ceuse, and Verdon in Provence, where by 1980 "sport climbers" set new difficulties in free climbing. Hudon and Jones reversed the equation that brought Bev Johnson to Yosemite: the "rock is our apparatus; climbing is our routine." Bachar winced. Verdon "felt like an insult to your climbing intelligence." The routes were technically hard, but there were too many bolts and too few risks. Beat values were imperiled, and Bachar wanted respect for "the guy who sticks it out. Seriousness and danger are . . . as deeply-rooted in climbing as technical difficulty." Yosemite seemed "in a spiritual league far beyond these other areas," but partisans were talking past each other. As Jardine put it, "We were astronauts"; Bachar "was Siddhartha."[25]

Bruce Morris depicted a battle between "maximum technical difficulty" and "maximum terror," but it was also about whether Yosemite was a sacred or secular space. Those dedicated to Beat ideals heaped scorn on new ways. Morris complained that "means have replaced ends" and that "personal self-worth has begun to be measured exclusively in terms of the free-climbing standard at which an individual performs." Werner Braun said it showed "the degeneration of society." Bridwell quoted Albert Einstein about "a perfection of means and a confusion of ends." Tom Higgins damned the "preposterous assertions" of sport climbers, whom he called "tricksters." Chouinard ranted about specialists "who have only one trick" and "take the soul out of any sport." All conceded that the tactics elevated difficulty, but critics—like the era's telemark skiers, "soul surfers," and fly fishers—so equated technique with sporting and environmental virtue that any breach was a slight of nature and community. Daniel Duane likened debates to "scriptural disputes between apostles." It made perfect sense for Bachar to argue: "You're destroying the rock when you put a bolt in on lead, but you're putting it in because you need it at that moment, or you'll get badly hurt or die if you fall. When a bolt is put in on rappel it's for some future pseudo-first ascent. It's contrived."[26]

Defenders of tradition went beyond carping. In print they figuratively erased apostates' deeds by heralding "ground-up" ascents and disparaging or ignoring suspect climbers. *Climbing* celebrated "the first legitimate lead" of one route previously ascended by a less admirable climber. New terms were invented to capture the relative spontaneity and virtuosity of ascents. "On-Sight," "Flash," "Redpoint," and "Pinkpoint"—the latter linking a feminine color to climbs on which gear had been pre-placed—became metrics of ethical rigor. Individuals were also targeted. Bachar and Kauk seconded one Jardine route, pointedly using only chocks rather than cams. Bachar implied that Jardine was angered "because we had floated it," but Jardine called it "equally significant." When Kauk got up another Jardine route, partisans credited him with the first ascent. By 1981, Jardine was gone. Whether driven out, as some argued, or drawn to other adventures, as he claimed, *The Nose* debacle punctuated his era. Other wayward climbers had ropes cut and equipment stolen. In one particularly ugly incident, locals bombed nonlocals with bags of human excrement. There were very real costs to defying the traditionalists.[27]

Pressure was even brought at the national level. In 1986 the American Alpine Club hosted a "Great Debate" pitting Bachar, Kauk, and Henry Barber against several sport climbers who dubbed themselves "eurodogs." The meeting was framed as a discussion of American and European traditions, but the audience saw it as a struggle between good and evil. Chouinard gave away t-shirts with the phrase "The Devil Is a Hangdog"; others read "Sport Climbing Is Neither." The debate resolved nothing, however, so *Climbing*'s editor tried to codify culture: "In *traditional style,* the climber starts from the bottom of the proposed route, with the eventual goal of free climbing to the top without falling. When falls are taken, the leader typically lowers to the ground or to a no-hands or similarly relaxed stance, commonly leaving the rope through the last piece of protection. This is known as *yo-yoing.* All protection is placed on lead."[28]

This was less about describing than inventing tradition. Even a casual

Figure 11.2. The "Great Debate" at the 1986 annual meeting of the American Alpine Club. *From left:* Henry Barber, Rob Robinson, Randy Vogel, Ron Kauk, Lynn Hill, John Bachar, Todd Skinner, Christian Griffith, and Alan Watts debated sport and traditionalist rules, but pre-arranged protest t-shirts such as Kauk's bearing the slogan "The Devil Is a Hang-Dog" suggested an unwillingness to compromise. Ironically, within a year Kauk would switch sides, arguing that sport climber tactics were the wave of the future.

glance at recent ascents revealed that siege tactics never completely disappeared from big walls. Moreover, the ethical distinctions between yo-yoing, which allowed one or several climbers to fall repeatedly without relinquishing their high point, and hang-dogging, which did the same but allowed a climber to examine a crux and practice moves, were philosophically arbitrary. Nor was Yosemite innocent to "Eurotactics." Bridwell had done "minor reshaping" to several routes, including installing a bolt before free climbing *Wheat Thin,* and like nearly everyone in the valley, he had gardened extensively. Even Bachar blurred the line by hanging from hooks while drilling on *Bachar/Yerian,* and he, too, used an electric drill. There were no unbroken legacies in the sport, especially in the previous two decades. "Purity," Don Mellor observed, "was a relative thing."[29]

Tradition was a shaky bulwark. Its logic had so many holes that Bachar turned defensive even before interviewers questioned him. Self-identified "traditionalists," a term first invoked by British critics of aid climbers, could not talk their way to victory, so they turned from words to deeds. It was not that principle ceased to matter, but it was always only one of several concerns. Debates about style were also battles over turf among a group Lito Tejada-Flores called "creative elitists." More specifically, they were battles among those few who needed first ascents to attain status. Morris explained that the "number and varieties of potentially great [routes] are eternally fixed," and Bachar later admitted, "All I wanted was a little rock saved for me." When logic failed the traditionalists, they turned to another tradition: cold chisels. Bachar was only the most conspicuous of several in Yosemite, Joshua Tree, City of Rocks, and other areas who erased routes by chopping, pulling, and plugging bolts, most of which were replaced by equally righteous sport climbers. One traditionalist reasoned, "Chopping the bolts won't totally solve the problem, but it will let those who shit on the altar know that it won't be tolerated."[30]

Nothing was settled and Bachar began to brood. His mentor Bridwell admitted that the "first rule of climbing is there are no rules." Then Ron Kauk went over to the dark side. Kauk, the incredibly talented high-school dropout who persuaded Bachar to leave UCLA. Kauk, Bachar's climbing blood brother and his only free climbing equal. Kauk, the stalwart ally who held the line at the AAC panel. Kauk, the champion of Camp 4 who wore jeans to a bouldering event and taunted sport climbers: "John Wayne never wore Lycra." Kauk went to Europe in the mid-1980s, climbed sport routes, and said, "bolts could revive the stagnating scene in Yosemite." It was too much. By Bachar's own admission he had "a big chip on [his] shoulder," so in 1988 when Kauk rap-bolted a line Bachar coveted, Bachar chopped a Kauk route. Kauk and Mark Chapman confronted him in Camp 4's parking lot. Friends divided. Tempers flared. Bachar yelled "punch me." Chapman complied with a blow to the neck. Bachar fell and was rushed to the hospital, his left arm numb. Chapman was arrested and taken to jail, dazed by what had happened.[31]

Vandalism erupted, and Yosemite seemed to deflate. There had been whispers for years that valley climbers were behind the curve. Traditionalists were incapable of climbing the hardest grades, and for all their vaunted talk about risk, most valley climbs paled in comparison to routes elsewhere. Tony Yaniro hang-dogged up North America's first 5.13 elsewhere in the Sierra, and Frenchman Jíbe Tribout put up North America's first 5.14 at Oregon's Smith Rocks. Outsiders blew by. Bachar called it a "slander," sulked off to a canyon, and cranked up a ghetto blaster to drive away his demons and everyone else. Chouinard counseled Camp 4 to forget Europe. The über traditionalist wanted to "change the rules. Let's play our own game." For the first time since before Mark Powell, Camp 4 lacked a leader. Traditionalists championed Peter Croft, who seemed Bachar's heir when he free soloed several major routes including the Rostrum's *North Face* (5.11.c), *Astroman* (5.11c), and *Cosmic Debris* (5.13a), but they had the wrong man. A transplant from Squamish, Croft was an incredibly ethical climber, exposing his own breaches when no one else caught them, but he was humble to a fault. He lacked the necessary zeal to be Camp 4's bully.[32]

Traditionalists also overplayed their caricature of sport climbers. They had not, as John Long said, "completely disowned the past." Climbing had a powerful inertial effect on everyone. Even the most radical aspirants had to honor historical figures and values to gain legitimacy. New routes were still subject to peer review, and new climbers did not deny ground-up values. Like traditionalists, sport climbers insisted that true first ascents proceeded from the ground. Hang-dogging and rap-bolting were for training. A "red point" ascent, in which the climber placed gear while moving up, remained the threshold of success. Even the traditionalists' emphasis on risk lost ground. During an exchange visit to Europe, a group of American women climbers steeped in Camp 4 values warmed to "Eurotactics." "Instead of worrying about risk," one wrote, she "could focus on pure difficulty." Chouinard had it backward. The only way that traditionalists could win was by engaging apostates, and victory could be achieved only by prevailing both in terms of better ideas and better performances.[33]

Chouinard's savior was not an alpha male but a five-foot-nothing, hundred-pound rock nymph who had already fled Yosemite for the East coast. Like Beverly Johnson, Lynn Hill had been a gymnast before becoming a climber, but whereas Johnson had been weak, Hill was possibly the top woman athlete in the world. Yet she was not a firebreather. At the "Great Debate" she annoyed both sides by honoring the values she had learned from Bridwell but denying that hang-dogging "hurt anyone." Despite the angst, by the mid-1990s none of this mattered. A new generation had found a way to compromise and take climbing in new directions, making it at once more extreme, secular, and popular. Yosemite Valley also came out of its doldrums. Old climbers gained new respect, and Camp 4 experienced a surprising renaissance. Valley walls were once more cutting-edge sites. Hill set the stage in the most ironic of ways by traveling to Europe and climbing plastic holds on temporary walls before television cameras and thousands of spectators. It took a women's pro-climbing competition to prove that masculine adventure in Yosemite still mattered.[34]

12. CONSUMERS

Having read the same news and editorials, climbers across the
country share the same information, if not the same values.
—Don Mellor

Like other parts of society, climbing was growing more complex and
commodified. Tensions between traditionalists and sport climbers were
but one of many schisms that had emerged during the 1970s and 1980s. The
battles included elitist versus moderate, amateur versus pro, solitary versus
social, and indoor versus outdoor climbers. The sport was really a microcosm of the "segmented society," just another "system of insular units each
maximizing its power and rewards" to the exclusion of others. Thus modern climbers, who had long tried to distance themselves from the masses,
showed that they were not so different. Each clash bared another subset
within their ever more fractured community.[1]

Traditionalists rued this hiving, but their torment was old. Heterodoxy
had been grist for jeremiads since the 1860s, and by 1970 it was filling the
pockets of righteous traditionalists. The ensuing accusations of hypocrisy
were bad enough. Even worse was the way Madison Avenue had anticipated
it. By 1956 analysts realized that social splintering—their term was "market
segmentation"—was good business. By 1970 they foresaw ever more disag-
gregation "of consumers by age group, income, education, geography, ethnic
background, and use patterns." One notable opportunity was the lifestyle
market. "Today," declared *Business Week,* "people want to do things, rather
than have things." This was the essence of "postmodern tourism," "a self-
referential and trend-driven" rush to consume nature as experience. By 1980
outdoor sports was a growth market. Participation reached critical mass,
filled by those well-educated, relatively wealthy, aggressively consuming
professionals who claimed wilderness as a private playground.[2]

Here were paradoxes: splintering was traumatic yet change had been
climbing's one constant, and for all their differences, climbers were ever
more connected to one another by an ecology of consumption. The more
traditionalists promoted the joys of climbing through books, photos, clothing, and technologies, the more they spread the word, profited, and drew
people to nature. In the process they eroded the closed society and ancient

taboo against professionalization. Even traditionalists dedicated to amateur ideals found it hard to hold out when leading lights cashed in. The ambitious coordinated ascents with photographers and writers so audiences could consume their feats. Elite climbs took on aspects of spectacle that contrasted sharply with older ideals, and the traditionalists were as implicated in these changes as any group.[3]

Lynn Hill's career—the very relevance of that word marks a remarkable shift—revealed these contradictory forces at the end of the twentieth century. Like many climbers, Hill embraced "climbing as therapy" when her parents divorced, and by her late teens she identified less with her imperfect family in Orange County than with an "imperfect family of friends" at climbing areas. Like Beverly Johnson, Hill learned through gymnastics how to truncate complex choreography into units of movement, a crucial technique in the hang-dogging era. Like most post-1960 climbers, she also learned outside the club system, starting with friends on climbs that would have appalled the RCS, and advancing with tutors such as the Stonemasters in Joshua Tree and Jim Bridwell in Yosemite. Unlike Johnson, Hill entered a world now mediated by mentors such as Maria Cranor and Mari Gingery. And although she, too, suffered a lot of patriarchal insults, in no way was she alone.[4]

Hill was a pathbreaker of a different sort. Blessed with "a lucky combination of genetics, personality, and environment" that produced athleticism and determination, she was a great gymnast, runner, and climber. This stellar athlete could, in an unqualified sense, compete with anyone. She climbed Half Dome and El Capitan in her teens. By her early twenties she had climbed a 5.13. Her diminutive body could not reach the same holds as tall climbers, but her thin fingers gained proportionally better purchase on the hardest routes' tiny cracks and nubbins. Her strength-to-weight ratio enabled her to move with unusual grace. John Long remarked, "We normally would have growled like wolves at having our male luster dimmed by a woman. But Lynn shattered the gender barrier so thoroughly that no one could put the pieces back together." Long was wrong. Sexism did persist, but Laura Waterman also oversimplified when she boasted that "Women had caught up." In reality, "only Lynn Hill" had pulled even.[5]

In one respect Hill was thoroughly typical. For Hill as for everyone else in Camp 4, money was tight and the sport's ancient conceit still held sway. As late as the 1980s, one of the world's best climbers still struggled with turning play into work. Although friends had cashed in, Bridwell still "didn't know for sure what to do. Making the money would make it easier to live, but I had grown up with this tradition," and tradition was everything. Climbers could push technique and technology only so far before breaking with the past, and that was sin. Reputations depended on historical continuity. This is what vexed the sport climbers. No matter how well they climbed, their deviant methods damned them, but traditionalists were also straying.[6]

It had always been the case that climbers who took lucre for their love were whores. In the nineteenth century almost all the best European climbers were guides, yet the Alpine Club categorically ignored their role in first ascents. That stigma lasted into the 1950s when heroes such as Armand Charlet, Gaston Rébuffat, Emilio Comici, Cesare Maestri, and Walter Bonatti were given backhanded praise as "guide-amateurs"—mountaineering's equivalent to the asterisk in baseball. Even in the 1960s, when the Beats worked as guides, entertainers, and entrepreneurs, they adamantly opposed publicizing climbs because it adulterated the sport. So Bridwell emulated his heroes by working odd jobs and oil rigs, doing time as a guide, and giving the occasional talk. Earnings were meager and intermittent.[7]

More opportunities emerged in the 1970s. Bridwell began to receive free gear in exchange for endorsements. He also rigged for Hollywood, trained Navy SEALS, competed in the made-for-TV *Battle of the Fittest,* and joined a trans-Borneo expedition. Payoffs were still paltry, however. There was little money in televised competitions, and Bridwell nearly died from one of Borneo's intestinal parasites. Life was so thin he yanked and filed his own teeth after a falling rock cracked his mouth. Bridwell scraped and scrapped, slept in tents and trailers, and was never a pro in any modern sense. As such, he was an ironic emblem of Yosemite. Although the valley still boasted the top climbers in the world, it was a cultural backwater. Elsewhere the masculine ideal of the "Brotherhood of the Rope" had frayed under the forces of competition and commodification. Not until after 1980 did Camp 4 finally embrace professionalization.[8]

Yosemite climbers only sensed their idiosyncrasies when they ventured outside the valley. It was fine for the RCS to mock-climb Disneyland's Matterhorn for the ride's grand opening in 1959, but when Royal Robbins went to Britain in the mid-1960s to experience the pure sport, he was chagrined to learn that he had been scheduled as a "guest star" with several legendary English climbers for a televised first ascent on the sea cliffs of South Stack. This had been entertainment in Britain since the mid-1950s, and to Joe Brown the "thought of being offered money to do something that bore no resemblance to work in my eyes was ecstasy." To Robbins it was anathema. Similarly, when John Bachar attended Germany's Sportklettern International in

1985, he imagined an "avant-garde" gathering with climbers discussing "ethics, philosophy, spiritual aspects, concentration." Instead, he was hounded by autograph seekers and saddened by the competitiveness. When Robbins returned he purified his trip by writing only about English climbing ethics; when Bachar came home, he had a rope sponsorship and several modeling gigs.[9]

It was not so much that fame became fungible—that was old news. Rather, the ways to make money had expanded. Bev Johnson had worked as a climbing ranger, ski instructor, and seamstress, but by 1974 she was also a member of the Screen Actors Guild, acting in commercials and shows, rigging cameras for studios, and recording sound for her partner Mike Hoover's outdoor and adventure films. Bridwell and Bachar made $30,000 for a soft drink commercial. Bachar earned another $38,000 for a shaving commercial after *Rolling Stone, Life, Newsweek,* and *Playboy* ran features on him, while Ron Kauk and Jerry Moffatt free climbed Lost Arrow Spire for a live broadcast of ABC's *Wide World of Sports.* Still, these were opportunistic payouts that did not alter basic lifestyles. Only Hill managed to find steady income by winning *The Survival of the Fittest* each of the four years that NBC staged the event, and like Johnson, who had invited her to compete, Hill performed stunts such as climbing untethered over a hot air balloon 6,000 feet above the ground for the show *That's Incredible.*[10]

Critics howled. Bachar discounted Kauk and Moffatt's first free climb of Lost Arrow Spire. Walt Unsworth called such spectacles "peepshow[s] for the proletariat," yet many top climbers were implicated. Some who competed before cameras made less money than those rigging or operating cameras. Every climber needed to eat, and no one not independently wealthy could easily reject the money. As Trip Gabriel observed, "With many superb climbers roughly on a par, true advances are made by leaps of imagination and skill. . . . Rock climbing, understand, is a sport well into an end game." Even Werner Braun and Tucker Tech maintained their dirtbag cred by serving on the Yosemite Search and Rescue (YOSAR) squad. Some top climbers elided these contradictions through a form of rhetorical jujitsu. Bridwell called himself an artist. Peter Croft insisted his spectacular solo link-ups were motivated by a shortage of vacation time. Asked about his growing income from climbing-related activities, Bachar replied, "Money doesn't do much for me."[11]

Others were more candid about their own or others' careers. John Roskelley was America's most driven climber since John Harlin. Robert Roper observed, "To be invited on more climbs, to attract sponsors, press coverage, book contracts, all the goods and services of such a career, [Roskelley] needs to get the great summits. He needs to get them by diabolical new routes, to prove to the world how good he is." Rock climbers were less calculating, but many had complex motives. Australian Louise Shepherd regarded professionalism "with ambivalence" because it had "unfortunate whiffs of . . . 'honest harlotry.' I'd rather go grape-picking." Instead of resorting to stoop labor, however, she described her sponsored climbs as "Olympic amateurism." Others were comfortable admitting "there is money and glory to be had." Todd Skinner asked, "Why train so hard to repeat somebody else's route? Why not find your own and be known for that?" Bill Davidson confessed, "Why then was I trying [El Capitan] solo? I could give the usual answer, but mainly I knew what it would mean if I succeeded—FAME!" Climbing was a job Hill worked at "five days a week, eight hours a day, and we put in a lot of overtime." Such remarks would have scandalized the Victorians, but this was the 1980s.[12]

Beats had redefined the sport's relationship to the market, and they melded the two ever more in middle age. Galen Rowell said climbing was "a wonderful metaphor for life. If you risk too much, you'll eat it and die; if you don't risk enough, you won't get anything out of it." Chouinard did not "care if it's a great financial risk or a physical risk. . . . People who take risks on a daily basis are more successful people, both mentally and physically, and, I think, are more content." Rick Ridgeway said "Businesspeople have their own K2's." These were not crass rationalizations for selling out. Chouinard, Robbins, Rowell, Tom Frost, and Doug Tompkins had always mongered both goods and ideals. Technology, sport, and values were ecologically linked. Profit was not inimical to principle, and many consumed them as a seamless whole. Moreover, outdoor sports grew rapidly as prosperity rose, especially in individualistic, "high-status" sports such as mountaineering and skiing. There were 60,000 rock climbers in the United States by 1980 and over 100,000 by 1995.[13]

They were all consumers, both of goods and of transcendental rhetoric. Mountaineers, according to R. L. G. Irving, hoped "to give personality to these objects of our devotion, and so making our small contribution to the gradual permeating and final replacement of the material and perishable by the non-material and indestructible." Of course, Irving argued this in at least six very material books, but to single him out is to miss his utter typicality. Many elites discussed spiritual liberation while advising readers on gear needed to attain enlightenment. Edward Whymper, Annie Peck, and Geoffrey Winthrop Young traced the fine points of technology, clubs created economies of scale for merchants, and consuming climbers helped build Sporthaus Schuster, Holubars, Eddie Bauer, Recreational Equipment Co-Op, and Ski Hut into commercial successes.[14]

In the decades after 1965, the industry's structure grew more complex. At the top of the food chain were multinational corporations gobbling brands and stores when not merging as new species. Kenneth Klopp bought Tompkins's North Face in 1968 and made it a clothing brand. Odyssey Holdings Inc. bought out North Face and its ten stores, and when OHI went bankrupt, its holdings were acquired by investors who were then leveraged by VF Corporation, which owned many clothing labels and apparel licenses for sporting merchandise. Royal Robbins lent his name to his wife's clothing line. By the mid-1980s their company grossed $7 million. In 2003, Phoenix Footwear Group branched into outdoor apparel by acquiring Royal Robbins Inc. The brand generated $30 million in sales by 2007, so a Missouri-based apparel maker that also owned Kelty and Sierra Designs bought Royal Robbins.[15]

One way to survive this feeding frenzy was to evolve into a top predator. Recreational Equipment Co-Op incorporated as REI in 1956 and then after 1970 expanded its retail operations. By 1990 it had twenty-two stores in thirteen states; by 2005, anchored by its 100,000-square-foot flagship store in Seattle, REI owned several subsidiary companies and seventy-seven stores. It had 1.7 million member-customers and over $1 billion in sales. In the late 1960s Yvon Chouinard added corduroy shorts and rugby shirts to his catalog. When clothing proved more lucrative than gear, he established Patagonia. Meanwhile Malinda and Yvon bought out the Frosts' share in Chouinard Equipment, and by 1978 the company controlled 80 percent of the gear market. By 1984, Lost Arrow Corporation, the holding company for the Chouinards' equipment, clothing, catalog, and retail operations, grossed $20 million. By 1990 sales topped $100 million. Meanwhile, Doug Tompkins invested profits from the sale of North Face in his wife's sporty line of women's clothing. By the mid-1980s Plain Jane, rebranded as Esprit, brought in more than $1 billion in sales.[16]

Many more inhabited the ecosystem at lower trophic levels. Colorado's Greg Lowe made climbing gear, backpacks, and camera cases under Lowe Alpine and LowePro, selling Lowe Alpine to the British textile firm William Baird in 1990 for $34 million. Ray Jardine patented his cams, cut a deal with Wild Country for his Friends, and exited the valley with enough "spare change in my pockets" to sail and backpack for the rest of his life. John Bachar and Mike Graham netted $65,000 their first year selling Fíres, and profits doubled the next year. Charles Cole, another valley climber, developed his own sticky-soled shoe, established Five Ten, and gained a share of the metastasizing market. Even the former dirtbag John Middendorf found a niche making gear for the demographically tiny but intensely consuming big-wall climber. When that market grew, North Face purchased his A5 brand. Moreover, every outfit relied on climbers as laborers.[17]

Mountain art was another growth area. Yosemite had long been both muse and cash cow for the likes of Albert Bierstadt, Eadweard Muybridge, Carleton Watkins, and Ansel Adams, but rock climbers were slow to capitalize. Cameras were initially tools used to document passage. A more artistic vision emerged when Henry Kendall's landscape aesthetic influenced Frost, Glenn Denny, and eventually *Ascent*. Yosemite climbers began to shoot with one eye on the public. Bridwell recorded every move for slide shows, while Chouinard collaborated in commercial films of his Yosemite and Patagonia ascents. The result was artistic and fiscal success. Roger Brown's *Sentinel: The West Face* won first prize at the 1968 Trento Film Festival, and Lito Tejada-Flores's *Fitzroy: First Ascent of the Southwest Buttress* won the same in 1969. Mike Hoover's 1972 *Solo* was nominated for an Oscar, and Fred Padula's 1978 *El Capitan* won the grand prize at the Banff Mountain Film Festival. Galen Rowell and Jeff Foott used their adventures to hone their craft as famed outdoor and wildlife photographers. Much of this work shared two key traits: a dedication to the Beat ideals of adventure, and an assumption that nature was separate from civilization. Others were drawn to art by money. Rick Ridgeway had an epiphany on a film project: "we were all doing the same thing—climbing the mountain. There was one difference, however. [The cameramen] were getting paid for it. This big light bulb came on in my head and I said, 'The movies are for me.'"[18]

Words were another industry. Mountaineers had transcribed private adventures into profitable tales since Edward Whymper, Leslie Stephen, Clarence King, and John Muir, but the library grew immensely in the 1970s. From 1975 to 1980, 169 English-language guides, memoirs, and histories were published. The pace slackened in the 1980s and then doubled after 1990. Most were about the Himalaya and Mount Everest, and Südtirol's Reinhold Messner and England's Chris Bonington were conspicuous authors. The two most prolific writers, however, were John Long and Galen Rowell. Long's eleven and, if we include his photography texts, Rowell's fifteen books, along with Messner's and Bonington's works, all revealed several departures from the Victorian canon. Messner had crafted a bullying voice, boasting of how he was the first to climb Everest without oxygen, to solo Everest, and to climb every 8,000-meter peak. He mocked lesser climbers and criticized those who

used bolts for carrying their "courage in [a] rucksack." He also sensationalized with terms like "edge" and "extreme," a trend one skiing author called
"Extremitis."[19]

The climbing essay also evolved. Before 1955 climbers had relied on patrons to sing their praises. Alfred Mummery had William Coolidge, George
Mallory had Geoffrey Young, and the individualists had Dick Leonard. When
Beats broke from clubs they exchanged patronage for new promotional
tools. *Summit, Ascent, Mountain, Vulgarian Digest, Climbing, Descent,* and
Off Belay became platforms for the unaligned. At first magazines functioned
like journals. Younger climbers still had to climb well *and* invest "time and
ingenuity buttering up" influential figures like Royal Robbins, who edited
Summit. To curry favor, Chuck Kroger and Scott Davis patronized Robbins's
shop and wrote fawning letters about all "he had done in promoting climbing ethics and alpine-style climbing." The sentiments were sincere and calculated. Kroger and Davis were committed climbers, but the Stanford grads
also "knew how to get good grades." The new order was not so different. As
Steve Roper recalled, even the Beats "couldn't slack off lest we be thought incompetent by our 'bosses.'" The games within the game continued.[20]

By the time Galen Rowell edited the *American Alpine Club Newsletter*
in 1973, this broadened publishing apparatus created additional changes.
Rowell wanted to discuss ethics, ecology, and waning interest in clubs, but
the editors of *Climbing* and *Mountain* had other concerns. Commercial rags
lived and died by advertising revenue. Editors gauged bottom lines, and
marketing shaped coverage. Like *Summit, Mountain* and *Climbing* favored
personality-driven essays, interviews, and tales about firsts and extremes.
They borrowed *Ascent's* aesthetic because dynamic composition and color
captured the buyer's eye. By 1980 slick-sheet magazines were the norm, and
polished photographs dominated the genre. Chuck Kroger remarked that
the slides he showed to clubs "don't seem to pack that much of a wallop anymore, compared to the stuff you see in *Climbing Magazine*." Yosemite remained a constant, however. *Mountain's* fourth issue featured the valley,
as did half of *Climbing's* covers in its first two years. Both magazines had
broader coverage, but the Yosemite aesthetic was applied to Arizona, Colorado, New York, and Nepal, as well as to skiing and surfing magazines such as
Tracks.[21]

Ads also reflected these cultural shifts. Gear manufacturers and clothing
merchants had advertised since the 1800s, but as late as 1960 newsletters
such as the *Yodeler, Mugelnoos,* and *American Alpine Club News* still used
typescript ads. Photo and line art began to appear in the late 1950s, and off-

set printing in the 1960s introduced duotone and halftone ads for Sporthaus Schuster, *Mountain World*, REI, and Chouinard Equipment. Because they were among the first commercial outdoor periodicals, *Summit* and *American Whitewater* were important labs for refining outdoor ads, yet *Summit's* founders, two devout Seventh Day Adventists, balked at trends such as an essay suggesting Earth was older than six thousand years or ads with sexual content. Second generation magazines had fewer qualms. After 1969 scantily clad women were used to market many products, including a series of ads for the German ropemaker Edelrid that featured a naked woman barely concealed by rope wrapped around her arms, torso, and leg. Bondage-themed ads were an extreme version of sexualized product promotion, but the practice ran across the industry.[22]

The Edelrid ads underscored Beats' assumptions that climbing was a heterosexual, male-dominated sport, but by the early 1970s the market had to adjust. As clubs waned entrepreneurs took over the training of novices. In 1968, Robbins founded Rockcraft Climbing School in Modesto. In 1969, Bob Culp started a self-named school in Boulder. In the 1970s, Chouinard ran workshops on rock and ice technique. The most prominent operation was the Yosemite Mountaineering School, founded in 1969 by the park concessionaire to profit from tourists' growing fascination with climbers. Wayne Merry was its director because, as a former ranger and first ascensionist of *The Nose*, he bridged the worlds of the Yosemite Park and Curry Company, NPS, and Camp 4. The YMS began by playing to masculine fantasy. Its first brochure was a paean to imperial climbing, complete with photos of solitary men in dynamic, wild settings. It poetically invited consumers to "Climb into a new dimension." One need not "be an experienced mountain climber to plant your own flag." The "'hard men' of Yosemite climbing—men who have forged the toughest new routes"—would provide the "opportunity to enjoy Yosemite's unrivaled alpine environment on a completely new plane of experience."[23]

The first brochure was a pitch-perfect rendition of Beat values, but by 1975 it was out of tune. The adventure rhetoric continued. A 1978 leaflet beckoned, "What greater challenge to the mountaineer than the granite walls and peaks of Yosemite?" but the accompanying imagery revealed a more complex gendering. In the early 1970s the YMS taught many aspiring adventurers, but most clients were less ambitious. Brochures were reworked to appeal to consumers rather than guides. Photos focused on groups of women and men rather than lone heroes. In one, the key image foregrounded an attractive blond (the director's wife) in a climbing class. The

Figure 12.1. This rope ad, part of a series devised by the editor of *Mountain* magazine, photographer Leo Dickinson, and a fellow student from Dickinson's art school, pushed the edges of sexuality, yet using women's bodies to market outdoor gear to an assumed male clientele was widespread in the 1970s. Within a few years the industry had to adjust to a rapidly broadening consumer base that, by the early 1990s, included enough women to constitute their own market segment.

Climb

into

a

new

dimension.

You don't have to go very far to do it.

Adventurers from all over the world come right here to America every year to meet one of its greatest and most interesting challenges—Yosemite.

Now, you don't have to be an experienced mountain climber to plant your own flag.

Because Yosemite has its own mountaineering school and guide service.

With the endorsement of the National Park Service, the Yosemite school will provide any park visitor with a safe means to learn mountain climbing under expert instruction and supervision.

If you have never climbed but have wanted to, this is your chance to learn. The Yosemite Mountaineering School and Guide Service will give you an opportunity to enjoy Yosemite's unrivaled alpine environment on a completely new plane of experience. If you've never "belayed in slings," or climbed a "chimney" or stood just above the clouds, you've yet to experience a whole new set of sensations in mountain climbing.

Figure 12.2. The first brochure for the Yosemite Mountaineering School was a pitch-perfect rendition of Beat values with images of lone men in challenging vertical landscapes and allusions to conquest, but within a half-decade the YMS had reconfigured the brochure to emphasize a heterosocial experience with women and men alike participating in classes.

YMS commissioned articles in tourist periodicals and promoted an explicitly heterosocial and heterosexual experience. Its most successful ad was a t-shirt with the empowering slogan, "Go Climb a Rock." Consumers bought it, and the ubiquitous shirts adorned many a body that never touched granite. By the mid-1970s the YMS had become synonymous with Yosemite fun.[24]

Climbing schools, gear stores, and rescue squads were the means by which many climbers earned their keep. On its surface they seemed like an emerging sporting proletariat, but economic relationships were more symbiotic. If climbers needed merchants to subsidize their lifestyles, entrepreneurs needed climbers as more than consumers. Climbers were the beta testers who abused gear and suggested refinements, and only when top climbers used gear on hard routes could makers distinguish their products from competitors. Chouinard asked Steve Roper not only to "beat the hell out of [a prototype] and tell me how it works" but to write "a testimonial . . . on my pitons & carabiners." These were not just favors among friends but key marketing tactics. Lawrence Hamilton noted that the most effective advertisers were "not the Madison Avenue flacks but the serious climbers themselves." Reputations counted. When Chouinard Equipment revised its piton lines the year it introduced clean climbing, the catalog had a photo of Royal Robbins at a picnic table covered in Chouinard pitons to imply that this gear was the choice of the greats.[25]

Unfortunately, implied messages no longer necessarily worked. Photos might speak for themselves within the homosocial world of Camp 4, but middling climbers had become both the most important trophic level of this evolving ecology, perhaps its keystone species, and an unwieldy cultural and material force. Consumers funded upward mobility. The lessons, books, gear, and clothing they bought enriched entrepreneurs and helped dirtbags escape their bottom-feeding ways. Middendorf established A5 Adventures and then another brand under his own name, and Russ Walling marketed tools by his nickname of "Fish." "Local" increasingly applied to climbers who owned property in or near the park, not just the wastrels of Camp 4. But better standards of living came at a price. Although elites profited from this growth, they lost cultural power in the exchange.[26]

Consumers were not mere purses and wallets. They produced meaning as well. When Steve Roper griped about pitons on girls' key chains and that "more rurps are sold for reasons of status than for actual use," or Chouinard moaned that "the average guy on the street was running around with a carabiner hanging off his belt," they saw consumers commandeering esoteric technology. Surfers, skiers, and kayakers suffered similar appropriations.

Owning a RURP, board, or paddle no longer secured distinction, so participants redefined the basis of identity. In climbing this coincided with ever
more extreme articulations of risk by Bridwell and Bachar. Surfers turned "to
'attitude' as a way of maintaining collective 'difference' and an 'alternative'
image," most importantly by embracing the "masculinisation of surfing and
the progressive exclusion of women." In every sport young men aggressively
excluded outsiders to maintain their sense of difference, but in taking consumers' money, they also eroded the divide between an "us" and a "them."
All were now linked by a market ecology that no one could disentangle.[27]

This complex relationship between tradition-bound elitists and heterodox consumers bursts from the pages of the *Chouinard Equipment* and
Great Pacific Iron Works catalogs, which were a sort of gearhead porn. Climbers could lust over and buy nearly anything for a day hike, big-wall epic,
or extreme expedition. Chouinard's Great Pacific Iron Works store sold his
wares and specialty items by other makers. Climbers could buy Shoenards, a
co-branded climbing shoe made by Vasque, Chouinard ropes made under a
license agreement by another manufacturer, and an array of hammers, ice
axes, training devices, and other tools, all of which Chouinard obsessively refined. The same held for "soft goods." A growing line of under- and outer-
wear crowded the *GPIW* catalog until 1981, when Patagonia and Chouinard
Equipment were separated for practical and legal reasons. Every catalog featured a new or redesigned something for adventure, but climbers could also
show their brand loyalty with t-shirts, posters, tote bags, and decals bearing the Great Pacific Iron Works or Patagonia logos. In these ways Chouinard
and the whole industry's tactics differed little from those of mainstream mar-
keters.[28]

To nurture this lucrative ecosystem retailers and makers formed the Outdoor Industry Association (OIA), but Beats never measured themselves solely
by income. Even as he benefited from consumption Chouinard tried to discipline its appetite. Catalog biographies of Chouinard the climber and gear
maker heralded his values and fostered a powerful cult of personality, but
ambition went beyond personal aggrandizement. Pithy epigrams reinforced
cultural agendas. Consumers could ogle a new tool or sweater while bask-
ing in the wisdom of Albert Einstein, Mick Jagger, Henry David Thoreau, Han
Shan, or Robert F. Scott, who became an icon of masculinity because he died
well while racing Amundson to the South Pole. Essays schooled consumers
in the use of gear, the Beat philosophy of minimalism and risk, and the need
for environmental sensitivity. Chouinard's complex and often contradictory
ideals permeated texts, but they were perhaps most sharply etched in a 1981

essay encouraging consumers to move from "the AeroSpace age" back "to primitive times" by buying a tump line made of petroleum byproducts. Catalogs were complex didactics, entrepreneurial extensions of an evangelizing voice Chouinard had long cultivated.[29]

Trouble was, readers had their own agendas. Participation in outdoor sports grew worldwide, mostly from outside the club system, yet by the early 1990s there were eighty-two national organizations. Climber surveys revealed a spectrum of motives from personal quests and risk-taking to fun and flirtation, yet all were authentic climbers. This broadened sporting culture did not obliterate Beat values. Many still sought spiritual self-testing in nature. Psychologist Mihály Csíkszentmihályi studied climbers to develop his concept of flow, a mental state in which athletes merged seamlessly with their environments. As Daniel Duane argued, "A love for the sport, therefore, is a love of extreme physical discomfort and a hunger for tasks so stupidly difficult they can obliterate your self—the ostensible point of the enterprise."[30]

Duane's experiences illuminate both the continuing pull and shifting fortunes of Beat ideals. Son of Richard Duane, a club-era climber from the Bay Area, Daniel was one of many nonelites trying to navigate Yosemite's legendary climbingscape: "I . . . thought how thirty years ago El Capitan was a barely charted Louisiana Purchase; now it was impregnated with stories and route names: The Shield, Genesis, the Muir Wall, the Heart Route, Jolly Roger, and Magic Mushroom. . . . A climber of the sixties may have had the fear and pleasure of the unknown, but now the psychic universe of the wall was overwhelmingly rich." Becoming a valley climber resembled an apprenticeship. Duane had to master many techniques and formations before reaching the epitome of adventure, El Capitan. Propelling him was a familiar goal. More than anything Duane wanted "to epic," to overcome a desperate jam and give meaning to a painfully ill-defined sense of self. As such he offers an astonishingly candid glimpse into the trials of young adulthood and poverty of wilderness ideology.[31]

The reality of El Capitan differed greatly from what Duane imagined, and his errand seemed contrived. "If wilderness is anywhere something could eat you, then I'd been putting in the predator myself: gravity." The result was often unsatisfying. Much of big-wall climbing involved mundane tasks like whacking, hauling, and sitting. Glory was at best fleeting. "In one of my exhausted rotating pauses [while ascending a rope], I looked up and laughed out loud. I realized I'd arrived—all those great old photographs of climbers jumaring in space at dawn"—but the moment passed. Soon the immensity of the task closed in. "Suddenly coming unglued," he retreated repeatedly, telling himself "to stop imagining that authentic experience can be found only by climbing El Capitan. I've got to stop deceiving myself that, *Yeah, that'll do it. Then I won't hate myself anymore.*" Instead, he tried again and again. In a genre that built toward clichéd moments of insight and redemption, Duane's narratives dwelt on confusion, impotence, and failure, and although he eventually succeeded, by then he knew it resolved nothing.[32]

As well as any author, Duane captures the Sisyphean quest for manly moments, what Mo Antoine called "feeding the rat," but this was not climbers' sole or even paramount motive. Most were satisfied by a fun, moderate route. This exacerbated the queues which had been growing since holiday outings in the 1950s, and moderates no longer deferred to elites. They discussed ethical debates but concluded they were irrelevant. Indeed, some even complained when their betters passed them on routes. They also mocked self-appointed ethical authorities and celebrated more modest adventures. One wrote that "the do-something-not-too-often-done reason is just as important as meeting any particular challenge. What matter if the one person who ascended your mole hill last year was a ten year old kid? Is he not as much of an adventurer as the fifty who climbed the Salathé Wall?"[33]

Others were less kind. One story parodied E. Van Chin-Hard as the General Motors of climbing, Warren Harding as a "Hardy boy," Royal Robbins as "a pure and venturesome prince from the climbing aristocracy," and Reinhold Messner as an idiot. The hero was an impossibly brilliant climber who viewed everyone as unworthy until "they adopt my terrific mind set":

> Most climbers today are gutless, nervous low-landers with no respect for the rock environment and no knowledge of what real exposure is. They use old pitons as hand trowels and scrape the vegetation out of the cracks in order to insert their destructive chocks. Me, I leave the plants there and often incorporate them into my protection system. When I anchor to the edelweiss, I leave the flower undisturbed as I lovingly place my microsling around the tiny stem. I savor the texture of the delicate petals. Once you have this kind of mystical appreciation for the vertical world, my standards are easy to achieve.

Underlying the satire was an unsubtle refusal to bow to betters and palpable proof that there were "no consistent answers" to why climbers climbed or what their experiences meant.[34]

Reading the era's magazines and journals, though, one might easily miss this. Climbing literature dwelled on extreme forms of adventure. Writers obsessed about current ethical disputes or practiced a solipsistic form of reportage from the vertical front. The fate of clubs also suggested that moderate climbing was fading. The Rock Climbing Section and Stanford Alpine Club had struggled since the 1960s. RCS programs increasingly reflected an aging membership, and the RCS and Mountaineering Section were suspended for want of qualified leaders. The SAC struggled because fewer students joined clubs, nor did they need outings to escape campus once Stanford ended its signout system in the mid-1960s. By 1970 stronger members no longer taught or led beginners. They were, as Roger Gocking noted, "off doing their own things." Novices had to rely on commercial schools. The end of the club era seemed imminent, yet this was exactly when social climbing rebounded.[35]

Even as the SAC spasmed out of existence in 1984 and the Sierra Club killed the RCS in 1988, their terminations were less an end than a reorganization. In fact sporting clubs were one of the few types of associations people flocked to after 1970. In 1967 the Loma Prieta Chapter formed a Peak Climbing Section that thrived during these years, and members of the defunct Bay Area RCS revived the old Cragmont Climbing Club. By the 1990s women had more women-only clubs, homosexual climbers formed the Stonewall Climbers, rock gyms offered a whole new experience, and the Internet helped climbers network more effectively than ever. Social climbing survived, but the new associations revealed the sport's continuing segmentation. Climbers grew more cosmopolitan and visited more places, but expanded participation also created ever more subsets. The more populous and diverse the community, the easier it was to socialize only with those who exactly mirrored each other in identity, values, and ambitions.[36]

Consumption also reshaped the ecosystem. For a long time liability had been an afterthought. For diehards the risks were both obvious and an attraction. The notion of liability seemed absurd to all but the lawyerly Richard Leonard, who first bought insurance for SC outings in 1937. Instead clubs managed risk by testing members and technology. In 1948 the American Alpine Club formed a Safety Advisory Council to publish annual analytical summaries of major accidents, and in 1960 the Union Internationale des Associations d'Alpinistes established a testing committee. Still no one sued a climber, club, or manufacturer if things went bad, even though climbers were often at least careless, if not negligent, in the lack of skill, neglect of safety, and misuse of equipment. This changed in the 1970s as society and the courts reexamined longstanding assumptions about personal and product liability. Fewer consumers accepted the notion of *caveat emptor* when it came to their bodies, especially when objective information was imperfect. Outdoor sports were a conspicuous testing ground for the boundaries of proper risk. Climbers sued climbers, hikers sued parks, and everyone, it seemed, sued gear manufacturers.[37]

For a time the litigation chilled the industry and sport. Manufacturers got their first scare in 1962 when Rick Litterick died after a piton broke on a Bay Area RCS outing. The inquiry within the community—no suit was filed—pointed to the nature of the piton as a contributing factor, so Gerry Cunningham, the maker, suspended sales and offered refunds for the return of his products. Gerry stopped making gear, and other manufacturers continued with a heightened sense of the exposure, especially after several gear related accidents in the mid-1970s, including three who died when a bolt hanger broke while they were rappelling from *The Nose*. No one wanted their "ass sued," and entrepreneurs such as Leeper and Chouinard withdrew problematic pitons, harnesses, and tump lines. They also enhanced product reliability. In 1967 REI created THAW Corp. to test items, while Chouinard Equipment and Patagonia kept production local to maintain quality control. The OIA also formed a tort liability committee to study issues, and gear makers posted prominent warnings that climbing was dangerous and that it was consumers' responsibility to learn how to use gear properly.[38]

None of this stopped the lawsuits. Popular perception was that businesses were victimized by predatory lawyers, frivolous claims, and usury insurers, and the fate of Chouinard Equipment seemed to confirm impressions. During the 1980s the company was hammered by product criticism and at least six lawsuits, many of which involved blue-collar workers using gear in unintended and incompetent ways. Uncertainty about courts led Chouinard to settle several cases, and the remaining suits and skyrocketing insurance led him to file for bankruptcy. The result was more restructuring. Liability and premiums precipitated termination of the SAC and RCS and closure of climbing areas by landowners. In 1989, employees bought Chouinard Equipment, moved it to Salt Lake City, and changed the name to Black Diamond to commemorate the insignia Chouinard had borrowed from John Salathé. Other manufacturers went further. Concerned about aging bolt hangers, Ed Leeper published recall notices that warned: "LEEPER HANGERS NOW IN PLACE CAN BE DANGEROUS" and should be replaced. Athletes also suffered. Producer costs were passed to retail consumers, underwriters refused to insure risky activities, and landowners narrowed access for bungee-jumpers, climbers, kayakers, skiers, skateboarders, and skydivers.[39]

Participants further altered outdoor recreation. Although risky play survived and endless suits did not follow, neither was it business as usual. Liability fears altered technological innovation. Gear makers offered fewer devices to enable risk taking (as hangers and bashies had done in the 1970s) and board, kayak, and ski designs grew more stable and easier to use. The volatile legal environment also coincided with another round of consolidation. Then things calmed. By the 1990s courts had settled on the principle that "primary assumption of risk" fell to consumers, not to entrepreneurs. This reduced exposure for guides, manufacturers, and landowners when negligence was not an issue, yet it also made risks more explicit because consumers had to sign liability waivers before taking classes or entering lands. Climbers also voluntarily lessened the risks. In 1986 the American Professional Mountain Guides Association formed to certify members and the AAC established an Access Committee to negotiate with landowners. In 1998, Chris McNamara founded the American Safe Climbing Association to proactively replace aging quarter-inch bolts with sturdier three-eighths-inch bolts. By community volition, the sport became less risky and more predictable.[40]

It was also more consumable. In 1962, Henry Kendall called the camera "one of the last pieces of nonessential equipment to be discarded." By 1980 even the photographer was mandatory for top traditionalist and sport climbers. Regardless of whether bolts were placed on rappel or ascent, cameras were preplaced to ensure a crux move was captured from the best angle. Ascents were staged for consumption. Sport climbers were stereotypically framed in closely cropped photos of heroes making desperate moves, while traditionalist imagery emphasized sweeping vistas, often with climbers as tiny specks in swelling seas of granite. Similar canons divided soul and hotdog surfers, backcountry and freestyle skiers, and adventure and rodeo kayakers. This voyeuristic side was not new, but it was more commercialized. The photos that so dazzled Kroger appeared in articles and ads and literally fulfilled Guy Debord's insight that spectacle "is *capital* accumulated to the point where it becomes image."[41]

Spectacle had been around since the days of club practices, but now it was also capital. The ecosystem did not process it, however, in any consistent manner nor for any single end. The quest for firsts continued, but they were coordinated more and more with book and film projects. Opportunity sometimes emerged without intent, as when Mike Corbett helped paraplegic Mark Wellman climb El Capitan to unsought media coverage, but other events were highly calculated. First traverse and the ever evolving first or youngest Fill-in-the-Blank up El Capitan, Mount Everest, or the highest summits of the seven continents revealed climbers' continuing ability to reinvent challenge. Categorical firsts also shaped other sports, including first ski descents of Mount Everest and, eventually, the first woman to ski Mount Everest, but novelty had its limits. The merit of being first to climb Everest in shorts was not quite like being the first paraplegic, and George Willig's ascent of the World Trade Center in 1977 or Dan Goodwin's 1981 climb of the Sears Tower were never more than stunts. Likewise, Bill Briggs's 1971 ski descent of Grand Teton earned praise, but Rick Sylvester's 1972 descent of El Capitan by skiing off the summit with a parachute or Mark Newcomb's and Stephen Koch's 1972 descent of Grand Teton's *Black Ice Couloir* with belays and crampons drew heated criticism that Sylvester only enflamed by repeating his leap for film. Traditionalists regarded these antics as another "gimmick" to "demean" the mountain.[42]

Critics missed the mark; the point was to be seen. Goodwin stopped partway up the Sears Tower so cameramen could film him eating a plankton-based food he marketed. In 1976 a Las Vegas stuntman strung and walked a cable above Yosemite Falls. The NPS arrested him, yet it celebrated when the Project Bandaloop dance group performed on Yosemite's big walls. They said their choreography combined "natural history and cultural history," but it was virtual theater. Neither dancers nor music were perceptible to anyone except the film crew dangling from skeins of ropes hung across the faces of El Capitan and Yosemite Falls. It did matter that Bandaloop, unlike the stuntman, had obtained permits, but taste also mediated the reception of acts that corresponded poorly to historical ideals about legitimate play. Nor did top climbers always respect traditions. When Wolfgang Güllich doubled for Sylvester Stallone in *Cliffhanger,* or Ron Kauk for Tom Cruise in *MI II,* or Rick Sylvester for James Bond in *The Spy Who Loved Me,* they all sensationalized climbing, as did the guides who helped David Lee Roth dangle from Half Dome for an album cover and Jack Osbourne get in shape to climb El Capitan for a reality show.[43]

Although mostly harmless hustle, spectacle did have a dark side. The publication surge contained the usual tales of great deeds and doers and many many how-to books. The tone differed little from previous eras, but a new genre sensationalized the most morbid moments. Thus unlike *The Games Climbers Play,* which offered a "selection of one hundred mountaineering articles," *The Armchair Mountaineer* promised "Triumphs and Tragedies of Ascent." This was mild compared to the grisly back-from-the-dead stories about permanent disfiguration, the latest of which is Aron Ralston's account of severing his hand to escape a Utah canyon. But for outright spectacle, nothing beat *The Mammoth Book of Mountain Disasters,* and it seems more than coincidental that Heinrich Harrer's grim chronicle of the Eiger's north face, *The White Spider,* stayed in print after 1959, or that bookstores now shelve the AAC's *Accidents in North American Mountaineering,* or that journalists only cover skiing, surfing, climbing, and kayaking when someone is hurt or dies, or that accident videos on YouTube are disturbingly popular. When the tourists in El Capitan Meadow train their scopes on climbers, a cultural space opens that is all too reminiscent of a NASCAR race.[44]

For the sheer complexity of consequences, little matched the sponsorship of climbers. This began in the 1950s as a "supra-national ideal of mountain brotherhood" among Europeans and in the 1960s as a nationalistic American agenda. Massive, military-like expeditions lost favor due to politicization, ecological impacts, and an unsporting tendency to prevail through sheer numbers, and clubs filled the gap, supporting younger climbers in the great ranges. Thus even as the American expedition took nineteen climbers, thirty-seven Sherpas, 400 sponsors, and 900 porters to Mount Everest, Jim McCarthy, Layton Kor, Dick McCracken, and Royal Robbins used a modest AAC grant to make a first ascent in the Yukon's Cirque of the Unclimbables. Small groups evoked the spirit of Eric Shipton and Bill Tilman, whose journeys off the maps of Asia, South America, and the Southern Ocean captivated young adventurers. Ensuing grants enabled more cutting-edge routes, but they also fueled greater reliance on petroleum. In 1935 and 1936, the RCS flew to Knight Inlet en route to Mount Waddington, as had teams traveling to the Cirque of Unclimbables in the 1950s and 1960s, but from there teams humped their loads. In 1971, AAC grant recipient Dennis Hennek used snowmobiles from Pangnirtung Fjord to Mount Asgard on Baffin Island. The next year Italians used helicopters, as did Hugh Burton and Steve Sutton in British Columbia's Bugaboos in 1973. By 1980, Denali's Kahiltna Glacier was a landing strip.[45]

The use of machines in the wilderness raised criticism, yet it paled before the disgust aimed at formal competitions. Donald Calhoun seriously misread rock climbing culture when he argued that it was "the exact antithesis of the American preoccupation with spectator sport." Climbers had always shown an intense if passive-aggressive competitiveness. The sin for traditionalists was in being overt. Other cultures regarded competition quite differently. The genesis of the professional climbing circuit that brought fame and money to Lynn Hill, ironically enough, was the Mountaineering Federation of the USSR. Since the 1940s it had held competitions to rank members, yet as Vitaly Abalakov noted in 1975, the Soviets believed "alpinism is naturally an extremely collective activity. . . . teamwork means more than competence for climbing with companions on one rope." Almost every Anglo climbing assumption inverted beyond the Iron Curtain.[46]

When détente policies encouraged exchanges between Soviets and Americans in the 1970s, ideas followed bodies across tense borders. At the Fifth Rock Climbing Championships in Yalta in 1974, Marek Brniak found a nearly objective form of sport. The routes were new to all competitors—no home court advantage—and pitches, or "control sections," were timed before a breathless audience. Flying away, Brniak wondered whether "those crazy competitive climbing lovers [would] turn the wonderful valleys into stadiums of concrete with rambunctious crowds of the mob, noisy cheap music, shrieking vendors of hot dogs, chewing-gum, soda pop inside the screaming stands?" The gap between this nightmare and daytime in Yosemite, where dirtbags played Hendrix on boomboxes while climbing El Capitan, was less than Brniak knew, yet the threat seemed dire enough that the AAC editorialized against it. Echoing Alfred Mummery and Geoffrey Young, William Putnam counseled members to "demonstrate our love for our mountains rather than our rivalry among men. Mountaineering . . . provides an escape from the super-competitiveness and hectic pace of day-to-day existence." Competition "can destroy this essential ingredient of the mountain experience without bringing in its place any beneficial result to the individual or society."[47]

It is hard to find a text more prescient about the prospect of change or more wrong about its effect. Putnam distilled many myths, all of which simplified past and future. His possessive yet altruistic rhetoric echoed the enlightened disinterest that mountaineers had cultivated since the Alpine Club. He tried to will back into being a genteel pastime wholly divorced from the world of Yosemite, Baffin, and Baltistan, and his nihilistic future did not anticipate the individual and communal benefits that flowed from competition. When surfers began to compete in 1954, the sport grew more popular and lucrative for entrepreneurs and athletes without extinguishing the anticompetitive soul surfer culture. Skiing thrived *because* of television. Skateboarding grew rapidly with competition-based publicity. Younger climbers who knew these sports did not necessarily share traditionalists' fears. Todd Skinner regarded the Russian Speed Climbing Championships as a stage for demonstrating American prowess. Alison Osius argued that "competition might help women's climbing" by providing more exposure for top women.[48]

The first American meets in the 1980s mirrored the Soviet system. Contestants were barred from routes beforehand, speed counted more than style, and events such as the Phoenix Bouldering Competition and California Bouldering Championships took place on natural rock. Europeans competed in England and across the continent. By mid-decade the circuit included Arco di Trento, Bardonecchia, and other sport-climbing havens, money prizes, a championship, and intense media coverage. In 1986 the contests moved indoors. Much like the skateboard parks of the American West in the 1970s, the "climbing gym" was a perfect venue for capturing consumers. Then in 1988 the circuit came to Utah's Snowbird ski resort. The event, held on a temporary, twelve-story structure attached to the lodge, was a financial bath but cultural watershed. Organizers lost their shirts. Vulgarian Dave Craft declared it "not climbing." Chouinard sarcastically remarked that it was "pretty sexy to see a well-honed woman in turquoise Lycra flowing up a difficult climb." David Roberts disliked the "overtly rivalrous" atmosphere, yet by the end he was "standing on my feet cheering wildly with the rest of the crowd." The spectacle had captivated. Ice climbers staged a contest by piping water from a reservoir near Telluride to make frozen waterfalls when nature did not comply, and sponsors in Europe and North America increased their financial backing.[49]

Lynn Hill, who in the early 1980s left California for love and fun in New York's Shawangunks, entered competitive climbing by chance during a trip to Europe in 1986. Her athletic gifts and competitiveness quickly shone. She placed well at the first Arco meet and nearly won the Sport Roccia title. The next year she did prevail, and by 1989 she was ranked the top woman in the world. In 1990, Hill ascended *Masse Critique* in Provence to become the first woman to climb 5.14. Then in a superfinal at Lyon, she was one of three competitors, and the only woman, to reach the top of the wall, and the only climber to complete the hardest move. At that moment Lynn Hill was arguably the best climber in the world, male or female. *Life, Newsweek,* and the *New York Times Magazine* featured her and her training methods, including a custom climbing wall in her attic.[50]

Artificial climbing walls had a long history. Climbers had scaled campus buildings for decades before Geoffrey Young wrote *A Roof-Climber's Guide to Trinity* in 1899. The Stanford Alpine Club and Caltech Climbers drove campus security to distraction in the 1950s. Europeans had built climbing structures since at least the 1940s, and Paris had an outdoor wall before 1960 for public demonstrations. In the 1970s Tacoma and the University of Washington poured aggregate concrete walls for local buffs. The public walls were made of masonry, stone, or wood, but a different technology emerged indoors. Quietly, many climbers were, like Hill, building training walls in garages, attics, and bedrooms. By the 1970s, English climbers formed modular holds from sand-embedded resins and glued them in place. Although this led the climber further from organic nature, the molded plastic holds often had the shape and texture of real rock. French climbers refined the system by making holds interchangeable with bolts. It was a short leap for entrepreneurs to open indoor gyms so urban-based climbers could train year-round, and competitions quickly increased their popularity and profitability.[51]

Outdoor sports such as kayaking were also popular, but none matched the growth of indoor climbing. Belgium had two gyms in 1985 and fifty by 1990. Seattle's Vertical Club was North America's first gym in 1987. By 1990 more operated in Portland, Boulder, and New York, and participation rose to perhaps 150,000 active climbers in the United States; by 2004 there were 7.6 million, 1.6 million of whom were classified as enthusiasts. Most telling, the indoor climbers outnumbered the outdoor climbers. By the millennium hundreds of gyms studded Europe and North America, ranging from socially exclusive venues to an abandoned chicken barn and iced-over silo in Iowa. Indoor climbers read a journal called *Urban Climber*, and gym owners formed the Climbing Wall Association to support their corner of the ever more complicated "outdoor" sports industry.[52]

What happened inside gyms only furthered segmentation. In some ways gyms seemed to revive club culture. Once past the ubiquitous waiver, women and men socialized as much or more than they climbed, yet gyms were not like clubs. There was no *us* at a gym, and the range of skills and ambitions was, in most senses, much narrower than the heterosocial RCS and SAC. There was diversity. For one thing gyms catered to families. Many firms accommodated parents and kids, but it was segregated play. There was family time, but there were also times when personnel and music catered to the hardcore, single, female, or aging athlete. There were times to play, practice, compete, and party, but nothing like the old mixing occurred in what was more accurately the serially homosocial world of the gym. For all its artificiality and tribalism, however, gyms were a binding agent. Requisite belay instruction, top ropes, and overhanging walls ensured that the falling climber dangled harmlessly. Gyms domesticated the sport, and their minimization of risk was why so many men, women, and children preferred to climb inside.[53]

Gyms allowed people to push limits without injurious falls, but their protective nature created novel threats. Gyms were ultimate environments. Hang boards and weight equipment enabled urban climbers to train muscles and tendons. Customizable holds and overhanging walls—which were a function of liability concerns—helped tune techniques on small holds that tested toe and first-knuckle strength. The result was a dramatic rise in overuse injuries. Tendonitis in hands and wrists affected 74 to 89 percent of sampled climbers. They were also plagued by new manifestations of the old "climber's finger" injury, known as "digital pulley injuries," which occurred when tendons shifted under extreme torque. Females suffered soft tissue injuries at higher rates than males, but even John Bachar's career was curtailed by chronic elbow pain from overtraining.[54]

Gyms consumed bodies, yet when gym rats ventured outdoors, which was not a given, they threatened much more. These were the sport climbers who traveled in packs, cavorted, and generally pissed off traditionalists. Their very presence exposed radically different ways of being in nature. Climbing was a boisterous social activity for sport climbers, but the cacophony of music, gabbing, laughing, and swearing was inimical to those seeking solitary adventure. As Lawrence Hamilton noted, the problems were "not only physical. Crowds of climbers in the mountains detract greatly from each individual's experiences; the illusions of wilderness and adventure can be irreparably damaged." The resulting battles were as much about the environmental aesthetics of play as the sporting implications of techniques. A primary worry, as one ranger said, was the fear that "if you bolt it, they will come." In other ways all climbers shared key traits. As gear and bodies improved, they all pushed themselves to the breaking point. Major accidents did not increase above the long-term average, but stress-related injuries rose sharply. Greg Child thus got it right when he declared, "We are the ibuprofen generation."[55]

Climbers were alike in other ways as well. Dick Jones once told the RCS that competitive climbing was "taboo." "To climb against the time records of others is absolutely wrong," yet it was a part of the game. With the advent of competitions, traditionalists seemed to drop pretense. Valley climbers had accelerated up El Capitan since the second ascent of *The Nose*. When Bridwell, Long, and Westbay climbed it in a day, the route became a kind of vertical dash. In 1992, Peter Croft and Hans Florine set the time at 4:22, which was cut to 3:24 in 2001 and to 2:45:45 in 2007. The next step was to link routes. In the 1940s RCS member Harriett Parsons criticized this practice, but in 1986 über traditionalists John Bachar and Peter Croft "enchained" *The*

Nose and *Northwest Face* in 20:40. Some mourned the diminution of routes. Others sought to be the fastest man, woman, women, or other categorical first. Contests were explicit. When Dean Potter soloed El Cap and Half Dome in 23 hours, two days later Florine dropped it to 21:03. There *was* room for humor. When Potter and Steph Davis climbed the *Northwest Face* in 3:59, Potter declared, "That pretty much blows away the male/female record." Davis replied, "Ah—the x and y chromosome record."[56]

As speed and enchainments became popular feats, even the traditionalists joined the spectacle. Peter Croft insisted it was "not the times and records that count, but the adventure," yet when he and Bachar linked El Capitan and Half Dome, an alerted friend breathlessly reported the ascent in *Climbing*. Photographers regularly documented the pair, proving that publicity and adventure were no longer mutually exclusive. Meanwhile, sport climbers searched the valley for prizes. When Ray Jardine left Yosemite, Mark Hudon, Max Jones, and Stefan Glowacz took over the quest to free El Capitan, settling on *The Salathé Wall* as a likely route because some cracks on *The Nose* were too thin for fingers. Eventually Todd Skinner and Paul Piana succeeded in 1989, but their ascent was noteworthy as much for their methods as for the achievement. Both were outsiders, especially after Skinner hang-dogged a coveted route in 1985, so the two secretly plotted an array of sport tactics. Skinner built a special gym to perfect hard moves, and the team made "camping trips" up the wall to work pitches with top ropes, draw notes and arrows with chalk, and even mend their shredded hands with Super Glue. After a month of reconnaissance, they returned to ground to make a "first" free ascent in one continuous push, photographer in tow.[57]

Other climbers freed additional big-wall routes, but none garnered more acclaim than Lynn Hill's free ascents of *The Nose*. After retiring from competition, Hill was at loose ends, seeking the next big thing when former boyfriend John Long remarked that *The Nose* was "one of the last great problems in American free climbing." It was a good fit. Hill had climbed the route in her teens, she was as talented as anyone, and as Long noted, her tiny fingers were "secret weapons." As in women's gymnastics, flexibility, strength-to-weight ratios, and sheer small size had become advantages in the climbing world of the late 1980s and early 1990s. Sue McDevitt, five feet tall and "103 pounds soaking wet," similarly tiny Beth Rodden, and preadolescent Tori Allen became top climbers indoors and out for similar reasons. In 1992, Hill and Florine reconnoitered *The Nose* while setting the X and Y chromosome record at 8:40. Hill then worked it with nonlocal partners, and sure enough her slender fingers got purchase where men clawed in vain. Hill wired the moves and in September 1993 made a ground-to-summit ascent in four days with Brooke Sandahl. "The next obvious challenge," she remarked, was to repeat it "faster or in better style," so in 1994, Hill freed *The Nose* in one day, leading all pitches herself.[58]

Hill's feats were called "burly" and "among the world's great rock-climbing accomplishments," but her remarks embodied tensions that had long stalked the sport. She said the ascents were about "the spirit of liberation, of following what felt natural to me, regardless of the expectations or judgments of others," yet she was part of a great chain of being. "My own inspiration and achievements . . . are simply an extension of the experiences, passion and vision of others." Her desire to honor and escape the past collided. Hill said it was dishonest to claim "the first free ascent of a climb that had been made easier by chiseling holds," yet like everyone else she had used Jardine's holds. There was also the spectacle. Hill contrasted the "contrived, scripted form of grace" in gymnastics with her "beautifully free-form and spontaneous" climbs, yet she staged film and support crews at key points to capture the spontaneity of her one-day ascent. The result was a fiasco. Cameramen balked, batteries failed, and Hill bonked. She succeeded her next try, without most of the photographers, beginning at 10 P.M. and ending twenty-three hours later with an amazing do-or-forget-it lunge into the dark at 9 P.M. The point is not to diminish her feat, nor to dismiss her attempt at recognition for it, but rather to notice that her ascent, like every other elite climb in the waning decades of the twentieth century, was intended as a consumable experience. The line between climbers and consumers no longer existed. They were us and we were them.[59]

13. SURVIVORS

It was Me Me I I Me Me.
—ERIC PEHOTA

Like most people, climbers vacillated between embracing and resisting the past. They all venerated the founders, but traditionalists tended to act like fundamentalist preachers, admonishing sinners to follow sacred texts literally. They, along with other wilderness advocates, imagined an immaculate past, and it was no coincidence that they shared many saints. Muir, Adams, Brower, Chouinard, and Rowell formed a sporting and spiritual genealogy extending back to a seminally pure beginning, and values were essential, singular, and timeless. I once witnessed the power of this mindset when a screaming match erupted between friends, spittle flying wildly, over whether one had rested on a piton. The sin was a supposed breach of faith, a trespass of sport and nature. It was then that I realized Chuck Pratt was correct: climbers do have a religion, but it is one that has thrived by simplifying a very messy past.

This selective vision was on full display one evening in September 1999. The event was a celebration. The National Park Service had suggested converting Sunnyside Campground—the name climbers had long ignored in favor of Camp 4—into much-needed employee dorms, whereupon Tom Frost, Richard Duane, Pat Ament, and others nominated the site to the National Register of Historic Places, while Steve Roper reminded younger generations of Camp 4's past. Lawsuits, petitions, and negotiations reversed the NPS decision. That moment represented nothing less than a federal validation of the sport, and climbers wanted to party. In a park that annually hosted 4 million visitors, 1.5 million cars, and 13,000 buses, six hundred climbers gathered to reminisce. The NPS capped the night by announcing it would revert to calling the site *Camp 4*.[1]

The celebration was recorded for posterity, while a second film narrated by Yvon Chouinard's climbing buddy Tom Brokaw wove the evening into a history that married John Muir to "no trace," climbing to environmentalism, and mountaineering to Camp 4. The valley was narrowed to a tale about elites by elites. Clubs and women vanished, as did the tangled relationships among climbers, concessionaires, constables, consumers, and contexts. The commemoration reduced Camp 4 to a hermetic Eden of vertically bound Adams. The gaps between forgiving memory and inconvenient evidence were not new. Previous debates over the 1950 French ascent of Annapurna, the 2000 kidnapping of four Americans in Kyrgyzstan, and Southern California surf and skate shops revealed an uneasy melding of memory and history. Valley climbers remembered NPS oppression but forgot the many moments of mutual accommodation.[2]

These elisions extend to climbers' impact on environmental culture. Michael Cohen has argued that "the men who opened up routes on the high peaks were expressing their love for the mountains," and that some matured into "conservation warriors" and the SC's "most energetic campaigners for conservation." This is true as far as it goes. Muir, Adams, Leonard, Robinson, Brower, Chouinard, Rowell, and Tompkins were influential, but this explains neither the sources nor effects of love. Pilgrims of the vertical exhibited a passion that seemingly paralleled other pilgrims. All risked life for spiritual quests, and all romanticized death. Climbers denied they harbored death wishes, and indeed very few were suicidal. Less easy to answer is why they willingly took risks and what their priorities revealed about their relationship to nature and to society.[3]

First an easy retort. Climbers are simply wrong when they insist that climbing is no more dangerous than, say, driving a car. The actuarials were nowhere near the same. Chouinard admitted, "I stopped counting when the death toll for my friends reached 50," and Rowell lost twice as many. Most deaths happened at elevation on bigger, more dangerous mountains, as when Rob Slater, Alison Hargreaves, and five others died during a storm on Pakistan's K2, or when an avalanche buried Alex Lowe on Tibet's Shishapangma. Still, in Yosemite fifteen climbers died from 1990 to 2000, while twenty-two people died in vehicular accidents, yet the latter pool was vastly larger. Climbing *was* lethal, even in Yosemite. Exploring the vertical required navigating slick terrain, dodging debris, and trusting uncertain technology. Climbers slipped while descending trails or were struck by rocks. Bolts failed, or bolts held but granite failed. The soloing deaths of Derek Hersey, Tobin Sorenson, Michael Reardon, and John Bachar were obvious examples of how even elites could miscalculate risk, as were the deaths of Todd Skinner and Dan Osman when their equipment broke on Yosemite's Leaning Tower. The single-engine planes that carried climbers also posed risks, as when Galen and Linda Rowell died while returning from Alaska.[4]

Yosemite's fatalities represent a milder version of the tragedies that have stalked outdoor sports. Mountaineering deaths around the world grew as the sport became more popular, and big-wave surfing, extreme skiing, and storm kayaking resembled athletic forms of Russian roulette. Thus while everything in life carried risks, outdoor athletes marked themselves by eagerly embracing it. Royal Robbins insisted "climbing requires that there be danger," and that "risk is in the final analysis an essential ingredient." Rowell said "joy comes from overcoming risk without killing yourself," yet he "definitely" believed "it's better to live a short life and push yourself." Extreme skier Bill Briggs was blunt: "If there's no risk, there's no adventure," but as one surfer noted, danger was "like a drug. You get the thrill fairly easily at first, but then it becomes harder to achieve and you have to ride larger and larger waves in order to get that feeling back." The insidious escalation of risk in Yosemite was endemic to all outdoor sports, as was athletes' intensely self-centered focus. Big-wall climber Pete Takeda told himself, "I am my own god. I live life. Life doesn't live me." Skier Eric Pehota admitted, "It was Me Me I I Me Me. . . . You just wanted to keep pushin' it. See how big and steep you could go without killing yourself." Overcoming risk gave Chouinard "an incredible elation to being alive." Stefano DeBenedetti felt like "a little Superman."[5]

This sense of self-possession, of embracing risk to assert one's mastery of life hinged on monumental nature. Daniel Duane called El Capitan his "ten-megaton Old Testament God." Others were similarly drawn, and most were no more articulate than when George Mallory told reporters he coveted Mount Everest "Because it is there." Modern climbers dismiss the remark as unreflective of Mallory's intellect, proof of how difficult it is to express something deep, but Mallory's biographers see instead a succinct answer to "a fundamental truth." Mallory wanted Everest because it was the biggest thing around; if there had been a higher peak he would have gone there instead. Mallory tested himself on Everest the way others climbed El Capitan or surfed Mavericks or skied Mont Blanc: because monumental nature was there and, as DeBenedetti said, because it "was my way to become a man."[6]

The result was a powerful fusion of nature and the self. Athletes, like many environmentalists, anchored their identities to "transcendent experiences of unity with nature." An extreme example was Timothy Treadwell, who sought out grizzly bears and eventually, with partner Amie Huguenard, died when one attacked. Extreme athletes were less extreme, but they, too, maintained a bubble by telling themselves their avocations were "something only somebody fairly smart could do," that their "self-reliance and independence" set them apart, that risk enabled them "to reach creatively to the most elusive core of the most complex problems," and that "survival sharpens their perceptions and increases their love of life." It made perfect sense for

Mark Twight to equate "maturity as a climber" with maturity as "a human being," but this individualistic view could go too far. When stories filtered down
from Everest of climbers ignoring the dead and dying to reach the top, the
community disowned such trespasses.[7]

Ostracism did not follow from any abiding dedication to the fallen.
Climbers were just as quick to distance the dead. The core value of self-
control permeated disaster debriefings. The AAC's annual *Accidents in North
American Mountaineering* and the "Staying Alive" essays in valley guidebooks, while concerned with safety, also sustained a conceit that climbers
could, with sufficient study, "actually control the risk." Like early test pilots,
climbers blamed victims for not having the right stuff. Ruth Dyar said those
who died "were not 'real mountaineers' and did not know what they were
doing." The RCS told *Time*, "failure . . . was due to poor judgment, and lack of
experience, skill and equipment . . . this is typical of most mountaineering
accidents in the U.S." Within the community expertise trumped all. Thus real
climbers could legitimately dispense with ropes and other, as Roper put it,
"impedimenta." David Brower told Will Siri, "I don't like a helmet and won't
wear one if I can help it when I am climbing for fun." The alternative gets
"yourself mixed up with steel workers, soldiers and crash drivers." The point
was to takes risks to prove mastery of the self and nature.[8]

Unfortunately, shit happened. Nature, gear, and judgment did fail. Even
close calls underscored the limits of control. In 1986, I made a roped solo
of the relatively easy *Snake Dike* route on the southwest face of Half Dome.
The hard moves were low, followed by easy dikes and low-angle slabs. Bored,
I went exploring, traversing off route toward a big roof near the south face.
I was so engrossed in the adventure I ran out of rope 155 feet from my anchor with no intervening protection. The farther I went, the closer I was to
my limits. A slip would have led at least to an uncontrolled 160-foot skin-
grinding, bone-punishing pendulum. I got scared and began to retrace my
moves, doing the best bit of climbing I never recounted until now. I was
lucky but hardly alone. Yvon Chouinard fell 160 feet before his belay held,
but he was on one of the Tetons' few overhanging walls. Rowell had a hold
break and by the time his belay held, he was "upside down, my head three
feet from a pointed rock." Lynn Hill fell seventy feet after her rope came un-
tied, but a tree broke her fall and she landed miraculously between two boulders. Mark Melvin had a bolt snap, resulting in a "sudden five foot static fall"
that loaded huge forces onto the only other bolt holding him and his belayer.
None were slackers like me, yet all owed as much to chance. David Roberts
said few climbers "really accept the role of sheer luck in our survival." Talk of
self-control was a "smug recipe" for "pure rationalization."[9]

These were the messy details outdoor athletes overlooked. My first wife met me on top of Half Dome. We spent the evening watching the Perseid meteor showers and discussing the day. I never mentioned my idiot adventure—that was my business. She would only have worried about things that had not happened, and the discussion would only have complicated my fun. Again, I was not alone. Roberts wrote, if "one reads only the books and articles of climbers themselves, one might never suspect that the choice to risk life and limb had any moral consequences." Climbers were not unique. To do almost anything well we must specialize, forswearing some paths to take advantage of others, but risk takers rarely acknowledged the implications of their choices. Only in middle age did Lynn Hill admit it was her "ability to focus single-mindedly [that] enabled me to climb fiercely hard routes," but the result was "a rather restricted experience in life." In fact most people dwelled only on the positive traits. In one opinion survey respondents said climbers were "ambitious," "determined," and "striving," all the things Hill personified.[10]

They could also be intensely loyal. Alison Osius found "a bonding with people—trusting, sharing, communicating" that made "your life much richer." Climbers were there for each other in good times and bad, but they could also stifle. Belonging meant rites of passage and an expectation of conformity, and personal relationships were increasingly limned by a group that in some ways was literally an extended family. Julie Brugger remembered that "climbing isolated us from other people and other experiences that would have allowed us to grow in different ways." These were among the things climbers did not discuss.[11]

Thus traits like "selfish," "insular," and "incurious" also fit. Risk takers could even rationalize death as a validation. Doug Coombs once remarked,

> I remember being really shocked when a friend died skiing and then the next friend died skiing and then the next . . . you just become numb to it. It's still terrible, and you don't like it, but it doesn't make you stop. I hate seeing people that I know die, but I know it's going to happen. I mean, that's just part of it. It's like saying you know someone who's died in a car accident. You know, what's worse: the car accident or falling off the mountain? . . . I think the car accident is worse. At least when they're falling off the mountain, they love what they were doing.

When Coombs fell off the Couloir de Polichinelle, his widow said "We never questioned our life. . . . We knew that the risks that we encountered were worth every bit of it." Left unsaid was how Coombs's son felt about those risks.[12]

That may seem harsh, but outdoor athletes have excelled at externalizing costs. Families who worried were ignored. Survivors who criticized were marginalized. Take for example the partners of Alex Lowe, Peter Boardman, and Joe Tasker. When Lowe died, friend and partner Conrad Anker married his widow and parented his kids. Jennifer Lowe-Anker stayed in the community, but Maria Coffey and Hillary Boardman represented "a reality which [climbers] preferred to turn away from. They had spouses, lovers, families who would suffer if they died in the mountains. It seemed that by going to Everest we were somehow stepping into their arena and bringing with us tangible proof of the pain they risked inflicting by indulging in such a dangerous sport."[13]

Discussing those costs opened a Pandora's box. One of the sport's most introspective voices, Tom Hornbein admitted that he had "dexterously ignored" these issues. When Coffey revealed "what it was like to be in love with someone who came home from an expedition, dallied briefly in the pleasure of loving and being loved, but, restless, was soon off," it was like "a dash of cold water." Hornbein had "pursued dreams, grown confident, learned to survive, acquired a love of the wilderness, and shared special moments with kindred spirits," but Coffey placed those gifts in context. For others, facing the realities of life on the mountain only strengthened their resolve. When a friend died on Minya Gonga in China, Chouinard "went into an incredible depression. But when I came out of it I had lost all fear of dying. And it's helped me to cope with my feeling that mankind as a species has ended its day. That thought used to really get me down. Now I think, hey, we're all gonna die. Maybe all at once, and so be it. We're an incredibly damaging species, and we're pulling all these other beautiful species down with us, and maybe we ought to just get out of here. You do what you can. Then—even if you're burning gasoline to get there—you just have to say fuck it, let's go surfing."[14]

For the less nihilistic, survivors were ethical Rubicons. Hornbein conceded that climbing was "hard to justify to loved ones and others who hold some stake in the climber's continued existence." It was "about as far from selfless sacrifice as one can get." John Thackray accused climbers of falling "in love with themselves every time they elude death. They have a narcissistic relationship to death, and preen in front of those dark mirrors. At each escape . . . there's a little infantile voice within that shouts gleefully: 'Hey, look at me! I'm terrific!'" Even Roberts, who had long defended risk-taking, concluded that such inspiring books as William O. Douglas's *Of Men and Mountains* and Gaston Rébuffat's *Starlight and Storm* were "intellectually flaccid." Roberts had climbed in many places yet regarded himself as "a culturally insensitive and incurious traveler with a monomaniacal passion for mountain walls." Lynn Hill rued missing so "many other aspects of the world around me." Pete Takeda admitted, "I created much pain, for myself and others." As climbers had kids or lost friends, new perspectives emerged. Eventually Jim Beyer, Roger Breedlove, Charlie Clarke, John Evans, Sibylle Hechtel, Bev Johnson, Jean Ruwitch, and Andrew Todhunter all concluded, like Roberts, that "climbing made a very poor model for how to get through 'normal' life."[15]

This was especially true for relationships. Hill's successes "made it difficult to maintain a stable personal life." Brooding about "what mountaineering cost me," Roberts wondered "whether I might have been a better husband" and "a better son." In an essay titled "Growing Up Scared," Valerie Mendenhall Cohen needed "to say there was a definite downside" to having parents who prioritized climbing. "Now that I have been a mother myself, I think my parents' leaving me so often and for so long with other people . . . cold." In my case, mom always requested I call her after trips. The obvious implication was to know I had survived. I used to think this silly, but no longer: I have a daughter. Similarly, when former climber Steve Friedman learned his sister's dirtbag boyfriend would soon become his dirtbag brother-in-law, he confessed, "I feel a kinship with you. It is not a good feeling." Even if nothing bad happened, every departure was a little death, every leaving an occasion to hold one's breath. The emotional costs strained families and lovers, and like Maria Coffey, many concluded they were "glad to be distanced from that world. . . . It taught me enough."[16]

Risk-taking was not essentially gendered. Bev Johnson said she loved the "amazing" feeling of "the edge. . . . incredible calmness, no panic, no fear—completely controlled but without tension," but how climbers interacted did reveal differences. Few men devoted ink to nonclimbers. Joe Brown's wife earned a photo and paragraph in his autobiography; Dougal Haston's wife merited a sentence. Women climbers, by contrast, wove people into their tales. Sue Giller described women climbers as "willing to make communications . . . a goal," but men "tend[ed] to be a little bit more closed." This begs context. While men did say little and even reveled in "the feeling that very little needed saying," this was partly because climbing separated and exhausted in a gender-neutral manner. Even the cheerful Molly Higgins admitted, "I don't swear anymore, it takes too much energy. I don't even sing. When

I'm belaying I just sit with my head against the rock and doze." A stunned Barbara Eastman replied, "You nap when you're belaying me?"[17]

Parenting also divided. While men could climb childless or as parents without censure, women were judged either way. Bev Johnson wanted to "love someone . . . [and to] have children" but was "afraid to cast about in that sea." As friends built families, she found the "ties with them were less and less." Conversely, Alison Hargreaves was assailed by the British press as a bad mother after dying on K2. Her defenders noted that fathers who died on mountains suffered no comparable rebuke, yet insisting that women should be just as free simply lowered the bar. Similarly, Jon Krakauer's *Into the Wild* elided the ethical lapses of Chris McCandless's tragic quest in Alaska to instead linger on a final self-photo, "at peace, serene as a monk gone to God." It took nonclimber Sean Penn's film version to expose the visceral effects of loss. Both men and women increasingly regard risk-taking as an individualistic right, yet a century ago Samuel Turner wrote, "if I had known what I would have to go through, I should have decided that it was not right for a married man to take such risks which . . . took all the pleasure away, and gave me, instead, that unreasonable, unsatisfying thirst for adventure which leads to fatal results."[18]

Individualistic and experientialist athletes have reigned in the United States since 1955, redefining risk as a benefit and transforming outdoor sports from a communal to a private engagement with nature. These pilgrims of the vertical embraced nature for its symbolic values. The goods, stories, and wilderness they consumed were the means to a personal relationship with nature. To sustain it, they extended their tunnel vision about social relationships to their material interactions with nature. Climbers' ecological impacts were as problematic as their risk-taking, and the evolving environmental culture was just as dependent upon ignoring the messy details.[19]

No discussion of environmental impacts can proceed without attention to demography. By 2000 over 145 million Americans played outdoor sports. About 8.8 million (>4 percent) climbed, 14 million kayaked, 68.8 million camped, and 71.8 million hiked. Hunting and angling continued long declines from peak levels in the 1950s, while snowboarding and surfing grew by 51.2 and 25.6 percent just from 2000 to 2001. Early magazines still thrived because of their established reporting and advertising networks. Climbers bought *Climbing* and *Rock & Ice,* surfers *Surfing* and *Tracks,* kayakers *American Whitewater,* and skaters *Skateboarder,* but now these periodicals were networked. Action Sports Group owned *Bike, Canoe & Kayak, Fantasy Surfer, Powder, Skate, Snow, Surfer, Surfing,* and *Wavewatch. Urban Climber* teamed with Big City Mountaineers. Growth and segmentation produced economies of scale for even niche publications such as *Speed Climbing, Alpinist, She Sends,* and *Surf Girl.*[20]

By 2003 the industry generated $50 billion in sales, and contests for market position were fierce. As Jim Bridwell noted in 1974, innovation had been "a two-sided coin: a nuisance to climbers and a boon for manufacturers," but his efforts to stop the trend through "decreation" were in vain. Technology was intrinsic to the sport. By the mid-1970s it took $150 to get started; by the mid-1980s the baseline was $250. Cams, which cost several to ten times a piton, only accelerated inflation. Warren Harding boycotted the devices on principle, yet the trend toward ever more sophisticated gear only accelerated. After 1990 many outdoor magazines published special annual "Gear Guide" issues. The stakes could be high. When two writers left *Climbing* to run the rival *Rock & Ice,* their former employer sued for conspiracy. Rainier Mountaineering Incorporated, which had a guiding monopoly at Mount Rainier since the 1960s, complained when the NPS proposed to open the peak to other guide services.[21]

As consumption mainstreamed climbing, climbers entered pop culture. Mountain Dew leveraged the ennui of extreme athletes who had "Climbed that . . . Skied that" and needed reenergizing by sugar- and caffeine-saturated drinks. Real climbers hocked airlines, batteries, beers, deodorants, haute couture, SUVs, and war. In 1995, Comcast launched Outdoor Life Network to televise extreme sports. Starbucks used an inspiring quotation from climber Ed Viesturs on its cups. The teen Tori Allen hocked an action figure doll. Hollywood even made climbing an emblem of feminist empowerment when Kelly Preston shouted, "I did the 23-hour Nose-Route to the top of El Capitan in 6 hours!" and then punched Tom Cruise. When parsed, these messages revealed less about the sport than the market's ability to domesticate. Advertisers used climbers to project desires and fears consumers already nurtured. Climbers were just another signifier of toned bodies, nice scenery, and "possessive individualism."[22]

It all exacerbated pressures. The guidebooks one climber called "ego books" became maps leading outsiders to Yosemite, and NPS Golden Eagle Passes made coming more affordable. Climbing ranger Mead Hargis noted "that anyone who has taught a friend to climb, written an article, manufactured or sold equipment has contributed towards this increase." Others wanted to keep new routes secret and make climbers explore on their own, but egos were irrepressible. Most climbers liked the recognition, but some peaks were overrun when Fred Beckey, Steve Roper, and Allen Steck published *Mountains of North America* and *Fifty Classic Climbs*—the latter satirized as "Fifty Crowded Classics"—to highlight important routes. Even Baffin Island experienced more helicopters and tourists. Climbing had always been a density-dependent sport, but the aesthetic concerns of adventure were increasingly accompanied by ecological issues.[23]

Actually, climbers have always packed an environmental wallop. By the 1890s Alfred Mummery saw "large quantities" of "broken glass and sardine boxes" on the Matterhorn, and in 1938 Lord Schuster complained that the Riffelhorn was "so polished by the thousands of feet that had trodden [it] that I was in fear of slipping at every step." Fifty years later human excrement and trash littered routes from Yosemite to the Himalaya. Ledges smelled of "sewage" and water seeps were septic. Climbers had to adopt backpacking practices, carrying out what they brought in. Some even organized garbage runs. In 1973 they filled many trash bags at the base of Half Dome, seventeen more in 1980, and twenty-two in 1990. Even after decades of stewardship, in 1995 volunteers stuffed thirty bags just on *The Nose*. Rangers blamed "a small group," but as I walked El Capitan's base one spring, I was struck by how my daypack slowly filled with bits of duct tape, gear, and trash from all along the cliff.[24]

Nature is no simple victim. Earthquakes rearranged valley features and human psyches, and rockfall from Middle Brother has forced the NPS to close routes that had been popular since the 1930s. Most spectacularly, two granite blocks fell from Glacier Point in 1996, creating an air blast that flattened trees and killed a hiker. Another deadly slide killed a climber in 1999 and spurred a lawsuit that ended all climbing on Glacier Point. But usually nature suffered worse. When not gardening cracks, stripping bryophytes, or wire-brushing rock, climbers trampled vegetation and disrupted habitat. Skeins of "volunteer trails" killed plants and exacerbated physical and chemical erosion. Land managers diverted budgets to consolidate trails, replant slopes, and channel runoff. The NPS prohibited camping atop Half Dome and closed routes to protect endangered species. Soles polished granite, hands greased holds, and bodies scraped lichen. Routes slowly turned into white vertical stripes; walls began to resemble zebras. One conspicuous example is *Nutcracker Suite*, whose zigzag course can be seen a mile away because of the lightning-bolt scar thousands of climbers have created retracing Royal Robbins's pioneer effort at clean climbing.[25]

These adverse impacts reignited old fires. Still incensed about bolts, rapbolting, and hang-dogging, traditionalists blamed sport climbers and argued that traditionalist values should be official values. By 1991, though, environ-

Figure 13.1. The ecological impact of outdoor sports became ever more apparent as participation grew after World War II. Some instances of harm were spectacular, such as the discovery of this trash dump on El Capitan's Thanksgiving Ledge by clean-up volunteers in 1998, yet of far greater impact were the bits of trash, the human waste, and the relentless traffic over the bases and faces of every climbing area in the world by the late 1990s.

mentalists were criticizing all climbers. Citing provisions in the 1964 Wilderness Act that prohibit "motorized equipment" and "permanent installations," the Wilderness Society informed the Forest Service and NPS that bolts and other fixed gear were illegal. Meanwhile, Yosemite planners so expanded official wilderness boundaries that all land more than a quarter mile from, or one hundred feet above, a roadway was restricted. Climbers feared being evicted by bureaucratic legerdemain, so several formed the Access Fund, surveyed Yosemite's diverse climbing constituency, and with the Sierra Club —which had parted with the Wilderness Society on fixed gear—lobbied to ameliorate environmental impacts *and* ensure that climbing remained a legitimate activity in parks and wilderness areas.[26]

Negotiations were tortured and tortuous across many public lands. Correspondence among managers at Arizona's Superstition Mountains, Joshua Tree National Monument, Idaho's City of Rocks, Colorado's Front Range, St. Lawrence Valley's cliffs, and New York's Shawangunks revealed a continental conversation about climbing, yet plans were ultimately organic to each community. Rangers considered zoning Yosemite like a city, allotting spaces to climbers using different methods, but this proved biased and unenforceable. Climbers were often no help. Some claimed a libertarian right to climb anytime and anywhere; others were just as certain that fixed gear was illegal and that climbing had one true tradition. The only thing they shared was a fear of government regulation, but that was enough to force a grudging consensus: ban motorized drills, accept manual drills, and end bolt-chopping. Many doubted that climbers could manage themselves, but rangers did not want the job. In an era of falling budgets and rising crime, the Yosemite Association had to fund a climbing ranger privately to mediate among climbers and the NPS.[27]

Other sports experienced similar access problems. BASE jumpers were reviled because they tended to die when leaping off tall places with parachutes, and cavers, hang gliders, kayakers, and snowmobilers incited an array of aesthetic and environmental concerns. Still, no sport had an issue that matched climbers' fixation with bolts. Sport climbers continued to view bolts as advancing standards, especially on face climbs where traditional protection was unavailable, while traditionalists continued to see bolts as the root of all evil. One traditionalist claimed that bolts accelerated exfoliation. Another dismissed trash and erosion as "temporary" issues but viewed tolerance of bolts as eroding "our respect for the environment." Fixed gear clearly undermined what Lawrence Hamilton called "the illusions of wilderness and adventure," but traditionalists' ecological arguments were suspect. One biologist concluded that "Anchors in no way, shape, or form are affecting biodiversity." Bolts did enable usage, but most damage was caused by simple traffic. This was vexing because impacts could be worse on traditionally protected routes than on heavily bolted, very difficult sport climbs. On popular routes flora was gouged, habitat trampled, and lichen scrubbed, bolts or no bolts. *High Country News* asked, "Have rock climbers turned from environmental crusaders into an environmental menace?"[28]

Beyond their immediate impacts on rock, climbers only gradually became aware of the environmental costs of the technology they brought to the mountains. The backpackers' mantra, "Leave No Trace," was echoed best by Doug Robinson in 1972: "Clean is climbing the rock without changing it; a step closer to organic climbing for the natural man." In practice, though, such environmental sensitivity required an increasing array of consumer goods. One advocacy campaign even counseled climbers to buy and carry ever more stuff to fulfill these clean climbing goals. Clean was achieved by using the right gear, but this made sense only by externalizing some costs. The shift to chocks and cams involved not only a change in designs but in materials and energy. New tools were made from aluminum and titanium, which were forged with electricity that produced fewer emissions than coke furnaces but far more BTUs, and ore from foreign mines created unregulated environmental damage. Full-cost accounting complicated clean climbers' arguments. Broader perspective led Ray de Sassure in 1952, Mike Loughman in 1958, and Al Errington, Galen Rowell, and Chip Salaun in the 1970s to suggest that bolts were environmentally better because they reduced consumption. Bolted routes enabled climbers to carry less gear, and vertical ecology— aside from lichen—got a break.[29]

For anyone other than bolt manufacturers this held no sway. Resistance was not purely materialistic, yet pecuniary interests did matter. Many outdoor manufacturers integrated environmental values with corporate images. Surfboard makers sought greener materials and processes, entrepreneurs supported environmental organizations, and climbers lent their names to issues. Royal Robbins funded causes. Galen Rowell spoke on China's oppression of Tibet. These were good works, yet they hinged on resources derived from consumption. Outdoor athletes were invested in contradictory relationships with nature. No one more clearly illustrated this than Yvon Chouinard.[30]

Yvon and Malinda Chouinard were extraordinarily successful entrepreneurs, widely admired for innovations in design, the workplace, and marketing. Their adaptation of piled polyester and polypropylene for rugged, lightweight, quick-drying garments made Patagonia, Inc. the industry standard. In the 1970s, Malinda made the company more family friendly with a childcare center and novel flextime policy so employees could schedule work around play. Escalating sales and profit sharing made the then Lost Arrow, Inc. the envy of many. Analysts were fascinated by the company's understated pitch, what one reporter called "anti-marketing," and its dedication to environmental advocacy. In the 1990s, Patagonia, Inc. shifted to organic cotton and, when assessments revealed this was still ecologically damaging, to recycled cotton and synthetics from recycled plastic bottles. The Chouinards also instituted a tithing program, giving 2 percent of pretax profits to causes at first and rising to 10 percent by 1985 and 1 percent of net sales by 1996. In 2001, they and Craig Matthews founded 1% for the Planet Alliance to foster similar tithing programs around the business world.[31]

Yvon Chouinard backed his words like few others, but it was through business, not climbing, that he gained influence. His concern for wild nature was longstanding, but for two decades he had been known primarily as a cranky traditionalist, not an environmental firebrand. When his image did shift in the 1980s, he quickly distinguished himself by confronting consumption. Patagonia, Inc.'s policies on cotton and synthetics were one example; another was his self-critique. He told a reporter, "we're part of the problem, too. . . . There's no such thing as making sustainable clothing, any of that stuff. We're causing a lot of pollution and causing a lot of waste. That's just the way it is and we recognize that and that's why we . . . do our penance." He even advised shoppers to buy used clothing. If climbing was an economy of spectacle, then Chouinard used his capital to make people pause. Like its rivals, Patagonia, Inc. sponsored athletes, but its ambassadors wrote more on environmentalism than clothes. John Sherman called dirtbags model nonconsumers. Ron Kauk backed contemplative climbing. Chouinard lectured on corporate responsibility. Many admirers did not know he had climbed. To them he was, to use *Time*'s phrase, "A Hero of the Planet."[32]

But Patagonia, Inc. was not an environmental organization; it was a business that competed for customers. When it signed Dean Potter as an ambassador, Patagonia, Inc. hoped he would enhance the bottom line. At first it was a good bet. Potter was ambitious, setting speed records on Half Dome and El Capitan, and in 2002 free soloing the difficult and dangerous Cerro Fitzroy and Cerro Torre in the Southern Patagonian Ice Field. Potter was called soulful and spiritual and likened to Stylite monks for his fanaticism and exhibitionism. That volatile combination served both until May 2006, when Potter soloed Delicate Arch. The climb was announced by his handler at Patagonia, Inc., and just as quickly Arches National Park rewrote its rules to prevent a repeat. Other climbers were outraged. Potter climbed the arch perhaps six times to rehearse and film moves with help from friends who ascended a fixed rope to the top. He said he was inspired to climb as an artistic expression and to commune with nature. Critics focused on rope marks in the soft sandstone and noted that locals had abstained from the arch so they could climb elsewhere in the park. Now they, not Potter, faced new restrictions. Potter also seemed oblivious to the fact that the arch was an icon, emblazoned on Utah license plates and Olympic medals. Company officers encouraged Potter to apologize, but he turned petulant, insisting he did nothing wrong and regretting only "the negative publicity."[33]

The climb was a debacle. Even close friends called Potter a publicity seeker, but the rougher the comments, the more he dug in, insisting he was perfectly in his right as "a climber. I feel compelled to climb most everything I see." Neither did he apologize for the publicity. He was "a professional athlete" and "recognition of what I do is part of the job." If anything, he was a victim "deeply hurt" by the "split this has put in our climbing community." His only apology went to Patagonia, Inc. "for the injury this has caused the company and the brand." The harm was real. The company scrambled to distance itself, denying any prior knowledge of the climb. Otherwise it had "no position." Within the company there was no consensus. Some officers sympathized because Potter broke no law; others felt he defied the law's spirit. The longer Patagonia, Inc. stayed silent, the worse the optics seemed. Rick Ridgeway, the vice president of environment and marketing, admitted that it was "a blow against Patagonia's reputation for having a strong environmentally oriented mission." When the fiscal year ended, the company severed its ties to Potter and his wife Steph Davis, who had been his adamant defender. Each lost perhaps $50,000 in sponsorships. The damage to Patagonia, Inc. was less calculable but probably greater.[34]

Setting aside the things he did not grasp, Potter bared the tensions between industrial and romantic orientations to nature. Like most athletes, he wanted to escape society for a solitary engagement with wilderness. He explained, "more so than I want to be on top of that or I want to conquer that, it's I want to be a part of that, . . . I want to become one with that." Yet like most outdoor athletes, Potter's errand into the wild was only half the experience; the other half was telling the world. Although not all taped their endeavors for a feature film, Potter's story was common. Like Alfred Smith or John Muir, George Mallory or David Brower, Royal Robbins or John Bachar, Potter's adventure was not over until his tale was told, and like other climbers, part of the story dwelled on how he had established a moral claim to nature. His labors, like any backpacker, kayaker, skier, or surfer, had forged a special bond with nature that needed to be recognized. The community was a shadow companion, always at some level shaping how outdoor athletes interacted with nature, and part of nature's importance was as a seemingly pristine stage upon which they defined themselves and inscribed messages to society.[35]

This is an essential, although not exclusive, context for understanding the role of climbers in the wilderness movement. Climbing clubs had been in the vanguard of restricting access to nature since Leslie Stephen wrote *The Playground of Europe* and the Alpine Club spoke out against funicular railways. The Appalachian Mountain Club, Seattle Mountaineers, and American Alpine Club had advocated for wildness since the late nineteenth century, and when not assaulting urban boulders or Sierra peaks, RCS members fought for trees in the Butano Forest, protested roads and resorts on San Gorgonio, and decried pollution during the mid-twentieth century. The NPS was initially "manned almost entirely by" the Sierra Club, whose climbers and ex-climbers staffed positions in parks, administrations, and commissions. Climbers' genteel ideas about nature and advocacy held sway for a century. Mountains, as R. L. G. Irving said, were "cathedrals" that generated "a new spirit," yet as Dan Thropp and other RCS members noted, preservation's "basic purpose" was "to fight to the last ditch to preserve places to have fun in." Climbers passionately opposed developing wilderness for rival uses, but they were not above refining it for their own needs.[36]

Environmental advocacy grew more complex after 1945. Bob Marshall bequeathed his fortune to the Wilderness Society. Aldo Leopold moved readers to "think like a mountain." Arne Naess and George Sessions traded anthropocentrism for "deep ecology." The early postwar era was also when the Sierra Club's focus shifted from peaks and trees to ecosystems. Even RCS members said "wilderness areas . . . are absolutely essential for our further understanding of how the various plants and animals of a community maintain a self-controlled, though fluctuating, balance."[37]

What did not change was wilderness's role as a stage for identity. Lobbying for the 1964 Wilderness Act, Secretary of the Interior Stewart Udall reminded the Carpenters Union that preserving the "last remnants of the grandeur that once was. . . . means a chance for young and old to pit their human resources against the earth and the elements." People who played in the wild were some of its most passionate defenders. Lawyer Joseph Sax made this circular when he argued that wilderness existed for people to test themselves, and "the preservationist [was] the only spokesman we have for the tradition of man-in-nature." Marshall and Leopold valued wilderness as a site for frontier fantasies, and Marshall, Naess, and Sessions regularly climbed in the Sierra Nevada, Brooks Range, Himalaya, and Antarctica to recreate their identities. The Sierra Club was founded as both an environmental group *and* a climbing club.[38]

Preservation, play, and identity come into sharp focus with Yvon Chouinard and Doug Tompkins. The two had known each other since at least 1964, when Chouinard nominated Tompkins for AAC membership, and they first visited the Patagonian wilderness together in 1968, driving six months in a VW bus to climb Cerro Fitzroy and film *Fitzroy*. The experience was life-changing. Chouinard named his business for the region and became a corporate magnate. In the 1970s he and other aging athletes formed "The Do Boys" and went "fun hogging." Brokaw, Ridgeway, Robbins, Tompkins, and others took up kayaking and sailing, made first descents of rivers, and emulated Bill Tilman and Joshua Slocum. These absentee CEOs preferred to identify by play, and the subtitle to Chouinard's autobiography, *The Education of a Reluctant Businessman*, evoked perfectly the psychic tensions of an aggressive entrepreneur ill at ease with his day job. The wilderness of southern South America was where Chouinard escaped himself.[39]

Tompkins went further, literally investing himself in the landscape. After his divorce and sale of Esprit, Tompkins used the proceeds to establish the Foundation for Deep Ecology and Conservation Land Trust, then moved to Chile to buy land that extended from the Pacific over the Andean spine into Argentina. By 2007 he owned over 3,000 square miles in Palena Province, Chile, dubbed Parque Pumalín for its wild pumas. Tompkins had planned to deed it to Chile. Meanwhile, Conservacion Patagonica, an organization run by his second wife Kristine McDivitt, the former general manager and CEO of Patagonia, Inc., bought and rehabilitated land for a planned national park in Argentina. To complete the circle, the Chouinards and Ridgeway used Patagonia, Inc. catalogs to promote the Tompkins' causes, raise money, and help Patagonia, Inc. employees assist Tompkins and McDivitt in South America.[40]

How one felt about these activities depended entirely upon perspective. For those involved these were good works. They preserved rare habitat and gave "back to the place that gave us our name." Their efforts inspired environmentalists, and the reserves materialized their devotion to deep ecology. To locals this was more northern hemispheric imperialism. Most of Tompkins's holdings were purchased from multinational corporations. When pieced together they literally split Chile in two, blocking a road and national development. These acquisitions also erased history, evicting most residents and employing the remainder to deracinate domesticated plants and animals or to service a new ecotourism economy. In their drive to save imperiled nature, Tompkins and Chouinard reenacted the worst excesses of North American preservationism, creating wilderness through dispossession. They epitomized a paternalistic form of environmentalism that doubted the capacity of aboriginal and working-class people to appreciate and steward nature. It should come as no surprise that Tompkins and McDivitt polarized Chilean politics.[41]

Patagonian preservationism was cast as a stand for nature, but it was also about play. Chouinard wrote passionately about habitat and species, but he was also an adventurer who loved Patagonia as an edgy place to climb and kayak. When discussing his causes he was a bundle of contradictions. Chouinard spoke in terms of "good" and "evil," spent little time in the office, and liked to rub elbows at cocktail parties in Buenos Aires. He spoke eloquently about the complexities of consumption yet spent so much on recycled materials for a surfing shack that a writer called it "conspicuous denial" and wondered whether Chouinard's gripes about consumerism were "honest despair or just the rhetoric of a privileged evangelist." Similarly, Parque Pumalín was serious ecosystem preservation, something both Tompkins and Chouinard viewed in apocalyptic terms, but it was also high-end ecotourism with exclusive lodgings, vegan meals, and more untrod peaks than Tompkins could climb.[42]

But to conclude that these successful entrepreneurs were hypocrites misinterprets the thread of their lives and how adventurers related to nature. The identities of outdoor athletes were intrinsically linked to their landscapes of play. They were the mountains or waves or rivers or snow, and wild nature was them. It was why a young David Brower wrote at the end of a backpacking trip, "This person was not coming home—he had just left it!" Preservation was always also about saving the self. That they said they were serving the greater good was less a function of deceit than of a blinding self-centeredness.[43]

Ultimately, though, fun-hogging was self-defeating. By casting wilderness as a playground, athletes invited in the hordes. Every visitor not only altered ecology but filled landscapes with new meanings. Simply loving nature adulterated it. Named a World Heritage Site by UNESCO, Yosemite Valley has been both an unparalleled example of sublime nature and a cathedral overrun since at least the 1880s, when tourists first complained of too many visitors, yet there was never consensus about the loss or the culprits. Climbers in Camp 4, patrons of the Ahwahnee, and families at Camp Curry saw different sins. They blamed motor homes, tour buses, snobbish hotels, usurious concessionaires, officious rangers, dirtbag climbers, and every other heathen in this itinerant city of 60,000 souls. Moreover, every passionate denunciation incited a passionate defense. The skating rink was no less adored than the waterfalls; the grocery store was reviled almost as much as it was patronized.[44]

Underlying the grousing was an abiding love of place. The backpacker rhapsodizing about wilderness from a foot-deep rut in the John Muir Trail was no less ironic than the rafter gushing about sublime scenery from an inner tube in the Merced River, six-pack perched on his belly. Both were right, but those invested in "pure" nature were doubly vexed. First, the idea of wilderness was both real ecology and a cultural construct that erased the past, and equating it with landscapes that retained a "primeval character and influence," as the 1964 Wilderness Act stated, made wild nature chimerical. History undermined ideals of purity because the past was always more complicated than imagined. Second, climbers have long influenced environmental culture, but they are a shrinking portion of those in nature. Participation in outdoor sports has fallen since 2000, and the few growing activities tend to be "physically not very challenging." Meanwhile Dow, Exxon, Wells Fargo, and other companies have begun to support national parks, yet their values, like those of Chouinard and Tompkins, are complex and contradictory. Even when corporate officers do care about nature, they also care about bottom lines, which means encouraging consumption.[45]

Thus if purity, defined as nature untouched by humans and experiences unsullied by apostates, is the litmus test of an authentic experience, then complex places like Yosemite can only lose value over time, and sanctuaries such as Pumalín will only displace and intensify consumption elsewhere. This is the conundrum that pilgrims of the vertical face as they seek sacred nature. The more they yearn for unmediated adventure, the more they bump up against the wider world. There will be no end to frustration until they reexamine first assumptions and adopt more complex historical perspectives. Although adventurers believed that nature was, or should be, separate and unadulterated, and they were, or should be, outside society, they never did escape their contexts, and nature never was a hermetic refuge. We must also acknowledge what was gained and lost as a result. Individualizing outdoor sports and valorizing its risks led to peak physical and aesthetic performances, yet the social, cultural, and ecological costs were steep. How we assess that tradeoff is as idiosyncratic as any issue in outdoor sports, but for those who think the costs too dear, then maybe a little nostalgia is in order. Maybe there is a place for heterosocial values, and maybe equating respectability with restraint—in social and ecological relations—has merit. And maybe, just maybe, we should let go of a few fantasies and grow up a bit.[46]

ABBREVIATIONS

AAC   Henry S. Hall Jr. American Alpine Club Library, Golden, Colorado

AACN   *American Alpine Club News*

AAJ   *American Alpine Journal*

AINAM   *Accidents in North American Mountaineering*

Bancroft   Bancroft Library, University of California, Berkeley

Beardsley   Irene Beardsley, Rendez-vous Hautes Montagnes, Department of Special Collections, Stanford University Libraries, Stanford, California

CDWOYNP   Climbing Drawer, Wilderness Office, Yosemite National Park

Clyde   Norman Asa Clyde Papers, Bancroft Library, University of California, Berkeley

Colby   William E. Colby Papers, Bancroft Library, University of California, Berkeley

Dawson   Glen Dawson Private Papers, Pasadena, California

Evans   John Evans Climbing Journal, 2 vols., copies in author's possession

Farquhar   Francis P. Farquhar Papers, Bancroft Library, University of California, Berkeley

Frost   Tom Frost, Photographs, Oral History, Articles, ca. 1960–1998, Department of Special Collections, Stanford University Libraries, Stanford, California

GPIW *Great Pacific Iron Works* catalogs, Patagonia Company Records, Patagonia Headquarters, Ventura, California

Hob Nail   *Berkeley Hiking Club Hob Nail,* Bancroft Library, University of California, Berkeley

JCCC   *Journal of the Cragmont Climbing Club,* also published as "Cragmont Climbing Club, Founded on March 13, 1932," 2 vols., Carton 7:30, Sierra Club San Francisco Bay Chapter Records, Bancroft Library, University of California, Berkeley

Matthes   François Emile Matthes Papers, Bancroft Library, University of California, Berkeley

Menocal   Armando Menocal Private Papers, Moose, Wyoming

Mugelnoos   *The Mugelnoos,* newsletter of the Southern (Angeles) Chapter of the Sierra Club, Henry S. Hall, Jr. American Alpine Club Library, Golden, Colorado

NARASB   National Archives and Records Administration, San Bruno, California

Parsons   Marion and Edward Parsons Papers, Bancroft Library, University of California, Berkeley

PCR   Patagonia Company Records, Patagonia Headquarters, Ventura, California

Roper   Steve Roper Private Papers, Oakland, California. Portions reprinted with permission of Yvon Chouinard. Copyright 1961–1964, 1966. All rights reserved to Yvon Chouinard.

SAC   Stanford Alpine Club Files, Department of Special Collections, Stanford University Libraries, Stanford, California

SACJ   *Stanford Alpine Club Journal,* Department of Special Collections, Stanford University Libraries, Stanford

SAC Scrapbook   Stanford Alpine Club Scrapbook, c. 1947–1958, Department of Special Collections, Stanford University Libraries, Stanford, California

SCB   *Sierra Club Bulletin*

SCR   Sierra Club Records, Bancroft Library, University of California, Berkeley

SCMP   Sierra Club Members Papers, Bancroft Library, University of California, Berkeley

SCMRR   Sierra Club Mountain Registers and Records, Bancroft Library, University of California, Berkeley

SCSFBCR   Sierra Club San Francisco Bay Chapter Records, Bancroft Library, University of California, Berkeley

SupAR   Superintendent's Annual Reports for Yosemite National Park, Yosemite Research Library

SupMR   Superintendent's Monthly Reports for Yosemite National Park, Yosemite Research Library

Southern Campus   *Southern Campus,* University Archives, Powell Library, University of California, Los Angeles

T&T   *Trail and Timberline*

Yodeler   *The Yodeler,* newsletter of the Bay Area Chapter of the Sierra Club, Sierra Club Research Library, San Francisco

YOSAR   Search and Rescue Files, Search and Rescue Office, Yosemite National Park

YPCCP   Yosemite Park & Curry Company Papers, 1970–Present, Yosemite Research Library

YRL   Yosemite Research Library, Yosemite National Park, California

NOTES

1. Adventurers

The epigraph is quoted in Richard F. Fleck, *John Muir: Mountaineering Essays* (Salt Lake City: Gibbs M. Smith, 1984), 103.

1. For "hardship" see Patrick F. McManus, "The Big Trip," in *A Fine and Pleasant Misery* (New York: Holt, Rinehart and Winston, 1978), 34; Maurice Herzog, *Annapurna* (New York: E. P. Dutton, 1952).
2. For "pilgrims" see "Talus of Yosemite," *Summit* (June 1968), 33. For insular, noncompetitive activity and "seriously" see John Macaloon and Mihály Csíkszentmihályi, "Deep Play and the Flow Experience in Rock Climbing," in *Play, Games, and Sports in Cultural Contexts*, ed. Janet Harris and Roberta Park (Champaign, Ill.: Human Kinetics Publishers, 1983), 361–62, 381. For escape, timeless, and "history" see Leslie Stephen, *The Playground of Europe* (London: Longmans, Green, 1871), 67, 68, 271; also Mark Twight, "The Rebel Yell," *Climbing* (Eyewitness Special Edition, 2001–2002), 108. For "products" see Maurice Isserman, "The Ethics of Mountaineering, Brought Low," *Chronicle of Higher Education*, 5 May 2006, B15. For "individual" see Michael D. Rooks, Richard B. Johnston III, Cindy D. Ensor, Bobbi McIntosh, and Susan Johnson, "Injury Patterns in Recreational Rock Climbers," *American Journal of Sports Medicine* 26 (November–December 1995), 683. For "tangle" see Roselyn Elizabeth Stone, "Meanings Found in the Acts of Surfing and Skiing" (Ph.D. diss., University of Southern California, 1970), 116. For "communion" see Mikel Vause, ed., *Mountains and Mountaineers* (La Crescenta, Calif.: Mountain N' Air, 1993), 12. For critiques of escape see Lawrence C. Hamilton, "Modern American Rock Climbing: Some Aspects of Social Change," *Pacific Sociological Review* 22 (July 1979), 289; David Robbins, "Sport, Hegemony and the Middle Class: The Victorian Mountaineers," *Theory, Culture & Society* 4 (1987), 588; Neil Lewis, "The Climbing Body, Nature and the Experience of Modernity," *Body & Society* 6 (November 2000), 59. For climbing as an extended discourse on style see Peter H. Hansen, "British Mountaineering, 1850–1914" (Ph.D. diss., Harvard University, 1990), 138; Margaret Mary Dillon, "H. Adams Carter's Editorship of *The American Alpine Journal*, 1960–1995" (Ph.D. diss., Ohio University, 1997), 8; Reuben Ellis, *Vertical Margins: Mountaineering and the Landscapes of Imperialism* (Madison: University of Wisconsin Press, 2001), 177, 185.
3. For "ourselves" see Geoffrey Winthrop Young, *On High Hills: Memories of the Alps* (London: Methuen, 1933), 363; Peter Gillman and Leni Gillman, *The Wildest Dream: The Biography of George Mallory* (Seattle: Mountaineers, 2000). For "heavy" see *Recollections: The Wall of Early Morning Light, an Interview with Warren Harding* (Trey Solberg and Roger Derryberry, Downward Bound Productions, 2001); Warren Harding, *Downward Bound: A Mad! Guide to Rock Climbing* (Englewood Cliffs, N.J.: Prentice-Hall, 1975). For climbing as a social experience see Richard G. Mitchell Jr., *Mountaineering Experience: The Psychology and Sociology of Adventure* (Chicago: University of Chicago Press, 1983). For environmental advocates see Jennifer Hattan, "First on Top," *Sierra* (May–June 2001), 51–52.
4. Edward Whymper, *Scrambles amongst the Alps*, ed. and rev. H. E. G. Tyndale (Exeter, U.K.: Webb & Bower, 1986), 11; Charles S. Houston, "Foreword," in *Why I Climb: Personal Insights of Top Climbers*, ed. Steve Gardiner (Harrisburg, Pa.: Stackpole Books,

1990), ix–x; Macaloon and Csíkszentmihályi, "Deep Play," 364; Vause, *Mountains and Mountaineers*, 16; Michael P. Cohen, *The History of the Sierra Club, 1892–1970* (San Francisco: Sierra Club Books, 1988), ix; Hansen, "British Mountaineering," 7.

5. For "commonplace" see Stephen, *The Playground of Europe*, 66. Richards's "belong" remark quoted in Hansen, "British Mountaineering," 380. For "maximum" and "mastering" see Pierre Bourdieu, *Distinction: A Social Critique of the Judgement of Taste*, trans. Richard Nice (Cambridge, Mass.: Harvard University Press, 1984), 219; Trevor Williams and Peter Donnelly, "Subcultural Production, Reproduction and Transformation in Climbing," *International Review for Sociology of Sport* 20 (1985), 3–16; Hugo van der Poel, "Leisure and the Modularization of Daily Life," *Time & Society* 6 (July 1997), 171–94; Harvey C. Perkins and David C. Thorns, "Gazing or Performing? Reflections on Urry's Tourist Gaze in the Context of Contemporary Experience in the Antipodes," *International Sociology* 16 (June 2001), 185–204; Eric de Léséleuc, Jacques Gleyse, Anne Marcellini, "The Practice of Sport as Political Expression?" trans. R. Anthony Lewis, *International Sociology* 17 (March 2002), 73–90; Lise Kjølsrød, "Adventure Revisited: On Structure and Metaphor in Specialized Play," *Sociology* 37 (2003), 459–76. For recreation and class see R. C. White, "Social Class Difference in the Use of Leisure," *American Journal of Sociology* 61 (1955), 145–50; Alfred C. Clarke, "The Use of Leisure and Its Relation to Levels of Occupational Prestige," *American Sociological Review* 21 (June 1956), 301–7; Rabel J. Burdge, "Levels of Occupational Prestige and Leisure Activity," *Journal of Leisure Research* 3 (1969), 262–74; Benjamin G. Rader, "The Quest for Subcommunities and the Rise of American Sport," *American Quarterly* 29 (1977), 355–69; Pierre Bourdieu, "Sport and Social Class," *Social Science Information* 17 (December 1978), 819–40. For historical analysis see Robert A. Stebbins, *Amateurs: On the Margin between Work and Leisure* (Beverly Hills: Sage, 1979); Robert A. Stebbins, *Amateurs, Professionals, and Serious Leisure* (Montreal: McGill-Queen's University Press, 1992); John Lowerson, *Sport and the English Middle Classes, 1870–1914* (New York: Manchester University Press, 1993); Neil Wigglesworth, *The Evolution of English Sport* (Portland, Ore.: Frank Cass, 1996); Roland Naul, "History of Sport and Physical Education in Germany, 1800–1945," in *Sport and Physical Education in Germany*, ed. Roland Naul and Ken Hardman (New York: Routledge, 2002), 15–27. For the hegemonic position of class and race in recreation see Mark Spence, "Grinding the Gears on the Roads that Ruin," *Reviews in American History* 31 (March 2003), 125; Robbins, "Sport, Hegemony and the Middle Class."

6. Harvey Manning, ed., *Mountaineering: The Freedom of the Hills* (Seattle: Mountaineers, 1960). For sport as structure see Elliott J. Gorn and Michael Oriard, "Taking Sports Seriously," *Chronicle of Higher Education* (24 March 1995), A52; Kevin Young and Philip White, "Sport, Physical Danger, and Injury: The Experiences of Elite Women Athletes," *Journal of Sport and Social Issues* 19 (February 1995), 55.

7. On social structures see Bruce C. Johnson, "Climbing Games and Danger," 8 (paper given at American Sociological Association, San Francisco, September 1978); Hamilton, "Modern American," 285–90, 296; Robbins, "Sport, Hegemony and the Middle Class," 579–601.

8. For key texts see Joan W. Scott, "Gender: A Useful Category of Historical Analysis," *American Historical Review* 91 (December 1986), 1053–75; James Eli Adams, *Dandies and Desert Saints: Styles of Victorian Manhood* (Ithaca: Cornell University Press, 1995); Gail Bederman, *Manliness and Civilization: A Cultural History of Gender and Race in the United States, 1880–1917* (Chicago: University of Chicago Press, 1995), 7–24; James Gilbert, *Men in the Middle: Searching for Masculinity in the 1950s* (Chicago: University of Chicago Press, 2005), 15–33; Robyn Longhurst, "Geography and Gender: Masculinities,

Male Identity and Men," *Progress in Human Geography* 24 (September 2000), 439–44; J. A. Mangan and James Walvin, eds., *Manliness and Morality: Middle-Class Masculinity in Britain and America, 1800–1940* (Manchester: Manchester University Press, 1987); David Morgan, "Masculinity, Autobiography and History," *Gender and History* 2 (Spring 1990), 34–39; Karen D. Pike, "Class-Based Masculinities: The Interdependence of Gender, Class, and Interpersonal Power," *Gender and Society* 10 (October 1996), 527–49; Michael Roper and John Tosh, "Historians and the Politics of Masculinity," in *Manful Assertions: Masculinities in Britain since 1800*, eds. Michael Roper and John Tosh (New York: Routledge, 1991), 1–24; John Tosh, "What Should Historians Do with Masculinity? Reflections on Nineteenth-Century Britain," *History Workshop Journal* 38 (Autumn 1994), 170–202; Bryce Traister, "Academic Viagra: The Rise of American Masculinity Studies," *American Studies* 52 (June 2000), 274–304. For performative gender see David Brown, "Pierre Bourdieu's 'Masculine Domination' Thesis and the Gendered Body in Sport and Physical Culture," *Sociology of Sport* 23 (June 2006), 162–88; Gerald R. Gems, *The Athletic Crusade: Sport and American Cultural Imperialism* (Lincoln: University of Nebraska Press, 2006); Hugh Klein, "Adolescence, Youth, and Young Adulthood: Rethinking Current Conceptualizations of Life Stage," *Youth & Society* 21 (June 1990), 446–71; J. A. Mangan, ed., *Making European Masculinities: Sport, Europe, Gender* (Portland: Frank Cass, 2000); Michael Messner, "Boyhood, Organized Sports, and the Construction of Masculinities," in *Men's Lives*, eds. Michael S. Kimmel and Michael A. Messner, 2nd ed. (New York: Macmillan, 1992), 161–76; Michael A. Messner, *Power at Play: Sports and the Problem of Masculinity* (Boston: Beacon Press, 1992); Steven A. Riess, "Sport and the Redefinition of American Middle-Class Masculinity," *International Journal of the History of Sport* 8 (May 1991), 5–27; Steven P. Schacht, "Misogyny On and Off the 'Pitch': The Gendered World of Male Rugby Players," *Gender and Society* 10 (October 1996), 550–65; Young and White, "Sport, Physical Danger, and Injury," 48. For gender in mountaineering and other outdoor sports see Kristin L. Anderson, "Snowboarding: The Construction of Gender in an Emerging Sport," *Journal of Sport & Social Issues* 23 (February 1999), 55–79; Donald W. Calhoun, *Sport, Culture, and Personality* (Champaign, Ill.: Human Kinetics Publishers, 1987), 313–14; Bruce Erickson, "The Colonial Climbs of Mount Trudeau: Thinking Masculinity through the Homosocial," *Topia* 9 (Spring 2003), 67–82; Bruce Erickson, "Style Matters: Explorations of Bodies, Whiteness, and Identity in Rock Climbing," *Sociology of Sport Journal* 22 (September 2005), 373–96; Susan Frohlick, "The 'Hypermasculine' Landscape of High-Altitude Mountaineering," *Michigan Feminist Studies* 14 (1999–2000), 83–106; Jon Gertner, "The Futile Pursuit of Happiness," *New York Times Magazine*, 7 September 2003, 44–47, 86–91; Johnson, "Climbing Games and Danger," 6; David Le Breton, "Playing Symbolically with Death in Extreme Sports," *Body & Society* 6 (March 2000), 1–11; Lewis, "The Climbing Body"; Sherry B. Ortner, *Life and Death on Mt. Everest: Sherpas and Himalayan Mountaineering* (Princeton: Princeton University Press, 1999); Richard Phillips, *Mapping Men and Empire: A Geography of Adventure* (New York: Routledge, 1997); Kevin Young, Philip White, and William McTeer, "Body Talk: Male Athletes Reflect on Sport, Injury, and Pain," *Sociology of Sport Journal* 11 (June 1994), 190.

9. William James, "The Moral Equivalent of War," in *The Writings of William James: A Comprehensive Edition*, ed. John J. McDermott (New York: Random House, 1967), 660–71; George E. Johnson, "Play as a Moral Equivalent to War," *The Playground* 6 (1912), 111–23. For "will" see Whymper, *Scrambles amongst the Alps*, 215. For "need" see Gardiner, *Why I Climb*, 88.

10. For "virgin" see Edward Whymper, "A New Playground in the New World," *Scribner's*

Magazine 33 (June 1903), 646. For imperialism see Ellis, *Vertical Margins;* Peter L. Bayers, *Imperial Ascent: Mountaineering, Masculinity, and Empire* (Boulder: University of Colorado Press, 2003); Peter H. Hansen, "Coronation Everest: The Empire and Commonwealth in the 'Second Elizabethan Age,'" in *British Culture and the End of Empire,* ed. Stuart Ward (New York: Manchester University Press, 2001), 57–72; Peter H. Hansen, "Confetti of Empire: The Conquest of Everest in Nepal, India, Britain, and New Zealand," *Comparative Studies in Society and History* 42 (April 2000), 307–32; Maurice Isserman and Stewart Weaver, *Fallen Giants: A History of Himalayan Mountaineering from the Age of Empire to the Age of Extremes* (New Haven: Yale University Press, 2008). For "prestige" and "sensuous" see Hansen, "British Mountaineering," 149, 288–89. For "abated" and "coquette" see Whymper, *Scrambles amongst the Alps,* 35, 119. Biesheuval quoted in Jose Burman, *A Peak to Climb: The Story of South African Mountaineering* (Cape Town: C. Struik, 1966), 165. For "Matterhorn" and "acme" see Valerie Mendenhall Cohen, ed., *Woman on the Rocks: The Mountaineering Letters of Ruth Dyar Mendenhall* (Bishop, Calif.: Spotted Dog Press, 2006), 174–75, 259. For metaphorical sexualization of nature see Annette Kolodny, *The Lay of the Land: Metaphor as Experience and History in American Life and Letters* (Chapel Hill: University of North Carolina Press, 1975); Annette Kolodny, *The Land Before Her: Fantasy and Experience of the American Frontiers, 1630–1860* (Chapel Hill: University of North Carolina Press, 1984).

11. For "competent" and "glory" see Cohen, *Woman on the Rocks,* 12, 174. For risk see Hamilton, "Modern American," 302; Lito Tejada-Flores, "The Games Climbers Play," *Ascent* (May 1967), 23–25.

12. For "love" see Stephen, *Playground of Europe,* 68. For "edge" and "ultimate" see Gardiner, *Why I Climb,* 41. For "Ulysses" see A. F. Mummery, *My Climbs in the Alps and Caucasus* (New York: Chas. Scribner's Sons, 1895), 325. For other sports see Annie Gilbert Coleman, *Ski Style: Sport and Culture in the Rockies* (Lawrence: University Press of Kansas, 2004), 134; Roselyn Elizabeth Stone, "Meanings Found in the Acts of Surfing and Skiing" (Ph.D. diss., University of Southern California, 1970), 15. For risk and gender see Calhoun, *Sport, Culture, and Personality,* 311. I thank Mike Lansing for help with this.

13. For "interpose" see Lunn, *A Century of Mountaineering,* 160. For "fellowship" see Houston, "Foreword," ix. For "spoil" see Sam Moses, "Stone Walls, Stout Hearts," *Sports Illustrated* (6 March 1978), 69. For "wild" see "Take Out the Pitons," *Yodeler,* 14 May 1940, 7.

14. For skiing and surfing see Stone, "Meanings in the Acts of Surfing and Skiing," 60–61, 78, 88, 108; Douglas Booth, "Surfing: The Cultural and Technological Determinants of a Dance," *Culture, Sport, Society* 2 (Spring 1999), 36; Coleman, *Ski Style,* 125–26, 213. For "rewarding" see Bill Birkett and Bill Peascod, *Women Climbing: 200 Years of Achievement* (Seattle: Mountaineers, 1989), 172. For debates see J. H. Doughty, "The Conventions of Mountaineering," in *Hill-Writings of J. H. Doughty,* ed. H. M. Kelly (Manchester: Rucksack Club, 1937), 48–49; Lawrence Hamilton, "The Changing Face of American Mountaineering," *Review of Sport & Leisure* 6 (Summer 1981), 33; Hamilton, "Modern American," 287, 316n18.

15. For worn see Lord Schuster, *Mountaineering: The Romanes Lecture Delivered in the Sheldonian Theatre, 21 May 1948* (Oxford: Clarendon Press, 1948), 21. For "history" see Rebecca Solnit, *Savage Dreams: A Journey into the Landscape Wars of the American West* (Berkeley: University of California Press, 1994), 230. For nature and technology see Jeffrey K. Stine and Joel A. Tarr, "Technology and the Environment: The Historian's Challenge," *Environmental History Review* 18 (Spring 1994), 2.

16. For technology as context see David Rothenberg, *Hand's End: Technology and the Limits of Nature* (Berkeley: University of California Press, 1993), xiv–xvi, 29–30, 56, 90, 110–11;

Claude S. Fischer, *America Calling: A Social History of the Telephone to 1940* (Berkeley: University of California Press, 1992), 17–19, 230, 254, 260, 269–70; Wiebe E. Bijker, Thomas P. Hughes, and Trevor J. Pinch, eds., *The Social Construction of Technological Systems: New Directions in the Sociology and History of Technology* (Cambridge, Mass.: MIT Press, 1987), 3–4; Ruth Schwartz Cowan, "The Consumption Junction: A Proposal for Research Strategies in the Sociology of Technology," in *The Social Construction of Technological Systems,* 261–80.

17. For "paradaisical" see François Matthes, "The Yosemite . . . ," carton 133:23, SCMP. For geology see N. King Huber, *The Geological Story of Yosemite National Park,* U.S. Geological Survey Bulletin 1595 (Washington, D.C.: United States Government Printing Office, 1987); François E. Matthes, *The Incomparable Valley: A Geological Interpretation of the Yosemite,* ed. Fritiof Fryxell (Berkeley: University of California Press, 1950). I thank Brian Coffey for this.

18. For "secular" see Lynn Hill with Greg Child, *Climbing Free: My Life in the Vertical World* (New York: W. W. Norton, 2002), 82. For "singular" see James Hutchings, "California for Waterfalls!" *San Francisco Daily California Chronicle,* 18 August 1855. For "Israelites" and "Born" see Kevin Starr, *Americans and the California Dream, 1850–1915* (New York: Oxford University Press, 1973), 101, 186; David Robertson, *West of Eden: A History of the Art and Literature of Yosemite* (Berkeley: Yosemite Natural History Association and Wilderness Press, 1984), xv–xvii. For script see Hal K. Rothman, *Devil's Bargains: Tourism in the Twentieth-Century American West* (Lawrence: University Press of Kansas, 1988), 20; Mark David Spence, *Dispossessing the Wilderness: Indian Removal and the Meaning of the National Parks* (New York: Oxford University Press, 1999), 101–32; Stephen Germic, *American Green: Class, Crisis, and the Deployment of Nature in Central Park, Yosemite, and Yellowstone* (Lanham, Md.: Lexington Books, 2001), 41–65. For landscape sensibilities see Arnold Berleant, *The Aesthetics of Environment* (Philadelphia: Temple University Press, 1992); Arnold Berleant, *Living in the Landscape: Toward an Aesthetics of Environment* (Lawrence: University Press of Kansas 1997); Derek Gregory, *Geographical Imaginations* (New York: Blackwell, 1993); David M. Wrobel and Patrick T. Long, eds., *Seeing and Being Seen: Tourism in the American West* (Lawrence: University Press of Kansas, 2001); Robert B. Riley, "The Visible, the Visual, and the Vicarious: Questions about Vision, Landscape, and Experience," in *Understanding Ordinary Landscapes,* ed. Paul Groth and Todd W. Bressi (New Haven: Yale University Press, 1997), 200–9; Simon Schama, *Landscape and Memory* (New York: Vintage, 1995); Dell Upton, "Seen, Unseen, and Scene," in *Understanding Ordinary Landscapes,* 174–79.

19. The starting place for spirituality is Maria Coffey, *Explorers of the Infinite* (New York: Jeremy P. Tarcher/Penguin, 2008). For "majesty" and "tenfold" see Stephen, *Playground of Europe,* 272–73, 282. For "cosmic" see Daniel Duane, *Looking for Mo* (New York: Washington Square Press, 1998), 135. For "peeled" see Whymper, *Scrambles Amongst the Alps,* 134. For "cripple" see Lunn, *A Century of Mountaineering,* 26.

20. For "lived" see Cohen, *Woman on the Rocks,* 189. For similar expressions through time see Stutfield, "Mountaineering as a Religion," 245; Schuster, *Mountaineering,* 29. For other sports see Stone, "Meanings in the Acts of Surfing and Skiing," 7, 71–72, 116; Coleman, *Ski Style,* 220. For knowing nature see Richard White, "'Are You an Environmentalist or Do You Work for a Living?': Work and Nature," in *Uncommon Ground: Toward Reinventing Nature,* ed. William Cronon (New York: W. W. Norton, 1995), 171–85; Thomas G. Andrews, "'Made By Toile?': Tourism, Labor, and the Construction of the Colorado Landscape, 1858–1917," *Journal of American History* 92 (December 2005), 837–63.

21. For "influence" see Theodore Roosevelt, "John Muir: An Appreciation," in *Wild Yosemite:*

Personal Accounts of Adventure, Discovery, and Nature, ed. Susan M. Neider (New York: Skyhorse Publishing, 2007), 26. For "unofficial" see Nicholas Clinch, "Francis Farquhar: Personification of Tradition," *SCB* (February 1975), 21. For "effective" see John McPhee, *Encounters with the Archdruid: Narratives about a Conservationist and Three of His Natural Enemies* (New York: Farrar, Straus & Giroux, 1971), 5. For Sessions see Bill Devall and George Sessions, *Deep Ecology: Living as If Nature Mattered* (Layton, Ut.: Gibbs Smith, 1985). For "Heroes" see Roger Rosenblatt, "Reaching the Top by Doing the Right Thing," *Time* (11 October 1999). For awards see Mountain Light, "Galen Avery Rowell, August 23, 1940–August 12, 2002," http://www.mountainlight.com/rowellg.html (accessed 12 August 2008); Changemakers, "Nomination Details for the Geotourism Challenge: Mountain Travel Sobek," http://www.changemakers.net/en-us/node/5838 (accessed 12 September 2008).

22. For "prepared" see Marjorie Hope Nicolson, *Mountain Gloom and Mountain Glory: The Development of the Aesthetic of the Infinite* (Seattle: University of Washington Press, 1997 [1959]), 1.

23. Several scholars have pleaded for more attention to gender in environmental history. Carolyn Merchant, "Gender and Environmental History," *Journal of American History* 76 (March 1990), 1117–21; Melissa Leach and Cathy Green, *Environment and History* 3 (October 1997), 343–70; Virginia Scharff, "Man and Nature: Sex Secrets of Environmental History," in *Human Nature: Biology, Culture, and Environmental History,* eds. John P. Herron and Andrew G. Kirk (Albuquerque: University of New Mexico Press, 1999), 31–48. For works that elaborate this theme see Carolyn Merchant, *Ecological Revolutions: Nature, Gender, and Science in New England* (Chapel Hill: University of North Carolina Press, 1989); Vera Norwood, *Made from This Earth: American Women and Nature* (Chapel Hill: University of North Carolina Press, 1993); Glenda Riley, *Women and Nature: Saving the Wild West* (Lincoln: University of Nebraska Press, 1999); Conevery Bolton Valençius, *The Health of the Country: How American Settlers Understood Themselves and Their Land* (New York: Basic Books, 2002). The most recent contribution is Susan R. Schrepfer's *Nature's Altars: Mountains, Gender, and American Environmentalism* (Lawrence: University Press of Kansas, 2005). For gender and recreation see Rosie Andrews, "No Spare Rib: The Advent of Hard Women Rock Climbers," in *Rock and Roses,* 7–10; Susan K. Cahn, ed., *Coming on Strong: Gender and Sexuality in Twentieth-Century Women's Sports* (Cambridge, Mass.: Harvard University Press, 1994); Coleman, *Ski Style,* 60, 211; Terry Gifford and Rosie Smith, comp., *Orogenic Zones: The First Five Years of the International Festival of Mountaineering Literature* (West Bretton, UK: Bretton Hall College of the University of Leeds, 1994), 27–43, 225–32; Sherrie A. Inness, *Tough Girls: Women Warriors and Wonder Women in Popular Culture* (Philadelphia: University of Pennsylvania Press, 1999); David A. Mazel, *Mountaineering Women: Stories by Early Climbers* (College Station: Texas A&M University Press, 1994), 3–26; Vera Norwood, "Constructing Gender in Nature: Bird Society Through the Eyes of John Burroughs and Florence Merriam Bailey," in *Human Nature,* 49–62; Margaret Talbot, "Being Herself Through Sport," in *Leisure, Health and Wellbeing,* Leisure Studies Association Conference Papers No. 44, ed. Jonathan Long (Eastbourne, UK: Leisure Studies Association, 1990–1991), 95–104. Schrepfer offers a tripartite gendering of mountains as Masculine, Feminine, and Domestic Sublimes. This tends to reify gender into essentialized and timeless relations, and it does not explain why someone such as Ruth Dyar Mendenhall switched effortlessly from the Feminine Sublime when describing mountain flora and "beauty" (Cohen, *Woman on the Rocks,* 116, 126, 263, 299) to intensely competing with other women (ibid., 43, 52–53, 100, 309–10) to admitting she went on one trip because

she "couldn't think of any manly way to get out of it" (ibid., 49). Missing are the contexts of behavior. My argument is that homosocial and heterosocial help to contextualize the social and personal dynamics of gendered expressions and actions, especially concerning risk and technology. For an explication of homosocial see Eve Sedgwick, *Between Men: English Literature and Male Homosocial Desire* (New York: Columbia University Press, 1985); Bruce Erickson, "The Colonial Climbs of Mount Trudeau." For discussions of the social context of risk and play see Barbara Humberstone, "Re-Creation and Connections in and with Nature: Synthesizing Ecological and Feminist Discourses and Praxis?" *International Review for the Sociology of Sport* 33 (December 1998), 387; Messner, "Boyhood, Organized Sports, and the Construction of Masculinities," 169; Young and White, "Sport, Physical Danger, and Injury," 55–56; Mellor, *American Rock,* 36; Stone, "Meanings in the Acts of Surfing and Skiing," 119. For a fuller discussion see Joseph E. Taylor III, "The Social Contexts of Gendered Play" (paper presented at the annual meeting of the Canadian Historical Association, Vancouver, British Columbia, June 2008).

24. For "striking" see Engel, *A History of Mountaineering in the Alps,* 183. For "real" see Birkett and Peascod, *Women Climbing,* 174; Phil Bettler, "Gleanings of a Climber," *Yodeler,* 17 October 1949, 5; Rachel da Silva, Jill Lawrenz, and Wendy Roberts, "A Brief History of Women Climbing in the Coast and Cascade Ranges," in *Leading Out: Women Climbers Reaching for the Top,* ed. Rachel da Silva (Seattle: Seal Press, 1992), 84.

25. For "mysterious" see Georg Simmel, *Simmel on Culture: Selected Writings,* eds. David Frisby and Mike Featherstone (Thousand Oaks, Calif.: Sage Publications, 1997), 232. For "extremities" see George Leigh Mallory, "The Mountaineer as Artist," *Climbers' Club Journal* (March 1914), 34. For "separated" see Gabriela Zim, *The View from the Edge: Life and Landscapes of Beverly Johnson* (La Crescenta, Calif.: Mountain N' Air, 1996), 43.

2. Victorians

The epigraph is from "On the Use and Management of the Rope in Rock Work," *SCB* (1931), 68.

1. For "surmounted" and "value" see Underhill, "On the Use and Management," 68. For "accolades" see Ed Webster, "A Conversation with Robert Underhill," *Climbing* 82 (February 1984), 22. For 1931 see Francis P. Farquhar, "The Sport of Mountain-Climbing," *SCB* (1931), 90; Glen Dawson, "Mountain-Climbing on the 1931 Outing," *SCB* (1932), 113–15; Robert L. M. Underhill, "Mount Whitney By the East Face," *SCB* (1932), 53–58. For histories see, e.g., Kenneth A. Henderson, "In Memorium: Robert Underhill, 1889–1983," *Appalachia* (Winter 1984–1985), 116.

2. For early rope use see Don Mellor, *American Rock: Region, Rock, and Culture in American Climbing* (Woodstock, Vt.: Countryman Press, 2001), 67–68. For technical instruction see Geoffrey Winthrop Young, ed., *Mountain Craft* (New York: Charles Scribner's Sons, 1920); "Noted Alpine Mountaineer to Lecture at Wolcott School on Swiss Customs," c. 1923, Colorado Mountain Club Scrapbook, vol. 4, 1919–1923, p. 102, CMC. For western climbs see Chris Jones, *Climbing in North America* (Seattle: Mountaineers, 1997), 43–124.

3. For Underhill see Henderson, "In Memorium: Robert Underhill, 1889–1983," 114–17; phone conversation with Brian Underhill, 20 August 2003. For "golden" see C. D. Cunningham and W. Abney, *Pioneers of the Alps* (London: Sampson Low, Marston, Searle, and Rivington, 1887), 23. "Ages" are overstated. See Peter H. Hansen, "British Mountain-

eering, 1850–1914" (Ph.D. diss., Harvard University, 1991), 190. For silver and iron see Arnold Lunn, *A Century of Mountaineering, 1857–1957* (London: George Allen & Unwin, 1957), 82–84.

4. For insecurity see Leslie Stephen, *The Playground of Europe* (London: Longmans, Green, 1871), 270; Arnold Lunn, ed., *The Englishman in the Alps: Being a Collection of English Prose and Poetry Relating to the Alps* (London: Oxford University Press, 1913), 208; Steve Gardiner, ed., *Why I Climb: Personal Insights of Top Climbers* (Harrisburg, Pa.: Stackpole Books, 1990), 4.

5. For urban context see Hansen, "British Mountaineering," 84, 88–89.

6. For "redefining" see Steven A. Riess, "Sport and the Redefinition of Middle-Class Masculinity in Victorian America," in *The New American Sport History: Recent Approaches and Perspectives,* ed. S. W. Pope (Urbana: University of Illinois Press, 1997), 190. For "preeminently" see Hansen, "British Mountaineering," 441. For British sport see Neil Wigglesworth, *The Evolution of English Sport* (Portland, Ore.: Frank Cass, 1996), 1–107. For American sports see Jennie Holliman, *American Sports, 1785–1835* (Durham, N.C.: Seeman Press, 1931); Steven A. Reiss, *City Games: The Evolution of American Urban Society and the Rise of Sports* (Urbana: University of Illinois Press, 1989), 1–48.

7. For ascent of Mont Blanc and bounty see Fergus Fleming, *Killing Dragons: The Conquest of the Alps* (New York: Atlantic Monthly Press, 2000), 1–63, 81. For its importance see Hansen, "British Mountaineering," 40. For earlier mountaineers see Walther Kirchner, "Mind, Mountain, and History," *Journal of the History of Ideas* 55 (April 1994), 303–5.

8. For "minority taste" see Hansen, "British Mountaineering," 48. For "idiot" and early climbing see Fleming, *Killing Dragons,* 75, 137. For science see Bruce Hevly, "The Heroic Science of Glacier Motion," *Osiris* 11 (1996), 66–86.

9. For sporting motives see Fleming, *Killing Dragons,* 75, 95, 100–5. For Grand Tour see Jim Ring, *How the English Made the Alps* (London: John Murray, 2000), 15–16, 25, 63. For promotion see Peter Hansen, "On the Edge of a Cliff: Mont Blanc and the French Revolution" (paper presented at the American Society for Environmental History," Baton Rouge, 2 March 2007); Peter H. Hansen, "Albert Smith, the Alpine Club, and the Invention of Mountaineering in Mid-Victorian Britain," *Journal of British Studies* 34 (July 1995), 300–24.

10. For social and technological change see David Robbins, "Sport, Hegemony and the Middle Class: The Victorian Mountaineers," *Theory, Culture & Society* 4 (1987), 586. For middle-class see Fleming, *Killing Dragons,* 64–65, 74–75, 83, 101, 144–45, 204. For aesthetic shifts see Marjorie Hope Nicolson, *Mountain Gloom and Mountain Glory: The Development of the Aesthetics of the Infinite* (Seattle: University of Washington Press, 1997), 3, 33, 271–323.

11. For Ruskin see John Ruskin, *Sesame and Lillies,* 2nd ed. in *The Works of John Ruskin,* ed. E. T. Cook and Alexander Wedderburn (New York: Longmans, Green, 1905), 89–90; Fleming, *Killing Dragons,* 140, 294–95. For sport and class see Wigglesworth, *The Evolution of English Sport,* 85–86, 89–103. For economics see Lowerson, *Sport and the English Middle Classes,* 14. For manly sport see Reuben Ellis, *Vertical Margins: Mountaineering and the Landscapes of Imperialism* (Madison: University of Wisconsin Press, 2001), 12. For "represented" see Hansen, "British Mountaineering," 2.

12. For early ascents see Roger Frison-Roche and Sylvain Jouty, *A History of Mountain Climbing,* trans. Deke Dusinberre (New York: Flammarion, 1996), 49–59, 318. For guides see Peter H. Hansen, "Partners: Guides and Sherpas in the Alps and Himalayas, 1850s–1950s," in *Voyages and Visions: Towards a Cultural History of Travel,* ed. Jaś Elsner and Joan-Pau Rubiés (London: Reaktion Books, 1999), 213–14. For Wills and the Wetterhorn

see D. F. O. Dangar and T. S. Blakeney, "The Rise of Modern Mountaineering and the Formation of the Alpine Club, 1854–1865," *Alpine Journal* 62 (November 1957), 16.

13. For socializing see Hansen, "British Mountaineering," 232–33. For milieu see Edward Whymper, *Scrambles amongst the Alps*, ed. and rev. H. E. G. Tyndale (Exeter, U.K.: Webb & Bower, 1986), 134. For Whymper's opportunism see Robbins, "Sport, Hegemony and the Middle Class," 594. For AC see Dangar and Blakeney, "The Rise of Modern Mountaineering," 16–38. For literature see Matthew S. Willen, "Composing Mountaineering: The Personal Narrative and the Production of Knowledge in the Alpine Club of London and the Appalachian Mountain Club, 1858–1900" (Ph.D. diss., University of Pittsburgh, 1995).

14. For "beyond," "exerted," and "country club" see Hansen, "British Mountaineering," 107, 112, 120–21. For club demography, "upper class," and outlook see Lunn, *A Century of Mountaineering*, 43–44, 98, 98–101.

15. For "suicide" see Ring, *How the English Made the Alps*, 78, 218. For "curious" see Ruskin, *Sesame and Lillies*, 21–22n2.

16. For "unjustifiable" see Hansen, "British Mountaineering," 351. For "exclusivity" and "prejudice" see Wigglesworth, *Evolution of English Sport*, 87, 89, 103. For "amateur" and "natives" see Lunn, *A Century of Mountaineering*, 49, 92.

17. For "pointers" and role of guides see Whymper, *Scrambles amongst the Alps*, 35, 100–6, 129–41. Mummery even referred to it as "my crack." A. F. Mummery, *My Climbs in the Alps and Caucasus* (New York: Chas. Scribner's Sons, 1895), 139. For "conformed" see Hansen, "British Mountaineering," 339. For motivation see Dangar and Blakeney, "The Rise of Modern Mountaineering," 19, 22; Walt Unsworth, *Hold the Heights: The Foundations of Mountaineering* (Seattle: Mountaineers, 1994), 53, 74, 91, 94, 99. For celebration of identity see Claire Éliane Engel, *A History of Mountaineering in the Alps* (Westport, Conn.: Greenwood Press, 1977).

18. For "Cockneyism," "communism," and war see Hansen, "British Mountaineering," 104, 333. For "Mont Blanc" see Peter H. Hansen, "Albert Smith, the Alpine Club, and the Invention of Mountaineering in Mid-Victorian Britain," *Journal of British Studies* 34 (July 1995), 308. For "disbelief" see Fleming, *Killing Dragons*, 98–99. For "King" and "objectionable" see Ring, *How the English Made the Alps*, 139.

19. For "courage," "self-respect," "manliness," and "manhood" see Hansen, "British Mountaineering," 286–87, 333. For "spice" see Ring, *How the English Made the Alps*, 157. For "fever" see George Meredith, *The Adventures of Harry Richmond*, rev. ed. (Westminster: Archibald Constable, 1897), 539–40.

20. For "vigorous," "brute force," and "battle" see Whymper, *Scrambles amongst the Alps*, 215. For Whymper and "worth" see Fleming, *Killing Dragons*, 215–20, 247, 252. For criticism of Whymper see Lunn, *A Century of Mountaineering*, 58–60.

21. For glory see Whymper, *Scrambles amongst the Alps*, 22, 63, 197–216.

22. For "violated," "desperate," "selfish," and reactions to accidents see Hansen, "British Mountaineering," 184, 190, 195.

23. For "morality" see John Tyndall, *Hours of Exercise in the Alps* (New York: D. Appleton, 1897), 155–56. For "mystic" and "tones" see Ring, *How the English Made the Alps*, 117–18. For "obsessively" see Robbins, "Sport, Hegemony and the Middle Class," 589; Stephen Heathorn, "How Stiff Were Their Upper Lips? Research on Late-Victorian and Edwardian Masculinity," *History Compass* (2004), B1 093, 4. For "and-so" see Ellis, *Vertical Margins*, 31. For exploration see Hansen, "British Mountaineering," 143–45, 152–53, 161, 172, 213–14.

24. For mountaineering trends and "stones" see Unsworth, *Hold the Heights*, 99, 102. For

beyond Alps see Peter H. Hansen, "Vertical Boundaries, National Identities: British Mountaineering on the Frontiers of Europe and the Empire, 1868–1914," *Journal of Imperial and Commonwealth History* 24 (1996), 48–71.

25. For growth of tourism see Ring, *How the English Made the Alps*, 84, 112, 140, 145–46. For European sports see J. A. Mangan, ed., *Making European Masculinities: Sport, Europe, Gender* (Portland, Ore.: Frank Cass, 2000). For clubs and demography see Hansen, "British Mountaineering," 310, 465, 471–75; Erik Weiselberg, "The Cultural Landscape of the Alps: British and German Mountaineering in the Nineteenth Century" (M.A. thesis, University of Oregon, 1994), 32–33, 36–43. For decline of British see Olivier Hoiban, *Les Alpinistes en France, 1870–1950: Une Histoire Culturelle* (Paris: L'Harmattan, 2000), 20–21.

26. For Cust see Hansen, "British Mountaineering," 353. For "community-oriented" and club activities see Weiselberg, "Cultural Landscape of the Alps," 30, 31–32, 34, 44–48. For nationalism see Unsworth, *Hold the Heights*, 113–16.

27. For Europeans and "mastery" see Lunn, *A Century of Mountaineering*, 90, 92. For "real" see Hansen, "British Mountaineering," 352. For reactions see Unsworth, *Hold the Heights*, 125.

28. For "commonplace," "refuge," and "wandered" see Stephen, *The Playground of Europe*, 66, 67–68. For "Cockney" see Mummery, *My Climbs in the Alps and Caucasus*, 116. For "vulgarizing" see Fleming, *Killing Dragons*, 324–25, 329. For "trippers" and "Holy" see Hansen, "British Mountaineering, 1850–1914," 160, 270. For Lake District see James Winter, *Secure from Rash Assault: Sustaining the Victorian Environment* (Berkeley: University of California Press, 1999); Harriet Ritvo, *The Dawn of Green: Manchester, Thirlmere, and Modern Environmentalism* (Chicago: University of Chicago Press, 2009). For European acceptance see Georg Simmel, *Simmel on Culture: Selected Writings*, ed. David Frisby and Mike Featherstone (Thousand Oaks, Calif.: Sage Publications, 1997), 219.

29. For "mastered" and "knowledge" see Mummery, *My Climbs in the Alps and Caucasus*, 358, 359; for contradictory behavior see ibid., 100, 106, 134, 176, 194–95, 333. For masculinity see Patrick McDevitt, *"May the Best Man Win": Sport, Masculinity, and Nationalism in Great Britain and the Empire, 1880–1935* (New York: Palgrave Macmillan, 2004), 1–13.

30. For "free," "aesthetic," "right thing," "goddess," "worthy," "effeminacy," and "manliness" see Mummery, *My Climbs in the Alps and Caucasus*, 113, 138–39, 325, 327, 331–32, 358. For "gymnast," "reckless," and "essentially" see "In Memoriam: A. F. Mummery," *Alpine Journal* (November 1895), 566, 567, 568. For potshots see Unsworth, *Hold the Heights*, 131. For influence see Yves Ballu, *Les Alpinistes* (Grenoble: Glénat, 1997), 155–67.

31. For "morality" see Unsworth, *Hold the Heights*, 133; but also F. W. Bourdillon, "Another Way of (Mountain) Love," *Alpine Journal* 24 (1908), 148–61. For Dent du Géant see Lunn, *A Century of Mountaineering*, 83. For aid see Kerwin Klein, "Into the Steep: The Eastern Alps and the Culture of Modern Alpinism, 1880–1939," *Sinnhaft* 21 (2008), 54–69.

32. For "uncanny," Dolomites, and "Un-English" see Engel, *A History of Mountaineering in the Alps*, 150–51, 212. For "self-consciously" see Klein, "Into the Steep," 54. For British unease see Fleming, *Killing Dragons*, 310. For Young and pitons see Lunn, *A Century of Mountaineering*, 130. Young's "everything" quoted in Mellor, *American Rock*, 34. For aid see John Middendorf, "The Mechanical Advantage: Tools for the Wild Vertical," in *Ascent: The Climbing Experience in Word and Image*, ed. Allen Steck, Steve Roper, and David Harris (Golden, Colo.: American Alpine Press, 1999), 153–57, 159. For sporting cul-

ture see Thomas L. Altherr, "The American Hunter-Naturalist and the Development of the Code of Sportsmanship," *Journal of Sport History* 5 (Spring 1978), 7–22.

33. For ascents see Middendorf, "The Mechanical Advantage," 156–58; Frison-Roche and Jouty, *A History of Mountain Climbing*, 90–120. For quotes see Lunn, *A Century of Mountaineering*, 130, 170; C. F. Meade, "The Perversion of Mountaineering," *Quarterly Review* 267 (1936), 14–25; Schuster, *Mountaineering*, 32; Irving, *A History of British Mountaineering*, 135; Engel, *A History of Mountaineering in the Alps*, 223; Unsworth, *Hold the Heights*, 114; Hansen, "Modern Mountains," 192; Ring, *How the English Made the Alps*, 245. For distinguishing German from Nazi culture see Thomas M. Lekan, *Imagining the Nation in Nature: Landscape Preservation and German Identity, 1885–1945* (Cambridge, Mass.: Harvard University Press, 2004).

34. For "die" see Lunn, *A Century of Mountaineering*, 90. For "danger" see Unsworth, *Hold the Heights*, 132.

35. For clubs see Jose Burman, *A Peak to Climb: The Story of South African Mountaineering* (Cape Town: C. Struik, 1966), 14–16; Hansen, "British Mountaineering," 473–81. For elitists see Unsworth, *Hold the Heights*, 338. For badges see Hansen, "British Mountaineering," 369–73. For internal rifts see Lunn, *A Century of Mountaineering*, 98–101; Hoiban, *Les Alpinistes en France*, 127, 199, 330.

36. For Americans see Hansen, "British Mountaineering," 353, 417–20, 430, 455; Howard Palmer, "Early History of the American Alpine Club," *AAJ* (1944), 175; Annie S. Peck, "A Woman's Ascent of the Matterhorn," *McClure's* (July 1896), 127–35. Any discussion of influence hinges on its definition. For physical achievement, Conrad Kain and Fritz Wiessner were most impressive. Chic Scott, *Pushing the Limits: The Story of Canadian Mountaineering* (Calgary: Rocky Mountain Books, 2000), 188–92; Jonathan Waterman, *Cloud Dancers, Portraits of American Mountaineers* (Golden, Colo.: American Alpine Club Press, 1993), 9–21. In terms of culture, Underhill's impact was greater at the time.

37. For urbanization see Eric H. Monkkonen, *America Becomes Urban: The Development of U.S. Cities and Towns, 1780–1980* (Berkeley: University of California Press, 1988), 69–130. For Harvard see Kim Townsend, *Manhood at Harvard: William James and Others* (New York: W. W. Norton, 1996), 22, 35–44, 75–78, 117, 176, 180–81, 193, 245. For "expectations" see Gail Bederman, *Manliness and Civilization: A Cultural History of Gender and Race in the United States, 1880–1917* (Chicago: University of Chicago Press, 1995), 13. For health, identity, and conservation see Gregg Mitman, "In Search of Health: Landscape and Disease in American Environmental History," *Environmental History* 10 (April 2005), 195–202; also Bryce Traister, "Academic Viagra: The Rise of American Masculinity Studies," *American Studies* 52 (June 2000), 274–304.

38. For leisure see Lawrence W. Levine, *Highbrow/Lowbrow: The Emergence of Cultural Hierarchy in America* (Cambridge, Mass.: Harvard University Press, 1988), 177, 202–5; Earl Pomeroy, *In Search of the Golden West: The Tourist in Western America* (New York: Knopf, 1957). For primitive and "danger" see Anthony Rotundo, *American Manhood: Transformations in Masculinity from the Revolution to the Modern Era* (New York: Basic Books, 1993), 227. For woodcraft see James Morton Turner, "From Woodcraft to 'Leave No Trace': Wilderness, Consumerism, and Environmentalism in Twentieth-Century America," *Environmental History* 7 (July 2002), 462–84.

39. For James see Townsend, *Manhood at Harvard*, 35–36, 183, 262. For Muir see John Muir to J. B. McChesney, 10 December 1872, in *The Life and Letters of John Muir*, ed. William Frederic Badé (Boston: Houghton Mifflin, 1924), 182; John Muir, *The Mountains of California* (New York: Penguin, 1985), 37–46; Michael P. Cohen, *The Pathless Way: John Muir and American Wilderness* (Madison: University of Wisconsin Press, 1984), 83–84. For

King see Clarence King, *Mountaineering in the Sierra Nevada,* ed. Francis P. Farquhar (rpt. 1935; Lincoln: University of Nebraska Press, 1997), 20, 94, 305–6. For earlier adventurers see Monica Rico, "Sir William Drummond Stewart: Aristocratic Masculinity in the American West," *Pacific Historical Review* 76 (May 2007), 190. For rivalry see Francis P. Farquhar, *History of the Sierra Nevada* (Berkeley: University of California Press, 1965), 145–87.

40. For "muscular Christianity" see H. E. M. Stutfield, "Mountaineering as a Religion," *Alpine Journal* 32 (1918), 243. For Case see Laura Waterman and Peter S. Lewis, *Yankee Rock & Ice: A History of Climbing in the Northeastern United States* (Harrisburg, Pa.: Stackpole, 1993), 15–26. For antimodernism and leisure see Jackson Lears, *No Place of Grace: Antimodernism and the Transformation of American Culture, 1880–1920* (New York: Pantheon, 1981), xii, xv, 5, 117–23.

41. For early American mountaineering see David Mazel, ed., *Pioneering Ascents: The Origins of Climbing in America, 1642–1873* (Harrisburg, Pa.: Stackpole Books, 1991). Other clubs forming at the turn of the century included the British Columbia Mountaineering Club in 1907 and the Colorado Mountain Club in 1912. For "prominent" see Michael P. Cohen, *The History of the Sierra Club, 1892–1970* (San Francisco: Sierra Club Books, 1988), 9, 51. For other clubs see Erik Weiselberg, "Ascendancy of the Mazamas: Environment, Identity and Mountain Climbing in Oregon, 1870 to 1930" (Ph.D. diss., University of Oregon, 1999); Jim Kjeldsen, *The Mountaineers: A History* (Seattle: Mountaineers, 1998), 11–22; Hugh E. Kingery and Elinor Eppich Kingery, *The Colorado Mountain Club: The First Seventy-Five Years of a Highly Individual Corporation, 1912–1987* (Evergreen: Cordillera Press, 1988), 13–49. For American tourism see Ring, *How the English Made the Alps,* 212. For European influences see Charles E. Fay, "Mountain Climbing as an Organized Sport," *The Outlook* 71 (7 June 1902), 378, 380. For clubs see Palmer, "Early History," 173–74, 188–90; Weiselberg, "Ascendancy," 213, 224–25, 343; Cohen, *History,* 44; Kjeldsen, *Mountaineers,* 11–12; "Edward Whymper," *SCB* (January 1912), 213.

42. For "pleasure" see Fay, "Mountain Climbing as an Organized Sport," 383.

43. For "moral stamina" see Palmer, "Early History of the AAC," 168. Sholes quoted in Weiselberg, "Ascendancy," 170. For "over-civilized" see Michael Kimmel, *Manhood in America: A Cultural History* (New York: Free Press, 1996), 136.

44. For Underhill see Henderson, "In Memorium: Robert Underhill," 114–17; phone conversation with Brian Underhill, 20 August 2003. For AMC see Marjorie Hurd, Walter D. Howe, and William R. Diamond, "The Development of A.M.C. Rock Climbing," *Appalachia* (1951), 345–47; Membership application for Robert L. M. Underhill, November 26, 1926, Membership Application Files, Henry S. Hall Jr. Library, American Alpine Club, Golden, Colorado. For essays see, e.g., Robert Underhill, "The Technique of Rock Climbing," *Appalachia* (December 1933), 565–90. For Tetons see Fritiof Fryxell, "The Grand Teton by the North Face," *AAJ* (1932), 465–69.

45. For circle see Harvard Alumni Association, *Harvard Alumni Directory: A Catalogue of Former Students Now Living: Including Graduates and Non-Graduates, and the Holders of Honorary Degrees* (Cambridge, Mass.: Harvard Alumni Association, 1919), 228, 324, 566; membership application for Robert L. M. Underhill, November 26, 1926. For "respected" see Frison-Roche and Jouty, *A History of Mountain Climbing,* 106. For "lover" see Webster, "Closing the Circle," 120.

46. Willa K. Baum, "Francis P. Farquhar: On Accountancy, Mountaineering, and the National Parks," Bancroft, 1–3, 143, 166–68; Harvard Alumni Association, *Harvard Alumni Directory,* 228, 723; phone conversation with Peter Farquhar, 5 September 2003.

47. For "culminating" see Underhill, "Mount Whitney By the East Face," 53. For "correct"

and "aid" see Dawson, "Mountain-Climbing on the 1931 Outing," 113. For trip see Francis P. Farquhar, "Some Climbs of the North Palisade," *SCB* (1932), 124–25.

48. For "virtue," "propriety," and "amateur" see Underhill, "On the Use and Management," 67–68, 73. For other literature see Young, *Mountain Craft*, 1–55, 103–8, 123–24, 140, 192, 200–3, 216–55; Engel, *A History of Mountaineering in the Alps*, 205–6.

49. For "master" see Dick Jones, "The Rock Climbing Section—Then Up to Now," *Mugelnoos*, 25 May 1939, 2. Steve Roper sees Muir as "among the pioneers of California mountaineering," but he does not perceive a cultural chain. Steve Roper, *A Climber's Guide to Yosemite Valley* (San Francisco: Sierra Club, 1964), 19.

50. For "trace" and "sacredness" see Bernadette McDonald and John Amatt, eds., *Voices from the Summit: The World's Great Mountaineers on the Future of Climbing* (Washington: Adventure Press, 2000), 95, 191. For "bum" see Gary Arce, *Defying Gravity: High Adventure on Yosemite's Walls* (Berkeley: Wilderness Press, 1996), 40.

51. For "orthodox" and Muir's background see Dennis C. Williams, *God's Wilds: John Muir's Vision of Nature* (College Station: Texas A & M University Press, 2002), 6. For Tulare see David Igler, "When Is a River Not a River? Reclaiming Nature's Disorder in *Lux v. Haggin*," *Environmental History* 1 (April 1996), 55. For "right" see Muir, *Mountains of California*, 64; Kevin DeLuca and Anne Demo, "Imagining Nature and Erasing Class and Race: Carelton Watkins, John Muir, and the Construction of Wilderness," *Environmental History* 4 (October 2001), 541–60.

52. For "drilled" see John Muir, "The South Dome," in *Sacred Summits: John Muir's Greatest Climbs*, ed. Graham White (Edinburgh: Canongate, 1999), 110. For mystic see Kevin Starr, *Americans and the California Dream: 1850–1915* (New York: Oxford University Press, 1973), 418. For rhetorical parallels see John P. O'Grady, *Pilgrims to the Wild: Everett Ruess, Henry David Thoreau, John Muir, Clarence King, Mary Austin* (Salt Lake City: University of Utah Press, 1993), 90–91, 96, 104; Emil Zsigmondy, *In the High Mountains* (Glasgow: Ernest Press, 1992), 137–53, 275–84. For veneration see Barry Greer, "Mountain Solitaire: The Origins of American Solo Climbing," *Appalachia* (15 June 1992), 12–23; Terry Gifford, *Reconnecting with John Muir: Essays in Post-Pastoral Practice* (Athens: University of Georgia Press, 2006), 150.

3. Pioneers

The epigraph is from "The Rock Climbing Section—Then Up to Now," *Mugelnoos*, 25 May 1939, 4.

1. For peak bagging see Robert C. Pavlik, *Norman Clyde: Legendary Mountaineer of California's Sierra Nevada* (Berkeley: Heyday Books and Yosemite Association, 2008), 23–43. For "Grand Tour" see Robert Cates and Glen Dawson, comp., "Ernest Dawson and the Sierra Club: Exploration of the Southwest" (Pasadena, 1999), 10, Dawson. For other climbers see Bill Oliver, "A Tribute to the Honorary Members of the Sierra Peaks Section—Past & Present: Norman Clyde, Glen Dawson and Jules Eichorn; Part 1: On the Way to Whitney," *The Sierra Echo* 33 (November–December 1989): 3–15; Richard Searle, "Nathan C. Clark: Sierra Club Leader, Outdoorsman, & Engineer," pp. 1–3, Sierra Club History Committee, 1976, Bancroft.

2. For "another" see Norman Clyde, "First Ascent Up The East Face Of Mt. Whitney," folder 90, box 2, Clyde. For "learning," "best," and "experience" see Glen Dawson to Father and Mother, 10 August 1931, Dawson. For public statements see Glen Dawson, "Mountain-Climbing on the 1931 Outing," *SCB* (1932), 113–15; for Dawson's climbing experiences

see Richard Searle, "Glen Dawson: Pioneer Rock Climber and Ski Mountaineer," pp. 4–5, Sierra Club History Committee, 1975, Bancroft.

3. For Leonard see "Richard Leonard Interview Transcripts," 10 November 1972, carton 82:6, pp. 2–7, SCMP.

4. "Richard Leonard Interview," ii–vi, 4–6. For Marshall see James M. Glover, *A Wilderness Original: The Life of Bob Marshall* (Seattle: Mountaineers, 1986), 41–42.

5. Doris Leonard, "Early Days at Cragmont," *The Yodeler,* 7 February 1939, 7.

6. For readings see "Climber's Record for Richard Leonard," c. 1939, Menocal. For "British considered" and "better way" see "Richard Leonard Interview," 6.

7. For "futile" and views on pitons see Geoffrey Winthrop Young, ed., *Mountain Craft* (New York: Charles Scribner's Sons, 1920), 202, 219–20, 246–55. For "treatise" see Robert L. M. Underhill, "On the Use and Management of the Rope in Rock Work," *SCB* (1931), 80.

8. For "infinitely," "fallacy," and testing see Richard Leonard, "Piton Technique on the Cathedral Spires," *Appalachia* 20 (December 1934), 178–79. For "kill you" and innovations see "Richard Leonard Interview," 7.

9. For training, "standard," "impossibility," and "must not" see Young, *Mountain Craft,* 65–73, 148, 149, 261–62. For "inborn" see Underhill, "On the Use and Management of the Rope," 67, 84. For "considerably" see Richard M. Leonard, "Values to Be Derived from Local Rock-Climbing," *SCB* (1934), 28. For long falls see "Indian Rock, Coming & Going," *Yodeler,* 30 October 1939, 7.

10. For "neglect" and "confessing" see Young, *Mountain Craft,* 201. For early club activities see Leonard, "Early Days at Cragmont" and JCCC 1:1–5, carton 7:30, SCSFBCR.

11. JCCC 1:1–5; Rock Climbing Committee, "A Climber's Guide to Local Rock-Climbing," *Yodeler* 1, 19 January 1939, 7; Dick Leonard, "Part III. Indian Rock," *Yodeler* 1, 13 November 1939, 5; Dick Leonard, "A Climber's Guide to Local Rock-Climbing: Part IV. Pinnacle Rock," *Yodeler* 1, 24 November 1941, 4.

12. For "preserve" see JCCC 1:1. For records see "CCC Climbing Record—First Edition—Nov 1, 1932," carton 7:29, SCSFBCR.

13. JCCC 1:5–6; "Richard Leonard Interview," 3–4; Ansel F. Hall to Oliver Kehrlein, 14 July 1934, box 2, Farquhar.

14. JCCC 1:7–9. For Husted see "Membership of the Cragmont Climbing Club on October 23, 1932," carton 7:30, SCSFBCR.

15. For "competition" see Gary Arce, *Defying Gravity: High Adventure on Yosemite's Walls* (Berkeley: Wilderness Press, 1996), 23. Leonard's table is undated photocopy of document provided by Mike Corbett in Roper. For competition see "Ascents Made by Members of the Cragmont Climbing Club," carton 7:30, SCSFBCR. For women competing see Ann Lage, "Marjory Farquhar: Pioneer Woman Rock Climber and Sierra Club Director," 7–17, Sierra Club History Committee, 1977, Bancroft; Valerie Mendenhall Cohen, ed., *Woman on the Rocks: The Mountaineering Letters of Ruth Dyar Mendenhall* (Bishop, Calif.: Spotted Dog Press, 2006), 25, 100, 309–10.

16. For Eichorn see JCCC 1:1; Steve Roper, *Camp 4: Recollections of a Yosemite Rockclimber* (Seattle: Mountaineers, 1994), 20; Leonard, "Early Days at Cragmont." For RCS as insular see Chris Jones, *Climbing in North America* (Seattle: Mountaineers, 1997), 127–28.

17. JCCC 1:9–16; "By-Laws of San Francisco Bay Chapter of the Sierra Club," c. 1933, RCC Reports, Menocal.

18. Lewis F. Clark, "A Rock-Climbing Section of the San Francisco Bay Chapter," *SCB* (1932), 161–62; *Oakland Tribune,* 28 November 1932, 1.

19. For "passed out" see Leonard, "Early Days at Cragmont," 7. For membership and atten-

dance see "CCC Climbing Record—First Edition—Nov 1, 1932" and "RCS Climbing Records, Third Edition—January 1, 1934," carton 7:29, SCSFBCR. For dissolve see Minutes of RCC, 15 February 1933, RCC Reports, Menocal.

20. For growth see "Climbing Area Table for First 14 Half-Years of RCS," carton 7:26; attendance registers for the Rock Climbing Section in carton 7:25; and "Membership of the Cragmont Climbing Club on March 13, 1933," carton 7:30, SCSFBCR. For transit systems see Anthony Perles, *The People's Railway: The History of the Municipal Railway of San Francisco* (Glendale: Interurban Press, 1981); Harre W. Demoro, *The Key Route: Transbay Commuting by Train and Ferry, Part Two* (Glendale: Interurban Press, 1985); Harre W. Demoro, *Electric Railway Pioneer: Commuting on the Northwestern Pacific, 1903–1941* (Glendale: Interurban Press, 1983). For urban transportation elsewhere see Thomas R. Dunlap, *Nature and the English Diaspora: Environment and History in the United States, Canada, Australia, and New Zealand* (New York: Cambridge University Press, 1999), 108–17. I thank Tom Dunlap for this.

21. Glen Dawson, "Climbing the Face of Eagle Rock," *SCB* (1933), 155; Dick Jones, "The Rock Climbing Section—Then Up to Now," *Mugelnoos,* 25 May 1939, 4. For seasonal rhythms see "Mixed Nuts and Dates," *Mugelnoos,* 1 December 1938, 3. For ski industry see Annie Gilbert Coleman, *Ski Style: Sport and Culture in the Rockies* (Lawrence: University of Kansas Press, 2004), 35–72. For ski mountaineering see Bob Brinton, "History of the Ski Mountaineers," *Mugelnoos,* 4 October 1945, 4. For transportation see Ruth Dyar Mendenhall, "Women on the Rocks, Way Back Then," in *Rock and Roses: An Anthology of Mountaineering Essays,* ed. Mikel Vause (La Crescenta, Calif.: Mountain N' Air Books, 1990), 83.

22. For correspondence see Bill Rice to [Dick Leonard], c. 1936, carton 1:1, SCMRR. For visits see "Yodeler Snoops at Stony Point," *Yodeler,* 30 October, 1939, 6; "Devil's Slide—September 21," *Yodeler,* 33 September 1941, 4. For operations see "RCC Meeting Notes," *Yodeler,* 28 May 1940, 4. For "play safe" see "Rock Climbers' Safety First," *Mugelnoos,* 5 May 1938, 5. For technology see Max M. Strumia, "Old and New Helps to the Climber," *AAJ* 1 (1932), 526–27. For nationalism see Geoffrey Winthrop Young, *On High Hills: Memories of the Alps* (London: Metheun, 1933), 340, 357, 362. For "good deal" see Lilian E. Bray, "The Kaisergebirge," *Alpine Journal* 37 (1925), 281–82. For "too easy" see J. H. Doughty, "The Conventions of Mountaineering," in *Hill-Writings of J. H. Doughty,* ed. H. M. Kelly (Manchester: Rucksack Club, 1937), 54.

23. For new technologies see Strumia, "Old and New Helps to the Climber," 526–9. For "natural climb" see Lage, "Marjory Farquhar," 24. For "acrobatics" see Ansel Easton Adams, "Retrospect: Nineteen-Thirty One," *SCB* (1932), 7. For Sholes quote see Erik L. Weiselberg, "Ascendancy of the Mazamas: Environment, Identity and Mountain Climbing in Oregon, 1870 to 1930" (Ph.D. diss., University of Oregon, 1999), 237. For "fun" see "Rock Climbers' Safety First," 5. For playground see Jim Kjeldsen, *The Mountaineers: A History* (Seattle: Mountaineers, 1998), 31. For sexual allusions see Ralph Arthur Chase to O. Kehrlein, 8 March 1934, carton 1:14, SCMRR. For manly conquest see Francis Farquhar's eulogy to Peter Starr in William Alsup, *Missing in the Minarets: The Search for Walter A. Starr, Jr.* (Yosemite: Yosemite Association, 2001), 111–12.

24. For "morals" see Richard Leonard interview by Pieter Crow, 25 October 1983, tape recording, San Francisco, California, Bancroft. For Yosemite trip see "Yosemite Valley Trip, First Annual Climbing Trip of the Rock Climbing Section of the Sierra Club," carton 7:30, SCSFBCR.

25. For "spikes" see "Richard Leonard Interview," 9. For "protractor" see Bestor Robinson,

"First Ascent of the Higher Cathedral Spire," *SCB* (June 1934), 34. For reconnaissance see Leonard, "Piton Technique," 178. For failed attempt see Jules Eichorn to Glen Dawson, 11 September 1933, Dawson.

26. For pitons see Richard Leonard and Arnold Wexler, "Belaying the Leader," *SCB* (December 1946), 86–87. For Sporthaus see "Expenditures Authorized by the Executive Committee," 13 December 1932 to 28 June 1933, RCC Reports, Menocal. For pendulum, chipping, and boosting see Leonard, "Piton Technique," 181–83; Robinson, "First Ascent," 36–37.

27. For "freely" see Eichorn to Dawson, 11 September 1933, Dawson. For "satisfaction" see Robinson, "First Ascent," 37. For "nailing" see Leonard, "Piton Technique," 178. For "not been climbed" and "amused" see "Richard Leonard Interview," 11–12. For "most technical" see John Middendorf, "The Mechanical Advantage: Tools for the Wild Vertical," in *Ascent: The Climbing Experience in Word and Image,* ed. Allen Steck, Steve Roper, and David Harris (Golden, Colo.: American Alpine Press, 1999), 161. For "German" see "Letters From Abroad," *Yodeler,* 7 June 1943, 3. For training see Edward W. Koskinen, "When Is a Piton Not a Piton?" *Yodeler,* 24 April 1939, 7.

28. Peter Holger Hansen, "British Mountaineering, 1850–1914" (Ph.D. diss., Harvard University, 1991), 264–65.

29. Richard M. Leonard and the Committee on Mountaineering, "Mountain Records of the Sierra Nevada," typed mss., Sierra Club, 1937, Bancroft.

4. Members

The epigraph is from "Yosemite Valley Trip, First Annual Climbing Trip of the Rock Climbing Section of the Sierra Club," p. 4, carton 7:30, SCSFBCR.

1. Susan Frohlick, "The 'Hypermasculine' Landscape of High-Altitude Mountaineering," *Michigan Feminist Studies* 14 (1999–2000), 83–106.

2. For women segregated see Jose Burman, *A Peak to Climb: The Story of South African Mountaineering* (Cape Town: C. Struik, 1966), 144–48. For sex-segregated history see Janet Robertson, *The Magnificent Mountain Women: Adventures in the Colorado Rockies* (Lincoln: University of Nebraska Press, 1990). For encouragement see Robert C. Pavlik, *Norman Clyde: Legendary Mountaineer of California's Sierra Nevada* (Berkeley: Heyday Books and Yosemite Association, 2008), 62.

3. For "simple" see Robertson, *Magnificent Mountain Women,* xii. For "Wimmin" see Glenda Riley, *Women and Nature: Saving the 'Wild' West* (Lincoln: University of Nebraska Press, 1999), 1. For Hood see Erik L. Weiselberg, "Ascendancy of the Mazamas: Environment, Identity and Mountain Climbing in Oregon, 1870 to 1930" (Ph.D. diss., University of Oregon, 1999), 125–26. For Lyell see Bertha Gorham Pope, "With the Sierra Club in 1914," *SCB* (January 1915), 247–57.

4. For "undermined" and gendering see Peter Hansen, "British Mountaineering, 1850–1914" (Ph.D. diss., Harvard University, 1991), 293, 312–24, 479–80.

5. For "equal" see Charles E. Fay, "Mountain Climbing as an Organized Sport," *The Outlook* 71 (7 June 1902), 377. For journals see Matthew S. Willen, "Composing Mountaineering: The Personal Narrative and the Production of Knowledge in the Alpine Club of London and the Appalachian Mountain Club, 1858–1900" (Ph.D. diss., University of Pittsburgh, 1995), 261–71. For "social" see Weiselberg, "Ascendancy," 115.

6. For "malignant," "telescope," and new clubs see Weiselberg, "Ascendancy," 113–14, 346–52.

7. For histories see Allen H. Bent, "The Literature of Mountain Climbing in America," *Appalachia* (June 1918), 268–80. For LeConte see Weiselberg, "Ascendancy," 115, 213. For Parsons see Edward Taylor Parsons, "Report of an Investigating Trip to the Yosemite Valley," 21 May 1900, carton 3, Parsons. For Curtis see Jim Kjeldsen, *The Mountaineers: A History* (Seattle: Mountaineers, 1998), 9–12. For "gulag" see Greg Child, *Postcards from the Ledge: Collected Mountaineering Writings of Greg Child* (Seattle: Mountaineers, 1998), 94. For joint see William A. Brooks, "With Sierrans and Mazamas—July, 1905," *Appalachia* (May 1906), 114–25. For Iowa see Sylvanus J. Ebert to Secretary, 9 March 1938, Arthur H. Blake to Ebert, 19 April 1938, carton 1:14, SCMR. For Matthes see correspondence, boxes 1 & 2, Matthes; Glen Dawson to William Colby, 2 May 1955, D-miscellany, box 1, Colby.

8. For Europeans see Hansen, "British Mountaineering," 275–324. For individuals see Bill Birkett and Bill Peascod, *Women Climbing: 200 Years of Achievement* (Seattle: Mountaineers, 1989), 19–31. For categorical see Lawrence C. Hamilton, "Modern American Rock Climbing: Some Aspects of Social Change," *Pacific Sociological Review* 22 (July 1979), 294, 302–3. For North American women see Rachel da Silva, Jill Lawrenz, and Wendy Roberts, "A Brief History of Women Climbing in the Coast and Cascade Ranges," in *Leading Out: Women Climbers Reaching for the Top*, ed. Rachel da Silva (Seattle: Seal Press, 1992), 84–85; Valerie Mendenhall Cohen, ed., *Woman on the Rocks: The Mountaineering Letters of Ruth Dyar Mendenhall* (Bishop, Calif.: Spotted Dog Press, 2006); Karen Routledge, "'Being a Girl Without Being a Girl': Gender and Mountaineering on Mount Waddington, 1926–36," *BC Studies* 141 (Spring 2004), 31–58. For moderates see Weiselberg, "Ascendancy," 197–98, 297. For Bullock and Peck see Rebecca A. Brown, *Women on High: Pioneers of Mountaineering* (Boston: Appalachian Mountain Club, 2002), 143–200. For genderings see Susan R. Schrepfer, *Nature's Altars: Mountains, Gender, and American Environmentalism* (Lawrence: University Press of Kansas, 2005), 72, 82.

9. For "equality" see Annie S. Peck, *A Search for the Apex of America* (New York: Dodd, Mead, 1911), xi. For banners see Reuben Ellis, *Vertical Margins: Mountaineering and the Landscapes of Neoimperialism* (Madison: University of Wisconsin Press, 2001), 95–97. For women-only see Birkett and Peascod, *Women Climbing*, 23, 34; Glen Dawson, "Mountain-Climbing on the 1934 Outing," *SCB* (1935), 105–6.

10. For "responsibility" see Miriam Underhill, *Give Me the Hills* (Riverside, Conn.: Chatham Press, 1956), 150; Miriam E. O'Brien, "Without Men: Some Considerations on the Theory and Practice of Manless Climbing," *Appalachia* (December 1932), 187–203.

11. For "gone" and priorities see Underhill, *Give Me the Hills*, 158, 169. For celebration see Hansen, "British Mountaineering," 79.

12. On membership see Kjeldsen, *Mountaineers*, 13, 19; Ann Lage, "Marjory Farquhar: Pioneer Woman Rock Climber and Sierra Club Director," pp. 40–43, Sierra Club History Committee, 1977, Bancroft. For outings see Anne Farrar Hyde, "Temples and Playgrounds: The Sierra Club in the Wilderness, 1901–1922," *California History* 66 (September 1987), 208–19; Weiselberg, "Ascendancy," 153, 272. For ceremonies see Kevin S. Blake, "Colorado Fourteeners and the Nature of Place Identity," *Geographical Review* 92 (April 2002), 155–79; Kjeldsen, *Mountaineers*, 37, 41.

13. "Cragmont Climbing Club, Founded on March 13, 1932, by Richard M. Leonard—Sierra Club, and Kenneth May—Sierra Club," carton 7:30, SCSFBCR.

14. For attendance see attendance registers in carton 7:25, SCSFBCR.

15. JCCC 2:4, carton 7:30, SCSFBCR.

16. For "support" and "marvelous" see JCCC 2: 6, 19. For spectating see "Or Are They?" *Yo-*

deler, 22 December 1938, 5. For film see Ralph Yearly, "More Benefits of Local Climbing," *Yodeler,* 11 September 1939, 6.

17. For picnics see "Rock Climbing Practice," *Mugelnoos,* 15 September 1938, 5. For swimming see "Pinnacle Rock," *Yodeler,* 8 September 1941, 5. For talking see "Seen Here and There at St. Helena Palisades," *Yodeler,* 20 March 1939, 4. For resting see "Cragmont Rock-Sunday May 10," *Yodeler,* 11 May 1942, 3. For radio see "Hunters Hill," *Yodeler,* 30 October 1939, 5. For Easter see "Current Event," *Mugelnoos,* 6 April 1939, 3. For "skin" and "Underhill" see JCCC 2:5, 17, 44. For knitting see entry for 25 May 1935 in "Sierra Club Rock Climbing Section, Attendance Record 3rd Year, 11/25/34–11/17/35," carton 7:25, SCSFBCR. For "worthy" see Cohen, *Woman on the Rocks,* 47.

18. For "business" see Barbara Norris, "Rock Climbers Found to Be Sane: Will Walk a Mile for a Meal," *Yodeler,* 22 December 1938, 5. For dancing see "A Day with the Rock Climbers" and "Pine Canyon Climb, October 26," *Yodeler,* 27 October 1941, 5. For singing see Helena Nelson, "Neophyte Narrative," *Yodeler,* 30 April 1940, 5. For films see Yearly, "More Benefits of Local Climbing." For scavenger and music see Norris, "Rock Climbers Found to Be Sane," 5. For night climbing see "Technique for the Benighted," *Yodeler,* 8 May 1939, 4. For dress, wrestling, and pillow see JCCC 2:5, 11, 45.

19. For Base Camp see Richard Searle, "John and Ruth Mendenhall: Forty Years of Sierra Club Mountaineering Leadership," pp. 7–10, Sierra Club History Committee, 1979, Bancroft.

20. For banquets see "After the Brawl Is Over," *Mugelnoos,* 10 November 1938, 4. For slumber see "Cragmont Rock-Sunday May 10," *Yodeler,* 11 May 1942, 3. For films see "Climbing Movie," *Mugelnoos,* 27 July 1939, 2. For other activities see Jules Eichorn to Fellow Sierrans, 26 January 1934, Menocal.

21. For newsletters see Richard Searle, "Glen Dawson: Pioneer Rock Climber and Ski Mountaineer," Sierra Club History Committee, 1975, Bancroft, pp. 11–13; Barbara Norris Bedayn, "Yodeler's First Decades: A Glance Back," *Yodeler,* 5 January 1948, i–ii. For features see "Who's Who and Why," *Mugelnoos,* 20 April 1939, 3. For health see *Yodeler,* 24 April 1939, 2. For teasing see "Hynters Hill," *Yodeler,* 15 January 1940, 3; "Third Hand for Rock Climbers," *Yodeler,* 18 December 1939. For "authority" see Weiselberg, "Ascendancy," 128. For "forum" see Richard G. Mitchell Jr., *Mountain Experience: The Psychology and Sociology of Adventure* (Chicago: University of Chicago Press, 1983), 100.

22. For weddings see "Romance Department," *Mugelnoos,* 24 August 1939, 2. For domestic outing see entry for April 25–26, 1936, "Rock Climbing Section Attendance Record, Sierra Club, 4th Years, 11/24/35–11/15/36," carton 7:25, SCSFBCR. For "Get your Man" see Elizabeth Lewis, "What to Wear When on the Rocks," *Mugelnoos,* 4 May 1944, 2. For competition see Cohen, *Woman on the Rocks,* 25–26, 43, 52–53. For "wives" see "To-Moro and To-Moro and To-Moro," *Mugelnoos,* 14 September 1939, 1. For Weeks see "Who's Who on Rocks and Skis No. 52—Ivan Weeks," *Mugelnoos,* 30 October 1947, 2.

23. For "Mass Honeymoon" see "Who's Who No. 36—Bob MacConaghy," *Mugelnoos,* 10 July 1941, 2. For weddings and births see "Married Couple Department," *Mugelnoos,* 10 August 1939, 2. For "social club" see Weiselberg, "Ascendancy," 193. For "joining" see "Romance Dept." *Mugelnoos,* 20 March 1941, 2.

24. For "proselytes" see "Human Fly Convention," *Mugelnoos,* 11 May 1939, 4. For "boys" and training see JCCC 2:24. For articles and talks see "Speech on Rock Climbing Technique," *Mugelnoos,* 18 August 1938, 4. For films see "Two-Twine Technique and Traverse," *Mugelnoos,* 9 November 1939, 1.

25. For scheduling see "Climbing Leaders—Trips Led," c. 1934; for locations see "Committee on Rock Climbing Meeting Choices," 1 October 1935; for leaders see Carolyn Crow-

ley to Doris [Leonard], 17 August 1937; for committees see [RCC] to Ellen Gammack, 3 September 1937; for access see "Minutes of RCC Meeting, 27 November 1940, all in Menocal. For Strawberry see "The First Straw(Berry)," *Mugelnoos*, 8 June 1939, 4. For Bonita see "Lytle," *Mugelnoos*, 22 June 1939, 4.

26. For committees see "Rock Climbing Committee List," c. March 1952, Menocal. For other clubs see John D. Scott, *We Climb High: A Thumbnail Chronology of the Mazamas, 1894–1964* (Portland: Mazamas, 1969), 42; Kjeldson, *Mountaineers*, 46. For Leonard see "Notes—12/20/36," Menocal.

27. For "Mexico" see "Membership Register," RCS, SF Bay Chapter, SC, May 1939," Menocal. For management see "RCS Members Unroped," *Mugelnoos*, 10 August 1939, 4. For meetings see "RCS Meeting," *Mugelnoos*, 23 June 1938, 3; "R.C.S. General Meet Held," *Yodeler*, 20 March 1939, 4. For pins see "R.C.S. Pins Arrive," *Yodeler*, 8 March 1939, 8. For discipline see Mitchell, *Mountain Experience*, 81–88.

28. For accidents see William E. Colby, "Report of the 1921 Outing," *SCB* (1922), 307–8; "Florence Hendra," *SCB* (1934), xvii–xviii. For Starr see William Alsup, *Missing in the Minarets: The Search for Walter A. Starr, Jr.* (Yosemite: Yosemite Association, 2001).

29. Farquhar quoted in Alsup, *Missing*, 111–12.

30. For "occurrences" and "quick" see Mitchell, *Mountain Experience*, 73. For "Self-control" see Dick Jones, "Rock Climbers' Safety First," *Mugelnoos*, 5 May 1938, 5. For tracking see A. M. Binnie, "Western Canada in 1933," *Alpine Journal* (1934), 81–88; "Dyer Barely Escapes Black Book," *Yodeler*, 5 March 1945. For soloing see "Tahquitz," *Mugelnoos*, 27 July 1939, 4. For safety measures see "Rock Climbing Section Meeting," *Mugelnoos*, 19 April 1938, 1. For first aid see 12 April and 10 May in "Rock Climbing Section Attendance Record, Sierra Club, 4th Years, 11/24/35–11/15/36," carton 7:25, SCSFBCR.

31. For AMC see Robert L. M. Underhill, "On the Use and Management of the Rope," *SCB* (1931), 84. For "more difficult" see "Rock Climbing Section Meeting," *Mugelnoos*, 19 April 1938, 1.

32. For monitoring see Glen Dawson to Dick Jones, 2 September 1935, in Glen Dawson, comp., "Dick & Glen: Selected Correspondence [of] Richard Jones and Glen Dawson," 2001, 4, Dawson. For records see "Climber's Record" in Menocal; "Climbing Record of Doris F. Leonard, September 19, 1935," carton 7:29, SCSFBCR.

33. For inconveniences see "Save Miraloma," *Yodeler*, 12 March 1940, 6; "Mt. Hamilton Party Runs into Hornet's Nest," *Yodeler*, 30 April 1940, 3. For unstable rock see "Devils Slide," *Yodeler*, 21 October 1940, 5. For "failed" see "Arrowhead Revisited," *Yodeler*, 10 April 1939, 5. For Babenroth see correspondence in carton 1:3, SCMRR. For Nelson and Rice see Chet Errett, "To the Members of the Sierra Club of California," *Mugelnoos*, 16 July 1942, 5–6.

34. For expenses see "Ropes and Members," *Mugelnoos*, 23 May 1938, 2. For rope lengths see "R.C.C. Meeting Notes," *Yodeler*, 9 April 1940, 7. For managing see "Detailed History of All Ropes," c. late 1933, Menocal. For texts see "Loan List for 'On the Use and Management of the Rope in Rock Work,'" Menocal. For delay see "Indian Rock, Coming & Going," *Yodeler*, 30 October 1939, 7.

35. For technology see John Middendorf, "The Mechanical Advantage: Tools for the Wild Vertical," in *Ascent: The Climbing Experience in Word and Image*, ed. Allen Steck, Steve Roper, and David Harris (Golden: American Alpine Press, 1999), 156, 160. For ropes see "Household Hints for Rock Climbers," *Mugelnoos*, 8 June 1939, 2. For hunting and fishing see Graeme Caughley, *The Deer Wars* (Auckland: Heinemann, 1983), 36–40. I thank for Tom Dunlap for this. For inquiries see Kenneth May, Richard Leonard, and Elliot Sawyer, "Comparative Table of Ropes for Climbing," June 1933, Menocal. For other

clubs see Underhill, "On the Use and Management of the Rope," 69. For tests see Dutch [Leschke] to Dick [Leonard], c. April 1934, "Record of Pitons Placed by the Rock Climbing Section on Local Climbs," Menocal; "The 'Dondero'—A Noble Experiment," *Yodeler*, 22 May 1939, 3.

36. For "quite possible" see Dutch to Dick, c. April 1934. For debate see Richard M. Leonard, "German Pitons," *Yodeler*, 20 March 1939, 4; "Letters to the Editor," *Yodeler*, 8 May 1939, 7.

37. For innovation see Edward Whymper, *Scrambles amongst the Alps*, ed. and rev. H. E. G. Tyndale (Exeter, U.K: Webb & Bower, 1986), 52. For consuming see "Rock Climbing Section Piton Account," May 1938, Menocal.

38. For inquiries see Harland Frederick to Richard Leonard, 31 October 1938. For markets see Leonard, "German Pitons." For innovation see Bob Hansen, "The Wafer Piton: Hardtack," *Yodeler*, 9 April 1940, 4. For demand see "Pitons for a Pittance," *Mugelnoos*, 29 August 1940, 3. For "trusted" see "For Piton Pounders to Ponder," *Yodeler*, 30 September 1940, 3.

39. For order see "Rock Climbing Section Piton Account," May 1938, Menocal. For male-dominated committees see "R.C.C. Meeting Notes," *Yodeler*, 9 April 1940, 7.

40. For women and pitons see Cohen, *Woman on the Rocks*, 127. For women climbing see Lewis F. Clark, "Climbing on the 1933 Sierra Club Outing," *SCB* 18 (1933), 152. For committee activity see "Committee on Rock Climbing Meeting Choices," 1 October 1935, Menocal. For other clubs see Kjeldsen, *Mountaineers*, 14–16. Committee gendering grew more rigid after the war. See "Minutes of RCC meeting," 2 December 1948, Menocal. For Pridham see "Who's Who and Why No. 7—May Pridham," *Mugelnoos*, 27 May 1939, 2. For cartoons see 1938 *Mugelnoos* for 8 July, p. 4; 3 August, p. 4; 18 August, p. 3; 1 September, p. 2; 15 September, p. 6; 29 September, p. 2; 13 October, p. 2; 27 October, p. 2; 29 December, p. 3.

41. For high trips see Michael P. Cohen, *The History of the Sierra Club, 1892–1970* (San Francisco: Sierra Club, 1988), 62–64, 90–92. For government infrastructure see "USNPS Announce Yosemite Activities," *Yodeler*, 4 June 1945. For transportation see Weiselberg, "Ascendancy," 141–47, 334. For lodges see Kjeldsen, *Mountaineers*, 37. For cables see Robertson, *Magnificent Mountain Women*, 56; M. Hall McAllister, "The Half Dome Trail and Stairway," *SCB* (January 1920), 101–3.

42. For Pinnacles see David Brower, "PART II Pinnacles National Monument," *Yodeler*, 20 March 1939, 6–7. For "U-ropia" see "First Tahquitz Climb," *Mugelnoos*, 11 May 1939, 1. For prerequisites see "Rock Climbing Section Meeting," *Mugelnoos*, 19 April 1938, 1.

43. For trip arrangements see "Sierra Club R.C.S. Yosemite Valley May 1937," carton 7:26, SCSFBCR. For "HARD" see "Yosemite: Everybody Came But the Rain," *Yodeler*, 11 June 1940, 3. For numbers see "Yosemite Valley Trip, First Annual Climbing Trip of the Rock Climbing Section of the Sierra Club"; "Yosemite Statistics," *Mugelnoos*, 5 June 1941, 1. For Camp 4 see Harlan D. Unrau, "Evaluation of Historical Significance and Integrity of Sunnyside Campground, Yosemite Valley, Yosemite National Park, California," (National Park Service, Denver Service Center, Resource Planning, 1997), 3–4.

44. For ledgers see "Rock-Climbers Sign-Up List, Sat. May 27, 1939," carton 7:26, SCSFBCR. For Starr see Alsup, *Missing*, 131. For "abilities" see "Yosemite: Everybody Came But The Rain," *Yodeler*, 11 June 1940, 1, 3.

45. For "purpose" and "explore" see RCC to unknown, May 1934; for "walls" see RCC to Randolph and Ken May, 20 August 1933, both in Menocal. For climbs see Richard Leonard, "Rock Climbing in Yosemite," *SCB* (April 1938), 116–19. For "error" see "Foreign Correspondence with W. Kenneth Davis," *Yodeler*, 21 February 1939, 3. For "unsolved" see Pi-

eter Crow, "Interview with Richard Leonard," 25 October 1983, San Francisco, California, Bancroft. For reconnoitering see "Seen Here and There about Yosemite," *Yodeler*, 5 June 1939, 3.

46. For apart see Ethel Boulware, "Afoot with the Sierra Club in 1934," *SCB* (1934), 9. For history see Steve Roper, *Camp 4: Recollections of a Yosemite Rockclimber* (Seattle: Mountaineers, 1994), 21–29. For Higher Spire see Bestor Robinson, "First Ascent of the Higher Cathedral Spire," *SCB* (June 1934), 35. For other ascents see "Higher Cathedral Spire Overrun," *Yodeler*, 30 April 1940, 4; "Seen About Yosemite," *Yodeler*, 13 November 1939, 6; "Pundt, Brower, Leonard, Adam First Ascent," *Yodeler*, 13 October 1941, 5. For "avoidance" and women see Roper, *Camp 4*, 28–29; Lage, "Marjory Farquhar," 16.

47. For spectating see "Seen Here and There about Yosemite," *Yodeler*, 5 June 1939, 3. For Bridge, Brower, and Leonard stories see "Unfit to Be Told," *Yodeler*, 27 February 1940, 7.

48. For "tale is told" see Mitchell, *Mountain Experience*, 72. For "A Night on the Diving Board" see "Newest RCS Song," *Yodeler*, 11 June 1940. For camp life see "Seen about Yosemite," *Yodeler*, 13 November 1939, 6.

49. For "wooing" see "While at Yosemite Did You See————?" *Yodeler*, 2 June 1941, 4. For Dyar/Mendenhall story see "Who's Who and Why No's. 9 and 10," *Mugelnoos*, 14 September 1939, 5. For "pass" and sleep see "Yosemite Valley Trip, First Annual Climbing Trip of the Rock Climbing Section of the Sierra Club," 1, 6–7.

50. For "entirely" see Robert Macfarlane, *Mountains of the Mind* (New York: Pantheon, 2003), 213.

51. Ruth Dyar Mendenhall, "Women on the Rocks, Way Back Then," in *Rock and Roses: An Anthology of Mountaineering Essays*, ed. Mikel Vause (La Crescenta, Calif.: Mountain N' Air Books, 1990), 79–80.

5. Soldiers

The epigraph is from "RCS Anniversary Observed: Dick Leonard Writes from Washington," *Yodeler*, 30 October 1942, 1.

1. For western history see Richard White, *"It's Your Misfortune and None of My Own": A New History of the American West* (Norman: University of Oklahoma Press, 1990), 463–531. For membership see Kenneth D. Adam, "Rock Climbers Look Toward Revival," *Yodeler*, 4 September 1945, special supplement 4, 9.

2. John McPhee, *Encounters with the Archdruid* (New York: Farrar, Straus and Giroux, 1971), 26–34.

3. For Voge, "ego," and sponsorship see David R. Brower, *For Earth's Sake: The Life and Times of David Brower* (Salt Lake City: Peregrine Smith Books, 1990), 29, 31, 64. For climbs see David Brower, "First 1300 Miles in the Sierras, Dave Brower," carton 7:29, SCSFBCR. For joining RCS see JCCC 2: 40.

4. For "lecturing" see Gabrielle Morris, "Bernice Hubbard May: A Native Daughter's Leadership in Public Affairs," p. 101, Sierra Club History Committee, 1976, Bancroft. For activities see Michael P. Cohen, *The History of the Sierra Club, 1892–1970* (San Francisco: Sierra Club, 1988), 395–434. For skills and spirituality see McPhee, *Archdruid*, 28–29.

5. For pitons and ropes see Richard M. Leonard, "German Pitons," *Yodeler*, 20 March 1939, 4; "National Priorities," *Yodeler*, 22 September 1941, 4.

6. For early lobbying see McKay Jenkins, *The Last Ridge: The Epic Story of the U.S. Army's 10th Mountain Division and the Assault on Hitler's Europe* (New York: Random House, 2003), 23–33. For skiing see Annie Gilbert Coleman, *Ski Style: Sport and Culture in the*

Rockies (Lawrence: University of Kansas Press, 2004). For AAC see "Proceedings of the Club" and "National Defence," *AAJ* (1940), 263, 304. For expertise see Susan R. Schrepfer, "Bestor Robinson: Thoughts on Conservation and the Sierra Club," p. 51, Sierra Club Oral History Project, 1974, Bancroft.

7. For "perfect" and "necessary" see "Sierra Club in Washington, D.C.," *Yodeler,* 22 September 1941, 2; "Robinson Urges RCS to Perfect Technique for Army Mountaineers," *Yodeler,* 2 June 1941, 1. For recruitment see "Skiing and National Defense," *Yodeler,* 29 December 1941, 1, 8; "Western Men Wanted," *Mugelnoos,* 1 January 1943, 1. For pulling strings see "Former Sierra Club Director Heads New Office," *Yodeler,* 23 August 1943, 1. For patrol see "Ski Mountains and Rock Climbers Patrols," *Mugelnoos,* 8 October 1942, 5.

8. For "anyone" see "From Porthole to Plantation," *Yodeler,* 27 April 1942, 2. For Army details see Schrepfer, "Bestor Robinson," 51; "Richard Leonard Interview transcripts," 10 November 1972, pp. 39–40, carton 82:6, SCMP. For RCS committee see "New Rock Climbing Committee," *Yodeler,* 27 October 1941, 1. For field tests see "RCS Pioneers in Testing Program," *Yodeler,* 27 October 1941, 1.

9. For surfing see Douglas Booth, "Surfing: The Cultural and Technological Determinants of a Dance," *Culture, Sport, Society* 2 (Spring 1999), 39. For weights see "Equipment Notes for Reference," c. 1941, Menocal. For manuals and movies see "The Technique of Rock Climbing," carton 23:36, SCMP; David R. Brower, ed., *Manual of Ski Mountaineering* (Berkeley: University of California Press, 1942).

10. For rumor see "R.C.C. Notes—November 27: A New Rope, R.C.S. Belay Technique," *Yodeler* 2, 16 December 1940, 4. For "superior" see "RCS Anniversary Observed," 1, 7. For "considerable" and data see Captain Leonard to Lt. Colonel Robinson, "SUBJECT: Rope, Climbing (Nylon)," 20 March 1943; for "posterity" see Richard M. Leonard to Francis P. Farquhar, 24 March 1943, both in carton 44:1, SCMP. For testing see "Minutes of RCC Meeting, 3 July 1942," and "Minutes of RCC Meeting, c. early September 1942," both in Menocal.

11. For Himalayan parallels see Peter H. Hansen, "Coronation Everest: The Empire and Commonwealth in the 'Second Elizabethan Age,'" in *British Culture and the End of Empire,* ed. Stuart Ward (New York: Manchester University Press, 2001), 61–63.

12. For "light-weight" and "postpone" see [Richard Leonard], "Priority," *Yodeler,* 27 October 1941, 5. For rationing see United States, *Battle Stations for All: The Story of the Fight to Control Living Costs* (Washington: Office of War Information, 1943). For ropes see "National Priorities," *Yodeler,* 22 September 1941, 4. For restricted RCS schedules see "RCS Summer Schedule," *Yodeler,* 8 September 1942, 2; "Calendar," *Mugelnoos,* 19 August 1943, 1. For Harris see "Minutes of RCC Meeting, 2 November 1942," Menocal.

13. For enlistments see *SCB* (1946), 102–11; "More Mountaineers en Route to Mountain Regiment," *Yodeler,* 9 February 1942, 2. For base camp see Richard Searle, "John and Ruth Mendenhall: Forty Years of Sierra Club Mountaineering Leadership," p. 9, Sierra Club History Committee, 1979, Bancroft. For *Mugelnoos* see "Editorial," *Mugelnoos,* 5 March 1942, 2. For "100%" see "Minutes of RCC Meeting, 30 September 1942," Menocal. For "ceased" and qualifications see "Minutes of RCC Meeting, 20 October 1941," Menocal.

14. For Bay Area RCS see "R.C.S.—Grizzly Caves—January 13," *Yodeler,* 26 January 1942, 3. For Southern RCS see "Rock Climbing Boom," *Mugelnoos,* 14 May 1942, 1. For leave see "Spring Revives Rock Climbing," *Yodeler,* 13 March 1944, 1. For wartime activities see "Climbers to Aid in Trail Work," *Yodeler,* 2 April 1945, 1.

15. For visitor figures see SupAR. For "duration" see "Yosemite Climbing," *Yodeler,* 8 September 1942, 3. For "mecca" and visits see "Yosemite Rock Climbing," *Mugelnoos,* 5 No-

vember 1942, 4; William Shand, Jr., "Some Yosemite Rock-Climbs," *AAJ* (1944), 210. For Tahquitz see "Bus-Ride for Tahquitz Climb," *Mugelnoos*, 14 May 1942, 2. For "takers" see *Yodeler*, 29 March 1943, 5.

16. For "disappointed" and "babysitter" see Valerie Mendenhall Cohen, ed., *Woman on the Rocks: The Mountaineering Letters of Ruth Dyar Mendenhall* (Bishop, Calif.: Spotted Dog Press, 2007), 202, 206.

17. For "highlights" see "RCS Summer Schedule," *Yodeler*, 8 September 1942, 2. For banquets see "Banquet Big Success," *Mugelnoos*, 14 May 1942, 1. For tracking see "Who's Where and Why," *Mugelnoos*, 19 August 1943, 2.

18. For "ten weeks" see "Service Notes," *Mugelnoos*, 23 April 1942, 4. For officers see "Army Wives Head for Washington," *Yodeler*, 19 October 1942, 4. For Camp Hale see "Mountain Men 1942," *Mugelnoos*, 10 September 1942, 1; Jack A. Benson, "Skiing at Camp Hale: Mountain Troops during World War II," *Western Historical Quarterly* 15 (April 1984), 169.

19. For carefree see "Still More Letters," *Yodeler*, 23 February 1943, 7. For crises see Benson, "Skiing at Camp Hale," 165–70.

20. Brower, *For Earth's Sake*, 87, 89, 95–96.

21. For Camp Hale see "Army-Bound Brower Visits East Bay," *Yodeler*, 19 October 1942, 4; David R. Brower, "Artur Argiewicz, Jr.," *SCB* (December 1945), 86–89. For training see "The Technique of Rock Climbing," carton 23:36, SCMP. For "affinity" and "shuddering" see "Instructor Describes Climbing Accident," *Yodeler*, 1 May 1944, 8.

22. For 10th Mountain Division see C. Minot Dole, *Adventures in Skiing* (New York: Franklin Watts, 1965). For "battalion" and "strip-tease" see Robert A. Bates, "The Pay-Off on Winter Training," *AAJ* (1946), 254. For warfare see Albert H. Jackman, "The Tenth Mountain Division," *AAJ* (1946), 187–92.

23. For Leonard see "Former Sierra Club Director Heads New Office," *Yodeler*, 23 August 1943, 1; "Richard Leonard Interview transcripts," p. 43; "Yodelears Hear," *Yodeler*, 13 August 1945, 7; "Yodelears Hear," *Yodeler*, 4 September 1945, 4. For POWs see "Rock Climber Arrives in England," *Yodeler*, 25 May 1942, 1; "Message Received from Leland Chase," *Mugelnoos*, 27 May 1943, 1; "Prisoner of War," *Mugelnoos*, 17 June 1943, 1; "Jack Arnold Liberated," *Yodeler*, 21 May 1945, 2; "Prisoners of War Rescued," *Mugelnoos*, 4 October 1945, 1. For joys and sorrow see "Flying Climber Decorated," *Yodeler*, 29 March 1943, 1; "Mountain Infantryman Killed in Action," *Yodeler*, 19 February 1945, 1.

24. For western clubs see Erik L. Weiselberg, "Ascendancy of the Mazamas: Environment, Identity and Mountain Climbing in Oregon, 1870 to 1930" (Ph.D. diss., University of Oregon, 1999), 8, 21, 72, 104–5, 109, 222, 228, 236, 252–53, 359, 362; Cohen, *History*, 7, 19–29, 39–40, 62–63, 94–100; Lawrence Rakestraw, "Before McNary: The Northwest Conservationist, 1889–1913," *Pacific Northwest Quarterly* 51 (1960), 56.

25. For "proving-ground" see Ansel Easton Adams, "Retrospect: Nineteen-Thirty One," *SCB* (1932), 7. For "ten" see Brower, *For Earth's Sake*, 57.

26. For gardening see "New Rock Grounds Discovered," *Mugelnoos*, 23 June 1938, 2. For snakes see David R. Brower, "St. Helena Miscellany: How a Rock Climber Saw It," *Yodeler*, 30 April 1940, 5. For huts see "San Jacinto Tramway Bonds Approved," *Mugelnoos*, 10 May 1945, 1. For wilderness values see Paul Sutter, *Driven Wild: How the Fight Against Automobiles Launched the Modern Wilderness Movement* (Seattle: University of Washington Press, 2002), 54–99, 194–238.

27. For "energetic" see Cohen, *History*, 71.

28. For Brower see *Yodeler*, 19 March 1945. For Leonard see *Mugelnoos*, c. February 1945. Al Baxter found the Alps "quite civilized, no back packing, *no bushes*, huts and all modern conveniences." "In the Editor's Mail," *Yodeler*, 17 October 1949, 4.

29. For "undesecrated" see Cohen, *History,* 64. For "happy few" and debate see Kenneth May, "Tenth Division Man Tells of Value of Previous Mountain Experience," *Yodeler,* 7 May 1945, 4; "Riegelh Praises Big Bend Country," *Yodeler,* 20 November 1944, 2; Dick Leonard, "Conservationist Writes From I-B Jungle," *Yodeler,* 4 December 1944, 3; Arthur H. Blake, "Re Conservation—The Race Is On," *Yodeler,* 8 January 1945, 1, 4; Major Richard M. Leonard, "Threats to Wilderness Arising from Unexpected Sources; Need for Vigilance Seen," *Yodeler,* 17 September 1945, 1, 8; David Brower, "How to Kill a Wilderness," *SCB* (August 1945), 2–5. For climbs see David Brower, "Some GI Climbs in the Alps," *SCB* (December 1945), 79–85. For Marsh see David Lowenthal, *George Perkins Marsh, Prophet of Conservation* (Seattle: University of Washington Press, 2000).

30. Both Adams and Brower used the phrase "proving ground." See Adams, "Retrospect," 7; Cohen, *History,* 81. For wilderness values see William Cronon, "The Trouble with Wilderness or, Getting Back to the Wrong Nature," in *Uncommon Ground: Toward Reinventing Nature,* ed. William Cronon (New York: W. W. Norton, 1995), 69–90. For sport and gender see Wanda Ellen Wakefield, *Playing to Win: Sports and the American Military, 1898–1945* (Albany: State University of New York Press, 1997), 136–37. For postwar wilderness see Lawrence S. Brown to David Brower, 29 March 1947, carton 23:36, SCMP.

31. For returns see "Special Victory Edition," *Yodeler,* 4 September 1945. For "old times" see "Pine Canyon Revisited," *Yodeler,* 4 June 1945, 4. For practices and parties see "The Social Climber," *Yodeler,* 13 August 1945, 4. For "unchanging" see "The Social Climber," *Yodeler,* 2 July 1945, 4; SupMR, July 1945; Adam, "Rock Climbers Look Toward Revival," 4, 9. For statistics see "Army Wedding," *Mugelnoos,* 4 February 1943, 4; "Preferred Stork," *Mugelnoos,* 20 December 1944, 3.

32. For "baby production" see Ann Lage, "Marjory Farquhar: Pioneer Woman Rock Climber and Sierra Club Director," p. 22, Sierra Club History Committee, 1977, Bancroft. For "came along" and "lead" see Richard Leonard Interview by Pieter Crow, 25 October 1983, San Francisco, California, Bancroft.

33. For "lives" see Richard White, "'Are You an Environmentalist, Or Do You Work for a Living?' Work and Nature," in *Uncommon Ground,* 174. For retreat see Cohen, *Woman on the Rocks,* 232. For masculinity see Zygmunt Bauman, "Postmodern Adventures of Life and Death," in *Modernity, Medicine and Health: Medical Sociology towards 2000,* eds. Graham Scambler and Paul Higgs (New York: Routledge, 1998), 216–31.

6. Individualists

The epigraph is from the minutes of the Rock Climbing Committee, 21 April 1941, Menocal.

1. Muir quoted in Michael P. Cohen, *The History of the Sierra Club, 1892–1970* (San Francisco: Sierra Club Books, 1988), 104. For Ritter see John Muir, *The Mountains of California* (New York: Penguin, 1985), 37–46. For existential see Michael P. Cohen, *The Pathless Way: John Muir and American Wilderness* (Madison: University of Wisconsin Press, 1984), 82. For "frowned" see Dick Jones, "The Rock Climbing Section—Then Up to Now," *Mugelnoos,* 25 May 1939, 4.

2. For early ascents see Hubert Dyer, "Camping in the Highest Sierras," *Appalachia* (January 1892), 273–89; Joseph N. LeConte, "Scrambles About Yosemite," *SCB* (January 1914), 126–35. For Michael see C. W. Michael, "First Ascent of the Minarets," *SCB* (1924), 28–33.

3. For Clyde see Robert C. Pavlik, *Norman Clyde: Legendary Mountaineers of California's Sierra Nevada* (Berkeley: Heyday Books and Yosemite Association, 2008). For tragedies

and "walks" see William Alsup, *Missing in the Minarets: The Search for Walter A. Starr, Jr.* (Yosemite: Yosemite Association, 2001), 47–49.

4. "Mountaineering Notes, *SCB* (1930), 109–10; "Some Sierra Ascents in 1931," *SCB* (1932), 120–21; David R. Brower, "Some Climbs in the Sierra—1933," *SCB* (1934), 97–98.

5. For Ritter see Muir, *Mountains of California*, 45. For "over-civilized" see Michael Kimmel, *Manhood in America: A Cultural History* (New York: Free Press, 1996), 136. For "limpid" see Norman Clyde, "The First Ascent of the Highest of the Minarets and of Mt. Ritter: The Sierra Nevada," folder 56, box 1; for "corpuscles" and "jaded" see Norman Clyde, "Mountain Climbing as a Means of Physical Training," folder 104, box 2, both in Clyde. For "shouted" see Muir, *My First Summer in the Sierra* (Boston: Houghton-Mifflin, 1998), 115–16, 118–20.

6. For "aesthetic" see Cohen, *History*, 65–66. For "climb" see John Muir to Mrs. Ezra S. Carr, 16 October 1873, in *The Life and Letters of John Muir*, ed. William Frederic Badé, 2 vols. (Boston: Houghton Mifflin, 1924), 1:293–94. For Brower see "First 1300 Miles in the Sierras, Dave Brower," carton 7:29, SCSFBCR; David R. Brower, "Some Climbs in the Sierra—1933," *SCB* (1934), 97–98. For Marshall see James M. Glover, *A Wilderness Original: The Life of Bob Marshall* (Seattle: Mountaineers, 1986), 30–42, 50–51, 79, 114–15.

7. For "Agassizjoch" see David R. Brower, *For Earth's Sake: The Life and Times of David Brower* (Salt Lake City: Peregrine Smith Books, 1990), 29. For lists see the RCS Climber's Records in Menocal. For "invited" see Bruce Barcott, "Our Son of a Bitch," *Outside* 26 (February 2001), 53.

8. Jim Kjeldsen, *The Mountaineers: A History* (Seattle: The Mountaineers, 1998), 45–50; Erik L. Weiselberg, "Ascendancy of the Mazamas: Environment, Identity and Mountain Climbing in Oregon, 1870 to 1930" (Ph.D. diss., University of Oregon, 1999), 333–34, 345.

9. For Cathedral see Bestor Robinson, "First Ascent of the Higher Cathedral Spire," *SCB* (June 1934), 34–37. For other climbs see Oliver Kehrlein to Norman Clyde, 16 June 1933, folder 7a–m, box 4, Clyde; Lewis F. Clark, "Up Tenaya Cañon in the Spring," *SCB* (1934), 101.

10. For beyond see Bestor Robinson, "The Ascent of El Picacho Del Diablo," *SCB* (1933), 56–62; Glen Dawson, "Rock-Climbing in Oregon," *SCB* (1935), 109. For RCS elsewhere see "Climbing in the Grand Teton Nat'l Park," *Mugelnoos*, 15 September 1938, 5; "The Crimson Canyons of the Kolob," *Mugelnoos*, 21 August 1941, 5; "Alaska Blitzed," *Yodeler*, 8 September 1941, 5. For Telescope see "No Count," *Mugelnoos*, 8 June 1939, 2. For "rock climb" see Susan R. Schrepfer, "Richard M. Leonard: Mountaineer, Lawyer, Environmentalist," 2 vols., Bancroft, 1975, 14.

11. For conditions and "lucky" see Schrepfer, "Richard M. Leonard," 15.

12. For backgrounds see Schrepfer, "Richard M. Leonard," 11, 28–31; Richard Searle, "Glen Dawson: Pioneer Rock Climber and Ski Mountaineer," Bancroft, 1975, 6; George Sinclair, "Interview with Jules Eichorn," AAC, 12–14. For generations see "Climb C-17 Proven Possible," *Yodeler*, 25 September 1939, 5.

13. For "old guard" see "Rock Climbing Notes," *Yodeler*, 18 November 1946, 3. For "scramming" see "And Here, in a Few Words, Are the Rock Climbers," *Yodeler*, 15 December 1941, 3. For speed and link-ups see Don to Dick, 11 October 1937, carton 1:14, SCMRR. For new climbs see "Pulpit Again," *Yodeler*, 14 May 1940, 7; "Kat's Pinnacle Topped," *Yodeler*, 18 November 1940, 4. For beyond Yosemite see "New Climb Made at Pinnacles," *Yodeler*, 16 October 1939, 4.

14. For mockery see "Climb C-17 Proven Possible," *Yodeler*, 25 September 1939, 5. For "grandmother" see *Yodeler*, 8 September 1942, 2. For "middle-aged" see *Yodeler*, 21 September 1942, 2.

15. For "yours" see Chris Jones, *Climbing in North America* (Seattle: Mountaineers, 1997), 156. For "formal" see "RCS Climbers Scale Bugaboo, Mt. Louis," *Mugelnoos*, 1 September 1938, 1. For "cannot" and "nailing" see "What's Next?" *Yodeler*, 30 January 1940, 5.

16. For first ascent see "Snowpatch Spire Climbed," *Yodeler*, 26 August 1940, 1. For return see "Snowpatch Again," *Yodeler*, 8 September 1941, 4–5. For "training" and "better" see "Double Spires Causes Comments," *Yodeler*, 31 March 1941, 2.

17. For confidence see "Bugaboo Boys Back," *Mugelnoos*, 15 September 1938, 2. For "toughest" and "monster" see Robert Ormes, "A Piece of Bent Iron," *Saturday Evening Post*, 22 July 1939, 13. For "Intelligence" see "CORRESPONDENCE FILE OF Richard M. Leonard," carton 82:27, SCMP.

18. For "sudden" see Ormes, "A Piece of Bent Iron," 13. For "only" and "home-ground" see Jones, *Climbing in North America*, 134–35.

19. For "military" see Cohen, *History*, 75. For data see "CORRESPONDENCE FILE OF Richard M. Leonard." For celebrations see "Shiprock Sunk After Long Battle," *Yodeler*, 16 October 1939, 1, 5–6; "Don't Rock the Boat," *Mugelnoos*, 26 October 1939, 1.

20. For equipment see Raffi Bedayan, "Shiprock Finale," *T&T* (February 1940), 23. For "bombproof" see Edward W. Koskinen, "When Is a Piton Not a Piton?" *Yodeler*, 24 April 1939, 7.

21. For overseas see F. H. Keenlyside, "American Alpine Journal, Volume VI, No. 3, 1947, Canadian Alpine Club Journal, Volume XXX, 1947, Mountain Club of East Africa, Bulletin, Nos. 3, 4, and 5, 1947, Mountain Club of South Africa, Journal, No. 49, 1946, Sierra Club Bulletin, Volume 32, No. 5, 1947," *Climbers Club Journal* 8 (1948), 387–90. For "Rocking-Chair" see D.R.B., "Lament of a Rocking-Chair Mountaineer," *Yodeler*, 12 May 1940, 3. For "engineer" see Bestor Robinson, "The First Ascent of Shiprock," *SCB* (1940), 3. For "further" see Carl Melzer, "American Alpine Journal" *T&T* (April 1940), 58; "Was Shiprock Climbed?" *Yodeler*, 30 October 1939, 3; Art Blake, "Rock Engineers Hasten Erosion," *Yodeler*, 12 May 1940, 2, 3.

22. David Brower, "It Couldn't Be Climbed," *Saturday Evening Post*, 3 February 1940, 24–25, 72–75.

23. Schrepfer, "Richard M. Leonard," 53–54; Frank A. Kittredge, "Memorandum for the Files," 27 October 1939, Superintendents' Conference 10/27/38–12/31/41, box 1; Richard M. Leonard to Arno B. Cammerer, 1 February 1940, Conference Data 1939 Santa Fe, N.M., Confidential, box 11, Central Classified Files, 1925–1953, General Records, NARASB.

24. For rescues see SupMR," August 1925 and July 1931; Memo to Supt. Col Thompson, 8 August 1935, Miscellaneous Accidents, 1925–1937, file 801-01.1, YRL.

25. For "rough" see SupMR, December 1927. For "ladders" see SupMR, June 1930. For "excellently" see SupAR, 1933. For "high," "cries," and "exposed" see SupMR, May 1934; "STATEMENTS OF MR. ALFRED SOARES . . . [and] OF MR. OCTAVIO JOHN CAMARA," 23 May 1934, Miscellaneous Accidents, 1925 to 1937, 801-01.1, YRL.

26. For defense see Bestor Robinson, "First Ascent of Higher Cathedral Spire," 37; President [of the Sierra Club] to Col. C. G. Thomson, 17 October 1934, carton 40:26, SCMP. For bragging see "Personals and Personalities," *Mugelnoos*, 27 July 1939, 2. For "beneficial" see Superintendent to Director, 12 August 1935, Miscellaneous Accidents, 1925 to 1937, 801-01.1, YRL. For "gawking" see "To-Moro and To-Moro and To-Moro," *Mugelnoos*, 14 September 1939, 1. For "stunts" see "Stunt Mountain Climbs Should Be Discouraged," *Yodeler*, 16 October 1939, 4.

27. For climbing reports see SupMRs for July 1932, January 1933, February 1934, February 1936. For socializing see Horace Albright to Francis Farquhar, 28 July 1922, box 1, Far-

quhar. For joint climbs see SupMR for March 1932. For "nothing" see B. F. Manday to
Frank Kittredge, 30 September 1939, Conference Data 1939 Santa Fe, N.M., Confidential, box 11, Central Classified Files, 1925–1953, General Records, NARASB.

28. For policy see "Climbing Rangers Urded [*sic*] for Parks," *Yodeler,* 11 September 1939, 1.
    For Eichorn see "Jules M. Eichorn," Hiring Cards file, YRL. For training see "Pitons for
    the NPS," *Yodeler,* 11 September 1939, 1. For later rangers see "Thomas H. Rixon," Hir-
    ing Cards file, YRL; "National Park Service Rock Climbing Training Conference, Yosemite
    National Park, November, 1955: Lesson Plans," "Rock Climbing," Vertical Files, YRL.

29. For "facilitate" see "Climbing Rangers Urded [*sic*] for Parks." For "efficiency" see SupAR
    1945; SupMR August 1940.

30. For early records see "Sierra Club—San Francisco Bay Chapter—Rock Climbing Section,
    Climbers Record—an index to rock climbing progress—," carton 7:26, SCSFBCR. For "in-
    dividualistic" see Morgan Harris, "Classification of Climbers," *Yodeler,* 11 June 1940, 6, 7.
    For refinements see "Minutes of RCC Meeting," 20 October 1941, Menocal; Dave Brower
    to Charles H. Wilts, 13 January 1955, carton 23:36, SCMP. For suspension see "Rock
    Climbing Section Abolished," *Yodeler,* 1 April 1946, 5. For "proficiency" and debate see
    "RCS By-Laws," *Mugelnoos,* 13 June 1946, 3; "RCS Safety Committee Meeting," *Mugel-
    noos,* 13 December 1951, 1. For tests and routes see "Proposed RCS Membership Test,"
    Mugelnoos, 13 June 1946, 1. For leader list see "Qualified Leaders and Members of the
    Sierra Club Rock Climbing Section, San Francisco Bay Chapter—January, 1956," carton
    193:12, SCMP.

31. For systems see "C.M.C. Earmarks Climbers," *Mugelnoos,* 18 July 1940, 3; Kjeldsen,
    Mountaineers, 43–45; "Summary of Annual Mountaineering Reports from Areas Admin-
    istered by the National Park Service, 1958," Mountaineering file, Vertical Files, YRL.

32. "Minutes of RCC Meeting," 21 April 1941, Menocal.

33. For "independent" and "patronize" see "Minutes of RCC Meeting," 21 April 1941; for
    "crack down" see "Minutes of RCC Meeting," 17 June 1948, Menocal. For "protection"
    see "Mountaineering Notes," *Yodeler,* August 1961, 4. For loans see "Equipment Round-
    Up," *Mugelnoos,* 8 November 1951, 4.

34. For RCS purchases see "Nylons," *Mugelnoos,* 13 June 1946, 1; "Minutes of RCC meeting,"
    20 December 1955, Menocal. For "legitimate" see "Twentieth Annual National Park Ser-
    vice Conference, Yosemite National Park, October 16–20, 1950," National Park Service
    Conference, Oct. 1950–Feb. 1952 folder, box 12, Central Classified Files, 1925–1953,
    NARASB. For "stunt" see Carl Russell to Roy Gorin, 23 September 1952; for "delicately,"
    problems, and lobbying see Richard Leonard to Gorin, 4 October 1952, carton 93:25,
    SCR. For interventions see Leonard to Gallwas, 27 May 1954, carton 93:25. For "never"
    see Wayne A. Merry and Warren J. Harding to Dick Leonard, 16 December 1958, carton
    88:27, SCR.

35. For nexus see SupMR for September 1948. For sign-out see "Summary of Annual Moun-
    taineering Reports from Areas Administered by the National Park Service, 1958," carton
    88:27, SCR. For institutional approach see "Climbing Problems in National Parks Dis-
    cussed," *Mugelnoos,* 11 November 1948, 2.

36. For visitors see "The Printed Word," *Mugelnoos,* 2 October 1947, 2; SupARs for 1946 to
    1959; SupMRs for July 1945, July 1958. For "noticeable" see SupMR January 1931. For
    "vigilance" and resources see SupAR, 1946. For development and criticism see Alfred
    Runte, *Yosemite: The Embattled Wilderness* (Lincoln: University of Nebraska Press,
    1990), 181–200.

37. For "new people" see "Minutes of RCC meeting, 10 March 1953, Menocal. For growth
    see "Atomic Event?" *Mugelnoos,* 16 May 1946, 1; "Men v. Mountains," *Time,* 10 October

1949, 44; Martin Litton, "Rock Climbers Practice on Valley 'Peaks,'" *Los Angeles Times*, 31 May 1951, 2:1. For domesticity see Joanne Meyerowitz, "Beyond the Feminine Mystique: A Reassessment of Postwar Mass Culture, 1946–1958," in *Not June Cleaver: Women and Gender in Postwar America, 1945–1960*, ed. Joanne Meyerowitz (Philadelphia: Temple University Press, 1994), 230–62. For generations see "The Social Climber," *Yodeler*, 1 October 1945, 4. For socializing see Howard Frohlich, "Rock Climbers' Party," *Yodeler*, 18 October 1954, 3. For mobility see Sylvia Kershaw, "The Lost Climb," *Yodeler*, 3 January 1949, 3. For global growth see Jim Ring, *How the English Made the Alps* (London: John Murray, 2000), 265. For "hospitality" see "The Social Climber," *Yodeler*, 15 October 1945, 4. For "white-man's" see "Tires for Fires," *Yodeler*, 5 February 1951, 3. For safety see "Rescue on Rocks," *Yodeler*, 20 December 1948, 1. For romance see "Beaumont-Wilts Wedding," *Mugelnoos*, June 1947, 3.

38. For "guard" see "The Social Climber," *Yodeler*, 1 October 1945, 4. For SC officers see "Officers Elected," *Mugelnoos*, 16 May 1946, 1. Raffi Bedayn shortened his last name in the early 1940s. See "Climbers Enjoy McKinley Pictures," *Yodeler*, 21 June 1943, 1. For other sections see Ray de Saussure, "Caving in California & Nevada," *Yodeler*, 20 October 1952, 6; "Knapsackers! Reconsider Unique Offer!" *Yodeler*, 19 January 1953, 7–8. For tensions see Thomas R. Dunlap, *Saving America's Wildlife: Ecology and the American Mind, 1850–1990* (Princeton: Princeton University Press, 1988), 84–88, 92–96, 132–37. I thank Tom Dunlap for this.

39. For growth see "Sierra Club News," *Mugelnoos*, 10 May 1956, 1. For political decline see Hervey Voge to Alexander Hildebrand, n.d., and D.R.B., "*CONFIDENTIAL* Mountaineering Committee," carton 31:35, SCMP. Prominent in the Southern RCS were Roy Gorin, George Harr, Ivan Weeks, Don Wilson, and Charles and Ellen Wilts. Leaders in the Bay Area RCS included Oscar Cook, Ray de Saussure, Bill Dunmire, Joe Firey, Dick Houston, Bill Long, Dick Long, Anton Nelson, John Salathé, Allen Steck, Bob Swift, and Frank Tarver.

40. For "horseback" see "Yosemite National Park," *Mugelnoos*, 16 May 1946, 1. For "population" and "reducing" see Polly Dyer, "Who Mist Yosemite?" *Yodeler*, 7 June 1948, 3. For 1950s see Ray DeSaussure, "'Easter West' Or Which Route Do You Want?" *Yodeler*, 21 April 1952, 8.

41. For western clubs see "Mountaineers Hear—," *Yodeler*, 17 January 1955, 4. For eastern clubs see "!NOTICE!" *Yodeler*, 7 May 1951, 2. For AAC see *AACN*, 16 June 1952, 4. For WFOC see "Conventional Weekend," *Mugelnoos*, 14 July 1955, 1. For joint see "Tahquitz—September 29, 30," *Mugelnoos* 11 October 1951, 1. For foreign clubs see Robin Hansen, "As Others See Us," *Yodeler*, 21 March 1949, 5. For colleges see "Colleagues Plan Outings," *Yodeler*, 7 April 1947, 4; "Brief History of the Berkeley Hiking Club?" *Hob Nail*, 25 January 1947, 1; John Rawlings, *The Stanford Alpine Club* (Stanford: CSLI Publications, 1999); *Southern Campus* (1951), 143, University Archives, Powell Library, UCLA; Hall Leiren, "Students Really Climb the Walls at Caltech at Night," *Los Angeles Times*, 27 December 1970, SG B1. For blurring see *Hob Nail*, 20 August 1947.

42. For SAC see Rawlings, *Stanford Alpine Club*, 3–8, 35, 56. For "impressive" and "sharp" see John Rawlings, "Alfred W. Baxter: An Interview for the Stanford Oral Histories Project" (1997), 2, 5, SAC. For technology and coordination see "Minutes of RCC meeting," 22 April 1947, Menocal. For private trips see Ax Nelson, "Stanford Alpine Club Active in Yosemite," *Yodeler*, 17 March 1947, 3–4.

43. For "purpose," "boys," "camaraderie," and "pressures" see Rawlings, *Stanford Alpine Club*, 38, 56, 57, 58. For relationships see John Rawlings, "Mary (Sherrill) Baxter: An Interview for the Stanford Oral Histories Project," (1997), 12, SAC. For supportive see John

Rawlings, "Ellen Searby Jori, An Interview for the Stanford Oral History Project" (1988), 1, 24, SAC. For officers see *SACJ* (1955), 2. For manless see Rawlings, *Stanford Alpine Club*, 7, 25, 55.

44. For "sorely" and "youth" see Robert C. Brooke Jr., "The Problem of the College Mountaineering Club," *SACJ* (1955), 72–76. For "educate" see "Editorial," *Mugelnoos*, 12 February 1953, 2.

45. For "generations" see Ed Morse, "Dick Leonard to Lead RCS 30-Year Reunion," *Yodeler*, February 1962, 5. For private trips see Demera G. Corombus, "Yosemite Challenges Climbers," *Yodeler*, 15 November 1948, 4; "Wilting in Yosemite," *Mugelnoos*, 8 November 1951, 4. For firsts see "Watkins Pinnacle Climbed," *Yodeler*, 6 January 1947, 5; Bob Swift, "Phantom Pinnacle Phalls," *Yodeler*, 18 September 1950, 5.

46. For "chust" see Nicholas B. Clinch to John Rawlings, 9 February 1994, "Nicholas B. Clinch: An Interview for the Stanford Oral Histories Project" (2001), n.p., SAC. For Salathé see Steve Roper, *Camp 4: Recollections of a Yosemite Rockclimbers* (Seattle: Mountaineers, 1994), 31–49. For partners see "A Record to End All Mountain Records," *Yodeler*, 7 May 1945, 3. For RCS see "The Social Climber," *Yodeler*, 17 May 1948, 4.

47. For Half Dome see Ax Nelson, "First Ascent of West Wall," *Yodeler*, 4 November 1946, 4. For "best ever" see "More on the Pinnacles—February 23," *Yodeler*, 17 March 1947, 3. For Lost Arrow Chimney and Lost Arrow see Warren Breed, "303 Sierra Peaks Still to Be Climbed, Yosemite 'Lost Arrow' Can't Be Scaled, Say Experts," *Oakland Post Enquirer*, 23 September 1941; "Nylons Ascend Lost Arrow," *Yodeler*, 16 September 1946, 5; Anton Nelson, "Five Days and Nights on the Lost Arrow," *SCB* (March 1948), 103–8.

48. For "agonizing" see Allen Steck, "Ordeal By Piton," *SCB* (May 1951), 5. For Sugarloaf see Cliff Hopson, "Sugar Loaf's South Face Licked," *Yodeler*, 8 January 1951, 5.

49. For "technical" see Steck, "Order By Piton," 1. For Salathé's legacy see Galen Rowell, *The Vertical World of Yosemite* (Berkeley: Wilderness Press, 1973), 15. For Castle Rock Spire see Bill Long, "First Ascent of Castle Rock Spire," *Yodeler*, 15 May 1950, 5. For Yosemite climbs see Allen Steck, "Yosemite Point Buttress," *SCB* (December 1952), 91–93; Allen Steck, "The 430-Foot Tree, *SCB* (December 1952), 93–94. For speed see Don Evers, "Puffs of a Pinnacle Prowler," *Yodeler*, 17 October 1949, 3.

50. For "bunny" see John Rawlings, "Ellen Serby Jori," An interview for the Stanford Oral History Project, conducted by John Rawlings," p. 22, 1988, SAC. For "challenge" see Brooke, "The Problem of the College Mountaineering Club," 73. For "exploration" see Paul Revak, "Club Activities in North California," *SACJ* (1955), 60.

51. For Baxter accident see Rawlings, "Alfred Baxter," 9–10. For classification and accidents see Rawlings, *Stanford Alpine Club*, 15, 72–73. For fatalities see "Memorandum for the Chief Ranger. Fatal Climbing Accident: Yeazell and Haines," 24 March 1949, carton 44:26, SCMP. For minor accidents see "Two Weekends Ago . . . ," c. 1950, SAC Scrapbook.

52. SupMR, April 1955; *AINAM* (1956), 16–18; Rawlings, *Stanford Alpine Club*, 72–73; "Minutes of RCC meeting," 26 April 1955, Menocal.

53. For Pottinger see SupMR, June 1947. For other SAC accidents see SupMRs for December 1947, May 1948, April 1954, April 1955, May 1955; "The Lost Arrow," *Mugelnoos*, 13 November 1952, 3; William W. Dunmire to Richard M. Leonard, 27 November 1952, carton 59:1, SCR. For "impressively" see "Yosemite Valley May 28–30," *Mugelnoos*, 14 July 1955, 1. For RCS accidents see Phil Bettler, "Two Climbing Accidents," *Yodeler*, 25 August 1947, 3; Don Evers, "Narrow Escape at Devils Slide," *Yodeler*, 18 April 1949, 5; Dave Cudaback, "A Rappelling Incident," *Yodeler*, 20 February 1950, 4; "Accident While Descending Tahquitz Rock June 19th," *Mugelnoos*, 8 July 1954, 1; John B. Thune, "Tragedy in the Bugaboos," *Yodeler*, 30 August 1948, 1, 4.

54. Only two deaths occurred in 1955—a normal year. For statistics see "Summary of Annual Mountain Climbing Reports from Areas Administered by the National Park Service, 1955," carton 88:27, SCR. For "lights" and meeting see Rawlings, *Stanford Alpine Club*, 74; *Mugelnoos*, 12 May 1955, 6. For training, qualification, and register see Don Wilson, "Yosemite Climbing and the Park Service," *Mugelnoos*, 14 July 1955, 4. For climbing rangers see "Minutes of RCC meeting," 14 April 1959, Menocal. For rescue see "Mountain Rescue," *Yodeler*, 6 June 1955, 3. For safety see Richard M. Leonard, Arnold Wexler, William Siri, Charles Wilts, David Brower, Morgan Harris, and May Pridham, *Belaying the Leader* (San Francisco: Sierra Club, 1956).

55. For "risk" see Rawlings, *Stanford Alpine Club*, 74. For "individual" see "Minutes of RCC meeting," 16 April 1955, Menocal.

56. For "fun" see Dan L. Thropp, "Conservation for Mugelnoos," *Mugelnoos*, 14 July 1955, 4. For "different" see Cohen, *History*, 142.

57. For Europe see "Harr Times in the Alps," *Mugelnoos*, 11 September 1952, 1. For North American club imperialism see Weiselberg, "Ascendancy," 3–4, 90–92, 188–91, 232, 260, 272, 297, 326; Janet Robertson, *The Magnificent Mountain Women: Adventures in the Colorado Rockies* (Lincoln: University of Nebraska Press, 1990), 44; Raymond Huel, "The Creation of the Alpine Club of Canada: An Early Manifestation of Canadian Nationalism," *Prairie Forum* 15 (1990), 25–43. For Canada and Alaska see Richard C. Houston, "Attempt on West Buttress of Mt. McKinley—1952," *Yodeler*, 6 October 1952, 4–5; John Evans and Allen Steck, "Mount Logan's Hummingbird Ridge," *AAJ* (1966), 8–18. For Andes and Antarctica see "Yourney to Yerupaja," *Yodeler*, 4 June 1951, 4; "People in the News," *Yodeler*, 6 January 1958, 3. For Himalaya see Will Siri, "Makalu: The First Attempt," *SCB* (October 1954), 3–4.

58. For "one-sided" see Revak, "Club Activities in Northern California," 59. For "gymnasium" see "Two weekends ago . . ." For clique see "Add Labor Day Doings in Yosemite," *Mugelnoos*, 12 September 1957, 6. For "separate" see remarks by Phil Bettler in "Minutes of RCC meeting," 29 September 1949, Menocal. For *Yodeler* and *Rotten Log* see "Minutes of RCC meeting" for 26 March 1958, 13 January 1959, and 14 April 1959, all in Menocal.

59. For "elite," "margin," and "ragged" see *Mugelnoos*, 12 May 1955, 6. For "hero" and "downgrade" see "R.C.C.," 26 April 1955, Menocal. For youth culture see George Lipsitz, "Who'll Stop the Rain: Youth Culture, Rock 'n' Roll, and Cultural Crisis," in *The Sixties*, ed. David Farber (Chapel Hill: University of North Carolina Press, 1994), 206–34. For recruitment see Joanne Klein, "The Rock Climbing Section," *Yodeler*, 7 May 1956, 8. For membership see "Minutes of RCC meeting," 19 January 1954, Menocal. For alienation see Roper, *Camp 4*, 92. For exclusivity see "Minutes of RCC meeting," October 1959, Menocal.

7. Experientialists

The epigraph is quoted in John Rawlings, *The Stanford Alpine Club* (Stanford: CSLI Publications, 1999), 13.

1. For "tigerish" see Warren Harding, *Downward Bound: A Mad! Guide to Rock Climbing* (Englewood Cliffs, N.J.: Prentice-Hall, 1975), 105. For "dominating" see Gary Arce, *Defying Gravity: High Adventure on Yosemite's Walls* (Berkeley: Wilderness Press, 1996), 40. For "God" see Mark Powell to Steve Roper, 2 March 1966, Roper.

2. For "pure" see William James, "A World of Pure Experience," in *Essays in Radical Empiricism* (Cambridge, Mass.: Harvard University Press, 1976), 21–44. For postwar society see

David Riesman, *The Lonely Crowd* (New Haven: Yale University Press, 1950), 236–41. For Beat-era climbers see Michael P. Cohen, *The Pathless Way: John Muir and American Wilderness* (Madison: University of Wisconsin Press, 1984), 82, 379n31.

3. Personal conversation with Mark Powell, Woodland Hills, California, 14 May 2002.

4. Chris Jones, *Climbing in North America* (Seattle: Mountaineers, 1997), 191–94.

5. For climbs see Steve Roper, *Camp 4: Recollections of a Yosemite Rockclimber* (Seattle: Mountaineers, 1994), 58–59, 83–87. For "philosophy" see Chuck Pratt, "The South Face of Mt. Watkins," *AAJ* (1965), 346.

6. For Durrance see Jones, *Climbing in North America,* 122. For Conns see Beth Wald, "Herb and Jan Conn," *Climbing* (December 1988), 95. For Beckey see Gary Speer, "Profiles of Fred Beckey," *Climbing* (February 1986), 24. For European bums see Lee Wallace Holt, "Mountains, Mountaineering and Modernity: A Cultural History of German and Austrian Mountaineering, 1900–1945" (Ph.D. diss., University of Texas at Austin, 2008). I thank Peter Hansen for help with this. For "resident" see Roper, *Camp 4,* 84.

7. For regulars see "Yosemite Trip," *Mugelnoos,* 11 June 1953, 3.

8. For "tall" see Roper, *Camp 4,* 58.

9. For "Winter Camp" see SupMR, April 1931, YRL. For boulders see Doug Robinson, "Camp 4," *Mountain* (July 1969), 24. For "trailers" see Galen Rowell, "Salathé Wall," in *Beyond the Vertical: Layton Kor,* ed. Bob Godfrey (Boulder: Alpine House, 1983), 203.

10. For ties to clubs see "Active RCS Members—December 1961," carton 7:27, SCSFBCR. For "elite" see Penny Carr to Roper, 19 May 1964; for "modify" see Chuck Pratt to Roper, 18 March 1965; for "greatest" see Pratt to Roper, 12 December 1958; for "white" and "beautiful" see Layton Kor to Roper, 17 February 1963, all in Roper.

11. For athletic gifts see Pat Ament, *A History of Free Climbing in America: Wizards of Rock* (Berkeley: Wilderness Press, 2002), 11; Yvon Chouinard, *Let My People Go Surfing: The Education of a Reluctant Businessman* (New York: Penguin, 2005), 9–10. For "oddballs" see Kor, *Beyond,* 13.

12. For ties to Beats see Royal Robbins, "Foreword," in *Beyond,* 8. For "modes" see Craig Leavitt, "On The Road: Cassady, Kerouac, and Images of Late Western Masculinity," in *Across the Great Divide: Cultures of Manhood in the American West,* eds. Matthew Basso, Laura McCall, and Dee Garceau (New York: Routledge, 2001), 221. For "hell," "vows," and "bodily" see Gilbert Rogin, "An Odd Sport . . . and an Unusual Champion," *Sports Illustrated,* 18 October 1965, 106.

13. Jack Kerouac, *The Dharma Bums* (New York: Viking, 1958), 97.

14. For "rebellion" see Michael Kimmel, *Manhood in America: A Cultural History* (New York: Free Press, 1996), 242–43. "Dog-eared" remark by Jeff Foott, personal conversation with author in Jackson, Wyoming, 18 August 2002. For Oahu see Matt Warshaw, *Mavericks: The Story of Big-Wave Surfing* (San Francisco: Chronicle Books, 2003), 30–36.

15. For working-class see Chouinard, *Let My People Go Surfing,* 7–15; Harding, *Downward Bound,* 98; Ament, *Royal Robbins,* 2–15. For European analogs see Arnold Lunn, *A Century of Mountaineering, 1857–1957* (London: George Allen & Unwin, 1957), 218–20. For Hemming see Mirella Tenderini, *Gary Hemming: The Beatnik of the Alps,* trans. Susan Hodgkiss (Glasgow: Ernest Press, 1995), 24–33. For education see Rawlings, *Stanford Alpine Club,* 127–29; Roper, *Camp 4,* 89–90, 93, 183–84; Rowell, "Salathé Wall," 203. For heroes see Royal Robbins to Roper, 16 January 1969, Roper.

16. For "uncommon" see Royal Robbins to Roper, 23 August 1972; for "death" see Yvon Chouinard to Roper, 22 May 1963, both in Roper.

17. For "ecstatic" see Barbara Ehrenreich, *The Hearts of Men: American Dreams and the Flight from Commitment* (Garden City, N.Y.: Anchor Books, 1983), 54; also Richard Can-

dida Smith, *Utopia and Dissent: Art, Poetry, and Politics in California* (Berkeley: University of California Press, 1995), 145–211. For drugs as new see Geoffrey Childs, "The Bird," in *30 Years of Climbing Magazine* (Carbondale, Colo.: Primedia Special Interest Publications, 1999), 243. For "escapism" see Kor, *Beyond*, 13, 152. For "orgies" see Mark Powell to Roper, 2 May 1963, Roper. For drugs see Tenderini, *Gary Hemming*, 25, 134; Pete Sinclair, *We Aspired: The Last Innocent Americans* (Logan: Utah State University Press, 1993), 166; Roper, *Camp 4*, 217–18. For earlier usage see Bob Swift, "Santa Trains in Pinnacles Caves," *Yodeler*, 18 December 1950, 3. For medicating see A. F. Mummery, *My Climbs in the Alps and Caucasus* (New York: Chas. Scribner's Sons, 1895), 104. For drunks see Don Whillans and Alick Ormerod, *Don Whillans: Portrait of a Mountaineer* (London: Heinemann, 1971), 246. For psychedelics see Beck to Roper, 1 February 1968, Roper.

18. For service generation see James T. Patterson, *Grand Expectations: The United States, 1945–1974* (New York: Oxford University Press, 1996), 598–99, 613–33. For military see Ament, *Royal Robbins*, 23–29; Chouinard, *Let My People Go Surfing*, 20–21. For "fictitious" see Pratt to Roper, 18 March 1965; for "Fuck" see Chouinard to Roper, 22 May 1963; for "PISSWATER" see Chouinard to Roper, 21 May 1964, all in Roper.

19. For "mentioned" see Pratt to Roper, 18 March 1965; for personal growth see Yvon Chouinard to Roper, 31 December 1963; for "illusions" see Chouinard to Roper, 31 December 1963; for "trick" see Komito to Roper, 6 January 1964; for misery see Roper to Allen Steck, 11 June 1964; for readings see Robbins to Roper, 27 April 1964, all in Roper.

20. For "ass" see Eric Beck to Roper, 19 May 1965; for deferments see Eric Beck to Roper, c. May 1964, both in Roper. For Harding and Long see Galen Rowell, "Twenty-Five Days on the South Face of Half Dome," *Summit* (December 1970), 2–3; Dick Long to Roper, 9 February 1968, Roper.

21. For bonding see Roper, *Camp 4;* Candida Smith, *Utopia and Dissent*, 167. For hierarchy see Rowell, "Salathé Wall," 203. For "brotherhood" see Steve Komito to Roper, 11 February 1966; for "circle" see Chuck Pratt to Roper, 18 March 1965, both in Roper. For "belonged" see Kor, *Beyond*, 151. For "sacred" see interview with Tom Frost, Tape 1 of 3:4–5, Frost. For nicknames see Layton Kor to Roper, 23 March 1964; Steve Komito to Roper, 7 August 1964; Mark Powell to Roper, 20 July 1965, all in Roper; Marco Jacquemet, "Name-chasers," *American Ethnologist* 19 (November 1992), 736. For surfing and skateboarding see Tom Wolfe, *The Pump House Gang* (New York: Bantam, 1968), 4–6, 15–30; *Dogtown and Z-Boys*, DVD, dir. Stacy Peralta (Agi Orsi Productions, 2001).

22. For "joyfully" see Rowell, "Salathé Wall," 204. For "captures" see Eric Beck to Roper, 2 March 1964; for reunions see Chuck Pratt to Roper, 12 December 1958; for "sucker" see Eric Beck to Roper, 1 January [1964], all in Roper.

23. For "proves" see Yvon Chouinard, "Modern Yosemite Climbing," *AAJ* (1964), 325. For hazing see Whillans and Ormerod, *Don Whillans*, 245–49; Michael W. Borghoff, "Of Salamanders and Bongbongs," *Summit* (June 1962), 13–15. For laugh see Steck to Roper, 1 June 1964; for mocked see Kor to Roper, 11 December 1967, both in Roper. For violence see Penny Carr to Roper, 19 May 1964, Roper. For "mind problems" see Steve Roper, *A Climber's Guide to Yosemite Valley* (San Francisco: Sierra Club, 1964), 24. For "hoots" and "coward" see Roper, *Camp 4*, 131. For "vulnerable" see Carr to Roper, 18 April 1964, Roper. For discipline see Peter Donnelly and Kevin Young, "Rock Climbers and Rugby Players: Identity Construction and Confirmation," in *Inside Sports*, ed. Jay Coakley and Peter Donnelly (New York: Routledge, 1999), 67–76.

24. For "lost" see Roper, *Camp 4*, 157. For Kor see Steve Roper, "West Buttress," in *Beyond*, 148. For Robbins see Ament, *Royal Robbins*, 35. For Chouinard and Yosemite see Choui-

nard, "Modern Yosemite Climbing," 325. For "DESTROY" see Chouinard to Roper, 23 May 1966; for compulsory see Layton Kor to Roper, 11 February 1967; for deaths see Eric Beck to Roper, 4 July 1964; for lovesick see Jim Baldwin to Roper, 18 April 1964; Steve Komito to Roper, 7 August 1964; for marriage see Chuck Pratt to Roper, 12 December 1958, all in Roper. For religion see Robbins, "Foreword," 8.

25. For "deeply" see Ehrenreich, *The Hearts of Men*, 54. For "painfully" see Roper, *Camp 4*, 158–59. For Kor see Denny, "The Nose," 148. For "defeatist" see Komito to Roper, 24 February 1971, Roper. For "sexless" personal conversation with John Waterhouse, 10 November 2005, Burnaby, British Columbia. For closeted see Steve Roper to author, "Re: Sexuality," 20 July 2006, personal email, 20 July 2006.

26. For women and Beats see Wini Breines, "The 'Other' Fifties: Beats and Bad Girls," in *Not June Cleaver: Women and Gender in Postwar America, 1945–1960*, ed. Joanne Meyerowitz (Philadelphia: Temple University Press, 1994), 382–408. For women's experiences and Baker see telephone conversation with Malinda Chouinard, 13 September 2007; Laura Waterman, "When Women Were Women in the Northeast," in *Rock and Roses: An Anthology of Mountaineering Essays*, ed. Mikel Vause (La Crescenta, Calif.: Mountain N' Air Books, 1990), 121; Jan [Sacherer Turner], "Re: The Chick History Thread," 9 May 2009, www.supertopo.com/climbing/thread.html?topic id=53589&msg=855364#msg855364 (accessed 22 July 2009). For afterthought see Art Gran to Roper, 15 January 1964; for "baby" see Steve Komito to Roper, 11 February 1966, both in Roper. For "love" see Roper, *Camp 4*, 158. For competitive see Rawlings, *Stanford Alpine Club*, 60. For clubs see Francisco Walcott, "Mountaineering Notes," *Yodeler*, March 1962. Rearick quoted in Ament, *Royal Robbins*, 36. For "haul" personal conversation with Lloyd Price, Yosemite Valley, March 2002.

27. For women climbers see Roper, *Camp 4*, 158–59; Dorene Frost Climbing Résumé, folder 1, Beardsley; "Irene Ortenberger Climbing Record" in John Rawlings, "Irene Beardsley: An Interview Conducted by John Rawlings," Stanford Oral Histories Project, 1997, Department of Special Collections, Stanford University Libraries, Stanford, California. For "carabiners" and "sex" see Chouinard to Roper, 7 December 1962 and c. mid-December 1962, both in Roper. For "agenda" see Roper, *Camp 4*, 158. For women's networks see Janice Sacherer Turner to author, "Re: Layton Kor's Email," 26 June 2009, personal email, 26 June 2009; Penny Carr to Sharon and Steve Roper, 26 March 1965; Liz Robbins to Steve Roper, 1 October 1965, both in Roper. For breakups see Ament, *Royal Robbins*, 21; Chouinard, *Let My People Go Surfing*, 20–21.

28. For Carr see Rawlings, *Stanford Alpine Club*, 30, 60, 63; Roper, *Camp 4*, 159. For hunger see Carr to Roper, 21 December 1961, 17 November 1962, 19 May 1964, and 17 December 1964; for "casual" see Carr to Roper, 18 April 1964, all in Roper.

29. For "uncomfortable" and "walls" see Carr to Roper, 9 November 1965, Roper; Roper, *Camp 4*, 159–60.

30. For "constantly" see Kor to Roper, 30 December 1964; for "do" see Glen Denny to Roper, 6 March 1964; for "wild" see Kor to Roper, 23 February 1963; for "desire" see Kor to Roper, 17 February 1963; for "hot" see Denny to Roper, 13 February 1963, all in Roper. For "virgin" see Royal Robbins, "The North America Wall," *Summit* (May–June 1965), 3. For "Don Juan" see Robbins, "Foreword," 9. For "orgasm" and "pure" see Denny to Roper, 29 November 1962 and 19 August 1963, Roper. For "Aphrodite," "lust," and "flesh" see Royal Robbins, "The Prow," *Summit* (July–August 1970), 5. For "love" and "mother" see Tom Higgins, "In Thanks," *Ascent* (1975–1976), 23. Contrast with Susan R. Schrepfer, *Nature's Altars: Mountains, Gender, and American Environmentalism* (Lawrence: University Press of Kansas, 2005), 203.

31. For Robbins see Ament, *Royal Robbins*, 34–35, 52, 57. For "oneness" see Chouinard to Roper, 16 January 1964; for "freedom" see Pratt to Roper, 18 March 1965, both in Roper.

32. Yvon Chouinard to Roper, 16 January 1964, Roper.

33. For *"violence"* and *"combine,"* see Chouinard to Roper, 16 January 1964, Roper. George Leigh Mallory, "The Mountaineer as Artist," *Climbers Club Journal* (March 1914), 28–40; also Doug Robinson, "The Climber as Visionary," *Ascent* (May 1969), 6–9.

34. For orientalist see Chouinard to Roper, 14 April 1963; for "truth" see Chouinard to Roper, 16 January 1964, both in Roper. For orientalism and Beats see Michael K. Masatsugu, "'Beyond This World of Transiency and Impermanence': Japanese Americans, Dharma Bums, and the Making of American Buddhism during the Early Cold War Years," *Pacific Historical Review* 77 (August 2008), 435–41. For safety see Morgan Harris, "Safety Last?" *SCB* (August 1942), 65–78.

35. For defiance and soloing see Ament, *Royal Robbins*, 7, 36, 235; personal conversation with Gail Wilts, Pasadena, California, June 2001; Michael Borghoff, "A Song of Stone," *Summit* (January 1960), 12–15. For reactions see "Using a Rope for Safer Climbing," *Summit* (June 1956), 3–6.

36. For "searching" see Royal Robbins, "The North America Wall," *AAJ* (1965), 336. For "experience" see Glen Denny to Roper, 29 November 1962; for "right" see Chuck Pratt to Roper, 18 March 1965; for "bug" see Eric Beck to Roper, 2 March 1964; for "righteousness" see Mark Powell to Roper, 2 March 1966, all in Roper. For "real" see Rawlings, *Stanford Alpine Club*, 128. For "amenities" see Kor, *Beyond*, 138.

37. For communities see "RCS Newsletters," c. summer 1968, carton 7:28, SCSFBCR. For declining popularity see "Liaison with Young Climbers," *AACN*, 6 November 1959, 1. For AAC see Carl and Helen Weisner, "Rock Climbing Section," *Yodeler*, 1 June 1959, 3; *AACN* (January 1968), 1, 2.

38. For "resurgent" see Powell to Roper, 24 March 1964, Roper.

8. Moralists

The epigraph is from "Mountaineering as a Religion," *Alpine Journal* (1918), 243.

1. Steve Roper, *Camp 4: Recollections of a Yosemite Climber* (Seattle: Mountaineers, 1994), 59–232.

2. Lawrence Hamilton, "The Changing Face of American Mountaineering," *Review of Sport & Leisure* 6 (Summer 1981), 15.

3. For "ruin" see C. F. Meade, "The Perversion of Mountaineering," *Quarterly Review* 267 (1936), 25.

4. Pat Ament, *Royal Robbins: Spirit of the Age* (Mechanicsburg, Pa.: Stackpole, 1998), 2–7; Royal Robbins to author, "Re: Research question on early years," 19 August 2006, personal email (20 August 2006); Royal Robbins, *To Be Brave* (Ojai: Pink Moment Press, 2009), 80. For photo see James Ramsey Ullman, *High Conquest: The Story of Mountaineering* (Philadelphia: J. B. Lippincott, 1941), 120.

5. For "imagine" see Peter H. Hansen, "Albert Smith, the Alpine Club, and the Invention of Mountaineering in Mid-Victorian Britain," *Journal of British Studies* 34 (July 1995), 305. For "clinging" see Ament, *Royals Robbins*, 7. For climbers see Layton Kor, *Beyond the Vertical*, ed. Bob Godfrey (Boulder: Alpine House, 1983), 14; Warren Harding, *Downward Bound: A Mad! Guide to Rock Climbing* (Englewood Cliffs, N.J.: Prentice-Hall, 1975), 98; Yvon Chouinard, *Let My People Go Surfing: The Education of a Reluctant Businessman* (New York: Penguin Press, 2005), 12; John Rawlings, *The Stanford Alpine Club*

(Stanford: CSLI Publications, 1999), 86; John Long, *Rock Jocks, Wall Rats, and Hang Dogs: Rock Climbing on the Edge of Reality* (New York: Simon & Schuster, 1994), 18.

6. For reaction see Royal Robbins, "Standing on the Shoulders: A Tribute to My Heroes," in *Voices from the Summit: The World's Great Mountaineers on the Future of Climbing*, ed. Bernadette McDonald and John Amatt (Washington: National Geographic Society and The Banff Centre for Mountain Culture, 2000), 190. For literature see Walt Unsworth, *Hold the Heights: The Foundations of Mountaineering* (Seattle: Mountaineers, 1994), 105. For Anglophilic literature see G. R. De Beer, *Alps and Men: Pages from Forgotten Diaries of Travellers and Tourists in Switzerland* (London: Edward Arnold, 1932). For "suicidal" and "aflame" see Ullman, *High Conquest*, 73. For Nazi symbolism see Robert Jewett and John Shelton Lawrence, *Captain America and the Crusade Against Evil: The Dilemma of Zealous Nationalism* (Grand Rapids: Wm. B. Eerdmans, 2004), 6–7, 34.

7. For "get you," "history," and *"men"* see Ulman, *High Conquest*, 18, 22. For "romantic" see John Cleare, *Mountains* (New York: Crown, 1975), 102.

8. For bullfighting see Royal Robbins to Steve Roper, 17 June 1966, Roper; Daniel Duane, *El Capitan: Historic Feats and Radical Routes* (San Francisco: Chronicle Books, 2000), 34.

9. Royal Robbins, "Introduction," in *Woman on the Rocks: The Mountaineering Letters of Ruth Dyar Mendenhall*, ed. Valerie Mendenhall Cohen (Bishop, Calif.: Spotted Dog Press, 2006), 11. Pat Ament, *A History of Free Climbing in America: Wizards of Rock* (Berkeley: Wilderness Press, 2002), 51–53, 61–62.

10. Ament, *Free Climbing*, 51–53; Chris Jones, *Climbing in North America* (Seattle: Mountaineers, 1997), 187–88.

11. For Robbins see Ament, *Royal Robbins*, 11; Roper, *Camp 4*, 153; Duane, *El Capitan*, 35. For licentious see Jones, *Climbing in North America*, 195–96, 261.

12. For bookkeeper see Ament, *Royal Robbins*, 15. For 1955 see D[on] W[ilson], "N.W. Face of Half Dome," *Mugelnoos*, 14 July 1955, 3; Ken Wilson, Allen Steck, and Galen Rowell, "Mountain Interview: Royal Robbins," *Mountain* (November 1971), 27–28; Harding, *Downward Bound*, 107.

13. For competitiveness see Wilson et al., "Mountain Interview: Royal Robbins," 28–31. For denial see Cleare, *Mountains*, 103. For other efforts see "Show Me the Way to Go Dome!" *Yodeler*, 18 June 1956, 3; Mirella Tenderini, *Gary Hemming: The Beatnik of the Alps*, trans. Susan Hodgkiss (Glasgow: Ernest Press, 1995), 42–43; Harding, *Downward Bound*, 106–8. For ascent see Royal Robbins, "Half Dome—The Hard Way," *SCB* (December 1957), 12–13. For rope arrangement see Michael P. Sherrick, "The Northwest Face of Half Dome," *SCB* (November 1958), 22.

14. Robbins, "Half Dome—The Hard Way," 13.

15. For "arduous" see Robbins, "Half Dome—The Hard Way," 13. For temptations see Sherrick, "Northwest Face," 23.

16. Don Mellor, *American Rock: Region, Rock and Culture in American Climbing* (Woodstock, Vt.: Countryman Press, 2001), 213; Wayne Merry to author, "Details," 20 April 2003, personal email (20 April 2003); Wayne Merry, "The Longest Climb," *Mariah* (1979), 24.

17. For "aimless" and "wolf" see Harding, *Downward Bound*, 98, 172. For RCS see "Applications for Membership in the San Francisco Chapter of the Sierra Club, Listed November 1, 1949—Date of Election January 2, 1950," *Yodeler*, 21 November 1949. James Ramsey Ullman, *The White Tower* (Philadelphia: J. B. Lippincott, 1945).

18. For climbs see Warren Harding, "Worst Error," *SCB* (October 1959), 76; Roper, *Camp 4*, 75, 86–87, 99–104. For later reputation see Steve Gardiner, ed., *Why I Climb: Personal Insights of Top Climbers* (Harrisburg, Pa.: Stackpole Books, 1990), 100. Harding's partners

were Rich Calderwood, Gerry Czamanske, Jack Davis, Bill Feuerer, Craig Holden, Wayne Merry, Mark Powell, Chuck Pratt, Wally Reed, Bob Swift, Frank Tarver, Bea Vogel, John Whitmer, and George Whitmore. Robbins's partners were Jerry Gallwas, Joe Fitschen, Tom Frost, Mark Powell, Chuck Pratt, and Mike Sherrick.

19. For "grumbling" see Harding, *Downward Bound*, 108. For "pouting" see Rawlings, *Stanford Alpine Club*, 63.

20. For "send" see "Bug-Ears on El Cap," *Yodeler*, 19 July 1943, 5; "Rock Climbers' Day Dream—Or Night Mare," *Mugelnoos*, 14 October 1948, 5–6. For ascent see Warren J. Harding, "El Capitan," *AAJ* 11 (1959), 184–89.

21. For "tactics" see Harding, *Downward Bound*, 108–16; also Glen Denny to Steve Roper, 19 August 1963, Roper; Jones, *Climbing in North America*, 326.

22. For accident see "Powell's Climbing Accident," *Mugelnoos*, 14 November 1957, 3. For team see Harding, *Downward Bound*, 108–16; personal conversation with Mark Powell, 14 May 2002, Woodland Hills, California; Mark Powell, Warren Harding, Ken McNutt, Dick Sykes, and Don Lauria, "The Dolt—A Eulogy," *Climbing* 37 (July–August 1976), 28–32; Merry, "The Longest Climb," 23–24. For "staggered" see Harding, "El Capitan," 184.

23. For credit see Harding, "El Capitan"; Steve Roper, *A Climber's Guide to Yosemite Valley* (San Francisco: Sierra Club, 1964), 59–60; Jeremy Collins and Timmy O'Neill (Jer-Co Studios), *A Brief Biased History of Big Wall Climbing*, http://www.alpinist.com/doc/ALP19/video_history_cartoon (accessed 7 May 2007). For 1957 see Harding, *Downward Bound*, 111–12. For immense see John Sheard, "Pilgrimage," in *Yosemite Climber*, ed. George Meyers (Modesto: Robbins Mountain Letters, 1979), 17.

24. For delay see Dick Leonard to John G. Preston, 3 October 1957, carton 77:11; Wayne A. Merry and Warren J. Harding to Dick Leonard plus cover sheet, 16 December 1958, and Hal F. Olson to Sierra Club, 16 December 1958, carton 88:27, all in SCR. For roles see John Rawlings, "Ellen Searby Jori: An Interview for the Stanford Oral History Project, Conducted by John Rawlings," p. 5, 1988, SAC. For 1958 see Roper, *Camp 4*, 76–80. For club reports see "El Capitan Cliff-Hangers Put on Show for Tourists," *Mugelnoos*, 12 September 1957, 2; Mark Powell, "El Capitan???" *Mugelnoos*, 9 October 1958, 6; Howard Frohlich, "President El Capitan Warren Harding," *Yodeler*, 17 November 1958, 1–2. For media see "El Capitan Climb, November-1958, OFFICIAL HISTORY FILE" in "Rock Climbing," Vertical Files, YRL.

25. For support see SupMR, December 1957. For opposition see E. T. Scoyen to Dave Brower, 29 January 1959, carton 88:27, SCR; "Park Service May Ban Climbing Aids," *Fresno Bee*, in "Rock Climbing," Vertical Files, YRL. For defenders see Wm. D. Loughman to Secretary of the Interior, 28 January 1959, Warren Harding, Wayne Merry, George Whitmore, and Searby to Conrad L. Wirth, 29 January 1959, both in carton 88:27, SCR. For order see Wayne Merry to Gary Colliver, 19 March 1993, "Wayne Merry," Biographical File, YRL. For resentment see Wilson et al., "Mountain Interview: Royal Robbins," 28; personal conversation with Mark Powell, 14 May 2002. For threat see Doug Robinson, "Grand Sieges and Fast Attacks," *Mariah* (September 1979), 26. For "slight" and "prompted" see Merry and Harding to Leonard, 16 December 1958; Warren Harding and Wayne Merry, "We Conquered El Capitan," *Argosy* 348 (April 1959), 24–28, 104–7. For criticism see Roper, *Camp 4*, 74, 186, 231.

26. For "fear" see Wilson et al., "Mountain Interview: Royal Robbins," 28. Ament, *Free Climbing*, 90, 107–8; Roper, *Camp 4*, 130, 181–84. For aid see Steve Roper, "Washington Column Climbers Encounter Rats, Thirst, Overhangs," *Summit* (October 1959), 16–17; Royal Robbins, "The Royal Arches Direct," *SCB* (October 1961), 56–57; Roper, *Camp 4*, 108.

27. For elsewhere see Ament, *Free Climbing,* 55, 196–97; Mellor, *American Rock,* 136, 233, 235. For "greatest" see Kor to Roper, 17 February 1963, Roper. For AAC see Art Gran to Steve Roper, 7 May 1964, Roper; personal conversation with Nicholas Clinch, 24 May 2002, Palo Alto, California. For "hard" see John S. Humphreys to Yvon Chouinard, 10 April 1963, AAC Archives Membership, Box C-L, AAC. For "influential" see Roper, *A Climber's Guide to Yosemite Valley,* 23. For "Mecca" see Don Whillans and Alick Ormerod, *Don Whillans: Portrait of a Mountaineer* (London: Heinemann, 1971), 244, 249. For joining see *AAC By-Laws and Registers,* AAC. For "elite" see Kor, *Beyond,* 151.

28. For "ridiculous" and "standard" see "Labels 'Trick Climbing' Charge As Ridiculous." For hamming see "Perpendicular Yosemite Peak Scaled for First Time." For hiding see Jones, *Climbing in North America,* 325.

29. For "determination" see Royal Robbins, "Climbing El Capitan," *SCB* (December 1960), 47–55. For animosity see Jones, *Climbing in North America,* 258–59; R[oyal] R[obbins], "El Capitan—First Continuous Ascent," *Mugelnoos,* 13 October 1960, 4. For peer review see Layton Kor to Roper, 20 December 1964, Roper; also Jim Bridwell and Keith Peall, *Climbing Adventures: A Climber's Passion* (Merrillville, Ind.: ICS Books, 1992), 28; John Long, "Foreword," in *Climbing Free: My Life in the Vertical World,* by Lynn Hill with Greg Child (New York: W. W. Norton, 2002), xi; Joseph E. Taylor III, "Mapping Adventure: Map ping Class and Gender in Yosemite Valley's Climbing Landscapes," *Journal of Historical Geography* 32 (January 2006), 209–11.

30. For innovations see Anton Nelson, "Five Days and Nights on the Lost Arrow," *SCB* (March 1948), 104; Charles Wilts, "The Knife-Blade Piton," *SCB* (June 1954), 71–77; "Rope Dope," *Mugelnoos,* 16 May 1946, 1; Chouinard, "Modern Yosemite Climbing," 322–23; Steve Roper to author, "Re: Army pitons," 4 February 2007, personal email (4 February 2007). For vanadium see Roper, *Camp 4,* 33; Christopher W. Wells, "The Road to the Model T: Culture, Road Conditions, and Innovation at the Dawn of the American Motor Age," *Technology and Culture* 48 (July 2007), 518n41.

31. For individual manufacturing see "Hardware Hard Wear," *Mugelnoos,* 20 April 1939, 3; *Yodeler,* 16 December 1949, 2; Rawlings, *Stanford Alpine Club,* 57, 59; Sherrick, "The Northwest Face of Half Dome," 19–20; Chuck Wilts to Dave [Brower], 6 May 1954, and Brower to Wilts, 28 May 1954, carton 23:36, SCMP; Powell et al., "The Dolt—A Eulogy," 28–31.

32. Steve Roper tells the stove leg story well in *Camp 4,* 69–70, 72–73, 75. The number of the original stovelegs was unsettled, so I asked Frank—whose wife Julidta edited my first book—to clarify details. Phone conversation with Frank Tarver, 31 January 2007. Some did still craft tools. See Eric Beck to Steve Roper, 16 March 1964, Roper. For second ascent see Robbins, "Climbing El Capitan," 49–50; "Seven and a Half Days on the Face," *Summit* (September 1960), 6. For doubts see Arthur C. Lembeck, "Are Ring Pitons Safe?" *Summit* (December 1960), 8–9. Robbins wanted guidebooks to note first continuous ascents. Royal Robbins to Steve Roper, 22 December 1962, Roper.

33. For "powerful" see Susan R. Schrepfer, "Richard M. Leonard: Mountaineer, Lawyer, Environmentalist" (Bancroft Library, University of California/Berkeley, Regional Oral History Office, Sierra Club History Series, 1975), 11. For training see Will Gadd, "John Salathé," *Climbing* (December 1988), 96; "Runners Seek Company," *Yodeler,* 18 December 1950, 6; Phil Arnot, "A Physical Conditioning Program for Mountain Climbing," *Summit* (January 1960), 20–21; Tex [Floyd] Bossier to Steve Roper, 15 January 1963, Roper.

34. For "Roper" see Kor, *Beyond,* 136. For Robbins see Royal Robbins to Roper, 31 May 1964, Roper. For reconnaissance see Ament, *Free Climbing,* 101. For adventure see Chouinard, *Let My People Go Surfing,* 15–18.

35. For Chouinard see Yvon Chouinard, "Are Bolts Being Placed by Too Many Unqualified Climbers?" *Summit* (March 1961), 10–11. For "values" see "Discussion on Bolts. . . ." *Summit* (June 1961), 25–27; Ray de Saussure, "Looking Ahead on Expansion Bolts," *Yodeler,* 3 March 1952, 7. For "no bolts" see R[oyal] R[obbins], "North Face of Lowe Cathedral Rock," *Mugelnoos,* 14 July 1960, 3. For chopping see "Winter (brrr) Ascent of the Lost Arrow," *Mugelnoos,* 8 January 1959, 4; Eric Beck to Roper, 19 May 1964, Roper.

36. For "outside" see Stutfield, "Mountaineering as Religion," 241. For Squirrels and "superfluous" see Lunn, *A Century of Mountaineering,* 157.

37. For YCC see Yvon Chouinard to Steve Roper, January 1960, and Chouinard to Roper, 23 February 1960, Roper. For elitist clubs elsewhere see Lunn, *A Century of Mountaineering,* 196. For "solely" see "Letters," *Summit* (July–August 1964), 23. For "cubic" see Robbins, "Climbing El Capitan," 49. For "prattle" see Bestor Robinson, "Shiprock," *AAJ* (1940), 56. For Robbins on *The Nose* and *Muir Wall* see Roper, *Camp 4,* 173; Royal Robbins, "Alone on the John Muir Wall, El Capitan," *AAJ* (1969), 322. Chouinard did not reject bolts or safety but wanted to control placement. See "Your Letters," *Summit* (June 1963), 28.

38. For usage see Ed Leeper, "Testing Drills and Anchors in Granite," *Summit* (April 1963), 18–23; "Your Letters," *Summit* (June 1963), 28–29. The principal free climbers were Pratt, Roper, Bob Kamps, Tom Gerughty, Frost, Mort Hempel, and Chris Fredericks. For "thrilling" and "harmless" see Royal Robbins, "North Wall of Sentinel Rock," *Summit* (March 1963), 9.

39. For "ruthlessly" see Glen Denny to Steve Roper, 14 January 1963, Roper. For climbs see Allan Macdonald, "Realm of the Overhang," *SCB* (December 1962), 5–22; Edward Cooper, "Direct Southwest Face of Yosemite Valley's El Capitan," *AAJ* (1963), 337–43. For reactions see Roper, *Camp 4,* 116.

40. For prearrangement see Chic Scott, *Pushing the Limits: The Story of Canadian Mountaineering* (Calgary: Rocky Mountain Books, 2000), 332–33. For "dead" see Glen Denny to Steve Roper, 29 November 1962; for "maniac," "schizophrenia," and "rape" see Denny to Roper, 14 January 1963; for Robbins's reaction see Mark Powell to Steve Roper, 18 June 1964 and 9 August 1964, Robbins to Roper, 9 August 1964 and 12 December 1964, Eric Beck to Roper, 12 October 1964, all in Roper.

41. For "expression" see Denny to Roper, 14 January 1963, Roper; Kor, *Beyond,* 142–48. For insider see Royal Robbins, "Foreword," in *Beyond,* 8.

42. For incidents see Roper, *Camp 4,* 173–74, original in italic; Jones, *Climbing in North America,* 329. For rules see Hill and Child, *Climbing Free,* 141.

43. For "clique" see Allen Steck to Steve Roper, 1 June 1964, Roper. For ranking see Kor, *Beyond,* 152. For competitiveness see "Bouldering," *Summit* (June 1961), 9–11; Wilson et al., "Mountain Interview: Royal Robbins," 28–29, 30. For speed see C[huck] W[ilts], "Classic Climb Conquered: Time Cut," *Mugelnoos,* 11 July 1957; R[oyal] R[obbins], "More Yosemite Ascents," *Mugelnoos,* 13 October 1960, 5. For seconding climbs see Doug Scott, *Big Wall Climbing* (New York: Oxford University Press, 1974), 150–51; Wilson et al., "Mountain Interview: Royal Robbins," 28–29. For England see Brown, *The Hard Years,* 67.

44. For "arrogance," "overt," and "noble" see Roper, *A Climber's Guide to Yosemite Valley,* 23–25; for demurral see Royal Robbins, "Summit Reviews," *Summit* (November 1964), 31. For "obligation" and "superiority" see Bob Kamps, "Bolt Ethics . . ." *Summit* 11 (July–August 1965), 28. For debate see Chouinard, "Modern Yosemite Climbing," 323–24; Steve Roper, "Overuse of Bolts," *Summit* (June 1964), 24–26. For "moral" and *"way"* see "Let-

ters," *Summit* (September 1965), 33, 34. For "shoot out" see "Letters," *Summit* (October 1965), 33. For "pity" see Steve Komito to Steve Roper, 11 February 1966, Roper.

45. Charles Pratt, "The South Face of Mount Watkins," *AAJ* (1965), 339–46.

46. For "crux" see Royal Robbins to Steve Roper, 12 December 1964, Roper. For "virgin" see Royal Robbins, "The North America Wall," *Summit* (May–June 1965), 3.

47. For "freedom" see Chouinard, "Sentinel Rock," 331. For "dominate" and "bond" see Pratt, "The South Face of Mount Watkins," 345–46. For "courage" see Royal Robbins, "The North American Wall," *AAJ* (1965), 336. For "dignity" see Roper, *A Climber's Guide to Yosemite Valley,* 25. For big walls see Royal Robbins, "Letters," *Summit* (April 1968), 35. For reactions see Joe Kelsey, "The Oceania Wall," *Summit* (April 1970), 24–27; Tom Higgins, "In Due Time," *Ascent* (1972), 18–22.

48. For Ribbon Falls see Charles Pratt, "Ribbon Fall, East Portal," *AAJ* (1965), 412–14. For "psyched" see Kamps to Bonnie, 6 July 1962, Kamps, Roper; Roper, *Camp 4,* 133, 182–84; Jim Bridwell, "Bird's Eye View," *Alpinist* (Winter 2006–2007), 68.

49. Chouinard's "crutch" quoted by Don Lauria in Harding, *Downward Bound,* 167; also Chouinard to Roper, c. June 1964, Roper. For "purer" see Yvon Chouinard, "Muir Wall—El Capitan," *AAJ* (1966), 46. For "brew" see Royal Robbins, "Arcturus—A New Route on Half Dome," *Summit* (April 1971), 6.

50. For hallucinations see Chouinard, "Muir Wall," 48–50. For "visionary" and "ingredients" see Doug Robinson, "The Climber as Visionary," *Ascent* (May 1969), 6, 9; Doug Scott, "On the Profundity Trail," *Mountain* (May 1971), 12–17; Ax Nelson, "First Ascent of West Wall," *Yodeler,* 4 November 1946, 4.

51. For "egoist" see Robbins, "Alone on the John Muir Wall," 319, 322; Royal Robbins, "Solo Ascent of El Capitan," *Summit* (March 1969), 13–15. For solos and influence see Lunn, *A Century of Mountaineering,* 172; Wilson et al., "Mountain Interview: Royal Robbins," 31; Chuck Pratt to Steve Roper, 18 March 1965, Roper; Steve Roper, "Mountaineering Notes," *Ascent* (May 1970), 45. For *In Cold Blood* see *AAJ* (1971), 359–60.

52. For "recover" see Meade, "Perversion of Mountaineering," 25. For testing see Hamilton, "Changing," 26. For comparison with skiing and surfing see Annie Gilbert Coleman, *Ski Style: Sport and Culture in the Rockies* (Lawrence: University Press of Kansas, 2004); Nick Ford and David Brown, *Surfing and Social Theory: Experience, Embodiment, and Narrative of the Dream Glide* (New York: Routledge, 2005). For technology see R. E. Stone, "Meanings Found in the Acts of Surfing and Skiing" (Ph.D. diss., University of Southern California, 1970), 60–61, 78, 86–88, 108. For "impedimenta" see Steve Roper, *Climber's Guide to Yosemite Valley* (San Francisco: Sierra Club, 1971), 18.

53. For "delight" and climbs see Royal S. Robbins, "Tis-sa-ack," *AAJ* (1970), 7–8; Robbins, "East Wall of Upper Yosemite Fall"; Royal Robbins, "The Prow," *Summit* (July–August 1970), 2–7; Royal Robbins, "Arcturus, Northwest Face of Half Dome," 358–59.

54. Comici's "falling" quoted in Roger Frison-Roche and Sylvain Jouty, *A History of Mountain Climbing* (New York: Flammarion, 1996), 100; also Warren Harding, "Reflections of a Broken-Down Climber," *Ascent* (July 1971), 34. For hooks see Galen Rowell, "Two New Yosemite Routes," *AAJ* (1970), 10; Wilson et al., "Mountain Interview: Royal Robbins," 33; also Glen Denny to Steve Roper, 28 August 1963, Roper.

55. For Half Dome see Galen Rowell, "Twenty Five Days, South Face of Half Dome," *Summit* (December 1970), 2–9. For "penchant" see Royal Robbins, "Incident on Half Dome," *Summit* (January–February 1969), 2. For "trend" see Steve Roper, "Mountaineering Notes," *Ascent* (May 1970), 45. For confusion see Royal Robbins, "Tis-sa-ack," *Ascent* (May 1970), 19.

56. "A Three-Week Trip Up El Capitan: Ordeal on a Sheer Rock Face," *Life,* 20 November 1970, 46–48; Harding, *Downward Bound,* 124–64; Royal Robbins, "The El Capitan Climb," *Summit* (December 1970), 30–31; Robert Grow, "The El Capitan Climb," *Summit* (December 1970), 31; "El Capitan, Wall of Morning Light," *AAJ* (1971), 360.

57. For "engineering" and "obvious" see *San Francisco Chronicle,* 1 December 1970. For "millions" see TM Herbert, "Comment on the Two Ascents of the Wall of Morning Light," *AAJ* (1971), 361. For "suction" and "shameful" see Wilson et al., "Mountain Interview: Royal Robbins." For "mad" see Yvon Chouinard, "Coonyard Mouths Off," *Ascent* (June 1972), 50. For similar scandals see *AACN,* November 1970, 3; Douglas Tompkins, "Second Thoughts on Cerro Torre," *Ascent* (July 1971), 47. For "adroit" see Robbins, "The El Capitan Climb," 30. For others cashing in see "Technical Rock Climbing Seminars," *Summit* 35 (May 1968), 35.

58. For media see Roper, *Camp 4,* 226–30. For Harding's denial see Harding, "Reflections," 33–34. For rescue see SAR Reports FY 70, Sept.–Dec., YOSAR; phone conversation with Pete Thompson, 25 March 2002.

59. For reactions see Don Lauria, "El Capitan, Wall of Early Morning Light," *AAJ* (1971), 360; *Summit* (December 1970), 30–31; *Summit* (May 1971), 41. For "eccentric" and "ripping" see Robbins, "The El Capitan Climb," 31. For "reckless" see Royal Robbins, "Toward a Climbing Ethic," *Summit* (October 1965), 34. For "police" see Royal Robbins, "T-I-M-E for a Change," *Summit* (November 1968), 2. Harding compared Robbins to Carrie Nation and Elmer Gantry in "Reflections," 35. For second ascent see *AACN,* May 1971, 1. For "difficult" see "Dawn Wall—Revisited," *Summit* (April 1971), 38.

60. For "rationalizing" see Harding, *Downward Bound,* 166–67. For "complicated," "essentially," "blot," and "rape" see Wilson et al., "Mountain Interview: Royal Robbins," 33–34. For "witnessed" see Herbert, "Comment on the Two Ascents of the Wall of Morning Light," 361. For principles see Royal Robbins, *Basic Rockcraft* (Glendale, Calif.: La Siesta, 1971), 62; Roper, *A Climber's Guide to Yosemite Valley,* 24–25. For reversal see Royal Robbins, *Advanced Rockcraft* (Glendale, Calif.: La Siesta, 1973), 79; Robbins, "A Review of 'Downward Bound,'" 314–16. For Robbins's reassessment see Gardiner, *Why I Climb,* 88.

61. For "Rat's," "Christians," "Inquisition," and Herbert see Harding, "Reflections," 33–35. For "best" see Harding, *Downward Bound,* 88; also Christian Bonington, "Too Cold for Ethics?" *Mountain* (May 1972), 17. For "morals" see Chris Jones, "Mountain Interview: Warren Harding," Mountain (May 1970), 16.

62. For support see "Letters," *Summit* (May 1971), 41. For "damn" see Harding, "Reflections," 34. For dismissal see Royal Robbins, "Yosemite Renaissance," *Summit* (November–December 1971), 31. For blank walls see Royal Robbins, "Incident on Half Dome," *Summit* (January–February 1969), 2. For "Joe" and "Art" see Chouinard, "Coonyard Mouths Off," 50. For "master" and "peers" see Roper, *Camp 4,* 104, 231. For Harding caring see Wilson et al., "Mountain Interview: Royal Robbins, 34. For "boys" see Harding, *Downward Bound,* 88. For "heavy" see *Recollections: The Wall of Early Morning Light, an Interview with Warren Harding* (Trey Solberg and Roger Derryberry, Downward Bound Productions, 2001). Harding's open letter quoted in Roper, *Camp 4,* 229.

63. For climbs see Royal Robbins, "El Cap Commentary," *Mountain* (January 1973), 32; "Basecamp," *Climbing* (November–December 1978), 4; Arce, *Defying Gravity,* 94–95; Kerry Drager, "Back on the Nose," *Outside* (November 1983), 17.

64. For continued weariness see *AACN* (May 1972), 2; *AACN* (November 1972), 3.

65. For "mastery" and "contemporary" see Duane, *El Capitan,* 40, 52. For "saying" see Jones, "Mountain Interview: Warren Harding," 16.

9. Entrepreneurs

The epigraph is from a letter to Steve Roper, c. June 1964, Roper.

1. For Beats see Barbara Ehrenreich, *The Hearts of Men: American Dreams and the Flight from Commitment* (Garden City, N.Y.: Anchor Books, 1983), 55; Craig Leavitt, "On the Road: Cassady, Kerouac, and Images of Late Western Masculinity," in *Across the Great Divide: Cultures of Manhood in the American West*, ed. Matthew Basso, Laura McCall, and Dee Garceau (New York: Routledge, 2001), 226.

2. For seasonal work see Layton Kor to Steve Roper, 29 April 1964; for school, teaching, and research see Powell to Roper, 18 June 1964, both in Roper; Robert Roper, *Fatal Mountaineer* (New York: St. Martin's Griffin, 2002). For NPS see Dave Dornan to Roper, 9 March 1960, Roper.

3. Yvon Chouinard, *Let My People Go Surfing: The Education of a Reluctant Businessman* (New York: Penguin, 2005).

4. Chouinard, *Let My People Go Surfing*, 7–12; Jeremy Bernstein, "Ascending," *New Yorker* (31 January 1977), 42.

5. Chouinard, *Let My People Go Surfing*, 12–18; Bernstein, "Ascending," 42–43; Ken Wilson, Allen Steck, and Galen Rowell, "Mountain Interview: Royal Robbins," *Mountain* 18 (November 1971), 28–29.

6. Chouinard, *Let My People Go Surfing*, 18. For Gallwas and Feuerer see Michael P. Sherrick, "The Northwest Face of Half Dome," *SCB* (November 1958), 22; Wayne Merry, "The Longest Climb," *Mariah* (1979), 24.

7. For "bitter" and "delay" see Bob Kamps to Bonnie, 6 July 1962, Kamps. For "studying," "super," "blueprints," and "think" see Yvon Chouinard to Steve Roper, 31 December 1963, Roper. For Army see Bernstein, "Ascending," 46–47.

8. For "evening," "biners," "concrete, "campaign," and Long see Chouinard to Steve Roper, c. June 1964; Dick Long to Roper, 4 June 1964, both in Roper. For producers see Tom Frost, "Yosemite & Frost, First Ascent of 'Rixon's West,'" *Mugelnoos*, 8 October 1959, 5; Gregg Blomberg to Roper, 10 April 1964, Roper; C. Don Widell, "Manufacturing an Alloy Piton," *Summit* (May–June 1965), 42–44. For surfing parallels see Douglas Booth, "Surfing: The Cultural and Technological Determinants of a Dance," *Culture, Sport, Society* 2 (Spring 1999), 41.

9. For growth see "More Climbers Scale U.S. Peaks, Step Up Equipment Spending," *Wall Street Journal*, 21 September 1960, 1. For retailers see Harvey Manning, *REI: 50 Years of Climbing Together* (Seattle: REI, 1988), 1–79; Bob Woodward, "Industry Trailblazers," *GearTrends® Outdoor* (Summer 2006), 14–19; Bob Woodward, "Industry Trailblazers, Part II," *GearTrends® Outdoor* (Winter 2007), 36–40.

10. For manufacturers see Woodward, "Industry Trailblazers," 14–19; Woodward, Industry Trailblazers, Part II," 36–40; Glen Denny to Roper, 6 March 1963, Roper. For shops see *Summit* (April 1960), 26 and (June 1961), 20; Pat Ament, *Royal Robbins: Spirit of the Age* (Mechanicsburg, Pa.: Stackpole, 1998), 218; Roper to Allen Steck, 11 June 1964, Roper. For prototypes see Mirella Tenderini, *Gary Hemming: The Beatnik of the Alps*, trans. Susan Hodgkiss (Glasgow: Ernest Press, 1995), 76; Gregg Blomberg to Steve Roper, 10 April 1964; Chouinard to Roper 18 June 1963 and 21 May 1964; Steve Komito to Roper, 20 January 1969, all in Roper. For hiring see Tex [Floyd] Bossier to Steve Roper, 21 December 1962; Steve Komito to Roper, 6 March 1965, both in Roper. Chouinard, *Let My People Go Surfing*, 23, 25, 29–30.

11. For "equal" and background see Steve Komito, "Normal Wear and Terror: My Three Decades Inside the Outside Industry," *The Mountain Yodel* (1998), 17–20. For climbs see Steve Komito, "Standing Rock," in Layton Kor, *Beyond the Vertical,* ed. Bob Godfrey (Boulder: Alpine House, 1983), 87–98. For work see Komito to Roper, 11 February 1966, 6 March 1966, and c. 1966, all in Roper.

12. For "discontent" see Komito to Roper, 6 January 1968; for debts see Komito to Roper, 6 January 1969, 20 January 1969, 18 February 1969, 24 February 1971, 7 June 1971, 26 December 1973, and 25 January 1974; for no climbing see Komito to Roper, 7 June 1971; for soles see Komito to Roper, 1 January 1967 and 20 January 1969; for pitons see Yvon Chouinard to Roper, 28 February 1961 and 18 March 1963; Gregg Blomberg to Roper, 10 April 1964, all in Roper; Lizzy Scully, "In the Business of Saving Soles," *Estes Park Trail-Gazette,* 17 October 2003, 10.

13. For "Chosen" see Komito to Roper, 9 October 1970; for "fix-a-shoe" see Komito to Roper, c. 1970; for "Bootmaker" see flyer attached to Komito to Roper, c. 1968; for branding see Komito to Roper, 1 January 1967, all in Roper; Mark Powell, Warren Harding, Ken McNutt, Dick Sykes, and Don Lauria, "The Dolt—A Eulogy," *Climbing* (July–August 1976), 28–32.

14. For European guiding see Peter H. Hansen, "Partners: Guides and Sherpas in the Alps and Himalayas, 1850s–1950s," in *Voyages and Visions: Towards a Cultural History of Travel,* ed. Jaś Elsner and Joan-Pau Rubiés (London: Reaktion Books, 1999), 210–31. For North America see Erik Weiselberg, "Ascendancy of the Mazamas: Environment, Identity and Mountain Climbing in Oregon, 1870 to 1930" (Ph.D. diss., University of Oregon, 1999), 29–30, 42, 49, 53–54, 324; Edward Whymper, "A New Playground in the New World," *Scribner's Magazine* 33 (June 1903), 643–44; "Mt. Rainier Guide Service," *Mugelnoos,* 14 July 1960, 6; Raye C. Ringholz, *On Belay! The Life of Legendary Mountaineer Paul Petzoldt* (Seattle: Mountaineers, 1997), 32–51. For Leysin see James Ramsey Ullman, *Straight Up: The Life and Death of John Harlin* (New York: Doubleday, 1968), 177–81, 195–98, 206–13; Ament, *Royal Robbins,* 181–97. For Exum see Glen Exum, *Never a Bad Word or a Twisted Rope,* ed. and comp. Charlie Craighead (Moose, Wyo.: Grand Teton Natural History Association, 1998). For "abhors" see Gaston Rébuffat, *Starlight and Storm: The Ascent of Six Great North Faces of the Alps with a Section on the Technique of Mountain Climbing,* trans. Wilfred Noyce, Sir John Hunt, and Roland Le Grand (New York: E. P. Dutton, 1957), 20–21. This blurs simple bifurcations of work and play. See Richard White, "'Are You an Environmentalist or Do You Work for a Living?': Work and Nature," in *Uncommon Ground: Toward Reinventing Nature,* ed. William Cronon (New York: W. W. Norton, 1995), 171–85; Joseph E. Taylor III, "The Social Contexts of Play" (paper given at the Canadian Historical Association annual meeting, Vancouver, June 2008).

15. For "talk" and "accomplishments" see Richard G. Mitchell Jr., *Mountain Experience: The Psychology and Sociology of Adventure* (Chicago: University of Chicago Press, 1983), 72–73. For photography and "Himalayas" see Hansen, "British Mountaineering," 219, 254. For lectures see Frank Hewitt, "Now We Know," *Yodeler,* 19 December 1949, 3. For tours see Anthony Brandt, "Introduction," in *Scrambles amongst the Alps in the Years 1860–1869,* by Edward Whymper (1871; Washington, D.C.: National Geographic Society, 2002), xvii; Peter Gillman and Leni Gillman, *The Wildest Dream: The Biography of George Mallory* (Seattle: Mountaineers, 2000), 217–21; "The Everest Party in Southern California," *Mugelnoos,* 11 March 1954, 1; "Starlight and Storm," *Mugelnoos,* 9 May 1957, 3; Steve Roper, *Camp 4: Recollections of a Yosemite Climber* (Seattle: Mountaineers, 1994), 88.

16. For photos and "pay" see Layton Kor to Steve Roper, 4 July 1964, Roper. For circuit see

AACN, 15 January 1965, 1–2; Ament, *Royal Robbins*, 196; *Climbing Cathedral Spires*, videotape copy of YOSE 97882 & 97895, YRL; William Siri, "PROPOSED SCENARIO FOR TRAINING FILM ON ROCK CLIMBING," 20 February 1955, carton 23:36, SCMP.

17. For European films see Kerwin Lee Klein, "Catholic Action: Luis Trenker and the Politics of Bergfilm," http://history.berkeley.edu/faculty/Klein/trenker/; Michael Childers, "Radical Reels: Film, Adventure, Identity, and Lifestyle on the Edge" (paper given at the annual meeting of the American Society for Environmental History, Baton Rouge, March 2007, copies in author's possession). For studio releases see *White Hell of Pitz Palu* (Dr. Arnold Fanck and G. W. Pabst, H. R. Sokal, 1929); *The White Tower* (Ted Tetzlaff, RKO Radio Pictures, 1950); "Annapurna," *Yodeler*, 4 January 1954, 3. For didactics see Carol Hall, "Stanford Alpine Club at Pinnacles National Monument," 1946, Department of Special Collections, Stanford University Libraries, Stanford, California. For Gmoser see "Vagabonds of the Mountains," *Yodeler*, 15 February 1960, 6. *Sentinel: The West Face* (Roger C. Brown, Summit Films, 1967). For "extravagant" and "star" see C. F. Meade, "The Perversion of Mountaineering," *Quarterly Review* 267 (1936), 22. For "hero" see Dave Rearick, "A Fine New Route in Yosemite," *Mugelnoos*, May 1960.

18. For "hypocritical" see Eric Beck to Steve Roper, 12 October 1964, Roper. For risk see Bruce Braun, "'On the Raggedy Edge of Risk': Articulations of Race and Nature after Biology," in *Race, Nature, and the Politics of Difference*, ed. Donald S. Moore, Jake Kosek, and Anand Pandian (Durham: Duke University Press, 2003), 179.

19. Warren Harding and Wayne Merry, "We Conquered El Capitan," *Argosy* 348 (April 1959), 24–28, 104–7; also Edwin Muller, "It's Foolish to Get Killed," *Saturday Evening Post* (9 June 1934), 22–23, 113–14; Robin Hansen, "They Climbed to Their Deaths," *Saturday Evening Post* (14 May 1949), 38–39, 142–148; Robert H. Bates, "We Met Death on K2," *Saturday Evening Post* (5 December 1953), 19–21, 166–70; Allen Steck, "Terror on Makalu," *Saturday Evening Post* (14 May 1955), 32, 65–66, 70–76; Nicholas B. Clinch, "We Scaled Doomsday Mountain," *Saturday Evening Post* (24 March 1961), 26–27, 91–94. For *Summit* see Chris Jones, *Climbing in North America* (Seattle: Mountaineers, 1997), 210n.

20. Although ignoring popular publications, see bibliography in Steve Roper, ed., *Ordeal by Piton: Writings from the Golden Age of Yosemite Climbing* (Stanford: Stanford University Libraries, 2003), 263–79.

21. Yvon Chouinard, "Coonyard Mouths Off," *Ascent* (June 1972), 50–52. For "important," "ethics," and equipment see Yvon Chouinard, "Modern Yosemite Climbing," *AAJ* (1963), 319, 324. For "prejudiced" see Yvon Chouinard to Steve Roper, 7 December 1962. For "cleaner" see John Middendorf, "The Mechanical Advantage: Tools for the Wild Vertical," in *Ascent: The Climbing Experience in Word and Image*, eds. Allen Steck, Steve Roper, and David Harris (Golden: American Alpine Press, 1999), 167; also Yvon Chouinard, "Chouinard on Ice," *Outside* (December 1977), 33; Yvon Chouinard, *Climbing Ice* (San Francisco: Sierra Club, 1978), 185–89. For no trace see James Morton Turner, "From Woodcraft to 'Leave No Trace': Wilderness, Consumerism, and Environmentalism in Twentieth-Century America," *Environmental History* 7 (July 2002), 462–84.

22. For "arbiters" see Weiselberg, "Ascendancy of the Mazamas," 281. For pre-*Bulletin* climbs see Theodore S. Solomons, "Mt. Goddard and Its Vicinity—in the High Sierra of California," *Appalachia* (January 1896), 41–57. For *SCB* see Edwin Bingham Copeland, "Ascent of Junction Peak," *SCB* (May 1900), 172–73. For distant climbs see LeRoy Jeffers, "Ascent of Mount Moran, Giant of the Tetons," *SCB* (January 1921), 161–66. For first ascents see Francis P. Farquhar, "First Ascent of the Middle Palisade," *SCB* (1922), 266–70. For histories see Francis P. Farquhar, "Some Early Ascents of Mount Dana," *SCB* (1931),

108–11. For growth see Richard M. Leonard, "Some Climbs in the Yosemite Region," *SCB* (1934), 99–100. For practice see Rock Climbing Committee, "A Climber's Guide to Local Rock-Climbing," *Yodeler,* 19 January 1939, 7. For guidebook see William Alsup, *Missing in the Minarets: The Search for Walter A. Starr, Jr.* (Yosemite: Yosemite Association, 2001), 127. For gatekeeping see Richard M. Leonard to Laura Brunner, 23 April 1934, carton 1:14, SCMRR.

23. For guidebooks see Alsup, *Missing,* 126–27; David R. Brower, ed., *A Climber's Guide to the High Sierra. Parts I–VI. Sawtooth Ridge, Ritter Range, Palisade Group, Yosemite Valley, Whitney Region, Evolution Group and the Black Divide, Preliminary Edition* (San Francisco: Sierra Club, 1949), Bancroft; Hervey Voge, ed., *A Climber's Guide to the High Sierra; Routes and Records for California Peaks from Bond Pass to Army Pass and for Rock Climbs in Yosemite Valley and Kings Canyon* (San Francisco: Sierra Club, 1954); Leigh Ortenburger, *A Climber's Guide to the Teton Range* (San Francisco: Sierra Club, 1956); "New Listing of Climbs at Tahquitz," *Mugelnoos,* c. September 1953, 5–6; "At Last It's Here," *Mugelnoos,* 12 July 1956, 1; "The Shawangunks," *Mugelnoos,* 10 December 1959, 3–4. For "print" see "Climbers Guide," *Yodeler,* 7 December 1953, 6. For usefulness see "They Had a Granite Time," *Mugelnoos,* 3 December 1942, 3. For hiving see "Climbers Guide to High Sierra," *Yodeler,* June 1961, 1.

24. For Yosemite authors see *AACN,* 29 September 1961, 5; Allan MacDonald, "A New Climbing Classification Proposal," *SCB* (June 1961), 11. For compiling see Royal Robbins to Roper, c. 1962, Roper; Al Macdonald and Chuck Pratt to Bruce Kilgore, c. 1963, carton 307:2, and Roper to Sid, 8 January 1964, carton 307:7, SCR. For "*real,*" "respect," and "normal" see Roper, *A Climber's Guide to Yosemite Valley* (1964), 25.

25. For second edition see Steve Roper, *Climber's Guide to Yosemite Valley* (San Francisco: Sierra Club, 1971). For Welzenbach see Alan Rouse, "Grading Systems," *Mountain* (May–June 1975), 35–36. For "spirit" see Meade, "The Perversion of Mountaineering," 25. Irving quoted in Jim Ring, *How the English Made the Alps* (London: John Murray, 2000), 242. For RCS see "Yosemite Valley Trip, First Annual Climbing Trip of the Rock Climbing Section of the Sierra Club," p. 3, carton 7:30, SCSFBCR. For SC system see "MOUNTAIN RECORD COMMITTEE MEETS: A New Classification Proposed," *Yodeler,* 29 February 1938, 6. For decimal see Chuck Wilts, "Further Discussion on Climbing Classifications," *Summit* (January 1958), 16–17.

26. For criticism see Mountaineering Committee to David R. Brower, 4 February 1956, carton 193:12, SCMP. For "common" and "contribute" see Leigh Ortenburger, "A National Climbing Classification Proposed," *Summit* (May 1963), 14; Leigh Ortenburger, "Corrected Climbing Charts of the NCCS," *Summit* (June 1963), 24–25.

27. For NCCS group see Ortenburger, "A National Climbing Classification Proposed," 14. For lobbying see "Your Letters," *Summit* (April 1963), 24–26; carton 67:56, SCMP; Royal Robbins to Roper, 18 March 1963; Yvon Chouinard to Roper, 14 April 1963; Jim Baldwin to Roper, 9 February 1963; Mark Powell to Roper, 21 May 1963, all in Roper. For resistance see Michael Loughman, "Climbing Decimals," *Summit* (March 1963), 25; "Your Letters," *Summit* (June 1963), 27. For "Liberty Ridge" see "Letters," *Summit* (May 1963), 37. For provincialism see Ortenburger, "A National Climbing Classification Proposed," 14–16. For tradition see Dick Long to Roper, 4 November 1964, Roper.

28. For decision see Nicholas Clinch to Edward Wayburn, 8 June 1963, carton 67:56, SCMP. For "stick" see Robbins to Roper, 14 April 1963; for begged and table see Chouinard to Roper, 22 May 1963; for cues see Art Gran to Steve Roper, 4 April 1963, all in Roper. For published ratings see Roper, *A Climber's Guide to Yosemite Valley* (1964), 29–32; Jones,

Climbing in North America, 189fn. For dogmatic see Roper to Allen Steck, 25 October 1964, Roper; also Joseph E. Taylor III, "Mapping Adventure: Mapping Class and Gender in Yosemite Valley's Climbing Landscapes," *Journal of Historical Geography* 32 (January 2006), 190–219.

29. For early pamphlets see Weiselberg, "Ascendancy of the Mazamas," 174. For prewar see, e.g., Robert L. M. Underhill, "The Technique of Rock Climbing," *Appalachia* (December 1933), 565–90; J. Monroe Thorington, "Artificial Aids in Early Mountaineering," *Appalachia* (December 1940), 181–93. For reading see "Two-Twine Technique and Traverse," *Mugelnoos,* 9 November 1939, 1. For war see Kenneth Henderson, ed., *The American Alpine Club's Handbook of American Mountaineering* (Boston: Houghton Mifflin, 1942); David R. Brower, ed., *Manual of Ski Mountaineering* (Berkeley: University of California Press, 1946). For postwar see Richard M. Leonard, Arnold Wexler, William Siri, Charles Wilts, David Brower, Morgan Harris, and May Pridham, *Belaying the Leader: An Omnibus on Safety* (San Francisco: Sierra Club, 1956); Harvey Manning, ed., *Mountaineering: The Freedom of the Hills* (Seattle: Mountaineers, 1960). For methodology see Yvon Chouinard, "Climbing Cracks," *AAJ* (1970), 15–18; Royal Robbins, "On Technique," *Summit* (April 1969), 24–27. For self-interest see Royal Robbins, *Basic Rockcraft* (Glendale, Calif.: La Siesta, 1971); Yvon Chouinard and Thomas M. Frost, "On New Rock-Climbing Equipment and Its Use," *AAJ* (1967), 334–42.

30. For "made" see Denny to Roper, 6 March 1964; for Pinnacles see Roper to Steck, 11 June 1964; for strategizing see Roper to Steck, 25 October 1964; for history see Chouinard to Roper, 31 December 1963; Roper to Steck, 20 June 1964, all in Roper.

31. For RCS trouble and *Rotten Log* see "Minutes of RCC Meeting," 13 January 1959, Menocal. For Robbins and *Summit* see *Summit* (January–February 1965), 1. For "pissed" see Denny to Roper, 6 March 1964, Roper. For divided views see "Editorial," *Yodeler,* April 1961, 1–2; "Letters" and "Rebuttal," *Yodeler,* June 1961, 1–2. For coverage see Aubrey Wendling to Randal F. Dickey Jr., 28 January 1961, carton 30:40, SCR. For frustration see Roper to Steck, 11 June 1964 and 25 October 1964, both in Roper.

32. For "matters" see Steck to Will Siri, 1 February 1966; for "defended" see William E. Siri to Brower, 30 March 1966, both in 193:35, SCMP. For resistance see Brower to Publications Committee, 24 March 1966, carton 193:35; for ties to climbers see Brower to Theodore Waller, 20 December 1965, carton 12:13, both in SCMP. For broader issues see Michael P. Cohen, *The History of the Sierra Club, 1892–1970* (San Francisco: Sierra Club Books, 1988), 291–99, 314–23, 339–65. For encouragement personal conversation with Allen Steck, Berkeley, California, June 2001; also Joseph E. Taylor III, "Climber, Granite, Sky," *Environmental History* 11 (January 2006), 130–35.

33. For mountain art see Hansen, "British Mountaineering," 220–26, 248–51; Greg Child, Ansel Adams, David Brower, Paul Kallmes, and Wendy M. Watson, *Summit: Vittorio Sella, Mountaineer and Photographers, the Years 1879–1909* (New York: Aperture, 1999); Jonathan Spaulding, "The Natural Scene and the Social Good: The Artistic Education of Ansel Adams," *Pacific Historical Review* 60 (January 1991), 15–42; Anthony Decaneous, ed., *Bradford Washburn: Mountain Photography* (Seattle: Mountaineers, 1999); Whymper, *Scrambles amongst the Alps.* For Beat aesthetic see John Rawlings, *The Stanford Alpine Club* (Stanford: CSLI Publications, 1999), 104, 127–28, 132; Harold Drasdo, "Reading the Big Wall Image," in *The Mountain Spirit,* ed. Michael Charles Tobias and Harold Drasdo (Woodstock, N.Y.: Overlook Press, 1979), 75–83. For guidebook see Glen Denny to Roper, 31 July 1963, Roper.

34. For "total" see *AACN* (November 1967), 5. For recruiting see Joe Fitschen and Allen

Steck, "Attention Mountaineers," undated, carton 193:35, SCMP; also Tom Adler, ed., *Glen Denny: Yosemite in the Sixties* (Santa Barbara: T. Adler Books and Patagonia, 2007); Joe Kelsey, ed., *The Climbing Cartoons of Sheridan Anderson* (High Peaks Press, 1989).

35. For reception see "Proposed Journal of Mountaineering," *Yodeler* (December 1966), 4; "RCS Newsletter," November 1967, carton 7:28, SCSFBCR. For 1970 see Roper, *Camp 4*, 211. For "hotcakes" see Komito to Roper, 7 August 1964; for "weekdays" see Robbins to Roper, 9 August 1964; for "Everyone" see Pratt to Roper, 18 March 1965, all in Roper. For percentage see *AACN*, 25 May 1966, 2. For "pilgrims" see Royal Robbins, "Talus of Yosemite," *Summit* (June 1968), 33. For "tremendous" see *AACN* (November 1970), 2.

36. Komito to Roper, 6 March 1965 and 25 December 1970, both in Roper; A. Woodward, "Lost Arrow Inc," in *International Director of Company Histories*, vol. 22, ed. Jay P. Pederson (Detroit: Thomson Gale, 2005), 324; Woodward, "Industry Trailblazers, Part II," 37–40; personal conversation with Allen Steck, Berkeley, Calif., June 2001; Galen Rowell, *Many People Come, Looking, Looking* (Seattle: Mountaineers, 1980), 43–47.

37. For "November" see Douglas Gantenbein, "The Battle of the Bolt," *Sports Illustrated* 81 (24 August 1994), 2–4; Steve Gardiner, ed., *Why I Climb: Personal Insights of Top Climbers* (Harrisburg, Pa.: Stackpole Books, 1990), 83.

10. Dirtbags

The epigraph is from a letter to Ken Wilson, 22 October 1971, Roper.

1. Nancy Moss, "The Psychology of the Aging Athlete," *Clinics in Sports Medicine* 10 (1991), 431–44; John E. Morley, "The Aging Athlete," *Journal of Gerontology* 55 (November 2000), M627–29.

2. For "Golden" see Steve Roper, *Camp 4: Recollections of a Yosemite Rockclimber* (Seattle: Mountaineers, 1994), 11–15.

3. For "played" see Chris Jones, "Mountain Interview: Warren Harding," *Mountain* (May 1970), 18. For "rang" and "wagon" see Jim McCarthy, "The Last Mountain Men and the Last Frontier," *Summit* (November–December 1971), 8–9. For "creaking" see Galen Rowell, "An Elegy for Yosemite," *Climbing* (May–June 1971), 11. For "idyllic" see Roper, *Camp 4*, 229. For "sorry" see Steve Gardiner, ed., *Why I Climb: Personal Insights of Top Climbers* (Harrisburg, Pa.: Stackpole Books, 1990), 107. For "inner" see Lawrence Hamilton, "The Changing Face of American Mountaineering," *Review of Sport & Leisure* 6 (Summer 1981), 18, 23. For heroes see Pete Sinclair, *We Aspired: The Last Innocent Americans* (Logan: Utah State University Press, 1993), 159, 163, 169.

4. For "virgin" see Lawrence C. Hamilton, "Modern American Rock Climbing: Some Aspects of Social Change," *Pacific Sociological Review* 22 (July 1979), 305n9. For "plowed" see Gardiner, *Why I Climb*, 107. For "lines" see Tom Higgins, "In Thanks," *Ascent* (1975–1976), 23. For figures see Laura Avedisian, "The Yosemite Riot: Changes in Policy and Management in the National Park Service" (M.A. thesis, San Jose State University, 1998), 14. For "malaise" see Lito Tejada-Flores, "Overpopulation and the Alpine Ego Trip," *Ascent* (June 1972), 53. For reform see John Stannard, "Rock Climbing in 1984," *AAJ* (1973), 337–38. For degradation see Bob Van Belle, "The Death of Yosemite," *Off Belay* (August 1977), 45. For defense see Edward Hardy, "Letter to the Editor," *Off Belay* (December 1977), 55–56.

5. For "dwelt" see Donald Worster, *Nature's Economy: A History of Ecological Ideas* (New York: Cambridge University Press, 1977), 378. For British see C. D. Cunningham and W. Abney, *Pioneers of the Alps* (London: Sampson Low, Marston, Searle, and Rivington,

1887), 23. For Anglophiles see James Ramsey Ullman, *High Conquest: The Story of Mountaineering* (Philadelphia: J. B. Lippincott, 1941), 41. For historians' acceptance see Walt Unsworth, *Hold the Heights: The Foundations of Mountaineering* (Seattle: Mountaineers, 1994), 75, 105.

6. For "paternity" and Norway see Peter H. Hansen, "Modern Mountains: The Performative Consciousness of Modernity in Britain, 1870–1940," in *Meanings of Modernity: Britain from the Late-Victorian Era to World War II*, ed. Martin Daunton and Bernhard Rieger (New York: Oxford University Press, 2001), 190. For "glory" see Peter H. Hansen, "British Mountaineering, 1850–1914" (Ph.D. diss., Harvard University, 1991), 204. I thank Peter Hansen for help with this. For Canada see Zac Robinson, "The Golden Years of Canadian Mountaineering: Asserted Ethics, Form, and Style, 1886–1925," *Sports History Review* 35 (May 2004), 1–19. For Cascades see Erik L. Weiselberg, "Ascendancy of the Mazamas: Environment, Identity and Mountain Climbing in Oregon, 1870 to 1930" (Ph.D. diss., University of Oregon, 1999), 211–12, 284, 329. For Sierra see Michael P. Cohen, *The History of the Sierra Club, 1892–1970* (San Francisco: Sierra Club, 1988), 81. For "golden days" see Royal Robbins, "Foreword," in *Beyond the Vertical*, by Layton Kor (Boulder: Alpine House, 1983), 9. For publishing see Galen A. Rowell, ed., *The Vertical World of Yosemite: A Collections of Writings and Photographs on Rock Climbing in Yosemite* (Berkeley: Wilderness Press, 1973). For historians' acceptance see Gary Arce, *Defying Gravity: High Adventure on Yosemite's Walls* (Berkeley: Wilderness Press, 1996), 35–78.

7. For "vulgar" and arrivals see Roper, *Camp 4*, 195.

8. For "kicks" see Steve Roper to Allen Steck, 11 June 1964; for "puppets" and "real" see Chuck Pratt to Roper, 8 August 1965; for "leads" and "indefinable" see Mark Powell to Roper, 18 June 1964, all in Roper.

9. For "best" and "found" see Geoffrey Childs, "The Bird," in *30 Years of Climbing Magazine* (Carbondale, Colo.: Primedia Special Interest Publications, 1999), 241, 242–43. For Kor see Huntley Ingalls, "We Climbed Utah's Skyscraper Rock," *National Geographic* 122 (November 1962), 705–21.

10. For "everywhere" see Steck to Roper, 21 June 1965; for "running out" see Pratt to Roper, 8 August 1965, both in Roper. For climbs see Royal Robbins, "Happenings in the Valley," *Summit* (December 1967), 26–27; Don Lauria, "Dihedral Diary," *Summit* (September 1968), 12–17; Chuck Kroger, "El Capitan—Heart Route," *Climbing* (January 1971), 6–9.

11. For ratings see Jim Bridwell, "The Innocent, the Ignorant, and the Insecure," *Ascent* (July 1973), 46–49. For climbs see Jim Bridwell, "Brave New World," *Mountain* (January 1974), 26–34.

12. Warren Harding, *Downward Bound: A Mad! Guide to Rock Climbing* (Englewood Cliffs, N.J.: Prentice-Hall, 1975), 36–37, 138–41; John Middendorf, "The Mechanical Advantage: Tools for the Wild Vertical," in *Ascent: The Climbing Experience in Word and Image*, eds. Allen Steck, Steve Roper, and David Harris (Golden, Colo.: American Alpine Press, 1999), 162–63.

13. Bill Westbay, "Team Machine," in *Yosemite Climber*, ed. George Meyers (Modesto: Robbins Mountain Letters, 1979), 86.

14. Middendorf, "Mechanical Advantage," 169–70, 172; Greg Lowe, "Half Dome in Winter," *AAJ* (1974), 269–73.

15. For "deck" see Chris McNamara, *Yosemite Big Walls: Supertopos* (San Francisco: Supertopo, 2000), 56. For "connoisseur" see Royal Robbins, "El Cap Commentary," *Mountain* (January 1973), 32.

16. For "super-sensitive" and "artist" see Robbins, "El Cap Commentary," 32. For "mediate"

and "creation" see Jim Bridwell, "Bird's Eye View," *Alpinist* (Winter 2006–2007), 70, 78. For "Michelangelos" see Daniel Duane, *El Capitan: Historical Feats and Radical Routes* (San Francisco: Chronicle Books, 2000), 91. Child's "submission" quoted in McNamara, *Yosemite Big Walls*, 92.

17. For "scared" and "believe" see Jim Bridwell and Keith Peall, *Climbing Adventures: A Climber's Passion* (Merrillville, Ind.: ICS Books, 1992), 79, 165. For "imagine" see Bridwell, "A Bird's Eye View," 73. For ascents see Westbay, "Team Machine," 82–90, and photo 44, p. 67. For surfing and skiing parallels see William Oscar Johnson, "It's Got Its Ups and Downs," *Sports Illustrated* 54 (30 March 1981), 60–68; Roselyn Elizabeth Stone, "Meanings Found in the Acts of Surfing and Skiing" (Ph.D. diss., University of Southern California, 1970), 62–63.

18. For "obsession" see Childs, "The Bird," 239. For risks see Pat Ament, *A History of Free Climbing in America: Wizards of Rock* (Berkeley: Wilderness Press, 2002), 208; John Sherman, "Life Without a Net," *Climbing* (February–March 1994), 126, 128–29.

19. For training Bridwell, "Brave New World," 30. For "pumping" and "crackerjack" see Trip Gabriel, "Valley Boys," *Rolling Stone*, 28 April 1983, 39. For "qualify" see Sheard, "Pilgrimage," 21. For "best" see Childs, "The Bird," 238.

20. Nicholas B. Clinch to John Rawlings, 9 February 1994, in "Nicholas B. Clinch: An Interview Conducted by John Rawlings," Stanford Oral Histories Project, 2001, Department of Special Collections, Stanford University Libraries, Stanford, California; Yvon Chouinard, *Let My People Go Surfing: The Education of a Reluctant Businessman* (New York: Penguin, 2005), 18–20; Layton Kor, *Beyond*, 152; Roper, *Camp 4*, 155. For camping see Penny Carr to Sharon and Steve Roper, 16 March 1965, Roper. For "spectrum" see Chris Jones, *Climbing in North America* (Seattle: Mountaineers, 1997), 330.

21. For coverage see Yvon Chouinard, "Modern Yosemite Climbing," *AAJ* (1963), 319–27; "Eine Masche aus den USA," *Alpinismus* (June 1966), 24–25; "Yosemite," *Mountain* (July 1969), 7–25. For foreigners see Royal Robbins, "El Cap Commentary," 31; Chic Scott, *Pushing the Limits: The Story of Canadian Mountaineering* (Calgary: Rocky Mountain Books, 2000), 243–51, 333–37. For pop culture see Sheard, "Pilgrimage," 24. For dirtbags see Craig Vetter, "Climbers," *Playboy* (November 1986), 176, 184; Jack Herrick, "Life at the Center of the Known Universe," *Climbing* (November–December 1997), 97. For theft see Bridwell and Peall, *Climbing Adventures*, 133.

22. For "equipment," drugs, and "recreation" see Childs, "The Bird," 243, 244–45. For "rebelliousness" see Bruce J. Schulman, *The Seventies: The Great Shift in American Culture, Society, and Politics* (New York: Da Capo, 2001), 146; George Lipsitz, "Who'll Stop the Rain: Youth Culture, Rock 'n' Roll, and Cultural Crisis," in *The Sixties*, ed. David Farber (Chapel Hill: University of North Carolina Press, 1994), 206–34.

23. For "epics" see Sheard, "Pilgrimage," 20. For medicate see Bridwell and Peall, *Climbing Adventures*, 51. For sitting see John Rawlings, "Charles Kroger 12/18/97 Telephone Conversation," pp. 3–4, Chuck Kroger folder, SAC. For Stonemasters see John Long, *Rock Jocks, Wall Rats, and Hang Dogs: Rock Climbing on the Edge of Reality* (New York: Simon and Schuster, 1994), 48–54. For Plan see Duane, *El Capitan*, 101. For Vulgarians see Susan Fox Rogers, "The Vulgarians Revisited," *Climbing* (April–May 1993), 110. For Squamish see Scott, *Pushing the Limits*, 245–50. For hippies see William J. Rorabaugh, *Berkeley at War: The 1960s* (New York: Oxford University Press, 1989), 130–45. For "sufficiency" see Leanne Stedman, "From Gidget to Gonad Man: Surfers, Feminists and Postmodernisation," *Australia New Zealand Journal of Sociology* 33 (March 1997), 80.

24. For "camper" and "unique" see Roper, *Camp 4*, 146, 162.

25. For Bridwell's rule and "loonies" see Childs, "The Bird," 239, 244. For "grandfather" see

Gardiner, *Why I Climb*, 82. For cajole see Westbay, "Team Machine." For bully see Kroger, "El Capitan—Heart Route."

26. For "friction" see Bill Stall, "Yosemite Poses Supreme Challenge to Climbers," *San Diego Union*, 3 November 1968, G2. For camping see *AACN*, 9 March 1962, 1; Glen Denny to Roper, 28 August 1963, Roper; Pete Sinclaire, "Behold Now Behemoth," *Ascent* (May 1968), 5–9. For tensions see Avedisian, "The Yosemite Riot," 18–43.

27. For "America" see John Roskelley, *Stories Off the Wall* (Seattle: Mountaineers, 1993), 55. For "didn't" see Avedisian, "The Yosemite Riot," 68.

28. For "cockney" see A. F. Mummery, *My Climbs in the Alps and Caucasus* (New York: Chas. Scribner's Sons, 1895), 116. For "awareness" and "flood" see Rowell, "The Yosemite Story," 20, 39. For "vandals" see epigraph. For "Paradise" see Bridwell and Peall, *Climbing Adventures*, 16–17. For academic reactions see Roderick Nash, *Wilderness and the American Mind*, 3rd ed. (New Haven: Yale University Press, 1982), 327–28, 376.

29. Avedisian, "The Yosemite Riot," 50–79; SupARs for 1972 and 1973.

30. For Camp 4/Sunnyside see Ian Wade, "Yosemite Notes," *Off Belay* (January–February 1972), 43. For Bedayn and ranger see *AACN* (November 1971), 2; Raffi Bedayn, "Yosemite's Camp 4 to Continue," *Off Belay* (June 1973), 35. For "symptom" and Yellow Pines see Avedisian, "The Yosemite Riot," 16, 73–76.

31. For "devoted" see SupAR 1972. For "Pandora's" and "manpower" see SupAR 1974; for crime statistics see SupARs for 1973–1977. For rangers see Avedisian, "The Yosemite Riot," 68. For report see Kenneth Tapman, "Investigation Report on July 4, 1970, Incident at Yosemite National Park" (Washington, D.C.: Department of the Interior, 1970), YRL.

32. For "flower-children" and "dream" see Roskelley, *Stories Off the Wall*, 47. "Ah Wilderness!" *Off Belay* (June 1973), 45; "John Muir Turns Over in His Grave," *Off Belay* (June 1975), 45. For crime wave see SupARs for 1972–1977. For crash see Michael P. Ghiglieri and Charles R. "Butch" Farabee, *Off the Wall: Death in Yosemite* (Flagstaff: Puma Press, 2007), 128–37.

33. The story has been fictionalized in Jeff Long, *Angels of Light* (New York: Beech Tree Books, 1987); Nevada Barr, *High Country* (New York: Putnam, 2004). For "gang" see Tyler Stableford, "The Wild Bunch," *Climbing* (November–December 1995), 96. For names see Marco Jacquemet, "Namechasers," *American Ethnologist* 19 (November 1992), 733–48. For "lifestyle," "stratification," "orthodoxy," and "abide" see Hamilton, "Modern American," 286, 288, 296. For denial see Roper, *Camp 4*, 216–17. For hierarchies see Gabriel, "Valley Boys," 29. For J-Tree see Long, *Rock Jocks*, 48–54. For Tetons see Sinclair, *We Aspired*, 159–67. For Shawangunks see Dick Williams, *The Climber's Guide to the Shawangunks: The Trapps* (New Paltz, N.Y.: Vulgarian Press, 2004).

34. For "autonomous" see Sherry B. Ortner, "'Burned Like a Tattoo': High School Social Categories and 'American Culture,'" *Ethnography* 3 (2002), 141. For "copperplate" see John Jay, *Skiing the Americas* (New York: Macmillan, 1947), 94. For "masters" see Tom Blake, "My Ride-to-Remember," in *Surf's Up*, ed. H. Arthur Klein and M. C. Klein (New York: Bobbs-Merrill, 1966), 93. For "destiny" see James Brooke, "In Colorado, Ice Climbers Surmount Legal Hurdles," *New York Times*, 2 March 1997, A18. For diverse experiences see Stone, "Meanings Found in the Acts of Surfing and Skiing," 15, 43, 66, 70–72, 73, 77–78, 92, 94, 97–99, 101, 104; Kristin L. Anderson, "Snowboarding: The Construction of Gender in an Emerging Sport," *Journal of Sport & Social Issues* 23 (February 1999), 55–79. For politics see Dean Scheibel, "'Making Waves' with Burke: Surf Nazi Culture and the Rhetoric of Localism," *Western Journal of Communication* 59 (Fall 1995), 253–69; Eric de Léséleuc, Jacques Gleyse, Anne Marcellini, trans. R. Anthony Lewis, "The Prac-

tice of Sport as Political Expression," *International Sociology* 17 (March 2002), 73–90; Isiah Helekunihi Walker, "Terrorism or Native Protest? The Hui `O He'e Nalu and Hawaiian Resistance to Colonialism," *Pacific Historical Review* 74 (November 2005), 575–602.

35. For all-season see "New Climb Reported," *Yodeler,* 4 March 1946, 4, 6. For "hasten" see Art Blake, "Rock Engineers Hasten Erosion," *Yodeler,* 12 May 1940, 2, 3. For loose flake see "Cathedral Spire in Danger," *SCB* (June 1946), 17–18. I thank Tom Dunlap for help with this.

36. For "problem" see Kor, *Beyond,* 136. For clean pitons see Middendorf, "Mechanical Advantage," 167. For damage see Tom Frost, "Preserving the Cracks!" *AAJ* (1972), 1–6; Royal Robbins, "Help Save South Crack," *Summit* (October 1972), 4–9.

37. For "deterioration" and "wilderness" see Yvon Chouinard and Tom Frost, "A Word . . . ," pp. 2–3; for "awareness" see Doug Robinson, "The Whole Natural Art of Protection," 16, both in *Chouinard Catalog* (1972), PCR; Andrew G. Kirk, *Countercultural Green: The Whole Earth Catalog and American Environmentalism* (Lawrence: University Press of Kansas, 2007), 198–201.

38. For hagiography see Sinclair, *We Aspired,* 163. Frost remembered the revolution as a seamless shift and himself as the agent of change. Tape 1 of 3, p. 1, Frost. For nuts see Stéphane Pennequin, "Nuts' Story 2001: A Nut Odyssey," trans. John Brailsford, *High Mountain Sports* 233 (June 2001), 40–45; Edward W. Koskinen, "When Is a Piton Not a Piton?" *Yodeler,* 24 April 1939, 7; Royal Robbins, "Nuts to You!" *Summit* (May 1967), 4. For "man's" see Robbins to Steve Roper, 17 June 1966, Roper.

39. For "craft" and "weaker" see Royal Robbins, "A Visit to Britain," *Summit* (December 1966), 5. For tech see Robbins, "Nuts to You!" 2–7. For routes see Roper, *Camp 4,* 214–15; Doug Robinson, "The Whole Art of Natural Protection," in *Contact: Mountain Climbing and Environmental Thinking,* ed. Jeffrey Mathes McCarthy (Reno: University of Nevada Press, 2008), 134–36.

40. For "Nuts," "satisfying," and photos see Robbins, "Nuts to You!" 2, 4, 6; Roper, *Camp 4,* 214. For support see "Letters," *Summit* (October 1967), 28. For "substitute" and "fanatics" see Bernstein, "Ascending," 38. For "Cocksucker's" see Vetter, "Climbers," 186.

41. For switch see Hamilton, "Changing," 17–18. For Feuerer see *Summit* (March 1969), 36–37. For "eternal" and advocacy see Neal H. Humphrey Jr., "The Book of the Crag (Reflections on a Chouinard Catalog)," *Off Belay* (October 1972), inside cover. For tech see "Chock Talk," *Off Belay* (February 1976), 6–8. For critics see Richard W. Tyrrell, "Still a Place," *Off Belay* (April 1978), 7–8. For safety see SAR Incident Report No. 8804-1033-100-97; SAR Incident Report No. 56 (3 October 1975); AAC-SAR Report No. 75-3836 (#60), all in YOSAR. For first clean see Bruce Carson, "Some Clean Wall Climbs in Yosemite," *AAJ* (1974), 58–61; Galen Rowell, "Climbing Half Dome the Hard Way," *National Geographic* (June 1974), 782–91.

42. For "footsteps" and "slings" see Bart O'Brien, "Climbing Half Dome—Twenty Years After," *AAJ* (1978), 468, 470. For litter see Yosemite Clean-Ups—A New Tradition?" *Off Belay* (October 1973), 50. For human waste see Merry, "The Longest Climb," 26; Amy Cilimburg, Christopher Monz, and Sharon Kehoe, "Wildland Recreation and Human Waste: A Review of Problems, Practices, and Concerns," *Environmental Management* 25 (May 2000), 587–98.

43. For scars see John Cleare, *Mountains* (New York: Crown, 1975), 112–15. For joys see Weiselberg, "Ascendancy," 89. *Solo* (Mike Hoover, Pyramid Home Video, 1973). For gardening see R[oyal] R[obbins], "Royal Arches Direct—First Ascent," *Mugelnoos,* 14 July 1960, 6. For trees and vines see Kor, *Beyond,* 152. For peregrines and salamanders see SupAR 1980; SupAR 1994.

44. For "abhorred" see Yvon Chouinard, "Modern Yosemite Climbing," *AAJ* (1963), 325. For storms see Merry, "The Longest Climb," 27. For "construction" and "ecology" see Daniel Duane, *Lighting Out: A Vision of California and the Mountains* (St. Paul: Graywolf Press, 1994), 118, 119. For starvation see Westbay, "Team Machine," 90.

45. For "serious" see Middendorf, "Mechanical Advantage," 168. For "begotten" see John Long, "Free Will," in *Yosemite Climber,* 28. For "blood" see Don Mellor, *American Rock: Region, Rock, and Culture in American Climbing* (Woodstock, Vt.: Countryman Press, 2001), 168. For aid see Westbay, "Team Machine," 86, 90. For chalk see *GPIW* (1975), 3, PCR. For tape see Bridwell and Peall, *Climbing Adventures,* 129. For benzoin, "courage," and criticisms see O'Brien, "Climbing Half Dome—Twenty Years After," 470.

46. For "business" and "atrophied" see Chouinard, *Let My People Go Surfing,* 31, 33. For "dirt" and "Ironmongery" see 1972 *Chouinard Catalog,* 30, 41–56; compare with *GPIW* (1986), 16; for bashies see *GPIW* (1983), 3, 24, all at PCR.

47. For "impossible," "Mecca," and "cosmic" see Bridwell, "Brave New World," 31. For "religion" see Chuck Pratt, "The View from Deadhorse Point," *Ascent* (May 1970), 41. For "Awareness" and catharsis see Westbay, "Team Machine," 86. For "nothing" see Pete Takeda, "Up Against the Wall," *Climbing* (June–July 1992), 132. For "addiction" see Bridwell and Peall, *Climbing Adventures,* 20. For cathartic and drug like see John Macaloon and Mihály Csíkszentmihályi, "Deep Play and the Flow Experience in Rock Climbing," in *Play, Games, and Sports in Cultural Contexts,* ed. Janet C. Harris and Roberta J. Park (Champaign, Ill.: Human Kinetics Publishers, 1983), 367, 382. For "control" see Sam Moses, "Stone Walls, Stout Hearts," *Sports Illustrated* (6 March 1978), 72. For "vertical" see Vetter, "Climbers," 186.

48. For "earth" see Chouinard, "Modern Yosemite Climbing," 327. For *"El Cap"* see *AACN,* 22 May 1964, 2. For bigwalls before Chouinard see Harry Tutton, "Ascent of the Diamond," *Yodeler* (September 1960), 3. For post-1963 superalpinism see *AACN,* 25 September 1964, 3; Bridwell and Peall, *Climbing Adventures,* 77–85; Galen Rowell, *Many People Come, Looking, Looking* (Seattle: Mountaineers, 1980), 125–56.

49. For Canadians and drugs see Scott, *Pushing the Limits,* 245–49, 333–36. For *Darkness* see Greg Child, *Mixed Emotions: Mountaineering Writings of Greg Child* (Seattle: Mountaineers, 1993), 102. For music see George Meyers, ed., *Yosemite Climber* (Modesto: Robbins Mountain Letters, 1979), 16; Gabriel, "Valley Boys," 39. For palimpsest see Bridwell, "Brave New World," 31.

50. For "surly" see Mellor, *American Rock,* 217. For Nose-in-a-day see Bridwell and Peall, *Climbing Adventures,* 125–33; Westbay, "Team Machine," 82–83; John Long, "The Nose," *Climbing* (June–July 1991), 60–64, 118–21. For cover photo see *Mountain* (January 1971).

51. For "easier" and complaints see Robbins, "El Cap Commentary," 32. For "punks" see Steve Roper, "Camp 4: Past & Present," *Climbing* (September 1998), 94. For "generation" see Bridwell, "Brave New World," 31. For "popular" see Sherman, "Life Without a Net," 130.

52. For unintentional climbers see SupMR, May 1956. For intentional see SupMR, June 1961. For technical climbers see SupMR, March 1958; Wayne Merry to Gary Colliver, 19 March 1993, "Wayne Merry," Biographical File, YRL; *AACN,* 25 September 1964, 2–3.

53. For "tremendous" see Stall, "Yosemite Poses Supreme Challenge," G2. For "rescue" see Chuck Pratt to Roper, 8 August 1965; for training see Allen Steck to Roper, 1 June 1964, both in Roper. For climbers see Stableford, "The Wild Bunch," 96; vol. 1: 22 June 1964, Evans. For development of YOSAR phone conversation with Pete Thompson, 25 March 2002; "Yosemite Rescue Group," *Off Belay* (June 1972), 45.

54. For training see Tim J. Setnicka, *Wilderness Search and Rescue: A Complete Handbook* (Boston: Appalachian Mountain Club, 1980). For rescuer accidents see Royal Robbins, "Scree," *Summit* (October 1968), 30; Tim Setnicka, "Mountain Insanity," *Off Belay* (February 1978), 8. For climber accidents see Royal Robbins, "Incident on Half Dome," *Summit* (January–February 1969), 2–5; "Yosemite Rescue," *Mountain* (September 1973), 38–42; Royal Robbins, "Yosemite Death Attributed to Rope Damaged by Fall," *Off Belay* (December 1976), 41; Tim Setnicka, "A 'Bombproof' Anchor: An Analysis of a Fatal Accident on El Capitan," *Off Belay* (August 1978), 15–16; Tim J. Setnicka, "Yosemite Rescues," 42 *Appalachia* (1979), 30–33; Tim Setnicka, "At Night on Mt. Watkins," 43 *Appalachia* (June 1980), 30–39.

55. For "hundreds" see Hamilton, "Modern American," 290. For easy see *AACN* 118 (November 1971) 2. For "hero" see Tejada-Flores, "Overpopulation and the Alpine Ego Trip," 53. For "fall" see Meyers, *Yosemite Climber*, 15, 16. For safe see Gardiner, *Why I Climb*, 106. For "Unthinking" see Setnicka, "Mountain Insanity," 8.

56. Rescue statistics compiled from SAR Incident reports for 1967–December 1979, YOSAR.

57. For "gang," "clique," "hope," and Russ Walling's spectacularly inappropriate behavior with corpses see Stableford, "The Wild Bunch," 96, 131. For "vibe" see Childs, "The Bird," 243. For "party" see Bridwell and Peall, *Climbing Adventures*, 200. For recent entitlement see Janet Reitman, "Soul Men," *Los Angeles Times*, 21 January 2001, 1. For stress of rescue see Jennifer Lois, "Peaks and Valleys: The Gendered Emotional Culture of Edgework," *Gender & Society* 15 (June 2001), 395–98.

58. For permission see Don Wilson, "The First Ascent of Spider Rock," *SCB* (June 1957), 45. For "water" see Donald J. Liska, "Shiprock," *Summit* (May 1960), 11. For other ascents see "Indian Country," *Mugelnoos*, 12 November 1953, 3; "Spy Rock Climbed," *Yodeler*, 2 April 1956, 3; "Mark, Pitony and Cleopatra," *Mugelnoos*, 11 October 1956, 3; "Rock and Rolled," *Mugelnoos*, 9 May 1957, 3; Mark Powell, "Four Californians Scale the Spectacular Totem Pole," *Summit* (April 1958), 8–11.

59. For detection, "conscience," lying, and "treading," see Kor, *Beyond*, 64–67, 76, 113, 102–3, 112–13. For resentment see Penny Carr to Roper, 17 November 1962, Roper. For "offer" see Pratt, "A View from Deadhorse Point," 37. For race see Eric Beck to Steve Roper, 19 November 1964; Kor to Roper, 23 March 1964, 11 February 1967, 11 December 1967, all in Roper. For objections see D[ave] R[earick], "Totem Pole—Second Ascent," *Mugelnoos*, 8 January 1959, 1.

60. For notification see Frank F. Kowski, "Letters," *Summit* (January–February 1968), 28. For "taboo," "gloating," and fooling see Bridwell and Peall, *Climbing Adventures*, 60, 113–22. For Hueco, Baboquivari, and others see Mellor, *American Rock*, 114–15, 186–88, 224–25, 275–77. For Devils Tower see Brenda L. Haes, "Devils Tower, Wyoming: An Examination of a Clash in Cultures," *Annals of Wyoming* 75 (Summer 2003), 2–7. For other affronts see Rawlings, *Stanford Alpine Club*, 80; Alison Osius, "Risky Business," in *Leading Out: Women Climbers Reaching for the Top*, ed. Rachel da Silva (Seattle: Seal Press, 1992), 200; Gardiner, *Why I Climb*, 123.

61. For "wondered" and "happened" see Child, *Mixed Emotions*, 114–15. For Miwoks see Mark David Spence, *Dispossessing the Wilderness: Indian Removal and the Making of the National Parks* (New York: Oxford University Press, 1999), 101–32. For "pursue," "mystical," and "respect" see David Kozak, "The Unclimbable Summits?" *AAJ* (1984), 124. For religion see Haes, "Devils Tower, Wyoming," 6. For "diplomacy" see Cameron M. Burns, "Shiprock's East Face," *AAJ* (1995), 72.

62. Child, *Postcards from the Ledge*, 104. For terms see Gabriel, "Valley Boys," 39; Roskelley, *Stories Off the Wall*, 49; Herrick, "Life at the Center of the Known Universe," 97.

63. For "gone" see *AAJ* (1995), 343. For later declension see Kevin Worrall, "A New Age in Old Camp Four," *Climbing* (May–June 1994), 78–89, 151–52.

11. Traditionalists

The epigraph is quoted in Trip Gabriel, "Valley Boys," *Rolling Stone* (28 April 1983), 36.

1. For Johnson see Gabriela Zim, *The View from the Edge: Life and Landscapes of Beverly Johnson* (La Crescenta, Calif.: Mountain N' Air Books, 1996), 21–35, 42–43, 90. For clubs see Julie Brugger, "A Mountain Experience," in *Rock and Roses: An Anthology of Mountaineering Essays*, ed. Mikel Vause (La Crescenta, Calif.: Mountain N' Air Books, 1990), 28–30. For gymnastics see "Who's Who and Why No. 18—Muir Dawson," *Mugelnoos*, 11 April 1940, 2; Pat Ament, *John Gill: Master of Rock*, rev. ed. (Mechanicsburg, Pa.: Stackpole, 1998), 18.
2. For see "Apron," "balance," and "girl" see Zim, *View*, 47, 50.
3. For "only," "5.10 Bev," and "command" see Zim, *View*, 50, 53, 54. For "get up" see Sibylle Hectell [*sic*], "Walls Without Balls: Memories of a California Climber During the '70s," in *Rock and Roses*, 64.
4. Prominent players included Julie Brugger, Barbara Eastman, Carla Firey, Catherine Freer, Ellie Hawkins, Sibylle Hechtel, Molly Higgins, Diane Hunter, Elaine Matthews, Donna Pritchard, Annie Rizzi, Judy Sterner, and Debbie Wolfe. See *AACN* (November 1971), 2; Hectell, "Walls Without Balls," 63, 65, 67; Zim, *View*, 46. For women's athletics see Susan K. Cahn, *Coming on Strong: Gender and Sexuality in Twentieth-Century Women's Sport* (Cambridge, Mass.: Harvard University Press, 1994), 248–54. For "categorical" see Lawrence C. Hamilton, "Modern American Rock Climbing: Some Aspects of Social Change," *Pacific Sociological Review* 22 (July 1979), 303. For "fiasco" see Hectell, "Walls Without Balls," 66. For "afraid" see Sibylle Hechtel, "Untitled," *AAJ* (1974), 63.
5. For female ascents see "Solo Ascent of El Capitan," *Summit* (October–November 1978), 4–5; Bill Birkett and Bill Peascod, *Women Climbing: 200 Years of Achievement* (Seattle: Mountaineers, 1989), 117–20; Janet Robertson, *The Magnificent Mountain Women: Adventures in the Colorado Rockies* (Lincoln: University of Nebraska Press, 1990), 154–55; Hectell, "Walls Without Balls," 64, 68; Irene Miller to Members RHM-USA, n.d., folder 4, Beardsley. For breadth of achievement by early 1970s see folders 6 to 8 in Beardsley. For Himalaya see Monica Jackson and Elizabeth Stark, *Tents in the Clouds: The First Women's Himalayan* Expedition (Seattle: Seal Press, 2000); Stephen Harper, *A Fatal Obsession: The Women of Cho Oyu* (London: Book Guild, 2007), 5–7; Birkett and Peascod, *Women Climbing*, 99–111. For Denali, peak bagging, and Annapurna see Arlene Blum, *Breaking Trail: A Climbing Life* (Orlando: Harcourt, 2005), 55–110, 125–77; Arlene Blum, *Annapurna: A Woman's Place* (San Francisco: Sierra Club, 1980), 17–18. For criticism see "Letters," *Outside* (August–September 1981), 10.
6. For "radical" see Sherry B. Ortner, *Life and Death on Mt. Everest: Sherpas and Himalayan Mountaineering* (Princeton: Princeton University Press, 1999), 217. For incorporation see Zim, *View*, 46–47. For accidents see Harper, *Fatal Obsession*, 79–92; Jocelyn C. Glidden, "USA-USSR Pamirs Expedition," *AAJ* (1975), 79–80; Blum, *Annapurna*, 218–33; John Roskelley, *Nanda Devi: The Tragic Expedition* (Harrisburg: Stackpole, 1987). For criticism see David Roberts, "Dangerous Routes," *Outside* (June–July 1981), 29–34, 85–87; Blum, *Breaking Trail*, 302–5.
7. For responses see "Letters," *Outside* (August–September 1981), 8–10. For membership see Irene Miller to RHM-USA, January 1976, folder 4, Beardsley; Rachel Da Silva, Jill

Lawrence, and Wendy Roberts, "A Brief History of Women Climbing in the Coast and Cascade Ranges," in *Leading Out: Women Climbers Reaching for the Top,* ed. Rachel Da Silva (Seattle: Seal Press, 1992), 73, 91, 100. For decline see Roberts, "Dangerous Routes," 85. Blum disputed Johnson but not Higgins; see "Letters," *Outside* (August–September 1981), 8–10; Zim, *View,* 49, 64. For empowerment see Elaine M. Blinde, Diane E. Taub, Lingling Han, "Sport as a Site for Women's Group and Societal Empowerment: Perspectives from the College Athlete," *Sociology of Sport Journal* 11 (March 1994), 51–59. For models and "speak" see Lynn Hill with Greg Child, *Climbing Free: My Life in the Vertical World* (New York: W. W. Norton, 2002), 32, 87, 125. For "sex-related," see Birkett and Peascod," *Women Climbing,* 177. For "bond" see Alison Osius, "A Tale of Two Countries: The French-American Women's Climbing Exchange," *Appalachia* (Winter 1983–1984), 72. For "fun" see Steve Gardiner, ed., *Why I Climb: Personal Insights of Top Climbers* (Harrisburg, Pa.: Stackpole Books, 1990), 91. Rowell quoted in Hill and Child, *Climbing Free,* 125.

8. For backgrounds see Hectell, "Walls Without Balls," 62–63; Da Silva et al., "Brief History," 96; Birkett and Peascod, *Women Climbing,* 113. For "tomboy" and "fraternity" see Hill and Child, *Climbing Free,* 22, 125. For "jock," "Sherwood," and "partners" see Zim, *View,* 33, 45, 46. For "prove" see Hechtel, "Untitled," 63; Lynn Hill, "I Didn't Dare Fall," in *The Stone Masters: California Rock Climbers in the Seventies,* ed. John Long and Dean Fidelman (Santa Barbara: Tom Adler Press and Stonemaster Press, 2009), 99–104. For "chalk" and proclaim see Gardiner, *Why I Climb,* 73, 90. For "schizoid" and "prerogative" see Jim Bridwell and Keith Peall, *Climbing Adventures: A Climber's Passion* (Merrillville, Ind.: ICS Books, 1992), 105. For "luscious" see Chic Scott, *Pushing the Limits: The Story of Canadian Mountaineering* (Calgary: Rocky Mountain Books, 2000), 333.

9. For drugs, "one man," "beast," "bonding," and sex life see Zim, *View,* 46–47, 48, 49, 50, and 40—42, 50, 51, 56, 57, 73–75. For porn see John Long, "Foreword," in *View,* 12–14. For "two," "coincidence," and "opposite" see Hectell, "Walls Without Balls," 66.

10. For panties see Scott, *Pushing the Limits,* 333. For dildo see Chris McNamara, *Yosemite Big Walls: Supertopos* (San Francisco: SuperTopo, 2000), 84. Hectell, "Walls Without Balls," 61. For climbingscape see Bruce Morris, "Method and Madness: Evolution of Yosemite Face-Climbing Standards," *AAJ* (1982), 45.

11. For "homogeneous" and "emancipatory" see Kevin Young, "Women, Sport and Physicality: Preliminary Findings from a Canadian Study," *International Review for the Sociology of Sport* 32/3 (1997), 298–99, 302. Arlie Anderson, "Climbing Down," *High Mountain Sports* (April 2001), 24–26. For independence see Brugger, "A Mountain Experience," 37. For difference see Eric Radack, "The Last Great Problem," *Appalachia* (Winter 1983–1984), 33–43. For solo and conservatism see Zim, *View,* 19–20, 54, 63, 91, 127. For "compromise" see Sam Moses, "Stone Walls, Stout Hearts," *Sports Illustrated* (6 March 1978), 70. For "anti-feminist" see Roberts, "Dangerous Routes," 87. For "arsenal" and "pig" see Hill and Child, *Climbing Free,* 85, 118. For "machine" see Jeanne Panek, "A Late Night on a High Wall," in *Leading Out,* 175. For acculturation see "Letters," *Outside* (August–September), 10; Kevin Young and Philip White, "Sport, Physical Danger, and Injury: The Experiences of Elite Women Athletes," *Journal of Sport and Social Issues* 19 (February 1995), 54. For sexuality see Valerie Mendenhall Cohen, ed., *Woman on the Rocks: The Mountaineering Letters of Ruth Dyar Mendenhall* (Bishop, Calif.: Spotted Dog Press, 2006), 181; Da Silva et al., "Brief History," 101; Cahn, *Coming on Strong,* 268; Michael A. Messner, "Becoming 100 Percent Straight," in *Inside Sports,* eds. Jay Coakley and Peter Donnelly (New York: Routledge, 1999), 104–10.

12. For gender models see Hill and Child, *Climbing Free,* 32. For "ambiguously," pain, and

acculturation see Young and White, "Sport, Physical Danger, and Injury," 55, 56. For injuries, illness, and "badges" see Zim, *View,* 25, 53, 54, 107; Molly Higgins, "First Time," in *Yosemite Climber,* ed. George Meyers (Modesto: Robbins Mountain Letters, 1979), 54, 55; Cohen, *Woman on the Rocks,* 51. For "deviance" see Robert Hughes and Jay Coakley, "Positive Deviance among Athletes: The Implications of Overconformity to the Sport Ethic," *Sociology of Sport Journal* 8 (December 1991), 307–25. For tough see Sherrie A. Inness, *Tough Girls: Women Warriors and Wonder Women in Popular Culture* (Philadelphia: University of Pennsylvania Press, 1999), 3, 19, 20–21, 177. For "stresses" see Birkett and Peascod, *Women Climbing,* 171.

13. For "legend," "professor," and background see Duane Raleigh, "Being Bachar," *Rock and Ice* (March 2008), 43, 45; John Steiger, "Johnny Rock," *Climbing* (October 1986), 31–39; Eric Perlman, "The Camp 4 Gym: Is that Junk at Yosemite the Most Sophisticated Health Club Ever?" *Backpacker* (May 1986), 40–43.

14. For free climbing see John Long, "Free Will," in *Yosemite Climber,* 28–51. For "coffin" see Hill and Child, *Climbing Free,* 58.

15. For Barber, "weird," Fowler, and Nabisco see Pat Ament, *A History of Free Climbing in America: Wizards of the Rock* (Berkeley: Wilderness Press, 2002), 188, 208, 219–20, 244. For "boldness" and "blow" see Steiger, "Johnny Rock," 31–32, 38. For "frontier," "nuts," and "altered" see Gabriel, "Valley Boys," 36, 40. For other sports see David Le Breton, "Playing Symbolically with Death in Extreme Sports," *Body & Society* 6 (March 2000), 4. For "borrowed" see John Long, "The Only Blasphemy," in *The High Lonesome: Epic Solo Climbing Stories,* ed. John Long and Hai-Van K. Sponholz (Helena: Falcon, 1999), 54.

16. For routes see Arce, *Defying Gravity,* 129–35; Ament, *Free Climbing,* 253–55; Huber and Zak, *Yosemite,* 123–24; Don Ried and Chris Falkenstein, *Rock Climbs of Tuolumne Meadows,* 3rd ed. (Evergreen, Colo.: Chockstone Press, 1992), 6, 45, 129, 130. For admiration see Alan Nelson, "The Path of the Master—Tuolumne," *AAJ* (1984), 109–15. For reward see epigraph.

17. For innovations see Douglas Booth, "Surfing: The Cultural and Technological Determinants of a Dance," *Culture, Sport, Society* 2 (Spring 1999), 39–44; Jennifer K. Chalsma and Kenneth J. Korane, "Engineering the Ultimate Ski," *Machine Design* (7 February 1991), 26–32; Craig R. Stecyk III and Glen E. Friedman, *Dogtown: The Legend of the Z-Boys* (New York: Burning Flags Press, 2000); Peter Noble, Michael Wadden, Timothy Bourke, David Williams, Knut Nordb, "An Introduction to Ethnotechnology for Naval Architects: Sea Kayak Design of Yesterday and Tomorrow," *Marine Technology* (October 1994), 309–14.

18. For Jardine and cams see Eric Perlman, "Prophet or Heretic?" in *The Best of Rock & Ice: An Anthology* (Seattle: Mountaineers, 1999), 129–38; Bob Dill, "Abalakov Cams," *Off Belay* (February 1978), 9–11; Stéphane Pennequin, "Expanding Protection, The Story of Nuts Part 2: Adjustables," trans. Paul Cartwright and John Brailsford, *High Mountain Sports* (October 2003), 76–80. For surfing see Booth, "Surfing," 39–40.

19. For nails see Geoffrey Winthrop Young, ed., *Mountain Craft* (New York: Charles Scribner's Sons, 1920), 153–55. For testing see Beebee Company to Norman Clyde, 29 December 1931, folder 7a–m, box 4, Clyde; "Some Technical Aspects of Friction Climbing," *Mugelnoos,* 11 August 1949, 3. For tennis see Joseph N. LeConte, "Scrambles About Yosemite," *SCB* (January 1914), 126–35. For Bramani see Edward Tenner, *Our Own Devices: The Past and Future of Body Technology* (New York: Alfred A. Knopf, 2003), 86. I thank Peter Hansen for help with this.

20. This discussion was aided immensely by Steve Komito and Steve Roper, *Camp 4: Recollections of a Yosemite Rockclimber* (Seattle: Mountaineers, 1994), 206. For crush see Phil

Macnaghten and John Urry, "Bodies of Nature: Introduction," *Body & Society* 6 (November 2000), 8–9. For different shoes see Robertson, *Magnificent*, 165.

21. For "slipped" see John Bachar to author, "Re: Fire history," 25 March 2008, personal email (25 March 2008); Raleigh, "Being Bachar," 80.

22. For "killing" see Gardiner, *Why I Climb*, 73. For rating impact see Alan Rouse, "Grading Systems," *Mountain* (May–June 1975), 35–36. For "desecration" see Ansel Adams with Mary Street Alinder, *Ansel Adams: An Autobiography* (Boston: Little, Brown, 1985), 57. For "boldness" see Hill and Child, *Climbing Free*, 85. For "predictable" see Lawrence Hamilton, "The Changing Face of American Mountaineering," *Review of Sport & Leisure* 6 (Summer 1981), 32. For "generation" see Ken Wilson, Allen Steck, and Galen Rowell, "Mountain Interview: Royal Robbins," *Mountain* (November 1971), 34.

23. Perlman, "Prophet or Heretic," 129–35; Ament, *Free Climbing*, 208–9, 219–21, 239.

24. For drills see "Drilling on Lead with Power Drills," *Climbing* (April–May 1988), 115; Morris, "Method and Madness," 44. For climbs see Max Jones, "Long, Difficult Free Climbs," *AAJ* (1981), 90. For "appalled" see Perlman, "Prophet or Heretic," 133.

25. For style see Morris, "Method and Madness," 42–48. Hudon and Jones quoted in James D. Bridwell, "Free Climbing, 1980," *AAJ* (1980), 467. For "intelligence," "spiritual," and "respect," see Steiger, "Johnny Rock," 33, 36, 37. For "Siddhartha" see Perlman, "Prophet or Heretic?" 131. For sport terms see Sylvia Fuller, "Creating and Contesting Boundaries: Exploring the Dynamics of Conflict and Classification," *Sociological Forum* 18 (March 2003), 21–22.

26. For "terror," "Means," and "self-worth" see Morris, "Method and Madness," 41, 46. For "degeneration" see Joseph Poindexter, "The Ultimate Dare," *Life* (September 1984), 58. For "perfection" see Bridwell, "Free Climbing, 1980," 467. For "preposterous" see Thomas Higgins, "Letter to the Editor—Climbing Ethics," *AAJ* (1983), 112; Tom Higgins, "Tricksters and Traditionalists: A Look at Conflicting Climbing Styles," *Climbing* (October 1984), 18–25. For "specialists" and "soul" see Yvon Chouinard, "Coonyard Mouths Off—Part II," *Climbing* (February 1987), 45–46. For "apostles" see Dan Duane, "Up on the Big Stone," *Outside* (October 2000), 82. For "destroying" see Steiger, "Johnny Rock," 36. For other sports see Booth, "Surfing," 52, 49; Steve Barnett, *Cross-Country Downhill and Other Nordic Mountain Skiing Techniques* (Seattle: Pacific Search Press, 1978), 6, 11–13, 89–91.

27. For debates see Higgins, "Tricksters." For partisan see Steve Schneider, "Sea of Domes: Purity, Boldness, and Change in Tuolumne Meadows," *Climbing* (August–September 1991), 61–66, 128–31. For "legitimate" see *Climbing* (June 1984), 6. For leaving see Perlman, "Prophet or Heretic," 131–32, 135–36; Gabriel, "Valley Boys," 36. For bomb see Richard Jensen, *Wings of Steel* (Hagerstown, Md.: Review and Herald Publishing, 1994), 76–80, 96.

28. For *"traditional"* and roundtable see Michael Kennedy and John Steiger, "Same Board, Different Rules," *AAJ* (1987), 53; "The Great Debate," *Climbing* (February–March 1987), 31.

29. For "Purity" see Mellor, *American Rock*, 212. For siege, bolting, and altering see Bridwell, *Climbing Adventures*, 16, 40, 96; Meyers, *Yosemite Climber*, 92. For yo-yo see Glen Denny to Steve Roper, 6 March 1963, Roper. For drilling see Steiger, "Johnny Rock," 33, 36. Eric Hobsbawm, "Inventing Traditions," in *The Invention of Tradition*, eds. Eric Hobsbawm and Terence Ranger (New York: Cambridge University Press, 1983), 1–14.

30. For roots see Arnold Lunn, *A Century of Mountaineering, 1857–1957* (London: George Allen & Unwin, 1957), 196–97. For "eternally," turf wars, and replacements see Morris, "Method and Madness," 41, 42–43. For "creative" see Lito Tejada-Flores, "Overpopula-

tion and the Alpine Ego Trip," *Ascent* (June 1972), 53. For "saved" see Raleigh, "Being Bachar," 80. For defensive see Gabriel, "Valley Boys," 73; Steiger, "Johnny Rock," 34–36. For "altar" see Mark Wilford, "The Chisel Speaks," *Climbing* (October–November 1985), 71.

31. For "revive" see Alexander Huber and Heinz Zak, *Yosemite: Half a Century of Dynamic Rock Climbing* (Birmingham, Ala.: Menasha Ridge Press, 2003), 76. For Kauk, "chip," "rules," and fight see Raleigh, "Being Bachar," 43, 46, 80–81; Sam Moses, "On The Rocks, Kauk Is It," *Sports Illustrated* (2 June 1986), 98–112. For "Lycra" see Hill and Child, *Climbing Free*, 202.

32. For deflate see "Valley Winds Down," *Climbing* (December 1986), 8–9. For Europeans see Dave Pegg, "What's Your Problem?" *Climbing* (December 1996–February 1997), 86–90. For "slander" see Steiger, "Johnny Rock," 36. For sulk see Raleigh, "Being Bachar," 81. For "rules" see Chouinard, "Coonyard Mouths Off—Part II," 48. For Croft see Jeff Smoot, "Peter Croft," *Climbing* (June 1986), 30–33; *Bachar: One Man, One Myth, One Legend* (Michael Reardon, Jumprunner Productions, 2005).

33. For "disowned" see *Bachar.* For continuity see Fuller, "Creating," 18–28; Hamilton, "Changing Face," 30. For "focus" see Hill and Child, *Climbing Free*, 188.

34. For "hurt" see Kennedy and Steiger, "Same Board, Different Rules," 56, 58; Fuller, "Creating," 12–17.

12. Consumers

The epigraph is from *American Rock: Region, Rock, and Culture in American Climbing* (Woodstock, Vt.: Countryman Press, 2001), 40.

1. For "insular" see Robert H. Wiebe, *The Segmented Society: An Introduction to the Meaning of America* (New York: Oxford University Press, 1975), 172; Lizabeth Cohen, *A Consumers' Republic: The Politics of Mass Consumption in Postwar America* (New York: Alfred A. Knopf, 2003).

2. For jeremiads see Peter H. Hansen, "British Mountaineering, 1850–1914" (Ph.D. diss., Harvard University, 1991), 362. For "consumers" and "things" see "Selling to the Hottest Market Ever," *Business Week*, 17 October 1970, 124, 126. For consumerism and recreation see Sam Binkley, *Getting Loose: Lifestyle Consumption in the 1970s* (Durham, N.C.: Duke University Press, 2007), 228–42. For "postmodern" and "self-referential" see Hal K. Rothman, *Devil's Bargain: Tourism in the Twentieth-Century American West* (Lawrence: University Press of Kansas, 1998), 339–40.

3. For consumption and community see Anthony E. Rotundo, *American Manhood: Transformations in Masculinity from the Revolution to the Modern Era* (New York: Basic Books, 1993), 284.

4. For sexism, danger, "therapy," and "family" see Lynn Hill with Greg Child, *Climbing Free: My Life in the Vertical World* (New York: W. W. Norton, 2002), 43–44, 45, 48, 53, 61, 189.

5. For "growled" and athleticism see Hill and Child, *Climbing Free*, xi, 24–26, 124, 129, 157–59, 160–70. For "genetics" see Steve Gardiner, ed., *Why I Climb: Personal Insights of Top Climbers* (Harrisburg, Pa.: Stackpole Books, 1990), 118. For "caught" see Laura Waterman, "When Women Were Women in the Northeast," in *Rock and Roses: An Anthology of Mountaineering Essays*, ed. Mikel Vause (La Crescenta, Calif.: Mountain N' Air Books, 1990), 125.

6. For "tradition" see Gardiner, *Why I Climb*, 83.

7. Robert A. Stebbins, *Amateurs, Professionals, and Serious Leisure* (Montreal: McGill-

Queen's University Press, 1992), 6–8. For "amateurs" see Arnold Lunn, *A Century of Mountaineering, 1857–1957* (London: George Allen & Unwin, 1957), 167; Douglas Kern, "Our Asterisked Heroes," *The New Atlantis: A Journal of Technology and Society* 6 (Summer 2004), 65–74. For Bridwell see Geoffrey Childs, "The Bird," in *30 Years of Climbing Magazine* (Carbondale, Colo.: Primedia Special Interest Publications, 1999), 247–48; Jim Bridwell and Keith Peall, *Climbing Adventures: A Climber's Passion* (Merrillville, Ind.: ICS Books, 1992), 209; Gardiner, *Why I Climb*, 85.

8. Childs, "The Bird," 247–48; Bridwell and Peall, *Climbing Adventures*, 209; Daniel Duane, *El Capitan: Historical Feats and Radical Routes* (San Francisco: Chronicle Books, 2000), 78.

9. For Disney see "Item #5. Matterhorn," *Mugelnoos*, 9 July 1959, 2. For "ecstasy" and BBC see Joe Brown, *The Hard Years* (Seattle: Mountaineers, 2001), 141, 243–46; John Cleare, *Mountains* (New York: Crown, 1975), 101. For Robbins's purism see Royal Robbins, "A Visit to Britain," *Summit* (December 1966), 5–9. For "avant garde" see John Steiger, "Johnny Rock," *Climbing* (October 1986), 33; Trip Gabriel, "Valley Boys," *Rolling Stone* (28 April 1983), 40.

10. For Johnson see Gabriela Zim, *The View from the Edge: Life and Landscapes of Beverly Johnson* (La Crescenta, Calif.: Mountain N' Air Books, 1996), 69–75, 91, 127. For commercials and shoes see Duane Raleigh, "Being Bachar," *Rock & Ice* (March 2008), 47, 79–80. For media see Gabriel, "Valley Boys." For ABC see Craig Vetter, "Climbers," *Playboy* (November 1986), 184. For Hill see Hill and Child, *Climbing Free*, 105, 132–39, 152–55.

11. For "peepshow" see Walt Unsworth, *Hold the Heights: The Foundations of Mountaineering* (Seattle: Mountaineers, 1994), 372. For insinuation and Braun see Vetter, "Climbers," 184. For "end" see Gabriel, "Valley Boys," 36, 73; Pete Takeda, "The Lifer," *Climbing* (June–August 1995), 110–15, 163–65. For resistance see Olivier Aubel and Fabien Oh, "The Denegation of the Economy," *International Review for the Sociology of Sport* 39 (June 2004), 131. For Bridwell and Croft see Gardiner, *Why I Climb*, 84; Chic Scott, *Pushing the Limits: The Story of Canadian Mountaineering* (Calgary: Rocky Mountain Books, 2000), 336. For "Money" see Joseph Poindexter, "The Ultimate Dare," *Life* (September 1984), 60.

12. For "invited" see Robert Roper, *Fatal Mountaineer* (New York: St. Martin's, 2002), 36. For "Olympic" and "harlotry" see Bill Birkett and Bill Peascod, *Women Climbing: 200 Years of Achievement* (Seattle: Mountaineers, 1989), 171, 177. For labeling athletes see Stebbins, *Amateurs, Professionals, and Serious Leisure*, 19, 35–36. For "glory" see Greg Child, *Postcards from the Ledge: Collected Mountaineering Writings of Greg Child* (Seattle: Mountaineers, 1998), 168. For "known" see Gardiner, *Why I Climb*, 124. For "FAME!" see Scott, *Pushing the Limits*, 335. For "overtime" see Hill and Child, *Climbing Free*, 105.

13. For "K2's" and "content" see Gardiner, *Why I Climb*, 10, 74. For growth see Maarten Van Bottenburg, *Global Games*, trans. Beverly Jackson (Urbana: University of Illinois Press, 2001), 32, 156–64; Sports Business Research Network, "Market Research Results, Category = Mountain/Rock Climbing Participation: Total vs. Frequent Participation," http://sbrnet.com/research.asp?subRID=94 (accessed 5 May 2008).

14. For "non-material" see R. L. G. Irving, *A History of British Mountaineering* (London: B. T. Batford, 1955), 231. For advising see Annie S. Peck, "Practical Mountain Climbing," *Outing* 38 (1901), 698–99. For clubs see Hansen, "British Mountaineering," 317–24; Richard M. Leonard, "Mountain Tent Zippers," *Yodeler*, 3 January 1949, 6.

15. For consolidate see "SIC 5091 Sporting and Recreational Goods and Supplies," in *Encyclopedia of American Industries*, vol. 2: Service and Non-Manufacturing Industries, 4th ed., ed. Lynn Pearce (Detroit: Gale, 2005), 602–5; Hoovers, "The North Face Apparel

Corp.," http://www.hoovers.com/company/The_North_Face_Apparel_Corp/hrtsti-1 .html (accessed 9 May 2010); "Kellwood Announces Agreement to Acquire Royal Robbins Inc." 18 June 2007, http://www.kellwood.com/news/article.asp?item=209 (accessed 6 May 2008).

16. Harvey Manning, *REI: 50 Years of Climbing Together* (Seattle: Recreational Equipment Incorporated, 1988), 109–74; Yvon Chouinard, *Let My People Go Surfing: The Education of a Reluctant Businessman* (New York: Penguin, 2005), 33–78; John Ryle, "Lord of All He Surveys," *Outside* (June 1998), 64.

17. Hoovers, "Lowe Alpine Company Description," http://www.hoovers.com/company/ Lowe_Alpine_Holdings_Limited/rfhtkti-1.html (accessed 10 May 2010); Eric Perlman, "Prophet or Heretic?" *Rock & Ice* (July–August 1995), 56–57; Raleigh, "Being Bachar," 80; Scott Doggett, "Where Rubber Meets the Rock: Ropes to Riches for Man Who Makes Top Climbing Shoes," *Denver Post,* 3 July 2005, 5L. For labor see John Rawlings, "Charles Kroger 12/18/97 Telephone Conversation," p. 6, Chuck Kroger folder, SAC.

18. For Yosemite artists see Rebecca Solnit, "Ghost River, Or Photography in Yosemite," in *Yosemite in Time: Ice Ages, Tree Clocks, Ghost Rivers,* by Mark Klett, Rebecca Solnit, and Byron Wolfe (San Antonio: Trinity University Press, 2005), 11–31. For document see Hermann Buhl, *Nanga Parbat Pilgrimage: The Lonely Challenge* (Seattle: Mountaineers, 1998), 328–33. For climber art see Glen Denny, *Yosemite in the Sixties* (Santa Barbara: Patagonia and T. Adler Books, 2007). For shows see Duane, *El Capitan,* 84. For films see *Sentinel: The West Face* (Roger C. Brown, Summit Films, 1967); *Solo* (Mike Hoover, Pyramid Home Video, 1973); *El Capitan* (Fred Padula, 1978). For photographers see Robert Roper, "Introduction," in *Galen Rowell: A Retrospective* (San Francisco: Sierra Club, 2006), 25. For "light bulb" see Gardiner, *Why I Climb,* 8.

19. Scott Herring, *Lines on the Land: Writers, Art, and the National Parks* (Charlottesville: University of Virginia Press, 2004). There were 169 English-language books from 1975 to 1980, 282 from 1981 to 1990, and 499 from 1991 to 2000. Figures from Library of Congress online catalog searches. For "courage" see Reinhold Messner, "The Murder of the Impossible," trans. Victor Fry, *Mountain* (May 1971), 27. For rhetorical shift see Walter Pause and Jürgen Winkler, *Extreme Alpine Rock: The 1000 Greatest Alpine Rock Climbs,* trans. Hugh Merrick (New York: Granada, 1979). For "extremitis" see Lou Dawson, "Extremitis," *Couloir Magazine* (February–March 1996), 27; Roselyn Elizabeth Stone, "Meanings Found in the Acts of Surfing and Skiing" (Ph.D. diss., University of Southern California, 1970), 83.

20. For patronage see Fergus Fleming, *Killing Dragons: The Conquest of the Alps* (New York: Atlantic Monthly Press, 2000), 333. For magazines see Margaret Mary Dillon, "H. Adams Carter's Editorship of *The American Alpine Journal,* 1960–1995" (Ph.D. diss., Ohio University, 1997), 214, 226–29. For other sports see Annie Gilbert Coleman, "From Snow Bunnies to Shred Betties: Gender, Consumption, and the Skiing Landscape," in *Seeing Nature through Gender,* ed. Virginia J. Scharff (Lawrence: University Press of Kansas, 2003), 195–217. For "buttering," "fawning," and "grades" see John Rawlings, *The Stanford Alpine Club* (Stanford: CSLI Publications, 1999), 157–58. For "bosses" see Steve Roper, "A Way of Life," *Summit* (Spring 1994), 60.

21. For Rowell see *AACN* (May 1972), 2. For membership see Chris Jones, "Who Needs the AAC?" *Ascent* (July 1971), 44–46. For personality-driven see Demetri Kolocotronis, "Hot Henry: An Interview with Henry Barber," *Climbing* (May–June 1974), 2–5. For "wallop" see Rawlings, "Charles Kroger 12/18/97 Telephone Conversation," 6; Stone, "Meanings in the Acts of Surfing and Skiing," 83.

22. For nineteenth century see Hansen, "British Mountaineering," 275–79, 375. For type-

script see "Shipment," Mugelnoos, 10 August 1939, 4. For published typescript see *AACN,* 13 April 1956, 5. For line art, duotone, and halftone see *AACN,* 11 November 1958, 4; *Summit* (April 1960), 26. For newsletters see *Yodeler* (January 1970), 3, 4, 6, 7, 8. For *Summit* see *Summit* (April 1956), 5; *Summit* (April 1968), 33–35; Chris Jones, *Climbing in North America* (Seattle: Mountaineers, 1997), 210n; Helen Kilness to William A. Long, 3 March 1969, letter facsimile printed in *Descent* (Summer 1972), 4. For adapting see Steven Lubar, "Men/Women/Production/Consumption," in *His and Hers: Gender, Consumption, and Technology,* eds. Roger Horowitz and Arwen Mohun (Charlottesville: University of Virginia Press, 1998), 13. For sex see *Climbing* (March–April 1974), 15. For Edelrid see *Mountain* (May 1970), 9; *Mountain* (July 1970), 9.

23. For decline see "Mountaineering Notes," *Yodeler* (June 1962), 3. For schools see Royal Robbins to Steve Roper, 17 June 1966; Liz Robbins to Jani Roper, 1 July 1971, both in Roper; *AACN* (May 1972), 8. For YMS see "Mountains of History," in "Climbing MT: History! YNP" folder, YRL. For brochure see "Yosemite Mountaineering [1970]," Box RL-E-073, YPCCP.

24. For "challenge" see "Spring Activities," c. 1978; for brochures see "Yosemite Mountaineering [1975]" and "Yosemite Mountaineering [1978]," all in box RL-E-073, YPCCP. For ads see "Yosemite National Park Schedules 'Rock Festival,'" *Mainliner Magazine,* n.d., "Rock Climbing," Vertical Files, YRL; "You, Too, Can Go Climb a Rock," *Motorland* 92 (May–June 1971), 16–20.

25. For working see *AACN,* 11 May 1969, 3. For "advertisers" and symbiosis see Lawrence Hamilton, "The Changing Face of American Mountaineering," *Review of Sport & Leisure* 6 (Summer 1981), 18; Lawrence C. Hamilton, "Modern American Rock Climbing: Some Aspects of Social Change," *Pacific Sociological Review* 22 (July 1979), 289. For "beat" see Yvon Chouinard to Steve Roper, 19 March 1963; for "testimonial" see Chouinard to Roper, 6 December 1961, both in Roper. For endorsements see Cleare, *Mountains,* 110; Hill and Child, *Climbing Free,* 141. For Robbins photo see *Chouinard Equipment Catalog* (1972), 41, 51, PCR.

26. Big Walls Web site, http://www.bigwalls.net/ (accessed 17 August 2009); Fish Site, http://www.fishproducts.com/index1.html (accessed 17 August 2009).

27. For "status" see Steve Roper, *Climber's Guide to Yosemite Valley* (San Francisco: Sierra Club, 1971), 36. For "carabiner" see Gardiner, *Why I Climb,* 72. For "attitude" and "exclusion" see Leanne Stedman, "From Gidget to Gonad Man: Surfers, Feminists and Postmodernisation," *Australian and New Zealand Journal of Sociology* 33 (March 1997), 75, 80–81; Coleman, "Shred Betties," 206–12. For consumers see Stuart Hall, "Encoding, decoding," in *The Cultural Studies Reader,* ed. Simon During (London: Routledge, 1993), 94, 99–103.

28. For hardware see *Chouinard Equipment* (1972), 26–40, 43, 45, 49, 51, 56; *GPIW* (1985), 2, 68. For "soft goods" see *Chouinard Equipment* (1972), 57; *Patagonia Catalog* (1981), 2–3. For logos see *GPIW* (Winter 1980), 26, all at PCR.

29. For OIA, http://www.outdoorindustry.org/about.over.html (accessed 9 May 2008). For gear history see *GPIW* (1983), 3; for company history see *GPIW* (1986), 2, 16; for lessons see *Chouinard Equipment GPIW* (1983), 39; for epigrams see *Chouinard Equipment* (1972), 1, 33, 72; *GPIW* (1975), 1, 16, 96; *GPIW* (1978), 1; *GPIW* (Winter 1980), 52; *GPIW* (1983), 2, 5; for philosophy see Yvon Chouinard and Tom Frost, "a word . . .", *GPIW* (1975), 2–4; for "AeroSpace" and "primitive" see Yvon Chouinard, "On Tump Lines," *GPIW* (1981), 17, 29, all at PCR.

30. For growth see Van Bottenburg, *Global Games,* 10, 32–33, 156–59, 163–6. For motivations see Brandon Wayne Rapelje, "Rock Climbing Sub-Worlds: A Segmentation Study"

(M.S. thesis, Texas A&M University, 2004); Amy L. Ackerman, "Differences in Motivation for Participation and Attitudes toward Management among Rock Climbing Sub Groups" (M.S. thesis, Old Dominion University, 2006). For flow see Mihály Csíkszentmihályi, *Flow: Studies of Enjoyment* (Chicago: University of Chicago Press, 1974), 24, 28, 45–49, 57–88. For "obliterate" see Dan Duane, "Up on the Big Stone," *Outside* (October 2000), 84–86.

31. For "epic" and "Louisiana," see Daniel Duane, *Lighting Out: A Vision of California and the Mountains* (St. Paul: Graywolf Press, 1994), 43, 121.

32. For "gravity," "photographs," "unglued," and failures see Duane, *Lighting Out,* 103, 154, 239. For "authentic" see Daniel Duane, *Looking for Mo* (New York: Washington Square Press, 1998), 13. For success see Duane, *El Capitan,* 13–29, 139–41, 225.

33. For "rat" see Al Alvarez, *Feeding the Rat: Profile of a Climber* (New York: Atlantic Monthly Press, 1988), 61. For queues see Larry Hamilton, "In the Valley," *Summit* (October 1970), 24–25. For debate see Sylvia Fuller, "Creating and Contesting Boundaries: Exploring the Dynamics of Conflict and Classification," *Sociological Forum* 18 (March 2003), 7n4, 13. For gripe see Alan Nelson, "Correspondence," *Climbing* (April 1984), 66; Duane, *Lighting Out,* 68–72. For "molehill" see Jon R. Beimer, "In Defense of Insignificance," *Off Belay* (February 1981), 18.

34. For "standards" see Robert A. Forrest, "The Chameleon: An Interview with a Daredevil Rock Gymnast," *Off Belay* (August 1978), 10–11. For "consistent" see Dillon, "H. Adams Carter's Editorship of the *AAJ,*" 12.

35. For clubs see Robert D. Putnam, *Bowling Alone: The Collapse and Revival of American Community* (New York: Simon & Schuster, 2000), 383–89. For RCS see *Yodeler* (March 1965), 1; *Yodeler* (January 1970), 6. For suspensions see Martin Friedman, "Report from Your Executive Committee," *Yodeler* (March 1964), 3; Bob Braun, "Rock Climbing Section Suspended," *Yodeler* (January 1967), 3. For "own" see Rawlings, *Stanford Alpine Club,* 163.

36. For terminate see Rawlings, *Stanford Alpine Club,* 168, 171; "The Molehill Club?" *Los Angeles Times,* 19 February 1989, V4. For growth see Putnam, *Bowling Alone,* 109–15. For new groups see "Peak Climbing Section Formed by Loma Prieta," *Yodeler* (March 1967), 4. For cosmopolitan see Hamilton, "Modern American," 286.

37. For afterthought see Gregg Blomberg to author, "Re: Research questions," 6 May 2007, personal email (7 May 2007). For liability see "Richard Leonard Interview transcripts, 10 November 1972," 30, carton 82:6, SCMP. For testing see *AACN,* 8 November 1963, 1–2; Helmut F. Microys, "Climbing Ropes," *AAJ* (1977), 130–47; UIAA, "Safety Labels," http://www.theuiaa.org/uiaa_safety_labels.php (accessed 28 May 2008). For early exposure see "Minutes of RCC Meeting," 10 July 1956, Menocal; Yvon Chouinard to Steve Roper, 28 February 1961, Roper. For suits see Janet Robertson, *The Magnificent Mountain Women: Adventures in the Colorado Rockies* (Lincoln: University of Nebraska Press, 1990), 161; "Camper Sues Government Over Stumble," *Portland Oregonian,* 4 August 2006. For law see David A. Moss, *When All Else Fails: Government as the Ultimate Risk Manager* (Cambridge, Mass.: Harvard University Press, 2002), 226–52.

38. For piton failure and withdraw see G. A. Cunningham, "Failure Analysis," *Summit* (June 1962), 3; Ed Leeper to author, "Re:Re:Recall Notice," 30 May 2007, personal email (30 May 2007). For "ass" and concerns see Ed Leeper to author, 30 April 2007, letter in author's possession; Gregg Blomberg to Steve Roper, 10 April 1964, Roper. For mid-1970s see "Edelrid Rope Not at Fault in Climber's Death," *Summit* (December 1976), 32; Ed Leeper, "An Epidemic of Broken Bolts," *Summit* (June–July 1977), 8–13; Tim Setnicka, "A 'Bombproof' Anchor: An Analysis of a Fatal Accident on El Capitan," *Off Belay* (August

1978), 15–16. For testing see "The REI Field Tests of Chocks," *Off Belay* (April 1977), 18–20. For waivers see "Is Sanity Returning to Outdoor Liability Law?" *Outside* (July 1993), 26.

39. For impressions see John Taladay, "First Thing We Do: Kill All the Plaintiffs," *Climbing* (August–September 1994), 176. For Chouinard see Jon Krakauer, "After the Fall: A Modern Rock Climbing Story," *Outside* (June 1990), 36–40, 108–9. For clubs see "Stanford Bans Climbing," *Climbing* (August 1986), 11. For closures see Donald P. Judges, "Of Rocks and Hard Places: The Value of Risk Choice," *Emory Law Review* 42 (Winter 1993), 30. For Leeper see "Paid Recall Notice," *Rock & Ice* (June 2004), 94. For prices see "Yosemite Mountaineering Schedule and Guide Fees Summer 1975," "Yosemite Mountaineering School and Guide Service 1991 Rates and Dates," Box RL-E-073, YPCCP; *GPIW* catalogs for 1975, 1989, PCR.

40. For litigation see Moss, *When All Else Fails*, 241–52. For innovation and guides see Judges, "Of Rocks and Hard Places," 30, 140n489; Seth Masia, "Evolution of Ski Shape," *Skiing Heritage* 17 (September 2005), 33–37. For "primary assumption" see David Horton, "Extreme Sports and Assumption of Risk: A Blueprint," *University of San Francisco Law Review* 38 (Summer 2004), 629–48. For responses see Richard Doel, "Fixed Protection: The Purists Were Right," *Summit* (October–November 1979), 10; Chris McNamara, "American Safe Climbing Association," *AAJ* (1999), 216–17.

41. For "essential" see Henry W. Kendall, "Climber's Camera," *SCB* (December 1962), 96. For photographers see Robertson, *Magnificent*, 165; "Hot Flashes," *Climbing* (October–November 1991), 42–43; Paul Piana, *Big Walls: Breakthroughs on the Free-Climbing Frontier* (San Francisco: Sierra Club, 1997). For aesthetics see Fuller, "Creating," 22. For other sports see Matt Warshaw, "Power Outage," *Surfer Magazine* 34 (July 1993), 48–65; Kelley MacAulay and Bobbie Kalman, *Extreme Skiing* (New York: Crabtree, 2006); John Foss, "Rapids and Ruins: Kayaking the Deepest Canyons in the World," *American Whitewater Journal* (May–June 1996), 49–60. For *"capital"* see Guy Debord, *The Society of the Spectacle,* trans. Donald Nicholson-Smith (New York: Zone Books, 1995), 24.

42. Mark Wellman and John Flinn, *Climbing Back* (Waco, Tex.: WRS Publishing, 1992). For continents see Dick Bass, Frank Wells, and Rick Ridgeway, *The Seven Summits* (New York: Warner Books, 1986). For categorical see "Dutch Iceman to Climb Everest in Shorts: It's All About the Inner Fire," MountEverest.net, http://mounteverest.net/news.php?news_15688 (accessed 7 March 2007). For traverse see Chris McNamara, "El Cap Girdle Traverse," in *Contact: Mountain Climbing and Environmental Thinking,* ed. Jeffrey Mathes McCarthy (Reno: University of Nevada Press, 2008), 64–71; Annie Gilbert Coleman, *Ski Style: Sport and Culture in the Rockies* (Lawrence: University Press of Kansas, 2004), 9. For descents see *The Man Who Skied Down Mt. Everest,* dir. Bruce Nyznik and Lawrence Schiller (Creative Films, 1975); Dave Hahn, "The No-Fall Zone," *Outside* (January 2007), 75–81, 107; Drew Simmons, "Not Afraid of the Dark," *Couloir Magazine* (October–November 1994), 56; Rick Sylvester to Jack Morehead, 29 February 1972, Biographical Files, YRL. For Willig and Goodwin see Sam Moses, "Stone Walls, Stout Hearts," *Sports Illustrated* (6 March 1978), 75; Hill and Child, *Climbing Free,* 147. For "demean" see Unsworth, *Hold the Heights,* 372.

43. For plankton see Hill and Child, *Climbing Free,* 147. For cable see SupAR (1976), YRL. For "combine" see Heather Millar, "Dancing on Air," *Smithsonian* (September 2000), 88. For movies see Breashears, *High Exposure,* 189–98; Scott, *Pushing the Limits,* 298.

44. For how-to see Doug Scott, *Big Wall Climbing* (New York: Oxford University Press, 1974); John Bachar and Steve Boga, *Free Climbing with John Bachar* (Mechanicsburg, Pa.: Stackpole Books, 1996). For anthologies see *The Mountaineers Anthology Series,* 2 vols.

(Seattle: Mountaineers, 2001). For maimed see Aron Ralston, *Between a Rock and a Hard Place* (New York: Atria, 2004). Heinrich Harrer, *The White Spider: The Story of the North Face of the Eiger*, trans. Hugh Merrick (New York: Dutton). For death see Hamish MacInnes, ed., *The Mammoth Book of Mountain Disasters: True Accounts of Rescue from the Brink of Death* (New York: Carroll & Graf, 2003); John Thackray, "The Pornography of Death: Climbing's Dark Embrace," *Climbing* (July–August 1981), 38–39.

45. For "supra-national" and European trends see Lunn, *A Century of Mountaineering*, 214–16. For Everest see James Ramsey Ullman, *Americans on Everest: The Official Account of the Ascent Led by Norman Dyhrenfurth* (Philadelphia: Lippincott, 1964), 17–32. For Shipton and Tilman see Peter Steele, *Eric Shipton: Everest and Beyond* (Seattle: Mountaineers, 1999); J. R. L. Anderson, *High Mountains and Cold Seas: A Biography of H. W. Tilman* (London: Victor Gallancz, 1980). For grants see *AACN*, 27 September 1963, 2–3. For transportation see David R. Brower, *For Earth's Sake: The Life and Times of David Brower* (Salt Lake City: Peregrine Smith Books, 1990), 47; Scott, *Pushing the Limits*, 265, 297, 301; Andy Selters, *Ways to the Sky: A Historical Guide to North American Mountaineering* (Golden, Colo.: American Alpine Club, 2004), 237.

46. "Rock-climbing" quoted in Donald W. Calhoun, *Sport, Culture, and Personality* (Champaign, Ill.: Human Kinetics Publishers, 1987), 312. For passive aggressive see Duane, *El Capitan*, 81–84, 90–92. For "alpinism" see Marek Brniak, "Abalakov's Comments on Soviet Alpinism," *Climbing* (March–April 1975), 19; Jim Mitchell, "The Soviet Mountaineering Program," *Summit* (October 1975), 20–21; *AACN* (May 1973), 1, 6.

47. For exchange see Mike Warburton, "Détente on the Salathe Wall," *Summit* (October 1975), 2–3, 20–21. For "crazy" see Marek Brniak, "Po Sportivnomu Skalolazaniju," *Climbing* (September–October 1974), 19. For "love" and "destroy" see "AAC Opposes Competitive Climbing," *Summit* (June–July 1977), 42.

48. For simplification see David Roberts, *On the Ridge Between Life and Death: A Climbing Life Reexamined* (New York: Simon & Schuster, 2005), 346; also Douglas Booth, "Surfing: The Cultural and Technological Determinants of a Dance," *Culture, Sport, Society* 2 (Spring 1999), 47–48, 50–51; Coleman, *Ski Style*, 198; Catherine Palmer, "Smells Like Extreme Spirit: Punk Music, Skate Culture and the Packaging of Extreme Sports," in *Musical Visions: Selected Conference Proceedings from 6th National Australian/New Zealand IASPM and Inaugural Arnhem Land Performance Conference*, ed. Gerry Bloustein (Kent Town, South Australia: Wakefield Press, 1999), 107–14. For acceptance, "women's," and Skinner see Gardiner, *Why I Climb*, 41, 115, 118, 120, 123.

49. For contests see *Climbing* (February 1985), 9–10. For organizations see "Competition Climbing History," http://new.ifsc-climbing.org/?page_name=history (accessed 10 June 2008); USA Climbing, "History," http://www.usaclimbing.net/rockcomps/resources/history.cfm (accessed 10 June 2008). For Snowbird see Michael Benge, "Off the Rocks," *Climbing* (August–September 1988), 44–56. For skate parks see Iain Borden, *Skateboarding, Space, and the City: Architecture and the Body* (New York: Berg, 2001), 57–88. For disaster see David Roberts, "A Mountain of Trouble," in *Escape Routes: Further Adventure Writings of David Roberts* (Seattle: Mountaineers, 1997), 94–113. For "not climbing" see Guy Waterman and Laura Waterman, *Yankee Rock & Ice: A History of Climbing in the Northeastern United States* (Harrisburg, Pa.: Stackpole Books, 1993), 321–22. For "sexy" see Yvon Chouinard, "A View from the Gallery," *Climbing* (August–September 1988), 52. For "rivalrous" and "cheering" see Roberts, *On the Ridge*, 346–47. For ice see James Brooke, "In Colorado, Ice Climbers Surmount Legal Hurdles," *New York Times*, 2 March 1997, A18. For gyms see Trip Gabriel, "Cliffhanger," *New York Times Magazine*, 31 December 1989.

50. Hill and Child, *Climbing Free,* 189–224. For coverage see "Upward Mobility: The Best Woman Climber in the World Gets Paid for Going Higher," *Life* (August 1989), 104–5.

51. For buildering Geoffrey Winthrop Young, *A Roof-Climber's Guide to Trinity: Containing a Practical Description to All Routes* (Cambridge: W. P. Spalding, 1899); Lucy Ames, "Mountaineering, Freedom of the Quad," *SACJ* (1964); Hall Leiren, "Students Really climb the Walls at Caltech at Night," *Los Angeles Times,* 27 December 1970, SG B1 (I'm indebted to Ellen Wilts for this). For U.S. rock walls see "Artificial Crag," *Summit* (July–August 1972), 29; Jack Wilkins, "Tacoma Builds Practice Mountain," *Off Belay* (February 1974), 37; Ron Brown, "Rock Climbing Fitness," *Off Belay* (April 1975), 8–13.

52. For kayaking see Outdoor Industry Foundation, *Outdoor Recreation Participation Study, Seventh Edition, for Year 2004: Trend Analysis for the United States* (Boulder: Leisure Trends Group, 2005), 234–54. For walls see "Climbing in the Club Rooms," *Yodeler,* 1 April 1946, 2; Karl Lukan, ed., *The Alps and Alpinism,* trans. Hugh Merrick (New York: Coward-McCann, 1968), 73. For gyms see Robin Mittelstaedt, "Indoor Climbing Walls: The Sport of the Nineties," *Journal of Physical Education, Recreation & Dance* 68 (November–December 1997), 27. For growth see Sports Business Research Network, "Wall Climbing (Artificial) Participation: Total vs. Frequent Participation," http://www.sbrnet.com/research.asp?subRID=95 and "Mountain/Rock Climbing Participation: Total vs. Frequent Participation," http://www.sbrnet.com/research/asp?subRID=94 (both accessed 5 May 2008; Matt Burbach, *Gym Climbing: Maximizing Your Indoor Experience* (Seattle: Mountaineers, 2004), 14. For Iowa see Mike Finkel, "Stretching the Imagination," *Sports Illustrated,* 11 November 1996; P. J. Huffstutter, "Like the Alps, But in Iowa," *Los Angeles Times,* 1 January 2007, A1.

53. For gym sociology see Mittelstaedt, "Indoor Climbing Walls," 27–29. For demography see SBRnet data in note 52.

54. For "illusions" see Hamilton, "Changing," 18. For "bolt it" personal conversation with Mark Fincher, 6 March 2002, Yosemite Village. For "overuse," "digital," and statistics see Michael D. Rooks, Richard B. Johnston III, Cindy D. Ensor, Bobbi McIntosh, Susan Johnson, "Injury Patterns in Recreational Rock Climbers," *American Journal of Sports Medicine* 26 (November–December 1995), 683–85.

55. For injuries see Williams S. Bowie, Thomas K. Hunt, Hubert A. Allen Jr., "Rock-Climbing Injuries in Yosemite National Park," *Western Journal of Medicine* 149 (August 1988), 172–77. While incidents rose, they remained "roughly in proportion to the increases in annual visitation." SupAR (1993), YRL. For Bachar see Vetter, "Climbers," 176. For gendered differences see Nick Paumgarten, "Dangerous Game," *New Yorker,* 18 April 2005, 100–20. For "ibuprofen" see Child, *Postcards from the Ledge,* 41.

56. For "taboo" and "wrong" see "Rock Climbers' Safety First," *Mugelnoos,* 5 May 1938. For speed see Yi-Wyn Yen, "The El Capitan Climbing War," *Sports Illustrated,* 5 August 2002. For criticize see Aunt Harriett [Parsons], "Double Spires Causes Comments," *Yodeler,* 31 March 1941, 2. For enchainment see Phil Bard, "Double Header: El Cap & Half Dome in a Day," *Climbing* (August 1986), 8. For mourn see Charles Cole, "El Cap and Half Dome, 1986," *Climbing* (October 1986), 48. For Potter and Florine see Pete Takeda, "The Milestone," *Climbing* (December 1999), 83. For "ah" see Steph Davis, "The X & Y Chromosome Record," http://www.bdel.com/bd/art_popup_chromosome.html (accessed 15 September 2001). Allen Guttman notes that "modern sports are characterized by the almost inevitable tendency to transform *every* athletic feat into one that can be quantified and measured." Climbing is neither immune nor new to this given the evidence of timed ascents of Mont Blanc by the 1820s, but the rise of stop-watch-timed ascents did mark a significant cultural turn in climbers' candor about competition. Allen Guttman,

From Ritual to Record: The Nature of Modern Sports (New York: Columbia University Press, 2004), 47.

57. For "adventure" see Scott, *Pushing the Limits,* 337. For promotion see Peter Croft and Steve Boga, *Lightweight Alpine Climbing with Peter Croft* (Harrisburg, Pa.: Stackpole Books, 1996). For *Salathé* see Mark Hudon, "Long, Hard, and Free," *Mountain* (May–June 1981); Paul Piana, "Salathé Wall, 1988," *Climbing* (October 1988), 52–60.

58. Alexander Huber and Heinz Zak, *Yosemite: Half a Century of Dynamic Rock Climbing* (Birmingham, Ala.: Menasha Ridge Press, 2003), 139–71; Steph Davis, *High Infatuation: A Climber's Guide to Love and Gravity* (Seattle: Mountaineers, 2007), 161–86. For gymnastics see Ann Chisolm, "Acrobats, Contortionists, and Cute Children: The Promise and Perversity of U.S. Women's Gymnastics," *Signs: The Journal of Women in Culture and Society* 27 (Winter 2002), 415–50. For "soaking" and climbers see Lisa Morgan, "Local Hero," *Climbing* (December–February 1995), 96; Katie Brown, *Vertical World: Conservations with Today's Masters of Rock* (Helena, Mont.: Falcon, 2007), 41–57; Sarah J. Murray, "Tori Allen: Going Up," http://www.womenssportsfoundation.org/Content/Articles/Athletes/About%20Athletes/T/Tori%20Allen%20Going%20Up.aspx (accessed 13 June 2008). For "problem," "weapons," and "challenge" see Hill and Child, *Climbing Free,* 225, 227, 240; Michael Benge, "The Nose Goes," *Climbing* (December 1993–January 1994), 56–57.

59. For "accomplishments" see Bernadette McDonald and John Amatt, eds., *Voices from the Summit: The World's Great Mountaineers on the Future of Climbing* (Seattle: Adventure Press, 2000), 113. For "liberation," "expectation," and "inspiration" see Lynn Hill, "First Free Ascent of the Nose in a Day," *AAJ* (1995), 65. For "burly" see Michael Benge, "Hill Docs Nose Free in a Day," *Climbing* (November–December 1994), 52. For "chiseling," "spontaneous," and filming see Hill and Child, *Climbing Free,* 132, 240, 242–46; *Free Climbing the Nose,* VHS, dir. Lynn Hill (Lynn Hill, 1997).

13. Survivors

The epigraph is from *Steep,* DVD, dir. Mark Obenhaus (High Ground Productions, 2007).

1. For NPS see SupAR (1997), April 9, YRL. For "Sunnyside" see Lynn Hill with Greg Child, *Climbing Free: My Life in the Vertical World* (New York: W. W. Norton, 2002), 81. For battle see Andrew Kirk and Charles Palmer, "When Nature Becomes Culture: The National Register and Yosemite's Camp 4, a Case Study," *Western Historical Quarterly* 37 (Winter 2006), 497–506. Steve Roper, "Camp 4, Past & Present," *Rock & Ice* (September 1998), 94–95. For visits see SupARs for 1990s. For celebration see Alison Osius, "Camp 4 Celebration: A Community Comes Together," *Climbing* (February 2000), 34–36; *Celebration at Camp 4: Highlights from the Climber's Reunion, 9/25/99,* VHS, dir. Christine Denton Cohen (Peloton Productions, 2000). For NHR see Linda McMillan, "Camp 4 Takes Its Rightful Place on the National Historic Register," *AACN* (Spring 2003), 10–11.

2. For "no trace" see Yvon Chouinard's remarks in *Vertical Frontier: A History of the Art, Sport and Philosophy of Rock Climbing in Yosemite,* VHS, dir. Christine Denton Cohen (Peloton Productions, 2002). For commemoration see Janet A. Wells, "Thanks for the Memories," *Climbing* (August–September 1993), 46–47; Michael Scott Moore, "100 Years of Hanging Ten," *Los Angeles Times,* 21 July 2007, A23; Martha Groves, "Shop's Past Has Wheels," *Los Angeles Times,* 12 February 2007, B1. For debate see David Roberts, *True Summit: What Really Happens on the Legendary Ascent of Annapurna* (New York: Simon & Schuster, 2002); Greg Child, *Over the Edge: The True Story of Four American Climbers'*

Kidnap and Escape in the Mountains of Central Asia (New York: Villard, 2002). For accommodation see "Yosemite," *Climbing* (December 1986), 66.

3. For "love," "warriors," and "energetic" see Michael P. Cohen, *The History of the Sierra Club, 1892–1970* (San Francisco: Sierra Club, 1988), 65–66, 71.

4. For driving see Steve Gardiner, *Why I Climb: Personal Insights of Top Climbers* (Harrisburg, Pa.: Stackpole Books, 1990), ix, 96, 106. For death wish see William Barry Furlong, "Doctor Danger," *Outside* (January 1981), 42. For "50" see Brett Johnson, "Yvon Chouinard, Climbing All the Way," *Inside VC,* http://www.insidevc.com/archives/02272000/ventura/268905.shtml (accessed 28 September 2000). For 100 see Steve Boga, *Climbers: Scaling the Heights with the Sport's Elite* (Harrisburg, Pa.: Stackpole Books, 1994), 55. For Slater and Hargreaves see Greg Child, *Postcards from the Ledge: Collected Mountaineering Writings of Greg Child* (Seattle: Mountaineers, 1998), 208–11. For Lowe see Jennifer Lowe-Anker, *Forget Me Not, A Memoir* (Seattle: Mountaineers, 2008). For statistics see Case Incident Reports (CIR) and tallies at YOSAR; Michael P. Ghiglieri and Charles R. "Butch" Farabee, Jr., *Off the Wall: Death in Yosemite* (Flagstaff: Puma Press, 2007), 266–67. For accidents see CIR 84-29720; CIR 931255/SAR #93-049; and SAR-074, 12 July 2001, all in YOSAR; "Two Climbers Die in Freak Yosemite Accident," *AACN* (November 1973), 3; *AINAM* 55 (2002), 32–33; Matthew Preusch, "Expert Climber Loses Footing on Trail, Dies," *Portland Oregonian,* 6 November 2007; Hill and Child, *Climbing Free,* 61; Steve Bechtel, "Climbing World Mourns Todd Skinner," *Rock & Ice* (January 2007), 26; National Transportation Safety Board, "Brief of Accident LAX02FA251," 30 March 2004.

5. For climber deaths see David Le Breton, "Playing Symbolically with Death in Extreme Sports," *Body & Society* 6 (March 2000), 2; also Andrew Todhunter, *Dangerous Games: Ice Climbing, Storm Kayaking, and Other Adventures from the Extreme Edge of Sports* (New York: Doubleday, 2000). For "requires" see Nicholas O'Connell, *Beyond Risk: Conversations with Climbers* (Seattle: Mountaineers, 1993), 96. For "essential," "joy," and "definitely" see Boga, *Climbers,* 53–54. For "adventure," "killing," "Me Me," and "Superman" see *Steep.* For "thrill" see Mark Stranger, "The Aesthetics of Risk: A Study of Surfing," *International Review for the Sociology of Sport* 34 (1999), 267–68. For "god" see Pete Takeda, "Heavy Weather," *Climbing* (February–March 1993), 64. For "elation" see Craig Vetter, "He's Not Worthy," *Outside* 22 (January 1997), 110.

6. For "megaton" see Daniel Duane, *Looking for Mo* (New York: Washington Square Press, 1998), 135, 202. For Mallory see Peter Gillman and Leni Gillman, *The Wildest Dream: The Biography of George Mallory* (Seattle: Mountaineers, 2000), 221–23; Walther Kirchner, "Mind, Mountain, and History Revisited," *Journal of the History of Ideas* 55 (April 1994), 304. For "become" see *Steep.*

7. For "anchored" see Stranger, "The Aesthetics of Risk," 273–74; Georg Simmel, *Simmel on Culture: Selected Writings,* eds. David Frisby and Mike Featherstone (Thousand Oaks, Calif.: SAGE Publications, 1997), 220. For Treadwell and Huguenard see *Grizzly Man,* DVD, dir. Werner Herzog (Discovery Docs and Lions Gate Films, 2005). For "smart" see Sam Moses, "Stone Walls, Stout Hearts," *Sports Illustrated* (6 March 1978), 75. For "self-reliance" see Jon Krakauer, "After the Fall: A Modern Rock Climbing Story," *Outside* (June 1990), 111. For "elusive" see Furlong, "Doctor Danger," 92. For "love" see Maria Coffey, *Fragile Edge* (London: Chatto & Windus, 1989), 182. For "human" see Mark Twight, *Kiss or Kill: Confessions of a Serial Climber* (Seattle: Mountaineers, 2001), 10. For Everest stories see Maurice Isserman, "The Ethics of Mountaineering, Brought Low," *The Chronicle of Higher Education,* 5 May 2006, B15.

8. For "control" see David Roberts, *On the Ridge Between Life and Death: A Climbing Life Reexamined* (New York: Simon & Schuster, 2005) 349. For "real" see Valerie Mendenhall

Cohen, ed., *Woman on the Rocks: The Mountaineering Letters of Ruth Dyar Mendenhall* (Bishop, Calif.: Spotted Dog Press, 2006), 155–59. For "typical" see Lee Todd, "Advice to Mountaineers," *Yodeler,* 18 September 1950, 2. Leslie Stephen, *The Playground of Europe* (London: Longmans, Green, 1871), 301. For astronauts see Tom Wolfe, *The Right Stuff* (New York: Farrar, Straus, & Giroux, 1979), 17–32; Kenneth J. Koka, Eric E. Schwarz, and Catherine Schwarz, "Risky Business: Observations on the Nature of Death in Hazardous Sports," *Omega: The Journal of Death and Dying* 21:3 (1990), 221; John Dill, "Staying Alive," in *Yosemite Climbs,* ed. George Meyers and Don Reid (Denver: Chockstone Press, 1987), 4–16. For "impedimenta" see Steve Roper, *Climber's Guide to Yosemite* (San Francisco: Sierra Club, 1971), 18. For "helmet" see David R. Brower to William Siri, 22 June 1955, carton 23:36, SCMP.

9. For accidents see Jeffrey Bernstein, "Ascending," *New Yorker,* 31 January 1977, 43; Hill and Child, *Climbing Free,* 1–12; Chris McNamara, "El Cap Girdle Traverse," in *Contact: Mountain Climbing and Environmental Thinking,* ed. Jeffrey Mathes McCarthy (Reno: University of Nevada Press, 2008), 67. For "upside" see Boga, *Climbers,* 53. For "smug," "rationalization," and "luck" see Roberts, *On the Ridge,* 350.

10. For "suspect" and heroes see Roberts, *On the Ridge,* 356, 358. For "focus" and "restricted" see Hill and Child, *Climbing Free,* 179, 221. For survey see Richard G. Mitchell Jr., "Public Opinion and Mountaineering," *Off Belay* (April 1980), 26–28.

11. For "trusting" see Gardiner, *Why I Climb,* 116; Peter Donnelly and Kevin Young, "Rock Climbers and Rugby Players: Identity Construction and Confirmation," in *Inside Sports,* ed. Jay Coakley and Peter Donnelly (New York: Routledge, 1999), 67–76. For "isolated" see Julie Brugger, "A Mountain Experience," in *Rock and Roses: An Anthology of Mountaineering Essays,* ed. Mikel Vause (La Crescenta, Calif.: Mountain N' Air Books, 1990), 31–32, 35.

12. For rationalizations see Gabriela Zim, *The View from the Edge: Life and Landscapes of Beverly Johnson* (La Crescenta, Calif.: Mountain N' Air Books, 1996), 62; Coffey, *Fragile Edge,* 181–82. For "shocked" and "worth" see *Steep.*

13. For dismiss see John Rawlings, "Charles Kroger 12/18/97 Telephone Conversation," p. 4, Chuck Kroger folder, SAC. For Lowe see Lowe-Anker, *Forget Me Not,* 187–272. For "indulging" and Boardman and Coffey see Coffey, *Fragile Edge,* 88.

14. For Hornbein see Tom Hornbein, "Foreword," in *Where the Mountain Casts Its Shadow: The Dark Side of Extreme Adventure,* by Maria Coffey (New York: St. Martin's Press, 2003), xi–xv. For "fuck it" see Vetter, "He's Not Worthy," 110.

15. For "selfless" and "essence" see Thomas Hornbein, "Heroes: Personal Ponderings," in *Voices from the Summit,* 185. For "narcissistic" see John Thackray, "The Pornography of Death: Climbing's Dark Embrace," *Climbing* (July–August 1981), 38–39. For older see Mitchell, "Public Opinion, and Mountaineering," 26–27. For "normal," "flaccid," and "incurious" see Roberts, *On the Ridge,* 341, 358, 362. For "world" see Hill and Child, *Climbing Free,* 174. For "pain" see Takeda, "Heavy Weather," 64. For others see Greg Child, *Mixed Emotions: Mountaineering Writings of Greg Child* (Seattle: Mountaineers, 1993), 218; Moses, "Stone Walls," 74–75; Coffey, *Fragile Edge,* 181–82; 22 June 1964, Evans; Sibylle Hechtel, "Ethics of Ambition," http://funclimbsaroundtheworld.com/?p=20 (accessed 13 February 2008); Zim, *View,* 60–61, 71; Janet Robertson, *The Magnificent Mountain Women: Adventures in the Colorado Rockies* (Lincoln: University of Nebraska Press, 1990), 160–61; Andrew Todhunter, "Of Odds and Angels," in *The Best of Rock & Ice: An Anthology,* ed. Dougald MacDonald (Seattle: Mountaineers, 1999), 198–200; Nick Paumgarten, "Dangerous Game," *New Yorker,* 18 April 2005, 100–20; Bruce Barcott, "Cliffhangers," *Harper's Magazine* (August 1996), 64–69.

16. See especially Coffey, *Where the Mountain Casts Its Shadow.* For "maintain" see Hill and Child, *Climbing Free,* 264. For "cost" and "better" see Roberts, *On the Ridge,* 363, 381–82. For "cold" and "important" see Cohen, *Woman on the Rocks,* 334, 336. For "kinship" see Steve Friedman, "Letter to My Future Brother-in-Law," *Outside* (October 1999), 107–8.

17. For "incredible" see Zim, *View,* 44. The lack of gender difference in values should not surprise. Sociologist Kevin Young notes that most athletes have "been socialized into . . . 'middle-class gender roles' emphasizing individualism and achievement. [Women] had been taught that their sex was not a handicap and did not feel socially obliged to be passive or acquiescent in sport or elsewhere." Kevin Young, "Women, Sport and Physicality: Preliminary Findings from a Canadian Study," *International Review for the Sociology of Sport* 32:3 (1997), 299, 301. Sibylle Hechtel observed that "Women's expectations of themselves and their predominantly male climbing partners changed as much as men's expectations of women climbers. . . . Today, if I go to a climbing area alone and ask a man if he'll climb with me, he usually asks what I can lead. Fifteen years ago a more likely response was the question, 'I guess, what can you follow?'" Hectell, "Walls Without Balls," 69. For wives see Joe Brown, *The Hard Years* (Seattle: Mountaineers, 2001); Dougal Haston, *In High Places* (Seattle: Mountaineers, 1972), 111. For women relating see Hill and Child, *Climbing Free,* 127–71; Zim, *View,* 73–184; Birkett and Peascod, *Women Climbing,* 110–11. For "communication" see Sue Giller, "Survival Mode," in *Women in the Antarctic,* ed. Esther D. Rothblum, Jacqueline S. Weinstock, and Jessica F. Morris (New York: Haworth Press, 1998), 63. For "saying" see Daniel Duane, *Lighting Out: A Vision of California and the Mountains* (St. Paul: Graywolf Press, 1994), 251. For "doze" and "nap" see Molly Higgins, "First Time," in *Yosemite Climber,* ed. George Meyers (Modesto, Calif.: Robbins Mountain Letters, 1979), 59.

18. For "cast" and "common" see Zim, *View,* 71, 177. For Hargreaves see Susan Frohlick, "'Wanting the Children and Wanting K2': The Incommensurability of Motherhood and Mountaineering in Britain and North America in the Late Twentieth Century," *Gender, Place and Culture* 13 (October 2006), 477–90. For "monk" see Jon Krakauer, *Into the Wild* (New York: Villard, 1996), 199; *Into the Wild,* DVD, dir. Sean Penn (Paramount Vantage, 2007). For "married" see Samuel Turner, *My Climbing Adventures in Four Continents* (New York: Charles Scribner's Sons, 1911), 17–18. Tim Egan reflected on these costs. His blog generated an extraordinarily passionate and heated 245 responses that fell into a few broad categories. Fifty-six supported Egan on the need to consider others before engaging in risk-taking sports, while only six fully opposed him (twenty-four were off message). The largest set of responses were by self-professed risk-takers who simply ignored Egan and instead sought to rationalize their avocation (or profession in a few cases) by focusing on the value to the self rather than seeing the self as part of social networks. Tim Egan, "Mountain Madness," *New York Times,* 21 July 2008, http://egan .blogs.nytimes.com/2008/07/09/mountain-madness/ (accessed 21 July 2008).

19. Leanne Stedman, "From Gidget to Gonad Man: Surfers, Feminists and Postmodernisation," *Australian and New Zealand Journal of Sociology* 33 (March 1997), 80; also *GPIW* (Winter 1980), 31, 34, 48, PCR.

20. For figures see OIA, *Human Powered Outdoor Recreation: State of the Industry Report* (Boulder: Outdoor Industrial Association, 2002). For segmentation see Lizabeth Cohen, *A Consumers' Republic: The Politics of Mass Consumption in Postwar America* (New York: Vantage, 2003), 309. For women see Victoria Carty, "Textual Portrayals of Female Athletes: Liberation or Nuanced Forms of Patriarchy?" *Frontiers* 26:2 (2005), 132, 136. For networking see Outdoor Industry Association, "Urban Climber Magazine Joins Forces with Big City Mountaineers," 22 September 2004, http://www.outdoorindustry.com/

media.outdoor.php?news_id=800&sort_year=2004 (accessed 6 May 2008). Circulation figures from *Ulrich's Periodicals Directory,* 1970 to 2005; Mick Ryan, "Climb Like a Girl, Parts 1–4," UKClimbing.com (April 2005), http://www.ukclimbing.com/articles/page .php?id=107 (accessed 25 June 2008).

21. For industry overview see OIA, *Human Powered Outdoor Recreation.* For "coin" and "decreation" see Jim Bridwell, "Brave New World," *Mountain* (January 1974), 31. For costs see John Byrd, "Climbing 1974: Growth, Money, Politics, and Hope," *Climbing* (Winter 1974–1975), 25. For Harding see Gardiner, *Why I Climb,* 101. For lawsuit see "Climbing Magazine Sues *Rock and Ice,*" 18 June 2002, http://www.camp4.com/news .index.php?newsid=340 (accessed 11 June 2007). For Rainier see Craig Welch, "The Battle to Be King of the Mountain," *Seattle Times,* 29 December 2002.

22. For Mountain Dew see Reuben Ellis, *Vertical Margins: Mountaineering and the Landscapes of Imperialism* (Madison: University of Wisconsin Press, 2001), 6. For climbing ads see Thai Airlines in *Life* (January 1989), back cover; "Style; Boulder Dash," *New York Times Magazine,* 23 April 2006, http://www.nytimes.com/slideshow/2006/04/20/ magazine/20060420.html (accessed 26 March 2007); other television commercials by Eveready, Old Spice, Suzuki, Toyota, and U.S. Marine Corps. For "Nose" see *Jerry Maguire,* DVD, dir. Cameron Crowe (Gracie Films, 1996). For Viesturs see Starbucks cup "The Way I See It #140," c. February 2008. For Allen see Fat Brain Toys, "Huck Doll—Tori Allen Rock Climber," http://www.fatbraintoys.com/toy_companies/huck_doll/huck_doll _tori_allen_rock_climber.cfm (accessed 26 June 2008). For market see Carty, "Textual Portrayals," 133, 135, 139–40.

23. For "contributed" see Mead Hargis, "Climbing 1974," *Off Belay* (February 1974), 17–21. For "ego" see Lawrence Hamilton, "The Changing Face of American Mountaineering," *Review of Sport & Leisure* 6 (Summer 1981), 31, 33. For Golden Eagle see *AACN* (May 1971), 4. For guidebooks see Lito Tejada-Flores, ed., "The Guidebook Problem," *Ascent* (July 1974), 80–85. Fred Beckey, *Mountains of North America: The Great Ranges of the Continent* (New York: Bonanza, 1982); Steve Roper and Allen Steck, *Fifty Class Climbs of North America* (San Francisco: Sierra Club, 1979); George Bell Jr., "Fifty Crowded Classics," in *Ascent: The Mountaineering Experience in Word and Image,* ed. Allen Steck and Steve Roper (San Francisco: Sierra Club, 1989), 129–37. For Baffin see Chic Scott, *Pushing the Limits: The Story of Canadian Mountaineering* (Calgary: Rocky Mountain Books, 2000), 297.

24. For "sardine" see A. F. Mummery, *My Climbs in the Alps and Caucasus* (New York: Chas. Scribner's Sons, 1895), 22. For "polished" see Lord Schuster, *Mountaineering: The Romanes Lecture Delivered in the Sheldonian Theatre, 21 May 1948* (Oxford: Clarendon Press, 1948), 21. For impacts see Amy Cilimburg, Christopher Monz, and Sharon Kehoe, "Wildland Recreation and Human Waste: A Review of Problems, Practices, and Concerns," *Environmental Management* 25 (June 2000), 587–98. For "sewage" see John Daniel, "Climbing Into Life," in *Contact,* 144. For advise see John Hart, "Humpty Dumpty Shat on a Wall: A Guide to Responsible Elimination," *Climbing* (February–March 1992), 111–15. For litter see Bart O'Brien, "Climbing Half Dome—Twenty Years Later," *AAJ* (1978), 466–70; Greg Donaldson, "Cleaning Half Dome—Twenty-Two Years After," *AAJ* (1980), 549–50. For "small" see Mark Fincher, "Climber Impacts," in *Yosemite Big Walls,* 16.

25. For loose rock see Troy Johnson, "Many Wall Routes Go But El Cap Fights Back," *Climbing* (September 1989), 21. For quakes see Brock Wagstaff, "Earthquake on El Cap," *AAJ* (1981), 95–97. For Middle Brother see SupAR 1987. For Glacier Point see Gerald F. Wieczorek et al., "Unusual July 10, 1996, Rock Fall at Happy Isles, Yosemite National Park,"

GSA Bulletin 112 (January 2000), 75–85; "Falling Rock Lawsuit Might Block Rock Climbing in Parks," *Parks & Recreation* 40 (October 2005), 27. For "gardening" see Dick Dorworth, "Doin' the Dog," *Climbing* (May–June 1971), 5–6. For impact see Stephen D. Blackwell, "Environmental Impacts of Rock Climbing in Yosemite National Park" (M.A. thesis, San Diego State University, 2001). I thank Sarah Elkind for this. For salamander see SupAR (1994); for peregrine see SupAR 1980. For trails see "CLMBMGMT: Yosemite Fund Proposal" and "CLMBMGMT: Restoration/Rehabilitation" folders, CDWOYNP.

26. For adverse see Barbara R. Johnston and Ted Edwards, "The Commodification of Mountaineering," *Annals of Tourism Research* 21 (1994), 473. For Wilderness Society see Joan Reiss to Jim Riley, 29 January 1991, "CLMBMGMT: Wilderness Society"; for Sierra Club see Jeff Widen, "Conservations for Developing Policies on the Use of Permanent Climbing Anchors (bolts) in Federally Designated Wilderness Area," 1 May 1991, "CLMBMGMT: Sierra Club"; for surveys see "CLMBMGMT: USE SURVEY: Ingraham & Tuttle" and "CLMBMGMT—USE SURVEY—Access Fund" at CDWOYNP. For boundaries see National Park Service, "General Management Plan: Visitor Use/Park Operations/Development, Yosemite National Park, California, September 1980" (Washington, D.C.: National Park Service, 1980), 26–29.

27. For planning process see "CLMBMGMT: MGMT Plans: YNP-1989," "CLMBMGMT: Impact Assessment: Studies: Other Parks," "Climbing MGMT: Correspondence WASO-Western Region," "CLMBMGMT: Correspondence Chronological," "CLMBMGMT: Public Comments," "CLMBMGMT: Impact Assessment: Studies: Other Parks," "CLMBMGMT: Working Group: 1992–1993," "CLMBMGMT: Mgmt Plans—Other Parks," "CLMBMGMT: Nat'l Parks & Cons. Assoc. Meeting, 11/93," "CLMBMGMT: National Policy: ANPRM," "CLMBMGMT: Impact Assessment: LAC," "CLMB: Liability," "CLMB-MGMT: MGMT. PLANS: YNP, Dec '93 Sup. Docs," "CLMBMGMT—Resource Mgmt. Plan," "CLMBMAGMT: USFS," all at CDWOYNP. For ranger see Kimberly Lisagor, "The Life-Expanding, 24/7, Work-and-Play (& Change the World) Adventure Plan," *Outside Magazine* (September 2005).

28. For "illusions" see Hamilton, "Changing Face," 18. For access see Michael J. Yochim, "Kayaking Playground or Nature Preserve? Whitewater Boating Conflicts in Yellowstone National Park," *Montana, The Magazine of Western History* 55 (Spring 2005), 52–64. Hang-gliding and BASE jumping were briefly regulated in Yosemite; see SupARs for 1974–1976, 1980–1983, 1985, 1990, 1992–1993, 1997–2000. For exfoliation see Hannah Gosnell, "The Electric Climber," *Yosemite* (Winter 1991), 3. For "respect" and "slip" see Robin Ingraham Jr., "The Numbers Game," *Climbing* (August–September 1990), 24. For "biodiversity" see Beth Baker, "Controversy Over Use of Rock-Climbing Anchors May Be Missing the Mark," *BioScience* 49 (July 1999), 529. For "menace" see Robyn Morrison, "Invasion of the Rock Jocks," *High Country News*, 7 July 2003.

29. For early no trace see "Climbing Problems in Nationals Parks Discussed," *Mugelnoos*, 11 November 1948, 2. For "Clean" see Doug Robinson, "The Whole Natural Art of Protection," in *Chouinard Catalog* (1972), 12, PCR. For advocacy see "The New Iron," *Climbing* (August 2000), 104–7. For accounting see Chris T. Hendrickson, Lester B. Lave, and H. Scott Matthews, *Environmental Life Assessment of Goods and Services: An Input-Output Approach* (Washington, D.C.: Resources for the Future, 2006), 3–20. For bolts see Ray de Saussure, "Looking Ahead on Expansion Bolts," *Yodeler* (3 March 1952), 7; Mike Loughman, *Summit* (April 1958), 21–22; "Yosemite," *Summit* (July–August 1970), 36; Tejada-Flores et al., "The Guidebook Problem," 83; Al Errington, "Piton Removal Techniques," *Off Belay* (April 1972), 38–39; Chip Salaun, "A Hole in the Clean Climbing Philosophy," *Off Belay* (June 1976), 33–37. A remark by Arthur Johnson suggested that debates about

fixed gear's ecological implications date at least to the 1930s. Eric Redd, "Arthur B. Johnson: Climbing and Conservation in the Sierra Club's Southern California Chapter, 1930–1960s," 17, Sierra Club History Committee, 1980, SCMP.

30. For values see Jenni Mintz, "'Green' Surfboards Are More Environmentally Friendly," *Seattle Post-Intelligencer,* 12 August 2007. For Robbins see Stuart Gordon, "Derring-Do Requires 3 Volumes," *Modesto Bee,* 5 May 1996, A1. For Rowell see Robert Roper, "Introduction," in *Galen Rowell: A Retrospective* (San Francisco: Sierra Club, 2006), 25–45.

31. Joseph P. Kahn, "Lost Arrow," *Inc.* (December 1984), 72–74; Paul B. Brown, "The Anti-Marketers," *Inc.* (March 1988), 62–69. For reforms see Yvon Chouinard, *Let My People Go Surfing: The Education of a Reluctant Businessman* (New York: Penguin, 2005), 81–252.

32. For Chouinard see Bernstein, "Ascending," 36 52; Fleming Meeks, "The Man Is the Message," *Forbes* (17 April 1989), 148–52; Roger Rosenblatt, "Reaching the Top by Doing the Right Thing," *Time,* 11 October 1999. For "penance" see Robert Smith, "Patagonia Clothing Company and Founder Yvon Chouinard," 12 November 2002, Morning Edition, National Public Radio. For advocacy see "The Cleanest Line," Patagonia Employees Weblog, http://www.thecleanestline.com/ (accessed 14 April 2008); Andrew G. Kirk, *Countercultural Green: The Whole Earth Catalog and American Environmentalism* (Lawrence: University Press of Kansas, 2007), 200–3. Historian David Steigerwald argues that the "act of consumption is trivial in the most basic sense: It has no larger social meaning beyond the subjective impulse of the individual consumer," and that "whether as an individual act of choice or as an expression of a particular group's value system, [it] cannot carry the weight of history." David Steigerwald, "All Hail the Republic of Choice: Consumer History as Contemporary Thought," *Journal of American History* 93 (September 2006), 399, 401. For environmental historians and environmentalists, consumption has been a core problem shaping everything from urban blight to rural dispossession and climate change. For historical studies see Matthew W. Klingle, *Emerald City: An Environmental History of Seattle* (New Haven: Yale University Press, 2007); Matthew Klingle, "Spaces of Consumption in Environmental History," *History & Theory* 42 (December 2003), 94–100; John Soluri, *Banana Cultures: Agriculture, Consumption, and Environmental Change in Honduras and the United States* (Austin: University of Texas Press, 2005); Mark David Spence, *Dispossessing the Wilderness: Indian Removal and the Making of the National Parks* (New York: Oxford University Press, 1999). For environmentalist discussions see "The Cleanest Line."

33. For Potter see Rob Buchanan, "Climbing at the Speed of Soul," *Outside* (December 2002). For Delicate Arch see Tim Neville, "How Delicate Was Dean?" *Outside* (June 2006); "Dean Potter Solos the Delicate Arch," http://www.aerialistmovie.com/arch/index.html; "Climbing Utah's Delicate Arch," SummitPost.com, http://www.summit post.org/phpBB2/viewtopic.php?t=19511 (accessed 15 July 2008). For "negative" see Melissa Block, "Utah Park Officials Fret Over Climb of Delicate Arch," *All Things Considered,* National Public Radio, 2 June 2006.

34. For "blow" see Neville, "How Delicate Was Dean?" For "compelled" and "job" see "Official Statement from Patagonia and Dean Potter on the Delicate Arch Climb," (June 2006), http://outside.away.com/outside/features/200606/patagonia-dean-potter-delicate-arch-statement.html (access 10 June 2008); Angus M. Thuermer Jr., "Climber Potter, Patagonia Agree to Split the Synchilla," *Jackson Hole News & Guide,* 21 March 2007.

35. For "conquer" see Block, "Utah Park Officials Fret Over Climb of Delicate Arch." I thank Rick Braithwaite, Nick Clinch, Tom Dunlap, Matt Klingle, Mike Lansing, and Mark Spence for help with this.

36. For RCS participation see "Hearing Finally Heard," *Mugelnoos,* 13 March 1947, 4; "A Vote for 'F' Is a Vote for Conservation," *Yodeler,* 18 October 1948, 1; Barbara Tilden, "The Day We Saw Half Dome from Mt. Hamilton," *Yodeler,* 4 February 1952, 3. For "entirely," "impartial," and impact see Cohen, *History of the Sierra Club,* 44, 61, 67. For "cathedral" and "spirit" see R. L. G. Irving, *A History of British Mountaineering* (London: B. T. Batsford, 1955), 231. For "basic" and "fun" see Dan L. Thropp, "Conservation for Mugelnoos," *Mugelnoos,* 14 July 1955, 4.

37. For Leopold and Marshall see Paul S. Sutter, *Driven Wild: How the Fight Against Automobiles Launched the Modern Wilderness Movement* (Seattle: University of Washington Press, 2002); Arne Naess, "The Shallow and the Deep, Long Range Ecology Movements: A Summary," *Inquiry* 16 (1973), 95–100; George Sessions, "Nickel Pinnacle" and "Kings Canyon Climbs," *SCB* (October 1955), 80–81. For "essential" see Wilfred Ward, "Why Wilderness," *Yodeler,* 7 March 1955, 7.

38. For "pit" see Stewart Udall, "We Must Save the Beauty of Our Land," *Carpenter Magazine* (April 1964), quoted in Tom Miller, "The West's Defender of Wild Places," *Los Angeles Times,* 12 July 2005, F1. For "spokesman" see Joseph L. Sax, *Mountains Without Handrails: Reflections on the National Parks* (Ann Arbor: University of Michigan Press, 1980), 54.

39. "The American Alpine Club Proposal for Membership [Douglas Tompkins]," 18 September 1964, box R–Z, AAC Archives Membership, American Alpine Club Archives, Henry S. Hall Jr. Library, Golden, Colorado. For Do Boys and "hogging" see Chouinard, *Let My People Go Surfing,* 46–48; Yvon Chouinard, *Climbing Ice* (San Francisco: Sierra Club, 1978), 170–71; Pat Ament, *Royal Robbins: Spirit of the Age* (Harrisburg, Pa.: Stackpole, 1998), 242–46; Yvon Chouinard, "Lessons from the Edge," in *Extreme Landscapes,* ed. Bernadette McDonald (Washington, D.C.: National Geographic, 2002), 239–47. For escapism see Vetter, "He's Not Worthy," 52, 108–10.

40. For Tompkins see John Ryle, "Lord of All He Surveys," *Outside* (June 1998), 57–68, 167–69; William Langewiesche, "Eden: A Gated Community," *Atlantic Monthly* 283 (June 1999), 84–105; Rick Ridgeway, "Patagonia Dreaming," in *Extreme Landscapes,* 187–205.

41. For "giving" see Patagonia, "Creating a National Park in Patagonia: All a Part of the Job at Patagonia," Holiday 2007, http://www.patagonia.com/usa/patagonia.go?assetid =27057 (accessed 14 April 2008). For opposition see "Now He Is Buying in Argentina," *Santiago [Chile] Times,* 27 August 2001, http://test.chirongroup.com/splash/stimes/index/php?nav=story&story_id451 (accessed 3 December 2003). For paternalism see Ryle, "Lord of All He Surveys," 60, 68, 167; Vetter, "He's Not Worthy," 50, 108. Cooperation in Argentina was easier, but the context differed. Whereas Tompkins literally divided Chile with his purchases, Argentina acquisitions were less extensive, and Tompkins and Chouinard worked with Parques Nacionales de Argentina. A historical analogy can be drawn between Tompkins's efforts in Chile and the Rockefeller family's consolidation of holdings in Jackson Hole for Grand Teton National Park, but the scale and imperial implications place Parque Pumalín in a different category. Robert W. Righter, *Crucible for Conservation: The Creation of Grand Teton National Park* (Boulder: Colorado Associated University Press, 1982). Seeing nature as separate is a North American trait. The rest of the world does not cultivate such bifurcated views. See Ramachandra Guha, "Radical American Environmentalism and Wilderness Preservation: A Third World Critique," *Environmental Ethics* 11 (Spring 1989): 71–83; Louis S. Warren, *The Hunter's Game: Poachers and Conservationists in Twentieth-Century America* (New Haven: Yale University Press, 1997); Theodore Catton, *Inhabited Wilderness: Indians, Eskimos, and National Parks in Alaska* (Albuquerque: University of New Mexico Press, 1997); Spence, *Dispos-*

sessing the Wilderness; Karl Jacoby, *Crimes Against Nature: Squatters, Poachers, Thieves, and the Hidden History of American Conservation* (Berkeley: University of California Press, 2001); Alan MacEachern, *Natural Selections: National Parks in Atlantic Canada, 1935–1970* (Montreal: McGill-Queen's University Press, 2001); Theodore Binnema and Melanie Niemi, "'Let the Line Be Drawn Now': Wilderness, Conservation, and the Exclusion of Aboriginal People from Banff National Park in Canada," *Environmental History* 11 (October 2006), 724–50; John Sandlos, *Hunters at the Margin: Native People and Wildlife Conservation in the Northwest Territories* (Vancouver: University of British Columbia Press, 2007).

42. For trips see Chouinard, "Lessons from the Edge." For "evangelist," "evil," and "conspicuous" see Vetter, "He's Not Worthy," 50, 108–9. For Tompkins see Ryle, "Lord of All He Surveys," 63, 169.

43. For "home" see David R. Brower, "Far From the Madding Mules: A Knapsacker's Retrospect," *SCB* 20 (1935), 77.

44. For "fun-hogging" see Johnston and Edwards, "The Commodification of Mountaineering," 473–75. For debate see Alfred Runte, *Yosemite: The Embattled Wilderness* (Lincoln: University of Nebraska Press, 1990), 49; National Park Service, *Final Yosemite Valley Plan, Supplemental Environmental Impact Statement,* Volume 3: Public Comments and Responses (Yosemite: National Park Service, United States Department of the Interior, 2000).

45. For "primeval" see United States, "Wilderness Act," Public Law 88-577 (16 U.S.C. 1131–1136), 88th Cong., 2nd Sess., 2c; William Cronon, "The Trouble with Wilderness, Or, Getting Back to the Wrong Nature," *Environmental History* 1 (January 1996), 7–28. For "challenging" see H. Ken Cordell, "The Latest on Trends in Nature-Based Outdoor Recreation," *Forest History Today* (Spring 2008), 10; Oliver R. W. Pergams and Patricia A. Zaradic, "Evidence for a Fundamental and Pervasive Shift Away from Nature-Based Recreation," *Proceedings of the National Academy of Sciences* 105 (19 February 2008), 2295–300. For corporations see "Symposium: Corporate Social Responsibility and the Environment," *Review of Environmental Economics and Policy* 2 (Summer 2008), 219–75. For Yosemite see SupARs for 1990 and 1991.

46. Richard White, "The Problem with Purity," in *The Tanner Lectures on Human Values,* vol. 21, ed. Grethe B. Peterson (Salt Lake City: University of Utah Press, 2000), 213–28; Michael Bess, *The Light-Green Society: Ecology and Technological Modernity in France, 1960–2000* (Chicago: University of Chicago Press, 2003), 237–90.

ACKNOWLEDGMENTS

How did this happen? All I remember now is that it was about 1 A.M. in a St. Paul hotel, Mark Spence was proposing a boondoggle conference panel, and whiskey was involved. S.P.E.N.C.E. promised surfing in Hawaii, and I foolishly believed him. For the record, Kaanapali had six-inch swells that week. Then Matt Klingle backed out because he "had to finish the dissertation," which just wasn't plausible if you knew Matt at the time. Tiring of my own topic, I poached Klingle's and wrote about climbers and bolts, the research amounting to rereading the journals of my youth. In the course of that paper a larger question emerged about how people have related to nature through outdoor sports—in other words this book. Since then an extended family of intellectual parents, siblings, children, friends, and, for lack of a better word, more than friends have kept me going. Most will remain nameless— you *know* who you are—but several require outing. Joel Orth and Shannon Patrick helped my research immensely at Iowa State University, and Lara Braithwaite, Michael Cohen, Tom Dunlap, Peter Hansen, Kerwin Klein, and Mike Lansing encouraged me even after reading draft chapters. I thank them all despite their atrocious lack of judgment.

I must also thank the many people and institutions that aided and abetted this project, including Keith Benson, Bruce Seely, and Mike Sokal at the National Science Foundation; Jared Ficker, Russ Galipeau, and Cyndi Mattiuzzi at the National Park Service; Barbara Beroza and Linda Eade at the Yosemite Research Library; John Dill at Yosemite Search and Rescue; Ellen Byrne, Becky Evans, and Caitlin Lewis at the Colby Memorial Library and the Sierra Club for use of its historical archives; Glen Denny, Aimee Morgan, John Rawlings, and Mattie Taormina at Stanford University; Peter Stevens at the University of Washington; Scott Mackenzie, John Ng, Sonny Wong, and Vera Yuen at Simon Fraser University; Susan Snyder at the Bancroft Library of the University of California Berkeley; Andrew Patterson of the Dundee University Rucksack Club; Ben Anderson of the Manchester University Mountaineering Club; Mike Dent of the Manchester Rucksack Club; Lloyd Athearn and Janet Miller of the American Alpine Club; Beth Heller, Gary Landeck, Fran Loft, and Michael Wejchert at the Henry S. Hall, Jr. Library of the American Mountaineering Center; Lowell Skoog of the Seattle Mountaineers; Robert Cates, Dan Richter, John Ripley, and Yvonne Tsai of the Southern California Mountaineering Association; and Robert Graver, April Miller, Wilson Riley, and Shirley Schulz of the Potomac Appalachian Trail Club.

I am especially fortunate that Bob Connor, Geoffrey Harpham, Kent Mullikan, and Lois Whittington of the National Humanities Center helped get this rolling with a John D. and Catherine T. MacArthur Fellowship; and the librarians Betsy Dain, Jean Houston, and Eliza Robertson were amazing. The entire 2002–2003 class made Lara's and my time enjoyable, and they gave Bell Braithwaite Taylor a very warm welcome. Since then, Kathleen McDermott has encouraged me despite my flakiness, while Joyce Seltzer, Kate Brick, Peter Holm, and the anonymous reviewers for Harvard University Press helped transform this into a more readable work.

In truth every book incurs debts, and I thank everyone from the bottom of my very shallow heart, but none more so than the climbers. Despite all the printed words, mountaineering is still an oral culture performed and reproduced in small circles around the globe. Gaining access to that discourse is essential even if, as in my case, only to locate the written materials. I soon learned that being welcomed by the community meant engaging not so much a bunch of climbers as an extended family that now sprawls across five continents. I owe everyone a huge debt of gratitude.

Sadly, some of the most generous have passed on, including John Bachar, Alfred Baxter, Warren Harding, Bob Kamps, Doris Leonard, Galen Rowell, Todd Skinner, and Ellen Wilts. For their kind contributions of materials, time, and advice, I also thank Michael Anderson, Brian Baldwin, Dave Banks, Dimitri Barton, Mary Baxter, Eric Beck, Gregg Blomberg, Greg Bombeck, Bert Brown, Malinda Chouinard, Yvon Chouinard, Nick Clinch, Kristi Cohen, Michael Cohen, Valerie Cohen, Gary Colliver, Herb Conn, Peter Croft, Scott Davis, Glen Dawson, Glen Denny, Margaret DeStaebler, Leo Dickinson, John Dill, Dave Dornan, Daniel Duane, John Evans, Peter Farquhar, Dean Fidelman, Mark Fincher, Jeff Foott, Tom Frost, Doug Gantenbein, John Gill, Art Gran, Larry Hamilton, Mead Hargis, Bonnie Kamps, Joe Kelsey, Steve Komito, Layton Kor, Don Lauria, Ed Leeper, Dick Long, George Marks, Peter Mayfield, Jim McCarthy, Chris McNamara, Wayne Merry, George Meyers, Mike Osborn, Mark Powell, Lloyd Price, John Rawlings, Don Reid, Elizabeth Robbins, Royal Robbins, Renny Russell, Craig Sabina, Kim Schmitz, Sebastian Straub, Andy Selters, Ray Smutek, Gary Snyder, Allen Steck, Sara Steck, Bob Swift, Anne Tarver, Frank Tarver, Pete Thompson, Bea Vogel, Mike Warburton, Duke Watson, and Ken Wilson.

Three people deserve special mention. First, in Yosemite Ken Yager showed me documents and gear that are destined for a museum in Yosemite Valley (http://www.yosemiteclimbing.org/). He also dragged my sorry, forty-something butt up many cliffs to improve my sense of Yosemite's vertical nature. Next, when I met Armando Menocal in Jackson, he immediately dropped in my lap three binders of irreplaceable documents about the early RCS. I dearly hope he will donate them to the AAC's Henry Hall, Jr. Library. Last, Steve Roper has been astonishingly generous, offering access to a trove of correspondence that needs to be archived. He also linked me to the community and responded to many emails and drafts. Without his and their help, the present book would not have been possible.

Finally, there is my family. Yes, I know, this is the boring part: the love, the devotion, yadda yadda yadda. Clearly, you do not live in my world. It is despite these people, not because of them, that I ever finished this. I cannot count the times that Rick distracted me with "projects" and then publicly humiliated me on the world's most sadistic golf course, or Sue egged me on about funding for public education, or Craig lured me into talking about Bay Area sports, or Mom, well . . . all I will say is she needs to stop watching Glenn Beck. It is a wonder that I wrote anything at all given how often Bell demanded a spin in what I mistakenly view as *my* office chair. Do these people not know that I am a Serious Scholar? Lara at least had the decency to hit the save button before pulling the plug on the computer. For that, among other reasons, I dedicate this waste of paper to her.

MAP AND ILLUSTRATION CREDITS

Maps 1.1, 3.1, and 3.2. Cartography by John Ng, Department of Geography, Simon Fraser University.

Figure 1.1. "Yosemite Valley, Winter," 1940. Photograph by Ansel Adams. © 2009 The Ansel Adams Publishing Rights Trust and the Center for Creative Photography.

Figure 2.1. *Alpine Journal* (1872), frontispiece. Courtesy Henry S. Hall, Jr. Library of the American Alpine Club.

Figure 2.2. Ellis Carr, "Two Days on a Ice Slope," *Alpine Journal* (August 1893), 428. Courtesy Henry S. Hall, Jr. Library of the American Alpine Club.

Figure 2.3. Robert L. M. Underhill, "On the Use and Management of the Rope in Rock Work," *Sierra Club Bulletin* (1931), plate XXX. Courtesy Henry S. Hall, Jr. Library of the American Alpine Club.

Figure 3.1. Courtesy Sierra Club's Colby Memorial Library.

Figure 3.2. Courtesy Ken Yager and Yosemite Climbing Association.

Figure 4.1. Courtesy Sierra Club's Colby Memorial Library.

Figure 4.2. Courtesy the Bancroft Library, University of California, Berkeley.

Figure 4.3. *Mugelnoos,* 27 October 1938, p. 1. Courtesy Henry S. Hall, Jr. Library of the American Alpine Club.

Figure 4.4. *Mugelnoos,* 27 October 1938, p. 2. Courtesy Henry S. Hall, Jr. Library of the American Alpine Club.

Figure 4.5. Courtesy Herb Conn and Potomac Appalachian Trail Club.

Figure 5.1. *Mugelnoos,* 4 February 1943, p. 2. Courtesy Henry S. Hall, Jr. Library of the American Alpine Club.

Figure 5.2. Courtesy Duke Watson and Seattle Mountaineers.

Figure 5.3. Courtesy Renny Russell and Henry S. Hall, Jr. Library of the American Alpine Club.

Figure 6.1. Courtesy Yosemite Research Library, Yosemite National Park.

Figure 6.2. Courtesy Bob Swift.

Figure 6.3a & b. Card courtesy the Bancroft Library, University of California, Berkeley; tool photo courtesy the Sierra Club's Colby Memorial Library and the Pirkle Jones Foundation.

Figure 6.4. Courtesy Yosemite Research Library, Yosemite National Park.

Figure 7.1. Photo courtesy Glen Denny.

Figure 7.2. *Ascent* (1969), 14. Courtesy Michael Anderson.

Figure 8.1. *Yodeler,* 19 July 1943, p. 5. Courtesy Sierra Club's Colby Memorial Library.

Figure 8.2. Courtesy Ken Yager and Yosemite Climbing Association.

Figure 8.3. *Off Belay* (April 1976), 43. Courtesy Greg Bombeck and Sierra Club's Colby Memorial Library.

Figure 9.1. Photo courtesy of Glen Denny.

Figure 9.2. Photo courtesy of Glen Denny.

Figure 10.1. Photo courtesy of George Meyers.

Figure 10.2. Photo courtesy of Glen Denny.

Figure 10.3. Courtesy Michael Anderson and Sierra Club's Colby Memorial Library.

Figure 10.4. Courtesy Jim Bridwell.

Figure 10.5. *Ascent* (1970), 43. Courtesy Michael Anderson and Sierra Club's Colby Memorial Library.

Figure 11.1. *Summit* (November 1970), 34. Courtesy Michael Anderson and Sierra Club's Colby Memorial Library.

Figure 11.2. Courtesy Henry S. Hall, Jr. Library of the American Alpine Club.

Figure 12.1. Courtesy Leo Dickinson, Ken Wilson, and Sierra Club's Colby Memorial Library.

Figure 12.2. Courtesy Yosemite Research Library, Yosemite National Park.

Figure 13.1. Courtesy Chris McNamara.

INDEX

Abalakov, Vitaly, 225–226, 253
Adam, Kenneth, 72, 79, 97
Adams, Ansel, 12, 44, 57, 92, 102, 122, 130, 170, 187, 227, 239, 259–260
Alaska, 15, 94, 113, 131, 140, 159, 210, 260, 266; Mount McKinley (Denali), 15, 77, 94, 252
Alpine Club (London), 5, 22–25, 27–34, 36–37, 39, 41, 43, 59–60, 64–65, 67, 102, 180, 235, 253, 273
Alpine Club of Canada, 34, 65, 131
Alpine Journal, 22, 46, 50, 79
Alps, 64, 67, 102–104, 112, 134, 149, 194, 204, 206; Dolomites, 16, 31, 38; Eiger, 32, 210–211; Grépon, 24, 23, 67; Matterhorn (Il Cervina), 17, 26–27, 29–30, 32, 44, 57, 67, 73, 81, 191, 267; Mont Blanc, 18–20, 28, 31, 34, 38, 67, 149; Wetterhorn, 17, 22, 191
American Alpine Club, 34, 38, 45, 50, 93, 99, 115, 123–124, 147, 157–158, 185, 188, 201, 215, 229–231, 248, 250, 252–253, 262, 273
American Whitewater, 182, 241, 266
Anderson, Sheridan, 143, 188, 207, 216, 220
Appalachian Mountain Club, 37–38, 65, 78, 80, 123, 273; *Appalachia*, 38, 67, 79
Argiewicz, Artur, 79, 82, 99–100, 113, 154–155
Ascent, 2, 186–188, 239–240

Bachar, John, 218, 223–231, 256, 260; background, 223–224; climbing philosophy, 224, 229, 235–236, 245; climbs, 196, 256–257, 273; entrepreneur, 227, 236, 238
Baffin Island, 195, 252–253, 267
Baldwin, Jim, 163, 192–193, 212
Baltistan, 253; K2, 73, 118, 237, 260, 266; Trango Tower, 210
Baxter, Alfred, 124, 128, 131
Bay Area RCS, 60, 73, 75, 115, 123–124, 183, 246; committees, 76, 129; creation, 52–54; discipline, 77; growth, 76–77; innovations, 58–60, 80–83; newsletter, 69; outings, 85–86, 122; Rock Climbing Committee, 76, 107, 119–120; safety, 52–53, 77–84, 249;

systematization, 52–53, 76–80, 183. *See also* Cragmont Climbing Club; Practice sites; *Yodeler*
Beat culture, 133, 137, 180, 197. *See also* Climbing culture
Beck, Eric, 140, 146, 168, 190, 197, 212
Beckey, Fred, 134–135, 267
Bedayan (Bedayn), Raffi, 54, 74, 79–80, 82, 113–115, 122, 147, 159, 175, 180, 182, 201, 308n.38
Blake, Arthur, 92, 202–203
Blum, Arlene, 7, 220–221
Bonatti, Walter, 138, 168–169, 235
Brevoort, Meta, 34, 65–66
Bridge, Marjory, 51, 57, 66, 74, 82, 87, 92, 112. *See also* Farquhar, Marjory Bridge
Bridwell, Jim, 45, 136, 190, 192–200, 213–215, 228, 230–232, 234–236, 239; background, 193, 219, 222, 224, 235; climbing philosophy, 198–199, 245, 267; climbs, 196–197, 210–212, 256
Briggs, Bill, 251, 261
Brower, David, 45, 54, 81, 109, 113, 120, 133, 147, 157, 163, 184–185, 206, 262, 276; Army experiences, 96, 99–100, 102; background, 58, 91–92; climbs, 79, 86–87, 110–111, 114–115, 273; environmental advocacy, 12, 102–103, 110, 122–123, 130–131, 181, 259–260; SC officer, 103, 122–123, 186–187
Brown, Joe, 138, 235, 265
Brugger, Julie, 218, 263, 333n.4
Bruhl, Etienne, 67–68
Bugaboos, 113, 252; Snowpatch Spire, 113

Calderwood, Rich, 135, 156, 159, 316n.18
Caltech Climbers, 124, 254
Camp 4 (Sunnyside), 13, 85, 123, 127, 133, 135–138, 144, 148, 188, 201, 208–209, 214, 224, 234–235, 244; boulders, 127, 135, 226, 259–260, 276; education, 138; intoxication, 138, 197–199, 201, 210, 222; reputation, 158; sexuality, 138, 141–144, 222; social dynamics, 140–141, 163–165, 169–171, 192–193, 197–199, 202, 212, 214, 218–223, 229, 232

Canyon de Chelly National Monument, 214–215

Carr, Penny, 136, 141, 144, 147

Carter, Tom, 219, 221–222

Cathedral Spires, 58–60, 81, 86–87, 107, 111–112, 125, 160, 169, 212; Higher Spire, 58–59, 62, 128–129, 151, 161, 163, 185, 203; Lower Spire, 59, 128, 203

Chamonix (France), 18, 37, 180

Charlet, Armand, 38–39, 235

Child, Greg, 66, 195, 210, 215–217, 256

Chouinard, Malinda, 223, 238, 271, 275

Chouinard, Yvon, 42–43, 135, 137–138, 140–142, 147, 149, 157–158, 160, 168–170, 182, 185–186, 193, 197, 247; background, 176–177, 209, 221–222, 237, 274; climbing philosophy, 145–146, 160–163, 167, 173, 182–183, 188–189, 204, 225, 227–229, 231–232, 244–246, 254, 264, 275–276; climbs, 157, 163, 166, 168, 181, 206, 210; entrepreneur, 175–179, 181, 183, 188, 209–210, 226, 237–239, 241, 244–246, 249, 271, 274–275; environmental advocacy, 12, 259–262, 271–272, 274–277, 352n.41; innovator, 157, 203

Chouinard Equipment, 177, 180, 188, 203; catalog, 203, 206, 209, 238, 241, 244–245. *See also* Great Pacific Iron Works; Lost Arrow Corporation; Patagonia (company)

Cirque of the Unclimbables, 210, 252

Clark, Lewis, 39, 43–44, 51–52

Class, 4, 7, 19–25, 29–30, 32, 34–39, 41–43, 138, 233

Climber's Guide to Yosemite Valley, A, 183–185

Climbing, 2, 229, 240, 257, 266

Climbing accidents, 79, 128, 249, 260–263. *See also* Climbing culture

Climbing business: Climbing Wall Association, 255; competitions, 232, 252–254; gyms, 254–256; liability, 179, 245, 248–250; marketing, 240–246, 267; Outdoor Industry Association, 245, 249

Climbing culture: acculturation, 63, 68, 223, 273; adventure, 2–3, 15, 22, 25, 36–37, 39, 41–42, 58, 64, 68, 75, 96, 108, 115, 122, 137, 138, 142, 144, 146, 148–150, 152–153, 158–160, 166–167, 173, 179, 180, 182, 194, 203–204, 209, 232, 239, 241, 245–248, 256–257, 261, 266, 268, 270, 273, 276–277; amateurism, 24, 41–42, 234–235; anglophilia, 150, 153, 192, 204; authenticity, 3, 13, 23, 36; Beats, 138–139, 141, 145–148, 158, 179, 181–182, 184, 186–188, 190–193, 198, 212, 217, 228, 235, 237, 239, 241, 243, 245–246; bolting wars, 115, 157–158, 160–166, 174–175, 227, 229–232, 268–270; categorical firsts, 34, 51, 195, 251, 254; clean climbing, 42, 183, 203–209, 244, 270–271, 330n.38; clubs, 248, 259; competitiveness, 51, 113, 148, 252–253, 256–258, 344–345n.56; dirt-bagging, 197–198, 215–217; discipline, 162, 165, 173; environmental advocacy, 29, 37–38, 200, 232, 239, 256, 259, 268–277; ethics, 31–33, 41, 43, 148, 173–174; genteel values, 151; golden age, 17, 22, 190–192; growth, 188, 191, 237, 255, 266; gymnastics, 218–219, 232, 234, 257; heterosocial, 29–30, 34, 42, 51, 53, 61–75, 84, 86, 90, 124–125, 136, 140, 145, 147, 182, 184, 247, 255; homosocial, 30, 34, 136, 144–145, 181–182, 189, 219–221, 244, 248, 255; imagery, 63, 71, 149–150, 164, 187–188, 193, 240–243, 246, 250; knowing nature, 4, 11, 19–20, 103, 105–106, 168–169, 322n.14; no trace, 42, 259; peer review, 158–159, 163; professionalization, 24, 179, 181, 190; publications, 191, 193, 234–237, 239–241, 248, 251–252, 266–267; publicity, 156–157, 170, 180–181, 186, 234–235, 240, 257–258, 272; risk, 7, 23–24, 26–31, 49, 77, 90, 130, 141, 145–147, 152, 157, 160, 167–169, 195–196, 224–225, 227–228, 237, 248–250, 255, 260–266, 348n.18; safety, 17, 90, 162; sexism, 64–65, 67, 219, 234, 241–242; sexualizing nature, 6, 102, 166, 169, 171, 195–196, 204, 220; speed climbing, 210–212, 256–258, 267; spiritual quest, 209; traditionalism, 17, 60, 162, 218, 225, 229–231, 233–234, 250, 256, 258, 268, 270; Victorianism, 34, 37–38, 41–42, 151, 225, 237

Climbing films, 181, 236, 239, 272; *Climbing Cathedral Spires,* 181; *El Capitan,* 208, 239; *Fitzroy: First Ascent of the Southwest Buttress,* 239; *Mountaineering in the Sierra Nevada,* 181; *Sentinel: The West Ridge,* 181–182, 239; *Sky-Land Trails of the Kings,*

181; *Solo,* 206, 239; *The Taking of Seneca Rock,* 181

Climbing schools, 180, 241, 243–244, 248; Yosemite Mountaineering School, 241, 243–244

Climbing techniques: aid climbing, 9, 31–34, 57, 59–60, 157, 185, 194–196, 207, 209; belaying, 5, 32–33, 40–41, 46–47, 78, 255; first free ascents, 151, 157, 163, 168, 194, 227–228; free climbing, 5, 8, 31, 33–34, 157, 184, 193–194, 219, 318n.38; hang-dogging, 227–228, 232, 268; ice climbing, 202, 212, 254; pendulums, 32; rap-bolting, 228, 231–232, 268; rappelling, 32; soloing, 140, 146, 168, 224–225, 260, 272; sport climbing, 228, 232, 250, 256–257, 268; yo-yoing, 229–230

Climbing technology, 79, 94–96, 148, 153, 159–160, 183; attitudes about, 36, 59–60; bashies, 194, 205, 209; BAT Hooks, 169, 194; bodies, 134, 160, 196, 208–209, 218–219, 223–224, 226, 256–257; bolts, 8, 17, 43, 115, 153–154, 169–172, 196, 199, 208, 227, 260, 268, 270–271, 350–351n.29; cameras, 180, 187–188; cams, 8, 225–226, 239, 250, 267; carabiners, 8, 17, 32, 53, 80–82, 111, 176, 244; chocks, 5, 8, 9, 203–205, 207, 209; climbing walls, 254–256; clubs, 9, 107, 246, 248, 252; dowels, 194; drills, 8, 43, 115, 153, 155–156, 194–195, 203, 225, 228, 230, 270; drugs, 256; fixed ropes, 28–29, 31, 157–159, 163–164, 166, 272; guidebooks, 156, 183–186, 222, 262, 267–268, 317n.32; hauling, 158, 186, 195; hooks, 81, 194, 205, 219; information systems, 9, 160; pitons, 8, 9, 17, 31–32, 36, 53, 58–59, 80–83, 111, 159, 176, 203–205, 207, 209, 244, 317n.32; rating systems, 184–185, 194, 206, 227, 229, 232; rope ascenders, 225, 229; rope ladders, 32; ropes, 8, 9, 17, 47, 79–80, 95–96, 111, 159, 178; RURPS, 157, 160, 169, 176–177, 196, 205, 244–245; shoes, 8, 9, 180, 195, 225–227; sleeping platforms, 194–195, 225; topos, 160–161, 227; transportation, 54, 69–70, 85, 96–97, 111

Club Alpin Français, 28, 24, 37, 67

Clubs, 9, 36–37, 62–68, 107, 183, 221; auxiliaries, 64–67, 221. *See also individual clubs*

Clyde, Norman, 43–44, 58; background, 108–109; climbs, 39–41, 54, 108–109, 182

Cohen, Michael, 103, 109, 114, 218, 260

Colorado Mountain Club, 65, 68, 84, 114–115, 119

Compagnie des Guides de Chamonix, 22, 25

Consumerism, 9, 38, 82, 85, 161, 174, 233, 237–238, 244–246, 248–250, 253, 258

Consumption, 174, 233, 248, 256; environmental impacts, 266, 268–272, 275–277, 351n.32

Cooper, Ed, 163–165, 181–182, 187–188

Corcoran, Doris, 53, 62, 69–72, 74–75. *See also* Leonard, Doris

Cragmont Climbing Club, 45, 47–54, 61, 68, 248; innovations, 46–49; journal of, 50, 68–71, 74. *See also* Bay Area RCS

Croft, Peter, 232, 236, 256–257

Cunningham, Gerry, 178, 249

Dawson, Glen, 43, 54, 59, 112; climbs, 41, 44, 54, 109, 113

Denny, Glen, 144, 146–147, 163, 186–188, 212, 239; climbing philosophy, 164

Dent, Clinton, 24, 28, 192

Diving Board, 88; *Porcelain Wall,* 173

Duane, Daniel, 11, 174, 194, 229, 246–247, 261

Dyar, Ruth, 51, 72, 74, 82, 87–88, 90, 262. *See also* Mendenhall, Ruth Dyar

Eichorn, Jules, 43, 50–53, 59, 68, 71, 88, 107; climbs, 41, 44, 86–87, 109, 111–112, 118, 182

El Capitan, 9, 77, 120, 125, 129, 136, 152, 164, 213, 222, 227–228, 234, 246–247, 251–253, 256–258, 261, 268–269; *Dawn Wall,* 170–171, 173, 190–192, 194–197, 217, 219–220; *Dihedral Wall,* 163–164, 220, 223; *Heart Route,* 193, 246; *Magic Mushroom,* 246; *Muir Wall,* 163, 168, 193, 246; *North America Wall,* 166–167, 170, 193, 195–196, 222; *Nose,* 144, 147, 154–159, 163, 169–170, 176, 187, 195, 206, 210–212, 219, 228–229, 241, 249, 256–258, 267–268; *Pacific Ocean Wall,* 196; *Salathé Wall,* 163, 187, 210, 219, 247, 257; *Sea of Dreams,* 196; *West Buttress,* 164; *Wyoming Sheep Ranch,* 210, 212, 222

Environmentalism, 259, 275, 352n.41; wilderness ideology, 103–104, 246, 277

Farquhar, Francis, 12, 15, 16, 39–41, 43–44, 51–52, 74, 77, 92, 95, 103, 117, 130, 181–182
Farquhar, Marjory Bridge, 74, 105, 130. *See also* Bridge, Marjory
Federation of Western Outdoor Clubs, 102, 116, 123
Feuerer, Bill, 135, 154–157, 159, 176, 316n.18; entrepreneur, 177, 180, 204
Fitschen, Joe, 135, 158, 162–163, 188, 316n.18
Frost, Tom, 140, 146, 149, 182, 225, 259, 316n.18; climbs, 157–158, 163, 166, 168, 187, 204, 210, 318n.38; entrepreneur, 177, 203, 209–210, 237–238; innovator, 157, 160, 176–177, 203, 239, 330n.38

Gallwas, Jerry, 134–135, 151–152, 159, 176, 181, 316n.18
Gardening, 11, 102, 206–209, 268. *See also* Vertical nature
Gender, 5–7, 13, 17–18, 20, 23, 25–26, 29, 32, 35–36, 41, 43, 44, 63–68, 82, 91–92, 104–106, 124, 138, 140–141, 145–146, 150, 166–167, 171, 191, 195, 204, 206, 209, 219–223, 231–232, 234–235, 240–248, 252, 254, 257–259, 261–262, 265–267, 273, 276, 282–283n.8, 284n.10, 286–287n.23, 348n.17; heterosocial, 13, homosocial, 12–13
Glacier Point, 86, 112, 219, 268
Great Pacific Iron Works, 209, 245
Guiding, 22, 24–25, 28, 180, 250, 267
Guttman, Allen, 344–345n.56

Half Dome, 9, 84, 116–117, 125, 169, 188, 194–195, 213, 220, 234, 251, 262–263, 268; *Arcturus,* 164–165; *Northwest Face,* 152, 157, 159, 168, 175, 206, 257; *Snake Dike; South Face,* 169–170; *Southwest Face,* 58, 111, 126, 168; *Tis-sa-ack,* 169
Hamilton, Lawrence, 219, 227, 244, 270
Hansen, Bob, 82, 88, 112–113, 119–120
Hansen, Peter, 18, 60
Harding, Warren, 120, 133, 135, 138, 140, 147–149, 151–160, 164, 169–174, 182, 190,

194–195, 200, 247, 315–316n.18; background, 3, 153–154; climbing philosophy, 158, 169, 173, 267; climbs, 147, 163, 166, 169–170, 195, 210; rivalries, 159, 171–173, 197
Hargreaves, Alison, 260, 266
Harris, Morgan, 51, 54, 81, 96, 119, 213
Hechtel, Sibylle, 219, 222, 265, 333n.4, 348n.17
Hennek, Dennis, 181, 192, 206, 210, 252
Herbert, TM, 135, 141, 149, 163, 167–168, 170–171
Heterosocial. *See* Climbing culture; Gender
Higgins, Molly, 219–223, 265–266, 333n.4
Higgins, Tom, 144, 165, 191, 217, 228
Hill, Lynn, 9, 221, 223, 230, 236, 253–255; background, 234, 254, 265; climbing philosophy, 227, 232, 237; climbs, 234, 257–258, 262–263
Himalaya, 206, 220, 268, 274; Annapurna, 2, 220–221, 260; Mount Everest, 2, 18, 57, 77, 150, 181, 220, 239, 251–252, 261–262, 264
Homosocial. *See* Climbing culture; Gender
Hoover, Mike, 206, 236, 239
Hornbein, Tom, 2, 264

Irving, R. L. G., 32, 184, 237, 274
Isserman, Maurice, 3

Jardine, Ray, 225–229, 238, 257
Johnson, Beverly, 218–223, 228, 232, 234, 236, 265–266; background, 218, 223; climbs, 219–220
Jones, Chris, 51, 114, 191
Jones, Dick, 42, 44, 54, 58, 78, 256
Joshua Tree National Monument, 183, 202, 224, 231, 234, 269

Kamps, Bob, 144, 149, 157, 165, 182, 215, 318n.38
Kat Pinnacle, 86, 112, 157
Kauk, Ron, 214, 227, 229–232, 236, 251; climbing philosophy, 229, 272; climbs, 225, 231
Kehrlein, Oliver, 51, 74, 92, 109, 111, 117
Kendall, Henry, 187, 239, 250
Kerouac, Jack, 137, 168
King, Clarence, 36, 43, 108, 239

Knowing nature. *See* Climbing culture, knowing nature

Komito, Steve, 175, 179–180

Kor, Layton, 136, 138, 140–141, 144, 146, 149, 158, 160, 164–165, 175, 181–182, 187, 193, 197, 210, 215, 252

Kroger, Chuck, 193, 198, 240, 250

Lauria, Don, 171, 192–193

Leaning Tower, 9, 163, 168–169, 260

LeConte, Helen, 62, 87, 110

Leeper, Ed, 175, 177, 180, 249

Leonard, Doris, 51, 74–75, 79, 87, 114. *See also* Corcoran, Doris

Leonard, Richard, 40, 51, 60–61, 69–70, 73, 75–76, 81–82, 92, 105, 107, 109, 112, 133, 149, 157, 161, 180, 182, 193, 213, 240, 248; Army experiences, 46, 91, 93–96, 98, 100; background, 45–46, 72, 79; *Belaying the Leader*, 130, 213; climbing philosophy, 58, 86, 181; climbs, 50, 53, 58–60, 79, 86–87, 110–112, 114; dynamic belay, 47–48; environmental advocacy, 103, 123, 130, 260; liaison, 115–116, 120–121, 147, 156; SC officer, 45, 103, 112, 116, 122–123; systematizer, 45–52, 78–79, 112, 118, 129, 183

Liberty Cap, 134, 152, 169

Lippmann, Fritz, 112–113, 119–120, 124

Loma Prieta RCS, 122, 193, 248

Long, Dick, 140, 167, 175, 177, 308n.39

Long, John, 45, 150, 198, 208, 210–212, 224–225, 232, 234, 239, 256–257

Longs Peak, 16, 84, 210, 220

Lost Arrow Chimney, 86, 125–126, 154, 160, 168, 194, 212

Lost Arrow Corporation, 238. *See also* Chouinard Equipment; Great Pacific Iron Works; Patagonia (company)

Lost Arrow Spire, 125–128, 160, 169, 236

Lowe, Greg, 195, 225–226, 238

Lower Brother, 62

Lower Cathedral Rock, 134

Lunn, Arnold, 8, 11, 22, 24, 31

Madsen, Jim, 193–194, 213

Mallory, George, 13, 43, 77, 90, 145–146, 180–181, 209, 240, 261, 273

Marshall, Robert, 45, 58, 102, 110, 274

Massachusetts Institute of Technology, 80, 94

Mazamas, 15–16, 37–38, 65–66, 68, 75–76, 84, 119, 123; environmental advocacy, 102. *See also* Oregon Alpine Club

McCarthy, Jim, 190, 210, 212, 252

McCracken, Dick, 165, 210, 252

Mendenhall, John, 16, 72, 74, 88, 97–98, 103, 106

Mendenhall, Ruth Dyar, 6, 7, 11, 74, 90, 97–98, 103, 106, 286–287n.23. *See also* Dyar, Ruth

Merry, Wayne, 120, 135, 156–157, 175, 241, 316n.18

Messner, Reinhold, 157, 239–240, 247

Michael, Charles, 77, 108, 116

Middendorf, John, 239, 244

Middle Brother, 268

Middle Cathedral Rock, 154, 163, 194, 212

Military, 213; and Camp 4, 133, 139–140, 158, 170, 180; Camp Hale, 98–100; 87th Infantry, 94, 98; Seneca Rocks, 99–101, 181; 10th Mountain Division, 93, 98–101, 104, 155; World War II, 90, 93, 113

Mitchell, Richard, 87

Modernity, 17, 19, 35

Morris, Bruce, 228, 231

Mount Hood, 16, 64–65, 119

Mount Rainier, 98, 118, 185, 267

Mount Ritter, 108–109

Mount Waddington, 92, 111–113, 252

Mount Watkins, 9, 152, 166, 194, 213

Mount Whitney, 15, 41, 44, 73, 78, 84, 87

Mountain, 2, 210–211, 240

Mugelnoos, 74, 83, 93, 96, 98, 100, 104, 240

Muir, John, 1, 3–4, 10, 11, 15, 25, 27, 37–38, 239; and climbing, 36, 42–43, 78, 108–110, 182, 201, 206, 273, 293n.49; environmental advocacy, 12, 42–43, 102, 110, 259–260

Mummery, Alfred F., 7, 24, 30, 45, 77, 90, 109, 181, 200, 240, 253, 267

National Geographic, 122, 206

National Park Service, 45, 50, 61, 85, 90, 108, 116, 118, 120–121, 130–131, 147, 156, 170–171, 175, 183, 188, 197–203, 214, 241, 259–260, 267–270, 273–274, 276. *See also* individual parks

National Ski Patrol Committee, 93, 99
Native Americans, 114, 214–216. *See also* Race
Nelson, Anton, 126–127, 160, 168, 308n.39
Nicholson, Marjorie Hope, 12
North Face, The, 178, 188, 238–239
Nutcracker Suite, 1–2, 4–5, 8, 13, 204, 268

O'Brien, Miriam, 38, 66–68, 82, 220
Oregon Alpine Club, 37, 65. *See also* Mazamas
Ortenburger, Leigh, 183–185
Ortner, Sherry, 220
Outdoor play, 16, 18, 20, 35–36
Outdoor sports: angling, 229, 266; backpacking, 203; hiking, 266; hunting, 266; kayaking, 8, 94, 202, 225, 244–245, 250, 260, 266, 270, 273; skateboarding, 225, 250, 253–254, 260; skiing, 8, 168, 202, 225, 229, 236, 244–245, 250, 253, 260, 273; surfing, 8, 94, 137–138, 168, 198, 202, 225, 229, 244–245, 253, 260, 266, 273

Padula, Fred, 208, 239
Parque Pumalín, 275–277
Parsons, Harriet, 87, 113, 256
Patagonia (company), 238, 245, 249, 271–273, 275
Patagonia (region), 170, 239, 272, 274–277, 352n.41
Peck, Annie, 35, 66–67, 237
Pinnacles National Monument, 73, 84, 112, 115, 122, 126, 183, 186
Potter, Dean, 257, 272–273
Pottinger, Anne, 128, 130
Powell, Mark, 133–135, 138, 141, 146–147, 151–152, 154–155, 157, 190, 193, 224, 316n.18; background, 133–134, 175; climbs, 134–135
Practice sites: Cragmont Rock, 46–47, 49, 51–53, 78, 94, 96; Devils Gate, 55, 83, 96; Devils Slide, 54, 79; Dutchmans Rock, 54; Eagle Rock, 55, 96; Hunters Hill, 54, 249; Indian Rock, 46, 48–49, 94, 96; Miraloma Rocks, 54, 79; Mount Diablo, 54; Mount Tamalpais, 54, 69, 75; Pinnacle Rock, 46, 49, 96; Stony Point, 57, 96, 135; Strawberry Peak, 76; Tahquitz Rock, 73, 78, 83–84, 97, 135, 151, 183–184, 204

Pratt, Chuck, 134, 136, 140, 143, 145–147, 149, 157–158, 166–167, 175, 181–182, 188, 192–193, 204, 209, 259, 316n.18, 318n.38; climbs, 163, 166, 215, 219
Pulpit Rock, 86–87, 112, 125

Race, 7, 43, 150, 190, 214–216. *See also* Native Americans
Rébuffat, Gaston, 180–181, 235, 265
Recreational Equipment Co-operative, 177–178, 238
Recreational Equipment Incorporated (REI), 178, 238, 241, 249
Ridgeway, Rick, 237, 273–275
Riegelhuth, Jack, 74, 118, 155
Risk. *See* Climbing culture, risk
Rixon's Pinnacle, 125, 206
Robbins, Elizabeth, 7, 204, 238
Robbins, Royal, 2, 7, 26, 42–43, 45, 128, 135, 138–139, 141–153, 159, 166, 182, 184–186, 188, 190–193, 195, 212, 221, 237, 240, 247, 316n.18, 317n.32; background, 149, 151–152, 174, 274; climbing philosophy, 4–5, 6, 150, 152–153, 158–159, 161–164, 167, 171–174, 182, 195, 204, 235–236, 261, 268; climbs, 134, 146, 154, 157, 163, 168–169, 210, 252, 268, 273; entrepreneur, 178, 180–181, 186, 226, 237–238, 241; environmental advocate, 200, 271; rivalries, 159, 164–165, 169–171, 181, 197
Roberts, David, 210, 254, 262–265
Robinson, Bestor, 43, 51, 54, 59, 92, 105, 107, 109, 130, 163, 182; Army experiences, 93–94, 98–99; climbs, 41, 44, 86, 111, 114–115, 117, 180; SC officer, 103, 122, 260
Robinson, Doug, 136, 168, 203, 206, 270
Rock Climbing Sections, 13, 45, 57, 61, 90–94, 96, 108, 114–115, 118, 129, 131, 133–135, 146–147, 180, 234, 248, 249, 252, 255–256, 262, 273–274; annual banquet, 73, 76, 82, 93, 98; climber classification, 85, 118–120; discipline, 88, 119–120, 183; environmental advocacy, 103–104; as gatekeeper, 78, 119, 183; generational tensions, 113, 131–132, 146–147; outings, 84–90; safety, 5, 47–53, 84, 90, 117, 119–120, 125, 129–130, 181, 195; social functions, 72, 75, 98, 100, 104–105; systematization, 112; technology, 94–95, 97, 115, 203; termination,

54, 131, 248–249. *See also individual sections*

Roper, Steve, 51, 87, 133, 139–142, 147, 149, 158, 160, 163–165, 168–170, 173, 175, 178, 191–193, 198, 212, 240, 259, 293n.49, 317n.32, 318n.38; Army experiences, 139–140; climbing philosophy, 161, 244, 262; as writer, 183–188, 259, 267

Roskelley, John, 198, 200–201, 221, 236–237

Rostrum, 86–87, 206, 232

Rowell, Galen, 164, 169–170, 187–188, 191, 193–194, 206, 221, 237, 239–240, 271; environmental advocacy, 12, 200, 259–262, 271

Royal Arches, 86, 157, 169; *Royal Arches,* 87

Ruskin, John, 20–21, 23, 25, 28, 102, 187

Sacherer, Frank, 147, 149, 182; climbing philosophy, 167, 210, 225; climbs, 157, 163, 167, 192–193, 196, 210

Salathé, John, 125–128, 130, 133, 151–152, 168, 308n.39; climbs, 125–127, 160, 182, 194; pitons, 125–127, 159, 176, 180, 203, 249

Sax, Joseph, 274

Schrepfer, Susan, 286–287n.23

Searby (Jori), Ellen, 127, 156–157

Seattle Mountaineers, 16, 37, 68, 76, 84, 119, 123, 185, 273

Sentinel Rock, 9, 125, 151, 169, 206, 212, 220; *In Cold Blood,* 168; *Steck-Salathé,* 126, 151, 168, 194, 224

Sequoia National Park, 112; Moro Rock, 87, 117

Sessions, George, 12, 135, 156, 175, 274

Sexuality, 2, 124, 248, 255, 267

Shawangunks, 183, 202, 206, 218, 222, 269

Shepherd, Louise, 8, 13, 223, 237

Sherrick, Mike, 134–135, 152, 316n.18

Shiprock, 114–115, 163, 210, 214–215

Sierra Club, 5, 11, 34, 37, 39, 44, 46, 52, 60, 62, 64, 66, 68, 74–77, 84, 90–92, 99, 108, 116, 119–120, 183–185, 248, 260; environmental advocacy, 11–12, 102, 123, 130–131, 181, 186, 269; ski mountaineers, 55, 91, 93, 96, 105, 124, 185

Sierra Club Bulletin, 39, 41, 50, 79, 89, 92, 109, 127, 183, 186, 188

Siri, Will, 123, 127, 186, 262

Ski Hut, The, 177–178, 188, 238

Skinner, Todd, 230, 237, 253, 257, 260

Slater, Rob, 196, 210, 212, 260

Southern RCS, 72–73, 75, 113, 117, 123, 175; Base Camp, 72–74, 80, 96; creation, 54–57; growth, 122; safety, 57, 78–79; systematization, 57, 76–80. *See also Mugelnoos*

Spectacle, 250–254, 257–258

Spider Rock, 134, 214–215

Split Pinnacle, 86, 112

Sport, 17–18, 20, 35–36, 60, 202, 223, 237. *See also* Outdoor sports

Sporthaus Schuster, 59, 81–82, 125, 176–177, 238, 241

Squamish (British Columbia), 198, 232

Stanford Alpine Club, 121, 124, 130–131, 135, 159, 240, 248–249, 254–255; accidents, 125, 128–130, 187, 193; and RCS, 124, 129

Starr, Peter, 77–79, 85, 181

Steck, Allen, 126–127, 131, 151, 156, 167, 182, 227, 308n.39; entrepreneur, 12, 178, 181, 186, 188, 193, 267

Steigerwald, David, 351n.32

Stephen, Leslie, 2–3, 4, 7, 11, 22, 24–25, 27–29, 64, 67, 109, 239, 273

Stutfield, H. E. M., 30, 36, 148, 162

Summit, 182, 185–186, 204, 207, 240–241

Swift, Bob, 127, 308n.39, 316n.18

Tarver, Frank, 159, 308n.39, 316n.18, 317n.32

Technology, 7, 81–82, 159, 168, 176–177, 212, 225, 227, 237, 250, 267, 270–271. *See also* Climbing technology

Tejada-Flores, Lito, 135, 191, 213, 231, 239

Tetons, 140, 176, 183–185, 188, 202, 262, 352n.41; Grand Teton, 16, 38, 251

Tompkins, Doug, 178, 188, 237–238, 260, 274–277, 352n.41

Udall, Stewart, 12, 274

Ullman, James Ramsey, 146, 149–150, 216

Underhill, Robert L. M., 15–17, 34, 38–42, 44, 46–47, 52, 60, 62–63, 68, 71, 78, 80, 90, 102, 109, 133, 170, 291n.36; background, 16, 38–39; climbing philosophy, 15–16, 34, 41; climbs, 35

Vertical nature, 6, 31–32, 59, 81, 202–203, 206–209; degradation, 8–9, 203, 270, 272, 350–351n.29; geology, 9, 226; lichen, 207;

Vertical nature *(continued)*
  menace of, 208; pollution, 206, 208, 268–
  269; weather, 9–10, 166, 195, 208. *See also*
  Gardening
Victorian culture, 19–20, 22–35
Vogel, Bea, 124, 154, 316n.18

Washington Column, 85–86, 154, 157, 169,
  206, 212; *Astroman,* 210, 220, 232; *Lunch
  Ledge,* 62, 87
Weiselberg, Erik, 183
Westbay, Billy, 209–212, 256
White, Richard, 105
Whitmore, George, 135, 156, 195, 316n.18
Whymper, Edward, 6, 21, 24, 26, 36, 45, 73,
  81, 90, 180, 187, 191, 194, 237, 239
Wiessner, Fritz, 35, 42, 112–114
Wilderness Society, 46, 269, 274
Wills, Alfred, 22, 24, 191
Wilson, Don, 134–135, 151–152, 184, 214,
  308n.39
Wilts, Chuck, 74, 97, 124, 135, 159, 162, 184,
  308n.39
Wilts, Ellen, 74, 97, 135, 142, 308n.39
Workman, Fanny Bullock, 35, 66–67

Yodeler, 74, 85, 92–93, 97–98, 100, 104, 112–
  113, 131, 183, 214, 240

Yosemite National Park, 10–11, 84–86; Camp
  9, 85–87, 122–123, 133, 135–136, 188;
  climber registration system, 118–119, 121;
  climbing ranger, 118, 129, 270; drugs, 199–
  202; Hetch Hetchy, 191, 200; relations with
  climbers, 117–118, 199–201; rescue operations, 108, 116–119, 128–130, 170, 212–
  214, 344n.55; riot, 199–200; Tenaya Canyon, 111, 166; Tuolumne Meadows, 77,
  224; visitation, 97, 104, 121–123; Yellow
  Pines Campground, 201; Yosemite Search
  and Rescue (YOSAR), 213–214, 236. *See
  also* Camp 4
Yosemite Park and Curry Company, 92, 197,
  241; under Music Corporation of America
  management, 200. *See also* Climbing
  schools
Yosemite Valley, 9–12. *See also individual
  formations*
Young, Geoffrey Winthrop, 2, 24, 31–32, 34,
  39, 41, 46–47, 49, 109, 165, 237, 240, 253,
  254
Young, Kevin, 223, 348n.17

Zsigmondy, Emil, 29, 31–33, 43